Hermeticism
and the
Renaissance

FOLGER INSTITUTE SYMPOSIA

Compiled by the Folger Institute and
Published by the Folger Shakespeare Library

An influential collaborative enterprise founded in 1970 and now cosponsored by twenty-two major universities, the Folger Institute is a rapidly growing center for advanced studies in the humanities. Through support from such agencies as the National Endowment for the Humanities and the Andrew W. Mellon Foundation, the Institute offers a complex interdisciplinary program of seminars, workshops, symposia, colloquia, and lectures. The physical center of the Institute is the Folger Shakespeare Library, an independent research library administered by the Trustees of Amherst College and located on Capitol Hill in Washington.

Hermeticism and the Renaissance

Intellectual History and the Occult in Early Modern Europe

**Edited by
Ingrid Merkel and Allen G. Debus**

Folger Books
Washington: The Folger Shakespeare Library
London and Toronto: Associated University Presses

Associated University Presses
440 Forsgate Drive
Cranbury, NJ 08512

Associated University Presses
25 Sicilian Avenue
London WC1A 2QH, England

Associated University Presses
2133 Royal Windsor Drive
Unit 1
Mississauga, Ontario
Canada L5J 1K5

The paper used in this publication meets the requirements of the American National Standard for Permanence of Paper for Printed Library Materials Z39.48-1984.

Library of Congress Cataloging-in-Publication Data

Hermeticism and the Renaissance.

  (Folger Institute symposia)
  "Folger books."
  Papers presented at a conference held in March 1982
at the Institute for Renaissance and Eighteenth-Century
Studies in the Folger Shakespeare Library in Washington,
D.C.
  Includes bibliographies.
  1. Hermetism—History—Congresses. 2. Occult
sciences—Europe—History—Congresses. 3. Renaissance—
Congresses. I. Merkel, Ingrid. II. Debus, Allen G.
III. Folger Institute of Renaissance and Eighteenth-
Century Studies. IV. Series.
BF1586.H47 1988   135'.4   85-45616
ISBN 0-918016-85-1 (alk. paper)

Printed in the United States of America

Contents

Introduction

INGRID MERKEL and ALLEN G. DEBUS

The present book is the end result of the conference, "Hermeticism and the Renaissance," which was held in March 1982 at the Institute for Renaissance and Eighteenth-Century Studies in the Folger Shakespeare Library in Washington, D.C. The idea had originated in the Washington Collegium for Humanistic Studies and Research, an informal confederation of Washington area institutions. The conference itself was developed by Susan Zimmerman, then Associate Chairman of the Folger Institute, and by Ingrid Merkel of the Catholic University of America. The National Gallery of Art, through its Center for Advanced Study in the Visual Arts, provided for an exhibition of Hermetic materials from Washington museums and libraries, which were on display at the time of the conference.

The meeting was organized for the purpose of discussing the role of Hermeticism in Renaissance thought. Much interest in the subject had been generated by the publications of Frances Yates, who had emphasized this in her *Giordano Bruno and the Hermetic Tradition* and in all of her later books.[1] Indeed, so influential had her books been that Hermeticism was being detected in "virtually every aspect of sixteenth-century thought," as one of her followers writes in this volume in an essay on Hermetic architecture. Such prominent attention paid to a phenomenon not normally considered to be in the mainstream of European thought provoked considerable opposition among scholars. One of the goals of the conference, therefore, had been to evaluate charges advanced (particularly by traditional historians of science) that Dame Frances's conclusions had been accepted uncritically by too many scholars and that the role of Hermeticism had been vastly overstated. To be sure, few of her critics question that Hermeticism was a strand of Renaissance Neoplatonism or that her research—continuing as it did in the tradition of the earlier investigations by Kristeller, Garin, Festugière, and others—had done much to promote the recognition of this fact. But these critics argued that claims to a seminal importance or to an exclusive impact on Renaissance thought had yet to be substantiated.

The issue has been complicated and sometimes entirely obscured by the fact that Hermeticism has been understood in a bewildering variety of ways, often without recognition of its meaning or of its historical context. Yates used the term *Hermeticism* for a wide range of occult and mystical writings and reserved *Hermetism* for texts and documents immediately related to the *Corpus Hermeticum*. This distinction has rarely been employed by others. A second object of the conference, consequently, had been to explore further and to clarify the meaning and use of these terms. *Hermeticism* was chosen for the title of the conference because it allowed for a wider range of discussion. Most of the textual studies were based on and were centered around the Hermetica in the stricter sense of the word. Any discussion of Renaissance Hermeticism was thus anchored in the Hellenistic tradition of the texts or their purported medieval adaptations.

Third, the conference was to promote investigations of Hermetic phenomena in diverse areas of Renaissance culture with the purpose of detecting a coherence in the many *disjecta membra* of the tradition. Scholars were encouraged to present arguments for or against the validity of Hermeticism as a self-contained and independent body of ideas that had exerted a well-defined influence. With his interest in mind, the conference was divided into studies of the origins and of the transmission of texts and into examinations of Hermetic components in Renaissance philosophy and science, literature and art.

Habent sua fata libelli, and conferences have their fate, too. In 1980, on her last visit to the United States, Frances Yates had accepted an invitation to help in the planning and to deliver the keynote lecture of the conference, but by 1982 her attendance was no longer possible due to ill health. Still, she had emphasized in preliminary discussions the great need for scholarly rigor in this field that was so riddled with speculation. She had hoped that young scholars would study the texts with the same love that had inspired her throughout her own career as historian. It was indeed sad for all those associated with the organization of the conference to learn not only of the death of Dame Frances, but also that of yet another scholar of mysticism and the cabala, Gershom Scholem, shortly before the beginning of the meeting.

The book owes its structure to the conference. The editors—Ingrid Merkel and Allen G. Debus, a contributor to the conference who had been invited to a joint editorship—adopted the division into origins and transmission of texts as well as into papers on magic, science, philosophy, literature, and art with only slight modification. Three papers that were read at the conference were not included, whereas seven papers were commissioned afterward. Many of the original contributions have retained the flavor of their oral presentation, because the editors did not want to change or unify styles.

It had soon become evident that any effort to draw a more unified or sharper profile of Hermeticism (or Hermetism) in its uniqueness or in its interaction with other philosophies fell short of our expectations. The conclusive definition that would have brought the diverse and largely contradictory elements of the tradition into focus has remained as elusive as ever. A second problem was that while some papers address themselves vigorously to this question, others of equal interest touch on Hermetic problems only in passing or explore issues of the occult in general. These factors guided the editors in their decision to assign a more general subtitle to the collection of papers.

Lest the reader conclude that the conceptual evasiveness of Hermeticism is endemic to the system and clearly betrays its fallacy, the editors wish to assert that scholarly interest in the subject is not declining and that it does not show any slackening in rigor. Indeed, the fact that Hermeticism reflected so many aspects of other philosophies and adapted them to its own mold may prove to be its saving grace in the end. Even if Yates's claims regarding the positivistic impact of Rosicrucian alchemy on the genesis of modern science have now been questioned by some of her most ardent admirers, there are few who would now dispute that, taken in context, the Rosicrucian tracts were of great concern to seventeenth-century scientists and physicians representing many schools of thought. Or if Newton's fascination with traditional transmutative alchemy and his interest in theological speculation remain an embarrassment to many scientists and historians of science who would prefer to emphasize the "real" achievements to be found in the *Principia mathematica,* they must now admit—if reluctantly—that the study of Hermeticism in the sixteenth and seventeenth centuries will lead them to a fuller understanding of their hero.

It is the richness and the critical acumen of the documentation rather than a matter of conclusiveness that led the editors to believe that the collected papers would be of value for many concerned with this aspect of the Renaissance. Most papers concentrate either on trends or details of the tradition, but all probe into the chiaroscuro of early modern thought of which Hermeticism is one colorful strand.

The bulk of the papers, as mentioned before, are grouped into three major sections: background of the Renaissance; magic, philosophy, and science; and art and literature. The introductory part of the book highlights the early stages of Hermeticism in Hellenistic Alexandria, junction of Greco-Roman, Egyptian, and Jewish thought (John Scarborough). The studies once again confirm the great diversity and richness in religiophilosophical as well as in astrological, alchemical, and magic sources. The *Corpus Hermeticum,* of course, remains as fragmented as ever, and its eighteen *libelli* still have not found their historical author or authors. The abundant and certainly incongruent Hermetic elements nevertheless seem to have interacted easily and frequently, at least in a popular circumstance, for the use by religious circles or schools or to the advantage of individual practitioners of magico-science. As denigrated as this amalgam of religion, science, and magic has been by scholars, it is most symptomatic of the spirit of late antiquity, whose waning it survived by its own strength to pass into the Middle Ages and into the Renaissance. In any event, the history of Hermetic thought emerges as much more complex and much richer than had been recognized before (William Grese). Judeo-Hellenic philosophy, in particular, might have been an important factor for the conception of the Hermetica (Moshe Idel). *Asclepius,* one of the prominent and more controversial texts of the corpus, shows great affinity to the *Books of Enoch* of Jewish tradition, a fact that would have facilitated its transmission and proliferation by Judeo-Arabic philosophers in medieval times and in the Renaissance when pagan thought merged with cabalistic speculation and the Christian tradition to form the *prisca theologia* of Renaissance Hermeticism.

Manifestations of Hermetic mysticism and magic in various areas of human interest from the time of Ficino's translations of *Poimandres* and *Asclepius* through the demise of the pristine theology to an afterglow of Hermeticism in the eighteenth century form the main arguments of the book. Premonitions of what, in the eighteenth century, was to become an issue of reason over faith emerged in the sixteenth century as an argument between the confessions—namely, the role of miracles in the proof of divine revelation (D. P. Walker). While this battle was won by Protestant rationalism, the basic struggle was replayed in the controversy surrounding the notions of magia and magus, or the theory and practice of magic by Renaissance Hermeticists. *Asclepius* is vigorously refuted in the first paper of the second part of this volume as the single source for *De vita coelitus comparanda* by Ficino and subsequently for Agrippa's *De occulta philosophia* (Brian Copenhaver). Claim is made instead that Ficino drew on *De sacrificiis* by Proclus and that the Hermetic text, therefore, exerted less influence on the formation of the concept of magia.

This corrective view of the importance of one Hermeticum is followed by two examinations of witchcraft, one of which treats its specific relation to Hermeticism. In medieval times, witchcraft had drawn on popular Hermetic—for the most part, spurious—texts. In the Renaissance, however, witchcraft became erudite (Paola Zambelli). The almost contemporary publication of the *Malleus Maleficarum* and the *Corpus Hermeticum* are significant in this context. Renaissance Hermeticists insisted shrewdly and with good reason on the difference between *magia naturalis* and all other magical practice. This distinction between black and white magic, good and bad witches, proved most beneficial to the many scientific heretics, astrologers, and wise men who only rarely figured as objects of witch-hunts, which were advocated by learned demonologists like the English Puritan theologian William Perkins. Men like Perkins failed in spite of their lucid expositions on the subject. The chief victims of the witch-craze were persecuted rather for social maladjustment or eccentricities than for actually proven devil worship (Leland Estes).

One of the believers in and a possible practitioner of the art, Giordano Bruno, suggests some of the obvious ambiguities of the magus-scientist. Before, scholars believed that his interest in Lullian mnemonics had been an adolescent, ludicrous, and foolish preoccupation. Now it seems that it was in Paris that he embraced Lullism as well as Copernicanism (Edward Gosselin). In fact, both tendencies might have been linked with religious reformism, even reunionism. He might well have been sent to England as an agent of Henry III on a mission to introduce there the "supper disguised." Furthermore, Bruno might have seen himself "on mission" in 1591 in Italy, proposing to cure "troubles in religion" through mystical Lullism and the teachings of Copernicus.

It is this extraordinary mixture of speculative, scientific, and religious fervor that puzzles the modern observer of the magi. The most distinguished and certainly the most influential early modern scientist exposes the same complex features. Isaac Newton's study of alchemy and his lifelong interest in the occult has become a subject of much recent scholarship (B. J. T. Dobbs). His commentary on the *Emerald Tablet,* that most obtuse of Hermetic documents, confirms Newton's preoccupation with the theory of matter. He looked for answers to his questions, such as concerned the divine activating spirit of matter, in this sacred and much heralded treasure of Hermeticism. From the circle of Newtonians and the fringes of their new mathematics, committed to millenary reform, came the extraordinary Dr. Cheyne, who proved to be an important purveyor of Hermetic mysticism in the early eighteenth century (G. S. Rousseau).

Alchemy and chemical medicine also showed an impressive strength well into that century. Numerous arguments for and against alchemy and Paracelsian medicine were made by scientists who worked both within the academic establishment and outside of it. The history of these disciplines is much more stratified than if viewed exclusively from the angle of "progressive" science (Allen Debus). Some recent developments suggest that the relation of science and magic might be undergoing a reevaluation. In a qualitative sense (that is, when judged by its own presumptions), magic might not at all be regressive, but progressive.

Hermetic manifestos such as the *Fama fraternitatis* or the *Confessio fraternitatis* proclaim the Rosicrucian dream of a perfectible science in the service of mankind (Karin Johannisson). That dream became a concrete program and helped the institutionalization of science in the seventeenth and eighteenth centuries. The Royal Academy fostered not only an official science but also encouraged widespread magico-scientific activities. Freemasonic societies practiced and supported enterprises that were also deeply attached to the idea of a radical transformation of society. The chief notions of institutionalized science—collective enterprise, transnational communication, and commitment to an utilitarian purpose—were shared, if not instigated, by the magic tradition of the seventeenth and eighteenth centuries.

From these revisions of historiography, Hermeticism emerges as a prescientific system with an undisputed affinity to our science, although some still consider this affinity disreputable. But whatever troubles the relation of magic and science also encumbers the historiography of art, literature, and philosophy. In spite of the attention given to science, Hermeticism is most pervasive and most elusive in literature and in the arts. One of the chief arguments in the third part of this volume concerns the ambiguity of Hermetic representations, or their lack of precise, unequivocal linguistic and iconographical formulations. The thrust of the first argument, therefore, is directed toward a critique of the epistemology of the occult, particularly of the use of analogy (Brian Vickers). Stress is put on the hierarchical, a priori system of correspondences that are based on identity, as opposed to the open system of similarity/dissimilarity used in the genuine literary metaphor or in the progressive sciences.

Similar criticism is applied subsequently to the method of defining influences of Hermeticism in actual works of literature (Wayne Shumaker). Examples from Milton and Shakespeare demonstrate the ambivalence of interpretations in the Hermetic vein. This ambiguity and the constraints imposed by the use of Hermetic allegory are confirmed by a confrontation of Jakob Böhme's open and dynamic concept of reality with his mystical linguistics. *Aurora,* in particular, demonstrates the struggle within the confines of the closed system of occult analogy, a conflict that Böhme resolved via a millenary theory of signatures that he adopted from

Paracelsus (Ingrid Merkel). His "Rosicrucian linguistics" contributed largely to heterodox linguistic speculation among Puritans and alchemists in mid-seventeenth-century England. Their view of words was at odds with the conventional, Aristotelian view of language and nature held by the experimental scientists of that day. In this controversy of two rival views of language and reality, modern scientific notions of language and probability disengaged themselves from the "obscurantist" signaturism of the Rosicrucians (Hugh Ormsby-Lennon).

The abundance of materials in architecture and sculpture, in painting and book illumination also need to be examined with discrimination. One paper on art takes issue with the tendency to overrate the influence of Hermeticism in the hieroglyphic iconography of the Renaissance. It suggests that Renaissance interest in hieroglyphs was predominantly humanistic and linguistic. A Hermetic fascination with hieroglyphs gained the upper hand only in the later seventeenth and eighteenth centuries (Charles Dempsey). In the early eighteenth century, pictorial Hermeticism affiliated itself with Rosicrucian social and political ideology. In the service of these ideas it survived well into the nineteenth century, particularly in connection with Freemasonic humanism. Frescoes in a Palladian villa at Piombino near Venice were commissioned by the Venetian nobleman Andrea Cirnaro and were executed in 1716 by Mattia Bortoloni (Douglas Lewis). They constitute a curiosity inasmuch as Freemasonic activities were documented heretofore in Italy only after 1731. This cycle of rare artistic quality, furthermore, was ordered by a high-ranking member of the ultraconservative Venetian Republic.

Discussion of the influence of Hermeticism on architectural design and theory of the Renaissance typically has focused on esoteric and occult elements, such as statues of the planets or of the four humors. An example of a larger mode of Hermetic thought is the reconstruction by Juan Bautista Villalpando, a Spanish Jesuit, of the temple described in Ezekiel's vision (Robert Jan van Pelt). That reconstruction—in *Ezechielem explanationes*—offered a new theory of the orders as well as a theory of harmonic proportions in accordance with musical consonances. Villalpando's temple does not resemble a sanctuary but rather presents the image of an ideal city. This conception coincides with the Hermetic notion of spiritualized matter and with man's deification through the image of the magical city Adocentyn, which was founded by Hermes Trismegistus, according to *Asclepius*. In Villalpando's explanations, the temple of God has developed into the palace of man and into the city of the future.

The concluding paper of this volume traces some of the legacies of Hermes Trismegistus in the centuries following the waning of the Renaissance. Emphasis, however, is given to the survival of Hermeticism in the twentieth century. A variety of beliefs, and the recovery of alchemy in the psychology of Carl Gustav Jung, indicate that Hermeticism did survive in new forms (Antoine Faivre).

The richness of the documentation on magical and Hermetic phenomena certainly justify a sustained interest in these arcana. However they may be related to our science and art and to the rise of the modern world, they have remained a challenge to contemporary thought. Ambiguities notwithstanding, the work of Frances Yates, particularly in the areas of an overlap in art and politics, or literature and philosophy, has stimulated research that might lead to a more comprehensive understanding of a lost mentality that is much needed for us to make sense of the world in which we live. It is out of respect for her contribution to the search for meaning, and in anticipation of future recoveries, that the editors dedicate this volume to her memory.

Note

1. Frances Yates, *Giordano Bruno and the Hermetic Tradition* (Chicago, 1964). See also, *The Art of Memory* (London, 1966); *Theatre of the World* (Chicago, 1969); *The Rosicrucian Enlightenment* (London, 1972); *The Occult Philosophy in the Elizabethan Age* (London, 1979).

Hermeticism
and the
Renaissance

PART 1
Background to the Renaissance

1

Hermetic and Related Texts in Classical Antiquity

JOHN SCARBOROUGH

The priesthood has been testing the novitiate for several days. As the son of a king, it might be thought that the Prince was worthy to be a member of the select on his name alone, but he, too, has to undergo strenuous and serious probing of his character. Exposed to magic, the Prince does not flinch, keeping mind and eye on his goal of purity. The Grand Master of the Mysteries of Isis assembles his fellows to consider the Prince's cool valor, pure heart, and request to enter the sacred precinct, and intones:

Ihr, in dem Weisheitstempel eingeweihten Diener der grossen Götter Osiris und Isis! Mit reiner Seele erklär' ich euch,daß unsere heutige Versammlung eine der wichtigsten unserer Zeit ist.- Tamino, ein Köngissohn . . .	Ye servants of the Great Gods Osiris and Isis, consecrated in the Temple of Wisdom, I declare to you that our gathering today is of the greatest importance. Tamino, son of a king . . .

(Wolfgang Amadeus Mozart [German lyrics by
Emanuel Schikaneder], *Die Zauberflöte,* Zweiter Akt:im Palmenwald)

Opera aficionados will immediately have recognized the words and generalized plot from Mozart's *Magic Flute,* but the same fans of the gorgeous music may not have noticed the peculiar mixture of the fantastic, the intellectual, and the evil somberness that adds to the exotic dreaminess and power of the opera. As Grand Master of the Mysteries of Isis, Sarastro must continually wage a battle of wits and emotions against the Queen of the Night. Her daughter, Pamina, is torn between loyalties: The Queen of the Night has destined Prince Tamino for Pamina, but the evil mother demands that Pamina murder Sarastro and bring back a powerful symbol of the sun—a "mächtigen Sonnenkreis"—worn by Sarastro. Good eventually prevails, and the music is unforgettable.

Isis and Osiris in a German opera of 1791?

The Renaissance Look Back: Recovery of Ancient Hermeticism

The pseudo-Egyptian trappings of *The Magic Flute* are part of a constant fascination for things Egyptian in western Europe since the Renaissance. *The Magic Flute* simply paraded contemporary Freemasonry with its pretended antiquity, in keeping with what "everybody knew": Ancient wisdom could ultimately be traced back to the Egyptians, a pervasive assumption strongly reinforced by many intellectuals continuing the search for an archetypal religion and science, hidden but promising true renewal when discovered and understood. Once magic had emerged from the depths of a medieval necromancy and risen to a vaunted respectability, equipped with classical philology, philosophy, exegesis, and an aesthetic balance, it took on the role of a desired path through which Renaissance savants could rediscover the very ancient sources of pre-Christian knowledge. And although there were scholars who pondered Greek and Roman magical, astrologic, and quasi-Egyptian texts before the fifteenth century, a major focus for such studies was the Platonic Academy at Florence and its two principle students of ancient magic and Hermeticism, Marsilio Ficino (1433–99) and Giovanni Pico della Mirandola (1463–94). The search was not new: Egyptian Gnostics had in their day also sought to incorporate Platonism and a Roman Neoplatonism into a Christian doxography, but the Renaissance found that Aristotle, the medieval Scholastics, and ancient Jewish, Arabic, Indian, and Persian sources could also be marshaled to the defense of a Christian mysticism. The rediscovery of purported ancient Egyptian wisdom in Greek, in the form of revelations by Hermes Trismegistus, an ancient sage easily predating the earliest Greek philosophers and at least contemporary with the earliest Jewish traditions, only added impetus. Combined with the cabala, an ancient Jewish fount of mystical Gnosticism and magical interpretations, this new Hermeticism gleamed brilliantly for a time as one of Renaissance scholarship's most dazzling rediscoveries, a rediscovery that displayed a patina far older than Greco-Roman sources. Ficino and Pico became major players on this stage of reviving the Old Wisdom, and it is due to the careful modern scholarship of Frances Yates, as well as D. P. Walker, that one is now able better to comprehend the intellectual gymnastics of the Florentine Platonic academicians, seeking to put this new Hermeticism into the mainstream of western European thought.[1]

Ficino's magic, which he claimed was absolutely rational, found good religious foundations in his Latin translation of the Greek texts of Hermes Trismegistus, which had become part of Ficino's personal collection in about 1463. The Neoplatonism of the Greek revelations especially appealed to Ficino; coupling it with the appearance of a creation story in the texts, he could launch a search for support of a gentile genealogy of prophecy connecting Hermes to the Old Testament Prophets, then to Orpheus (the link with the Greeks), and finally to Pythagoras and Plato. Plato could then become *the* Christian philosopher.[2] As Yates has shown, Hermes Trismegistus was known in late Roman antiquity, long before Ficino "restored" him to an honored place among classical sources. Many magical and alchemical tracts in Greek allude to Hermes, and a complete Hermetic work existed in Latin by the ninth century, although its author was thought to be Apuleius.[3]

Pico added the parallels of Jewish magic and Gnosticism, known from the cabala, to Ficino's Hermeticism. Pico believed that the cabala was a secret revelation by God to Moses on Mount Sinai, given orally only to leaders of the migration out of Egypt.[4] Yates details this curious admixture of Hebrew magic and mysticism, Christian magic, assumptions of magical effects from Hebrew letters, and even a farfetched deduction that Christ's divinity could be seen in the cabala's functions on divine names. The Christian Scriptures were indeed magic in their own right.[5] Pico's Hebrew-Christian magic made Church authorities uneasy, and they harassed Pico when he attempted to present his thesis of Christian and Jewish magic in Rome in 1486.[6] But it was Giordano Bruno (1548–1600) who expressed the most influential doctrine of the Renaissance looking back to Hermeticism for a firm renewal of true ancient knowledge.[7] Ficino had taught that the Hermetic texts had forecast the coming of Christianity, but Bruno simply accepted the pseudo-Egyptian religion of the Hermetics as the true religion, discarding Ficino's idea of Hermes Trismegistus as a gentile prophet. Bruno saw signs of a return of this true religion all around him; an important aspect was Copernicus's heliocentric theory, itself quoting Hermes Trismegistus on the sun as a visible god (from the Hermetic *Asclepius*). When Bruno defended Copernicus against the Aristotelians at Oxford, he said that Copernicus was just a mathematician who had not understood the true meaning of heliocentrism. Bruno asserted that Copernicus's theory portended a return to magical insight into a living nature, a magical animism. Sooner or later, the Church would take notice, even though Bruno firmly believed his new religion could be encompassed within a Catholic framework. Tricked into returning to Venice in 1592, Bruno was burned at the stake as a dangerous heretic on the Campo de' Fiori in Rome, 17 February 1600.

The Hermetic Texts: Context, Content, and History

Although many classical scholars tend to denigrate the Greek, Latin, and Coptic texts that have come down to this century under the rubric of "Hermetic" or "magical" works, it is quite clear that many tracts formed an important portion of a large circulating literature in the Roman Empire, a literature that proclaimed its venerable origins and secret or semisecret subjects. Most often cited as Hermetic texts are those which are thought to be religious or philosophic in nature, with other Hermetic works which address astrology, magic, stone lore, alchemy, and similar topics simply relegated to "the masses of rubbish."[8] That Scott and similar scholars have missed the full value of the range of Greco-Roman Hermetic tracts is signaled by a summary of Hermetic goals, preserved by Stobaeus (early fifth century A.D.) in an anthology of extracts, now classed as Fragment 23 in the standard Greek text of the *Corpus Hermeticum*.[9] The anonymous writer, quoted by Stobaeus, at one point says, "Men pull up the roots of plants and they determine the properties of their juices. They examine the natures of stones and they cut open those animals lacking the power of reason."[10] Hermetics were intrigued by the total range of human curiosity, indicated by the frequent references to astrological lore,[11] magic that has many affinities to the texts called the

Papyri Graecae Magicae, alchemy, medical astrology, and similar topics. In spite of a modern tendency to separate the scientific materials from what one might call the occult, classical antiquity did not have the rigid boundaries between aspects of knowledge which have become characteristic of the sciences and humanities in the West since the nineteenth century, and one should not be surprised to find Galen of Pergamon (A.D. 129–after 210) citing (through Pamphilus) a tract on medical botany by Hermes Trismegistus which was well known in the first century.[12] Pamphilus had prepared a glossary of plant nomenclature,[13] especially to the listings in Dioscorides' *Materia Medica* of the mid-first century, so that Pamphilus—as noted by Galen—had used one of a number of "Egyptian books" by Hermes, extant in the first century.

The interrelationships among the Greco-Roman magical works and the Hermetic tracts is not unintentional.[14] Magic is one of the oldest of human assumptions and has close affinities to what later becomes science. There is an understanding of a natural (or unnatural) order that pervades the universe, so that man is continually on a quest to divine the secrets of that organization, revealed openly— as in astrology's assertions of the links between the stars and the fate of man—or through solutions to the constant puzzles surrounding man in his physical setting. Moreover, magic claimed a venerated heritage—"sacred writings" would have, by definition, an authorship which was semidivine, and as interpreted by Roman imperial times, a certain knowledge which could be comprehended only by those who knew the codes. It is quite ordinary that the Hermetic tracts should be intermingled with the codes of alchemy, astrology, magic in its myriad forms, as well as the presumably more legitimate pursuits of philosophy and religion.

Pamphilus in Galen records one of the earliest citations of a literature by Hermes "the Egyptian," but there are numerous other mentions of this body of writing in pagan antiquity that show its wide dispersion. The Egyptian god Thoth (or Tehuti) was by the fifth century B.C. identified in Greek, as Thōuth, Thōth, or Tat, and associated with the Greek Hermes.[15] The epithet "Three-Times-Great"[16] is probably derived from the Egyptian *aā aā,* "the Great Great," which gives the usual citation in English as Hermes Trismegistus. A firmly identified theological literature by Hermes Trismegistus was known to Tertullian in the second century, and his reference in *De anima* (33.2) may, in turn, derive from the physician, Soranus of Ephesus (fl. A.D. 98–117).[17] Athenagoras (fl. A.D. 138–161 in Alexandria) writes that "Hermes who is called Trismegistus link[s] [his] own family with the gods. . . ,"[18] and that he was regarded as a god because he had been a king. Athenagoras's aside has close similarity to the citations of the Egyptian king, Nechepso,[19] and his advisor, the prophet Petosiris, which turn up in Galen, Vettius Valens, and other technical Greek texts of the second century.[20] If Reitzenstein's deductions on the Ptolemaic origins of such a Hermetic astrology are correct, one may then connect the semilegendary astrology of Nechepso with the extant Hermetic book called the *Poimandres.*[21]

Ammianus Marcellinus lists Hermes Trismegistus among the great sages of the past,[22] along with Pythagoras, Socrates, Numa Pompilius, Apollonius of Tyana, and Plotinus, all of whom had supposedly written on astrology, elements of the soul, and the divinities of destiny.[23] Zosimus the alchemist (fourth century?)[24]

seems to know something of the mystic hymn of Hermes Trismegistus,[25] but even with the good summary of the "books" by Hermes Trismegistus in the *Stromata* (6.4) of Clement of Alexandria (ca. A.D. 150–200) and the *De mysteriis* (1.1 and 8.1–4) by the Neoplatonist Iamblichus (fl ca. A.D. 315), there is grave confusion by the fourth century concerning separate topics. Clement says that forty-two books by Hermes are said to be essential: ten considered law, the gods, and the training of priesthoods, and were termed hieratic; ten recounted the rituals of worship in Egyptian religion; two were hymns to the gods and precepts to be followed by the king; six books were medical, containing descriptions of the structures of the human body, accounts of diseases, some surgical and related instruments, remedies and drugs for ophthalmological ailments, and an account of women; four books were about astrology and astronomy; and the final ten books recounted cosmography, geography, priestly garments, and objects necessary for the correct administration of the sacred rites and rituals. But it is Iamblichus who tells that, even though many works passed under the name of Hermes Trismegistus, most were not written by him, but were simply circulated under that name (*De mysteriis* 8.4). Iamblichus had previously written (*De mysteriis* 1.1) that earlier generations had "inscribed" their works with the name of Hermes, one assumes for the purpose of gaining a respectful readership.

One gains only a vague notion of an ancient textual history of the Hermetic works, which presumably stemmed from records on stone, inscribed by a "first" Hermes. These tablets escaped the destruction of the Flood, according to Syncellus (d. A.D. 826), and then the "second" Hermes (namely, Hermes Trismegistus) put down this collected wisdom on scrolls.[26] Syncellus has recorded a tradition that the works of Hermes Trismegistus were translated from the hieroglyphic into Greek by Manetho during the reign of Ptolemy II Philadelphus (283–45 B.C.). Scott, however, points out not only the corruption of the Greek text of Syncellus, but also the parallel legend recorded by Flavius Josephus, *Jewish Antiquities* 1.71: Ancient wisdom was set down on tablets of clay and stone—the clay to survive the coming devastation of the world by fire, the stone to escape destruction by a future deluge.[27] According to Josephus, the inscriptions were engraved by the family of Seth, son of Adam. To be sure, Seth and Enoch were occasionally identified or confused in the tradition with Hermes and Agathodaemon,[28] but such cross-identifications generally emerge from later testimonia, particularly those in Arabic.[29] Any attempt to recover a "real" Hermes must be dismissed, even though Pseudo-Manetho says that Ptolemaic Egypt had concocted a reasonable pedigree for the extant texts under the name.

Even though there are some instances of correspondence among the extracts of Stobaeus, Psellus, and other Byzantine compilers,[30] the manuscripts which have survived of the *Corpus Hermeticum* emerge from separate traditions than those which seem to have been known in Roman and Byzantine antiquity.[31] The earliest witnesses among the manuscripts are of the fourteenth century (Cod. Laurentianus 71.33 with *Corpus Hermeticum* 1–14, and Vaticanus Graecus 237 with *Corpus Hermeticum* 1–18), Parisinus Graecus 1220 (*Corpus Hermeticum* 1–18) emerging probably in the context of the fourteenth century.[32] A majority of the twenty-eight manuscripts of the Greek texts of the *Corpus* are of the fifteenth and sixteenth centuries, and although the readings can be improved through collations, many passages remain speculative since a number of books have suffered mutilation. The texts, therefore, are generally of a late date, supplemented only on occasion by papyrological fragments.[33] One is forced to conclude, as did Reitzenstein before Nock and Festugière, that these Hermetic texts may be subject to widespread corruption and interpolation by scribes of the High Middle Ages and early Renaissance, and that what one studies as the Hermetic corpus may preserve only parts of an "authentic" ancient tradition. Nonetheless, the careful explication of Reitzenstein, Scott, Ferguson, Nock, Festugière, and other modern scholars has allowed a recovery of the ancient Hermetic writings, a recovery somewhat different than that experienced in the Renaissance. Currently standard Greek and Latin texts of ancient Hermeticism suggest a lively activity in Hellenistic, Roman, and early Byzantine times in the debate about religiophilosophic traditions and related facets of human knowledge, including astrology, alchemy, medical botany, and stone lore.

Much as one first discovers philosophy before medicine as a base in Greco-Roman medical practice,[34] so also the cautious modern observer of the Hermetic tracts meets philosophy before other approaches to knowledge, albeit in a vague manner, generally reflective of the Neoplatonism of the Roman Empire. Continually hovering in the background seems to be Plato's *Timaeus,* but open quotations and allusions to known Platonic works are relatively rare, so that one cannot assume a linear descent of the Hermetic treatises from Plato. Likewise, no other ancient philosopher can be claimed as the originator of the Hermetic works, but there does appear a carefully presented linear descent, mapped clearly in the ancient traditions: If so-and-so espoused a doctrine, he *must* have gained it from a teacher, who in turn gained it from *his* teacher, and so on as far back as the traditions would permit. It was the habit of Greco-Roman compilers of philosophic doctrines (Diogenes Laertius in the third century, for example) to assume a heritage of some sort from the great names of the classical past. Plato and Pythagoras figure prominently, so that one could assume that Plato's notions of the soul somehow went back to Pythagoras, even though Pythagoras left nothing in writing. But where—given this basic premise of teachers and their pupils—did Pythagoras receive his ideas? Traditions spoke of Pythagoras's time in Egypt, and the answer was found in that venerable land of ancient wisdom, badly perceived by resident Greeks after the beginning of the Ptolemaic era (ca. 301–30 B.C.). It had long been accepted as a historical fact that both Plato and Pythagoras had studied in Egypt, and they surely had studied in the establishments of the Egyptian priesthoods. Only the Egyptian priests knew what Plato and Pythagoras might have learned, and the priests insured secrecy by their arcane manner of recording data in the hieroglyphic. When Manetho is credited with translating the writings of Hermes Trismegistus into Greek sometime during the reign of Ptolemy II Philadelphus, the continuation of a teacher-to-pupil linkage was assured, since *a* Hermes (probably number two in the traditions) obviously had taught the Greek visitors—or at least Greeks had received a version of the ancient Egyptian wisdom through the resident priesthoods. Moreover, once the name Hermes had been attached to this body of literature, now in Greek, it had the stamp of absolutely firm authority. The wisdom was semidivine, and no mere mortal could hope to compete with such holy works.

The nature of these Hermetic texts can be well illustrated by considering two separate tracts: the Latin *Asclepius* and the Greek text called the *Poimandres*. In the *Asclepius*,[35] the Greek god of medicine is the student of Hermes, and one reads in the prologue the words of Hermes Trismegistus that

> It is God that has brought you to me, Asclepius, to hear a teaching which comes from God. My discourse will be of such a nature, that by reason of its pious fervour it will be rightly deemed that there is in it more of God's working than in all I have spoken before—or rather that God's power has inspired me to speak. And if you understand my words, and thereby come to see God, your mind will be filled with all things good,—if indeed there are many goods, and not rather one Good, in which all goods are comprised . . .[36]

Asclepius is bidden to fetch Tat (Thoth), and Asclepius suggests that Ammon also be included for the forthcoming instruction,[37] but Hermes says that only Ammon may be added to the divine company of himself, Tat, and Asclepius, "but summon no one else, lest a discourse which treats of the loftiest of themes, and breathes the deepest reverence, should be profaned by the entrance and presence of a throng of listeners."[38] Such knowledge is not for the masses, probably contrasted to an emerging Christianity, which the author of *Asclepius* (3.24–25) says will bring the destruction of Egypt and the abolition of piety.[39] In fact, the *Asclepius* contains a most ringing assertion of Egypt as the finest land on earth, and the fountain of all knowledge:

> Do you not know, Asclepius, that Egypt is an image of heaven, or to speak more exactly, in Egypt all the operations of the powers which rule and work in heaven have been transferred to earth below? Nay, it should rather be said that the whole Kosmos dwells in this our land as in its sanctuary.[40]

The lessons in the Hermetic *Asclepius* are what one might expect as a vague summary of pagan religion and philosophy, perhaps as taught in the fourth century: the immortality of the soul; the doctrine of elements; the origin of forms and matter, and ". . . though all kinds are immortal, not all individuals are immortal";[41] man as a reflection of God, with the attributes of God; the nourishment of the soul; the concept of mind and intelligence; God as perceivable and imperceptible; man and his recognition of divinity; man's ranking (third) behind God and the Cosmos; the fit subjects of study, expressed in the following manner:

> Philosophy is nothing else than striving through constant contemplation and saintly piety to attain the knowledge of God; but there will be many who will make philosophy hard to understand, and corrupt it with manifold speculations . . . by a cunning sort of study, in which philosophy will be mixed with diverse and unintelligible sciences, such as arithmetic, music and geometry . . . the student of philosophy undefiled . . . ought to direct his attention to the other sciences only so far as he may learn to see and marvel how the returns of the heavenly bodies to their former places, their halts in pre-ordained positions, and

the variations of their movements, are true to the reckonings of number; only so far as, learning the measurements of the earth, the depth of the sea, [the . . . of air], the force of fire, and the properties, magnitudes, workings, and natures of all material things, he may be led to revere, adore, and praise God's skill and wisdom. And to know the science of music is nothing else than this—to know how all things are ordered, and how God's design has assigned to each its place.[42]

There are touches of Plato, Aristotle, the Stoics, Neoplatonists, and other brands of philosophy that characterize this mélange, much as one notes more openly Plato, the Stoics, an idealized Hippocrates, and Aristotle in the writings of Galen—for instance, *On the Usefulness of the Parts*,[43] and *On the Doctrines of Hippocrates and Plato*.[44] The unknown writer's venom against arithmetic (here is probably meant the "theory of number") may have its opposite represented by the open embrace given to Greek arithmetic by later Christian authors including Boethius,[45] and the antipathy toward music may reflect the increasingly sterile works on musical theory exemplified by the third-century *On Music* composed by Aristides Quintilianus.[46] One wonders what could qualify the learning of the *Asclepius* as particularly special, except for its Egyptian and divine pedigree.

Both Scott and Nock and Festugière print the Greek text and provide translations of a Hermetic work called the *Poimandres*.[47] Most specialist scholars have agreed that this tract is one of the more sophisticated of the Hermetic treatises, and it has received much attention in attempts to connect it with other writings of the late Roman Empire, Christian and non-Christian.[48] As the apparatus criticus in the Nock-Festugière edition indicates, there are a number of parallel texts and testimonia which show a fairly wide knowledge of the *Poimandres* in the Roman Empire, and this work suggests the basic nature of the "revelations" of Hermes Trismegistus as they were understood in late antiquity. *Poimandres* begins as a story should, with "Once upon a time, when I was beginning to think about the things as they are, and my thoughts were floating into a very high plane,"[49] followed by what can only be described as a vision. The writer "explains" that his senses were as if under the influence of sleep, but not a sleep which resulted from exhaustion or an excess of food, a state necessary for obtaining a true knowledge of God, so says the writer of another treatise in the Hermetic corpus.[50]

It seemed to me that there appeared before me a Being of enormous size, who appeared limitless in dimension, and who called me by my name, and said to me, "What do you want to hear and see, and to learn and know through thought?" I said, "Who are you?" "I," he said, "I am Poimandres, the Mind *(nous)* of the Absolute Sovereignty: I know what you want, and I am with you everywhere." I said, "I want to be instructed in the matters of metaphysics *(ta onta),* and to comprehend the nature of existing things and to know God *(gnōnai ton theon)*."[51]

Poimandres agrees to teach. Having demanded the revelation, the visionary is shown various aspects of cosmogony, beginning with a limitless light that descends into a gloom, followed by the creation of water, steaming as if it were smoking, and giving off a sound of deep sorrow, not exactly heard but perceived only by the intellect. Then a vision within the vision appears: light that produces a holy word *(logos hagios)*,[52] active with fire and water, shortly revealed with breaths of air and a sort of swampy earth. Poimandres interprets for the visionary: The light is the Mind, and the word issuing from the light is the son of God. The remainder of the *Poimandres* is a series of visions, interpreted for the dreamer, showing how the light engendered all other matter in the world, including a Second Mind (the Demiurge), stars, animal life, man and woman, and an eschatology of dissolution. Of interest is the parallel in the *Poimandres* (24)[53] to the notion of *thymos* in Plato's *Timaeus* and *Cratylus*.[54]

Comparison with classical dream manuals is instructive. In the *Oneirocritica* of Artemidorus (late second century A.D.), one reads that there is a tendency to inquire after the hidden meanings in dreams—a useless pursuit says Artemidorus, since the gods would not be bothered with the smallish matters of individuals.[55] Yet Artemidorus says that Plutarch (presumably the well-known author of the *Parallel Lives*) had had a dream in which Hermes appeared to conduct Plutarch into the heavens,[56] a forecast of imminent death. If the author of the *Poimandres* represents the mystical in crypto-Hellenic and Egyptian learning, by contrast Artemidorus will have none of the visions or interpretations: He seeks simple meanings, shorn of arcane learning accessible only to a few. Moreover, Artemidorus thought "cosmic" dreams were impossible for someone of no public status: Only a king, a magistrate, or at the very least a member of the nobility could have such visions.[57] But Artemidorus may not be typical, if one considers the dream classifications provided by Macrobius (early fifth century) in the famous *Commentary on the Dream of Scipio* (1.3).[58] There is, indeed, a place for the apparition (in Greek, *phantasma*) *hoc est visum*,[59] which

comes upon one in the moment between wakefulness and slumber, in the so-called "first cloud of sleep." In this drowsy condition [the dreamer] thinks he is still fully awake and imagines he sees specters rushing at him or wandering vaguely about, differing from natural creatures in size and shape, and hosts of diverse things, either delightful or disturbing.[60]

The Hermetics, however, have even more in mind than Artemidorus's "cosmic dream" reserved for kings, or the apparition of Macrobius (or his Stoic source), which consists of imaginations. Hermes Trismegistus showed a true revelation, whereby the person underwent a change in both self-perception and in his view of the corporeal and noncorporeal world.

The Hermetics and Alchemy

Olympiodorus the alchemist (fourth or fifth century?) quotes Zosimus's work *Concerning Physical Property*,[61] in which is found a passage from Hermes Trismegistus speaking of a line by one Achaab the Farmer, who had noted that planting wheat was the origin of wheat. Olympiodorus's quotation of Zosimus continues with Hermes' comments that "matter is colored by matter, as it is written; according to the hue, it is not divided from itself, unless physical and incorporeal: but the skill *(technē)* itself is of both kinds."[62] Alone this peculiar excerpt from a Hermetic tract might not make too much sense were it not for two independent manuscripts, titled *Isis the Prophetess to Her Son Horus,* which incorporate Achaab (the manuscripts are dated to the fifteenth and seventeenth centuries),[63] which in turn link with a Hermetic tradition of addresses of Isis to Horus, documented by Stobaeus.[64] The formal analogy, coupled with a Hermetic axiom, shows that this bit of evidence, buried in Olympiodorus's quotation of Zosimus, is ultimately of Hermetic origin.[65] Achaab the Farmer, however, points to another extract in the alchemical texts, which fuses Hebrew and Greek theories in a matrix clearly Hermetic: the short tract is entitled *True Book of Sophē* [= Cheops] *the Egyptian God, and God of the Hebrews, Lord of the Powers, Sabaōth,*[66] and it combines two methods of making gold, the first "Democritean," and the second "the tincture of Isis, made known by Heron."[67] Heron is probably another name for Horus,[68] so that the *Book of Sophē* is again connected with the Hermetic excerpts of Isis to Horus in Stobaeus.

An unknown Hermetic writer—Festugière thinks of the third century[69]—had drawn up the *Book of Sophē* in response to the conflicting claims of Greek and Hebrew-Egyptian alchemical methods for making gold.[70] By placing both in a Hermetic context, the writer was able simultaneously to show the differences and to smooth them into a composite account of tincture-of-gold techniques, finally incorporated into the alchemical books of Zosimus. As a whole, the Greek alchemical texts have a number of references to Hermes, and there are many clipped quotations from Hermetic alchemy embedded in Zosimus, Olympiodorus, Cleopatra the Jewess, and similarly quasi-bogus authors named in the alchemical traditions from Egypt.[71] Hermetic revelations functioned importantly for the Greco-Egyptian alchemists, and by using the cryptodivine ancestry purportedly given in alchemical books "by" Hermes Trismegistus, these dimly perceived seekers after the philosophers' stone could give their writings a literary patina of respectability. The texts frequently suggest the crucial matrix of Hermetic pronouncements in alchemy,[72] and although the technical matter often outweighs Hermetic interpretations (for example, in the fundamental *Papyrus Holmiensis,* or "Stockholm Papyrus"),[73] the Hermetic approach to alchemy provided a convenient justification for both the methodology and premises of Greco-Egyptian alchemy. By the third century, Gnosticism and several traditions of drug lore and mineralogy had, in their turn, become intertwined with alchemy,[74] so that the welter of authorities with their mutually contradictory claims would eventually receive a further smoothing, best seen in the Arabic reworking of Greco-Egyptian alchemical writings and theories.[75]

Hermetic Medical Astrology and Herbal Pharmacology

The Hermetic medical revelations take on multiple facets, again apparently to reconcile several varying traditions using an underlying presumption of an archetypal basis. Although there are instances of Egyptian medical learning sandwiched in Galen and other medical sources from the Roman Empire,[76] the Hermetic mold of medical thinking is better illustrated by the astrological-pharmacological tract by Thessalus, called *Powers of Herbs.*[77] Until the appearance in print of the several Greek and Latin recensions of *Powers* as edited by Hans-Veit Friedrich in 1968, one depended upon the preface to the work, known as Thessalus's *Letter to Claudius* (or perhaps Nero), initially published in volume 8 of the *Catalogus Codicum Astrologorum Graecorum* (Brussels, 1912).[78] Even in the truncated form of the documents in the *CCAG*, Thessalus's *Letter* demonstrated the intermeshing of medical astrology, magic, and plant lore, but the two texts—one in Greek and one a medieval Latin translation—added to the quandary concerning the date of the Thessalus quoted as author, as well as the date of the Caesar Augustus addressed in the *Letter.* Moreover, the *CCAG* texts following the *Letter* are compactions of three separate, short tracts, two by Thessalus, and a third by someone named Alexander. In the *Letter* itself, Thessalus wishes to tell the emperor about the revelation provided by Asclepius (stemming, of course, from an original revelation from Hermes Trismegistus),[79] and there is great affinity to the supposed writings of Nechepso-Petosiris, which had gained a large reading public in the Julio-Claudian era.[80] Hermes Trismegistus has revealed to Asclepius the herbs that are truly associated with the planets,[81] and the signs of the zodiac.[82] In spite of the challenges to the conclusions by Boudreaux and Cumont in their initial comments on the *Letter* of Thessalus,[84] current opinion has rejected the suggestion that the document should be called ". . . the so-called *Letter* of the astrologer Harpocration to Caesar Augustus."[84] Reitzenstein, in his lucid summary of the text and its implications,[85] had signaled an acceptance of the *Letter* as by Thessalus to either Claudius or Nero (sometime between A.D. 41 and 68), a view followed by Festugière and Friedrich.[86]

In the *CCAG* version of the texts that follow the *Letter* to the emperor, one first reads about the twelve plants associated with the twelve signs of the zodiac,[87] in turn followed by an exposition of seven planets linked with seven plants.[88] The third clipped treatise is not attributed to Thessalus but to an Alexander,[89] and this "work by Alexander" considers the same seven plants as in the preceding tract. Moreover, the *CCAG* texts merely suggest the wealth of Hermetic tracts which consider plants and herbs, and their relationships to the planets, the signs of the zodiac,[90] and the traditional three divisions of ten degrees within a sign of the zodiac (decans), and plants linked with the "fifteen fixed stars."[91] Medical astrology and pharmacology is well represented by Thessalus's *Letter* and by the full text of his *Powers of Herbs*—clearly of Hermetic inspiration and origin—but there are many instances of Roman physicians and scientists who believed that astrology was one of the most important diagnostic tools: Galen's *Crisis Days* (3.5–6)[92] makes the point that astrology aids in pinpointing both diagnosis and prognosis in diseases,[93] and his account is bereft of any of the mysticism that permeates corollary Hermetic works.[94] To Galen, medical astrology is a "science";[95] to the Hermetic writers, herbal and medical astrology were revelations explaining why certain plants have healing powers,[96] a problem that had defied Theophrastus's best efforts as he considered why herbs differed from ordinary plants in the classification scheme of the *Historia Plantarum.*[97] The Hermetic explanation

certainly did not replace the botany of Theophrastus, or the careful assessment of
drug lore assembled by Dioscorides (fl. ca. A.D. 65), or the massive assembly of
pharmaceuticals by Galen which provided a model for Byzantine pharmacy.[98] But
in place of Theophrastus's confusion, Dioscorides' brilliant but inapplicable 'drug
affinity' system,[99] and Galen's basic uncertainty about classifications of drugs, the
Hermetics could claim that their acceptance of divine power was an active way of
receiving it and thereby increase in strength, much as a person instructed by
Poimandres can say he ". . . has been invested with the power and instructed in
the Nature of the Whole and in the Greatest Divinity" *(tou pantos tēn physin kai
tēn megistē thean)*.[100] Herbal astrology by the Hermetics is marked by a
simplicity—a deceptive simplicity from the standpoint of modern pharmacology—
suggested by the following from Thessalus's *Powers of Herbs:*[101]

A Plant of the Sun: Chicory *(chichōrion)*[102]
[1] First named among the plants of the Sun is "heliotrope"; yet there are many
kinds of "heliotropes," and of all these the most efficacious[103] is the one called
chicory. [2] Its juice mixed with oil of roses is an ointment.[104] [3] It is suitable for
relieving heartburns,[105] and it releases tertians,[106] quartans, and intermittant
fevers,[107] and mixed with an equal part of the oil of unripe olives, it stops
headaches. [4] If someone looking toward the east [lit. "sunrise"] smears on the
juice of the chicory, invoking the presence of the [god] Helios, and begs to give
him praise he will be most favored among all men in that day.[108] [5] One prepares
from the chicory's root little pills *(katapotia)* for heartburns and disorders of the
stomach, in which the stomach is afflicted and will not accept foods, and for
disorders of the stomach in which the stomach receives nourishment but does
not promote digestion: downy woundwort,[109] 8 drachmai; saffron crocus,[110] 2
drachmai; Pontic honey, 14 drachmai; mastic flower,[111] 6 drachmai; ginger
[root],[112] 4 drachmai; pepper,[113] 4 drachmai; Dead Sea bitumen/mineral
pitch,[114] 2 drachmai; anise,[115] 4 drachmai; mastic gum/resin,[116] 4 drachmai; the
root of the chicory, 24 drachmai; pound these ingredients in a mortar with very
old mead (honey plus wine: *oinomeli*)[117] and make lozenges of 1 drachma. Drink
one with water for heartburns; drink one with the best wine for stomach
ailments.

There are some parallels with other known recipes and descriptions as found in
Pliny, Columella, Dioscorides, Galen, the *Papyri Graecae Magicae,* and the Byzantine *Geoponica,*[118] but this particular Hermetic use of a chicory stimulant for
digestion seems rather unusual among Roman prescriptions. At first, the botany
seems poor, with the heliotrope including the chicory, but the writer is not saying
that this is *the* heliotrope—he is speaking of a broad class of herbs attracted to the
sun, the literal meaning of the word. And except for the invocation of Helios after
anointing oneself with the juice of the chicory, the recipe is a fairly straightforward
listing of ingredients and preparation method, often encountered in the drug books
of Galen and later Byzantine pharmacy. Moreover, folk medicine still retains the
employment of mastic, anise, and chicory as stomach calmers, traditions backed
to some extent by the physiological chemistry of the herbs. Upon examination, the
Hermetic accounts of astrological herb lore suggest a number of traditions, includ-

ing the technical approach of Dioscorides and Galen, as well as the specifics of drugs and herbs found in the magical papyri. Festugière thinks that the Hermetic writers divided their astrological medicine into classes, according to which plant represented the sun[119]—chicory is Type B, with a special listing of herbs for the moon, Saturn, Jupiter, Mars, Venus, and Mercury.[120]

The inclusion of exotic Eastern substances—the ginger and pepper—suggests that Thessalus's *Powers of Herbs* dates from the first half of the first century. A flourishing drug trade with Far Eastern markets was in full revival,[121] and Dioscorides' *Materia Medica* indicates the fresh incorporation of Indian, Malayan, and some Chinese spices into the Roman pharmacopoeia,[122] as contrasted with their general absence in the drug listings of Theophrastus and Nicander.[123] Diocletian's famous *Price Edict* of A.D. 301 lists ginger,[124] showing that this substance had been valued in Roman pharmacy and the culinary arts for two centuries, and that it commanded high prices once it reached Roman territory.[125] The Hermetic writer is well aware of good ingredients for his drug formula, and there is a sophistication in *Powers of Herbs* that reflects a command of current literature as well as the expected elitism. *Powers of Herbs* (2.1) shows the context not only of a formal pharmacy, but also the magic papyri and certain phrases that were clichés in the koine Greek of the time, mirrored in the Christian New Testament,[126] as well as the complicated lore of medicoastrological stones seen in the Greek texts known as the *Kyranides*.[127]

The Cultural and Literary Context: "Egyptian" Pseudo-Learning in Greek Guise

The historic and cultural context of the Hermetic works helps explain why they should have achieved such popularity, even though they were intended for a pseudoeducated elite. If one recalls that the last hieroglyphic inscription, as known to modern Egyptologists, was engraved on the island of Philae in A.D. 394,[128] and then also remembers that by the end of the fourth century paganism had been officially banned in the Roman Empire, it becomes clear that a command of ancient Egyptian hieroglyphics was a thing of the past by A.D. 400. Hermetic Greek works, proclaiming their authentic Egyptian origins, are not the only remnants of attempts to revive a brand of paganism in the face of an age set for the spiritual revolution represented by Christianity. One may mention the curious *Hieroglyphica* by "Horapollo" probably composed sometime in the fourth century. The author's name is bogus, a typically Greco-Egyptian coinage joining Horus with his Greek equivalent Apollo, but an otherwise unknown Philip announces that he has translated into Greek the hieroglyphic of Horapollo,[129] a patent lie when one sees the interpretations of almost two hundred hieroglyphs (some real, some not) as mere allegories and symbols of ancient wisdom.[130] Philip—whoever he was—knew as little about the Egyptian language as had the unscrupulous tour guides in the Egypt of Herodotus's day.[131] Yet when the text of Horapollo was rediscovered in the early fifteenth century, it caused great excitement among would-be translators of the Egyptian picture writing,[132] and remained the basis of almost all debate and translation of Egyptian until J. F. Champollion published his *Lettre à M. Dacier* in 1822.[133] It seems that late Roman antiquity had its share of blatant pseudolearning and scholarly fraud, comparable to Kirchenhoffer's *Book of Fate*,[134] which appeared in English the same year as Champollion published his *Lettre*, or the nonsense of the likes of von Däniken and Crowley in the twentieth century.[135] Horapollo's supposed hieroglyphics apparently appealed to those desiring an easy path to the ancient wisdom, those who might have been unwilling to wrestle with the difficult premises of Plotinian philosophy,[136] or Hermetic fuzziness, or even the curious paradoxes that made up Christian orthodoxy after the Council of Nicaea in 325. It was the Egyptian setting that provided the appeal, similar to the appeal engendered by Hermetic literature after initial publication in 1471. As Walker and Yates have documented, the Hermetic literature suggested a reformed and learned magic and astrology, contrasted with demonology and black magic, and this "white magic" retained a respectability among scholars and writers for some centuries.[137]

Also surviving from the era of the Hermetics in the Egypt of the Roman Empire is a collection of materials called the *Papyri Magicae Graecae*.[138] Formerly scorned as simply a record of jumbled superstitions with a pseudopatina of Egyptian learning, these papyri have recently been restudied and translated with commentaries by a team of scholars, assembled by the School of Divinity at the University of Chicago.[139] Much as Thorndike had detailed the underpinnings of magic in early science, so also have the *PGM* yielded a trove of insights on how Jew, Christian, and pagan perceived of their world. The papyri show and record hundreds of drugs and spells that indicate how an ordinary person might think of magic and folk medicine, as well as the presence of amulets and magical tokens in everyday life. The following are illustrative:

[A remedy] against a scorpion sting: on a clean papyrus, write [the following] figures, and place it on the part which has the sting, and wrap the papyrus around it, and the sting will lose its pain immediately. The figures:

Make the figures eleven times.[140]
[A remedy] for runny eyes: write

on papyrus, and attach it as an amulet.[141]
Another remedy for coughs: on hyena-hide parchment, write these letters:

hand it around the neck as an amulet and wear it, but keep it from getting wet.[142] A contraceptive, the only one in the world: Take seeds of the bitter vetch (*orobos: Vicia orobus* DC), as many as you can through the years, as you wish for yourself, so that you would remain sterile; steep the seeds in the freshly expelled blood of a menstruating woman. Let the seeds become part of the nature of the menstrual blood. And take a living frog and throw the seeds of the bitter vetch into its mouth, so that the frog swallows them, and let the living frog go free at the place where you captured him. And take the seed of henbane (*hyoskyemos: Hyoscyamus niger* L.), steep it in mare's milk; and take the nasal mucus of a cow with grains of barley, put these into a leather bag made from the hide of a fawn, and on the outside bind it up with a bag of mulehide, and fasten it up during the waning of the moon in a female sign of the zodiac on a day of Cronos of Hermes. Mix also with the barley grains cerumin from the ear of a mule.[143]

At first glance, these Greek texts certainly do exude the odor of total superstition, but close analysis reveals correspondence with both the specifics and language of the Hermetics, Dioscorides, Galen and his sources, and similar authors. There is another "priestly" side to these papyri—an elitism that pervades the Hermetic works as well—but here in the *PGM*,[144] the "revelations" are given as secret codes, perhaps for the instructions of other members of a nameless Egyptian cult:

And we have drawn our revelations from the many copies and all secret writings. Thus:
A snake's head: a leech[145]
A snake's "ball of thread": this means soapstone[146]
Blood of a snake: hematite
A bone of an ibis: this is buckthorn[147]
Blood of a hyrax: truly of a hyrax[148]
"Tears"[149] of a hamadryas baboon:[150] dill juice
Crocodile dung: Ethiopian soil
Blood of a hamadryas baboon: blood of a spotted gecko[151]
Lion semen: human semen
Blood of Hephaestus: wormwood
Hairs of a hamadryas baboon: dill seed
Semen of Hermes: dill
Blood of Ares: purslane
Blood of an eye: tamarisk gall[152]
Blood from a shoulder: bear's breech [or stinking hellebore][153]
From the loins: chamomile[154]
A man's bile: turnip sap[155]
A pig's tail: leopard's bane [or heliotrope][156]
A physician's bone: sandstone
Blood of Hestia: chamomile
An eagle: [?]
Blood of a goose: a mulberry tree's "milk"
Cronos's spice: piglet's milk
A lion's hairs: "tongue" of a turnip[157]
Cronos's blood: . . . of cedar
Semen of Helios: white hellebore
Semen of Heracles: this is mustard rocket[158]
A Titan's blood: wild lettuce[159]
Blood from a head: lupine
A bull's semen: egg of a blister beetle[160]
A hawk's heart:[161] heart of wormwood
Semen of Hephaestus: this is fleabane

Semen of Ammon: houseleek
Semen of Ares: clover
Fat from a head: spurge
From the belly [or bowels]: earth apple [or chamomile]
From a foot: houseleek[162]

These "revelations" are even more opaque than the usual Hermetic ones, and one can observe that the code for special plants is a simple substitution system, perhaps borrowed from the format of similar pharmaceutical substitution lists known from late Roman and Byzantine medicine.[163] While the physicians compiled their substitution lists for the benefit of doctors and their patients who might be unable to procure certain drugs (and thereby be able to consult such a list for effective substitutes), the priestly revelations here in the *PGM* are obviously intended to baffle the uninitiated. One is tempted to see this magical substitution list as something more—perhaps a listing of what hieroglyphics mean in Greek, but the manner of the Greek text and its introduction suggests an intentional writing in Greek with only the compilation of a private code in mind. Again, one is struck by an elitism, also characteristic of the Hermetic revelations. A magical name for a common plant, herb, animal, or medicinal substance certainly would sound better to the uninitiated, so one can conclude that *PGM* 12.409–45 is an example of pseudo-Egyptian learning in Greek.

Added to the magical papyri are a number of phylacteries and gemstones which vividly illustrate the role of magic among the peoples of the Roman Near East,[164] and there are many points of contact between the Hermetic texts and the magical documents, especially in terms of the multiplicity of dieties so common in the religion of very ancient Egypt. This is not pseudolearning; it is rather a kind of updating of older traditions in Greek wrappings, albeit with the loss of many essential Egyptian concepts due to the Greek predilection for logical distinctions. Occasionally there have survived texts from Roman Egypt that may show a true Egyptian medicine or magic, but it is clear that modern understanding of these documents is woefully inadequate, exemplified by the recently published Crocodilopolis medical books, preserved in demotic.[165] The modern editor has forgotten the warnings of Frankfort, Morenz, and most recently Hornung,[166] regarding the dangers of assuming Egyptian analogues for modern religion, medicine, and pharmacology. Fortunately, a new edition of this priceless demotic text—which probably dates from Roman Egypt—has been undertaken by qualified scholars resident at the Oriental Institute of the University of Chicago.

Galen's "Egyptian Sciences": Prognostics and Astrology

Quite popular among medical historians is the vision of Galen as a medical scientist who looked beyond his own century and who thereby provides a good model for modern physicians. When such a view collides with Galen's espousal of medical astrology and Egyptian learning as fundamental for medical practice, such sections as are preserved in Galen's writings are dismissed as interpolations by later—and usually superstitious Christian—copyists.[167] To be sure, one can state that the *Prognostics from Astrology on When the Patient Will Leave His Bed,*[168] contained in the Galenic corpus, is at the very least a pseudo-Galenic tract from Byzantine times (if not the Renaissance), but when a second- or third-century Pseudo-Galen solemnly proclaims his respect (through Homer) for the venerability of Egyptian medicine,[169] one comprehends something of what the best intellects of the Roman Empire believed about the wisdom of old Egypt.[170] In doubtlessly genuine Galenic works, one reads how the polymath physician denied the utility of Pythagorean mystical numbers, noting along the way that the seven mouths of the Nile or the seven stars of the Pleiades have little connection with the seventh day of inflammation in the chest or lungs.[171]

On the other hand, Galen judged magical charms and amulets as having some power, reporting that green jasper helps sooth abdominal pains, but he thinks the prescription of King Nechepso is wrong: One can use the amulet without the engraving of a snake and a wreath of stars.[172] By mentioning that Nechepso had set down his findings in fourteen books, Galen indicates he either has read these tracts, or at the very least is well aware of their influence through a pharmacodox-ographical tradition, perhaps considering medically potent stones. It is, however, in his medical astrology that Galen comes closest to the contemporary Hermetic writings. He states that astrology was one of the greatest achievements of Egyptians astronomers,[173] and he believed that the position of the moon in relation to the good and evil planets had important power over his patients' conditions.[174] Illnesses were especially troublesome if the good stars were in Aries, and the bad stars in Taurus, and the moon in Taurus, Leo, Scorpio, or Aquarius at the birth of the patient; diseases were milder, however, for the patient born when the moon was crossing Aries, Cancer, Libra, or Capricorn.[175] Someone who "refused to observe these things," Galen writes, "or who refused to believe in the observation of others, was doubtlessly a sophist, noisily shouting down the opinions of others, and who proposes reasons for the obvious, and who does not attempt to proceed from understood phenomena to hidden things."[176] From one of the best medical minds of the second century, this is an unequivocal endorsement for medical astrology, fully in agreement with the Hermetics. Similarly, Galen agreed with the Hermetic writers on the dispersal of knowledge, as one can read in the Arabic text of Galen's *On Medical Experience:*

> If, however, you should tell me only of such things as are uttered by a man in the street, you would then say nothing suitable for men of quality . . . but you would only be setting forth the information of the lower and less intelligent class of the inhabitants.[177]

Galen would have rejected the data of the *PGM* on this basis, but would have accepted the coldly logical arguments of medical astrology by the Hermetics, especially since the Hermetic tracts included pharmacology. The sources of Hermetics drug lore and Galen's pharmaceutical data stemmed from the same sources and traditions, and other than the formulaic invocations found in Hermetic medical astrology, there is little to distinguish the methodology of preparation or the knowledge of specific ingredients.

Egyptian Drug Lore in Dioscorides' Materia Medica

Sometime around A.D. 65, Dioscorides of Anazarbus wrote his *Materia Medica,* one of the most influential tracts on drug lore ever composed.[178] In its various versions, this collection of pharmacology, medical botany, stone lore, and drugs made from animal sources remained a fundamental reference until well into the nineteenth century. Many parts of the Arab world still regard Dioscorides as *the* recipe book for drugs, even in this century of sophisticated pharmaceutical chemistry. Part of Dioscorides' medical botanizing included collecting plants and listening to traditional recipes in the Roman Egypt of the mid-first century, and there are again points of contact between Hermetic drug lore and what Dioscorides incorporated in his *Materia Medica.*

In addition to mentioning the Ptolemaic physiologist Erasistratus (fl. ca. 260 B.C.),[179] it appears that Dioscorides knew and reflected the works by Petosiris, if the annotations by Byzantine copyists are correct. In *Materia medica* (5.98),[180] Dioscorides discusses cupric sulfate (blue vitriol, $CuSO_4.5H_2O$; Greek *chalkanthos*);[181] another source named Peteēsios (Petosiris) had given it the name *pinarion.*[182] Normally this would mean mother-of-pearl, but the texts of Petosiris probably indicated the occasional similarity in purplish hues characteristic of both cupric sulfate and mother-of-pearl. The Greek texts of Dioscorides, before Wellmann's primary reediting of the *Materia Medica,* had included the phrase, "Peteēsios calls it pinarion," and it was so translated by Berendes.[183] Wellmann has relegated the reference to Petosiris to part of his apparatus criticus, indicating that he believed this to be a later interpolation or a Byzantine scribe's "commentary" *(scholion)* which had migrated into the body of Dioscorides' Greek after centuries of recopying. One may, however, note the striking parallel as recorded by the Byzantine scholiasts, even if Dioscorides had not quoted Petosiris directly. Although Wellmann has eliminated the phrase from the standard edition, one can also reflect on the strong traditions in the manuscripts that had included it. The Byzantine scribes were correct on one matter regarding *chalkanthos* (Dioscorides) and *pinarion* (Petosiris). Naming the substance moderns call blue vitriol or cupric sulfate was troublesome among Greek mineralologists and pharmacologists, and the Hermetic suggestion of this copper compound's resemblance to mother-of-pearl was intended either to clarify its identity or to provide a secret name for the substance. Dioscorides had encountered the texts under the name of Petosiris, and had rejected *pinarion* in favor of the more common and explicit *chalkanthos.*

Attached to Wellmann's edition to Dioscorides is a series of corollary Greek texts labeled RV, usually cited as "Pseudo-Dioscorides." Dioscorides, in *Materia Medica* (1.26),[184] considers saffron crocus (*Crocus sativa* L.), and Pseudo-Dioscorides has quoted Thessalus on the plant.[185] It is quite possible that Dioscorides had encountered Thessalus's *Powers of Herbs* among the many works circulating in the eastern half of the Roman Empire in the reign of Nero (A.D. 54–68), and the clear association of this Pseudo-Dioscorides with the main text of the *Materia Medica* may show that it is Pamphilus who has quoted Thessalus, and that the synonymn lists for plants in Dioscorides by Pamphilus contained extracts from Thessalus. Pamphilus has been mentioned above,[186] in connection with Hermetic tracts as recorded by Galen, but it is of interest to note that Pamphilus became rich as a physician in Rome,[187] even as he compiled an alphabetical listing of plants,[188] providing alternative nomenclatures as frequently set down in the Wellmann Greek text of Dioscorides as RV. Galen does not rate Pamphilus's abilities very highly as an herbal botanist, accusing him of describing plants he had never seen and of inserting superstitious botanical nonsense ("Egyptian insanities") into his writings.[189] The *Suda,* a Byzantine encyclopedia of ca. A.D. 1000, says that Pamphilus was a "grammarian of Alexandria,"[190] pointing to an Egyptian matrix for both the Hermetic quotations credited to Pamphilus and the botany so heavily criticized by Galen. Pamphilus probably flourished in Alexandria and Rome in the last decades of the first century,[191] and he provided glosses for 150 Egyptian plant names in the text of Dioscorides' *Materia Medica.*[192] If this welter of attributions and sources for botanical nomenclature delineates anything, it implies not only a quasi-Hermetic origin for an alphabetical rearrangement of Dioscorides' herbs, but also that Dioscorides must have been aware of contemporary Hermetic botanical lore. Much as Galen had accepted some of the current medical astrology that traditionally was assigned to Egyptian learning, Dioscorides had incorporated data from his Egyptian sources,[193] which consequently had been elaborated and reformulated by Pamphilus.

Hermetic science generally delineated an approach in conflict with the medical theories inherited by Galen and the painstaking and detailed pharmacology represented in Dioscorides' *Materia Medica.* Even though Galen was willing to accept the diagnostic premises of medical astrology, he had little but scorn for the mysticism in the works of Pamphilus, and the parallel traditions of Hermetic botany were rejected by Dioscorides in his original, nonalphabetical text, suggesting a similar assessment of Hermetic drug lore as understood in the Roman Egypt of the mid-first century. While Hippocratic medicine, coupled with certain aspects of an earlier philosophic tradition, had formulated notions of disease explained through nature itself and man's interpretations through nature's elements, qualities, and humors, the Hermetics had evolved a mystical medicine which invoked the latent power of the Old Gods in a crypto-Hellenistic guise. One may also note that the attempt by Ptolemy—the same Ptolemy who put together the brilliant synthesis of astronomy known by its Arabic title, the *Almagest*[194]—to place astrology on a scientific footing was badly aimed: His astrological manual, called the *Tetrabiblos*[195] descends into a curious vagueness quite at variance with his own *Almagest.* Compared with the precision of Vettius Valens's carefully organized guide to astrology,[196] or even the earlier *Phainomena* of Aratus,[197] or the Latin astrological manuals by Manilius and Firmicus Maternus,[198] the *Tetrabiblos* maunders in distinction from the *Almagest.* Indeed, the astronomical and astrological data came from common traditions, but astrology and its magical counterparts were solidly deterministic, bereft of the breathless wonder characteristic of the *Almagest,* a sense of continual discovery that hearkens back to the earliest pre-Socratic philosophers.

The Hermetics, and their purportedly Egyptian sources, represented the old way in more than one sense: Hermetic lore sought to revive something of the very ancient unity of religion with all aspects of human existence, a unity only foggily glimpsed by Hellenistic savants sitting in the Ptolemaic Egyptian city of Alexandria. That old certainty was continually challenged by Greek thinking, nicely typified by the anatomical and physiological research of Herophilus and Erasistratus at Alexandria from about 280 to 260 B.C.[199] The common folk held on to their trusted spells and incantations, perhaps now redone into Greek and Hebrew,[200] and later Coptic. And even though the Roman East had come to a greater acceptance of what moderns term mystery religions,[201] the careful choices of an organized Christianity insured a blending of an important mystery with Greek rhetoric, logic, philosophy, and (one may argue) science. Egypt was the center of Christian Gnosticism,[202] which exhibited similar roots to those of Hermeticism, but after much debate and quarreling, Christianity decided to reject the elitism of the Gnostics,[203] an elitism also forcefully affirmed by the Hermetics. If Hermeticism, alchemy, magic, and astrology continued to exercise influence after the final victory of Christianity, they would do so only as hidden writings and generally furtive adherents,[204] surfacing in times of change and doubt. Christianity had signaled its own style of social and intellectual revolution by admitting all who accepted the mystery, and the intellectual heart of this brilliant amalgam of Greek thinking, Jewish monotheism, and Roman organization and law also encouraged a continuation of the quest for knowledge, not necessarily hidden, mystical, or deterministic.

Astrology, magic, and a pseudo-Hermeticism may indeed be alive in the West today, but claims of their followers always founder on the insistence of hidden evidence. Modern pseudoscience resorts to identical claims, as contrasted to the one aspect of magic and alchemy which gave rise to modern science: If one *can* predict the future through repeatedly correct spells and formulas, then one should be able to design a system of thinking securely based upon observations of minerals and all of nature's substances which can be shared and likewise verified, as contrasted to being merely accepted. The unknown author of the Hermetic *Asclepius* had predicted the future accurately: The age had moved beyond a mystical certainty, and the Egyptian paradise would lose its importance in the mind of Western man.

Notes

Abbreviations and Short Titles Employed in the Text and Notes

Aetius, ed. Olivieri: Alexander Olivieri, ed., *Aetii Amideni Libri medicinales I–IV* (Leipzig, 1935) (*CMG* 8. 1)

Alchimistes, ed. Halleux: Robert Halleux, ed. and trans., *Les alchimistes grecs,* vol. 1, *Papyrus de Leyde, Papyrus de Stockholm. Fragments de recettes* (Paris, 1981) (Budé)

Artemidorus, ed. Pack: Roger A. Pack, ed., *Artemidori Daldiani Onirocriticon* (Leipzig, 1963) (Teubner)

Barb in *Legacy*: A. A. Barb, "Mystery, Myth and Magic," in *The Legacy of Egypt,* 2d ed., ed. J. R. Harris (Oxford, 1971), pp. 138–69

Berthelot, *Collection,* or *CAAG*: M. Berthelot, ed., *Collection des alchimistes grecs.,* 3 vols. (Paris, 1887–88; reprint, 3 vols. in 1, London, 1963)

CCAG: *Catalogus Codicum Astrologorum Graecorum,* 12 vols. (Brussels, 1898–1912)

CMG: *Corpus Medicorum Graecorum*

CML: *Corpus Medicorum Latinorum*

Corpus Hermeticum, ed. Nock and Festugière: A. D. Nock and A.-J. Festugière, eds. and trans., *Hermès Trismégiste,* 4 vols. (Paris, 1946–54; vols. 1–3 reprint, 1983; vol. 4 reprint, 1980) (Budé)

Corpus Hermeticum, ed. Scott: Walter Scott, ed. and trans., *Hermetica: The Ancient Greek and Latin Writings Which Contain Religious or Philosophic Teachings Ascribed to Hermes Trismegistus,* 4 vols. (Oxford, 1924–36; reprint, London, 1968) (vol. 4 has introd., addenda, and indexes by A. S. Ferguson)

Dioscorides, ed. Wellmann: Max Wellmann, ed., *Pedanii Dioscuridis Anazarbei De materia medica,* 3 vols. (Berlin, 1906–14; reprint, 1958)

Festugière, *Hermétisme:* A.-J. Festugière, *Hermétisme et mystique païenne* (Paris, 1967)

Festugière, *Révélation:* R. P. Festugière, *La Révélation d'Hermès Trismégiste,* 4 vols. (Paris, 1950–54; reprint, 4 vols, 1983)

Galen, ed. Kühn: C. G. Kühn, ed., *Claudii Galeni Opera omnia,* 20 vols. in 22 parts (Leipzig, 1821–33; reprint, Hildesheim, 1964–65) (cited by vol. and page)

Geminos, ed. Aujac: Germaine Aujac, ed. and trans., *Géminos: Introduction aux Phénomènes* (Paris, 1975) (Budé)

Horapollo, ed. Leemans: Conrad Leemans, ed., *Horapollinis Niloi Hieroglyphica* (Amsterdam, 1835)

LCL: Loeb Classical Library

Macrobius, ed. Willis: J. Willis, ed., *Ambrosii Theodosii Macrobii: Commentarii in Somnium Scipionis* (Leipzig, 1970) (Teubner)

Manetho, ed. Waddell: W. G. Waddell, ed. and trans., *Manetho* (Cambridge, Mass., 1940; reprint, 1964) (LCL)

PGM: Karl Preisendanz, ed. *Papyri Graecae Magicae: Die griechischen Zauberpapyri,* 2d ed., ed. Albert Henrichs, 2 vols. (Stuttgart, 1973–74) (Teubner)

Ptolemy, *Almagest,* trans. Toomer: G. J. Toomer, trans. and annot., *Ptolemy's Almagest* (London, 1984)

Ptolemy, *Tetrabiblos,* ed. Robbins: F. E. Robbins, ed. and trans., *Ptolemy: Tetrabiblos* (Cambridge, Mass., 1940; reprint, 1964) (LCL)

RE: *Real-Encyclopädie der classischen Altertumswissenschaft*

Reitzenstein, *Mysterienreligionen:* R. Reitzenstein, *Die hellenistichen Mysterienreligionen,* 3d ed. (Leipzig, 1927)

Reitzenstein, *Poimandres:* R. Reitzenstein, *Poimandres* (Leipzig, 1904)

Scarborough, *Medicine:* John Scarborough, *Roman Medicine* (London, 1969; reprint, 1976)

Stewart, ed., *Nock: Zeph Stewart,* ed., *Arthur Darby Nock: Essays on Religion and the Ancient World,* 2 vols. (Cambridge, Mass., 1972)

Suda, ed. Adler: Ada Adler, ed., *Suidae Lexicon,* 5 Vols. (Leipzig, 1928–38; reprint, Stuttgart, 1971) (Teubner)

Thessalus, ed. Friedrich: Hans-Veit Friedrich, ed., *Thessalos von Tralles: Griechisch und lateinisch* (Meisenheim am Glan, 1968)

Thorndike: Lynn Thorndike, *History of Magic and Experimental Science,* vols. 1 and 2 (New York, 1923)

Vettius Valens, ed. Kroll: G. Kroll, ed., *Vettii Valentis Anthologiarum libri* (Berlin, 1908)

---

1. Frances A. Yates, *Giordano Bruno and the Hermetic Tradition* (Chicago, 1964), esp. pp. 1–189; D. P. Walker, *Spiritual and Demonic Magic: From Ficino to Campanella* (London, 1958).

2. Yates, *Bruno,* pp. 1–83

3. Ibid., pp. 3, 9–10.

4. Ibid., p. 85.

5. Ibid., pp. 87–116.

6. Ibid., p. 112.

7. The following is adapted from *Dictionary of Scientific Biography* (1970), s.v. Frances A. Yates, "Bruno, Giordano."

8. *Corpus Hermeticum,* ed. Scott, 1:1.

9. *Corpus Hermeticum,* ed. Nock and Festugière, 4:1–22.

10. Ibid., p. 15 (Frag. 23.45); commentary in *Corpus Hermeticum,* ed. Scott, 3:539.

11. Festugière, *Révélation,* 1:89–185.

12. Galen, ed. Kühn, 11:798.

13. M. Wellmann, "Die Pflanzennamen des Dioskurides," *Hermes* 33 (1898): 360–422, at 373; John Scarborough and Vivian Nutton, "The Preface of Dioscorides' *Materia Medica*: Introduction, Translation, Commentary," *Transactions and Studies of the College of Physicians of Philadelphia,* n.s. 4 (1982): 187–227, at 189 with nn. 9–10.

14. Thorndike, 1:287–89.

15. Herodotus 2.67, 138.

16. But cf. Reitzenstein, *Poimandres*, p. 118; F. L. Griffith and H. Thompson, *The Leyden Papyrus: An Egyptian Magical Book* (1904; reprint, New York, 1974), p. 30n: Hermes (Thoth) is "five times great." In the Rosetta stone (196 B.C.) occurs "Thoth great-great," translated into Greek as Ἑρμῆς ὁ μέγας καὶ μέγας. English translation in E. R. Bevan, *The House of Ptolemy* (1927; reprint, Chicago, 1968), p. 265. Further refs. and discussion in *Corpus Hermeticum*, ed. Scott, 1:4–5.

17. Reitzenstein, *Poimandres*, p. 2; J. H. Waszink, ed., *Quinti Septimi Florentis Tertulliani: De anima* (Amsterdam, 1947), pp. 47; comm. p. 395.

18. William R. Schoedel, ed. and trans., *Athenagoras: "Legatio" and "De Resurrectione"* (Oxford, 1972), p. 68 (= *Plea*, 28.6).

19. Galen, ed. Kühn, 12:207; Scarborough, *Medicine*, p. 120; Vettius Valens, ed. Kroll, pp. 374–75; see also nn. 182–83 below; Aetius, ed. Olivieri, 2:18.

20. *Nechepsonis et Petosiridis fragmenta magica*, frags. collected and edited by E. Reiss (Göttingen, 1893), in *Philologus*, Supplementband 6:323–94.

21. Reitzenstein, *Poimandres*, pp. 4–9, followed by *Corpus Hermeticum*, ed. Nock and Festugière, 1:i–x.

22. Ammianus Marcellinus, 21, 14.5.

23. Ibid., 21.14.2–3.

24. M. Berthelot, *Les origines de l'alchimie* (Paris, 1885), p. 134.

25. Reitzenstein, *Poimandres*, pp. 266–70; cf. Berthelot, *CAAG*, 3:245 (= Zosimus, *Final Account*, p. 8).

26. Pseudo-Manetho in Syncellus, ed. Dindorf, p. 72 = appendix 1 in *Manetho*, ed. Waddell, p. 208.

27. *Corpus Hermeticum*, ed. Scott, 3:491–93.

28. Ibid., p. 493 n. 1.

29. *Corpus Hermeticum*, ed. Scott, 4:248–76, esp. 251; L. Massignon, in Festugière, *Révélation*, 1:384–400.

30. *Corpus Hermeticum*, ed. Nock and Festugière, 1:xxxvii–liii.

31. Ibid., 1:xi–xxxvi.

32. Ibid., 1:xi–xii.

33. E.g., from the Nag Hammadi documents; see J. P. Mahé, "Le sens et la composition du traité hermétique: L'ogdoade et l'ennéade, conservé dans le codex VI de Nag Hammadi," and "Remarques d'un latiniste sur l'Asclepius copte de Nag Hammadi," *Revue des Sciences Religieuses* 48 (1974): 54–65, 136–155.

34. Scarborough, *Medicine*, pp. 163–64.

35. A Greek original is known from the Papyrus Mimaut (ca. A.D. 300); Corpus Hermeticum, ed. Nock and Festugière, 2:275–76.

36. *Asclepius*, prol. 1a, trans. in *Corpus Hermeticum*, ed. Scott, 1:287 = French trans. in *Corpus Hermeticum*, ed. Nock and Festugière, 2:296.

37. *Asclepius*, prol. 1b, *Corpus Hermeticum*, ed. Scott, 1:287–89 = *Corpus Hermeticum*, ed. Nock and Festugière, 2:297.

38. *Asclepius*, prol. 1b, trans. in *Corpus Hermeticum*, ed. Scott, 1:287, 289.

39. *Corpus Hermeticum*, ed. Scott, 1:340–45 = *Corpus Hermeticum*, ed. Nock and Festugière, 2:326–29; cf. *Corpus Hermeticum*, ed. Scott, 1:178–87 = *Corpus Hermeticum*, ed. Nock and Festugière, 1:96–100.

40. *Asclepius*, 3.24b, trans. in *Corpus Hermeticum*, ed. Scott, 1:341; French trans. in *Corpus Hermeticum*, ed. Nock and Festugière, 2:326.

41. *Asclepius*, 1.4; trans. in *Corpus Hermeticum*, ed. Scott, 1:293.

42. *Asclepius*, 1.12b–14a; trans. in *Corpus Hermeticum*, ed. Scott, 1:308–11; French trans. in *Corpus Hermeticum*, ed. Nock and Festugière, 2:311–12.

43. G. Helmreich, ed., *Galenus: De usu partium*, 2 vols. (Leipzig, 1907–9; reprint, Amsterdam, 1968); M. T. May, trans., *Galen on the Usefulness of the Parts of the Body*, 2 vols. (Ithaca, 1968).

44. Phillip De Lacy, ed. and trans., *Galen on the Doctrines of Hippocrates and Plato*, 2 vols. (Berlin, 1978–80; *CMG* V 4, 1, 2).

45. See Michael Masi, *Boethian Number Theory: A Translation of the "De Institutione Arithmetica"* (Amsterdam, 1983).

46. Thomas J. Mathiesen, trans., *Aristides Quintilianus: On Music in Three Books* (New Haven, 1983).

47. *Corpus Hermeticum*, ed. Scott, 1:114–33; *Corpus Hermeticum*, ed. Nock and Festugière, 1:7–28.

48. The most important works are listed in *Corpus Hermeticum*, ed. Nock and Festugière, 1:1–2.

49. *Poimandres*, 1, *Corpus Hermeticum*, ed. Nock and Festugière, 1:7 (trans. Scarborough).
50. *Corpus Hermeticum*, ed. Nock and Festugière, 1:115.
51. *Poimandres*, 1–3, *Corpus Hermeticum*, ed. Nock and Festugière, 1:7 (trans. Scarborough).
52. *Poimandres*, 5, *Corpus Hermeticum*, ed. Nock and Festugière, 1:8.
53. *Corpus Hermeticum*, ed. Nock and Festugière, 1:15.
54. Plato, *Timaeus*, 70A–B; *Cratylus*, 419E.
55. Artemidorus (4.63), ed. Pack, p. 286.
56. Ibid. (4.72), ed. Pack, pp. 293–94.
57. Ibid. (1.2), ed. Pack, pp. 9–10.
58. Macrobius, ed. Willis, pp. 8–12, *Dream of Scipio*, 1.3.
59. Ibid., 1,3.7 (ed. Willis, p. 10).
60. Ibid., trans. William Harris Stahl, in *Macrobius: Commentary on the Dream of Scipio* (New York, 1952), p. 89; see also C. Blum, *Studies in the Dream-Book of Artemidorus* (Uppsala, 1936), pp. 57–60, who argues that Posidonius is the source of dream classification for both Artemidorus and Macrobius. The historical context for Artemidorus is suggested by Roger A. Pack, "Artemidorus and His Waking World," *Transactions of the American Philological Association* 86 (1955): 280–90.
61. Berthelot, *Collection*, 3:89.
62. Ibid. (trans. Scarborough).
63. Festugière, *Révélation*, 1:253.
64. *Corpus Hermeticum*, ed. Scott, 1:456–529 = Stobaeus Hermetic excerpts 23–26.
65. Reitzenstein, *Poimandres*, pp. 141–44.
66. Berthelot, *Collection*, 3:213–14 = Zosimus, 3.42.
67. *Book of Sophē*, 2 = Zosimus, 3.42.2 = Berthelot, *Collection*, 3:214.
68. Festugière, *Révélation*, 1:255, with nn. 1–2; cf. *PGM*, V.247ff.
69. Festugière, *Révélation*, 1; 254.
70. Cf. *PGM*, XII.193–201, which begins, "To make a tincture of gold. . . ."; see also commentary in *Alchimistes*, ed. Halleux, p. 71.
71. Berthelot, *Collection*, 3:462 [index reffs.]. For a presumably Hebrew text of herbal astrology, see the "Salomon" tract of *CCAG*, 8:2, 159–165; and the commentary by F. Pfister, "Pflanzenaberglaube," *RE*, vol. 19, pt. 2, (Stuttgart, 1938), cols. 1446–56 at col. 1452.
72. Festugière, *Révélation*, 1:217–82.
73. *Alchimistes*, ed. Halleux, pp. 110–51.
74. John Scarborough, "Gnosticism, Drugs and Alchemy in Late Roman Egypt," *Pharmacy in History* 13 (1971): 151–57.
75. Owsei Temkin, "Medicine and Graeco-Arabic Alchemy," *Bulletin of the History of Medicine* 29 (1955): 134–53.
76. E.g., Galen, ed. Kühn, 12:207.
77. Edited by Hans-Veit Friedrich.
78. *CCAG*, 8:3.
79. Festugière, *Hermétisme*, pp. 155–163: French trans. of *Letter;* cf. Festugière, *Révélation*, 1:150.
80. Reitzenstein, *Mysterienreligionen*, pp. 130–31.
81. Festugière, *Révélation*, 1:150.
82. Thessalus, ed. Friedrich, p. 43.
83. *CCAG*, 8:134–39, 253–57.
84. F. Boll, C. Bezold, and W. Gundel, *Sternglaube und Sterndeutung*, 4th ed. (Leipzig, 1927), p. 97.
85. Reitzenstein, *Mysterienreligionen*, p. 127.
86. But cf. Festugière, *Révélation*, 1:143, 145; and Pfister, "Pflanzenaberglaube," *RE*, vol. 19, [n. 71 above], col. 1451, in which Thessalus = Harpocration. For Harpocration, see Hans Gossen, "Harpokration (10)," *RE*, vol. 7, pt. 2, (Stuttgart, 1912), cols. 2416–17.
87. *CCAG*, 8:139–51.
88. Ibid., pp. 153–59.
89. Ibid., pp. 159–63; but cf. Pfister in *RE*, vol. 19, [n. 71 above], col. 1452.
90. Pfister in *RE*, vol. 19, pt. 2, esp. cols. 1449–51.
91. Festugière, *Révélation*, 1:137–86.
92. Galen, ed. Kühn, 9:908–13.
93. Scarborough, *Medicine*, p. 120.
94. Cf. Ptolemy, *Tetrabiblos*, 3.12, ed. Robbins, pp. 316–33.
95. A. D. Nock, "Posidonius," *Journal of Roman Studies* 49 (1959): 1–15, esp. 2; for Galen on Posidonius, see Stewart, ed., *Nock*, 2: 855–56.
96. A. D. Nock, *Conversion* (Oxford, 1933), pp. 108, 229; idem, "Studies in the Graeco-Roman

Beliefs of the Empire," *Journal of Hellenic Studies* 45 (1925): 84–101, esp. 87–88, nn. 29–30; Stewart, ed., *Nock*, 1: 37. Cf. Marcellus Empiricus, *De medicamentis*, 25,13 (ed. M. Niedermann, rev. as 2d ed. by E. Liechtenhan [Berlin, 1968; 2 vols.; *CML* V], vol. 2, p. 418): Sed hanc herbam ter, dum tenes, antequam colligas, praecantare debes sic: Terram teneo, herbam lego, (in nomine Christi,) Prosit ad quod te colligo.

97. John Scarborough, "Theophrastus on Herbals and Herbal Remedies," *Journal of the History of Biology* 11 (1978): 353–85.

98. John Scarborough, "Early Byzantine Pharmacology," in *Symposium on Byzantine Medicine* (Washington, D.C., 1985), pp. 213–32, esp. 215–21.

99. Explicated in detail by John M. Riddle, *Dioscorides on Pharmacy and Medicine* (Austin, 1985).

100. *Poimandres*, 1.27 = eds., *Corpus Hermeticum*, ed. Nock and Festugière, 1:16 (trans. Scarborough). Omitted from *Corpus Hermeticum*, ed. Scott, 1 129. *See* discussion in Nock, "Studies," p. 87 n. 24; Stewart, ed., *Nock*, 1:36.

101. *Powers of Herbs*, 2.1, Thessalus, ed. Friedrich, pp. 199, 203 (Greek text); trans. Scarborough. A French rendition in Festugière, *Révélation*, 1:151, seems to have been translated from a different Greek text, not clearly identified.

102. *Cichorium intybus* L. Cf. Theophrastus, *Historia Plantarum*, 7.7.1; Dioscorides, 2.132, ed. Wellmann, 1:205–6; Pliny, *Natural History*, 19.129; 20.73; 21.88; *Geoponica*, 12.28, ed. H. Beckh, (Leipzig, 1895), pp. 375–76) (from Didymus); Columella, *Agriculture*, 11.3.27, 12.9.2.

103. Apparently "as a drug" (Dioscorides, 1.98).

104. Cf. Dioscorides, 1.99; and Philumenus in Oribasius, 45.29.36, in *Oribasii Collectionum medicarum reliquiae*, 4 vols., ed. J. Raeder (Leipzig, 1928–33), 3:187; *CMG* 6.1.1–6.2.2, Philumenus is quoting Themison in part on ointments.

105. Cf. Galen, ed. Kühn, 6:604, 8:343.

106. Cf. *PGM*, 23, ed. Preisendanz, 2:159.

107. Ibid.; *PGM*, VII.211–12, and XVIIIb, ed. Preisendanz, 2:9, 141.

108. John 14:20 uses identical phraseology.

109. *Stachys germanica* L. (Dioscorides, 3.106; Pliny, *Natural History*, 24.136).

110. *Crocus sativus* L. (Dioscorides, 1.26; *PGM*, 4.1311, 1834, 2461).

111. *Pistacia lentiscus* L. (Theophrastus, *Historia Plantarum*, 9.1.2; *PGM*, 4.2581, 2647).

112. *Zingiber officinale* Rosc. (Dioscorides, 2.160).

113. *Piper nigrum* L. (Dioscorides, 2.159).

114. This is the famous *asphaltos* (Dioscorides, 1.73; *PGM*, VII.238, and XIII.243).

115. Here *glykanison* = *annēson*, which is *Pimpinella anisum* L. (*Scholia on Theocritus*, 7.63d; ed. C. Wendel, *Scholia in Theocritum vetera* [Leipzig, 1914; reprint, Stuttgart, 1967], p. 95).

116. Made from *Pistacia lentiscus* L., as in n. 111 above.

117. Cf. Dioscorides, 5.8; Galen, ed. Kühn, 10.356.

118. Parallel sources listed in n. 102 above.

119. Festugière, *Révélation*, 1:146–60.

120. Ibid., pp. 150–52.

121. John Scarborough, "Roman Pharmacy and the Eastern Drug Trade," *Pharmacy in History* 24 (1982):135–43.

122. Ibid., p. 137, with nn. 20–31.

123. Scarborough, "Theophrastus," [n. 97 above], pp. 360, 377–78.

124. Diocletian, *Price Edict*, 26.101–2, ed. Siegfried Lauffer, *Diokletians Preisedikt* (Berlin, 1971), p. 199.

125. J. Innes Miller, *The Spice Trade of the Roman Empire* (Oxford, 1969), pp. 53–57.

126. See n. 108 above.

127. The latest critical edition (Greek) is Dimitris Kaimakis, ed., *Die Kyraniden* (Meisenheim am Glan, 1976). The Hermetic overlay on this curious compilation (plants, stones, birds, etc.) has long been understood, but both its date and authorship remain very uncertain. Kaimakis, pp. 2–7, provides a short overview of the controversy, and lists the more important secondary works in his notes.

128. Barb in *Legacy*, p. 138.

129. Horapollo, *Hieroglyphica*, init., ed. Leemans, p. 1.

130. Allegories and symbols were very appealing to Renaissance students of classical art and forms; *see* the lucid introduction by George Boas to his translation of *The Hieroglyphics of Horapollo* (New York, 1950), pp. 15–54.

131. Herodotus, 2.125.

132. The text was discovered by Buondelmonte on the island of Andros in 1419; see Maurice Pope, *The Story of Decipherment* (London, 1975), pp. 11–13, with nn. 1–3.

133. The full title of this landmark in the history of Egyptology reads *Lettre à M. Dacier secrétaire*

perpetuel de l'Académie royale des Inscriptions et Belles-Lettres, relative à l'alphabet des hiéroglyphes phonétiques (Paris, 1822).

134. Barb in *Legacy*, p. 142.

135. Ibid., pp. 142–43; John Scarborough, "Von Däniken's New Myths," *Dictics* 10 (1974): 19–25.

136. *See* P. V. Pistorius, *Plotinus and Neoplatonism* (Cambridge, 1952), esp. 157–65; and the useful overview by W. R. Inge, *The Philosophy of Plotinus*, 3d ed., 2 vols. (London, 1948), 2:103: "The Immortality of the Soul" and "The Spiritual World".

137. This fascination seeped into English Victorian intellectual circles, far beyond those who might have known or studied the Hermetic tracts, and a "white magic" caught the fancy of many of the Pre-Raphaelite painters, as well as several novelists, e.g., George MacDonald, whose *Phantastes* (1858), *Lilith* (1895), and his children's novel *The Princess and the Goblin* (1872), still are pleasant reads.

138. Ed. Preisendanz, 2d ed. Henrichs (1974).

139. The first volume of an English translation of the *PGM* has been published: Hans Dieter Betz, ed., *The Greek Magical Papyri in Translation*, 1 (Chicago, 1985).

140. *PGM*, VII.193–96, ed. Preisendanz, 2:8, (trans. Scarborough).

141. Ibid., VII.197–98, ed. Preisendanz, 2:8 (trans. Scarborough).

142. Ibid., VIII. 206–7, ed. Preisendanz, 2:9 (trans. Scarborough).

143. Ibid., XXXVI.322–32, ed. Preisendanz, 2:174 (trans. Scarborough).

144. Ibid., XII.409–45, ed. Preisendanz, 2:84–85 (trans. Scarborough).

145. [Pseudo] Galen, ed. Kühn, 19:726.

146. A "snake's ball of thread" suggests the undigested hair in the feces of snakes. Lexicographers, (viz. Hesychius, s.v. *agathis*) note the "ball of thread" meaning, and it was also a term equivalent (in Byzantine Greek) for a mixture of roasted sesame seeds and honey *(sēsamis)*. The "soapstone" is suggested by readings in Pliny, *Natural History*, 37.153, and Theophrastus, *On Stones*, 7.42.

147. Probably among the *Rhamnus* spp., esp. *R. catharticus* L.

148. Probably the rock hyrax *(Procavia capensis),* sometimes called a coney.

149. *Dakrya* normally are the "tears" of trees, etc., as they produce gum exudates, saps, and the like. It may be that, since the scribes are listing the "tears" of the sacred baboon, we are seeing traces of a custom of collecting the "sleep sand" from the eyes of baboons.

150. The sacred baboon of ancient Egypt, *Papio hamadryas.*

151. The gecko is a lizard, and this particular gecko is probably *Tarantola mauritanica,* as in Aristotle, *Historia Animalium,* 538a27, 607a27.

152. Cf. Dioscorides, 1.75 RV, 1.89.

153. Text emended from *akanthis* to *akanthos*, either *Acanthus mollis* L., "bear's breech," or *Helleborus foetidus* L., "stinking hellebore."

154. Probably *Matricaria recutita* L.

155. Text emended from *bunis* to bounias, as in Dioscorides, 2.111. The turnip would be *Brassica napus* L.

156. Lit. "scorpion tail," probably a variety of "leopard's bane" in the genus *Doronicum,* or one of the heliotropes (e.g. *Heliotropium europaeum* L.). Cf. Theophrastus, *Historia Plantarum,* 9.13.6; Nicander, *Alexipharmaca,* 145; and Dioscorides, 4.190. *See also* Scarborough, "Theophrastus" [n. 97 above], pp. 373–74 with n. 120; idem, "Nicander's Toxicology, II: Spiders, Scorpions, Insects, and Myriapods," *Pharmacy in History* 21 (1979): 3–34, 73–92 [76 with nn. 269–279].

157. Emended as above in line 425; see n. 155 above.

158. Probably *Eruca sativa* Mill.

159. Dioscorides, 2.136 RV: "Wild lettuce: some call this hawkweed . . . priests Titan's blood." Cf. also Dioscorides. 4.34, and 33 RV.

160. *Kantharis* normally is one of the blister beetles, used in the manufacture of the infamous aphrodisiac known as Spanish fly; *see* John Scarborough, "Some Beetles in Pliny's *Natural History*" *Coleopterists Bulletin* 31 (1977): 293–96; idem, "Nicander's Toxicology," II [n. 156 above], pp. 20–21, 73–80, with nn. 215–230 and 238–325.

161. Cf. n. 159 above.

162. Dioscorides, 4.88: *chrysospermon* = aeizōon to mega, which makes this plant a houseleek.

163. Galen, ed. Kühn, 19.731–47 (a pseudo-Galenic work). Basically reproduced in *Paul of Aegina* (7.25), ed. I. L. Heiberg, 2 vols. (Leipzig, 1921–24); *CMG* 9.1, 2, 2:401–8.

164. Barb in *Legacy*, pp. 160–65; cf. Roy Kotansky, "Two Amulets in the Getty Museum: A Gold Amulet for Aurelia's Epilepsy and an Inscribed Magical-Stone for Chills and Headache," *J. Paul Getty Museum Journal* 8 (1980): 181–88.

165. E. A. E. Reymond, ed., *From the Contents of the Libraries of the Suchos Temples in the Fayyum,* 1: *A Medical Book from Crocodilopolis* (Vienna, 1976).

166. H. Frankfort, *Ancient Egyptian Religion: An Interpretation* (New York, 1948); Siegfried Mor-

enz, *Egyptian Religion,* trans. Ann E. Keep (Ithaca, 1973); Erik Hornung, *Conceptions of God in Ancient Egypt,* trans. John Baines (Ithaca, 1982).

167. An excellent example of the almost desperate wish to "cleanse" Galen of any irrationality is in Rudolph E. Siegel, *Galen's System of Physiology and Medicine* (Basel, 1968), p. 14 n. 47. A single line from Siegel's note gives a sense of the tone: "One may ask whether these strange prescriptions were later added to his treatises or whether [Galen] wanted to please the superstitious populace."

168. Pseudo-Galen, ed. Kühn, 19:529–73.

169. Pseudo-Galen, ed. Kühn, 14:675.

170. Jutta Kollesch, *Untersuchungen zu den pseudogalenischen Definitiones medicae* (Berlin, 1973), pp. 30–34.

171. Galen, ed. Kühn, 9:935.

172. Ibid., 12:207.

173. Ibid., 9:911.

174. Ibid., 9:910–11.

175. Ibid., 9:912.

176. Ibid., 9:913.

177. Galen, *On Medical Experience,* 26.6, in R. Walzer ed. and trans., *Galen On Medical Experience* (London, 1944), p. 142.

178. Scarborough and Nutton, "Preface" [n. 13 above], pp. 187–94.

179. Dioscorides, 4.64.

180. Dioscorides, ed. Wellmann, 3:68–69.

181. Cf. Pliny, *Natural History,* 34.123.

182. Dioscorides, 5.98.1, apparatus criticus line 13; cf. Papyrus Holmiensis, 3.12 *Alchimistes,* (ed. Halleux, p. 113.)

183. J. Berendes, *Des Pedanios Dioskurides aus Anazarbos Arzneimittellehre* (Stuttgart, 1902), p. 526.

184. Dioscorides, 1.26, ed. Wellmann, 1:29–31.

185. Dioscorides, ed. Wellmann, 1:30, lines 20–22.

186. See n. 13 above.

187. Galen, ed. Kühn, 12:839.

188. Ibid., 11:792.

189. Ibid., 11:792, 793, 796, 797, 798; 12:31.

190. *Suda* (delta), no. 1140, and (omicron), no. 835, ed. Adler, 2:101, 3:581.

191. Wellmann, "Pflanzennamen," [n. 13 above], p. 369.

192. Dioscorides, ed. Wellmann, 3:327–29.

193. Dioscorides, 4.162.4, ed. Wellmann, 2:308–9 tells of how those who dig the black hellebore stand and pray to Apollo and Asclepius, while keeping a sharp eye out for eagles flying over, since should an eagle see a hellebore digger, the "bird will give death." Lest a modern reader presume that this is an "Egyptian" superstition, one need only point out that Theophrastus (*Historia Plantarum,* 9.8.8) records an almost identical tradition, presumably from somewhere in the Greek Aegean world of the late fourth century B.C.

194. *See* the splendid translation by Toomer of Ptolemy, *Almagest.*

195. Ptolemy, *Tetrabiblos,* 1.2, ed. Robbins, pp. 4–19, admits limits.

196. Vettius Valens, ed. Kroll.

197. G. R. Mair, ed. and trans., *The Phaenomena of Aratus* (Cambridge, Mass., 1921 [LCL: in vol. with *Callimachus: Hymns and Epigrams* and *Lycophron*]).

198. G. P. Goold, ed. and trans., *Manilius: Astronomica* (Cambridge, Mass., 1977 [LCL]); cf. Geminos (ed. Aujac), pp. xxviii–xxxvi.

199. Scarborough, *Medicine,* pp. 33–35, with refs.

200. One needs to recall that Jews had settled in Egypt very early (aside from the Old Testament traditions); *see,* e.g., Bezalel Porten, *Archives from Elephantine: The Life of an Ancient Jewish Military Colony* (Berkeley, 1968). A garrison of Jewish soldiers was stationed on the island of Elephantine in the fifth century B.C.

201. Two recent books are recommended in this vast literature: Ramsay MacMullen, *Paganism in the Roman Empire* (New Haven, 1981); and Javier Teixidor, *The Pagan God: Popular Religion in the Greco-Roman Near East* (Princeton, 1977).

202. Still one of the best accounts is Hans Jonas, *The Gnostic Religion,* 2d ed. (Boston, 1963); *see* also the sprightly *Gnostic Gospels* by Elaine Pagels (New York, 1979).

203. Robert M. Grant, *Gnosticism and Early Christianity,* rev. ed. (New York, 1959), pp. 197–200.

204. Roman law had always viewed astrology with a jaundiced eye, so that later Christian condemnation did not depart from this long-standing heritage; Frederick H. Cramer, *Astrology in Roman Law and Politics* (Philadelphia, 1954).

2

Magic in Hellenistic Hermeticism

WILLIAM C. GRESE

One of the unsolved questions concerning the ancient Hermetic literature involves the relationship between the " 'religious' or 'philosophic' " Hermetica[1] and the astrological, alchemical, and magical texts that also circulated under the name of Hermes Trismegistus.[2] How one answers the question of the relationship between these two bodies of ancient Hermetic literature has a direct bearing on how one explains the origin and development of the Hermetic literature and on the type of Hermetic community that one sees as using the literature.

Present Status of the Question

Modern debate on the ancient Hermetica was inaugurated by Richard Reitzenstein in 1904 with his book *Poimandres*.[3] In that work Reitzenstein portrayed the Hermetica as a Hellenistic development of ancient Egyptian religion, and he used the Greek Magical Papyri as a means for clarifying earlier Greek-influenced developments in Egyptian religion. In other words, for Reitzenstein both the Hermetica and the Greek Magical Papyri result from the Hellenization of Egyptian religion, but the magical papyri preserve an earlier stage in that development, a link between ancient Egyptian religion and the " 'religious' or 'philosophic' " Greek Hermetica.

This attempt to explain the Hermetica as a Hellenistic development of ancient Egyptian religion has not been widely accepted by subsequent scholarship.[4] Instead, the predominant view is that the Hermetica are a Hellenistic development of Greek (especially Platonic and Stoic) philosophy, and the leading exponent of this position has been André-Jean Festugière.[5] For Festugière, the religious or philosophic Hermetica come from schools of *philosophic* thought and reflect in their dialogue form the discussions in such schools between teachers and their students. Sometimes Festugière even seems to suggest that the present written dialogues are the written records, though now pseudonymous, of actual periods of instruction within the schools.[6] This point is important for Festugière because it serves to underline the philosophic nature of the literature, a point that he argues in opposition to Reitzenstein.

Reitzenstein saw the Hermetica as religious literature coming from religious congregations, the origins of which were to be found in the worship led by Egyptian priests within Egyptian temples. The long history of these congregations could be traced to an extent, he felt, within the Hermetic literature.[7] There one could see evidence of the development from cultic ceremonies to literary texts, which by themselves were thought to accomplish the ends formerly achieved through cultic worship.[8]

Against Reitzenstein, Festugière argues that the liturgical elements in the texts are literary devices and do not reflect actual cultic worship experiences. In addition, he argues that the diversity within the *Corpus Hermeticum* would have made it impossible for that collection of religious or philosophic Hermetic texts ever to serve as a bible for a religious congregation.[9] It is in the context of this argument against Reitzenstein's interpretation of the Hermetica as the literature of a religious congregation that Festugière attempts to draw a line between the religious or philosophic Hermetica and the astrological and magical Hermetic texts.

It is not necessary to repeat here Festugière's extensive discussion, but I will consider one example Festugière discusses in detail, the *Liber Hermetis Trismegisti,* published in 1936 by Wilhelm Gundel under the title *Neue astrologische Texte des Hermes Trismegistos.*[10] The background of this work is complicated, to say the least. The Latin text is dated not earlier than the late fifth century A.D., but it seems to be only a portion of a larger and more detailed work written originally in Greek. The work is a poorly organized composite, made up of a number of pieces, some of which quote other astrologers and which can therefore be dated to the third or fourth centuries A.D. Other pieces that seem to antedate known Egyptian astrological works Gundel would date to the second or third centuries B.C. and trace back to the astrological material collected and used in the temples by Egyptian priests.

The first section of the book deals with the thirty-six decans, the powers that work their influence over a third of a sign of the zodiac, each affecting ten degrees of the zodiacal circle. This list gives the thirty-six decans, associates each decan with the proper sign of the zodiac, relates the decan to a planet, gives the name of the decan, describes the sign of the decan, and gives the geographic area and also area of the human body that is subject to the decan. The signs of the decans are characteristically Egyptian, some of the names are Egyptian, while others are Jewish or make use of the same strange letter combinations characteristic of the Greek Magical Papyri. According to Gundel, the geographic areas mentioned in the list show a knowledge of the third-century Roman Empire, yet reflect an Egyptian perspective.

This work, which names the decans and describes their influence, Festugière compares with the sixth excerpt of a Hermetic text found in Stobaeus.[11] The excerpt begins with a request by the disciple Tat in which he refers to the *Genikoi Logoi,* which apparently were a collection of Hermetic discourses.[12] "Since in the preceding *Genikoi Logoi* you promised to reveal to me about the thirty-six decans, now reveal to me them and their power" (6.1). In the following dialogue Hermes then discusses a number of astrological or astronomical phenomena, especially the thirty-six decans. These decans, Tat is told, are guards of all that is in the cosmos and preserve good order (6.5). All that happens is a result of these decans, specifically, changes of kings, revolts of cities, famines, plagues, tides, and earth-quakes (6.8). In addition, the decans produce daemons and stars as servants for themselves. From these stars, which have their own power, come the destruction of living beings and the animals that destroy fruits (6.12). The dialogue thus describes the role that the decans play in determining what happens in the world, and at the conclusion of the dialogue, this knowledge of the decans is made a prerequisite for the vision of God that brings an understanding of all reality (6.18).[13] For the author of this Hermetic text, the decans had an extremely important role in the cosmic system, and if one was to understand the cosmos and how it functioned, he had to be aware of the role played by these decans.[14]

This discussion of the power of the decans, a discussion that is part of the religious or philosophic Hermetica, provides the theoretical background for the specific information concerning the individual decans given in the *Liber Hermetis Trismegisti.* In excerpt 6 from Stobaeus, one is given a general picture of the cosmic role the decans play. In the *Liber Hermetis Trismegisti,* one is given the names of the individual decans and told what specific powers the individual decans have, information that the astrologer would need in order to make his specific forecasts.

For Festugière, such astrological texts as the *Liber Hermetis Trismegisti* are important aids in reconstructing the piety and world view of late antiquity, and thus they help to explain the intellectual context in which the religious or philosophic Hermetica were composed. The circles that produced the religious or philosophic Hermetica, however, were not, at least according to Festugière, the same groups that produced such astrological texts. The only thing that the two groups of Hermetica share is their common attribution to Hermes Trismegistus. Astrological texts, such as the *Liber Hermetis Trismegisti,* show a positive view of the cosmos. Their goal is to understand the cosmos and how it functions in order to live well and profitably within the cosmos. Such a view is the exact opposite of tractates 1 and 13 of the *Corpus Hermeticum.* For them the cosmos is in such a terrible state that the only hope for human beings is escape. This sharp contrast Festugière sees as making it impossible for the two bodies of Hermetic literature—the astrological texts and the religious or philosophic texts—to have come from the same group.[15]

Festugière's argument here, however, is refuted by his earlier argument that the *Corpus Hermeticum* was not the bible of a religious community. The tractates of the *Corpus Hermeticum,* to say nothing of the other religious or philosophic Hermetica, vary greatly. There is an optimistic, world-affirming group of Her-metica and a pessimistic, world-denying group of Hermetic texts. This lack of unity within the religious or philosophic Hermetica, a lack to which Festugière himself pointed,[16] makes it impossible to argue that because one group of this Hermetic corpus is at variance with the astrological Hermetica, there can there-fore be no connection between the astrological texts and all those which are called religious or philosophic. In fact, the frequent close connection with magical and astrological practices in the later history of the religious or philosophic Hermetica[17] should encourage one to look for a similar kind of connection in the early period as well.[18] But if one is to advance in the search, he must move beyond the shared concepts that Festugière has demonstrated to look for evidence of magical practice in the religious or philosophic Hermetica and for the use of this Hermetic literature by practicing magicians.[19]

Magical Practice in the Hermetica

Probably the most striking example of magical practice in the religious or philosophic Hermetica is the description of the invocation of spiritual beings to inhabit statues that is found in the *Asclepius,* sections 37–38.

> The most miraculous thing of all, which demands admiration, is that man has been able to discover the divine nature and to produce it. Since our ancestors by doubting and not observing the worship and divine piety often erred concerning knowledge of the gods, they discovered the art by which they could make gods. To this discovery they added an appropriate power *(virtus)* from the material of the world, and, inasmuch as they were not able to make souls, by mixing it and invoking the souls of daemons or angels they introduced the daemons or angels into their images by holy and divine mysteries. Therefore, their idols had the power to do both good and evil. (347.8–19)

This "power" *(virtus)*[20] that is used in the procedure is then identified as consisting of herbs, stones, and fragrances possessing a divine strength, and the reader is told that the daemons that are brought to dwell in the statues are kept happy by means of frequent sacrifices, hymns, and expressions of thanksgiving.[21] The parallels between this passage and Hellenistic magic have been frequently noted.[22] Even if the author intended to describe ancient Egyptian practice, he has, according to Jean-Pierre Mahé, interpreted it in terms of Hellenistic magic.[23] What is less clear is the intention of the author in mentioning the practice. On the one hand, he seems to view it as representing an inadequate understanding of the gods, while on the other hand, he also describes it as the greatest of human accomplishments.

Although the overall structure of the *Asclepius* is not obvious, there does seem to be a connection between the passage noted in sections 37–38 and one in sections 23–24. In the second passage, man is described as the creator of gods, but the method of that creation is not spelled out as it is in sections 37–38. In section 24 these gods that man makes are identified as statues filled with spirit, and the accomplishments of the statues are cited. They know in advance the future and predict it by means of the casting of lots, prophecy, dreams, and in many other ways.[24] In addition, they give to human beings sickness and cures, joy and sadness, all according to merit. As was the case in the previous section, so also here there are many parallels in the magical papyri to this description of humans creating material figures filled with divine power and to the many wondrous deeds that these images are able to accomplish.[25] Absent here, however, is the suggestion of a negative evaluation of the practice that was noted in the other section.

Such differences should not be suprising in view of the complicated history of the Hermetica as a whole, and also of the *Asclepius.* Although I have been describing the religious or philosophic Hermetica as a unit, the term actually refers to a collection of texts (*Corpus Hermeticum, Asclepius,* excerpts found in Stobaeus, and other fragments) that did not exist as one collection until the modern period.[26] The texts coming from Stobaeus and other writers are often fragments, even though some are quite lengthy, and the exact nature of the original relationships among the texts is unknown. The *Corpus Hermeticum* has come down to this day as an independent collection, but it is not known when the collection was made, why it was made, or what was excluded. The *Asclepius* also survived independently of the others. Thus, the history of the religious or philosophic Hermetica may be more complicated than has usually been recognized. This being the case, the lack of more references to magical practices may reflect more the selection of texts that have survived than the actual situation in antiquity. In fact, since Arthur Darby Nock has shown that the author of the *Asclepius* made use of a number of themes that also appear in other Hermetic texts that have survived,[27] these references to magical practices noted above could have come from another Hermetic work, or works, now lost.[28]

Another example of magical practice in the Hermetica can be found in one of these lost Hermetica that has been recovered, this one as part of the Nag Hammadi Coptic library. In addition to the Coptic version of two sections from the *Asclepius,* the sixth codex from the Nag Hamaddi library also includes a previously unknown Hermetic tractate that has been given the title *The Discourse on the Eighth and Ninth.* This tractate was originally written in Greek and has a number of parallels with the other religious or philosophic Hermetic texts, especially the thirteenth tractate of the *Corpus Hermeticum.*[29]

Like other Hermetic texts, this discourse is a dialogue between an initiate, here unidentified, and the mystagogue, Hermes Trismegistus. The dialogue begins with a request by the initiate for a vision of the eighth and ninth spheres, those spheres in which the god dwells above the seven spheres of the planets. After some instruction by the mystagogue, both mystagogue and initiate succeed by means of prayer in achieving visions of the eighth and ninth, and the prayer that is used names the deity with *voces magicae* (strings of vowels and consonants that make up magical words and phrases) in a way that is similar to usage in the Greek Magical Papyri.

I call upon thee, who rulest over the kingdom of power, whose word comes as a birth of light . . . the one mighty in power who is exalted above majesty, who is better than the honored (ones), Zoxathazo a ōō ee ōōō ēēē ōōōō ēē ōōōōōō ooooo ōōōōōō uuuuuu ōōōōōōōōōōōō ōōō Zoxazoth. Lord, grant us a wisdom from thy power that reaches us, so that we may describe to ourselves the vision of the eighth and ninth. (55.24–56.26).[30]

Here the powerful divine name is used in the prayer as a help in achieving the divine vision, and after the vision, the same vowels appear again in the expression of thanks.

> After these things I give thanks by singing a hymn to thee. For I have received life from thee, when thou madest me wise. I praise thee. I call thy name that is hidden within me. a ō ee ō ēēē ōōō iii ōōōō ooooo ōōō ōō uuuuuu ōō ōōōōōōōōō ōōōōōōōō ōō. (61.4–15)

That magical power is ascribed to the name is evident from the conclusion of the dialogue where an oath is added to keep those who read the book from misusing the name *(onomasia)*[31] by employing it to oppose the acts of fate. Those who read the book are made to swear that they will guard the secrets that Hermes has revealed, and the wrath of the god is promised to those who violate their oath.[32]

These same concluding instructions also provide for the erection of a record of the dialogue in the temple at Diospolis.

> Therefore I command that this teaching be carved on stone, and that you place it in my sanctuary. Eight guardians guard it with [ ] of the sun. The males on the right are frog-faced, and the females on the left are cat-faced. And put a square milk-stone at the base of the turquoise tablets and write the name on the azure stone tablet in hieroglyphic characters. (62.1–15).[33]

Further, the initiate is directed to erect the record at the astrologically most appropriate time. It is to be erected when Mercury (Hermes) is in his most powerful position.

> O my son, you will do this when I am in Virgo, and the sun is in the first half of the day, and fifteen degrees have passed by me. (62.16–20)

In commenting upon this passage, Mahé refers to *Kore Kosmu* (Stob. Exc. 23.29), where Hermes promises special assistance to those born under his sign, and Mahé suggests that the erecting of the record of this new birth of the initiate at just such a time would enable the initiate to share in these special benefits.[34] In any case, here is a concern for conformity to astrological powers that goes beyond the simple sharing of concepts to a reflection of practices that can also be paralleled in the Greek Magical Papyri.[35]

Use of Hermetic Material in the Greek Magical Papyri

When one turns to the Greek Magical Papyri, one finds a great number of magical spells attributed to Hermes, and some of them to Hermes Trismegistus.[36] In view of the magical activities attributed to Hermes (and to Thoth, his Egyptian counterpart) in both Egyptian[37] and Greek[38] mythology, one can hardly argue that these references to the name Hermes in the magical papyri must necessarily point to a connection between this literature and the religious or philosophic Hermetica. In a couple of cases, however, the connection seems to be more significant.

Papyrus XIII in the Greek Magical Papyri contains two versions of the Eighth Book of Moses, each of which includes a magic spell, the basic purpose of which is to require the creator god to appear and to give a revelation. The spell itself includes an account of the creation of the world and of the gods who control and direct it. This cosmogony is used in order to compel the creator god to appear before the magician who has demonstrated his knowledge of the secrets of creation, and one of the two editions of this spell identifies it as a "Hermetic" spell.[39] Although Hermes does appear within the cosmogony, the points of contact between this cosmogony and those in the religious or philosophic Hermetica are minimal.[40] Nevertheless, the Hermetic cosmogonies in *Poimandres* and *Kore Kosmu* also have little in common, and if they had not survived with a title attributing them to Hermes, one would have difficulty in including them within the Hermetic literature. Thus it is difficult to prove from the cosmogony itself whether it is Hermetic. What can be said is that at some point in the history of this magical spell it was felt to be Hermetic and was so described. The magician felt that he could use what he considered to be Hermetic material in his attempt to communicate with the god.

A somewhat clearer example of a relationship between the Greek Magical Papyri and the religious or philosophic Hermetica can be found in papyrus III, lines 494–611, which contain a spell that ends with the same prayer of thanksgiving as that which concludes the Hermetic *Asclepius* and follows *The Discourse on the Eighth and Ninth*.[41] The title of the spell is textually uncertain, but it is followed by a description of how the spell is to be used: "A procedure for every [ritual] and for [all things]. For whatever you want, make your invocation in this way" (lines 494–95). The power of the spell is such that it can be used for anything.[42]

The spell itself then begins with an invocation summoning the god and asking him to grant all the petitions of the prayer.

> [Come,] come to me from the four winds of the world, air-traversing, great god. Hear me in every rite which [I perform], and grant all the [petitions] of my prayer completely, because I know your signs, [symbols, and] forms, who you are each hour and what your name is. (Lines 496–501).[43]

The reason the magician can expect the god to hear the prayer and to grant the petitions is that the magician knows the god's "signs, symbols, and forms," who he is each hour and what his names are. The use of such knowledge to compel the deity is typical of such texts,[44] and here the magician demonstrates his knowledge in the lines that follow. He recites the god's signs, symbols, and names for each of the twelve hours:

> In the first hour you have the form and character of a young monkey, [the tree] you produce is the silver fir; the stone, the *aphanos;* the bird . . . your name is *phrouer.* In the second hour you have the form of a unicorn.

So the text continues on through twelve hours (lines 501–36).[45]

On the basis of the preceding list of the god's names, signs, and symbols, the magician asks the god to grant the petition he is seeking (lines 536–37). Four times he makes his request, and each time he couples it with a formula that is apparently expected to make the petition more efficacious. One of the requests is coupled with a tripartite identification of the god (lines 538–40). The other three requests contain references to the person praying. In the first he threatens to shake the heaven if his petition is not granted (lines 537–38),[46] in the third he claims to have the keys of the triangular paradise (lines 540–42),[47] and in the fourth he describes himself as the fatherless child of a widow—perhaps, as Preisendanz suggests, identifying himself with Horus, the son of Isis (lines 542–43).[48]

After a list of *voces magicae,* the spell continues with a hymnic section[49] summoning and praising the god as creator of the universe (lines 549–58). By identifying the god as the creator, the hymn praises the god for the power that will make it possible for him to give the material blessings that are to be requested in lines 577–81.[50] The hymnic summons is then followed by more *voces magicae* and by two more summonses for the god to come. The first of the two praises the god and asks him to listen (lines 564–75).[51] The second includes the list of specific blessings that the god is being asked to bestow:

> Come to me with a happy face to a bed of your choice, giving to me, [here the magician would identify himself], sustenance, health, safety, wealth, the blessing of children, knowledge *(gnosis),* a ready hearing, goodwill, sound judgment, honor, memory, grace, shapeliness, beauty to all who see me, you who hear me in everything whatsoever, give persuasiveness with words, great god. (Lines 575–82).[52]

Then there is another list of *voces magicae.*

So far nothing seems very different from other, similar magical spells. The god is summoned and asked to give material blessings, and various techniques are used by the spell to insure that the gifts requested will actually be given.

The whole direction of the spell changes, however, in what follows. After a twofold petition that the prayer be accepted (lines 583–90), the spell concludes with the same thanksgiving that concludes the *Asclepius* and follows *The Discourse on the Eighth and Ninth.*

> We give you thanks[53] with every soul and heart stretched out to [you], unutterable name honored with [the] appellation of god and blessed with the [appellation of father], for[54] to everyone and to everything you have shown fatherly goodwill, affection, friendship and sweetest power, granting us intellect, [speech] and knowledge; intellect so that we might understand you, speech [so that] we might call upon you, knowledge so that we might know you. We rejoice because you showed yourself to us; we rejoice because while we are [still] in bodies you deified us by the knowledge of who you are. (Lines 591–601)

The reason for the thanksgiving is the divine gift of knowledge *(gnosis).* In this section nothing is said about the other gifts that were requested. The thanksgiving continues:

The thanks of man to you is one: to come to know [you]. We have come to know, O [life] of human life. We have come to know, O womb of all knowledge. We have come to know, O womb pregnant through the father's begetting. We have come to know, O eternal continuation of the pregnant father. (Lines 601–6)

Of all the blessings requested earlier in the spell, the final thanksgiving singles out knowledge as the reason for the thanksgiving.

Those who composed the magical charms that have survived in the Greek Magical Papyri compiled their charms out of diverse materials from various religions.[55] The spell under consideration here was also most probably put together from a number of pieces.[56] The list of the signs, symbols, and names of the god and the hymnic portion may have been originally independent of each other.[57] But in adding this Hermetic conclusion, the author made knowledge the most important of the blessings requested, and he made the experience of knowledge the chief purpose of the spell. In doing so, he transformed a spell for various material blessings into a spell for knowledge.

This change in the purpose of the spell is demonstrated by the petition that the prayer be accepted, which follows the request for the material blessings and precedes the final thanksgiving.

I beg, master, accept my entreaty, the offering to you which you commanded. In order that you might now illuminate me with knowledge of things beloved by you even after the kind restoration of my material body, I pray, lord, accept this my request, [the] entreaty, the preliminary spell, the offering of my eloquent spirit. (Lines 582–88)

Here also one sees knowledge emphasized as the primary gift that is sought. No mention is made of the other gifts that were requested in the immediately preceding lines. Until this petition, the spell was typical of other magical spells requesting a variety of material blessings. This petition, however, concentrates the spell on the acquisition of knowledge for which the Hermetic thanksgiving offers thanks. What began as a spell for various material blessings has been changed into a spell to bring knowledge.

The acquisition of knowledge was important to the magician as well as to the Hermetist. The magician needed knowledge of the secret spells, formulas, names, powers, and gods that made it possible for him to perform his magic, and such knowledge was frequently seen as a divine gift.[58] For the Hermetist, knowledge meant knowing God, oneself, and one's place in the universe, and this knowledge was also seen as a gift of God.[59] Yet the line between the two types of knowledge was not so clear. The knowledge of the Hermetist could, as has been seen, include the knowledge of the cosmic powers of the universe that the magician needed to use,[60] and this particular spell shows how blurred the line between the two could become. For this spell functioned in both contexts.

That the final thanksgiving had its origin in the Hermeticism of the *Asclepius* and the *Corpus Hermeticum* seems certain,[61] and although the petition that precedes the final thanksgiving is not known in any other Hermetic version of the thanksgiving, the petition represents more the spirit of the final thanksgiving than the earlier magical spell for material blessings.[62] The knowledge requested is "knowledge of things beloved by you," and absent are those demands placed upon the god earlier in the spell. Here instead the god is begged to accept the petition. The prayer itself is said to have been commanded by the god, and it is identified as coming from the spirit. Both of these concepts occur in other Hermetic literature,[63] but neither is suggested by the earlier, non-Hermetic portion of the spell. In other words, when the original spell for material blessings was changed into a spell for knowledge, the kind of knowledge sought was the knowledge desired in the religious or philosophic Hermetica.

For the religious or philosophic Hermetica, knowledge is a gift given by the god, but it can be given in a variety of ways. In *Corpus Hermeticum* 1 knowledge comes through the revelation first of Poimandres and then of his disciple (1.27). In *Corpus Hermeticum* 4 knowledge is given by some sort of baptism (4.4), and in *Corpus Hermeticum* 13 by regeneration (13.8). In *The Discourse on the Eighth and Ninth* knowledge is a gift for which one prays (62.28–33). The person responsible for this Hermetic magic spell saw this spell as a way to achieve knowledge,[64] and in line with *Corpus Hermeticum* 1 (30–32), 13 (21), *Asclepius* (41), and *The Discourse on the Eighth and Ninth* (followed by *The Prayer of Thanksgiving,* 63.33–65, 7), the one who received the gift of knowledge responded to the god with an expression of thanks.

The use of magical techniques in order to persuade the god to give knowledge shows that the Hermetists were not limited to the options offered in the religious or philosophic Hermetica. Some could also make use of techniques that they shared with Greco-Egyptian magicians. The fact that this spell did not survive as part of the Hermetic corpora is a further demonstration that only a limited amount of ancient Hermetic literature did. That this spell survived instead as part of a magician's handbook testifies to a certain amount of sharing between Hermeticism and the magicians who produced the Greek Magical Papyri. And the sharing that it reveals went both ways. The Hermetic spell for knowledge is an adaptation of an earlier spell for material blessings, and after being made Hermetic, this spell was included in a magician's handbook as a way to acquire the knowledge necessary for magic.[65]

That not all were in favor of this sharing is suggested by the conclusion to *The Discourse on the Eighth and Ninth,* where the oath is added to keep those who read the book from abusing the name and using it to oppose the acts of fate (62.22–27). The author was aware of the uses to which the powerful names in his prayer could be put, and he sought to protect the names against their being used to escape what fate decreed. A similar rejection of *mageia* in favor of accepting what fate has to give was also, according to Zosimos, the position taken by Hermes in the no-longer-extant work, *On the Inner Life.*[66] Yet not all Hermetists shared this idea of what was proper. Iamblichus reports that Hermes revealed a method of theurgy that would allow one to ascend above fate to God,[67] and freedom from control by the zodiac was a benefit of the ceremony of regeneration discussed in *Corpus Hermeticum* 13.[68] The fear of the author of *The Discourse on the Eighth and Ninth* that the powerful names would be misused may very well have been a fear that they would be misused by other Hermetists.

This disagreement would only substantiate the point made earlier on the lack of unity among the religious or philosophic Hermetica. The sharing that I have shown between the religious or philosophic Hermetica and those which are astrological or magical is evidence that there was a certain amount of overlap between the circles that produced them.[69] Those who would ignore the overlap run the risk of distorting the history of ancient Hermeticism.

Notes

1. This terminology is taken from Walter Scott, *Hermetica: The Ancient Greek and Latin Writings Which Contain Religious or Philosophic Teachings Ascribed to Hermes Trismegistus*, 4 vols. (Oxford, 1924–36), 1:1, who used these terms to distinguish between the " 'religious' or 'philosophic' " literature he included in his collection of the Hermetica and the other Hermetic writings, which he identified as "masses of rubbish." In this essay, the phrase " 'religious' or 'philosophic' " Hermetica is used to refer to the Greek and Latin texts collected by Arthur Darby Nock and André-Jean Festugière, *Corpus Hermeticum*, 4 vols. (Paris, 1954–60), together with the new Coptic Hermetica from Nag Hammadi, in Douglas M. Parrott, ed., *Nag Hammadi Codices V, 2–5 and VI with Papyrus Berolinensis 8502, 1 and 4*, Nag Hammadi Studies, vol. 11, Coptic Gnostic Library (Leiden, 1979), pp. 341–451, which were not available to Nock and Festugière (See Nock and Festugière, *CH*, 4:150). Texts are cited on the basis of these editions.
2. For examples of such texts, see A.-J. Festugière, *La révélation d'Hermès Trismégiste*, 3d ed., 4 vols. (Paris, 1949–54) 1:89–308.
3. *Poimandres: Studien zur griechisch-ägyptischen und frühchristlichen Literatur* (1904; reprint, Darmstadt, 1966).
4. Reitzenstein himself later preferred to speak of an Iranian background. For a survey of the debate, see William C. Grese, *Corpus Hermeticum XIII and Early Christian Literature*, Studia ad Corpus Hellenisticum Novi Testamenti, vol. 5 (Leiden, 1979), pp. 35–40.
5. See esp. *Révélation*.
6. Ibid., 2:35–47.
7. *Poimandres*, pp. 211–16.
8. This interpretation is only mentioned in *Poimandres*, pp. 215–16 n. 2, but it is further developed in Richard Reitzenstein, *Die hellenistischen Mysterienreligionen nach ihren Grundgedanken und Wirkungen*, 3d ed. (1927; reprint, Darmstadt, 1966), pp. 51–52.
9. *Révélation*, 1:82–84.
10. *Neue astrologische Texte des Hermes Trismegistos*, ed. Wilhelm Gundel (1936; reprinted with corrections and additions by Hans Georg Gundel, Hildesheim, 1978).
11. *Révélation*, 1:118–20.
12. On the *Genikoi Logoi* see Grese, *Corpus Hermeticum XIII*, pp. 67–69.
13. Cf. the related view in excerpt from Stobaeus 2b.2; *Asclepius* 13.
14. References to other astronomical and astrological phenomena can be found in other of the religious or philosophic Hermetica; see Arthur Darby Nock, review of *Neue astrologische Texte des Hermes Trismegistos*, by W. Gundel, *Gnomon* 15 (1939): 366; reprinted, as "Astrology and Cultural History," in *Essays on Religion and the Ancient World*, ed. Zeph Stewart, 2 vols. (Cambridge, Mass., 1972), 1:500; also Maria Valvo, "Considerazioni su Manilo e l'Ermetismo" *Siculorum Gymnasium* 9 (1956): 108–17.
15. *Révélation*, 1:122–23.
16. Ibid., 1:83–84. For a fuller discussion of these different groups, see Wilhelm Bousset, review of *Die Lehren des Hermes Trismegistos*, by Josef Kroll, *Göttingische Gelehrte Anzeigen* 176 (1914): 697–755; reprinted with further notes in *Religionsgeschichtliche Studien: Aufsätze zur Religionsgeschichte des hellenistischen Zeitalters*, Supplements to Novum Testamentum, vol. 50 (Leiden, 1979), pp. 97–191.
17. For examples of such usage, see Francis A. Yates, *Giordano Bruno and the Hermetic Tradition* (Chicago, 1964).
18. Yates, *Bruno*, pp. 44–48, and Julius Ruska, *Tabula Smaragdina: Ein Beitrag zur Geschichte der hermetischen Literatur* (Heidelberg, 1926) pp. 34–37, criticized Scott for separating the two Hermetic corpora. Etiene Gilson, review of *La révélation d'Hermès Trismégiste*, vol. 1 (1944 ed.), in *Revue philosophique* 135 (1945): 180, disagreed with Festugière on the same point. Nock sees the religious or

philosophic Hermetica as a later development; see Nock and Festugière, *Corpus Hermeticum*, 1:i–v; Nock, *Essays on Religion*, 1:499–501.

19. It is beyond the scope of this essay to attempt a definition of *magic* or *magical*. When the terms are used here, they refer to practices or texts from a recognized body of Greco-Egyptian magical literature, the Greek Magical Papyri edited by Karl Preisendanz, *Papyri Graecae Magicae: Die griechischen Zauberpapyri*, 2d ed., ed. Albert Henrichs, 2 vols. (Stuttgart, 1973–74), here *PGM*. Texts will be cited by papyrus number (in roman numerals) and line number.

20. Following Festugière's explanation, Nock and Festugière, *Corpus Hermeticum*, 2:396 n. 325.

21. In line with this account of human practice in *Asclepius*, one should also consider the god's use of secret spells in creating souls, excerpt from Stobaeus 23 *(Kore Kosmu)*, 14–15, and the creation of the zodiac in 18.

22. See Nock and Festugière, *Corpus Hermeticum*, 2:378 n. 194; also Josef Kroll, *Die Lehren des Hermes Trismegistos* (Münster, 1928), pp. 90–95.

23. Jean-Pierre Mahé, "De l'Egypte à l'Afrique romaine: Remarques sur l'apocalypse d'Asclépius," *Revue des études latines* 53 (1975): 31.

24. Cf. the use of similar techniques to foretell the future in *Corpus Hermeticum* 12.19.

25. For examples, see *PGM* IV.1840–70, 1872–1927, 2373–2440; V.370–446; VII.862–918; XII. 14–95; also I.3–43; Theodor Hopfner, "Mageia," in Pauly/Wissowa, *Real Encyclopädie der classischen Altertumswissenchaft*, vol. 13, pt. 2 (1928), 347–51.

26. See the discussion of the history of this material in Scott, *Hermetica*, 1:25–30, 49, 82–111; also William C. Grese, "The Hermetica and New Testament Research," *Biblical Research* 28 (1983): 38–40.

27. Nock and Festugière, *Corpus Hermeticum*, 2:284–88.

28. Such a possibility would be supported by the reference to the worship of idols in paragraph 25 of "The Definitions of Hermes Trismegistus to Asclepius," an ancient Hermetic text that has survived only in Armenian. "Ceux qui (adorent les) idoles, adorent (de simples) images. Car, s'ils adoraient en connaissance (de cause), ils ne seraient pas égarés; mais faute de savoir ce qu'au juste ils adorent, ils se sont égarés (loin) de (la) piété." (The translation is by J.-P. Mahé, "Les Définitions d'Hermès Trismégiste à Asclépius," *Revue des sciences religieuses* 50 [1976]: 195–214. This passage, which seems to agree with the negative evaluation in *Asclepius* 37–38, does demonstrate a wider discussion of the practice in Hermeticism than can be seen in the Greek Hermetic texts.) A new edition of this Armenian text by Mahé has not been available to me. See J.-P. Mahé, *Hermès en Haute-Egypte*, vol. 2: *Le fragment du "Discours parfait" et les "Définitions" hermétiques arméniennes (NH VI, 8.8a)*, Bibliothèque copte de Nag Hammadi, Section "Textes," no. 7 (Quebec, 1982).

29. See the parallels cited by J.-P. Mahé, "Le sens et la composition du traité hermétique, 'L'Ogdoade et l'ennéade,' conservé dans le codex VI de Nag Hamadi," *Revue des sciences religieuses* 48 (1974): 54–65; also idem, *Hermès en Haute-Egypte*, vol. 1: *Les textes hermétiques de Nag Hammadi et leurs parallèles grecs et latins*, Bibliothèque copte de Nag Hammadi, Section "Texts," no. 3 (Quebec,1978), pp. 31, 38–47; Karl-Wolfgang Tröger, "On Investigating the Hermetic Documents Contained in Nag Hammadi Codex VI: The Present State of Research," in *Nag Hammadi and Gnosis: Papers Read at the First International Congress of Coptology (Cairo, December 1976)*, ed. R. McL. Wilson, Nag Hammadi Studies, vol. 14 (Leiden, 1978), p. 120.

30. Translations of this and other sections of *The Discourse* quoted here are by Peter A. Dirkse, James Brashler, and Douglas M. Parrott, in *Nag Hammadi Codices V and VI*, ed. Parrott. See the discussion of this passage in Mahé, *Hermès en Haute-Egypte*, 1:106–7. Cf. also the use of such magical words in theurgical unification with the deity cited in Hans Lewy, *Chaldaean Oracles and Theurgy: Mysticism, Magic and Platonism in the Later Roman Empire*, ed. Michel Tardieu, Etudes augustiniennes (Paris, 1978), p. 195.

31. The names mentioned above. See Mahé, *Hermès en Haute-Egypte*, 1:130–31.

32. Such secrecy is known elsewhere in the Hermetica (see *Corpus Hermeticum* 13. Title, 22; *Asclepius* 1.32) and in the magical papyri. See the secret name in *PGM* I.217; IV.1610; XII.237, 240; XIII.763; XXIIb.20; see also the requirements for secrecy in IV.254–55, 852–56, 922; XII.321–22. See also Pauly/Wissowa, 13.2:371–73.

33. Cf. "come to me . . . since I speak your names which thrice-greatest Hermes wrote in Heliopolis with hieroglyphic letters" (*PGM* IV.883–87). Cf. also the spell addressed to Hermes, *PGM* VIII.41–43.

34. Mahé, *Hermès en Haute-Egypte*, 1:129–30.

35. Cf. *PGM* III.275–81, 424–65; V.47–49; VI.4–4; VII.284–99; XIII.1026–37; Pauly/Wissowa, 13.2:354–58.

36. See *PGM* IV. 886, 2376; V.213; VII. 919; XXIVa.2–4; also the collection of texts in Festugière, *Révélation*, 1:283–308.

37. See Hans Bonnet, "Thot," in *Reallexikon der ägyptischen Religionsgeschichte* (Berlin, 1952), pp. 805–12.

38. See Stein, "Hermes," in Pauly/Wissowa, *Real Encyclopädie der classischen Altertumswissenschaft*, vol. 8, pt. 1 (1912), 773–92.

39. *PGM*, XIII.138. Hermes is also mentioned in XIII.14–16, where he is accused of having plagiarized a description of certain kinds of incense from this Mosaic book and having included it in a book of his own.

40. For example, in both an excerpt from Stobaeus 23 *(Kore Kosmu)* 10 and *PGM* XIII God's laugh or smile is involved in the creative activity. In *Kore Kosmu* 10 God smiles and says that Nature is to be. In *PGM* XIII.161–206, 471–530, God laughs seven times and various beings are created, but none called Nature.

41. The connection between the magic spell and the Hermetica was noted already by Reitzenstein *(Poimandres,* pp. 146–60), who extended the spell beyond what is now line 611 in Preisendanz's edition. By removing what he considered to be the magical accretions to the original spell, Reitzenstein claimed to have recovered a prayer from an Egyptian religious community. The parallelism between this recovered prayer and the language of the Hermetica was then taken by Reitzenstein to show the dependence of Hermeticism on that earlier form of Egyptian religion. Reitzenstein's analysis of the spell, however, is unconvincing, because once the magical elements are removed, little of the spell remains.

42. For similar claims concerning the power of a spell, see *PGM* IV.1167–68, 1275, 1331, 1596–97, 2153–78, 2622–26.

43. Such summonses are frequent in the magical papyri; for examples, see *PGM* I.163–66; III.51–53; IV.236–39, 1605–6; VII.555–56, 961–68; VIII.2–6; IX.1–4; XII.48–58, 147.

44. For examples of the use of such knowledge, see *PGM* I.181–83; III.106–9, 623–25; IV.884–87, 2321–25, 3270–72; VII.686–702, 786–94, 883–84, 892–93; VIII.6–21; IX.13–14; XIV.20–22.

45. On these various forms that are attributed to the Sun during its course through the Heaven, see Hans Georg Gundel, *Weltbild und Astrologie in den griechischen Zauberpapryi* (Munich, 1968), pp. 5–6.

46. For other examples of threats against the gods, see *PGM* II.54–55; IV.874–75, 2096–97, 2902–12; V.256–303; XII.140–42; LVII.1–13; LXII.8–16.

47. Cf. comparable claims by the magician in *PGM* IV.185–94, 3107–8; XII.92–94.

48. For other examples of the magician identifying himself with a god, see *PGM* I.251–52; IV.394, 2288–90.; V.247–49; XII.74–75, 227–36.

49. Such hymns occur throughout the *PGM*. See the collection of hymns at the end of *PGM*, vol. 2.

50. Cf. the similar technique in the prayer of *PGM* I.195–222. The god who is asked to provide the deliverance from spiritual powers is the one who established the powers.

51. Cf. the petitions that the god listen in *PGM* IV.870–72, 1281; VII.786–89, 898–99; XII.117–18.

52. Cf. the lists of blessings requested in *PGM* VIII.4–6; XII.69–71; XXXV.14–27; XXXVI.44–48, 221–27; cf. also the list in A.-J. Festugière, *L'idéal religieux des grecs et l'évangile* (Paris, 1932), pp. 290–93.

53. The translation of the thanksgiving follows, with the exception mentioned in n. 54 below, the text of Nock and Festugière, *Corpus Hermeticum*, 2:353–54.

54. Following the reading of Mahé, *Hermès en Haute-Egypte*, 1:161.

55. Cf. A. D. Nock, "Greek Magical Papyri," *Journal of Egyptian Archaeology* 15 (1929): 228–30; reprinted in *Essays on Religion and the Ancient World*, 1:188–90; also Hans Dieter Betz, "Fragments from a Catabasis Ritual in a Greek Magical Papyrus," *History of Religions* 19 (1980): 287–95.

56. Such a practice can be demonstrated elsewhere in the magical papyri. Cf., e.g., IV.930–1114, which was made by combining a lamp divination with a charm for direct vision and including an introductory *sustasis*. The repetition in 930–1114 (see esp. the two dismissals in lines 1057–65 and 1065–70 and the explanation in lines 1066–67) is a result of the inclusion of similar elements from both of the charms. Cf. also VIII.64–110, which combines material also found in IV.436–46, 1957–68; VII.233–48.

57. Related lists occur elsewhere in the magical papyri. Cf. IV. 1645–1704; XXXVIII. 15–26; and see Gundel, *Weltbild und Astrologie*, p. 6. Although this is the only occurrence in the papryi of this particular hymn, it is not unusual to find the same hymn used in different contexts. See n. 56 above on VIII.64–110, and see the collection of hymns, *PGM*, 2:237–66.

58. See Pauly/Wissowa, 13.2:367–71.

59. See *Theological Dictionary of the New Testament*, s.v. *"ginōskō ktl.,* B."

60. See the discussion above of excerpt 6 of Stobaeus and the *Liber Hermetis Trismegisti*.

61. On the Hermetic character of the thanksgiving, see Mahé, *Hermès en Haute-Egypte*, 1:148–50.

62. So Festugière, *L'idéal religieux des grecs*, p. 292 n.3.

63. See Grese, *Corpus Hermeticum XIII*, pp. 180–82.

64. The decision to use this particular magic spell as the basis of the Hermetic spell for knowledge may have been influenced by the association elsewhere between Hermes Trismegistus and the sympa-

thetic magic reflected in the opening list of the signs, symbols, and names of god. See Festugière, *Révélation,* 1:202–7; Franz Cumont, "Ecrits hermétiques, II: Le médecin Thessalus et les plantes astrales d'Hermès Trismégiste," *Revue de philologie de littérature et d'histoire anciennes,* n.s., 42 (1918): 105–8; Pauly/Wissowa, 13.2:315, 321.

65. See H. D. Betz, "The Formation of Authoritative Tradition in the Greek Magical Papyri," in *Jewish-Christian Self-Definition,* vol. 3: *Self-Definition in the Greco-Roman World,* ed. Ben F. Meyer and E. P. Sanders (Philadelphia, 1982), 164–65.

66. Howard M. Jackson, trans., *Zosimos of Panopolis on the Letter Omega,* Texts and Translations, no. 14, Graeco-Roman Religion, no. 5 (Missoula, Mont. 1978), p. 25; cf. also Nock and Festugière, *Corpus Hermeticum,* 4:118–19 (frag. 21).

67. *De mysteriis Aegyptiorum* 8.4. Cf. the comments of Festugière and Nock on this passage, *Corpus Hermeticum,* 4:115–16 n. 2.

68. See Grese, *Corpus Hermeticum XIII,* pp. 138–42.

69. In this connection, one might also refer to the points of contact between the magical papyri and the Neoplatonists, on which see S. Eitrem, "La théurgie chez les néo-platoniciens et dans les papyrus magiques," *Symbolae Osloenses* 22 (1942): 49–79; Clemens Zintzen, "Die Wertung von Mystik und Magie in der neuplatonischen Philosophie," *Rheinisches Museum für Philologie* 108 (1965): 71–100.

3

Hermeticism and Judaism

MOSHE IDEL

1

Renaissance thought may be described as confluence of medieval theology with some of the schools of thought of antiquity: Pythagoreanism, Platonism, Neo-platonism, Hermeticism, and, at the end of the Renaissance, even atomism. These trends of thought were adopted, at least partially, because of their concordance with the Jewish and Christian theologies which, according to thinkers like Marsilio Ficino and Pico della Mirandola, were foreshadowed in these allegedly pre-Christian theologies. Although this approach has already been analyzed in detail in the studies of D. P. Walker[1] and Charles Trinkhaus,[2] I should like to stress one particular aspect that seems to be significant enough to be mentioned here. The most important testimonies used by Renaissance thinkers in order to substantiate their theory of the existence of a *prisca theologia* are quotations from the writings of some ancient thinkers. Plato was described as an Attic Moses by Numenius,[3] Hermes Trismegistus was linked to Moses by the Jewish historian Artapanos,[4] and atomism was regarded as an ancient Jewish doctrine because of Flavius Josephus's assertion that Anaxagoras learned his theology from Jewish sources.[5] Common to all these ancient authors is the syncretistic climate of thought of late antiquity, as evinced by the attempts made by some Jewish Hellenistic authors to present Judaism as fully in accordance with, or as the origin of, Greek and Egyptian thought.[6] This syncretistic tendency obviously also influenced some of the church fathers, such as Lactantius and Eusebius of Caesarea,[7] who preserved some of its most important testimonies, adding to them their own views, namely that some ancient theologies also adumbrated the Christian tenets.[8] It seems to me that a full understanding of the structural assumption upon which Jewish Hellenistic thought[9] and some patristic views were based will substantially contribute toward a better evaluation of Renaissance syncretism. I shall focus on the particular type of syncretism relevant to this volume: Hermeticism. It appears that only upon this type of syncretism has the influence of Jewish views been recognized by scholars. Beginning with Causabon, a series of scholars have demonstrated the occurrence of Jewish material in the Hermetic corpus.[10] One must ask what the relation is between Artapanos's assertion of the identity of Moses with Hermes, three or four hundred years before the composition of the Hermetic writings, and the actual presence of Jewish elements in these works. Is it merely a coincidence?

In order to attempt to answer this question, I should like to analyze some motifs occurring in *Asclepius*. The first detailed scholarly attempt to prove the influence of a postbiblical Jewish work upon the *Asclepius* seems to be the short note of M. Philonenko, "Une allusion de l'Asclepius au livre d'Henoch."[11] This author convincingly pointed out the Enochic background of paragraph 25 of *Asclepius*. I should like here to expand upon this assertion. A perusal of this part of the Hermetic corpus will demonstrate that although Philonenko's note is correct, it does not state the whole truth. The influence of the Enochic myth of the descent of the angels who mingled with women and divulged secrets on *Asclepius* 25 is evident. The next paragraph, 26, deals with Hermes' prophecy on the aging of the world, the depravity of man and his future punishment by flood, fire, or disease and, following this, the renewal of the world.[12] It seems that the occurrence of the flood and the fire as two forms of punishment is not only influenced by the flood that follows the descent of the angels in the Bible, but also by the punishment by flood and fire mentioned in the Ethiopic *Enoch*.[13] Moreover, Hermes predicted the flood and fire exactly as Enoch predicted the end of the world in the Ethiopic version.[14] These similarities seem to point to an influence of the ancient Enochic literature which, at least partially, was written and disseminated in Egypt[15] on the *Asclepius* which presumably was also written in Egypt.[16] If this conclusion is correct, one must go a step further and reveal the real figure who is hidden under the name of Hermes: It is Enoch. In the *Asclepius,* Hermes tells the story of the creation of man and prophesies the descent of the angels and the flood. In biblical terms, Hermes seems to be an antediluvian prophetic figure, and this view clearly points to an identification of Hermes of the *Asclepius* with Enoch.[17] Such an identification is by no means new; it is shared by Hebrew,[18] Arabic,[19] and Christian[20] sources, and my short analysis of the *Asclepius* only confirms this widespread tradition. It seems, therefore, that the *Asclepius* includes not only some Jewish postbiblical motifs; its hero and its view of the history of mankind may properly be understood only against the background of the Enochic literature and the Jewish Hellenistic tendency to identify a central Jewish figure, like Moses, with Hermes.

With this conclusion in mind, let me compare the famous discussions of the animation of the statues in the *Asclepius* with material found in another Enochic work, the Hebrew *Enoch*. The Egyptian background of these passages (*Asclepius* 23–24, 37) is undeniable. It is worth pointing out, however, one particular detail that occurs in *Asclepius* 37: The invention of the art of creating gods came after the grave error of the ancestors regarding the nature of the gods, and after their negligence of the rituals. After the description of the way the gods are attracted into the idols, these idols are referred to as prone to doing good and evil. Moreover, the attraction of the gods into the statues is reported to be the result of man's incapacity to create souls. These rather negative attitudes toward the art of attracting the gods must be taken into consideration before one passes a final judgment on the use of the Egyptian sources. A comparison of *Asclepius* 37 with paragraphs 23–24 reveals that there are two somewhat differing views of man's creation of the terrestrial gods. This creation is referred to as the supreme proof of man's greatness in *Asclepius* 23, whereas in paragraph 37 this same action is the result of man's incapacity to create souls. This dichotomy may be the result of the influence of different sources: the Egyptian sources, where the technique of attracting gods was positively presented, and other sources in which this technique was connected with a theological error. To quote a passage found in the Hebrew *Enoch:*

When the Holy One, blessed be He, went out and went in from the Garden of Eden, from Eden to the Garden, and from the Garden to Raqia, and from Raqia to the Garden of Eden, then all and everyone beheld the splendour of this Shekina and they were not injured, until the time of the generation of Enosh who was the head of all idol worshippers of the world. And what did the generation of Enosh do? They went from one end of the world to the other, and each one brought silver, gold, precious stones and pearls in heaps like upon mountains and hills[21] making idols out of them throughout the world. And they erected idols in every quarter of the world: the size of each idol was 1,000 parasangs. And they brought down the sun, the moon, planets and constellations, and placed them before the idols on their right hand and on their left, to attend them even as they attend the Holy One, blessed be He, as it is written [1 Kings 22: 19]: "And all the host of heaven was standing by him on his right hand and on his left."[22] What power was in them that they were able to bring them down? They would not have been able to bring them down but for Uzza, Azza and Azziel who taught them sorceries whereby they brought them down and made use of them.[23]

I shall begin the examination of this passage with the final phrase—"made use of them." The Hebrew original, *mishtamshim bahem,* has an obvious magical overtone;[24] therefore, the sin of the generation of Enosh is not only idolatry, but more precisely theurgy—the idols were intended to serve magical purposes. The description of the building of these idols consists of two important features: First, the idols were composed of several elements, as were the Hermetic statues. And second, there are explicit astral implications linked to the function of these idols—in order to be efficient, the whole host of heaven must be brought down. This astral feature may be considered as a slight distortion of the bringing down of the powers of the planets in the Hermetic sources. Both *Asclepius* 37 and the Hebrew *Enoch* share a negative attitude toward this astral magic. One more detail occurs in these two books: in *Asclepius* 24–25, the divorce of the gods from man is mentioned immediately after the discussion of the animation of the statues. This is also the case in the Hebrew *Enoch,* chapter 5: the description of the presence of God in the

garden of Eden is followed by the above-mentioned passage on the idols; immediately afterward, one finds the angels' reproach to God:

> Why hast thou left the highest of the high heavens, the abode of thy glorious
> Name and the high and exalted Throne in Araboth on high and art gone and
> dwellest with the children of men who worship idols and equal thee to the idols?
> What hast thou to do with the inhabitants of the earth who worship idols?
> Forthwith the Holy One, blessed be He, lifted up His Shekina[25] from the earth,
> from their midst and the Shekina ascended to the high heavens.[26]

Is the occurrence of these two motifs in similar contexts mere chance? It seems
improbable; it would be more reasonable to infer that there is some historical
affinity between them. It appears that although the Hebrew *Enoch* is a relatively
late work, probably dating from the fifth or sixth century,[27] the material included in
it may be much older, and *Enoch* itself, or its sources, could have influenced the
somewhat negative attitude toward the creation of the gods in *Asclepius* 37.

The identification of Hermes with Moses in Artapanos could be only one
implication of a Jewish-Egyptian syncretistic tendency, whose most important
output may be the use of Jewish, Egyptian, and Hellenistic materials in the
Asclepius.

2

The first medieval Jewish reference to Hermes in Europe is to be found in Moses
ibn Ezra's early-twelfth-century work, *Maqalat al-Hadiqa,* (Treatise of the
garden), where a passsage preserved in Stobaeus's fragments is quoted.[28] More
important is the occurrence of the names of Hermes and Asclepius as two philosophers who attained union with the Active Intellect, in the *Book of Kuzari* 1, by
Judah ha-Levi.[29] A third author who mentions Hermes is Abraham ibn Ezra,
whose importance will be discussed later. However, before I deal with this Hermeticism, it is worth stressing that Moses ibn Ezra knew Judah ha-Levi and
Abraham ibn Ezra, and the latter was a close friend of ha-Levi.[30] These facts
cannot be mere coincidence; the only three thinkers in the first half of the twelfth
century who refer to Hermes had close personal relations.

I shall now discuss the Hermetic references in the works of Abraham ibn Ezra.
In one of his astronomical works, he mentions Henoch in three different ways:
"the ancient Henoch,"[31] "the Egyptian Henoch,"[32] and "the first Henoch,"[33]
always in an astrological context. It is obvious that Abraham ibn Ezra knew
Albumazar version of the legend about the triple Hermes,[34] the last of whom was
identified with Enoch. According to Albumazar, this identification apparently
existed among the Jews already before Albumazar's time.[35] Abraham ibn Ezra also
mentions Henoch in his commentary on the Pentateuch, where one learns that

> Perhaps Henoch saw, in a prophetic way, that Noah would revive the world, and
> that through him the curse would be relieved from the earth. [Henoch] saw this

in his [i.e., Noah's] constellation, since [Henoch] composed many books on many sciences which are still in existence today.[36]

Although the context of this discussion is astrological, it is obvious that Abraham ibn Ezra is referring to the Enochic, that is, Hermetic, books that deal with various subjects. It is therefore unlikely that the only Hermetic quotation found in Albumazar's works reached Abraham ibn Ezra. It seems more reasonable to suppose that Moses ibn Ezra's quotation of a Hermetic fragment preserved by Stobaeus and ha-Levi's mention of Hermes and Asclepius strengthen the assumption that Abraham ibn Ezra indeed saw several Hermetic treatises, which, presumably, also dealt with nonastrological topics. The direct astrological references to the Hermetic astrological literature are only the most obvious indication of Abraham ibn Ezra's new view of Judaism. This author seems to be the first Jewish thinker to interpret a significant number of biblical events in an astrological way and to interpret the Jewish commandments as intended, inter alia, to counteract the pernicious influence of the stars and to preserve their favorable effect.[37] This novel approach can be demonstrated by many examples, but I should like to elaborate on only one issue, which is Abraham ibn Ezra's astonishing interpretation of the episode of the golden calf. According to Abraham ibn Ezra,[38] Aaron's intention when building the calf was not idolatrous. He attempted to build a surrogate for Moses' missing leadership; the calf was intended to serve as a guide. However, according to Abraham ibn Ezra, Aaron's intention was misunderstood; part of the people conceived of the calf as an object of worship and fell into the sin of idolatry. This is why they were killed while Aaron remained alive and even continued to serve as a priest. When describing the nature of this surrogate, Abraham ibn Ezra writes, "It is a glory residing in a corporeal form."[39] In other words, Aaron built a calf that was intended to capture the glory and thus turn it into an angel that would lead the people of Israel instead of Moses. According to Abraham ibn Ezra, the form of the calf was intended to imitate an astral form, though he does not reveal what this form was.[40] Therefore, the making of the calf is conceived as astral magic. The construction was legal, but its aim was not properly realized. In order to better understand Abraham ibn Ezra's view, I quote his explanation of the nature of the teraphim:

The teraphim are built according to the forms of men and this form is made [in such a way as] to receive the power of the superior [beings].[41]

In both cases, Abraham ibn Ezra seems to imply that superior powers that will guide men are captured by corporeal forms made below for that purpose. This practice has, according to him, nothing to do with idolatry.

The combination of monotheism with astral magical intended to capture the supernatural powers seems to point to a Hermetic view of Judaism. The opposition between magic and Judaism was at least partially attenuated.

Before proceeding with my discussion of the history of Abraham ibn Ezra's natural magic, which seems to be Hermetic in its nature and sources, I would like to remark on a possible implication of his knowledge of Hermetic books. He was, like his friend Judah-ha-Levi, a native of Tudela.[42] Their knowledge of Hermeticism may be considered important new evidence that may strengthen the hypothesis of Henry and Renée Kahane on the Hermetic source of the Grail legend.[43] According to these scholars, Chrétien de Troyes and Wolfram von Eschenbach received the core of their literary works from a certain Kyot who was identified by them with William of Tudela. The latter transmitted to Chrétien and Wolfram several motifs that stem from the *Corpus Hermeticum;* moreover, these scholars alluded to the possibility that William could have been a converted Jew.[44] It is therefore interesting to add the discussion of the probable knowledge of Hermeticism by Jewish authors, natives of Tudela who flourished at the middle of the twelfth century, to the assumption of the Kahanes that Hermetic lore was known to a Jewish convert in Tudela in the second part of the twelfth century.[45]

It is worth noting that the first references to Hermes in twelfth-century Jewish authors are contemporaneous with the appearance of Hermetic motifs in Christian sources.[46]

3

Profoundly influenced by Abraham ibn Ezra's commentaries was the anonymous book entitled the *Book of Life,* written around 1200 in Germany or northern France.[47] In it one finds a recurring view, according to which

like the body which is composed of four elements so the soul which is a spirit is composed of four elements,[48] the source of wisdom, the source of understanding and the source of knowledge and the source of reason.[49]

This comparison of four material elements to four spiritual components might have been influenced by the following passage in the *Asclepius:*

By that part of man which, being made as of supernal elements, soul and intellect,[50] spirit and reason, he is divine, and has the possibility of ascending to heaven, whereas by virtue of his material body composed of fire and earth, water and air, he is mortal.[51]

As in this passage, the *Book of Life* links the conception of four elements of the spiritual part of man with his ascent. After another enumeration of the four spiritual elements, one reads:

But those [parts] which come from the intellectual soul shine by a supernal light, and on the paths of righteousness, fear and purity and bring the soul to the supernal world.[52]

Four decades after Abraham ibn Ezra's *floruit,* the most important Jewish medieval philosophical theology was formulated. Moses ben Maimon—Maimonides—vigorously interpreted Judaism in Artistotelian terms, and he rejected explicitly the Platonic and Neoplatonic tradition as well as the books of Hermes.[53]

His own view of the commandments was strictly intellectual, and he clearly rejected astrology, magic, and the astral magic of the Sabean,[54] the only living remnant of the Hermetic trend of thought. Maimonides' theology remained, during the thirteenth century and the first half of the fourteenth the dominant Jewish theology. However, around 1350, a clear-cut turn can be perceived: Abraham ibn Ezra returned to the forefront of Jewish theology; during the next fifty years, many "supercommentaries" on his commentary on the Pentateuch were written, mostly in Spain.[55] This is a tremendous phenomenon. Abraham ibn Ezra's commentary on the Pentateuch seems to be—after the Bible, Mishnah, and Talmud—the most commented Jewish text, much more so than any other philosophical text. This vast quantity of supercommentaries consists of thousands of folios, mostly still in manuscript form. The study of these manuscripts has not even begun. A perusal of part of this literature indicates that Hermetic works were known to some of the supercommentators who seem to be aware of the affinities of these works to Abraham ibn Ezra's views. One of these authors, Jehuda Mosconi, explicitly refers to a magical issue,[56] explained at length in the books of Hermes[57] and in the *Book of Agriculture*[58] and especially in the books of Zigarit.[59] Mosconi also mentions the *Book of the Talismans* by Hermes.[60]

What the context of such a *Book of the Talismans* may be is apparently learned from a passage found in another supercommentary on Abraham ibn Ezra, in Samuel ibn Sarsa's *Makor Hayyim* (The fountain of life). A quotation from a book of an earlier fourteenth-century author, David ibn Billya, maintains that

in the *Book of Talismans* it is written that . . . when a certain constellation occurs, you should pour any metal you wish into a mould of a beautiful man and the form composed of them [i.e., of the several stars of the constellation] will be successful in dignity and glory and it will foretell the future.[61]

This is alchemical and astral magic, intended to predict the future, whose affinity to Hermetic alchemical and magical literature is evident.[62] Ibn Sarsa also knew a book of the *Religion of the Prophets,* where it is stated that

Enoch was a great saint and sage who brought nations to the worship of God, blessed be He. At first he publicised the sciences of the stars and he gave each of the inhabitants of the seven climes a religion which conformed to the nature of that climate. He commanded them to observe festivals and offer sacrifices at particular times in accordance with the position of the stars and in keeping with the dominant star in the sky so that the star would guard the efflux of that particular climate.[63]

In ibn Sarsa's supercommentary, as well as in that of Samuel ibn Motot, a spurious book attributed to Abraham ibn Ezra is quoted, the *Book of the Substances.*[64] This is a magico-astral treatise that is based upon the supposition that causing the descent of the spiritual forces is the main magical technique. This view is also found in the *Picatrix,* a book influenced by Hermetic views.[65]

These occasional quotations are only part of the material that has certain affinities to the Hermetic views known to me.[66] It is reasonable to surmise that a systematic perusal of the vast literature on Abraham ibn Ezra will reveal much more material that will strengthen the hypothesis that the authors of the supercommentaries correctly perceived his views as close to astral magical views and searched for sources that would help them to interpret his writings. This was the avenue to the broadening of the Hermetic influence on Jewish texts.

4

One of the most important successors of the ibn Ezra tradition in the Renaissance was Yohanan Alemanno, one of Pico della Mirandola's Jewish teachers.[67] Alemanno quotes most of the above-mentioned works extensively. He was deeply influenced by these works,[68] and in his books he widened this approach in two important ways. First, he used additional Hermetic sources seemingly unknown in medieval Jewish texts.[69] Second, the Hermetic approach was used in order to interpret the most important elements of the Jewish tradition: the written and oral laws, the service in the Temple, prayer, and the performance of the commandments as intended (according to Alemanno) to cause the spiritual forces to descend.[70] The Temple was conceived of as a gigantic talisman constructed in order to induce the presence of God to descend upon it. There is in Alemanno's system a "Hermetic re-form" of Judaism; he himself describes the "ancient wisdom"[71] in these terms: It was so vast that they [the ancients] boasted of it in their books which they attributed to Enoch whom the Lord has taken (Genesis 6:4) and to Solomon who was wiser than any man and to many perfect men who performed actions by intermingling various things and comparing qualities in order to create new forms in gold, silver, vegetable, mineral, and animal that had never before existed, and to create divine forms that foretell the future, laws,[72] nomoi,[73] and spirits of angels, of stars and of devils." The similarity of this passage to the *Asclepius* passages on the creation of the gods is evident. Alemanno conceived of this technique as connected with Enoch and Solomon,[74] thereby implying that it was an ancient Jewish device. In light of my earlier discussion, it is clear why Enoch is mentioned in lieu of Hermes. But why Solomon? One answer may be the Hermetic perception of the Temple that was built by Solomon and his reputation as a magician. However, it seems that this is not the whole answer. The names of Enoch and Solomon appear together in a book where Hermetic traditions were reported in the names of Hermes alias Enoch. It is a particular version of *Sefer Raziel* (The book of Raziel)[75] into which important magical material, stemming from a Hermetic source in the Italian language, was inserted. According to this version of *Sefer Raziel,* Solomon received this book from the angel Raziel—the angel of the Divine Secrets—and furthermore, he had found "a book of Enoch, called Ermetis."[76] The manuscript of *Sefer Raziel* and its commentary were known to Alemanno, and there is clear evidence of the existence of Hermetic texts in Florence and even in the hands of Pico della Mirandola. Since the important parts of the manuscript are written in Italian, in Hebrew characters, it seems highly probable that it was also known to Alemanno's Christian contemporaries. However, this point deserves a more detailed study.

Let me return to the impact of Hermeticism on Alemanno's view of Judaism. I should like to discuss only two specific examples that may have some historical importance. When explaining the nature of the Tabernacle and its vessels, Alemanno writes:

> For the people [of Israel] were taught to believe in the possibility of causing spiritual forces and emanations to descend from above by means of preparations made by man for that purpose, such as talismans, garments, and certain objects whose purpose is to cause the descent of a certain spiritual power, as when our master, peace be with him,[77] prepared the golden calf. The intention was only to cause the spiritual forces[78] to descend by means of a physical body.[79]

Alemanno went so far as to ascribe to Moses the preparation of the golden calf, which is conceived in explicitly Hermetic terms, as an astrological talisman. This astonishing view of Moses as a Hermetic magician[80] seems to originate with Alemanno, and I was unable to find any Jewish parallel; nevertheless, it seems that a certain parallel existed, since Giordano Bruno writes:

> Cabalistorum doctrina confirmat et exemplum Mosis qui inferdum atque Jovis favorem comparandum virtulum aurem erexit ad Martis item temperandum simul atque Saturni violentem aeneum serpentem adorantum ofiecit.[81]

Bruno refers to a cabalistic conception of Moses as the builder of the calf in order to attract the gods. Are these two similar views of Moses a mere coincidence? It seems that the answer must be in the negative, since Bruno explicitly indicates that he adopted a cabalistic view. I assume, therefore, that the conception of Moses shared by Alemanno and Bruno is the result of a similar historical influence of a Hermetic cabala like Alemanno's. In the Nolan's eyes, Moses was the perfect Hermetic magician and Hermeticism was the perfect religion. A question may be asked about the way Alemanno's Hermetic interpretation of the cabala and Judaism could have reached Bruno. Alemanno's own view appeared in manuscripts in which only a few scholars were interested. However, there is a major exception; one particular cabalist was deeply influenced by Alemanno: Bruno's contemporary, Abraham Yagel.[82] This author was also influenced by Hermetic sources translated by Ficino.[83] Although I cannot cite any historical evidence of a link between Bruno and Yagel, a similar and quite astonishing statement made by Bruno (in the presence of the librarian of the Abbey of Saint Victor) has a parallel in one of Yagel's works. Bruno was reported to have asserted that[84] "he had heard it said that this duke [of Florence] wished to build a *civitas solis,* in which the sun would shine every day of the year, as it does in other cities etc." Yagel reports that[85] the great duke Cosimo de'Medici put woods of "lauro as walls of the city he built in Romania, which has the name of the City of the Sun." No third statement about a magical city of the sun built by a duke is known to me. Was Yagel the link between Alemanno's Hermetic interpretation of the cabala and Bruno's view of Moses as a Hermetic magician? Although I cannot supply a definitive answer and the question has to remain unsolved, I should like to point out a bibliographical detail. Alemanno's statement on Moses was copied from his *Collectanaea.* This manuscript was never published, and only a very few people could have read it. The only person that seems to have been influenced by Alemanno's notes was Abraham Yagel. He read the manuscript and even reacted to some opinions expressed in it.[86] I presume, therefore, that the only author besides Alemanno and Bruno who was acquainted with this idea was Yagel. This is the most I could discover concerning the possible relations among Alemanno, Yagel, and Bruno.

5

One of the most interesting cases of Hermetic influence on Renaissance magical praxis is the well-known initiation of Ferdinand of Aragon by Ludovico Lazarelli.[87] This passage has been discussed by Kristeller[88] and Walker,[89] who stressed the Hermetic overtones of the text. I should like to focus on one part of Lazarelli's discussion that deserves a longer analysis. Lazarelli quotes a passage from *Sefer Yezira* (Book of creation) that deals with the creation of the golem out of virgin earth by means of the pronunciation of combinations of letters.[90] The text referred to by Lazarelli cannot be located in the common versions of *Sefer Yezira*[91] since it is part of the commentary to this book written by the early thirteenth-century author Elazar of Worms. Gershom Scholem, who already pointed out this fact, was surprised by the very appearance of this text in a Christian work, since it was considered to be one of the most esoteric Jewish issues.[92] The text of Elazar is found in only three manuscripts listed by Scholem.[93] To his short list, I should like to make one highly significant addition. The text referred to by Lazarelli was also copied out in Yohanan Alemanno's *Collectanaea*. However, what seems more important than the mere occurrence of the text in two contemporary Italian authors is the affinity between the interpretation Lazarelli seems to give to this text and the interpretation alluded to in Alemanno's notes. Lazarelli saw this text as related to the secret alluded to in the *Asciepius*.[94] The exact nature of the Hermetic secret is not clear. According to Kristeller,[95] the text refers to the rebirth of Lazarelli through the initiated King of Aragon. According to Walker,[96] the text deals with Lazarelli's creation of the demons, or souls, and his providing the king with a good demon. I propose a slightly different interpretation. Lazarelli did not create demons, but attracted them into the body of the king. Such an interpretation is very close to the passage in the *Asciepius* concerning the incapacity of man to create souls,[97] but his ability to attract souls into already existing idols. The king played the role of an idol into which the divine soul was introduced. In Jewish terms, the king is conceived of as a golem, and Lazarelli's task was to vivify him by attracting the spiritual powers into the king's limbs by incantations of combinations of letters.

I support my interpretation of the Lazarelli text by an analysis of the sources quoted in one of Alemanno's folios of his *Collectanaea*. On the verso of folio 95, he quotes verbatim Elazar's text on the creation of the golem. No direct interpretation of the meaning of this process is suggested, but one can grasp Lazarelli's interpretation of the text from a passage copied out by Alemanno on the same page, immediately after the golem passage. It is a quotation from paragraph 9 of the *Centiloquium* of Claudius Ptolemaeus, with the commentary of Ali ibn Ragel.

Ptolemaeus said: The forms in the world of composition [i.e., in the world of generation and corruption] obey the forms of the spheres. This is why the masters of the talismans draw the forms of the spheres in order to receive the emanation of the stars in the object they intend to operate with.[98]

The Arab commentator of this text mentions "the masters of the idols who contemplate the efflux of the stars into the forms of the star."[99] Here, Alemanno added a marginal note of his own:

This is the secret of the world of the letters; they are forms and seals [made in order to] collect the supernal and spiritual emanation[100] as the seals collect the emanations of the stars.[101]

According to Alemanno, there are two ways of attracting the effluxes from above: the use of idols and seals in order to collect the efflux of the stars, and the use of Hebrew letters in order to collect the efflux from the world of letters, a place beyond the stars.[102] Since the passage quoted from Elazar of Worms was copied by Alemanno immediately before this note, I surmise that the combination of letters, which is a major part of the technique described in this text, was regarded by Alemanno as the way to attract spiritual efflux upon the golem made of clay.

This interpretation of Alemanno's view of the relationship between the supernal world of letters and the combination of letters in this world is corroborated by another passage found in Alemanno's *Collectanaea,* where the author asserts that

Moses . . . . had precise knowledge of the spiritual world which is called the world of Sefirot, and divine names, or the world of letters.[103] Moses knew how to direct his thoughts and prayers so as to improve the divine efflux . . . By means of that efflux, he created anything he wished, just as God created the world by means of various emanations. Whenever he wanted to perform signs and wonders, Moses would pray and utter divine names, words and meditations.[104] . . . The emanations then descended into the world and created new supernatural things.[105]

It is obvious that the names and words uttered by Moses were intended to derive an efflux from the world of letters or divine names. This is a parallel to the analysis of Alemanno's conception of the golem operation. Here, as in the golem technique, Alemanno conceived of the magical operation of attracting and collecting the supernal efflux as Hermetic astral magic.

So much for the magical part of the golem technique shared by Lazarelli and Alemanno. I should now like to focus on another aspect of the initiation text, emphasized by Paul Kristeller. According to this scholar, the main subject of the text is indicated by the words "mens mentem generet,"[106] or "syngenea mentis generatio."[107] The motif of spiritual rebirth is certainly Hermetic, whereas the Jewish text of the golem summarized by Lazarelli seems to deal only with the creation of an artificial man, not with the spiritual rebirth of the creator. However, Lazarelli interprets the details he quoted in a special way, forcing them to imply "generatio mentis."[108] Such an interpretation could be found in the discussions of the golem in the cabalistic school of Abraham Abulafia, the main proponent of the prophetic or ecstatic cabala.[109] According to this cabalist:

The greatest deed of the deeds is to make souls, which is the secret [meaning] of [the verse]: and the souls which they had made in Haran. Since God made man perfect, in the image of God He made him, and [therefore] this deed is with us the best of all deeds. This is why every learned person is obliged to make souls more than he is obliged to make bodies; his obligation to create bodies being intended to refer only to his making souls, this being the way a man can imitate his creator.[110]

This way of "imitatio dei" by "generatio animae" is proposed by one of Abulafia's students as the true meaning of the creation of the golem. According to this anonymous student, the real creation is the creation of souls by means of the combination of letters.[111] Was this view known to Alemanno and connected to the passage on the golem that he quoted in his *Collectanaea?* The answer to this question is quite positive. The quotation from Abraham Abulafia is found in his book the *Life of the World to Come,* which Alemanno knew very well. Alemanno quotes from this book several times,[112] but it is highly significant that a long quotation from this book is to be found immediately before the text of the golem in his *Collectanaea.*[113] This cannot be a mere coincidence for the two main subjects of Lazarelli's passage, which makes use of the golem text, are also found in Alemanno's *Collectanaea* immediately before and after the same text. Since both Alemanno and Lazarelli lived in northern Italy, at exactly the same period, and since Lazarelli's text is full of quotations from Hebrew sources, it is highly probable that he received the two interpretations of the golem passage from Alemanno.

To return to Alemanno's view of certain issues of Jewish tradition in order to explain properly discussions in Christian Hermetic texts: It seems that both Lazarelli and Bruno may be in debt to Alemanno's interpretation of the golem or the golden calf. But, whereas the Christian Hermeticists were also clearly influenced by the new emerging Hermeticism of the Renaissance period, Alemanno continues a tradition that seems to have begun with Abraham ibn Ezra. Therefore, one must reconsider the history of Renaissance Hermeticism; it is not only a confluence of the cabala and Hermeticism made by Pico della Mirandola and continued by the Christian cabalists like Francesco Giorgio or Cornelius Agrippa; it is also the result of the Hermetic interpretations of cabalistic doctrines based upon Hermetic motifs that stem from the Judeo-Arab tradition,[114] motifs that were well known long before Ficino undertook his Latin rendering of the *Corpus Hermeticum.* One must remember that the most important author of this Hermetic-cabalistic syncretism was Alemanno, the teacher of Pico della Mirandola.

Notes

1. D. P. Walker, *The Ancient Theology: Studies in Christian Platonism from the Fifteenth to Eighteenth Century* (London, 1972), pp. 1–21. See also Charles B. Schmitt, "Perennial Philosophy: From Agostino Steuco to Leibniz," *Journal of the History of Ideas* 27 (1966): 505–32.

2. Charles Trinkhaus, *In Our Image and Likeness,* 2 vols. (London, 1970), 2:739–40.

3. See J. G. Gager, *Moses in Greco-Roman Paganism* (Nashville, 1972), pp. 66–67.

4. See Eusebius, *Praeparatio Evangelica,* 9.27.6. For some suggestions on the possible influence of Hermes' functions on the image of Moses in Midrashic literature, see Samuel Kraus, "Moses, the Great Scribe of Israel," *HaGoren* 7 (1907): 30–34 (in Hebrew).

5. See *Contra Apionem*, 2.168; D. B. Sailor, "Moses and Atomism," *Journal of the History of Ideas* 25 (1964): 3–16.

6. See the references to the most important sources and studies in Norman Roth, "The Theft of Philosophy by the Greeks from the Jews," *Classical Folia* 32 (1978): 53–67, esp. pp. 61–65.

7. See note 4 above, and Roth, "Theft of Philosophy," pp. 65–66.

8. See Walker, *Ancient Theology*, p. 4.

9. See B. Z. Wacholder, *Eupolemus: A Study of Judeo-Greek Literature* (Cincinnati, 1974), pp. 75–96.

10. See B. A. Pearson, "Jewish Elements in *Corpus Hermeticum* I (Poimandres)," in *Studies in Gnosticism and Hellenistic Religions: Presented to G. Quispel*, ed. R. van de Broeck and M. J. Vermaseren (Leiden, 1981), pp. 336–48. This very important contribution is the dernier cri on the problem of Jewish influence on *Poimandres;* nevertheless, the final statements (p. 348)—"In the further development of the Hermetic tradition the Jewish elements gradually diminish. This diminution is quite noticeable in the later documents of the Hermetic corpus"—cannot be confirmed by the results of the present study.

11. *Christianity, Judaism and Other Graeco-Roman Cults: Studies for Morton Smith at Sixty*, 3 vols., ed. J. Neusner (Leiden, 1975), 2:11–163.

12. Some of the motifs occurring in the description of the end of the world were seemingly influenced by Egyptian materials, as P. Derechain has pointed out; see his article, "L'autenticité de l'inspiration égyptienne dans *Le Corpus Hermeticum*," *Revue de l'Histoire des Religions* 161 (1962): 192–93. However, the Egyptian source quoted by Derechain does not mention either the flood or the fire as punishments. See also his "Le Papyrus Salt 823 (BL 1005): Rituel pour la conservation de la vie en Egypt," *Academie royale de Belgique, Memoires* 58, nos. 1–2 (1965): 24–25.

13. *1 Enoch*, chaps. 12, 13; F. Martin, *Le livre d'Henoch* (Paris, 1975), pp. 22, 26. On the flood of water and fire in Hebrew and other ancient sources, see Louis Ginzberg, "The Flood of Fire," in *On Halakah and Haggadah* (Tel Aviv, 1960), pp. 205–19 (in Hebrew). See especially p. 293 n. 11a, where Hippolytus's *Philosophumena* (9.30) is adduced to prove the existence of two floods—the deluge and a flood of fire—among the ancient Jews; in that note, Ginzberg quotes also a Midrashic source where the generation of the deluge was also burned by fire! See also p. 206, where Ginzberg asserts that in Flavius Josephus's period there was already a view that Adam had predicted the destruction of the world by the floods of water and one of fire. In later sources preserved in Arabic, Hermes is explicitly referred to as living before the flood, and "he was the first to prophesy the coming of the flood and saw that heavenly plague by water and fire threatened the earth" (see Martin Plessner, "Hermes Trismegistus and Arab Science," *Studia Islamica* 2 [1954]: 51, quoting the ninth-century Albumazar). On the problem of the flood in Gnostic literature, see A. F. Klijn, "An Analysis of the Use of the Story of the Flood in the Apocalypse of Adam," *Studies in Gnosticism and Hellenistic Religions*, pp. 218–26. The author also discusses the subject of the flood of fire without being aware of Ginzberg's study referred to above.

14. *1 Enoch*, 19:3; Martin, *Livre d'Henoch*, pp. 53–54. See also A.-J. Festugière, *La Révélation d'Hermès Trismégiste*, 4 vols. (Paris, 1949–54), 1:334.

15. See J. T. Milik, *The Books of Enoch* (Oxford, 1976), p. 276.

16. See Derechain's discussions referred to in note 12 above.

17. See especially Martin Hengel's statement: "A comparison between Hermes-Thot in the Kore Kosmu and Enoch is astonishing . . . The parallels to the Enoch tradition are obvious. Thus, it is understandable that Enoch and Hermes-Thot were confused in the early Middle Ages" (*Judaism and Hellenism*, 2 vols. [London, 1974], 1:215; 2:141 n. 678.

18. See Semitic texts alluded to in P. S. Alexander, "The Historical Setting of the Book of Enoch," *Journal of Jewish Studies* 28 (1977): 166–67; Milik, *Books of Enoch*, pp. 114, 134. Hebrew identifications of the two figures will be discussed below.

19. M. Ullman, *Die Natur und Geheimwissenschaft im Islam* (Leiden, 1972), p. 371 and n. 2; David Pingree, *The Thousands of Abu-Mashar* (London, 1968), p. 15.

20. Charles S. F. Burnett, "The Legend of the Three Hermes and Abu Mashar's *Kitab al-Uluf* in the Latin Middle Ages," *Journal of the Warburg and Courtauld Institutes* 39 (1976): 231–32.

21. Compare to Song of Songs 2:8, which was interpreted in Midrash Rabba as referring to idolatry; see also Hosea 4:13.

22. This procedure is obviously intended to imitate the structure of the upper world; God is described as dancing before the righteous in the world to come in these terms: "[God] is dancing Himself in the banquet, and Sun and Moon and stars and constellations at his right and left, and [all these] are dancing with Him, in front of them [i.e., the righteous]" (*Otiot de R. Aqiva: Batei Midrashot*, 2 vols., ed. S. Wertheimer [Jerusalem, 1955], 2:375; in Hebrew).

23. *3 Enoch; or, The Hebrew Book of Enoch*, ed. and trans. H. Odeberg (New York, 1973), pp. 15–16; Hebrew text, pp. ix–x.

24. G. Scholem, *Jewish Gnosticism, Merkabah Mysticism and Talmudic Tradition* (New York, 1965), p. 54 n. 36; M. Gaster, *The Tittled Bible* (London, 1929), pp. 33–34. On the knowledge of the techniques of inducing spirits into idols among second-century Jews, see Saul Liberman, *Hellenism in Jewish Palestine* (New York, 1950), p. 121 n. 33; see also note 92 below.

25. Several ancient Jewish sources were adduced by Odeberg, *3 Enoch*, p. 18 n. 13, which deal with the removal of the Skekina because of idolatry; see also Alexander, "Historical Setting," p. 175 n. 38.

26. Odeburg, *3 Enoch*, pp. 17–18.

27. Alexander, "Historical Setting," p. 158.

28. Paul Fenton, "Gleanings from Moseh ibn Ezra's *Maqalat al Hadiqa*," *Sefarad* 36 (1976): 298, pointed out the source as Stobaeus, 1.1 (Nock and Festugière, *Corpus Hermeticum*, 3:182). Moses Ibn Ezra's book was written in Arabic; in the original, the name of Hermes is mentioned; in the Hebrew translation, made by Jehuda al Harizi, apparently at the beginning of the thirteenth century, the passage is referred to as Hermes' or Henoch's; see *Zion* 2 (Frankfurt, 1842): 123. This passage was quoted by Abraham Shalom in the second part of the fifteenth century; see his *Neweh Shalom* (Venice, 1574), fol. 73 v. Cf. M. Idel, *Kiryat Sefer*, vol. 50 (1975), p. 487 (in Hebrew). Isaak Heinemann, *Die Lehre von der Zweckbestimmung des Menschen im griechisch-römischen Altertum und im Jüdischen Mittelalter*, in *Bereich des jüdisch-theologischen Seminars* (Breslau, 1924), p. 29, asserts that Hermetic influence may be found in Bahya ibn-Paquda's *Duties of the Heart;* nevertheless, no hard evidence was adduced to confirm this assertion.

29. Judah ha-Levi, *Kitāb al-Radd wa-'l Dalīl Fi 'L-Din Al-Dhalīl*, ed. D. H. Baneth and H. Ben-Shamai (Jerusalem, 1977), pt. 1, para. 1, p. 5.

30. On the relations between the first two authors, see Hayyim Shirman, *Studies in the History of Poetry and Drama* (Jerusalem, 1979), pp. 253–54 (in Hebrew). On the relations between ha-Levi and Abraham ibn Ezra, see Hermann Greive, *Studien zum Jüdischen Neuplatonismus* (Berlin, 1973), p. 36; Naftali ben Menachem, "R. Jehuda Halevi we R. Abraham ibn Ezra," in *R. Jehuda Halevi—Qovetz Maamarim we-Haarakhot*, ed. J. Zemora (Tel Aviv, 1950), pp. 334–59 (in Hebrew); Asher Weiser, *Ibn Ezra's Commentary on the Pentateuch*, 3 vols. (Jerusalem, 1976), 1:7–8, 52–58.

31. *Book of the World* (Sefer ha-Olam), ed. J. L. Fleisher, in *Ozar ha-Hayyim*, vol. 13, pt. 5 (1937), p. 44: "omer Henoch ha-Kadmon." The "ancient Enoch" is mentioned, also in an astrological context, by Moses ben Samuel Kohen in his *Urim ve-Tumim* Vatican, Hebrew MS. 393, fol. 162. Cf. Moritz Steinschneider, *Die hebräischen Übersetzungen des Mittelalters* (Graz, 1956), p. 514 n. 95. The same phrase occurs also in the *Wisdom of the Chaldeans*—an old Hebrew astrological text, printed by Moses Gaster, *Studies and Texts*, 3 vols. (,1925–28), 1:348; 3:105. I should like to mention in this context that the *Book of Enoch*, referred to by Moses de Leon, and the *Book of Zohar*, the classic of the Jewish Cabala, may well have some affinity to Hermetic literature, as well as to Enochic texts that infiltrated in the thirteenth century. However, this highly complicated issue cannot be discussed in this framework.

32. *Book of the World*, p. 44, "amar Henoch ha-Mizri."

33. Ibid., p. 47, "amar Henoch ha-rishon."

34. This astrologer is mentioned more than once in Abraham ibn Ezra's astronomical works; see, e.g., *Book of the World*, p. 47.

35. Pingree, *Abu-Mashar*, pp. 14–15.

36. M. Friedlander, *Essays on the Writings of Abraham ibn Ezra* (London, n.d.), p. 44 (Hebrew part).

37. Ibn Ezra's view of the commandments was not properly analyzed; only a short digression on this most important issue may be found in Isaak Heinemann, *Taame ha-Mitzvot be-Sifrut Israel*, 2 vols. (Jerusalem, 1959), 1:65–72 (in Hebrew).

38. See the long excursus before Exodus 32 in Asher Weiser, *Ibn Ezra's Commentary*, 2:204–6.

39. Weiser, p. 205. There is a certain affinity between ibn Ezra's interpretation of the golden calf episode and that of Judah ha-Levi; both perceive the calf as the intended guide in lieu of Moses. This similarity was pointed out by Isaac Abrabanel, who defined the calf as being a talisman; see his *Commentary on Exodus*, 32.

40. Ibn Ezra, *Short Commentary on Exodus*, 32:5: "Whoever understands the secret of the construction of heaven will know why the form of the calf [was built]."

41. Weiser, *Ibn Ezra's Commentary*, 1:94 (Genesis 31:19). In his *Commentary on Zechariah*, 10:2, where the teraphim are also mentioned, ibn Ezra wrote: "To make a form like a certain zodiacal sign and this form is speaking." Cited by Weiser, p. 94 n. 16. Therefore, the teraphim have an explicit astrological nature, as one also learns from the end of ibn Ezra's *Commentary on Genesis*, 31:19.

42. Hayyim Shirman, "Where Was Jehuda Halevi Born?" *Tarbitz* 10 (1939): 237–39 (in Hebrew). Though Shirman's view that ha-Levi and Abraham ibn Ezra were born in Tudela was disputed by Salo W. Baron, *A Social and Religious History of the Jews*, 18 vols. (New York, 1957), 4:248 n. 34, no clear evidence was offered to disprove Shirman's assertion. The source quoted by Shirman to prove his view

was meanwhile published in the critical edition of A. S. Halkin, *Kitav al Mahadara wal Mudhakar—Liber Discussionis et Commemorationis* (Jerusalem, 1975), p. 158, where both versions—*Tudela* and *Toledo*—occur; the editor was, seemingly, unaware of Shirman's discussion, and therefore he chose Toledo as Judah ha-Levi's birthplace. But even if this version is the true one (and it seems that this is not the case), it is obvious from other sources that at least Abraham ibn Ezra lived in Tudela.

43. H. Kahane, R. Kahane and A. Pietrangeli, *The Krater and the Grail: Hermetic Sources of the Parzival* (Urbana, Ill., 1965). It seems highly significant that another Jew who received Christian baptism, Petrus Alphonsi—a contemporary of the above-mentioned Jewish thinkers—writes in his *Disciplina Clericalis:* "Enoch philosophus, qui lingua Arabica cognomitur Edric [i.e., Idris] dixit filio suo: Timor Dominem sit negotatio tua, et veniet tibi lucrum sine labore" (see Migne, *Patrologia Latina*, 157:672).

44. *Book of Kahane*, p. 126.

45. Ibid., pp. 125–26.

46. See M. D. Chenu, *Nature, Man, and Society in the Twelfth Century* (Chicago, 1968) index, s.v. "Hermetic Thought." It seems that an example of transmission of Hermetic lore from a Latin text to a Hebrew one can be found in the medico astrological discussion attributed to Enoch; see J. Shatzmiller, "In Search of the 'Book of Figures': Medicine and Astrology in Montpellier at the Turn of the Fourteenth Century," *Association of Jewish Studies Review* 7–8 (1982–83): 403.

47. On this treatise, see Joseph Dan, *The Esoteric Theology of Ashkenazi Hasidim* (Jerusalem, 1968), pp. 133–56, 230–35 (in Hebrew). Dan printed this work from the British Museum, Hebrew MS. 1055 in a mimeographic form in Jerusalem in 1973; the following references will be to this edition.

48. *Shorashim*. The meaning of this term is "element"; see, e.g., Abraham ibn Ezra's *Commentary on Ecclesiastes*, 5:2.

49. Ibid., p. 62; compare also p. 59.

50. *Sensu:* for the meaning of this term see Arthur Darby Nock and André-Jean Festugière, *Corpus Hermeticum*, 4 vols. (Paris, 1954–60), 1–2:367 n. 96; and A. J. Ferguson, *Hermetica*, 4:402–3.

51. *Asclepius*, in Nock-Festugière, *Corpus Hermeticum*, 1–2:308–9: "Unde efficitur ut, quoniam est ipsius una conpago parte, qua ex anima et sensu, spiritu atque ratione divinus est, velut ex elementis superioribus inscendere posse videatur in caelum, parta vero mundana, quae constat ex igne [et terra] aqua et aera, mortalis resistat in terra."

52. *Book of Life*, p. 61.

53. See his letter to Samuel ibn-Tibbon, the translator of the *Guide of the Perplexed:* "The books of Empedocles, the books of Pythagoras, the books of Hermes and the books of Porphyrius are all of them ancient philosophy on which [i.e., the book] is not worthy to spend the time" (A. Marx, "Texts by and about Maimonides," *Jewish Quarterly Review*, n.s., 25 (1934–35): 380.

54. See the introduction by Shlomo Pines in his translation of Maimonides, *Guide of the Perplexed* (Chicago, 1963), pp. cxxiii–cxxiv, and Leo Strauss's preface in ibid., pp. xxxiv–xxxvii.

55. On this body of literature, see the bibliographical essays of Moritz Steinschneider, "Supercommentare zu Ibn Ezra," *Jüdische Zeitschrift* 6 (1868): 121–31; Friedlander, *Essays*, pp. 212–51 (English part); Naftali ben Menachem, "The Commentators on ibn Ezra's Commentary on the Pentateuch," *Areset* 5 (1961): 71–92 (in Hebrew).

56. M. Steinschneider, "Jehuda Mosconi," in *Magazin fur die Wissenschaft des Judentums*, 20 vols., ed. A. Berliner and D. Hoffmann (Berlin, 1876), 3: 199.

57. *Sifra Hermes*.

58. Compare ibn Ezra's *Commentary on Exodus*, 4:10, where the *Book of Agriculture*, which was translated into Arabic from Egyptian, is mentioned.

59. Quotations that contain astral magic, attributed to this author, occur in *Picatrix*. See the Hebrew translation, New York, Jewish Theological Seminary MS. 247, fol. 3a.

60. Steinschneider, "Jehuda Mosconi," p. 199: "Sefer ha Talsimat le-Hermes"; compare note 114 below.

61. Printed in *Margaliot Tovah* (Ivano-Frankovsk, 1927), fol. 30v.

62. This quotation and its source, preserved in Hebrew manuscripts, will be analyzed in a separate study.

63. *Margaliot Tovah*, fol. 13v. See M. Idel, "The Magical and Neoplatonic Interpretations of the Kabbalah in the Renaissance," in *Jewish Thought in the Sixteenth Century*, ed. B. Cooperman (Cambridge, Mass., 1983), pp. 203–4 nn. 80–90. Ibn Sarsa's contemporary, Prophet Duran, quotes a similar view, which he ascribed to the "ancient Henoch who is Hermes." Duran's text was known and quoted by the Renaissance author Jehuda Muscato.

64. Idel, "The Magical and Neoplatonic Interpretations," p. 195.

65. Martin Plessner, *Picatrix: Das Ziel des Wissens von Pseudo-Magriti* (London, 1962), p. 194 n. 1.

66. E.g., Salomon ben Henoch al-Konstantini, who mentions, in the middle of the fourteenth century, in Burgos, Spain: "The ancient Hermes, who is called the ancient Henoch, has asserted that the evil soul becomes worse as it acquires more knowledge" (*Megalle Amukot*, Vatican, Hebrew MS. 59, fol. 10r). Cf. *Corpus Hermeticum*, 10.21: "The mind, when it has entered an impious soul, torments it." Cf. Walter Scott, *Hermetica* (Oxford, 1924), 1:201.

67. On Alemanno, see Arthur M. Lesley, *The Song of Solomon's Ascents: Love and Human Perfection according to a Jewish Associate of Giovanni Pico della Mirandola* (Ph.D. diss., Ann Arbor, Mich., 1976); Idel, "The Magical and Neoplatonic Interpretations."

68. Idel, "The Magical and Neoplatonic Interpretations," pp. 204–9.

69. See note 70 below.

70. Idel, "The Magical and Neoplatonic Interpretations," pp. 201–15.

71. Paris, Bibliothèque Nationale, Hebrew MS. 849, fols. 25r–25v.

72. *Torot.*

73. *Nimusin.*

74. On Alemanno's attempt to collect magical texts attributed to Solomon, in order to reconstruct the ancient Jewish magic lore, see M. Idel, "The Study Program of R. Yohanan Alemanno," *Tarbitz* 48 (1979): 321–25 (in Hebrew).

75. On this *Sefer Raziel,* see Idel, "The Study Program," pp. 310–11, n. 70; idem, "The Magical and Neoplatonic Interpretation," p. 194 n. 27.

76. New York, Jewish Theological Seminary, MS. 8117, fol. 66r.

77. The Hebrew verb is *hekhin.* From the paleographical point of view, the verb may also be *hevin,* i.e., "understood," and thus the meaning of the sentence will be totally different, since Moses would no longer be referred to as preparing the calf. However, my reading can be sustained for two reasons: The preparations of talismans were mentioned shortly beforehand and the golden calf was intended to play the same role as the talismans. Moreover, a few sentences before the quotation from Alemanno, the author writes: "[Exactly] as the heavens and the heavens of the heavens, because of their purity and sanctity, are the peculiar place for the angels and the God of Gods, so it is possible for the wise man, [who knows] the science of divinity and the science of nature, to prepare below on the earth a place which will be intended to preserve the presence of the angels and the God of Gods, and it is the tabernacle and its vessels." Here, the wise man seems to be Moses, and he is described as preparing the talismanic tabernacle.

78. *Bezurat geviah.* Alemanno's interpretation of this phrase of ibn Ezra as causing the descent of spiritual forces is clearly influenced by the supercommentaries of Samuel ibn Motot and Samuel ibn Sarsa on ibn Ezra. This continuation of the Hermetic motif, stemming from the middle of the twelfth century, is only one example of the way Hermetic views circulated in medieval Judaism and reached Renaissance Jewish authors, without any connection to Ficino's translation of the *Corpus Hermeticum.*

79. *Collectanaea,* Oxford, Bodleian, Reggio MS. 23 (Neubauer catalog no. 2234), fol. 22v.

80. Other texts in which Moses was described by Alemanno as a Hermetic magician were cited in Idel, "The Magical and Neoplatonic Interpretations," p. 203.

81. *De Imaginum, Signorum et Idearum Compositione,* in *Opere Latina Conscripta,* 3:102; see also Frances A. Yates, *Giordano Bruno and the Hermetic Tradition* (Chicago, 1979), p. 336; and pp. 353–54. In Bruno's view, the cabala was of Egyptian origin, and Moses learned it from the Egyptians; therefore, the cabala was presumably understood by Bruno as a kind of Hermetic lore: see *Spaccio de la Bestia Trionfante,* vol. 3, pt. 2 of *Dialoghi Italiani,* ed. Giovanni Aquilecchia (Florence, 1958), pp. 782–83: "Da questo parmi che derive quella Cabbala de gli Ebrei, la cui sapienza (qualunque la sia in suo geno) è procedura da gli Egizzi appresso de quali fu instrutto Mosé." Later on in the same work (p. 787), the worship of the golden calf and the brass serpent was presented as an Egyptian cult, but without any distinction between these two forms of "worship" being made.

82. The influence of Alemanno on Yagel has not yet been discussed in detail. This influence is profound, and I have hinted at it in some of my studies, but I shall elaborate on it in a study dedicated to this issue. For the time being, see Idel, "The Study Program," p. 330 n. 154; idem, "The Magical and Neoplatonic Interpretations," pp. 224–25; idem, "Prometheus in Jewish Garb," *Eshkolot,* n.s., 5–6 (1980–81): 124–25 (in Hebrew).

83. *Beer Sheva,* Oxford, Bodleian, Reggio MS. 11 (Neubauer caalog no. 1306), fol. 18r; *Gey ha-Hizzaion* (Alexandria, 1880), fols. 10r, 25r; *Beit Yaar ha-Levanon,* Oxford, Bodleian, Reggio MS. 9 (Neubauer catalog no. 1304), fols. 42v–48r.

84. Yates, *Bruno,* p. 233.

85. *Beit Yaar ha-Levanon,* fol. 9v. See also Moshe Idel, "Magic Temples and Cities in the Middle Ages and the Renaissance—A Passage of Mas'udi as a Possible Source for Yohanan Alemanno," *Jerusalem Studies in Arabic and Islam,* 3 (1981–82): 185–89.

86. Idel, "The Study Program," p. 330 n. 154.

87. *Testi Umanistici su l'Ermetismo,* ed. E. Garin, M. Brini, C. Vasili, and P. Zambelli (Rome, 1955), pp. 55–69.

88. Paul O. Kristeller, *Studies in Renaissance Thought and Letters* (Rome, 1956), pp. 236–42.

89. D. P. Walker, *Spiritual and Demonic Magic: From Ficino to Campanella* (London, 1958), pp. 64–72.

90. *Testi,* p. 68.

91. Kristeller, *Studies,* p. 23 no. 93; Walker, *Spiritual and Demonic Magic,* p. 68 n. 5.

92. Gershom G. Scholem, *Elements of the Cabala and Its Symbolism* (Jerusalem, 1976), pp. 405–6 and note 62 (in Hebrew); the whole discussion of Elazar's passage can be found in the English version of Scholem's paper on the golem in his *On the Kabbalah and Its Symbolism* (New York, 1965), pp. 184–86. But Lazarelli's text is not discussed there; his reference to the Renaissance author was cited only in the Hebrew version. I cannot analyze here the possibility of the golem techniques having a certain affinity to Hermetic traditions or that it might be an ancient Jewish view that was handed down from hoary antiquity; see note 24 above.

93. Ibid., p. 405 n. 61; three manuscripts are referred to.

94. *Testi,* p. 68: "Sed in dialogo ad Asclepium multo repertius narret."

95. Kristeller, *Studies,* pp. 238–39.

96. Walker, *Spiritual, and Demonic Magic,* pp. 68–69.

97. Para. 37, Scott, *Hermetica,* 1:358: "quoniam [enim] animas facere non poterant, evocantes animas demonum vel angelorum."

98. Reggio MS. 23, fol. 95*v*.

99. Ibid.

100. Compare to the view found in the *Picatrix,* where Aristotle allegedly asserts that "in ancient times, divine names had a certain ability to bring power to earth." (Munich, Hebrew MS. 214, fol. 51*r*).

101. Reggio MS. 23, fol. 95*v*.

102. On another distinction between astral magic and sefirotic magic—i.e., the capture of the efflux of the sefirot—see Idel, "The Magical and Neoplatonic Interpretation," pp. 200–202.

103. Alemanno distinguished between the realm of the sefirot and the world of the names or letters; see Moshe Idel, "The Letter of R. Isaac da Pisa in Its Three Versions," *Kovetz Al Yad: Minora Manuscripta Hebraica,* n.s., 10 (1982): 176–79 (in Hebrew).

104. For a further passage dealing with the power of attraction by prayers, see *Collectanaea,* Reggio MS. 23, fol. 3*v*, printed in Idel, "The Magical and Neoplatonic Interpretations," pp. 190–91; cf. Paris, Bibliothèque Nationale, Hebrew MS. 849, fol. 77*r*. In the above-mentioned article, I discussed a text found in Alemanno's *Collectanaea,* Reggio MS. 23, fol. 164*v*, where the Torah was conceived of as formed of divine names and capable of attracting spiritual powers from above. On the distinction between spiritual letters, which are engraved on the divine throne, and the letters that emerged by imaginary lines that connect the various stars, see Alemanno's long discussion in Hebrew MS. 849, fol. 68*r*–69*r*. On this type of alphabet, see Cornelius Agrippa, *De occulta philosophia* (1533), chap. 30; and the discussion of the various celestial alphabets by Israel Weinstock, "Metatron's Alphabet and Its Significance," in *Temirin,* 2 vols., ed. I. Weinstock (Jerusalem, 1982), 2:51–76 (in Hebrew).

105. Reggio MS. 23, fol. 17*r*.

106. Kristeller, *Studies,* p. 238.

107. Ibid.

108. *Testi,* p. 68: "Quod sic mea sententia est intelligendum: mentes deserti sunt divini sapientes, qui ideo deserti, nam vulgo despiciuntur, uxta illud sapientiae . . . Adam a vero, id est rubra et virgo ipsa sapientum mens est, quae vino messiae quod virgines germinat, virginea effecta est . . . Nam sapientum tantum mentes divinae generationis sunt compotes."

109. On this cabalistic school, see Gershom G. Scholem, *Major Trends in Jewish Mysticism* (New York, 1967), chap. 4.

110. Oxford, Bodleian, Mich. 143 (Neubauer catalog no. 1582), fol. 5*r*–5*v*: "The greatest dead of all is to make souls, [this is the] secret [of] and the souls which they had made in Haran. For thus did the Creator make man perfect in his own image. We consider this deed to be the most perfect of all, and thus the learned are obliged to make souls more than they are obliged to make bodies. The obligation to make bodies being intended to refer only to their obligation to make souls." Compare this text to Kristeller's paraphrase of a part of Lazarelli's text that is as yet unpublished: "Comme Dio è fecondo, cosi all'uomo immagine di Dio, spetta una, sua fecondità, la quala non riguarda soltano il corporo, ma anche l'intelleto" (*Studies,* p. 238).

111. See Munich, Hebrew MS. 10, fols. 172*v*–73*r*.

112. Idel, "The Study Program," p. 311 n. 68.

113. Reggio MS. 23, fol. 95*r*.

114. On the Hermetic knowledge of one of Alemanno's contemporaries, Abraham Farissól, see

David B. Ruderman, "Giovanni Mercurio da Correggio's Appearance in Italy as Seen through the Eyes of an Italian Jew," *Renaissance Quarterly* 28 (1975): 319–22. Farissol was acquainted with *Iggeret ha-Talisman* of Apollonius (see note 60 above) and was in contact with some leading figures of the Italian Renaissance; see David B. Ruderman, *The World of a Renaissance Jew: The Life and Thought of Abraham ben Mordecai Farissol* (Cincinnati, 1981), pp. 35–84, 98–118. Two of Alemanno's other contemporaries, Isaac Abrabanel and David Messer Leon, apparently knew Hermetic sources translated by Ficino; see, e.g., Abrabanel's *Yeshu'ot Meshiho* (Königsberg, 1861), fol. 9v; *Miphalot Elohim* (Lvov, 1863), fol. 59r. Recently, a study entitled "Dottrine [Ermetiche] tra gli Ebrei in italia Fino al Cinquecento," by Franco Michelini Tocci, was published. See *Italia Judaica: Atti del I Convegno internationale—Bari, 18–22 maggio, 1981* (Rome, 1983), pp. 287–301. However, none of the texts cited above is mentioned in this paper, which focuses upon quasi-Hermetic passages dealing with magic, astrology, or the Cabala, which have no substantial affinity to the *Corpus Hermeticum*.

PART 2

Magic, Philosophy, and Science

4

Hermes Trismegistus, Proclus, and the Question of a Philosophy of Magic in the Renaissance

BRIAN COPENHAVER

ῖνα φιλοσοφία μὲν καὶ μαγεία ψυχὴν τρέφῃ
Corpus Hermeticum, Excerpt. Stobaei 23.68

An important change in the writing of European intellectual history in our life-times can be dated from the publication of D. P. Walker's *Spiritual and Demonic Magic* in 1958, Frances Yates's *Giordano Bruno* in 1964, and Keith Thomas's *Religion and the Decline in Magic* in 1971, for such works finally established the study of occultism in the early modern period as a serious and autonomous topic of historical discourse.[1] No longer, for example, would historians of science see magical thought as a continuing embarrassment in the story of genuine science or as a primitive survival in otherwise modern currents of ideas, though such attitudes were not unusual as long as the chief guideposts to the occultist tradition were the invaluable volumes of Lynn Thorndike. Magic had been an object of critical, if not disinterested historical scholarship at least since Thorndike defended his dissertation at Columbia in 1905; but the more recent and remarkable reversal of opinion in the academic study of Western occultism demanded and still demands that such scholarship shed some of the burden of its ancestry—a triple burden.[2] First, the anthropology of the generations around the turn of the century, represented by such figures as Robertson Smith, Frazer, and Lévy-Bruhl, taught the twentieth century to think of magic as something distinctly primitive.[3] At roughly the same time, New Testament and classical scholars had begun to penetrate the secrets of Hellenistic magic, especially as they were revealed in the Greek Magical Papyri, but some of the best of this scholarship betrayed an anxiety to distinguish the magical from the religious as fixed and opposing categories and to find the exemplar of the religious in Christianity.[4] Most important, the amazing success of post-Newtonian science had long since relegated magic to the boneyard of unscientific" and "anti-progressive" species of human thought. And so a naive scientism, a learned piety, and an antiquated anthropology continue up to our own day to propagate a view of magic that makes little sense for the age of Marsilio Ficino. Far from being opposed to religion, Ficino's magic grew out of an impulse to reform Christianity; it was also part of his science, by no means something intrinsically unscientific; and above all it was erudite, as unlike anything that could be called primitive as one can imagine.[5]

For all students of Renaissance magic, Marsilio Ficino's *De triplici vita* (1489) is a cardinal text. Having seen more than thirty editions by the middle of the seventeenth century, it was by far the most popular of Ficino's original works, and its third book, *De vita coelitus comparanda,* was arguably the most significant statement on magic written in the Renaissance. Twenty-six years before the appearance of *De triplici vita,* Ficino had completed his translation of the first fourteen *logoi* of the Hermetic *Corpus,* which was published in 1471. In 1484 his translation of Plato appeared. Ficino's commentaries on and translations of Plotinus, Proclus, Iamblichus, and other Neoplatonists saw the light only in the 1490s, but he had read this body of Hellenistic philosophy by the time he wrote his major work on medical and astrological magic.[6] Given what he knew by 1489, it is not surprising that Ficino made good use of his philosophical learning in preparing *De vita coelitus comparanda,* as any page of that work will show. In Plato he found the doctrine of *anima mundi,* and he deduced from him the belief that number is the basis of magical harmony. Iamblichus showed him the effects of stellar influence on earthly matter, and Porphyry explained how images could be made to receive aerial demons through the magical use of smoke. A text of Plotinus on magic was the starting point for the work as a whole.[7] These and other, obscurer names from Ficino's pages make up a full roster of antique testimony on behalf of magic. At first glance, then, it may seem remarkable that the famous name of Hermes Trismegistus occurs in only two chapters of *De vita coelitus comparanda.*

The first passage that names the Hermes of Ficino's Hermetica is a single sentence from a list of ancient and modern authorities who explained how an astrological talisman could be made more efficacious if it were engraved under the influence of the celestial body whose image it was to bear. One of these witnesses, writes Ficino, was "Trismegistus [who] says that the Egyptians used to make such [moving images] from special terrestrial materials and then at the right moment implant the souls of demons and the soul of their ancestor Mercury into them."[8] This first reference to the famous god-making passages of the Hermetic *Asclepius* is repeated and extended throughout the ambiguous concluding chapter of *De vita coelitus comparanda.* I call it ambiguous because the reader leaves the work with less than a clear sense of Ficino's position on the role of decorated talismans in medicine. On the one hand, Ficino links Hermetic statue magic with the Plotinian metaphysics and cosmology that he so much admired; on the other hand, he associates the statues with a religious deception worked upon the Egyptian people by their priests, and he shows how Iamblichus preferred the purer religion of the *Chaldaean Oracles* to the demonolatry of the Egyptians.[9] Despite the appearance of Hermes in the concluding chapter of *De vita* and despite the relevance of the

Asclepius to Ficino's interest in talismans, Ficino's treatment of Hermes is not consistently positive nor is his presence indispensable for Ficino's overall argument.

Readers of the Hermetica will understand why Ficino treated Hermes as he did in *De vita*. It is because the Hermetica say rather little about magic, Ficino's topic. Ficino's analysis of magic in *De vita* consists primarily of what we would call philosophical and physical and even scientific arguments. *Natural philosophy,* however, is really a better term than *science* for Ficino's views on what we now call cosmology, physics, matter theory, geology, and biology, for in his day these were all within the province of *philosophia,* not yet autonomous sciences. As a humanist, Ficino naturally hunted out such materials in the remains of ancient wisdom, but it was difficult for him to find them in the Hermetica, where magic is only a matter of incidental comment, where most physical questions get even skimpier and more banal treatment, and where philosophy emerges at best eclectically, at worst incoherently. The intellectual disorder of the Hermetic tradition was known even to its original exponents: Asclepius opens *Logos* 16 by confessing to King Ammon that in his discourse "contradiction even of some of my own teachings may be apparent to you."[10]

No one familiar with the more systematic and extensive treatments of magic in ancient Neoplatonism or the Greek Magical Papyri or in the later works of Ficino and his followers will have trouble identifying allusions to ingredients of the magical world view scattered throughout the Hermetica: the cosmos is an organic unity whose parts affect one another as participants in the same life;[11] the unity of the cosmos is ascribed sometimes to the physical agency of πνεῦμα or δύναμις, referred at other times to the ability of immaterial νοῦς to penetrate all that exists;[12] the geography of the Hermetic universe corresponds loosely to the familiar post-Aristotelian conception, where things above are the causes of things below; more specifically, physical causality begins in the stars and is transmitted through the spheres to the earth;[13] the agency of the stars is as much personal as physical, so it is fitting that man's whole identity, not just his body, is the receptor at the nether end of this system of magical and celestial influences.[14]

Nothing from this catalog of magical and astrological commonplaces is a principal topic in any of the *logoi* translated by Ficino, whose leading themes are: *cosmogony,* the origin of the world and the question of a divine creation; *cosmology,* especially the nature of matter and place;[15] *theology,* the existence, attributes, and names of God;[16] *ethics,* the moral properties of God, cosmos, and man;[17] *anthropogony* and *anthropology,* man's origin, nature, and position in the universe;[18] *psychology,* the activities of mind and soul in man and elsewhere;[19] *soteriology* and *eschatology,* the return of man's soul to God, presupposing its fall and depending on revelation and contemplation as relations between man and the various hierarchies of being.[20] Ficino's great interest in these texts is explained not only by his mistaken and well-known views on their antiquity, provenance, and influence but also by the possibility of finding in some of them what has been called an "optimist gnosis" roughly compatible with Christianity. That is to say, one can read in the Hermetica the message that the human soul is immortal and a part of divine creation. Through sin and the allurements of matter, man has fallen, but man's fall can be redeemed because his evil is not absolute. The discovery of such a revelation in works thought to be Mosaic in age and context likewise redeemed not only Hermes, Asclepius, and other pagan sages in the tradition of *prisca theologia* but also Ficino and other humanists for whom erudition was a primary means to the perfection of Christendom.[21]

As part of the venerable heritage of antiquity, magic was also to be salvaged by this humanist undertaking, but insofar as the saving of magic required physical and philosophical arguments, it was not to be accomplished on the basis of the Hermetica. Ficino and others formulated theories of magical action that were altogether credible and respectable in terms of their physical and philosophical underpinnings, but the ingredients of such formulations were rarely to be found in what Hermes said to his disciples. There are only a few extensive passages in Ficino's Hermetica where such evidence might be discovered. Twenty lines of the compendious tenth treatise, called "The Key," speak of a community of actions among the hierarchies whose "operations are like rays of god, whose properties are like rays of the cosmos . . . and the operations work through the world and work upon man through the physical rays of the cosmos, while properties work through the elements." This text, which emphasizes the astrological unity of the cosmos, is also a possible basis for distinguishing occult properties based on celestial influence from manifest properties based on the elements.[22] In a passage near the beginning of the *Asclepius,* Hermes alludes to the kindred notion of ἐπιτηδειότης ("fitness"), which explains how two natural objects can be related in an occult manner without the intervention of a personal agent, and he also hints at something like the Neoplatonic idea of astrological σειραί or "chains":

> Heaven, the sensible god, is the minister of all bodies . . . , but heaven and soul itself and all things in the world are governed by the God who made them. From all these things I have mentioned, . . . influence passes continuously through the world. . . . But the world has been prepared by God as a receptacle for species of all forms, and Nature, using the four elements to make an image of the world through species, leads up to heaven all things made to be pleasing in the sight of God.

Festugière has shown how the larger context of this passage is a distinct section of the *Asclepius* (2–7), which depicts the cosmos as a continuous hierarchy. He has also connected *Asclepius* 19 with this "opening theme of *nexus*" and with the σειραί of the *Oracula chaldaica* and the Neoplatonists.[23] We can only guess how Renaissance readers, laboring without the benefit of Festugière's erudition, might have understood many of these allusions, but there is no doubt that they appreciated the magical import of the god-making texts of the *Asclepius,* where Hermes explains that the *qualitas* or magical power of the earthly gods that move the statues results from "plants, stones and spices that have in them a natural power of divinity" attuned to the heavens and sensitive to celestial prayer and music.[24] None of these passages, however, gives us clear instruction on the philosophical or physical grounds for belief in magic. From the Hermetica one cannot really learn *why* belief in magic is justified by philosophical reasoning or in terms of physical understanding, though one can discover in these and other passages *that* magic was part of what Hermes taught and so must be very old and hallowed by association with his name.

But the use of that name, especially in its adjectival and derived forms *(Hermetic, Hermetism,* and the inelegant *Hermeticism),* bears its own, ancient load of ambiguity. Writing about Hermetic astrological literature in the eighth book of *De mysteriis,* Iamblichus claimed that writings

> circulating under the name Hermes contain Hermetic (ἑρμαικὰς) notions, though these are frequently expressed in the language of the philosophers because they were translated from the Egyptian language by men who were not altogether ignorant of philosophy.

By the time Iamblichus (who died ca. A.D. 325) wrote these words, the origins of Hermetic astrology in genethlialogical manuals composed by Egyptian priests six centuries earlier had become so obscure that a Syrian writing in Greek could embrace with the word *philosophy* a body of practical, religious literature that bore little trace of the rational analysis still implied by φιλοσοφία, even after its long utilitarian career in the Hellenistic schools.[25] Iamblichus addressed an audience whose understanding of words such as *Egypt, Hermes,* and *philosophy* was colored as much by the special conditions of literary culture in late antiquity as by any consciousness that we might call historical. Likewise, our own use of expressions like *Hermetic magic* will have been conditioned by the modern cultural circumstances described above.[26] "Hermetic magic," "the magic of the Hermetica," and "the magical world picture of the Hermetic writings" all occur in an article by J. E. McGuire, which I cite not to debate its main arguments (as I have done elsewhere) but chiefly because it is a recent and well-known piece that illustrates problems arising from the use of such expressions. McGuire argues that these "traditions of magic . . . [have not] been an essential part of . . . Neoplatonism." Since the Cambridge Platonists and hence Newton were influenced by Neoplatonism, McGuire's aim is to exculpate Neoplatonic philosophy of interest in anything so dubious as magic, leaving the blame for magical influences with the mythical Hermes and removing it from Plotinus and his successors.[27] This argument fails on two counts. First, as I have already said, magic is not a central issue in the Hermetica. Second, the ancient Neoplatonists did in fact supply important physical and metaphysical support for belief in magic.[28]

Frances Yates recognized how the term "Renaissance Neo-Platonism may dissolve into a rather vague eclecticism," and to clarify the situation she argued "that the core of [this] . . . movement was Hermetic, involving a view of the cosmos as a network of magical forces with which man can operate."[29] While the idea of a *prisca theologia* certainly inspired Ficino and others to read Plotinus or even Plato as heirs of Hermes, there was also independent interest in the texts of the *Platonici,* without reference to any Hermetic "core." This autonomous reading of the Neoplatonists is evident in *De vita,* for example, where the *Platonici* are cited more often than Hermes and to greater effect as theoreticians of magic.[30] But in an article widely read by historians of science, Dame Frances emphasized "the Hermetic core of Ficinian Neoplatonism" and "the Hermetic attitude toward the cosmos . . . [as] the chief stimulus of that new turning toward the world and operating on the world which, appearing first as Renaissance magic, was to turn into seventeenth-century science."[31] She mentioned three texts from the Hermetica in her account of the Hermetic magus as operator-scientist. Her conclusion that it was "upon the magical passages in the *Asclepius* that Ficino based the magical practices which he described in *De vita*" in my view exaggerates the influence of those admittedly important passages at the expense of other sources, and her claim that "the 'Pimander' describes the creation, fall and redemption not of a man but of a magus" seems to me related to the cosmogonical, anthropological, and eschatological vision of *Corpus Hermeticum* 1, not textually but imaginatively.[32] And if Giordano Bruno's reading of a passage in *Corpus Hermeticum* 12 on a living and moving earth moved him to associate "Copernicanism with the animist philosophy of an extreme type of magus," then we must recognize the Hermetic component of any such magical philosophy to have been textually meager.[33] If one wishes to find the philosophical and scientific roots of Renaissance magical theory—as distinguished from the genealogy of the magus—one looks not to the eclectic pieties of Hermes Trismegistus but to the Neoplatonists.

In roughly the same sense that Platonic, Peripatetic, and Stoic teachings on substance, form, quality, matter, and motion provided theoretical frameworks for science in late antiquity, there also emerged by the time of Bolos Democritus (ca. 200 B.C.) what we can loosely call physico-philosophical theories of magic. The evidence for them is thin and scattered, though Plotinus in *Ennead* 4.4, Iamblichus in *De mysteriis*, Apuleius in his *Apology*, and various texts from Pliny, Galen, and others have been analyzed to show what they were like.[34] Some of this material was known to Ficino. In fact, until the work of Joseph Bidez in this century, Ficino seems to have been the only reader of the Greek original of perhaps the most important surviving statement of ancient magical theory, the work of Proclus that Ficino called *De sacrificio*. Titled Περὶ τῆς καθ' Ἑλληνας ἱερατικῆς τέχνης in Bidez's edition, this little tract of 105 lines is probably a précis made by Michael Psellus from a larger work of Proclus on magic. The art (τέχνη) described here by Proclus is called priestly (ἱερατική) because it derives from his deep interest in the theurgic magic of the *Chaldean Oracles*. The intent of this magic was religious—man's immortalization and union with the god—but its prerequisites were scientific and philosophical in as much as its procedures were based on distinct and coherent views of the nature of the cosmos.[35] Having made his copy of the Greek text of *De sacrificio* sometime after 1461, Ficino completed his Latin translation by 1489, around the time when he wrote *De vita*, but it was not published until 1497 along with Proclus's commentary on *Alcibiades 1*, Iamblichus's *De mysteriis*, and other, mostly Neoplatonic, works.[36] In 1901, Kroll undertook a reconstruction of Proclus's Greek on the basis of Ficino's Latin because the Greek manuscripts had fallen from view in the meantime. The relative success of Kroll's efforts speaks well of the accuracy of Ficino's rendering, but by 1928 Bidez had recovered the original Greek and had published his edition of it in volume 6 of the *Catalogue des manuscrits alchimiques grecs,* which unfortunately remains a relatively inaccessible collection.[37] In 1933, André Bremond prepared a wordy French translation, most of which Festugière reproduced in the first volume of his *Révélation*.[38] Garin,

Walker, and Yates have all noted the importance of Proclus's *De sacrificio* for the study of Renaissance occultism.[39] The Latin text in my appendix is based on a collation of the versions from Ficino's 1497 *Iamblichus,* from the Basel (1576) edition of Ficino's *Opera,* and from the two surviving Laurenziana manuscripts.[40] The English text in the appendix is my rough attempt at a translation of Proclus's Greek, not of Ficino's Latin—though the two are reasonably close at most points.

Without ever precisely identifying it, Ficino uses Proclus's *De sacrificio* some half-dozen times in *De vita coelitus comparanda,* most importantly in chapters 13 through 15 to show how celestial influence can be manipulated by the proper understanding and disposition of common terrestrial objects.[41] In these chapters Ficino amplifies essentially the same point made in the *Asclepius* about the magical power of "plants and stones and spices" used in the theurgic ritual of the statues, but in Proclus he finds a coherent physical and philosophical setting for what stands as a simple, isolated assertion in the Hermetic text. Ficino explains that the principle in question is "that most Platonic maxim, . . . that heavenly things exist on earth in an earthly condition, while earthly things in turn attain a heavenly dignity in heaven." This closely resembles the end of Proclus's first sentence (English appendix, lines 5–7), and the philosophical context for this principle emerges in lines 10 through 11 and 46 through 50, which must be read in terms of Proclus's longer writings, especially the *Elements of Theology.*[42] In that work, which does not concern itself directly with magic, Proclus sets forth a double hierarchical structure for all entities, described sometimes as σειραί or "chains," sometimes as "orders" or τάξεις. Both aspects of the hierarchy begin with higher entities called monads and henads, the latter identified with the various Olympian gods. In both parts of the structure, divine power from above is transmitted even to the lowest members of an order or chain. As Proclus puts it in proposition 145 of the *Elements,* "the distinctive character of any divine order (τάξεως) travels through all the derivative existents and bestows itself upon all inferior kinds."[43] This is what Ficino has in mind when he says at the beginning of chapter 14 that

> from each and every star there depends a series of things proper to it, even to the very lowest. Under the heart of Scorpio, after its demons and its men and the animal scorpion, we can also locate the plant aster, . . . which the physicians say has . . . wondrous power against genital diseases. . . . Under Sirius, a solar star, come first the Sun, then Phoebean demons as well, which sometimes appeared to men in the form of lions or cocks, as Proclus testifies. . . . And there is no reason why the lion fears the cock except that in the Phoebean order the cock is higher than the lion. For the same reason, says Proclus, the Apollonian demon, which sometimes appeared in the shape of a lion, immediately disappeared when a cock was displayed.

Lines 46 through 64 of *De sacrificio,* read once again in terms of the *Elements,* clarify Ficino's point. The lion and the cock are in the same solar series whose henad is Apollo or Phoebus—the lion probably because of the solar associations of the constellation Leo in astrology, the cock because he crows at sunrise. Since the cock is a creature of the air, he stands higher in the series, and his proximity and receptivity to the sun are reflected in his behavior.[44] Other members of the solar series enumerated here by Ficino—laurel, lotus, sunstone, sun's eye—also turn up in Proclus (lines 33–45, 65–67), and Ficino includes a long list of such heliotropia in the first chapter of De vita, thus again emphasizing the centrality of this solar series in his magic.[45]

It cannot be said too emphatically that this idea of chains or orders linking terrestrial to celestial entities and thereby providing a basis for astrological magic was a leading feature of a philosophy that was above all else systematic and rigorous. Proclus was no fatuous theosophist. Besides his original philosophy and his commentaries on Plato, he made important contributions in mathematics, physics, and astronomy. Unlike the Hermetica, his work cannot be dismissed as eclectic, inconsistent, or superficial. He shared with Porphyry and Iamblichus a stronger interest in magic than what is implied in the Enneads, but he was faithful to Plotinus in his desire to ground these interests firmly in theory. Thus, Proclus's high regard for theurgy, which Plotinus never mentions, is of a piece with his own ontology and psychology, the latter developed in conscious opposition to what Plotinus taught.[46] This disposition to theorize is evident throughout De sacrificio. His claim in line 20 that "likeness is sufficient to join beings to one another" depends on his philosophical rule that there can be no causality without similarity between cause and effect.[47] In Proclus's universe, moreover, the likelihood of discovering similarities is magnified by his belief "that all things are in all," the subject of lines 2 through 7 of De sacrificio and of proposition 103 of the Elements.[48] The intricate metaphor of lines 20 through 32 gives support to the possibility of a natural, nondemonic magic depending only on dispositions naturally present in objects.[49] Another philosophical rule—that unity is ontologically and causally prior to multiplicity—lies behind the advice to the magician in lines 69 through 80 that magic is a process of concentration, unification, and blending.[50] The signs or symbols (συνθήματα, σύμβολα) of lines 56 and 62, as we learn from Plotinus and Iamblichus, work ex opere operato and thus provide another alternative to the demonic magic implied by any specifically noetic act of the magician.[51] Surprisingly, throughout De sacrificio (lines 2–7, 15–18, 32–45, 69–72; cf. 54–56), Proclus also shows how empirical observation can serve the magician, not so much in saving the phenomena as in justifying magical theory in terms of phenomena alleged by tradition.[52]

But the most important philosophical context for Proclus's theory of magic is established by allusions at the beginning and end of De sacrificio to Diotima's conversation with Socrates in the Symposium. Diotima begins (202E–203D) by calling Love one of the spirits who mediate between heaven and earth and "form the medium of the prophetic arts, of the priestly rites of sacrifice (ἡ τῶν ἱερέων τέχνη τῶν τε περὶ τὰς θυσίας), initiation, and incantation, of divination and of sorcery (γοητείαν)." Love, she explains, is "an adept in sorcery, enchantment (δεινὸς γόης καὶ φαρμακεὺς), and seduction." Diotima ends her discourse (211B–D) with an account of Love's progress from sensible to abstract to authentic beauty. This makes sense of Proclus's comparing lovers and priests in lines 1 through 5 and also of his concluding (lines 88–95; cf. line 80) with an account of ascent to the ideal. The magic described in De sacrificio depends on the manipulation of sensible objects, but in this context natural magic becomes an erotic embrace of the insensible divine.[53] Ficino also identified love with magic and saw the operations of magic in terms which, if we hesitate to call them scientific, we should surely call cosmological. Because God's love had created and vitalized the world, knowledge of the world was a means of knowing God. Cosmology was propaedeutic to natural theology and justified by it. Let Ficino explain how magic, far from being unscientific or antireligious, was a central feature of such a cosmology. "Why," he asks in his *Commentary* on the *Symposium,*

> do we think that Love is a magician? Because all the power of magic consists in love. An act of magic is the attraction of one thing by another in accordance with a certain natural kinship. The parts of this world, members of one living being, all originating from the same maker, are joined together in the communion of one nature. Therefore, just as our brain, lungs, heart, liver, and other organs act on one another, assist each other to some extent, and suffer together when any one of them suffers, in just this way the organs of this enormous living being, all the bodies of the world joined together in like manner, borrow and lend each other's natures. Common love grows out of common kinship, and common attraction is born of love. This is true magic. Thus, out of an agreement of nature, fire is drawn upward by the hollow of the lunar sphere, air by the hollow of fire; earth is drawn to the depths by the center of the world, and water likewise is pulled by its place. The magnet does the same with iron, amber with chaff, and sulfur with fire. . . . Acts of magic, therefore, are acts of nature, and art is her handmaid. . . . Out of natural love all nature gets the name "magician."[54]

In the concluding chapter of *De vita,* Ficino treats the same question in a strikingly similar fashion, but this time he is commenting on the latter sections of *Ennead* 4.4, one of the primary inspirations of the whole treatise:

> Everywhere . . . nature is a magician, as Plotinus and Synesius say, everywhere baiting traps with particular foods for particular objects; this is no different from her attracting heavy things with the center of the earth, light things with the sphere of the moon. . . . Wise men in India claim that this is the attraction whereby the world binds itself together, and they say that the world is an animal throughout male and female alike, and that it joins with itself everywhere in the mutual love of its members. . . . Taking careful note of such things, the farmer prepares his field and seeds for gifts from heaven and uses various grafts to prolong life in his plant and change it to a new and better species. The physician, the scientist, and the surgeon bring about similar effects in our bodies, both to take care of our ills and to make a more fruitful disposition of the nature of the cosmos. The philosopher, who is learned in natural science and astronomy and whom we are wont rightly to call a magician, likewise implants heavenly things in earthly objects by means of certain alluring charms used at the right moment, doing no more than the farmer diligent in grafting, who binds the fresh sprout to the old stump. . . . The magician sets earthly things under heaven, subjects all things below to those above, so that everywhere feminine entities are fertilized by male entities suited to them.[55]

To the modern ear, talk about the physical world seems a strange context for a word like *love,* and Ficino's language sounds all the more bizarre when he makes *love* and *magic* near synonyms for the forces of kinship and attraction that grow out of the divine creative act and sustain the organic sympathies that bind the cosmos together. But the historian will listen more patiently to Ficino. Both his love and his magic are forces: They drive the motions of the heavenly bodies, cause the changes of elements, humors, and compounds, and support the mutual attractions of all these organs of the living cosmos. There is a real, if imperfect, analogy among the function of love in Ficino's physics, the function of πνεῦμα in Stoic physics, and the function of force in Newton's physics. Though Ficino's love lacked both the explanatory power of Newton's force and the systematic co-herence of the Stoic πνεῦμα, all three were terms of scientific intention in that they *aimed* to explain important features of the physical world.[56] Ficino's ideas about the role of erotic magic in the physical universe were not personal aberrations or idiosyncrasies peculiar to his historical moment. They were consistent develop-ments of his commitment to the sources of Neoplatonic philosophy. "Love is given in Nature," Plotinus argued, and "the qualities inducing love induce mutual approach: hence there has arisen an art of magic . . . [that] knit[s] soul to soul." In his most immanentist, anti-Gnostic moments, Plotinus insists on the organic unity of the world and on the erotic forces binding it together, just as Proclus does by specific assertion in *De sacrificio* and by that treatise's allusions to the *Sym-posium*.[57] Attention to the philosophical, cosmological, and theological contexts of such thinking about magic will be a healthy antidote to the impulse to view any interest in occultism as a deviation from religious probity or scientific rigor or philosophical depth. Such contexts are clearly evoked in *De sacrificio,* and, though their resonance has weakened in our own time, they rang loud for Ficino and his contemporaries.

In addition to the actual texts of *De sacrificio* and *De vita coelitus comparanda,* a third source of information for the influence of the former work on the latter exists in the Latin marginalia written by Ficino in the most important Greek manuscript of Proclus's treatise, Vallicellianus F20. Opposite lines 1 through 5 of *De sacrificio,* Ficino remarked that works of Porphyry, Mercurius, Plotinus, Iamblichus, and al-Kindi contain material akin to what he read in Proclus. ("Mer-curius," we note, appears as one author among five, all of whom are cited in *De vita;* below, I shall discuss the identity of Mercurius in another Renaissance text.)[58] Next, commenting on lines 15 through 32, Ficino uses the concept of *ordo* (cf. τάξις) to explain magical action as a system of attractions and repulsions within and among various sets *(ordines)* of corporeal and incorporeal entities in upper and lower regions of the cosmos. Since Ficino understood magic as an organic relation among the heavenly and earthly stones, plants, and animals of Proclus's treatise, he chose an organic and medical analogy to illustrate this relation. A lower entity in the cosmos, such as a human body, can be influenced by superior beings, such as stars, as one organ in the body can be affected by another, especially when the two organs are linked by objects bearing qualities appropriate to each. "Thus," writes Ficino,

> if you apply cerebral objects to the foot, it attracts power from the brain; if [you use] cardiac objects, [power comes] from the heart; if hepatic objects, from the

liver, etc. Likewise, if a particular nature is deficient in a man, you attract power from one star or another by bringing near to him what suits the star, especially a star at the peak of its influence.[59]

In the margins of lines 38 through 52 of *De sacrificio,* where Proclus describes chains, symbols, and the lion's fear of the cock, Ficino's notes treat the power of material objects, sounds, imagination, emotion, and reason to draw down natural and demonic powers from the heavens.[60] All this is familiar territory for students of Ficino. The marginalia most interestingly related to the text of *De vita,* however, are written opposite Proclus's account of the lotus, sunstones, and moonstones:

> I have seen a round stone marked with starlike dots which, when soaked in vinegar, moved first in a straight line for a bit and then wandered off on a curved course. I believe it was adapted to the firmament, especially after it was soaked in vinegar. For here it is fitting that art should finish what nature has begun. Why is the magnet suited to the Bear and the Pole? Why does it incline iron toward them, as in the sailors' instrument it seems to seek out the pole? Whence does an image of the Bear impressed on a magnet [and] hung about the neck on an iron necklace attract power from the [constellation] to us as it touches the flesh?[61]

This material is the seed of the first half of chapter 15 of *De vita,* which recounts two of Ficino's youthful experiences with talismans. Familiar with Proclus's descriptions of sunstones and moonstones and with the larger context of Neoplatonism, Ficino could draw the inference that begins this chapter—that carving images on such stones was needless since their effects emerged spontaneously from natural sympathies flowing through the chains and orders of the universe.[62] He wished, however, that solar and lunar stones were as powerful in their *ordines* as were the magnet and iron "under the series (cf. σειρά) of the North Pole," which is also "the order following the Bear." Ficino had been impressed by the magnet's lively behavior in the mariner's compass *(specula nautarum),* which he explained by the relative positions of magnet and iron in their *ordo.* Superior attracts inferior.[63] Moreover, he considered making a talisman of the magnet by carving the Bear on it under the influence of the Moon, but when he realized that the influences of the Bear were Saturnine and Martian and when he learned from the *Platonici* that the *daemones* of the North were usually evil, he dropped his plans. Meanwhile, in Florence he also saw what amounted to a natural talisman, "a stone . . . brought from India, extracted there from the head of a dragon, round, coin-shaped, naturally and symmetrically marked with many starlike dots."[64] Observing the circling motions of the stone in vinegar, Ficino reasoned that it was akin to the constellation Draco, a celestial neighbor of the Bear. Both the artificial Bear talisman and the natural Dragon talisman were joined in Ficino's mind with the magical sun- and moonstones of Proclus, though these associations become evident only through the notes Ficino left in the margins of Vallicellianus F20.

From such observations one can see how a theory of magic emerges much more clearly in the *De sacrificio* of Proclus and other Neoplatonic texts than in the Hermetica and how well Ficino was able to make use of such a theory. To test these findings, let us move to another influential exposition of Renaissance magical theory, the first book of *De occulta philosophia* by Cornelius Agrippa von Nettesheim, whose subject is natural magic.[65] Explicit citations of authority, though plentiful in this book, are not a full and precise guide to its sources. Despite his very heavy dependence on Ficino, for example, Agrippa gives his great predecessor no credit at all in book 1. Yet certain patterns of dependence are apparent. Of the hundred or so individual authors whom Agrippa cites by name, Pliny heads the list with more than a score of references.[66] And if we group Agrippa's citations by genre, period, and school, then the ancient Platonic philosophers emerge victorious, for they are named over forty times—more than a fifth of all direct citations in Agrippa's first book.[67] The eight references to Plato himself are the most numerous; Apuleius is mentioned seven times; Proclus five times.[68] But after Pliny's twenty-odd appearances, the second largest number of individual references (sixteen) goes not to one of Plato's followers but to the mythical sage whom Ficino knew as the fountainhead of all Platonic wisdom, Hermes Trismegistus.[69]

Who was Hermes Trismegistus or Mercurius Trismegistus or Mercurius or Hermes? Confusion over the various identities attached to the names Hermes and Mercurius was already a problem in antiquity—Cicero describes five gods named Mercurius: Augustine speaks of two called Hermes—and this confusion was only deepened by the complex transmission of the various species of Hermetic literature through the Middle Ages to Ficino, Agrippa, and their contemporaries.[70] Today, we have the advantage of Scott's and Festugière's distinctions between a "popular Hermetism" interested in astrology, alchemy, and magic and a "learned Hermetism" devoted to theology, cosmogony, anthropogony, soteriology, and eschatology. The latter, philosophical Hermetica have survived in the seventeen Greek treatises of the *Corpus Hermeticum,* the Latin *Asclepius* and the thirty-odd extracts found in the *Anthology* of Stobaeus. The former, occultist literature we know through modern editions of the *Kyranides* and related zoological, botanical, lapidary, and astrological texts; through fragments of such authors as Bolos of Mendes and Zosimus the Alchemist; through Pliny's considerable interest in the literature on φυσικὰ καὶ μυστικὰ inaugurated by Bolos; and through the discovery of the Greek Magical Papyri.[71] Some of this occultist material was unknown in Agrippa's time; practically none of it had been edited. Yet if we examine Agrippa's sixteen explicit citations of Hermes and Mercurius, we may detect a primitive version of Festugière's categories.

Five of these sixteen citations are attached to the names "Mercurius" and "Trismegistus," and four of these five can be traced to passages from the learned or philosophical Hermetica. These four deal with God's gifts of mind and speech to man, the demonic animation of statues, the presence of cosmic *(mundanus)* as opposed to supercelestial demons in the statues; and correspondences between celestial and terrestrial worlds.[72] The fifth occurrence of "Mercurius Trismegistus" is among a group of inventors of magic who followed in the footsteps of Zalmoxis and Zoroaster. Agrippa mentions this Mercurius in a subgroup of "the more famous masters . . . whose books Democritus of Abdera rescued from the tomb and clarified with his commentaries." The time-honored confusion between Democritus of Abdera (the atomist) and Bolos Democritus of Mendes (the occultist) is here complicated by the fact that some of the "masters" mentioned after Mercurius are historical figures who lived centuries after either Democritus—Plotinus, Porphyry, Iamblichus, and Proclus—while others like Gog Graecus and Germa Babylonicus are artifacts of the medieval Hermetica.[73]

The point is not that one expects philological or historical clarity from Cornelius Agrippa but that this is the only passage in book 1 of *De occulta philosophia* wherein the name "Mercurius Trismegistus" is associated with what we should now call *popular* as opposed to *learned* Hermetism. The converse obtains even more strictly. Nine of the eleven citations attached to the name "Hermes" are clearly linked with popular Hermetic sources such as the *Kyranides* or, more often, with medieval vehicles of popular Hermetism such as the *Liber aggregationis* attributed to Albertus Magnus, the *Picatrix,* or the *Secret of Secrets.* The most interesting of the eleven lists Hermes along with Bochus, Aron, Theophrastus, Thebit ben Qura, Zenothemis, Zoroaster, Evax, pseudo-Dioscorides, Isaac Judaeus, Zacharias Babylonicus, Albertus, and Arnaldus of Villanova as "authors who have published great volumes on the properties of things" but who have not discovered the sources of occult properties. Then Agrippa qualifies this allegation of failure, explaining that Alexander of Aphrodisias traced occult properties to the elements and qualities, the Platonists to formative ideas, Avicenna to the intelligences, Albertus to specific forms, and Hermes to the stars. All of this is very close to a passage from the *De mineralibus* of Albertus Magnus, and of the eleven "Hermes" passages, it is the only one of substantial theoretical interest.[74] The other ten either set forth specific correspondences between sets of heavenly bodies and sets of terrestrial objects (for example, the fifteen stars, stones and planets of the *Liber Hermetis de XV stellis*), or they describe the special magical effects of a particular substance or object (for example, the power to understand the speech of animals bestowed, according to the *Liber aggregationis,* by a fox's heart cooked with game).[75]

Most of Agrippa's references to Hermes, then, have nothing to do with the Mercurius Trismegistus made famous by Ficino, and neither the learned nor the popular Hermetica was of much theoretical value to this philosopher of natural magic. Of what use was Proclus? Three of Agrippa's five explicit citations of Proclus are of no greater significance than the material ascribed to Hermes and Mercurius. We learn that Proclus was one of the ancient masters of magic, that he recommended the use of a mole's heart in divining the future, and that he agreed with the *Asclepius* that demons could be induced to enter terrestrial objects.[76] The two remaining explicit citations are of much greater theoretical value. According to the first,

> it is obvious that all inferior things come beneath superior things and that somehow (as Proclus says) they are within one another, the upper within the lower and the lower within the upper, . . . earthly things in heaven but as it were causally and in a heavenly manner, and heavenly things on earth but terrestrially and as effects.

This is nearly an exact quotation from lines 5 through 7 (Latin) of Ficino's translation of Proclus's *De sacrificio,* and its meaning parallels Agrippa's earlier and unacknowledged use of the "Platonic maxim" on relations between archetypal and corporeal worlds from *De vita coelitus comparanda*.[77]

Agrippa's second direct and theoretical use of Proclus is to illustrate the operation of the principle of antipathy among spiritual beings, stars, animals, and other material objects. "Proclus," says Agrippa, "gives an example of [enmity and antipathy] in a spirit usually appearing in the form of a lion, which spirit quickly disappeared when confronted with a cock because the cock is antipathetic to the lion." That Agrippa returns to the case of the lion and the cock in at least four other passages of book 1 of *De occulta philosophia* is not surprising: after all, the cock's strange power over the lion was a commonplace in the ancient and medieval literature of magic. But we may connect these passages directly with Ficino's translation of Proclus because we have an explicit citation and because of similarities of language between Agrippa's texts and Ficino's.[78] Moreover, the five cases of direct reference to Proclus point us toward other, silent uses of *De sacrificio* numbering as many as seventeen.

Several of these concern heliotropic and selenotropic behavior in stones, plants, and animals, another commonplace of magical literature. Agrippa had to look no further than Ficino's *De vita* to find many instances of it. But of all the plants in Ficino's list of heliotropia, Agrippa singles out four, three of which (lotus, laurel, and palm) are the only botanical heliotropes specifically identified as such in Proclus's short text.[79] Likewise, there is nothing noteworthy in Agrippa's description of the heliotropic stone called sun's eye until we compare his language with lines 38 through 40 of Ficino's Latin translation of Proclus:

> [Agrippa] Lapis, qui dicitur Solis oculus, figuram habens similem pupillae oculi, ex cuius medio radius emicat, consortat cerebrum.
> [Ficino] Lapis autem qui vocatur coeli oculus vel solis oculus figuram habet similem pupillae oculi, atque ex media pupilla emicat radius.

Descriptions of the moonstone from Agrippa and from Ficino's Proclus also bear comparison:

> [Agrippa] Lapis selenites, id est lunaris, ex candido translucens, melleo fulgore, motum imitans lunarem, lunae figuram in se habens, reddensque eam in dies singulos crescentis, minuentisve numero.
> [Ficino] Lapis quoque selinitus, id est, lunaris, figura lunae corniculari similis, quadam sui mutatione lunarem sequitur motum.[80]

The cumulative weight of such evidence leads me to conclude that some important theoretical and descriptive elements in Agrippa's exposition of magic are at least in part owing to Proclus, though far fewer are directly ascribed to him. I have in mind especially a group of theoretical statements on sympathy and influence that occur within five pages of one another in *De occulta philosophia* and that may be found in Proclus as well: first, the comparison of a terrestrial object prepared for heavenly influence with a piece of wood prepared for lighting; second, the claim that *commixtio* or the combining of sympathetic substances is an excellent preparation for magical action; third, the claim that "the resemblance of natural to heavenly objects suffices for us to drink in their influence;" and finally, the assertion that the relationship in series of inferior and superior objects is "the source of the whole of magic and of all the more occult philosophy."[81] Earlier in his book Agrippa had attributed the idea "that all things are full of gods" to Democritus, Orpheus, and the Pythagoreans, yet it seems clear that he had also read at least one other text containing this commonplace, the *De sacrificio* of Proclus.[82]

Let me now draw five general and unequally significant conclusions about Proclus and Hermes in the Renaissance magical texts I have examined:

1. Ficino's Hermetica say little of theoretical interest about magic. Modern scholars should not use *Hermetic* and related terms as if they were vaguely synonymous with *magical* and its cognates.

2. The works of Plotinus, Porphyry, Iamblichus, Synesius, and Proclus are the most important ancient philosophical sources for the theory of magic in the Renaissance. Research on magic in the Renaissance should shift its attention to these texts and to their interpretation in the early modern period.

3. Magic cannot justly be made the victim of an indictment of Hermetism. Critics who believe that magic is not an important issue in early modern thought should not dismiss it for the same reasons used to belittle the Hermetica: eclecticism, incoherence, banality, the dating issue, and so on. New and better reasons for ignoring magic must be found. Moreover, the general reputation of Neoplatonic philosophy as an important foundation for magic must come to the fore in such debates along with the reputations of other ancient and medieval sources also important for Ficino's magic but not discussed here—Plato, Aristotle, Galen, Aquinas, and Albertus Magnus, to name some of the most important.[83] Any critique of Renaissance belief in magic must confront the weight of Ficino's learning in these sources, for his magic was part and parcel of his philosophical, theological, and medical erudition, not a throwback to some "primitive" way of thinking.

4. The Hermetica provided more genealogical or historical than theoretical justification for belief in magic. Association with the ancient theology may have made magic more admirable, but the "older" ancient theologians—Hermes, Zoroaster, Orpheus—were of little help in analyzing magic physically or philosophically. Hermetic allusions to magical ideas were frequent enough to associate magic with the *prisca theologia* but insufficiently rich in the relevant physical and philosophical arguments to provide the elements of a convincing, substantive theory of magic.

5. The popular Hermetica as transmitted through the Middle Ages were more important as a source of magical data than Ficino's Hermetica, but since they were mainly collections of recipes and curiosities unattached to any coherent philosophy, their theoretical value was not much greater. Their influence on Renaissance texts is evident in such writers as Agrippa and Symphorien Champier, and it should be investigated elsewhere.[84]

94   BRIAN COPENHAVER

Notes

1. D. P. Walker, *Spiritual and Demonic Magic: From Ficino to Campanella* (London, 1958); Frances Yates, *Giordano Bruno and the Hermetic Tradition* (London, 1964); Keith Thomas, *Religion and the Decline of Magic* (New York, 1971). For comments and criticism, I owe thanks to Michael Allen, Carol Kaske, Jill Kraye, P. O. Kristeller, George Matthews and D. P. Walker. Another friend from the Warburg Institute, Charles Schmitt, shared his enormous learning as generously in this effort as in so many others; all readers of this chapter will regret his untimely death in April 1986.

2. Lynn Thorndike, *The Place of Magic in the Intellectual History of Europe*, Ph.D. diss., Columbia University, 1905; idem, *A History of Magic and Experimental Science*, 8 vols. (New York, 1923-58). Though influenced by evolutionist anthropology, Thorndike from the beginning was too well informed about the Western tradition of learned magic to accept a total identification of the magical and the primitive (*History of Magic*, 1:4-5), but that his tolerance was limited is clear from his chapter on Marsilio Ficino (4:562-73), titled "Ficino the Philosopher." A longer perspective on the critical history of occultism emerges from descriptions of Gian Rinaldo Carli's *Dissertazione epistolare sopra la magia e stregheria* (1745) and Girolamo Tartarotti's *Del congresso notturno delle lamie libri tre* (1749) in *Magia e ragione: Una polemica sulle streghe in Italia intorno al 1750* by Luciano Parinetto (Florence, 1974), pp. 121-31, 165-76.

3. Mary Douglas, *Purity and Danger* (Harmondsworth, 1975), pp. 29-40, 73-89, 105-13; E. E. Evans-Pritchard, *Theories of Primitive Religion* (Oxford, 1965), pp. 26-47, 56-57, 78-79; idem, *A History of Anthropological Thought* (New York, 1981), pp. 95-169; Adam Kuper, *Anthropologists and Anthropology: The British School, 1922-1972* (Harmondsworth, 1975), pp. 13-50; Eric J. Sharpe, *Comparative Religion: A History* (London, 1975), pp. 72-96, 190-94. For a recent statement of the view that "the distinction . . . between primitive and Western modes of thought is similar in many ways to that between the occult and the scientific traditions," see *Occult and Scientific Mentalities in the Renaissance*, ed. Brian Vickers (Cambridge, 1984), pp. 33-45, 95-97, esp. p. 34.

4. Sharpe, *Comparative Religion*, pp. 149-51; John M. Hull, *Hellenistic Magic and the Synoptic Tradition* (Napierville, Ill., 1974), pp. 5-9; Morton Smith, *Jesus the Magician* (New York, 1978), pp. 1-7. Of all students of Hellenistic magic, A.-J. Festugière has most strongly influenced the study of magic in the Renaissance. For evidence of the "anxiety" mentioned above, see Festugière, "La valeur religieuse des papyrus magiques," in *L'idéal religieux des grecs et l'évangile* (Paris, 1932), pp. 281-328, esp. 327; idem, *Hermétisme et mystique païenne* (Paris, 1967), pp. 23-25, 27, 79-87; idem, "Contemplation philosophique et art théurgique chez Proclus," in *Studi di storia religiosa della tarda antichità pubblicati dalla cattedra di storia delle religioni dell'Università di Messina* (Messina, 1968), pp. 7-18; cf. A. H. Armstrong, "Salvation, Plotinian and Christian," *Downside Review* 75 (1957): 126-39; Martin P. Nilsson, "Die Religion in den griechischen Zauberpapyri," *Kungl. humanistiske Vetenskapssamfundets i Lund Arsberattelse* (1947-48): 59-93. The clearest expression of the opposite view is in David E. Aune, "Magic in Early Christianity," *Aufstieg und Niedergang der römischen Welt*, vol. 2: *Principat*, vol. 23, pt. 2, ed. Wolfgang Haase (Berlin, 1980), pp. 1507-16, 1536, 1557.

5. Paul Oskar Kristeller, *Eight Philosophers of the Italian Renaissance* (Stanford, Calif., 1964), pp. 48-50; Eugenio Garin, *Moyen Age et Renaissance*, trans. C. Carme (Paris, 1969), pp. 123, 129-31, 135-37, 142-43; idem *Italian Humanism: Philosophy and Civic Life in the Renaissance*, trans. Peter Munz (Oxford, 1965), pp. 88-96.

6. *Marsilii Ficini florentini . . . opera et quae hactenus extitere*, 2 vols. (1576; reprint, Turin, 1959), pp. 529-72; *Supplementum Ficinianum: Marsilii Ficini philosophi Platonici opuscula inedita et dispersa primum collegit et ex fontibus plerumque manuscriptis edidit auspiciis regiae scholae normalis superioris Pisanae Paulus Oscarius Kristeller . . .* 2 vols. (Florence, 1937), 1: lxxvii-clxvii; Kristeller, "Marsilio Ficino e Lodovico Lazzarelli: Contributo alla diffusione delle idee ermetiche nel rinascimento," in *Studies in Renaissance Thought and Letters* (Rome, 1956), pp. 223-24; Raymond Marcel, *Marsile Ficin (1433-1499)* (Paris, 1958), pp. 487-96, 747-49.

7. *Ti.* 34B-37C (Plot. *Enn.* 4.4.32; Ficino, *Opera*, p. 535); *Ti.* 53B, 69B-C (Ficino, *Opera*, p. 548); Iambl. *Myst.* 5.23 (Ficino, *Opera*, pp. 549, 1899; Synesius *Somn.* 132B-D; August. *De civ. D.* 21.6); Porph. *Ad Aneb.* in August. *De civ. D.* 10.11 (Ficino, *Opera*, p. 549); Plot. *Enn.* 4.3.11; 4.4.30-42 (Ficino, *Opera*, pp. 529, 570-72); Werner Beierwaltes, "Neuplatonisches Denken als Substanz der Renaissance," in *Magia Naturalis und die Entstehung der modernen Naturwissenschaften*, Symposion der Leibniz Gesellschaft, Hannover, 14-15 November 1975 (Wiesbaden, 1978), p. 8; A.-J. Festugière, *Personal Religion among the Greeks*, Sather Classical Lectures, vol. 26 (Berkeley, 1954), pp. 105-6; Theodor Hopfner, *Griechisch-Ägyptischer Offenbarungszauber . . . I Band*, Studien zur Paleographie und Papyruskunde, XXI, 2d ed. (Amsterdam, 1974), pp. 198-203; for the disagreement on whether Ficino was commenting on *Enn.* 4.3.11 or 4.4.30-45, see Marcel, *Ficin*, p. 495; Kristeller, *Supplementum*, 1: lxxxiv; and Eugenio Garin, "'Le 'Elezione' e il problema dell'astrologia," in *Umanesimo e esoterismo*, ed. Enrico Castelli (Padua, 1960), p. 18

(who all choose the former passage); and Walker, *Spiritual and Demonic Magic*, pp. 3, 41 (who prefers the latter).

8. Ficino, *Opera*, p. 548: Praeterea narrat Haly notum illic sibi virum sapientem industria simili fecisse imagines quae moverentur. . . . Quales et Trismegistus ait Aegyptios ex certis mundi materiis facere consuevisse et in eas opportune animas daemonum inserere solitos atque animam avi sui Mercurii; *Asclep.* 23–24, 37–38; cf. Plot. *Enn.* 3.6.19, 4.3.11. The *Asclepius*, the fourteen *logoi* of Ficino's translation, the three additional treatises translated by Lodovico Lazarelli, and the Hermetic fragments of Stobaeus, Lactantius, Cyril, and other ancient writers are best read in the *Corpus Hermeticum*, ed. and trans. A. D. Nock and A.-J. Festugière, 4 vols. (Paris, 1946–54); see below, n. 71.

9. Ficino, *Opera*, pp. 571–72; cf. *Asclep.* 37; although the phrase "magicum hoc illicitum" in the Basel (1576) text of chapter 26 of *De vita* has been seen as another evidence of Ficino's distrust of Hermetic statue magic, the editorial work of Carol Kaske and John Clarke on *De vita* has established that the better reading is "illicium"; thus, the phrase means "this magical charm," not "this illicit magic." For further analysis of the meaning of this phrase and of Hermes, Plotinus, Iamblichus, and the *Chaldaean Oracles* in chapter 26, see B. Copenhaver, "Synesius, Iamblichus and the *Chaldean Oracles* in Marsilio Ficino's *De vita*: Hermetic Magic or Neoplatonic Magic?" in *Festschrift for P. O. Kristeller*, ed. James Hankins et al. (forthcoming). Walker, *Spiritual and Demonic Magic*, p. 41 n. 2, points out a third allusion to the *Asclepius* in Ficino, *Opera*, p. 561, but Ficino does not name Hermes in this passage: Quanquam Arabes et Aegyptii tantum statuis imaginibusque attribuunt arte astronomica et magica fabricatis, ut spiritus stellarum in eis includi putent. . . . Spiritus igitur stellarum, qualescunque sint, inseri statuis et imaginibus arbitrantur. The beginning of chapter 8 of *De vita* (*Opera*, pp. 540–41: Tradunt astrologi maiores quasdam stellas a Mercurio compertas) refers not to Ficino's Hermetica but to the *Liber Hermetis de XV stellis*; compare Ficino's list of stars with those in Festugière, *La révélation d'Hermès Trismégiste*, 4 vols. (Paris, 1949–54), 1:160–86, esp. 169; likewise, the Mercurius who speaks at the end of chapter 14 (*Opera*, p. 550) about plants waxing and waning in phase with the moon seems to belong to the medieval literature *De virtutibus septem herbarum et septem plantarum*, for which see Festugière, *Révélation*, 1:146–60.

10. *CH* 16.1: φανήσεται γάρ, σοι καὶ τοῖς ἐμοῖς ἐνίοις λόγοις ἀντίφωνος. Festugière, *Hermétisme*, pp. 34–40, 53, 55, 66–67; idem, *Révélation*, 2: 5, 7, 14, 44–47; 4: 54–78.

11. Though *CH* 1.18 says that the bond among all things has been broken (ἐλύθη ὁ πάντων σύνδεσμος), *CH* 10.14 speaks of a single principle governing the cosmos (ἐκ μιᾶς δὲ ἀρχῆς τὰ πάντα ἤρτηται), and *CH* 12.15–16 argues for a universal vitalism (ὁ δὲ σύμπας κόσμος οὗτος, ὁ μέγας θεός . . . καὶ ἡνωμένος ἐκείνῳ καὶ συσσώζων τὴν τάξιν. . . . πῶς ἂν οὖν δύναιτο . . . ἐν τῷ θεῷ, ἐν τῇ τοῦ παντὸς εἰκόνι, ἐν τῷ τῆς ζωῆς πληρώματι νεκρὰ εἶναι;); for sympathy (συμπάθεια) as a binding force in the cosmos, see *CH* 8.5; cf. *Asclep.* 2–6.

12. *CH* 3.2: πυρὶ τῶν ὅλων διορισθέντων καὶ ἀνακρεμασθέντων πνεύματι ὀχεῖσθαι (cf. *CH* 2.11; 10.13); *CH* 1.27: δυναμωθεὶς καὶ διδαχθεὶς τοῦ παντὸς τὴν φύσιν; *CH* 10.23: καὶ αὕτη ἡ τοῦ παντὸς διοίκησις . . . διήκουσα δὶ ἑνὸς τοῦ νοῦ.

13. Arist. *Metaph.* 1071ᵇ3–1074ᵇ14; idem, *Mete.* 339ᵃ12–33; Pseudo-Arist. *De mundo* 397ᵇ–399ᵃ; *CH* 2.6: τὰς γὰρ σφαίρας ἔφης τὰς πλανωμένας κινεῖσθαι ὑπὸ τῆς ἀπλανοῦς σφαίρας; *CH* 1.11: ὁ δὲ δημιουργὸς Νοῦς . . . , ὁ περιίσχων τοὺς κύκλους καὶ δινῶν ῥοίζῳ, ἔστρεψε τὰ ἑαυτοῦ δημιουργήματα. . . . ἡ δὲ τούτων περιφορά . . . ἐκ τῶν κατωφερῶν στοιχείων ζῷα ἤνεγκεν ἄλογα . . . , ἀὴρ δὲ πετεινὰ ἤνεγκε, καὶ τὸ ὕδωρ νηκτά.

14. *CH* 1.9, 13, 25: ὁ δὲ Νοῦς ὁ θεός . . . ἀπεκύησε λόγῳ ἕτερον Νοῦν δημιουργόν, ὃς . . . ἐδημιούργησε διοικητάς τινας ἑπτά, ἐν κύκλοις περιέχοντας τὸν αἰσθητὸν κόσμον, καὶ ἡ διοίκησις αὐτῶν εἱμαρμένη καλεῖται. . . . [ὁ Ἄνθρωπος] ἠβουλήθη καὶ αὐτὸς δημιουργεῖν. . . . κατενόησε τοῦ ἀδελφοῦ τὰ δημιουργήματα, οἱ δὲ ἠράσθησαν αὐτοῦ, ἕκαστος δὲ μετεδίδου τῆς ἰδίας τάξεως. . . . καὶ οὕτως ὁρμᾷ λοιπὸν ἄνω διὰ τῆς ἁρμονίας, καὶ τῇ πρώτῃ ζώνῃ δίδωσι τὴν αὐξητικὴν ἐνέργειαν καὶ τὴν μειωτικήν, καὶ τῇ δευτέρᾳ τὴν μηχανὴν τῶν κακῶν, δόλον ἀνενέργητον [κ.τ.λ.]; *CH* 10.22: κοινωνία δέ ἐστι ψυχῶν, καὶ κοινωνοῦσι μὲν αἱ τῶν θεῶν ταῖς τῶν ἀνθρώπων. . . . ἐπιμελοῦνται δὲ οἱ κρείττονες τῶν ἐλαττόνων, θεοὶ μὲν ἀνθρώπων, ἄνθρωποι δὲ τῶν ἀλόγων ζώων, ὁ δὲ θεὸς πάντων.

15. *CH* 1.4, 11; 2.1–12; 3.1–3; 5.3–5; 8.1–4; 9.6–8; 10.10–11, 14, 22–23; 12.14–18; 14.2–3.

16. *CH* 1.24–26; 2.12–17; 3.1; 4.1–2, 10–11; 5; 6.1, 4; 8.2; 9.9; 10.1–14; 11; 14.4–10.

17. *CH* 1.20–21; 2.14–16; 4.1–2, 6–8; 6; 7; 9.4–5; 10.1–4, 10, 12; 12.5–11; 13.4, 12; 14.7–9.

18. *CH* 1.12–23; 3.3; 4.1–3; 5.6–8; 8.5; 9.1–5; 10.12–14; 12.19–20; 13.2.

19. *CH* 1.25; 9; 10.7–10, 13, 24–25; 12.1–4.

20. *CH* 1.24–26; 3.4; 4.6–10; 7.2–3; 10.7–8, 15–25; 11.22–23; 13.4–16.

21. Festugière, *Hermétisme*, pp. 37, 72–87; idem, *Révélation*, 1:83–85; 2:ix–xv; Yates, *Bruno*, pp. 2–12, 22, 398–403; D. P. Walker, *The Ancient Theology: Studies in Christian Platonism from the Fifteenth to the Eighteenth Century* (London, 1972), pp. 17–21; F. Purnell, "Francisco Patrizi and the Critics of Hermes Trismegistus," *Journal of Medieval and Renaissance Studies* 6 (1976): 155–78.

22. *CH* 10.22: καὶ τοῦ μὲν θεοῦ καθάπερ ἀκτῖνες αἱ ἐνέργειαι, τοῦ δὲ κόσμου ἀκτῖνες αἱ φύσεις. . . . καὶ αἵ μὲν ἐνέργειαι διὰ τοῦ κόσμου ἐνεργοῦσι καὶ ἐπὶ τὸν ἄνθρωπον διὰ τῶν τοῦ κόσμου φυσικῶν ἀκτίνων, αἱ δὲ φύσεις διὰ τῶν στοιχείων; on natures (φύσεις) and operations (ἐνέργειαι), cf. *CH* 16.13; Iambl. *Myst.* 8.7; Nock and Festugière, *Corpus Hermeticum*, 1: 134 nn. 75-76; 140-42; and for a similar distinction between occult *influxus* and manifest *lux* (both of which are natural) in Ficino, see *Opera*, p. 562.

23. *Asclep.* 3: caelum ergo, sensibilis deus, administrator est omnium corporum. . . . caeli vero et ipsius animae et omnium, quae mundo insunt, ipse gubernator est, qui est effector, deus. a supradictis enim omnibus . . . , frequentatio fertur influens per mundum. . . . mundus autem praeparatus est a deo receptaculum omniformium specierum; natura autem per species imaginans mundum per quattuor elementa ad caelum usque perducit cuncta dei visibus placitura; in *CH* (Nock and Festugière), 2: 299, this last phrase is translated "nature . . . prolonge jusqu'au ciel toute la série des êtres pour qu'ils plaisent aux regards de Dieu"; *Asclep.* 2-7, 19; *CH* 16.15: τὸ δὲ λογικὸν μέρος τῆς ψυχῆς . . . ἐπιτήδειον εἰς ὑποδοχὴν (fit as a receptacle) τοῦ θεοῦ; Iambl. *Myst.* 5.7, 12, 23; *Orac. chal.* 203; Procl. *El.* 39, 71-72, 79, 140, 143, 189; E. R. Dodds, ed. and trans., *Proclus, The Elements of Theology: A Revised Text with Translation, Introduction and Commentary* (Oxford, 1963), pp. 344-45; Festugière, *Révélation*, 2: 20-21; Festugière, *Hermétisme*, pp. 121-30; S. Sambursky, *The Physical World of Late Antiquity* (London, 1962), pp. 104-10; see below, n. 49.

24. *Asclep.* 23-24, 37-38: Et horum . . . deorum, qui terreni habentur, cuiusmodi est qualitas? Constat . . . de herbis, de lapidibus et de aromatibus divinitatis naturalem vim in se habentibus; Iambl. *Myst.* 5.23: ἡ θεουργικὴ τέχνη, κοινῶς τε οὕτωσὶ κατ' οἰκειότητα ἑκάστῳ τῶν θεῶν τὰς προσφόρους ὑποδοχὰς [receptacles] ἀνευρίσκουσα, συμπλέκει πολλάκις λίθους βοτάνας ζῷα ἀρώματα. It should be noted that *CH* 16, the *Definitiones Asclepii*, not published until 1507 in Lodovico Lazzarelli's translation, says a great deal about solar magic as a force against demonic powers; Kristeller, "Lazzarelli," pp. 224-29; Cesare Vasoli, "Temi e fonti della tradizione Ermetica in uno scritto di Symphorien Champier," in *Umanesimo e esoterismo*, pp. 242-43, 248-59. For another opinion on the importance of the Hermetica for Ficino's magic, see Eugenio Garin, *Astrology in the Renaissance: The Zodiac of Life*, trans. Carolyn Jackson et al. (London, 1983), pp. 40, 47, 65-66, 72; idem, "Postille sull'ermetismo del rinascimento," *Rinascimento* 16 (1976): 245-49; idem, "Divagazione ermetiche," *Rivista critica di storia della filosofia* 31: 462-26; idem, "Ancora sull' ermetismo," *Rivista critica della storia della filosofia* 32: 342-47; idem, *Il ritorno dei filosofi antichi* (Naples, 1983), pp. 67-77.

25. Iambl. *Myst.* 8.4: τὰ μὲν γὰρ φερόμενα ὡς Ἑρμοῦ ἑρμαϊκὰς περιέχει δόξας, εἰ καὶ τῇ τῶν φιλοσόφων γλώττῃ πολλάκις χρῆται· μεταγέγραπται γὰρ ἀπὸ τῆς αἰγυπτίας γλώττης ὑπ' ἀνδρῶν φιλοσοφίας οὐκ ἀπείρως ἐχόντων; Festugière, *Révélation*, 1: 106-7, 428-29; Festugière, *Hermétisme*, pp. 88-89.

26. See above, nn. 3-5.

27. J. E. McGuire, "Neoplatonism and Active Principles: Newton and the *Corpus Hermeticum*," in *Hermeticism and the Scientific Revolution: Papers Read at a Clark Library Seminar, March 9, 1974* (Los Angeles, 1977), pp. 100, 127, 131-32; B. P. Copenhaver, essay review of above article, *Annals of Science* 35 (1978): 530-31; cf. C. B. Schmitt, "Reappraisals in Renaissance Science," *History of Science* 16 (1978): 200-214; for *Hermetic magic* and similar terms, see Mary Hesse, "Hermeticism and Historiography: An Apology for the Internal History of Science," *Minnesota Studies in the Philosophy of Science*, vol. 5: *Historical and Philosophical Perspectives of Science*, ed. Roger H. Stuewer (Minneapolis, 1970), pp. 139, 147, 149; Paolo Rossi, "Hermeticism, Rationality and the Scientific Revolution," in *Reason, Experiment and Mysticism in the Scientific Revolution*, ed. M. L. Righini Bonelli and William R. Shea (New York, 1975), pp. 259-64; Allen Debus, *Man and Nature in the Renaissance* (Cambridge, 1978), pp. 13, 101, 133; Hugh Kearney, *Science and Change, 1500-1700* (New York, 1971), pp. 37-40; Brian Easlea, *Witch-hunting, Magic and the New Philosophy* (Sussex, 1980), p. 92; P. M. Rattansi, "The Intellectual Origins of the Royal Society," *Notes and Records of the Royal Society* 23 (1968): 132; these uses of *Hermetic* are accurate reflections of Yates's views in *Bruno*, pp. 44-82, but they do not, in my view, accurately represent the content of the philosophical Hermetica that Ficino translated.

28. Plot. *Enn.* 4.3.11; 4.4.32, 35, 38, 40, 42-44; Thorndike, *History of Magic*, 1: 290; E. R. Dodds, *The Greeks and the Irrational*, Sather Classical Lectures, vol. 25 (Berkeley, 1968), pp. 285-86; P. Merlan, "Plotinus and Magic," *Isis* 44 (1953): 341-48; Pierre Boyancé, "Théurgie et télestique néoplatoniciennes," *Revue d'histoire des religions* 147 (1955): 189-95; A. H. Armstrong, "Was Plotinus a Magician?" *Phronesis* 1 (1955-56): 73-79; Clemens Zintzen, "Die Wertung von Mystik und Magie in der neuplatonischen Philosophie," *Rheinisches Museum für Philologie*, N. F. 108 (1965): 71-100; J. Trouillard, "Le merveilleux dans la vie et la pensée de Proclos," *Revue philosophique* 163 (1973): 439-52; idem, *L'un et l'âme selon Proclus* (Paris, 1972), pp. 171-89; Andrew Smith, *Porphyry's Place in the Neoplatonic Tradition: A Study in Post-Plotinian Neoplatonism* (The Hague, 1974), pp. 81-150; B. P. Copenhaver, "Renaissance Magic and Neoplatonic Philosophy: *Ennead* 4.3.5 in Ficino's *De vita coelitus comparanda*," in *Marsilio Ficino e il ritorno di Platone: Studi e documenti*, ed. Giancarlo Garfagnini (Florence, 1986), pp. 351-69. Paola

Zambelli, "Platone, Ficino e la magia," in *Studia humanitatis: Festschrift für Ernesto Grassi* (Munich, 1973), pp. 126, 131–34.

29. Yates, "The Hermetic Tradition in Renaissance Science," in *Art, Science and History in the Renaissance*, ed. Charles S. Singleton (Baltimore, 1968), p. 255.

30. See above, n. 7; see also, for example, Ficino's *Phaedrus Commentary*, where Hermes is explicitly cited only once, while Hermias, Iamblichus, Plotinus, Proclus, Syrianus, and various unnamed *Platonici* are mentioned a total of twenty-seven times; Michael J. B. Allen, *Marsilio Ficino and the Phaedran Charioteer* (Berkeley, 1981), p. [268].

31. Yates, "Hermetic Tradition," pp. 255, 257, 261, 272.

32. Ibid., p. 257; Walker, *Spiritual and Demonic Magic*, pp. 36–42, assigns the *Asclepius* an important role, but also notes Ficino's considerable debt to the Neoplatonists; Yates seems to qualify her emphasis on the Hermetica on the last page (273) of her article; for other mentions of "man as magus" in the *Pimander*, see Yates, *Bruno*, pp. 28, 35, 137, but note that in her chapters on Ficino and Hermes (pp. 20–83), she does not make a strong case for magic in the Hermetica outside the *Asclepius*; for magical passages in the *Pimander*, see above, nn. 11–14.

33. Yates, "Hermetic Tradition," p. 31; idem, *Bruno*, pp. 241–46; *CH* 12.16–18; for an analysis of the views of Frances Yates and of the role of magic in early modern science, see B. P. Copenhaver, "Natural Magic, Hermetism and Occultism in Early Modern Science," in *Reappraisals in the Scientific Revolution*, ed. R. Westman and D. Lindberg, forthcoming.

34. Hopfner, *Offenbarungszauber*, 1: 255–61, 327, 542–46; 2: 1–39; some of the same material is more accessible in Hopfner, "Μαγεία," Pauly/Wissowa, *Real Encyclopädie*, 14/1, cols. 316, 367–73; Julius Röhr, *Der okkulte Kraftbegriff im Altertum*, Philologus, Supplementband 17, Heft 1 (Leipzig, 1923); Max Wellmann, *Die Φύσικα des Bolos Demokritos und der Magier Anaxilaos aus Larissa*, Abhandlungen der preussischen Akademie der Wissenschaften, Jahrgang 1928, philosophisch historische Klasse (Berlin, 1928), pp. 3–5, 9–16, 28, 42–51; Joseph Bidez and Franz Cumont, *Les mages hellenisés: Zoroastre, Ostanès et Hystaspe d'après la tradition grecque*, 2 vols. (Paris, 1938), 1: 107–17, 190–99.

35. Joseph Bidez et al., *Catalogue des manuscrits alchimiques grecs*, vol. 6: *Michael Psellus, Epître sur la chrysopée: Opuscules et extraits sur l'alchimie, la météorologie et la démonologie* (Brussels, 1928), pp. 139–51; Hans Lewy, *Chaldaean Oracles and Theurgy: Mysticism, Magic and Platonism in the Later Roman Empire* (Cairo, 1956), pp. 40–42, 70–74, 157, 177–78, 255–57, 464; Hopfner, *Offenbarungszauber*, 1: 205, 510–13; 2: 22–23.

36. *Index quae hoc in libro habentur. Iamblichus de mysteriis Aegyptiorum, Chaldaeorum, Assyriorum. Proclus in platonicum Alcibiadem de anima atque demone. Proclus de sacrificio et magia. Porphyrius de divino atque daemonibus. Synesius platonicus de somniis. Psellus de daemonibus* (Venice, 1497), sigs. hviir–hviiiv; Kristeller, *Supplementum*, 1: cxxxiv–cxxxv; Marcel, *Ficin*, pp. 489–95; Ficino, *Opera*, pp. 1928–29; Martin Sicherl, *Die Handschriften, Ausgaben und Übersetzungen von Iamblichos de Mysteriis: Eine kritisch-historische Studie*, Texte und Untersuchungen zur Geschichte der Altchristlichen Literatur, 62. Band (Berlin, 1957), pp. 23–26, 36.

37. Bidez, et al., *Catalogue*, 6: 140–41, 148–51; Joseph Bidez, "Un opuscule inédit de Proclus," *Académie des inscriptions et belles-lettres, Paris, Comptes-rendus des séances* (1927): 280–83; idem, "Proclus," *Annuaire de l'institut de philologie et d'historire orientales et slaves* 4 (1936); *Mélanges Franz Cumont*, pp. 85–100; I have been unable to obtain a copy of Kroll's reconstructed text, which is described by Bidez and others.

38. André Bremond, "Notes et documents sur la religion néo-platonicienne," *Recherches de sciences religieuses* (1933): 102–12; Festugière, *Révélation*, 1: 133–36.

39. Walker, *Spiritual and Demonic Magic*, pp. 35–36; Garin, "Problema dell'astrologia," pp. 19–20, 23–24; Garin, *Moyen Age et Renaissance*, p. 142 n. 1; Yates, *Bruno*, p. 67, n. 1.

40. MS Laurentianus Plut. 82.15, fols. 126v–128v; MS Laurentianus Strozz. 97, fols. 147v–151v; I have also seen the two Greek MSS of *De Sacrificio*: Laurentianus Plut. 10.32, fols. 119r–121v; and Vallicellianus F20, fols. 138r–140v; of which the latter is the basis of Bidez's edition; Kristeller, *Supplementum*, 1: xii, xv; Sicherl, *Handschriften*, pp. 23–26, 79–80, 184–88; see above, n. 36; Sicherl (p. 184) says that Laurentianus 82.15 "was made for the use of Lorenzo. According to Della Torre, this splendid codex is the comprehensive manuscript (*Komplexivcodex*) of Ficino's translations of the minor works of the Platonists, which the humanist sent to his patron Lorenzo toward the end of the year 1489 or the beginning of 1490."

41. The following uses of *De sacrificio*, whose line numbers are cited in the English translation of my appendix, seem fairly obvious in *De vita*:

P. 550: Nec alia ratione leo veretur gallum, nisi quoniam in ordine Phoebeo gallus est leone superior. Eadem ratione inquit Proclus, Apollineum daemonem, qui nonnumquam apparuit sub figura leonis, statim obiecto gallo disparuisse (lines 50–62).

P. 550: lapis Elitis radiis aureis Solem imitans. Lapis item qui Solis oculus appellatur, figuram habens pupillae, ex qua lumen emicat (lines 38–42).

P. 550: Inter plantas palma Phoebea est, et in primis laurus, qua virtute venenosa repellit et fulgur. . . . Loton esse Phoeboeam, rotunda tum poma testantur et explicatio foliorum eius die, replicatio vero nocte (lines 32–37, 65–67; cf. Iambl. *Myst.* 7.2).

P. 551: Multo vero potentiores in serie Lunae lapillos narrat Proclus. Primum quidem Selinitim, qui non modo figura Lunam imitetur, sed et motu, circumeatque cum Luna (lines 8–10, 43).

P. 551: Alterum vero recenset lapillum, helioselinon cognomento, qui Solis Lunaeque coniunctae Soli naturaliter habet imaginem (lines 44–45).

For other possible influences of *De Sacrificio*, see:

P. 531: ac si certe cuidam rerum speciei vel individuo eius rite adhibeas multa quae sparsa sunt sed etiam ideae conformia, mox in materiam hanc ita opportune paratam singulare munus ab idea trahes (lines 67–80).

P. 549: Iamblichus in materiis quae naturaliter superis consentaneae sint, et opportune riteque collectae undique, conflataeque fuerint, vires effectusque non solum coelestes, sed etiam daemonicos et divinos suscipi posse confirmat. Idem omnino Proclus atque Synesius (lines 88–96).

P. 552: Confirmatur dictum illud valde Platonicum, hanc mundi machinam ita secum esse connexam, ut et in terris coelestia sint conditione terrena, et in coelo vicissim terrestria dignitate coelesti, et in occulta mundi vita menteque regina mundi, coelestia insint, vitali tamen intellectualique proprietate simul et excellentia (lines 5–7, 14–19).

P. 549: Dixi equidem alibi, desuper ab unaquaque stella (ut Platonice loquar) seriem rerum illi propriam usque ad extrema pendere (lines 46–48).

P. 551: Superius autem in eodem rerum contextu trahit quidem quod est inferius et ad se convertit. . . . Sic in serie Solis inferior homo admiratur superiorem (lines 63–64).

P. 570: in universo esca quaedam sive fomes ad animam corpori copulandam est ille ipse, quem spiritum appellamus. Anima quoque fomes quidam est in spiritu corporeque mundi . . . quemadmodum summa quaedam in ligno siccitas ad penetraturum oleum est parata (lines 20–31).

On Proclus in the Renaissance, see Françoise Joukovsky, "Plotin dans les éditions et les commentaires de Porphyre, Jamblique et Proclus à la Renaissance," *Bibliothèque d'humanisme et renaissance* 42 (1980): 393–98; for other citations of Proclus in *De vita*, see Ficino, *Opera*, pp. 538, 548.

42. See above, nn. 24, 41.

43. Procl. *El.* 140–45: Πάσης θείας τάξεως [ἡ] ἰδιότης διὰ πάντων φοιτᾷ τῶν δευτέρων, καὶ δίδωσιν ἑαυτὴν ἅπασι τοῖς καταδεεστέροις γένεσιν; Dodds, *Elements*, pp. xvii, 129, 208–9, 257–60, 267, 273; Hopfner, *Offenbarungszauber*, 1: 95, 205; Festugière, *Hermétisme*, pp. 126–27; Lawrence J. Rosan, *The Philosophy of Proclus: The Final Phase of Ancient Thought* (New York, 1949), pp. 67, 85–87, 104; Dodds, *Elements*, p. 45, mentions a manuscript (Ambrosianus 329) written by Ficino and containing parts of the *Elements*; Walker, *Spiritual and Demonic Magic*, pp. 49–50, has analyzed a long passage from Ficino's commentary on Romans (*Opera*, p. 440) that also deals with *series numinum*.

44. Ficino, *Opera*, pp. 549–50: ab unaquaque stella . . . seriem rerum illi propriam usque ad extrema pendere. Sub ipso Scorpionis corde post eiusmodi daemonas atque homines, scorpiumque animal, collocare possumus etiam herbam Asterion . . . , quam medici tradunt qualitatem habere rosae vimque contra morbos genitalium mirabilem possidere. . . . Sub stella Solari, id est, Syrio, Solem primo, deinde daemones quoque Phoebeos, quos aliquando sub leonum vel gallorum forma hominibus occurrisse, testis est Proclus (etc., as in n. 41 above).

45. See above, n. 41; Ficino, *Opera*, pp. 532–33.

46. Dodds, *Elements*, pp. ix–xi, xx n. 4; Festugière, "Art théurgique," pp. 7, 17; Rosan, *Philosophy of Proclus*, pp. 213, 245–54; Zintzen, "Mystik und Magie," pp. 84, 94–96; Armstrong, "Was Plotinus a Magician?" p. 77; see above, n. 28.

47. Procl. *El.* 28, 29, 32; Dodds, *Elements*, pp. xxii, 216–19; Zintzen, "Mystik und Magie," pp. 77–79, n. 29; Rosan, *Philosophy of Proclus*, p. 73.

48. Procl. *El.* 103: Πάντα ἐν πᾶσιν, οἰκείως δὲ ἐν ἑκάστῳ; cf. Plot. *Enn.* 5.8.4: καὶ γὰρ ἔχει πᾶς πάντα ἐν αὐτῷ, καὶ αὖ ὁρᾷ ἐν ἄλλῳ πάντα; Dodds, *Elements*, p. 254.

49. See above, n. 23.

50. Procl. *El.* 5; *Orac. chal.* 224; Iambl. *Myst.* 5.23; Hopfner, "Μαγεία," cols. 314, 393; Garin, "Problema dell'astrologia," pp. 23–24.

51. Plot. *Enn.* 4.4.42: καὶ ὅτι δυνάμεις καὶ χωρὶς προαιρέσεως πολλαὶ καὶ αὗται καὶ ἄνευ μηχανῆς καὶ μετὰ τέχνης, ὡς ἐν ζώῳ ἑνί, . . . καὶ τέχναις καὶ ἰατρῶν καὶ ἐπαοιδῶν ἄλλο ἄλλῳ ἠναγκάσθη παρασχεῖν τι τῆς δυνάμεως τῆς αὑτοῦ; Iambl. *Myst.* 2.11: οὐδὲ γὰρ ἡ ἔννοια συνάπτει τοῖς θεοῖς τοὺς θεουργούς. . . . ἀλλ' ἡ τῶν ἔργων τῶν ἀρρήτων καὶ ὑπὲρ πᾶσαν νόησιν θεοπρεπῶς ἐνεργουμένων τελεσιουργία ἥ τε τῶν νοουμένων τοῖς θεοῖς μόνον συμβόλων ἀφθέγκτων δύναμις ἐντίθησι τὴν θεουργικὴν ἕνωσιν. . . . Καὶ γὰρ μὴ νοούντων ἡμῶν αὐτὰ τὰ συνθήματα ἀφ' ἑαυτῶν δρᾷ τὸ οἰκεῖον ἔργον; *Orac. chal.* 2.108, 109; Procl. *Ecl. de phil. chal.* 1.5; Zintzen, "Mystik und Magie," p. 91; Dodds, *Elements*, pp. 222–23; idem, *Irra-*

tional, pp. 292–93; Hopfner, *Offenbarungszauber*, 1: 200–203; Lewy, *Chaldaean Oracles*, p. 462; Rosan, *Philosophy of Proclus*, pp. 104–5; André Bremond, "Un texte de Proclus sur la prière et l'union divine," *Recherches de science religieuses* (1929): 460–62.

52. Hopfner, *Offenbarungszauber*, 2: 1–16; for catalogs of "empirical" data magically understood, see Wellmann, *Bolos Demokritos*, pp. 19–28; Röhr, *Kraftbegriff*, pp. 26–28, 56–64, 73, 76, 81, 86–87, 90–94; Plin. *HN* 9.79–80, 143; 20.1–2; 24.1–4; 25.72, 80, 81, 115, 145; 28.84, 90, 92, 101, 112–18; 32.1–2; 34.147, 150, 151; 36.126–27; 37.55–61, 134–35, 42, 45, 63; cf. Pl. *Resp.* 528E–530C; *Asclep.* 13; *CH* 9.4; 10.10; Festugière, *Révélation*, 1: 65, 84; 2: 45, 139, 150–52; Henri-Irenée Marrou, *St. Augustin et la fin de la culture antique*, Bibliothèque des écoles françaises d'Athènes et de Rome, fasc. 145 (Paris, 1938), pp. 233–35, 350–51, 454–57; see below, n. 75.

53. *Symp.* 202E–203D, trans. M. Joyce in *The Collected Dialogues of Plato, Including the Letters*, ed. E. Hamilton and H. Cairns, Bollingen Series, no. 71 (Princeton, 1961), pp. 555–56; Boyancé, "Théurgie," pp. 205, 207; Lewy, *Chaldaean Oracles*, p. 436; Hopfner, "Μαγεία," col. 308.

54. Marsile Ficin, *Commentaire sur le Banquet de Platon*, ed. and trans. Raymond Marcel (Paris, 1956), p. 220: Sed cur magum putamus amorem? Quia tota vis magice in amore consistit. Magice opus est attractio rei unius ab alia ex quadam cognatione nature. Mundi autem huius partes ceu animalis unius membra, omnes ab uno auctore pendentes, unius nature communione invicem copulantur. Ideo sicut in nos cerebrum, pulmones, cor, iecur et reliqua membra a se invicem trahunt aliquid seque mutuo iuvant et uno illorum aliquo patiente compatiuntur, ita ingentis huius animalis membra, id est, omnia mundi corpora connexa similiter, mutuant invicem naturas et mutuantur. Ex communi cognatione communis innascitur amor, ex amore, communis attractio. Haec autem vera magica est. Sic ab orbis Lune concavitate propter nature congruitatem sursum trahitur ignis, ab ignis concavitate aer, a mundi centro terra ad infima trahitur, a loco etiam suo rapitur aqua. Sic et magnes ferrum, electrum paleas, ignem sulphur. . . . Magice igitur opera nature opera sunt; ars vero ministra. . . . Et natura omnis ex amore mutuo maga cognominatur; ibid., pp. 65–66, 92; Zambelli, "Platone, Ficino e la magia," pp. 128–30; Paola Zambelli, "Le problème de la magie naturelle à la Renaissance," in *Magia, astrologia e religione nel Rinascimento: Convegno polacco-italiano* (Warsaw, 25–27 September 1972) pp. 60–61, 70.

55. Ficino, *Opera*, p. 570: Ubique igitur natura maga est, ut inquit Plotinus, atque Synesius, videlicet certa quaedam pabulis ubique certis inescans, non aliter, quam centro terrae gravia trahens, Lunae concavo levia. . . . Quo quidem attractu se cum ipso devinciri mundum testantur sapientes Indi, dicentes mundum esse animal passim masculum, simulatque foeminam, mutuoque membrorum suorum amore ubique coire secum. . . . Quod sane animadvertentes agricultura, praeparat agrum seminaque ad coelestia dona, et insitionibus quibusdam vitam plantae propagat, et ad speciem alteram melioremque perducit. Similia quaedam efficit et Medicus, Physicus, et Chirurgus in corpore nostro, tum ad nostram fovendam, tum ad universi naturam uberius comparandam. Idem quoque Philosophus, naturalium rerum astrorumque peritus, quem proprie Magum appellare solemus, certis quibusdam illecebris coelestia terrenis, opportune quidem, nec aliter inserens, quam insitionis studiosus agricola veteri recentem stipiti surculum. . . . Subiicit Magus terrena coelestibus, imo inferiora passim superioribus, ut proprias ubique foeminas suis maribus foecundandas; Plot. *Enn.* 4.4.40, 43, 44: Τὰς δὲ γοητείας πῶς; "Η τῇ συμπαθείᾳ. . . . ἡ ἀληθινὴ μαγεία ἡ ἐν τῷ παντὶ φιλία καὶ τὸ νεῖκος αὖ. . . . Καὶ γάρ, ὅτι ἐρᾶν πεφύκασι καὶ τὰ ἐρᾶν ποιοῦντα ἕλκει πρὸς ἄλληλα, ὁλκῆς ἐρωτικῆς διὰ γοητείας τέχνη γεγένηται προστιθέντων ἐπαφαῖς φύσεις ἄλλας ἄλλοις συναγωγοὺς καὶ ἐγκείμενον ἐχούσας ἔρωτα· καὶ συνάπτουσι δὲ ἄλλην ψυχὴν ἄλλῃ, ὥσπερ ἄν εἰ φυτὰ διεστηκότα ἐξαψάμενοι πρὸς ἄλληλα. . . . "Η ἑλκόμενος οὐ μάγων τέχναις, ἀλλὰ τῆς φύσεως τὴν ἀπάτην δούσης καὶ συναφάσης ἄλλο πρὸς ἄλλο οὐ τοῖς τόποις, ἀλλ' οἷς ἔδωκε φίλτροις. . . . Τοῦτο δὲ ἡ τῆς φύσεως γοητεία ποιεῖ; Synesius *Somn.* 132D: οἷς ὁμοιοπαθῶν εἴκει τῇ φύσει καὶ γοητεύεται; Zambelli, "Magic naturelle," pp. 60–61, 70; "Platone e la magia," pp. 128–30.

56. S. Sambursky, *Physics of the Stoics* (London, 1959), pp. 2, 5, 27, 66; idem, *Physical World*, pp. 3–4, 9–10, 102–3; David E. Hahm, *The Origins of Stoic Cosmology* (Columbus, Ohio, 1977), pp. 157–74. To note that the Stoic πνεῦμα is both material and animate is enough to indicate some of the differences between that idea and Ficinian *amor* or Newtonian force.

57. Plot. *Enn.* 4.4.40 (trans. S. MacKenna, *The Enneads* [London, 1962], p. 323); cf. Procl. *Comm. in Alc. 1* 52–53, 92; S. E. Gersh, *ΚΙΝΗΣΙΣ ΑΚΙΝΗΤΟΣ: A Study of Spiritual Motion in the Philosophy of Proclus*, Philosophia Antiqua, vol. 26 (Leiden, 1973), pp. 123–27; A. H. Armstrong, *The Architecture of the Intelligible Universe in the Philosophy of Plotinus: An Analytical and Historical Study*, Cambridge Classical Studies, 6 (Cambridge, 1940), pp. 58, 98–106.

58. MS Vallicellianus F20, fol. 138r: Eadem dixit Porphyrius in propositionibus. Vide Mercurium et Plotinum et Iamblicum et Alchindum; the work of Porphyry's referred to is the *Sententiae ad intelligibilia ducentes*, and is contained in the same manuscript; see Thorndike, *History of Magic*, 1: 642–46, on the *De radiis stellicis* or *Theorica magicae artis* of al-Kindi; Ficino, *Opera*, p. 562; see below, pp. 90–93.

59. MS Vallicellianus F20, fol. 138v: Sic si apponis pedi cerebralia, trahit vim a cerebro; si cordialia a

corde si epatica ab epate, etc. Similiter si natura propria in homine deficiat, trahes vim ab hac stella vel illa appropinquando huic quae conveniat cum stella, maxime stella vigente; the last word can also be read *ingente*, "large star"; Synesius *Somn.* 132B-D; see above, n. 54.

60. Ibid., fol. 139*v*.

61. Ibid., fol. 139*r*: Ego vidi lapillum rotundum et punctis quasi stellis insignitum qui aceto perfusus movebatur primo in rectum ali(quatenus), mox in girum oberrabat, quem credo firmamento esse accomodatum, maxime aceto perfusum. Oportet enim ibi quod natura incohavit arte compleri. Quid quod magnes convenit cum ursa et polo et illuc convertit ferrum, quod apparet in instrumento nautarum id polum explorandum? Unde imago ursae impressa magneti [   ] suspensa collo cum ferreo monili trah(eret) vim illius ad nos tangendo carnem? (Parentheses indicate doubtful readings; brackets indicate material illegible to me.)

62. Ficino, *Opera*, pp. 551-52; see above, n. 51.

63. See above, nn. 43-44.

64. Ficino, *Opera*, p. 551: Vidi equidem lapillum Florentiam advectum ex India, ibi e capite draconis erutum, rotundum, ad nummi figuram punctis ordine quamplurimis, quasi stellis naturaliter insignitum, qui aceto perfusus movebatur parumper in rectum, imo obliquum, mox ferabatur in gyrum, donec exhaleret vapor aceti. The markings Ficino saw on the stone and its reaction with acetic acid are consistent with the appearance and composition of a crinoid stem, a kind of carbonate echinoderm fossil.

65. *Henrici Cornelii Agrippae ab Nettesheym . . . opera quaecumque hactenus vel in lucem prodierunt* (Lyon, 1600?), 1: 1-148.

66. Ibid., pp. 8, 10, 21, 32, 37, 69, 75, 76, 82, 85, 86, 88, 92-94, 107, 109, 111, 115, 117, 132; Paola Zambelli, "Agrippa von Nettesheim in den neueren kritischen Studien und in den Handschriften," *Archiv für Kulturgeschichte* 51 (1969): 282; Yates, *Bruno*, pp. 132-33; Walker, *Spiritual and Demonic Magic*, pp. 86, 91-96.

67. Agrippa, *Opera*, 1: 4, 5, 13, 18, 23-24, 26-28, 31, 42, 43, 48, 56-57, 60, 66, 68, 69, 72, 77-79, 85, 89, 91, 107, 109, 116, 119, 121, 123, 140-42, 144.

68. Ibid., pp. 4, 5, 26-28, 43, 56-57, 68, 72, 79, 85, 89, 91, 109, 116, 121, 123, 142.

69. Ibid., pp. 5, 7, 26, 44, 57, 58, 64, 66, 68, 70, 80, 89, 109, 146; for these and other references to magical, psychological, ethical, anthropological, and eschatological themes from the *Hermetica*, see Paola Zambelli, "Cornelio Agrippa de Nettesheim: Testi scelti," in *Testi umanistici su l'ermetismo: Testi di Ludovico Lazzarelli, F. Georgio Veneto, Cornelio Agrippa di Nettesheim*, ed. Eugenio Garin, Archivio di Filosofia (Rome, 1955), pp. 107-18; idem, "Agrippa di Nettesheim: 'Dialogus de homine,' " *Rivista critica di storia della filosofia* 13 (1958): 58, 59, 65, 67, 68, 71; idem, "Cornelio Agrippa: Scritti inediti e dispersi," *Rinascimento*, 2d ser., 5 (1965): 201, 238, 296, 297, 303, 304; Wolf-Dieter Müller-Jahncke, *Magie als Wissenschaft im frühen 16. Jahrhundert: Die Beziehungen zwischen Magie, Medizin und Pharmazie im Werk des Agrippa von Nettesheim* (Marburg, 1973), pp. 32-33, 104 n. 5; Yates, *Bruno*, p. 137.

70. August. *De civ. D.* 8.26; Cic. *Nat. D.* 3.22; Walter Burkert, *Greek Religion* (Cambridge, Mass., 1985), p. 120.

71. Walter Scott, ed. and trans., *Hermetica: The Ancient Greek and Latin Writings Which Contain Religious or Philosophic Teachings Ascribed to Hermes Trismegistus*, 4 vols. (Oxford, 1924), 1: 1-2; Festugière, *Hermétisme*, p. 30; idem, *Révélation*, 1: 106-23, 137-87, 201-17, 225-96; K. H. Dannenfeldt, "Hermetica Philosophica," in *Catalogus translationum et commentariorum*, vol. 1, ed. P. O. Kristeller (Washington, D.C., 1960), pp. 137-56; *Die Kyraniden*, ed. Dimitris Kaimakis (Meisenheim am Glan, 1976); F. de Mely, ed., *Les lapidaires de l'antiquité et du moyen âge* (Paris, 1888), vol. 2: *Les lapidaires grecs*, pp. vii-lxxi, 3-133; Louis Delatte, ed., *Textes latins et vieux français relatifs aux Cyranides: La traduction latine du XIIe siècle; Le compendium aureum; Le De XV Stellis d'Hermès; Le livre des secrez de nature* (Paris, 1942); Max Wellmann, *Marcellus von Side als Arzt und die Koiraniden des Hermes Trismegistos* (Leipzig, 1934); Thorndike, *History of Magic*, 2: 229-35. For another opinion on the importance of "popular" and "learned" Hermetica in Renaissance magic, see the important writings of Garin cited above in note 24.

72. Agrippa, *Opera*, 1: 66: Dicunt Academici simul cum Trismegisto . . . omnia quae sunt sub lunari globo in hoc inferiori mundo generationi et corruptioni subiecta, eadem etiam esse in coelesti mundo, sed modo quodam coelesti; deinde etiam in mundo intellectuali, sed multo perfectiori et meliori nota, perfectissimo tandem in archetypo; cf. *CH* 1.9-16, 25; 4.2; 10.11; 16.5, 17; *Asclep.* 10; see above, nn. 11, 42; Festugière, *Révélation*, 1: 92-94.

P. 68: Mercurius Trismegistus scribit . . . compositam rite statuam, confestim per daemonem congruam animari. Cuius etiam meminit Augustinus de civitate Dei libro octavo; *Asclep.* 37-38; August. *De civ. D.* 8.23-24; see above, nn. 8-9.

P. 70: Nemo igitur dubitat simili modo certis quibusdam mundi materiis mundana numina quoque allici posse, vel saltem daemones horum numinum ministros sive pedissequos, ut inquit Mercurius, daemones aereos, non supercoelestes, nedum sublimiores; *Asclep.* 37-38; Ficino, *Opera*, p. 571.

P. 146: Dedit Deus homini mentem atque sermonem, quae (ut ait Mercurius Trismegistus) eiusdem virtutis, potentiae atque immortalitatis praemium censetur; *CH* 12.12.

73. Agrippa, *Opera*, 1: 4: Zalmoxis et Zoroaster . . . [quorum] vestigia secuti Abbaris Hyperboreus, Charmondas, Damigeron, Eudoxus, Hermippus; et clariores alii extiterunt antistites, ut Trismegistus Mercurius, Porphyrius, Iamblichus, Plotinus, Proclus, Dardanus, Orpheus Threicius, Gog Graecus, Germa Babylonicus, Apollonius Tyaneus, Osthanes: cuius libros e sepulchro erutos Abderites Democritus suis commentariis illustravit. Praeterea ad hanc artem Pythagoras, Empedocles, Democritus, Plato et plures nobilissimi philosophorum; Plin. *HN* 30.2.9–10; Thorndike, *History of Magic*, 1: 50, 58–67, 293, 558, 605, 777; 2: 177, 214–28, 353, 355, 430, 552, 557, 698, 706; Wellmann, *Bolos Demokritos*, pp. 3–5, 9–11, 14–17.

74. Agrippa, *Opera*, 1: 26–27: Verum undenam sint hae virtutes, nemo ex his prodidit qui de rerum proprietatibus ingentia volumina ediderunt, non Hermes, non Bochus, non Aron, . . . Orpheus . . . Theophrastus . . . Thebith . . . Zenothemis . . . Zoroaster . . . Evax . . . Dioscorides . . . Isaac Iudaeus . . . Zacharias Babylonicus . . . Albertus . . . Arnoldus. . . . Unde igitur haec veniant, altior speculatio requiritur. Opinatur Alexander Peripateticus . . . haec ab elementis eorundemque qualitatibus provenire. . . . Academici cum suo Platone ideis rerum formatricibus has virtutes attribuunt. Avicenna autem ad intelligentias, Hermes ad stellas, Albertus ad formas rerum specificas huiusmodi operationes reducunt; Albertus Magnus, *Book of Minerals*, trans. Dorothy Wyckhoff (Oxford, 1967), pp. 58–67.

75. The likelihood is that all eleven references to Hermes are traceable to the popular Hermetica and their medieval vestiges. The two possible exceptions are:
Agrippa, *Opera*, 1: 7: Ad omnium mirabilium operationem, ait Hermes, duo sufficiunt, ignis et terra; cf. *Asclep.* 2, 36; *CH* 10.18; 16.4; Müller-Jahncke, *Magie*, p. 58.
P. 78: Et dicit Hermes quod sperma ceti in suffitu non habet sibi par ad alliciendos daemones, quare si ex eo et ligno aloes, costo, musco, croco, thymiamate, cum sanguine upupae distemperatis fiat suffitus, valde cito congregat spiritus aereos; beyond noting that the materials mentioned here (the *upupa* or "hoopoe," especially) are favorites in the *Kyranides*, I can suggest no source.
The nine references remaining can either be traced to popular Hermetic sources or are associated by Agrippa with popular Hermetic authors:
P. 44: Ipse vero Hermes in animalis capite dicit esse foramina septem planetis distributa: videlicet aurem dextram Saturno . . . os autem Mercurio; Martin Plessner and Helmut Ritter, ed. and trans., *"Picatrix": Das Ziel des Weisen von Pseudo-Magriti* (London, 1962), pp. 157–63; Müller-Jahncke, *Magie*, p. 132 n. 5.
P. 57: Hermes, quem sequitur Albertus, planetis dat Saturno asphodelium . . . Lunae chenostacen; *The Book of Secrets of Albertus Magnus of the Virtues of Herbs, Stones, and Certain Beasts; Also a Book of the Marvels of the World*, ed. Michael R. Best and Frank H. Brightman (Oxford, 1973), pp. 18–23; Festugière, *Révélation*, 1: 146–50; Thorndike, *History of Magic*, 2: 233–34, 275.
PP. 57–58: Praeterea ex stellis insignioribus, iuxta Hermetis et Thebit doctrinam, hic aliquot enumerabo, quarum prima dicitur caput Algol, et praeest ex lapidibus adamanti, ex plantis elleboro nigro et Arthemesiae. . . . Decimaquinta cauda capricorni dicitur; haec tenet ex lapidibus chalcedonium, ex plantis maioranam . . . et radicem mandragorae; Delatte, *Textes latins*, pp. 241–75; Festugière, *Révélation*, 1: 165–69; Müller-Jahncke, *Magie*, p. 33.
P. 58: Amethystus autore Hermete subest Marti cum Iove et corde Scorpionis. . . . adamas Marti et capiti Algol; see above, as for pp. 57–58.
P. 64: facit quaedam mirabilia per unguenta, per collyria, per suffumigationes, per similia qualia videlicet leguntur in libris Chiramidis, Archytae, Democriti et Hermetis qui Alchorat inscribitur et aliorum plurium; Thorndike, *History of Magic*, 2: 727.
P. 80: Potentissimum autem suffitum describit Hermes ex septem aromatibus iuxta septem planetarum vires conflatum. Recipit nanque a Saturno costum, a Iove nucem muscatam . . . a Luna myrtum; for groupings of seven, see as for p. 57.
P. 89: Huiusmodi plures consimiles lychnos et lampades narrat Hermes et Plato et Chyrranides et ex posterioribus Albertus in quodam tractatu de hoc singulari; *Book of Secrets*, pp. 54, 102–12; cf. *Kyraniden*, ed. Kaimakis, 2.1.20; 31.22; 40.10, 13.
P. 109: Et ait Hermes: si quis certo die kalendarum Novembrium egressus ad venandum, primam avem quam ceperit coxerit cum corde vulpis, omnes qui ex hoc ederint avium caeterorumque animalium voces intellecturos; *Book of Secrets*, pp. 98–99; cf. *Kyraniden*, ed. Kaimakis, 2.2.31–36.

76. Agrippa, *Opera*, 1: 4 (see above, n. 73); p. 68: Tradunt Magi per inferiora superioribus conformia posse opportunis coeli influxus coelestia dona trahi, atque sic quoque per haec coelestia coelestes daemones. . . . dona non solum coelestia aut vitalia, verumetiam intellectualia quaedam demoniaca et divina desuper suscipi posse Iamblichus, Proclus atque Synesius cum tota Platonicorum schola confirmant, et Mercurius Trismegistus scribit (Procl. *De sacr.*, lines 15–17, 67–78, 88–96; see above, n. 72); p. 109: ipse Proclus Platonicus credidit tradiditque cor talpae ad praesagia conferre (Procl. *De sacr.*, line 83).

77. Agrippa, *Opera*, 1: 43: Manifestum est quod omnia inferiora subsunt superioribus et quodammodo

(ut inquit Proclus) sibi invicem insunt, scilicet in infimis suprema, et in supremis infima; sic in coelo sunt terrena, sed sicut in causa modoque coelesti; et in terra sunt coelestia, sed modo terrestri, scilicet secundum effectum (Procl. *De sacr.*, lines 5-7, 15-17; Latin appendix, lines 5-7, 16-18); Agrippa, *Opera*, 1: 18, 66 (see above, n. 42).

78. Agrippa, *Opera* 1: 78-79: Et est sciendum quod sicut contrarietas et inimicitia est in stellis et spiritibus, ita etiam in suffumigiis ad eosdem. . . . Quemadmodum exemplificat Proclus spiritum solitum apparere in forma leonis, obiecto gallo, mox disparuisse, quia gallus contrariatur leoni (see above, n. 44; Latin appendix, lines 57-59); Agrippa, *Opera* 1: 37-38, 99, 138; for accounts of the enmity between lion and cock in Aesop, Aelian, Pliny, Lucretius, Plutarch, Sextus Empiricus, the *Geoponica*, Alexander of Aphrodisias, Ambrose, and Pseudo-Albertus, see Wellmann, *Bolos Demokritos*, pp. 20-21; A. Orth, "Huhn," in Pauly/Wissowa, *Real Encyclopädie*, 8, cols. 2529-34.

79. Agrippa, *Opera*, 1: 46, 47, 49, 59-60; Procl. *De sacr.*, lines 12-14, 35-36, 65-67.

80. Agrippa, *Opera*, 1: 46, 49; Latin appendix, lines 38-41.

81. Agrippa, *Opera*, 1: 62-64: Nunc si optas ex aliqua mundi parte stellave virtutem accipere, adhibitis quae ad stellam hanc attinet, eius proprium subis influxum, velut lignum per sulphur, picam et oleam paratum ad suscipiendum flammam. . . . Virtus praeterea coelestis alibi quidem sopita iacet, ceu sulphur a flamma remotum; in viventibus autem corporibus saepe flagrat sicut sulphur accensum, tum vapore suo proxima omnia complet (Procl. *De sacr.*, lines 20-31; Ficino, *Opera*, p. 570); p. 63: aliquando necesse est in operationibus fieri mixtiones, ut si centum vel mille Solis virtutes per tot plantas, animalia et similia sparsae fuerint, possumus has simul conflare et in unum redigere formam. . . . Est autem in commixtione virtus duplex (Procl. *De sacr.*, lines 71-79; Latin appendix, line 72); p. 65: Congruitas enim rerum naturalium ad coelestia sufficit ut ab illis hauriamus influxum (Procl. *De sacr.*, line 20); pp. 66-67: Atque hac serie unumquodque infernum suo superiori, et per hoc supremo, pro suo genere respondere. . . . ex quorum serie tota magi et omnis occultior philosophia emanat. . . . omnis virtus superior inferiora longa et continua serie radios suos dispertiendo usque ad ultima fluat (Procl. *De sacr.*, lines 10-12, 44-50).

82. Agrippa, *Opera*, 1: 28: Democritus autem et Orpheus et multi Pythagoricorum . . . omnia plena diis esse dixerunt (Procl. *De sacr.*, line 46; Dodds, *Elements*, p. 276).

83. On various philosophical and medical authorities from Aristotle and Galen through Albertus Magnus and Thomas Aquinas who contributed to a philosophical theory of magic, see Brian P. Copenhaver, "Scholastic Philosophy and Renaissance Magic in the *De vita* of Marsilio Ficino," *Renaissance Quarterly* 37 (1984): 523-54; and for the influence of Ficino's philosophical magic from the late fifteenth through the early seventeenth centuries, see idem, "Magic and Astrology," in *The Cambridge History of Renaissance Philosophy*, ed. Charles Schmitt et al., forthcoming.

84. Agrippa, *Opera*, 1: 64, 89, 94; *Domini Simphoriani Champerii lugdunensis liber de quadruplici vita* (Lyon, 1507), sig. iii; Müller-Jahncke, *Magie*, pp. 31-32; Brian P. Copenhaver, *Symphorien Champier and the Reception of the Occultist Tradition in Renaissance France* (The Hague; 1978), p. 214; Tullio Gregory, "L'idea di natura nella filosofia medievale prima nell' ingresso della fisica di Aristotele: Il Secolo XII," in *La Filosofia della natura nel Medioevo: Atti del terzo congresso internazionale di filosofia medioevalae, Mendola, 31 August-5 September 1964* (Mendola, 1966), pp. 57-61; Wellmann, *Die Koiraniden*, pp. 4-9, 13, 19-23, 28-30.

Appendix

The three texts following are: first, an English translation of Proclus's Greek text; second, an edition of Ficino's Latin translation of Proclus; and third, the Greek text of Proclus from Bidez's edition. Notes to the English translation are keyed by line number to technical terms that require explanation; the reader should also consult Bidez's notes (*Catalogue*, 6: 148-51), some of which have been absorbed into mine.

The Latin edition collates two manuscript and two printed texts (see above, nn. 36, 40) to which the following *sigla* have been assigned:

P   MS Laurentianus Plut. 82.15, fols. 126*v*–128*v*
S   MS Laurentianus Strozz. 97, fols. 147*v*–151*v*
A   Ficino, *Index eorum . . . Iamblichus* (Venice, 1497), sigs. hviir-hviii*v*
B   Ficino, *Opera* (Basel, 1576), pp. 1928–29

B has no authority, but it is the most widely available edition. For reasons given by Sicherl (*Handschriften,* pp. 184–86; see above, n. 40) and because of its superior readings, I have chosen *P* as my copy text and have departed from it rarely. A full list of variants is supplied.

   The Greek text follows Bidez's edition (line numbers in parentheses), which I am not competent to improve. It is reprinted here because it is brief and relatively inaccessible and because the Greek is necessary for comparative and terminological purposes. Bidez based his edition on Vallicellianus F20. Sicherl (*Handschriften,* pp. 23–27, 79–81, 220) agrees with Bidez that the other Greek manuscript—Laurentianus Plut. 10.32—is a copy of the Vallicellianus made after Ficino's death, and he shows that Ficino wrote the text and marginalia of fols. 137–72 of the Vallicellianus; fols. 138–140*v* contain Περὶ τῆς καθ᾽ Ἑλληνας ἱερτικῆς τέχνης.Comparison of the first-person marginalia on fol. 139*r* with similar first-person material in Ficino's *De vita* (see above, nn. 61–64) confirms Sicherl's paleographic identification of the marginalia.

PROCLUS, ON THE PRIESTLY ART ACCORDING TO THE GREEKS

   Just as lovers systematically leave behind what is fair to sensation and attain the one true source of all that is fair and intelligible, in the same way priests—observing how all things are in all from the sympathy that all visible things have for one another and for the invisible powers—have also framed
5   their priestly knowledge. For they were amazed to see the last in the first and the very first in the last; in heaven they saw earthly things acting causally and in a heavenly manner, in the earth heavenly things in an earthly manner. Why do heliotropes move together with the sun, selenotropes with the moon, moving around to the extent of their ability with the luminaries of the
10   cosmos? All things pray according to their own order and sing hymns, either intellectually or rationally or naturally or sensibly, to heads of entire chains. And since the heliotrope is also moved toward that to which it readily opens, if anyone hears it striking the air as it moves about, he perceives in the sound that it offers to the king the kind of hymn that a plant can sing.
15   In the earth, then, it is possible to see suns and moons terrestrially, but in heaven one can also see celestially all the heavenly plants and stones and animals living intellectually. So by observing such things and connecting them to the appropriate heavenly beings, the ancient wise men brought divine powers into the region of mortals, attracting them through likeness.
20   For likeness is sufficient to join beings to one another. If, for example, one first heats up a wick and then holds it under the light of a lamp not far from the flame, he will see it lighted though it be untouched by the flame, and the lighting proceeds upward from below. By analogy, then, understand the preparatory heating as like the sympathy of lower things for those above; the

25 bringing-near and the proper placement as like the use made in the priestly
art of material things, at the right moment and in the appropriate manner; the
communication of the fire as like the coming of the divine light to what is
capable of sharing it; and the lighting as like the divinization of mortal
entities and the illumination of what is implicated in matter, which things
30 then are moved toward the others above insofar as they share in the divine
seed, like the light of the wick when it is lit.

The lotus also shows that there is sympathy. Before the sun's rays appear, it
is closed, but as the sun first rises it is slowly unfolded, and the higher the
light goes the more it is expanded, and then it is contracted again as the sun
35 goes down. If men open and close mouths and lips to hymn the sun, how does
this differ from the drawing-together and loosening of the lotus petals? For
the petals of the lotus take the place of a mouth, and its hymn is a natural
one. But why talk of plants, which have some trace of generative life? One
can also see that stones inhale the influences of the luminaries, as we see the
40 sunstone with its golden rays imitating the rays of the sun; and the stone
called Bel's eye (which should be called sun's eye, they say) resembling the
pupil of the eye and emitting a glittering light from the center of its pupil; and
the Moonstone changing in figure and motion along with the moon; and the
sun-moonstone, a sort of image of the conjunction of these luminaries,
45 imitating their conjunctions and separations in the heavens.

Thus, all things are full of gods: Things on earth are full of heavenly gods;
things in heaven are full of supercelestials; and each chain continues abounding up to its final members. For what is in the One-before-all makes its
appearance in all, in which are also communications between souls set
50 beneath one god or another. Thus, consider the multitude of solar animals,
such as lions and cocks, which also share in the divine, following their own
order. It is amazing how the lesser in might and size among these animals are
regarded with fear by those greater in both respects. For they say the lion
shrinks from the cock. The cause of this is not to be grasped from ap-
55 pearances but from intellectual vision and from differences among the
causes. In fact, the presence of heliacal symbols is more effective for the
cock: it is clear that he perceives the solar orbits and sings a hymn to the
luminary as it rises and moves among the other cardinal points. Therefore,
some solar angels seem to have forms of this same kind, and though they are
60 formless they appear formed to us held fast in form. Now if one of the solar
demons becomes manifest with the shape of a lion, as soon as a cock is
presented he becomes invisible, so they say, shrinking away from the signs of
greater beings, as many refrain from committing abominable acts when they
see likenesses of divine men.

65 In brief, then, such things as the plants mentioned above follow the orbits
of the luminary; others imitate the appearance of its rays (e.g., the palm) or
the empyrean substance (e.g., the laurel) or something else. So it seems that
properties sown together in the sun are distributed among the angels, demons, souls, animals, plants, and stones that share them. From this evidence
70 of the eyes, the authorities on the priestly art have thus discovered how to

gain the favor of powers above, mixing some things together and setting others apart in due order. They used mixing because they saw that each unmixed thing possesses some property of the god but is not enough to call that god forth. Therefore, by mixing many things they unified the aforemen-
75 tioned influences and made a unity generated from all of them similar to the whole that is prior to them all. And they often devised composite statues and fumigations, having blended separate signs together into one and having made artificially something embraced essentially by the divine through uni-fication of many powers, the dividing of which makes each one feeble, while
80 mixing raises it up to the idea of the exemplar. But there are times when one plant or one stone suffices for the work. Flax-leaved daphne is enough for a manifestation; laurel, box-thorn, squill, coral, diamond, or jasper will do for a guardian spirit; but for foreknowledge one needs the heart of a mole and for purification sulfur and salt water. By means of sympathy, then, they draw
85 them near, but by antipathy they drive them away, using sulfur and bitumen for purification, perhaps, or an aspersion of sea water. For sulfur purifies by the sharpness of its scent, sea water because it shares in the empyrean power.

For consecrations and other divine services they search out appropriate animals as well as other things. Beginning with these things and others like
90 them, they gained knowledge of the demonic powers, how closely connected they are in substance to natural and corporeal energy, and through these very substances they achieved association with the [demons], from whom they returned forthwith to actual works of the gods, learning some things from the [gods], for other things being moved by themselves toward accurate consid-
95 eration of the appropriate symbols. Thence, leaving nature and natural ener-gies below, they had dealings with the primary and divine powers.

Explanatory Notes

1–3 lovers . . . priests: see above, nn. 35, 53; Iambl. *Myst.* 8.4, 9.6; Bidez, "Proclus," p. 89 n. 1; Zambelli, "Magie naturelle," pp. 63–64.
3 all things are in all: see above, n. 48.
5–6 last . . . earthly: Procl. *Comm. Alc. I* 69; idem, *In Ti.* 1.26, 426; 3.141 (Diehl).
8, 12 heliotropes: see above, nn. 44, 45, 79, 80; Procl. *In Ti.* 1.111 (Diehl); idem, *Comm. Resp.* 2.161 (Kroll); Plin. *HN* 2.41.109; 16.36.87–88; 18.36.133, 67.251–53; 22.29.57–61; 26.42.69.
10 order: see above, nn. 43, 59–63; Procl. *In Ti.* 1.210–11 (Diehl).
10, 14 hymns: Procl. *Ecl. de phil. chal.* 2; *In Ti.* 1.18 (Diehl); cf. A.-J. Festugière, trans., *Commentaire sur le Timée,* 5 vols. (Paris, 1966–68), 2:114 n. 2; Rosán, *Philosophy of Proclus,* p. 189 n. 38.
11 heads of . . . chains: Proc. *In Ti.* 1.111 (Diehl); *Asclep.* 19.
18 ancient wise men: Plot. *Enn.* 4.3.11; Boyancé, "Théurgie," pp. 195–97, 204.
19–20 likeness: see above, n. 47.
32–38 lotus: cf. Iambl. *Myst.* 7.2.
39, 75 influences: Procl. *Comm. Alc. I* 69, 71; idem, *El.* 152.
38–45 stones: see above, nn. 61–64; Plin. *HN* 37.55.149, 60.165, 67.181; Mely, *Lapidaires,* 2:163, 182–83, 206; Albertus Magnus, *Book of Minerals,* p. 118.
46 all . . . gods: Arist. *De anima* 411ª7; Pl. *Leg.* 899B; Dodds, *Elements,* p. 276.
47–48 each . . . members: see above, n. 43; Procl. *In Ti.* 1.111–12, 210–11 (Diehl); idem, *Comm. Alc. I* 92–94; idem, *Comm. Parm.* 4.64.
49 communications: Procl. *In Ti.* 3.89 (Diehl); *Orac. chal.* 208; Iambl. *Myst.* 3.14.
50–62 lions and cocks: see above, nn. 41, 44; Porph. *Plot.* 10.
52 order: see above, 1. 10.

56 symbols: see above, n. 51; Procl. *In Ti.* 1.210–11 (Diehl): idem, *Comm. Resp.* 1.39 (Kroll); idem, *Comm. Alc. 1* 92–94.
59–60 form: Procl. *Comm. Resp.* 1.39–40; Trouillard, "Le merveilleux," pp. 444–45.
71–76 mixing: see above, n. 50; Boyancé, "Théurgie," p. 206 nn. 1–2.
73–74 call . . . forth: Lewy, *Chaldaean Oracles,* pp. 40–43.
76 statues: see above, nn. 8–9: Procl. *In Ti.* 1.51, 273; 3.155 (Diehl); Iambl. *Myst.* 5.23; *Orac. chal.* 101, 186 (bis); Dodds, *Elements,* pp. 292–93; Lewy, *Chaldaean Oracles,* pp. 291–93, 496.
81 flax-leaved daphne: Theophrastus (*Hist. Pl.* 1.10.4; 6.1.4; 6.2.2) mentions three plants named κνέωρος, which modern editors identify with *Daphne gnidium, Daphne oleoides* and *Thymelaea hirsuta.* The reading "cnebison" in both the 1497 and 1576 editions of Ficino's translation may be the product of a confusion with τὸ κνῆστρον (*s.v.,* Liddell, Scott, and Jones), which was another name for *Daphne oleoides;* cf. Plin. *HN* 13.35.114; 21.29.53–30.55.
82 manifestation: Lewy, *Chaldaean Oracles,* p. 246.
82–83 laurel . . . mole: Mely, *Lapidaires,* 2:36, 54, 164–65, 191, 198–99; Albertus Magnus, *Book of Minerals,* pp. 81, 100.
84–86 purification . . . sea water: Marinus *Vit. Proc.* 18; *Orac. chal.* 224; Dodds, *Elements,* p. 280.
87 empyrean: Proc. *Comm. Alc. 1* 113; idem, *In Ti.* 1.137 (Diehl).
88 consecrations: Procl. *In Ti.* 3.6 (Diehl); *Comm. Alc. 1* 9, 39–40, 61, 142; *Orac. chal.* 135; Dodds, *Irrational,* pp. 287, 291–95.

PROCULI OPUSCULUM DE SACRIFICIO INTERPRETE MARSILIO FICINO FLORENTINO

Quemadmodum amatores ab ipsa pulchritudine quae circa sensum apparet ad divinam paulatim pulchritudinem ratione progrediuntur, sic et sacerdotes antiqui, cum considerarent in rebus naturalibus cognationem quandam compassionemque aliorum ad alia et manifestorum ad vires occultas et omnia in
5 omnibus invenirent, sacram eorum scientiam condiderunt. Agnoverunt enim et in infimis suprema et in supremis infima: in coelo quidem terrena secundum causam modoque coelesti; in terra vero coelestia sed modo terreno. Nam unde putamus plantas illas quas heliotropias nominant, id est, solsequias, ad solis motum solem versus moveri, sed selinetropias, id est, lunise-
10 quas, ad lunam verti? Nempe cuncta precantur hymnosque concinunt ad ordinis sui duces, sed alia quidem intellectuali modo, alia rationali, alia naturali, alia vero sensibili modo. Itaque solsequia quomodocunque potest movetur ad solem. Ac si quis posset audire pulsationem ab ea in aeris circuitu factam, profecto illum quendam per eiusmodi sonum erga regem
15 suum compositum animadverteret qualemcunque potest planta conficere. Quamobrem in terra quidem aspicere licet solem et lunam sed pro qualitate terrena, in coelo autem plantas omnes et lapides et animalia pro coelesti natura vitam habentia intellectualem. Quae quidem veteres contemplati, aliis coelestium alia terrenorum adhibuerunt, unde divinas virtutes in locum in-
20 feriorem ob quandam similitudinem deduxerunt. Nempe similitudo ipsa sufficiens causa est ad res singulas invicem vinciendas. Si quis enim canapim sive papirum calefaciat, deinde subigat lucernae proximae, etiamsi non tangat videbit subito accensam canapim quamvis non tetigerit ignem accensionemque desuper ad inferiora descendere. Comparemus igitur canapim
25 calefactam sive papirum cognationi cuidam inferiorum ad superiora; appropinquationem vero eius ad lucernam opportuno usui rerum pro tempore, loco, materia; processum ignis in canapim praesentiae divini luminis ad id quod potest capere; accensionem denique canapis deificationi mortalium

materialiumque illustrationi, quae deinde feruntur sursum instar accensae
30   canapis ob quandam seminis divini participationem. Quid vero de lotho
dicam? Lothus implicat quidem in se folia ante solis exortum, oriente vero
sole explicat paulatim; et quatenus sol ad mediam coeli ascendit plagam,
eatenus pandit folia; quatenus vero a medio petit occasum, gradatim folia
contrahit. Videtur haec non minus dilatatione contractioneque foliorum hon-
35   orare solem quam homines genarum gestu motuque labiorum. Non solum
vero in plantis quae vestigium habent vitae sed etiam in lapidibus aspicere
licet imitationem et participationem quandam luminum supernorum,
quemadmodum helitis lapis radiis aureis solares radios imitatur. Lapis autem
qui vocatur coeli oculus vel solis oculus figuram habet similem pupillae oculi,
40   atque ex media pupilla emicat radius. Lapis quoque selinitus, id est, lunaris,
figura lunae corniculari similis, quadam sui mutatione lunarem sequitur
motum. Lapis deinde helioselinus, id est, solaris lunarisque, imitatur
quodammodo congressum solis et lunae figuratque colore. Sic divinorum
omnia plena, terrena quidem coelestium, coelestia vero supercoelestium,
45   proceditque quilibet ordo rerum usque ad ultimum. Quae enim super or-
dinem rerum colliguntur in uno, haec deinceps dilatantur in descendendo, ubi
aliae animae sub numinibus aliis ordinantur. Deinde et animalia sunt solaria
multa, velut leones et galli, numinis cuiusdam solaris pro sua natura par-
ticipes, unde mirum est quantum inferiora in eodem ordine cedant superi-
50   oribus quamvis magnitudine potentiaque non cedant. Hinc ferunt gallum
timeri a leone quamplurimum et quasi coli, cuius rei causam a materia
sensuque assignare non possumus sed solum ab ordinis superni con-
templatione. Quoniam videlicet praesentia solaris virtutis convenit gallo
magis quam leoni, quod et inde apparet quia gallus quasi quibusdam hymnis
55   applaudit surgenti soli et quasi advocat quando ex anthipodum medio coelo
ad nos reflectitur. Et quandoque nonnulli solares angeli apparuerunt formis
huiusmodi praediti, atque cum ipsi in se sine forma essent, nobis tamen, qui
formati sumus, occurrerunt formati. Nonnunquam etiam daemones visi sunt
solares leonina fronte quibus, cum gallus obiiceretur, repente disparuerunt.
60   Quod quidem inde procedit quia semper quae in eodem ordine constituta
inferiora sunt reverentur superiora, quemadmodum plerique intuentes virorum imagines divinorum hoc ipso aspectu vereri solent turpe aliquid per-
petrare. Ut autem summatim dicam, alia ad revolutiones solis correvolvuntur,
sicut plantae quas diximus; alia figuram solarium radiorum quodammodo
65   imitantur, ut palma dactylus; alia igneam solis naturam, ut laurus; alia aliud
quiddam. Videre sane licet proprietates quae colliguntur in sole passim
distributas in sequentibus in solari ordine constitutis, scilicet angelis,
daemonibus, animis, animalibus, plantis atque lapidibus. Quo circa sacer-
dotii veteris auctores a rebus apparentibus superiorum virium cultum adin-
70   venerunt dum alia miscerent, alia purificarent. Miscebant autem plura invicem quia videbant simplicia nonnullam habere numinis proprietatem, non
tamen singulatim sufficientem ad numinis ipsius advocationem. Quamobrem
ipsa multorum commixtione attrahebant supernos influxus, atque quod ipsi
componendo unum ex multis conficiebant, assimilabant ipsi uni quod est

75 super multa. Constituebantque statuas ex materiis multis permixtas, odores quoque compositos, colligentes arte in unum divina symbola reddentesque unum tale quale divinum existit secundum essentiam, comprehendens videlicet vires quamplurimas quarum quidem divisio unamquamque debilitavit, mixtio vero restituit in exemplaris ideam. Nonnunquam vero herba una vel

80 lapis unus ad divinum sufficit opus. Sufficit enim cnebron, id est, carduus, ad subitam numinis alicuius apparitionem; ad custodiam vero laurus, raccinum, id est, genus virgulti spinosum, cepa squilla, corallus, adamas, iaspis, sed ad praesagium cor talpae, ad purificationem vero sulphur et aqua marina. Ergo sacerdotes per mutuam rerum cognationem compassionemque conducebant

85 in unum, per repugnantiam expellebant, purificantes cum oportebat sulphure atque asphalto, id est, bitumine, aqua aspergentes marina. Purificat enim sulphur quidem propter odoris acumen, aqua vero marina propter igneam portionem. Et animalia in deorum cultu diis congrua adhibebant, caeteraque similiter. Quamobrem ab iis atque similibus incipientes, primum potentias

90 daemonum cognoverunt, videlicet eas esse proximas rebus actionibusque naturalibus, atque per haec naturalia quibus propinquant in praesentiam convocarunt. Deinde a daemonibus ad ipsas deorum vires actionesque processerunt, partim quidem docentibus daemonibus addiscentes, partim vero industria propria interpretantes convenientia symbola, in propriam deorum

95 intelligentiam ascendentes, ac denique posthabitis naturalibus rebus actionibusque ac magna ex parte daemonibus, in deorum se consortium receperunt.

Latin Variants

tit. Proculi] Opus Proculi *S,* Opus Procli *A,* Proclus *B;* opusculum *om. SAB;* sacrificio] + et magia *B*   8–9 solsequias] solisequas *AB*   9 selinetropias] selenetropias *S*   12 solsequia] solisequa *AB*   13 aeris] aere *AB*   18 aliis] alia *B*   20 deduxerunt] perduxerunt *B*   21 canapim] canabim   22 papirum] papyrum *AB*   23 canapim] canabim *AB;* quamvis] quantumvis *B*   24 canapim] canabim *AB*   25 papirum] papyrum *AB*   26 opportuno] oportuno *P*   27 canapim] canabim *AB*   28 canapis] canabis *AB*   30 canapis] canabis *AB*   30–31 lotho, Lothus] loto, Lotus *SAB*   40 selinitus] selenitus *AB*   41 figura] figure *AB*   42 helioselinus] helioseleneus *AB*   44 plena] + sunt *SAB*   45 quilibet] qualibet *B*   52 sensuque] sensuve *SAB*   55 anthipodum] antipodum   56 reflectitur] deflectitur *SAB*   57 huiusmodi] eiusmodi *SAB*   58 occurrerunt] occurrere *AB,* obcurrere *S;* visi] nisi *B*   60 quia *om. AB,* semper *om. A*   63 correvolvuntur] cor revolvuntur *A*   67 constitutis] constituti *B*   69 auctores] authores *B*   71 nonnullam] nonnulla *S;* numinis] + proprietatem *S*   72 ipsius] illius *AB*   73 commixtione] commistione *A;* supernos] super nos *AB*   75 permixtas] permistas *A*   77 comprehendens] comprehendes *P*   78 vires] viris *B;* quarum] quorum *PAB*   79 mixtio] mistio *A*   80 cnebron] cnebison *AB*   81 apparitionem] aparitionem *B*   82 cepa squilla] cepta, squilla *B*   83 sulphur et

aqua marina] sulfur atque marinam *B*   85 sulphure] sulfure *B*   87 sul-
phur] sulfur *SA*   88 in . . . diis] diis in deorum cultu *AB*   89 iis] aliis *B;*
incipientes] recipientes *AB*   90 cognoverunt] congnoverunt *S*   93 addis-
centes] ad discentes *A*   94 symbola] simbola *SA*

Πρόκλου περὶ τῆς καθ' Ἕλληνας ἱερατικῆς τέχνης

    ῝Ωσπερ οἱ ἐρωτικοὶ ἀπὸ τῶν ἐν αἰσθήσει καλῶν ὁδῷ προϊόντες ἐπ' αὐτὴν καταν-
(148.5) τῶσι τὴν μίαν τῶν καλῶν πάντων καὶ νοητῶν ἀρχήν, οὕτως καὶ οἱ ἱερατικοὶ ἀπὸ
τῆς ἐν τοῖς φαινομένοις ἅπασι συμπαθείας πρός τε ἄλληλα καὶ πρὸς τὰς ἀφανεῖς
δυνάμεις, πάντα ἐν πᾶσι κατανοήσαντες, τὴν ἐπιστήμην τὴν ἱερατικὴν
5 συνεστήσαντο, θαυμάσαντες τῷ βλέπειν ἔν τε τοῖς πρώτοις τὰ ἔσχατα καὶ ἐν τοῖς
(148.10) ἐσχάτοις τὰ πρώτιστα, ἐν οὐρανῷ μὲν τὰ χθόνια κατ' αἰτίαν καὶ οὐρανίως, ἔν τε
γῇ τὰ οὐράνια γηΐνως. ῍Η πόθεν ἡλιοτρόπια μὲν ἡλίῳ, σεληνοτρόπια δὲ σελήνη
συγκινεῖται συμπεριπολοῦντα ἐς δύναμιν τοῖς τοῦ κόσμου φωστῆρσιν; Εὔχεται γὰρ
πάντα κατὰ τὴν οἰκείαν τάξιν καὶ ὑμνεῖ τοὺς ἡγεμόνας τῶν σειρῶν ὅλων ἢ νοερῶς
10 ἢ λογικῶς ἢ φυσικῶς ἢ αἰσθητῶς· ἐπεὶ καὶ τὸ ἡλιοτρόπιον ᾧ ἔστιν εὔλυτον, τούτῳ
(148.16) κινεῖται καί, εἰ δή τις αὐτοῦ κατὰ τὴν περιστροφὴν ἀκούειν τὸν ἀέρα πλήσσοντος
οἷός τε ἦν, ὕμνον ἄν τινα διὰ τοῦ ἤχου τούτου συνῄσθετο τῷ βασιλεῖ προσάγοντος,
ὃν δύναται φυτὸν ὑμνεῖν.
(148.20)   ᾿Εν μὲν οὖν τῇ γῇ χθονίως ἐστὶν ἡλίους καὶ σελήνας ὁρᾶν, ἐν οὐρανῷ δὲ οὐρα-
15 νίως τά τε φυτὰ πάντα καὶ λίθους καὶ ζῷα, ζῶντα νοερῶς. ῝Α δὴ κατιδόντες οἱ
πάλαι σοφοί, τὰ μὲν ἄλλοις, τὰ δὲ ἄλλοις προσάγοντες τῶν οὐρανίων, ἐπήγοντο
θείας δυνάμεις εἰς τὸν θνητὸν τόπον καὶ διὰ τῆς ὁμοιότητος ἐφειλκύσαντο· ἱκανὴ
γὰρ ἡ ὁμοιότης συνάπτειν τὰ ὄντα ἀλλήλοις· ἐπεὶ καί, εἴ τις θρυαλλίδα προθερμήνας
ὑπόσχοι τῷ λυχναίῳ φωτὶ μὴ πόρρω τοῦ πυρός, ἴδοι ἂν αὐτὴν ἐξαπτομένην μὴ
20 ψαύουσαν τοῦ πυρός, καὶ τὴν ἔξαψιν ἄνωθεν τοῦ κατωτέρου γινομένην. ᾿Αναλόγως
(149.5) οὖν ἡ μὲν προθέρμανσις νοείσθω σοι τῇ συμπαθείᾳ τῶν τῇδε πρὸς ἐκεῖνα, ἡ δὲ
προσαγωγὴ καὶ ἐν καλῷ θεοῖς τῇ τῆς ἱερατικῆς τέχνης κατά τε καιρὸν τὸν πρέποντα
καὶ τρόπον τὸν οἰκεῖον προσχρήσει τῶν ὑλῶν, ἡ δὲ τοῦ πυρὸς διάδοσις τῇ παρουσίᾳ
τοῦ θείου φωτὸς εἰς τὸ δυνάμενον μετέχειν, ἡ δὲ ἔξαψις τῇ θειώσει τῶν θνητῶν καὶ
25 τῇ περιλάμψει τῶν ἐνύλων, ἃ δὴ κινεῖται πρὸς τὸ ἄνω λοιπὸν κατὰ τὸ μετασχεθὲν
(149.11) ὑπ' αὐτῶν σπέρμα θεῖον, ὥσπερ τὸ τῆς ἐξαφθείσης θρυαλλίδος φῶς.
    Καὶ ὁ λωτὸς δὲ παρίστησι τὴν συμπάθειαν, μεμυκὼς μὲν πρὸ τῶν ἡλιακῶν αὐ-
γῶν, διαπτυσσόμενος δέ πως ἠρέμα τοῦ ἡλίου πρῶτον φανέντος, καὶ ὅσον ὑφοῦ-
(149.15) ται τὸ φῶς, ἐξαπλούμενος, καὶ αὖθις συναγόμενος, ἐπὶ δύσιν ἰόντος. Τί δὴ οὖν
30 διαφέρει τοὺς ἀνθρώπους αἴροντας ἢ τιθέντας < τὰς > γένυς ἢ τὰ χείλη ὑμνεῖν τὸν
ἥλιον, ἢ τὸν λωτὸν τὰ φύλλα συμπτύσσοντα καὶ ἀναπλοῦντα; Γίγνεται γὰρ ἀντὶ
τῶν γενύων ταῦτα τῷ λωτῷ καὶ ὁ ὕμνος φυσικός. Καὶ τί δεῖ λέγειν περὶ φυτῶν
(149.20) οἷς ὑπάρχει ζωῆς ἴχνος τι γεννητικῆς; ᾿Αλλὰ καὶ λίθους ἔστιν ἰδεῖν ταῖς τῶν φωστήρων ἀπορροίαις ἐμπνέοντας, ὡς τὸν μὲν ἡλίτην ταῖς χρυσοειδέσιν ἀκτῖσιν ὁρῶμεν
35 τὰς ἡλιακὰς ἀκτῖνας μιμούμενον, τὸν δὲ βήλου προσαγορευόμενον ὀφθαλμὸν καὶ
σχῆμα παραπλήσιον ἔχοντα κόραις ὀφθαλμῶν καὶ ἐκ μέσης τῆς ἐν αὐτῷ κόρης
(149.25) στιλπνὸν ἀφιέντα φῶς, ὃν φασιν ἡλίου χρῆναι καλεῖν ὀφθαλμόν, τὸν δὲ σεληνίτην
τύπῳ τε καὶ κινήσει σὺν τῇ σελήνῃ τρεπόμενον, τὸν δὲ ἡλιοσέληνον τῆς συνόδου

τῶν φωστήρων τούτων οἷον ἄγαλμα ταῖς κατ' οὐρανὸν συνόδοις τε καὶ διαστάσε-
40   σιν ἀφομοιωθέν. Οὕτω μεστὰ πάντα θεῶν, τὰ μὲν ἐν γῇ τῶν οὐρανίων, τὰ δὲ ἐν
οὐρανῷ τῶν ὑπὲρ τὸν οὐρανόν, καὶ πρόεισιν ἑκάστη πληθυομένη σειρὰ μέχρι τῶν
ἐσχάτων· τὰ γὰρ ἐν ἑνὶ πρὸ τῶν πάντων, ταῦτα ἐν πᾶσιν ἐξεφάνη, ἐν οἷς καὶ ψυχῶν
συστάσεις ἄλλων ὑπ' ἄλλοις ταττομένων θεοῖς, ἔπειτα ζῴων ἡλιακῶν εἰ τύχοι
(150.4) πλῆθος, οἷον λέοντες καὶ ἀλεκτρυόνες, μετέχοντες καὶ αὐτοὶ τοῦ θείου κατὰ τὴν
45   ἑαυτῶν τάξιν. Καὶ τὸ θαυμαστὸν ὅπως ἐν τούτοις τὰ ἐλάττονα δυνάμει τε καὶ
μεγέθει τοῖς κατ' ἄμφω κρείττοσίν ἐστι φοβερά· ὑποστέλλεται γὰρ ὁ λέων, φασί,
τὸν ἀλεκτρυόνα. Τὸ δὲ αἴτιον ἀπὸ μὲν τῆς αἰσθήσεως οὐκ ἔστι λαβεῖν, ἀπὸ δὲ τῆς
νοερᾶς ἐπιβλέψεως καὶ τῆς ἐν τοῖς αἰτίοις διαφορᾶς. Ἐνεργεστέρα γοῦν ἐστιν ἡ τῶν
(150.10) ἡλιακῶν συμβόλων εἰς τὸν ἀλεκτρυόνα παρουσία· δηλοῖ δὲ τῶν ἡλιακῶν περιό-
50   δων συναισθανόμενος καὶ ᾄδων ὕμνον τῷ φωστῆρι προσιόντι τε καὶ ἐπὶ τὰ λοιπὰ
κέντρα τρεπομένῳ· διὸ καὶ ἄγγελοί τινες ἡλιακοὶ ὤφθησαν τοιαύτας ἔχοντες
μορφάς, καὶ ὄντες ἀμόρφωτοι, φαίνονται τοῖς ἐν μορφῇ κατεχομένοις ἡμῖν μεμορ-
(150.15) φωμένοι. Ἤδη δέ τινα τῶν ἡλιακῶν δαιμόνων λεοντοπρόσωπον φαινόμενον, ἀλεκ-
τρυόνος δειχθέντος, ἀφανῆ γενέσθαι φασὶν ὑποστελλόμενον τὰ τῶν κρειττόνων
55   συνθήματα· ἐπεὶ καὶ θείων ἀνδρῶν εἰκόνας ὁρῶντες πολλοὶ ἀνεστάλησαν ὑπ' αὐ-
ταῖς τι τῶν μιαρῶν ἐνεργεῖν.
(150.20)   Ἁπλῶς δὲ τὰ μὲν ταῖς περιόδοις τοῦ φωστῆρος συγκινεῖται, ὡς τὰ εἰρημένα
φυτά, τὰ δὲ τὸ σχῆμα μιμεῖται τῶν ἀκτίνων, ὥσπερ ὁ φοῖνιξ, τὰ δὲ τὴν ἐμπύριον
οὐσίαν, ὥσπερ ἡ δάφνη, τὰ δὲ ἄλλο τι. Ἴδιος ἂν οὖν τὰς συνεσπειραμένας ἰδιότητας
60   ἐν ἡλίῳ μεριζομένας ἐν τοῖς μετέχουσιν ἀγγέλοις, δαίμοσι, ψυχαῖς, ζῴοις, φυτοῖς,
(150.25) λίθοις. Ὅθεν οἱ τῆς ἱερατικῆς ἡγεμόνες ἀπὸ τῶν ἐν ὀφθαλμοῖς κειμένων τὴν τῶν
ἀνωτέρω δυνάμεων θεραπείαν εὑρήκασι, τὰ μὲν μίξαντες, τὰ δὲ οἰκείως ἀναιρού-
μενοι· ἡ δὲ μῖξις διὰ τὸ βλέπειν τῶν ἀμίκτων ἕκαστόν τινα ἔχον ἰδιότητα τοῦ θεοῦ,
οὐ μὴν ἐξαρκοῦν πρὸς τὴν ἐκείνου πρόκλησιν· διὸ τῇ μίξει τῶν πολλῶν ἑνίζουσι
65   τὰς προειρημένας ἀπορροίας καὶ ἐξομοιοῦσι τὸ ἐκ πάντων ἓν γενόμενον πρὸς ἐκεῖνο
(150.30) τὸ πρὸ τῶν πάντων ὅλον· καὶ ἀγάλματα πολλάκις κατασκευάζουσι σύμμικτα καὶ
θυμιάματα, φυράσαντες εἰς ἓν τὰ μερισθέντα συνθήματα καὶ ποιήσαντες τέχνῃ
ὁποῖον κατ' οὐσίαν τὸ θεῖον περιληπτικὸν καθ' ἕνωσιν τῶν πλειόνων δυνάμεων,
(151.4) ὧν ὁ μὲν μερισμὸς ἠμύδρωσεν ἑκάστην, ἡ δὲ μῖξις ἐπανήγαγεν εἰς τὴν τοῦ παραδείγ-
70   ματος ἰδέαν. Ἔστι δὲ ὅτε καὶ μία πόα καὶ λίθος εἷς ἀρκεῖ πρὸς τὸ ἔργον· ἀπόχρη
γὰρ πρὸς μὲν αὐτοφάνειαν τὸ κνέωρον, πρὸς δὲ φυλακὴν δάφνη, ῥάμνος, σκύλλα,
κουράλιον, ἀδάμας καὶ ἴασπις, πρὸς δὲ πρόγνωσιν ἡ τοῦ ἀσπάλακος καρδία, πρὸς
δὲ καθάρσεις τὸ θεῖον καὶ τὸ θαλάττιον ὕδωρ.
(151.10)   Διὰ μὲν οὖν τῆς συμπαθείας προσήγοντο, διὰ δὲ τῆς ἀντιπαθείας ἀπήλαυνον,
75   καθαίροντες εἰ τύχοι θείῳ καὶ ἀσφάλτῳ καὶ περιρραίνοντες θαλάττῃ· καθαίρει γὰρ
τὸ μὲν θεῖον διὰ τὸ δριμὺ τῆς ὀσμῆς, ἡ δὲ θάλαττα διὰ τὸ μετέχειν ἐμπυρίου
δυνάμεως.
(151.15)   Καὶ ἐν ταῖς τελεταῖς δὲ καὶ ταῖς ἄλλαις περὶ τοὺς θεοὺς θεραπείαις ζῷά τε
προσήκοντα ἐξελέγοντο καὶ ἕτερ' ἄττα. Ἀπὸ δὴ τούτων καὶ τῶν τοιούτων ὁρ-
80   μηθέντες, τὰς δαιμονίους δυνάμεις ἔγνωσαν, ὡς προσεχεῖς εἰσιν οὐσίαι τῆς ἐν τῇ
φύσει καὶ τοῖς σώμασιν ἐνεργείας, καὶ ἐπηγάγοντο δι' αὐτῶν τούτων εἰς συνου-
σίαν· ἀπὸ δὲ τούτων ἐπ' αὐτὰς ἤδη τὰς τῶν θεῶν ἀνέδραμον ποιήσεις, τὰ μὲν ἀπ'
(151.20) αὐτῶν διδασκόμενοι, τὰ δὲ καὶ αὐτοὶ κινούμενοι παρ' ἑαυτῶν εὐστόχως εἰς τὴν τῶν
οἰκείων συμβόλων ἐπίνοιαν· καὶ οὕτω λοιπόν, τὴν φύσιν καὶ τὰς φυσικὰς ἐνεργείας
85   κάτω καταλιπόντες, ταῖς πρωτουργοῖς καὶ θείαις ἐχρήσαντο δυνάμεσι.

5

The Cessation of Miracles

D. P. WALKER

I have not been working long on this Protestant doctrine of the cessation of miracles,[1] but I have done enough to realize how large the subject is and what a lot I still have to learn. I say this not so much to excuse the deficiencies of this paper as to make an appeal for all the relevant information my readers can give me. According to this doctrine miracles, such as were performed by Christ and his disciples and by Moses and the Prophets, ceased either soon after the Apostolic Age, or (it is more usually thought) when Christianity was firmly established, perhaps in the time of Constantine, or at the latest by about A.D. 600. They did not of course cease abruptly, but tailed off gradually. In any case, the evident purpose of the doctrine was to prove that all medieval and especially all contemporary Catholic miracles were either fakes or diabolic wonders, and to account for the lack of Protestant miracles. In the late sixteenth and early seventeenth centuries this doctrine was firmly and widely held by English Protestants. It is with this period and country that I shall be mainly concerned.

It is likely that in England the cessation of miracles became such a prominent and tenaciously held doctrine at this period partly because of the controversies arising out of Puritan attempts in the 1590s to cast out devils and the savage suppression of these attempts by Anglican prelates, as I suggested in my book, *Unclean Spirits*.[2] In these controversies both sides made explicit their basic assumptions about supernatural occurrences, and were thus led to a principle that they both accepted: the cessation of miracles. This principle is clearly and emphatically expressed in the *Dialogicall Discourses of Spirits and Divels* (1601) of John Deacon and John Walker,[3] and in the Puritan John Darrel's replies.[4]

But the doctrine certainly had earlier roots. Luther had sometimes preached the cessation of miracles. In a sermon of 1535 on Matthew 8: 1–14 (the cleansing of the leper and the healing of the centurion's servant),[5] he distinguished two kinds of miracles: first, miracles of the soul that is transformed by faith; and second, miracles of the body, such as these cures. The first kind is by far the greatest, for

Christ "marveled" at the centurion's faith; they are done daily and will continue until the Last Day. The second was always rare, and such miracles were done by God only to establish the new Church, its baptism and teaching. Now that Christianity rests securely on the Scriptures, these miracles of the body have ceased, just as, when the children of Israel had reached the Promised Land, the miracle of the Exodus no longer continued, and to ask now for miraculous signs (*Wunderzeichen*) would be to doubt the truth of the Gospels. But Luther does not here mention modern Catholic miracles, and may be thinking only of the lack of Protestant ones.

The wish to discredit contemporary Catholic miracles and to justify the lack of Protestant ones is conspicuous in Calvin's dedication to the king of France of his *Institutes,*[6] but here and elsewhere in the *Institutes*[7] and in his commentaries on the Gospels,[8] the cessation of miracles appears only as a recommended opinion, and not, as it later became, a dogmatically asserted principle. For example, on the end of Saint Mark's Gospel (16:15–20), where the resurrected Christ sends forth the Apostles to "preach the gospel to every creature," saying,

> And these signs shall follow them that believe; In my name shall they cast out devils; they shall speak with new tongues; They shall take up serpents; and if they drink any deadly thing, it shall not hurt them; they shall lay hands on the sick, and they shall recover.

Calvin comments cautiously:

> Although Christ does not express whether he wishes this to be a temporary gift, or to reside perpetually in his Church, it is however more probable that miracles, which were to make famous the new and still obscure gospel, were promised only for a certain time.[9]

Moreover, in this *Traité des reliques,* where one would certainly expect to find the doctrine, Calvin does not mention it.[10]

The English Protestants were divided on an important point. The Puritans believed that diabolic phenomena, such as possession and witchcraft, were still going on, whereas at least some Anglicans included these in the class of miracles and therefore maintained, cautiously but sometimes explicitly, that present-day demoniacs and witches could do nothing superhuman and were either diseased or deluded or fraudulent.[11] Although I consider this Anglican line extremely important, I am here concerned only with the general thesis, accepted by both Puritans and Anglicans, that the miracles in the Bible are historically true, but that no such miracles have occurred for about a thousand years.

Another reason that this doctrine was so prevalent in the two decades around 1600 was the Catholic use of contemporary miracles for anti-Protestant propaganda; this made it urgent to have a simple, compendious, and effective means of exploding all modern miracles. The Catholic exorcisms at Denham in 1585–86, closely connected with the Babington plot against Elizabeth, became widely known through Samuel Harsnett's book, *A Declaration of Egregious Popish Impostures* of 1603.[12] The exposure of the anti-Huguenot demoniac, Marthe

Brossier, as fraudulent in 1599 by the French physician Marescot was quickly translated into English.[13] In his anti-Protestant work, the *Disputationes de controversiis,* published in the 1580s and 1590s, the great Jesuit polemicist, Robert Bellarmin, used the continuance of Catholic miracles and the lack of Protestant ones as a God-given mark of the true Church.[14]

But the greatest boost to the Protestant interest in and anxiety about miracles was given by Justus Lipsius's two treatises, published in 1604 and 1605, shortly before his death, about miracles performed at two shrines of the Virgin Mary, one in the town of Hall, and one at Montaigu near Sichem, both in the Catholic Netherlands.[15] These two little books had enormous repercussions. They produced an immediate flood of polemical literature on both sides,[16] and in England Lipsius's miracles soon became the stock example of ridiculous but dangerous popish "lying wonders." Protestants everywhere were probably genuinely shocked that the great humanist scholar and historian, the apparently irenic promulgator of Christian neo-Stoicism, who had spent thirteen years teaching at the new Protestant university of Leiden, should not only return to the faith of his youth (if indeed he had ever left it), but should also publicly defend the most obviously superstitious and idolatrous practices of that degenerate faith. Moreover, although the two books were not violently polemical in tone, the miracles recounted in them were explicitly presented as divine proofs of the true Church, as evidence of God's approval of the cult of saints and of the Virgin, and of God's support for the Catholic side in the present wars in the Netherlands.[17]

These miracle books of Lipsius remain rather puzzling. On the one hand, I am inclined to accept his statement that he did have a sincere devotion to the Virgin Mary and a serene belief in the miracles worked by these two images of her. From his youth onward he had chosen Mary as his patron saint, and regularly prayed to her when he had to give an important public lecture, usually with good results *(felici ferè successu).*[18] He bequeathed his fur coat to a statue of the Virgin in a church at Louvain (unfortunately it did not fit her),[19] and on his deathbed, when his Jesuit confessor urged him to make a vow to visit the Virgin at Montaigu if he should recover, he replied, "Reverend Father, I no longer wish for life; but if the blessèd Virgin wishes to devote me to her service and the benefit of the Church, I will not refuse the task" *(non amplius R^{vde} Pater, mihi vita in voto est; si tamen velit me vovere Diva Virgo ad suum servitium et Ecclesiae utilitatem, non recuso laborem).*[20]

On the other hand, there are curious ineptitudes in the two books. For example, in the preface to the first of these—*Diva Virgo Hallensis* (The Virgin of Hall)—although he announces that in recounting these miracles he is exercising his usual profession of historian, he tells us that one of the daughters of the duke of Brabant, who brought the image to Hall in the thirteenth century, gave birth to 364 children at once. Lipsius comments, "This would seem more like fable than history, were it not that all our Annals agree in asserting it."[21] Indeed, in both books he is clearly not so much concerned with presenting convincing historical evidence that miracles did occur at these two shrines as with edifying and entertaining the reader. He is afraid that a long catalog of similar cures might become boring; he therefore puts some of them into verse,[22] and tells in elaborate detail any of the miracles that have the attractive fairy-tale quality of the *Golden Legend*.[23] The first miracles are, as Lipsius himself says, "both serious and funny" *(seria simul & jocosa)*. Two of these occurred at the siege of Hall in 1580, when a soldier, Jan Zwyck (Joannes Zwyckius), impiously said that he was going to cut off the nose of that little woman of Hall, "meaning the mother of God; but she had overheard the boast, and, devising a fitting punishment [*talionis poenam machinata*], procured that one of the first bullets fired took off his nose."[24] The unfortunate Zwyck then became the laughingstock of his comrades, who were always telling him to go to Hall and get back his nose. Another soldier said he would take the image to Brussels and burn it; he had his mouth and chin removed by a cannonball.

It is really not surprising that the Protestant adversaries of Lipsius should jeer at his miracles and constantly recall the wretched Zwyck's nose. Sir Edward Hoby, for example, a distinguished diplomat who had a controversy with an English Jesuit named John Floyd (who appears again in this story), in a pamphlet of 1609, having recalled some of the more entertaining of Lipsius's miracles, including "how she [the Virgin] made John Swickius lose the best nose in his face," concludes:

> But the truth is, we have too many of these alreadie, unlesse they were better; and yet I will not say, but that Lipsius is worth reading by the fireside, when men roste crabs, to drive a man out of a melancholic fit. For I thinke sobrietie it selfe could not chuse but change countenance to have him tell these ridiculous jests so seriouslie, as if he did verilie beleeve them to be true. For our parts, wee are not ashamed to confesse, that we have no other miracles, than those which were wrought by Christ, the Prophets, and Apostles[25]

The doctrine of the cessation of miracles had one glaringly weak spot: its lack of scriptural support. In the New Testament, when Christ confers wonder-working powers on the Apostles and those whom they should convert, as in Mark 16 (already quoted) and in John 14:12 ("He that believeth on me, the works that I do shall he do also; and greater works than these shall he do"), there is nothing whatever to indicate that these powers were limited in time. For Protestants, who had made Scripture the supreme—indeed nearly the sole—religious authority, this lack was a very grave defect. The doctrine therefore needed arguments to prop it up, arguments that could, if possible, be supported by biblical texts. The line of argument was as follows:

First, it is assumed, as has been seen in Luther and Calvin, that God does miracles only to establish a new religion, and that, as it becomes established, the miracles gradually cease. Richard Sheldon, a convert from Catholicism who had been a Jesuit, in his *Survey of the Miracles of the Church of Rome* (1616), gives this assumption a semblance of biblical authority by drawing the parallel, like Luther, with the Exodus: As the pillar of fire and manna ceased when the Jews entered Canaan, so Christians now no longer need the power of miracles given to Peter and Paul to guide the first believers through "the wilderness of Gentilisme, or of Pharasaicall pride."[26]

It follows from this assumption that the miracle-working faith proclaimed by Christ in Matthew 17:20 ("Verily I say unto you, If ye have faith as a grain of mustard seed, ye shall say unto this mountain, Remove hence to yonder place; and it shall remove; and nothing shall be impossible unto you")—that this faith is distinct from justifying faith and is no longer granted. James Mason, in his *Anatomie of Sorcerie* (1612), having stated that "it is more than probable that miracles are now ceased" and dated the cessation from the time of Constantine, when Christianity was publicly professed by godly emperors, quotes John Chrysostom on the above text.

> Since nowadays those miracles are not done in the Church, should we therefore say that Christians are bereft of faith? God forbid that we should have such a bad opinion of the people of God. Justifying faith is with us, but what is called the faith of miracles has ceased.[27]

I have not yet been able to find this comment on Matthew 17:20 in Chrysostom's works, either genuine or spurious, but it is also cited by Deacon and Walker and by Sheldon.[28]

This distinction between miraculous and justifying faith can also be supported by a famous text of Saint Paul in 1 Corinthians 13:2: "And though I have all faith, so that I could remove mountains, and have not charity, I am nothing." Calvin, in the *Institutes,* eager to deny the Catholic doctrine that faith without charity is unformed, explains that by "faith" Saint Paul here means merely the power to work miracles, which is a particular gift of God, "which a wicked man can have and abuse it" *(lequel un meschant homme peut avoir et en abuser).*[29] But commenting on Matthew 17 and the similar pronouncement in Matthew 21:21,Calvin dismisses these promises of miraculous powers as hyperbolic figures of speech *(hyperbolica loquendi forma).*[30]

The argument then goes on to show that those Catholic miracles which are not obviously faked or ridiculous, like Zwyck's nose, are the "lying wonders" of Antichrist, predicted by Saint Paul (2 Thessalonians 2:9) and by Christ in Matthew (24:24): "For there shall arise false Christs, and false prophets, and shall show great signs and wonders; insomuch that, if it were possible [εἰ δυνατόν] they shall deceive the very elect." Antichrist is named in the Bible only in the Epistles of Saint John (1 John 2 and 4; 2 John, verse 7), but other eschatological texts, such as the two just cited, and chapters 11 and 13 of Revelation, were taken to refer to him. From these sources, combined with early medieval prophecies, such as the Pseudo-Methodius *Revelations,* a full and relatively stable picture of Antichrist was built up.[31] He will be a diabolically inspired man who in the Last Days will both persecute Christians and try to mislead them by claiming to be Christ and performing wonders; after a short reign of about three and a half years, he will be destroyed by Christ or his agent. There was also a typology of Antichrist, the types being found both in the Bible and in later secular history. For example, a famous type of Antichrist as deceiver and wonder-worker was Simon Magus (Acts 8 and 18); of Antichrist as persecuting tyrant, Nero.

This tradition was radically transformed early in the Reformation. For Protestants, Antichrist was no longer an evil man in the future, but an existing institution, namely the papacy, and for many, the whole Roman Catholic church.[32] Although earlier heretics, such as Lollards, Hussites, and some Joachimites, had attacked particular popes as types of Antichrist, this firm identification of Antichrist with the Roman church was something new—new interpretation of the biblical texts in question. It raised many historical and eschatological problems. The various solutions of these resulted in great variety and vagueness about the beginning and duration of Antichrist's reign and the placing of the millennium, the binding of Satan for a thousand years, predicted in Revelation 20. John Foxe, for example, in the first edition of *Actes and Monuments* (1563), had a millennium in the past, lasting until A.D. 1000, when Satan was released, according to Revelation (20:3), "a little season," and Antichrist's reign began; but in the 1583 edition the millennium was shifted forward to last from the time of Constantine until the fourteenth century. But, although Antichrist's open reign began so late, with the persecution of Wycliffe and Huss, the corruption of the Church was far advanced long before this, by the seventh century at the latest, when, as has been seen, true miracles ceased. This early deprivation of church was generally agreed, in spite of many variations with regard to the exact phraseology of Antichrist's official reign and to the part played by the Turks and Islam as an Antichrist complementary to the papacy.[33]

One point about Antichrist on which nearly all Protestants and all Catholics were in agreement was that his satanic wonders were not supernatural, but only superhuman. This is a particular application of a general and widely held principle about the limitation of diabolic powers; it is, for example, the guiding thread of the Calvinist Johann Wier's careful investigations of demoniacs and witches.[34] The Devil cannot break the laws of nature, but can only move things about with superhuman speed; trouble men's animal spirits, thus producing illusions; and perhaps speed up natural processes. But he cannot create something out of nothing (such as manna), raise up the dead, or make the sun stand still.[35] The limitation was of course by no means clear-cut, since no one could be quite sure what the laws of nature were. But, be that as it may, it was agreed, as the Protestant convert Sheldon says, that all diabolic wonders are done "by the secret, hidden, quicke and speedy application of naturall causes."[36] And the Jesuit exegete Cornelius à Lapide comments on 2 Thessalonians 2:9:

> Neither Antichrist, nor the Devil, nor angels can do a true miracle, but only God. For a miracle is what is done above all power of nature, and what exceeds and transcends the powers of all natural causes and creatures. Antichrist therefore will not do true miracles but false and lying ones.[37]

This limitation of the Devil's powers is essential if miracles are to be taken as signs of divine approval of the person who performs them or of the church in which they are performed; for otherwise there is no way of distinguishing them from lying wonders. But from the Protestant point of view, it had the disadvantage that not all Catholic miracles could be quickly dismissed as the works of Antichrist, since some of them apparently did transcend the natural order—such as the raising of the dead. Hence one finds some Protestants who hold the view, already implied by Calvin, that God does sometimes allow Satan to perform supernatural miracles, and that the only way of detecting these is by seeing whether the doctrine of the performer is in conformity with Scripture. George Thomson, who published one of the earliest and most savage attacks on Lipsius's miracles, the *Vindex Veritatis* (1606), asserts that God does allow false prophets to do true miracles, in order to test the constancy of the faithful. He can quote, very appositely, Deuteronomy 13:1–4:

> If there arise among you a prophet, or a dreamer of dreams, and giveth thee a sign or a wonder, And the sign or wonder come to pass, whereof he spake unto thee, saying Let us go after other gods, which thou hast not known, and let us serve them; Thou shalt not hearken unto the word of that prophet.

Calvin could also cite Augustine writing against the Donatists, who are not to be believed even if they do perform miracles. He accepts the miracles done by Vespasian and Hadrian, vouched for by Suetonius and Tacitus, as evidence that God allows true miracles to occur among the heathen.[38] The wonders of Antichrist will be supernatural, for, in 2 Thessalonians 2:9 τέρασιν ψεύδους (literally "with wonders of a lie") means not lying false wonders (*prodigiis mendacibus* in the Vulgate), but true miracles used to back up false doctrine.[39] The true Church is founded, not on miracles, but solely on the canonical Scriptures.[40] Most Protestant writers against miracles do not take up this extreme position; for it has the serious defect of making the miracles in the New Testament quite pointless. The safer and more usual line was to state that the Church was founded on the canonical Scriptures and the miracles recounted therein, which are recognizably different from diabolic wonders.

After this brief sketch of the Protestant arguments in favor of the cessation of miracles, I now come to the Catholic answers to these arguments. My main sources are Bellarmin; Justus Lipsius; Robert Chambers—a Catholic priest living in Brussels who, in 1606, published an account and defense of the Virgin's miracles at Montaigu, and dedicated it to James I;[41] John Floyd (or Flood)—the English Jesuit whose *Purgatories Triumph over Hell* (1613) contains a chapter on Lipsius's and other modern miracles,[42] which sparked off Protestant replies such as Sheldon's *Survey of Miracles;* and finally, the French Jesuit Louis Richeome, whose *Trois discours pour la religion catholique: Des miracles, des saincts, et des images,* dedicated to Henry IV, appeared in 1597.[43] Richeome relies heavily on Bellarmin, but he is much fuller and more persuasively eloquent—his eloquence is highly praised by that connoisseur of French religious literature, Henri Brémond.[44]

In answering the argument that miracles have ceased because, now that Christianity is established, they are no longer necessary, Catholics are willing to make some concessions. Richeome admits that "the miracles that were only necessary at the beginning of the Church have ceased, the necessity having ceased"; but, he goes on, other miracles continue, "although less frequent, the necessity also being less." Of the first kind is the gift of tongues, which lasted only a few years. Nevertheless, even this gift still continues in a certain sense, in that members of the Church now speak all manner of tongues, from China to Peru, and yet the Church herself speaks only one language everywhere: Latin. Wherever a Catholic goes, "he hears God praised in the language of his mother." But the Protestants, having no missionaries, are confined to the few tongues of Europe, and they have no common liturgical language; they are neither catholic nor united.[45]

Bellarmin also accepts the principle that "miracles are necessary for persuading [people] to a new faith or [confirming] an extraordinary mission"; but he adds that this is not their only function. As witness given by God (testimonia Dei), they also often have the purpose of glorifying saints, proving their sanctity and the truth of their faith.[46] Moreover, like Richeome, Bellarmin claims that Calvin's doctrine is a new faith, and that he pretends to an extraordinary mission to reform the Church; on both counts he needs the confirmation of miracles.[47]

In general, the Catholics are in a strong position when maintaining that miracles are still necessary to guide Christians at a time when multiple heresies are rife and atheism is rearing its ugly head. According to Floyd, all ages have their scoffers at Divine Providence, and therefore their miracles, which, by punishing the wicked and rewarding the faithful, vindicate God's dominion, though these are carefully and sparingly distributed so as not to infringe on human free will. Then he asks, "Now in what age since the comming of Christ hath either piety more needed a spur, or impiety a curb, then in this we live in?" The world is full of wolves in sheeps' clothing—that is, of heretics. "Why then should we bynd the hands of God, that he may not send downe Miracles upon the world, which doth so need them? That he may not scarre ravenous wolves with thunderbolts from heaven in these days, as well as in former ages?"[48]

Another strong argument in favor of the continuing necessity of miracles was their use in converting the heathen. I have already shown Richeome taunting the Protestants with their lack of foreign missions. Bellarmin recalls the innumerable miracles of Saint Francis Xavier in the Far East, and then draws a series of contrasts between the saint's life and death and Luther's. One enters the Society of Jesus; the other deserts his monastery. One keeps his vow of chastity; the other breaks it and marries. One makes a special vow of obedience to the pope; the other attacks the Vicar of God. One has a "singular gift of miracles," and his body is preserved after death, "against the order of nature," with an odor of sanctity; the other could "not even resuscitate a fly" (ne muscam quidem resuscitare), and his corpse rotted in freezing weather, "against the order of nature," so that it stank through a metal coffin.[49]

The missionary argument was so strong that Protestants had to make some concessions to it. Sheldon, the former Jesuit, after implying that most of the missionaries' miracles are fakes, admits that the Jesuits begin by preaching the apostolic doctrine of faith in Christ and that it is quite possible that God does confirm this with miracles, though of course they later introduce their idolatrous superstitions.[50] Floyd quotes a similar concession in Philip Nicolai's De regno Christi, where the missionaries' miracles are admitted as credible because the Jesuits begin by preaching "as Lutherans or Evangelicals." The English Jesuit comments bitterly:

I think sobriety will smile at the Protestants felicity in this point, who may sit by the fire side, or ly quiet in their warme beds whilest the Jesuits go into barbarous countries to worke Miracles, to prove, forsooth their Ghospell that Fryars may marry Nunnes, and be saved in idle life by sole faith.[51]

With regard to the Protestant doctrine of Antichrist, the Catholics naturally keep to the traditional picture of him and his wonders. These wonders, Floyd and Richeome argue, will not be beneficial to body and soul, as are Catholic miracles, but merely astonishing tricks, such as are described in Revelation 13, "making the picture of a beast speak, bringing down fire from heaven, faygning himself dead and rising again."[52] Floyd also argues that if all present-day miracles are to be ascribed to Antichrist—to the powers of the Devil—then the love and fear of God will be greatly diminished. Recalling the vindictive miracles at the siege of Hall, he writes:

> If God when Hereticks blaspheme his *Mother,* and play with her *nose,* strike their tongues out of their heades, and their *best noses* from their faces, Heresy teacheth them to turne their hartes that want tongues, & their faces without noses against heaven, and call the Author of that miracle, Divell.[53]

Justus Lipsius, in the preface to his first miracle book, asks the question, Why are miracles nowadays not usually done in the name of God or Christ, but in that of saints, especially of the Virgin Mary? The answer is, There is no need now to prove the divinity of Christ, which all Christians accept; but the cult of saints and of the Virgin, attacked by so many new heretical sects, does need the support of God's approval expressed in miracles.[54] Lipsius here points to a very important aspect of modern Catholic miracles. They were of a kind that could be and was used, not only as a mark of the true Church, but also to validate practices and doctrines that were rejected by Protestants as idolatrous and superstitious: the Mass, the cult of the Virgin and of the saints as intercessors, and, going with this cult, the reverence of images and the magical power of relics.[55] For Protestants, of course, this use of miracles confirmed the belief that they were the lying wonders of Antichrist—not merely fake wonders, but deceiving and pernicious ones. But the Catholics could show, quite convincingly, that miracles of this type had frequently occurred before the supposed beginning of Antichrist's reign, which, as was shown, was usually dated by Protestants not earlier than A.D. 500.[56]

In this historical debate a crucial authority, respected by both sides, was Augustine, but he was a double-edged weapon. His pronouncements on miracles in some of his earlier writings, especially those against the Donatists (such as the *De unitate Ecclesiae*), could be used to support the Protestant contention that miracles are not a sufficient mark of the true Church,[57] and they were so used by Mason and by Sheldon.[58] In Augustine's *De vera religione,* written about 390, Sheldon and Thomson found almost the whole doctrine of the cessation of miracles:

> Since the Catholike Church hath been diffused over the whole world, neither are those miraculous things permitted to endure unto our times, lest the mind should alwaies seeke visible things, & by the custome of them, mankind should waxe cold, at the new appearance whereof, it was all on fire. (Sheldon's translation)[59]

But they forbore to mention Augustine's *Retractationes,* where he explains that he meant only that certain kinds of miracles—such as the gift of tongues—no longer happened, and that, when he wrote that book, he had already witnessed the healing of a blind man at the tombs of Ambrose and many other newly discovered martyrs at Milan.[60] Deacon and Walker, honestly but indiscreetly, cite both the book and the retraction.[61]

But, on the other hand, there is the long chapter in the last book of the *City of God* (22.8), in which Augustine recounts with great enthusiasm many miracles of his own day, including those wrought around Hippo by the newly arrived relics of Saint Stephen. This was a trump card in the Catholics' hand, and Bellarmin, Richeome, and Floyd all play it.[62] There was little the Protestants could do about it. However, since Augustine begins his chapter by stating the case he is going to refute—"But how comes it, say they, that you have no such miracles nowadays, as you say were done of yore?"—some of them had the impudence to cite this chapter as evidence of the early cessation of miracles, for example, Sir Edward Hoby and the editor of the eminent Puritan divine William Perkins's *Discourse of the Damned Art of Witchcraft* (1608).[63] Sheldon tries several ways out of the difficulty, none of them very convincing. He suggests that the chapter contains later interpolations, or alternatively, that these are not examples of pre-Antichrist miracles confirming the cult of saints, as Floyd claims, since the congregation may only have honored Saint Stephen, and not prayed for his intercession; or yet again, that even if they did pray to the saint, this does not justify present-day abuses of such prayers—just as the brazen serpent once cured snakebites, but was later rightly destroyed by Hezekiah because it was being worshiped as an idol.[64]

The Protestants, however firmly they held to the belief that modern Catholic miracles were either fraudulent or proofs that the Church of Rome was Antichrist, must have felt some anxiety about their own lack of miracles. By widening the connotation of the term *miracle,* it was possible to claim that they, too, had signs that God was on their side. I have shown Luther arguing that the invisible miracles of conversion and spiritual regeneration are greater than any physical wonders, and that they still continue in the true Church. This ancient doctrine is prominent in Saint Augustine, and it could also be used by Catholics. The same applies to the miracles of nature, which people fail to appreciate as such only through long habit; Richeome has an enormous digression on these.[65] More satisfying and reassuring was the extension of the term *miracle* to cover outstanding instances of Divine Providence. Sheldon, Hoby, and others claim as miraculous signs of God's approval of the English Reformation the preservation of Elizabeth's life in spite of all the popish plots to assassinate her, the Spanish Armada, and the Gunpowder Plot—quite an impressive little list.[66]

Bellarmin and Richeome maintain that both Luther and Calvin had attempted to perform miracles, but had failed ignominiously.[67] These highly suspect stories, which also appear in the Jesuit Thyraeus's monograph on demoniacs of 1596–98,[68] are taken from Catholic biographies of the two reformers. Luther is said to have tried in 1545 to exorcise a demoniac girl in a church at Wittenberg, but the possessing devil terrified him and locked him in the sacristy. The story about Calvin belongs to a class of miracles named by Richeome "miracles in reverse" *(miracles à reculons),* of which he gives several examples. The earliest of these is from Gregory of Tours, who tells of an Arian heretic who induced a man to feign blindness in order to confirm the truth of his heresy by performing a false miracle of healing; the man was struck with real blindness. Calvin, according to Jerome Bolsec's life of him (1577), persuaded a married couple, recent and impecunious immigrants to Geneva, in return for financial support to pretend that the husband was sick, and finally he was to feign death. Accompanied by many friends, Calvin then walked, as if by chance, near the house, heard the wails of the widow, and entered. Everyone knelt, and Calvin prayed that God would show his power by restoring the corpse to life, thus demonstrating Calvin's divine mission to reform the Church. He took the dead man's hand and commanded him in the name of the Lord to arise. But, by a just judgment of God, the simulated corpse was truly dead.

There was one kind of miracle that few disputed at the time but that raised insoluble problems for English and French Protestants: touching for the King's evil—the power of the French and English kings miraculously to cure scrofula. Here inevitably I rely heavily on Marc Bloch's fine study, *Les rois thaumaturges* (1924). Many Catholics—Richeome and Robert Chambers, for example—refer to the continuance of this ceremony of healing, so closely associated with the cult of saints.[69] But most Protestants ignored these awkward miracles and passed over them in silence.

I shall end this discussion by giving one example of the problems these miracles raised for a Protestant who was unable to evade the difficulty: the king of England, James I. James, in his *Daemonology,* first published in 1597 and reissued in 1603, the year he came to the throne, had proclaimed the now familiar doctrine: Since the establishment of Christ's "Church by the Apostles, al miracles, visions, prophecies & appearances of Angels or good Spirits, are ceased; which served only for the first sowing of faith, and planting of the Church."[70] Bloch quotes an anonymous letter, sent by an Italian to Rome in October 1603,[71] which clearly shows the painful conflicts produced by the rite of touching for a monarch who believed firmly both in the divine right of kings (which this ceremony was designed to confirm) and in the cessation of miracles. While his scrofulous subjects were waiting in an antechamber, James, before touching them, had a sermon preached by a Calvinist minister.

> Then he himself said that he found himself perplexed about what he had to do, that, on the one hand, he did not see how he could cure the sick without a miracle, and miracles had now ceased and were no longer wrought; and so he was afraid of committing some superstition; on the other hand, since this was an ancient custom and beneficial to his subjects, he was resolved to try it, but only by way of prayer, in which he begged everyone to join him. He then touched the sick. . . . It was noticed that while the king was making his speech he often turned his eyes towards the Scots ministers who were standing nearby, as if expecting their approval of what he was saying, having beforehand conferred with them on the subject.

James did what he could to cleanse the ceremony of popish superstition. He no longer made the sign of the cross when touching the sick person, and the gold coin that was hung around his neck no longer bore the cross or the inscription from

Psalm 118:23: "This is the Lord's doing; it is marvelous in our eyes" (*A Domino factum est istud, et est mirabile in oculis nostris*).[72]

Notes

1. So far as I know there is very little modern work on this subject; but see Keith Thomas, *Religion and the Decline of Magic* (London, 1971), pp. 80, 124, 256, 479, 485.

2. D. P. Walker, *Unclean Spirits: Possession and Exorcism in France and England in the Late Sixteenth and Early Seventeenth Centuries* (London, 1981), pp. 66–70, 72–73.

3. John Deacon and John Walker, *Dialogicall Discourses of Spirits and Divels* (London, 1601); idem, *A Summarie Answere to All the Material Points in Any of Master Darel His Bookes* (London, 1601).

4. John Darrel, *A Survey of Certain Dialogical Discourses* (n.p., 1602); idem, *The Replie of John Darrell, to the Answer of John Deacon, and John Walker* (n.p., 1602).

5. Martin Luther, *Werke*, 107 vols. (Weimar, 1910), 41:18–21.

6. John Calvin, *Institution de la religion chrestienne*, 5 vols., ed. J.-D. Benoit (Paris, 1957), 1:33–36.

7. Ibid., 4:473–74, 485–87.

8. John Calvin, *In Novum Testamentum commentarii*, 59 vols. (Brunswick, 1891), 1:400–401 (on Matt. 10:1–8), 973 (On Matt. 24:23: "Quum antichristos et mendaces prophetas Dominus miraculis armatos fore pronuntiet, non est cur tantopere superbiant papistae hoc obtentu, vel ipsorum jactantia territemur. Miraculis superstitiones suas confirmant: nempe quibus praedixit filius Dei, labefactandam esse multorum fidem. Quare tantum apud prudentes momenti habere non debent, ut per se sufficiant ad probandum hoc vel illud doctrinae genus. Si excipiant, hoc modo everti ac in nihilum redigi miracula, quibus tam legis quam evangelii sancita fuit autoritas: respondeo, certam spiritus notam illis insculptam fuisse, quae dubitationem et errandi metum fidelibus eximeret").

9. Ibid., p. 1211: "Quanquam autem non exprimit Christus, velitne hoc temporale esse donum, an perpetuo in sua ecclesia residere: magis tamen probabile est, non nisi ad tempus promitti miracula, quae novum et adhuc obscurum evangelium illustrent."

10. John Calvin, *Traité des reliques* (Geneva, 1543), in idem, *Three French Treatises,* ed. F. M. Higman (London, 1970).

11. See Walker, *Unclean Spirits,* pp. 66–70, 72–73.

12. See ibid., pp. 43–49.

13. Ibid., pp. 33–42, 65–66.

14. Robertus Bellarminus, *Disputationum . . . De controversiis Christianae fidei, adversus huius temporis haereticos,* 3 vols. (Ingolstadt, 1586–93), edition revised by Bellarmin, 4 vols. (Venice, 1596). I shall quote from *Disputationum . . .* (Ingolstadt, 1605), 2:348–62 (*De notis ecclesiae,* cap. 14, nota llma: Gloria miraculorum).

15. Justus Lipsius, *Diva Virgo Hallensis: Beneficia eius & Miracula fide atque ordine descripta* (Antwerp; 1604); idem, *Diva Sichemiensis sive Aspricollis: Nova eius beneficia & admiranda* (Antwerp, 1605); cf. *Bibliographie Lipsienne: Oeuvres de Juste Lipse,* 1st ser., 3 vols. (Gent, 1886), 1:535–98; 2:167–87.

16. Cf. *Bibliographie Lipsienne,* 1:535–98; 2:167–87; J. L. Saunders, *Justus Lipsius: The Philosophy of Renaissance Stoicism* (New York, 1955), pp. 51–53; Lipsius, *Opera omnia,* 4 vols. (Vesaliae, 1675), pieces at the beginning of vol. 1.

17. Lipsius, *Diva Virgo Hallensis,* pp. 15, 18; idem, *Diva Sichemiensis,* in *Opera omnia,* 3:1295, 1298–99.

18. Lipsius, *Diva Virgo Hallensis,* p. 1.

19. *La correspondance de Juste Lipse conservée au Musée Plantin-Moretus,* ed. A. Gerlo (Antwerp, 1967), p. 256 (account of Lipsius's death—23 March 1606—by Franciscus Van den Broek, Fr. Minor, an eyewitness).

20. Ibid., p. 259.

21. Lipsius, *Diva Virgo Hallensis,* p. 12: "Rem fabulae, quàm historiae propiorem, nisi eam Annales nostri constanti assensu tradidissent."

22. Lipsius, *Diva Sichemiensis,* in *Opera omnia,* 3:1296.

23. E.g., Lipsius, *Diva Virgo Hallensis,* pp. 25–27 (story of the servant about to be crucified for having lost a falcon).

24. Ibid., pp. 23–24: "See suis manibus Hallensi mulierculae (Dei parentem intelligebat) nasum abscissurum. . . . Diva audierat, & quasi talionis poenam machinata, procurat glande plumbeâ, inter primas excussâ, scurrae illi ipsi nasum auferri."

25. Edward Hoby, *A Letter to Mr. T. H. Late Minister: Now Fugitive* (London, 1609), pp. 100 (the falcon story cited in note 24 above), 101–2.

26. Richard Sheldon, *Survey* (London, 1616), pp. 50–51.

27. James Mason, *Anatomie* (London, 1612), p. 7: "Cùm hodie ista (sc. miracula in ecclesia non fiant, an propterea dicemus Christianos destitui fide? avertat deus, ut de populo dei tam male sentiamus. Adest fides justificans, sed ea quae miraculorum dicitur, jam desijt."

28. Deacon and Walker, *Dialogicall Discourses*, p. 300; Sheldon, *Survey*, p. 35.

29. Calvin, *Institution*, 3:25.

30. Calvin, *In Novum Testamentum*, 1:728: "Certum quidem est, hyperbolicam esse loquendi formam, quum fide pronuntiat transferri arbores et montes."

31. Richard Kenneth Emmerson, *Antichrist* (Manchester, 1981).

32. Ibid., pp. 206–ff.

33. See Katherine Firth, *The Apocalyptic Tradition in England, 1530–1645* (Oxford, 1979).

34. Johann Wier, *Histoires disputes et discours des illusions et impostures des diables*, 2 vols. (1579; reprint, Paris, 1885), 1:56–59.

35. Louis Richeome, *Trois discours pour la religion catholique: Des miracles, des saincts, et des images* (Bordeaux, 1597), pp. 182–85; Bellarminus, *Disputationum*, p. 349; Mason, *Anatomie*, pp. 16–18; Edward Hoby, *A Curry-Combe for a Coxe-Combe* (London, 1615), p. 221.

36. Sheldon, *Survey*, pp. 39–40.

37. Cornelius à Lapide, *Commentaria in Scripturam Sacram*, 21 vols. (Paris, 1857–63), 19:157, cap. 2, sec. 9: "Nec Antichristus, nec daemon, nec angeli possunt facere verum miraculum: sed solus Deus. Miraculum enim est quod fit super omnem naturae vim, quodque omnium naturalium causarum et creaturarum vires excedit et transcendit: Antichristus ergo faciet miracula non vera sed falsa et mendacia."

38. G. Thomson, *Vindex Veritatis: Adversus Iustus Lipsium Libri duo* (London, 1606), pp. 94–96.

39. Ibid., pp. 104–5.

40. Ibid., p. 99.

41. Robert Chambers, *Miracles Lately Wrought by the Intercession of the Glorious Virgin Marie at Mont-aigu* (Antwerp, 1606). This was answered by Robert Tynley, archdeacon of Ely, in *Two Learned Sermons . . . In the Seconde, Are Answered Many of the Arguments Published by Rob. Chambers Priest, concerning Popish Miracles; and Dedicated (Forsooth) to the Kings Most Excellent Maiestie* (London, 1609).

42. I. R. [Floyd], *Purgatories Triumph* (n. p., 1613), pp. 124–55 (chap. 5, "The miracles of the B. Virgin at *Hall*, and *Sichem*, and other Catholike Miracles are proved Authenticall, against the Prophane jestes of the *Letter*, and *Countersnarle*. And that they cannot be Antichrists Wonders"). Both works referred to are by Edward Hoby; for *Letter*, see note 25 above; the *Countersnarle* was published in 1613.

43. See note 35 above.

44. Henri Brémond, *Histoire littéraire du sentiment religieux en France*, 11 vols. (Paris, 1924), 1:18–67. He does not mention this work of Richeome.

45. Richeome, *Trois discours*, pp. 134–36; cf. pp. 123–24, on Protestants' lack of spiritual support.

46. Bellarminus, *Disputationum*, pp. 349–50; cf. Richeome, *Trois discours*, pp. 188–91.

47. Bellarminus, *Disputationum*, p. 353; Richeome, *Trois Discours*, pp. 192–94.

48. Floyd, *Purgatories Triumph*, pp. 130–31.

49. Bellarminus, *Disputationum*, pp. 356–57.

50. Sheldon, *Survey*, p. 185.

51. Floyd, *Purgatories Triumph*, p. 152.

52. Ibid., p. 151; Richeome, *Trois discours*, p. 213.

53. Floyd, *Purgatories Triumph*, pp. 148–49.

54. Lipsius, *Diva Virgo Hallensis*, p. 18.

55. Chambers, *Miracles Lately Wrought*, sigs. C3v–C4; Bellarminus, *Disputationum*, p. 357.

56. Floyd, *Purgatories Triumph*, pp. 144–47.

57. Augustine, *De unitate Ecclesiae, liber unus* (= *Ad Catholicos Epistola contra Donatistas*, in Migne, *Patrologiae Cursus, series Latina*, vol. 43, cols. 428–30, cap. 19), mentions also recent miracles at Milan, saying: "Quaecunque talia in Catholica (sc. ecclesia) fiunt, ideo sunt approbanda, quia in Catholica fiunt; non ideo ipsa manifestatur Catholica, quia haec in ea fiunt"; cf. idem, *De utilitate credeni*, cap. 16, and on this *Retractationum libri duo*, 1, cap. 14 (Migne, *PL*, vol. 42, col. 90; vol. 32, col. 606).

58. Sheldon, *Survey*, pp. 32–33.

59. Ibid., p. 121; Thomson, *Vindex Veritatis*, p. 79; Augustine, *De vera religione, liber unus*, cap. 25 (Migne, *PL*, vol. 34, col. 142): "Cum enim Ecclesia Catholica per totum orbem diffusa atque fundata

sit, nec miracula illa in nostra tempora durare permissa sunt, ne animus semper visibilia quaereret, et eorum consuetudine frigesceret genus humanum, quorum novitate flagravit."

60. Augustine, *Retractationum libri duo,* 1.13.7 (Migne, *PL,* vol. 32, cols. 604–5).

61. Deacon and Walker, *Dialogicall Discourses,* p. 333.

62. Bellarminus, *Disputationum,* pp. 359–60; Richeome, *Trois discours,* pp. 269, 288; Floyd, *Purgatories Triumph,* p. 145.

63. Hoby, *Curry-Combe,* p. 217; William Perkins, *A Discourse of the Damned Art of Witchcraft* (Cambridge, 1608), dedication signed by Thomas Pickering.

64. Sheldon, *Survey,* pp. 66–72.

65. Richeome, *Trois discours,* pp. 16–ff.

66. Sheldon, *Survey,* pp. 313–15; Hoby, *Curry-Combe,* p. 219.

67. Bellarminus, *Disputationum,* pp. 351–53; Richeome, *Trois discours,* pp. 149, 206.

68. Petrus Thyraeus, *Daemoniaci, Hoc est: De obsessis a spiritibus daemoniorum hominibus,* 2d ed. (Cologne, 1598), pp. 126–28.

69. Richeome, *Trois discours,* pp. 171–72; Chambers, *Miracles Lately Wrought,* sig. B4.

70. James I, *The Works* (London, 1616), p. 127.

71. Marc Bloch, *Les rois thaumaturges* (Strasbourg, 1924), p. 337: "Che se trovava perplesso in quel ch'haveva di fare rispetto, che dell'una parte non vedeva come potessero guarire i' infermi senza miracolo, et gia li miracoli erano cessati et non si facevano più: et cosi haveva paura di commettere qualche superstitione; dell'altra parte essendo quella usanza anticha et in beneficio delli suoi sudditi, se risolveva de provarlo, ma solamente per via d'oratione la quale pregeva a tutti volessero fare insieme con lui; et con questo toccava alli infermi . . . Si notava che quand'il Re faceva il suo discorso spesse volte girava l'occhi alli ministri Scozzesi che stavano appresso, com'aspettando la loro approbatione a quel che diceva, havendolo prima conferito con loro."

72. Ibid., p. 338.

6

Scholastic and Humanist Views
of Hermeticism and Witchcraft

PAOLA ZAMBELLI

Hermeticism and witchcraft, when considered from the point of view of intellectual and religious history, travel along paths that are almost parallel. They certainly are not absent in the Middle Ages; they surface then again and again. But it is particularly in the last decades of the fifteenth century that both undergo their decisive renewal and a kind of codification, in Italy as well as in Germany.

As for Hermeticism, it is a well-known fact that *Asclepius*—perhaps translated into Latin by Apuleius—had been circulating uninterruptedly ever since Lactantius had praised Hermes as a precursor of Christianity[1] while Augustine had condemned him as having inspired the demonic cult. In doing this, Augustine defined long in advance the terms that were later cited in the condemnation of witchcraft; he thus inspired the views of medieval and Renaissance demonologists all the way up to the *Decretum magistri Gratiani*.[2]

Hermetic themes going back to *Asclepius,* to Patristic sources, or to medieval pseudepigraphical texts (which for their part have close connections with the Hellenistic corpus so rich in alchemical and ritual passages) are of great importance to people like Hermann von Kärnten, Hildegard von Bingen, Thierry de Chartres, Bernardus Sylvester, Alain de Lille, Godefroiḍ de Saint-Victor, and Guillaume d'Auxerre, as has been shown by M.-T. d'Alverny, E. Garin, T. Gregory, and more recently by B. Stock.[3] However, a few authors of the middle of the thirteenth century whom I shall quote here as examples are closer to the problem of Hermeticism versus witchcraft. They have not been studied closely, from this point of view—except Albertus Magnus who has been recently studied "en face d'Hermès Trismégiste."[4] Guillaume d'Auvergne, as the great scholar Thorndike has pointed out, does indeed "display an intimate acquaintance" with Hermetic texts.[5] Apparently Guillaume had recourse to several medieval pseudepigrapha, like *Mercurius magnus in libro Veneris*[6] and a *Liber septem planetarum,* where Mercurius speaks of a *fabula saracena* regarding the catastrophe of incarnation

125

and fall of two angels.[7] Among the numerous passages—by no means complete—
that I found when first perusing the Guillaume d'Auvergne folio edition, there was
one that is unmistakable and fundamental, namely, the famous text from *Asclepius*
on theurgy (that is, the "creation of gods," that is, of statues that are alive and
endowed with divine powers).[8] Chapter 23 of *De legibus* quotes the entire passage
completely and verbatim and expressly names the source, Mercurius Trismegistus, in the book "quem scripsit de hellera, hoc est De deo deorum,"[9] and
shortly after that, chapter 25 narrates

> the destruction of the mistakes made by Mercurius where it is stated that by
> means of those execrations which he calls consecrations it was possible to turn
> statues into artificial gods, and to create gods by human ingenuity and power.[10]

Guillaume's attention to this text is so intense and so unceasing that he himself
acknowledges *Asclepius* as "the book we often referred to, [where] Mercurius calls
the world as well as the planets 'the sensitive God.' "[11]

Even though *Asclepius* is the main text in Guillaume's Hermetic library, it is not
the only one; the bishop of Paris makes use of all Hellenist Hermeticists,[12] and in
the particular context in which I am interested—when he discusses nature and the
veneration of demons (that is, sorcery) in his time.[13] On account of Guillaume's
pastoral duties he most certainly is one of the richest sources. He shows no
hesitation in examining closely the authenticity of the various parts of the *Corpus
Hermeticum*, whereas in the case of the young "sententiarius," Albertus Magnus,
an element of doubtful criticism, unusual for that time, becomes evident. Who was
that Trismegistus, the author of *Liber XXIV Philosophorum*, which he considered
a forgery?[14]

In the case of *Secretum secretorum*, a text of Arabic-Syrian origin, which was
attributed to Aristotle and commented on by Roger Bacon with "a defense of
legitimate divination," the repeated appearance of the names of Hermes or Her-
mogenes suffices for Albertus to classify the text as belonging in the works of
Trismegistus. Albertus finds in it one of the basic principles of witchcraft, namely
the ability of the *malefici* to reverse the *maleficium:*

> Indeed, necromancers teach that a *maleficium* can be superseded by another
> one, as it is clear from Hermes' book entitled *De secretis Aristotelis.*[15]

Albertus also quotes Hermes in other passages as being among those "certain
others dedicated to divination," a practice for which he prepared himself like a
hermit "in deserted places";[16] he often discusses secrets of alchemy[17] or of
horticulture[18] that he has taken from the *Libri incantationum Hermetis,* as well as
Hermes' general deliberations on astrology.[19] However, Loris Sturlese's recent
investigation points most emphatically to one passage that is quoted in *De animalibus* stemming from *Asclepius.* In this very quote, a dynamic conception of the
microcosmos becomes apparent, which is already very close to that developed by
Pico later on: "Hermes ad Asclepius scribens quod solus homo nexus est Dei et
mundi."[20] Yet it is even more interesting that Albertus links this concept with the

problematic nature of the *fascinatio* and the transitive faculties thanks to which some sorcerers (magi) are able to alter the bodies of others by means of the sorcerer's imagination:

> In those people who were born under the best [astral] conditions we see that they act with their souls transforming worldly bodies so that they are said to perform miracles. Hence originates *fascinatio* through which one person's soul causes in another's either obstacle or advantage, by means of his gaze or some other sense.[21]

Albertus was greatly impressed by that *Asclepius* passage, which later on was to inspire Pico's most stirring and suggestive passages of his *Oratio de dignitate hominis*. This can be seen in Albertus's recurring use of the same passages in his *De intellectu et intelligibili*.[22] Here, however, one lacks the concrete application to the case of the miraculous signs that can be performed transitively by those who, on account of the favorable constellation of their birth, possess faculties that elevate them above ordinary mortals. The analysis of phenomena such as somatization, *fascinatio,* and transitive faculties in general is of interest because it involves to a substantial degree the discussion as to the possibility and naturalness of certain effects, be they magical or due to witchcraft.[23] Therefore, the famous passage of the young and quite Hermetic-minded Giovanni Pico should be related not only to Albertus's passage taken from *Asclepius* and emphasized by Sturlese, but also to Avicenna's theory on the power of imagination.[24] It was certainly not by chance that this open-ended and noninquisitorial discussion on magic surfaced again and again, particularly in the case of thinkers who were greatly influenced by Hermes as well as by Avicenna, notably in Guillaume, Bacon, Albertus, and in the early Pico.[25]

In the fourteenth century, the frequent occurrence of Hermetic passages in Thomas Bradwardine's *De verbo Dei* and in the writing of German mystics has been noted.[26] But it is only in the century of humanism that a great qualitative change takes place. In 1463, Marsilio Ficino translated *Pimander,* Ficino's first work published as incunabulum in 1469. The interest in the fourteen dialogues grouped together under this title (and later added on to by another three—the *Definitiones Asclepii*—translated by Lazzarelli) did by no means eclipse the luster of the remaining *Corpus Hermeticum*. It continued to draw on traditional medieval pseudepigraphic sources, and the resounding success of *Pimander* was directly responsible for a series of reprints, commentaries, and translations into various languages of the *Asclepius;* it also led to original writings imbued with Hermetic spirit.[27] Here too Ficino opened the way to further research, both with his "Argumenta," which prefaced his translation, as well as with the *De amore in Platonis Convivium,* the *De vita,* and the theological writings themselves. Besides Pico and Lazzarelli, Ficino's successors at the beginning of the sixteenth century were Zorzi and Steuco in Italy; Lefèvre d'Etaples, Bovelles, Champier, and Postel in France; Reuchlin, Trithemius, and Agrippa in Germany, to name only the most important ones. Later on there followed the *Christianismi restitutio* (in which Servetus deals with the question whether "daemon ille Pimander" had known

Christ and whether he was capable of praising man in an adequate fashion),[28] and the tradition of Paracelsus, whom his publisher, Huser, called the "Trismegistus Germanus."[29]

But the crucial development occurred in 1486–87. In that year Pico and Ficino were forced to write the *Apologiae* of their magic theses—these form the central hub of both the *Conclusiones* with the introductory preface mentioned above and of the *De vita coelitus comparanda*—and two Dominican monks published in Cologne *Malleus maleficarum* ("the witch hammer"), which was directed against groups of adepts of magic who certainly had fewer speculative, dialectical, and political means at their disposal to defend themselves against persecution.[30] As is well known, Pope Innocence VIII, whom Raffael Volterrano characterized as being "ingenio tardo ac litteris procul,"[31] issued, shortly before condemning Pico, the famous bull against witches. The pope had been inveigled into it by the authors of the *Malleus*. In fact, the witch bull, *Summis desiderantes affectibus,* was printed as the most authoritative preface to Jacob Sprenger's and Heinrich Institoris's manual. It is, to be sure, more in the nature of a compilation, according to many historians. Yet for more than two centuries, it constituted the authorized code of repression.

I find it impossible to consider all this a mere chronological coincidence. Ficino and Pico de Mirandola undoubtedly moved on a level of culture and influence that cannot be compared with that of simple country women accused of witchcraft. Yet the concepts—Hermetic, no doubt—of these two men aimed at the establishment of a natural theory of magic; such a foundation appeared to be urgently needed in view of the first burning stakes. Only then could they continue to devote themselves—without incurring too much danger—to their readings and speculations, to their hymns and fumigations, which were fashionable already at the time when Gemistus Pletho was in Florence.[32]

The name of Gemistus Pletho brings to my mind the keen observation made by J. E. McGuire and C. B. Schmitt on the relative importance of the components of philosophy—it is no doubt "syncretistic"—of the two Florentines and their followers. According to the above-mentioned historians their conceptual framework is characterized mainly by Neoplatonism, not by Hermeticism, the mystical texts of which were too vague and would not have provided sufficient breadth to inspire an entire movement.[33] Here I shall mention only briefly the complex and at times distressing debate which, after an initial period of success in the departments of the history of science, almost led to an inquisitorial process against the late Frances Yates. She was, as Schmitt points out in fairness to her, primarily interested in other topics.[34] But I should like to express my opinion here without neglecting to mention this observation (which in my opinion was the keenest made in the course of the entire debate): I think the McGuire-Schmitt thesis is valid primarily in the field of the history of science; to be more specific, it is true of codification rather than the invention of science. For the person who is concerned with the codification of exact data and of theories, there is an absolute necessity to refer to a philosophical theory in the most complete and systematic manner possible. Undoubtedly Hermeticism, because of the mystical and literary vagueness of its dialogues, must necessarily lose something to Neoplatonism; in fact even more to Platonism proper and to Stoicism, with which the Hermeticist cosmology and psychology have so much in common. Not only that—all these considerations would be null and void vis-à-vis Aristotelianism if this criterion were univocal or, to be more realistic, if philosophy could always be so rigorous and pure. So far as theories dealing with religiosity and magic itself (from the Middle Ages to the Renaissance) are concerned, formal characteristics of systematics and completeness are not of great importance; on the contrary, they may even produce opposite effects.

In Ficino's *De amore,* there are some passages interpenetrated with magic—I analyzed them about ten years ago—written when the author was already considered an "alter Plato" and a disciple of Trismegistus. His translations of Plotinus, Porphyrius, Jamblichus, Proclus, Dionysius, and Psellus, however, were not yet planned. Therefore, when Pico arrived in Florence, he enjoined Ficino most urgently to undertake that task. Yet *De amore* remains Ficino's richest philosophical work and together with *De vita coelitus* his most magical work and masterpiece.[35]

In short, the unmistakably vague and mystical nature of *Pimander* and *Asclepius* only encouraged their literary success and their lasting influence on the piety of pre-Reformation times and of the radical Reformation itself. Finally, they accounted for the dominant presence in a debate that must be considered of great importance for the social problems of the Renaissance—the debate on the natural and demoniacal character of magic, on the distinctive features of natural magic and witchcraft—if they exist at all.

The reader who has had the patience to follow my presentation up to now will notice that I do not intend to maintain that the definition of natural magic by the two Florentine Platonists was entirely their own achievement—just as I would hardly maintain that the *Malleus Maleficarum* was totally devised by Sprenger and Krämer (who did not shrink from drawing on Apuleius). It is, however, quite evident that after Pico and Ficino there is much more emphasis on natural magic in all discussions since the threat of the approaching dark age became more and more evident and urgently called for the disavowal of any kind of ceremonial magic that might be denounced as witchcraft. Mention has already been made that such a definition had been current at the time of early Scholasticism (no need to go back so far as Apuleius!). But is is easy to see what kind of meaning a term like *natural magic* takes on in the mind of the Avicennian Guillaume d'Auvergne. In this source, so important for Pico, both words can be found, but they do not define a legitimate form of magic practiced by Christians experienced in nature, as claimed by E. Peter, an American historian of witchcraft.[36] When Guillaume speaks of *magia naturalis* he—being a true adherent of Augustinian terminology—has in mind the human nature that is corrupted by original sin and destined to sin again and again.

With the help of a very variable terminology—which in most cases indicates magic in its very negative sense, while in contradistinction praising "ars" or "via" or "scientia quintae essentiae"—another Avicennian, the mystic and scientist Roger Bacon, introduces the idea of legitimate and natural magic that is to be distinguished from the other kind commonly practiced. Legitimate magic constitutes fraudulent fiction ("fictum et fraudibus occupatum") if it does not make use of supernatural agents.[37] According to Roger Carton, the so-called Bacon experience of the exterior senses was part of an essentially Hermetic inspiration and would have to be traced all the way down to Campanella. Certainly his commentary on the *Secreta secretorum* must be mentioned here, as well as the *Epistola de secretis operibus artis et naturae et de nullitate magiae,* and the numerous excursus in his three *Opera.* These works need not be analyzed in detail, because his fundamental idea also influences Pico, in whose library Bacon's works were present. Suffice it to consider the relationship between art and nature:

> Given the fact that nature is powerful and marvelous, art, nevertheless, which employs nature as its instrument, is more powerful thanks to its natural virtue, as is shown in many instances.[38]

Bacon praises "the wonderful effects of art and nature . . . in which there is nothing of a magic nature, "so as to show how" all magical [necromantic] power is inferior to these effects and worthless altogether".[39] Bacon develops ideas of Guillaume d'Auvergne; particularly in his discussion on Asclepius's theurgy and on the famous statues magically revived, Guillaume had precluded that these "deos factitios esse et humano artificio atque potentia deos effici."[40] Bacon dismissed a contrast between art and nature in which preference seemed to be given to art.[41] Among the magic delusions, which are to be distinguished from futuristic (I am almost tempted to call them Leonardesque) miracles, which Bacon projects and describes, "non solum secumdum naturae possibilitatem, sed secundum artis complementum"[42], there are express references to necromantic practices (invocations, deprecations, sacrifices to demons) that are "all foreign to philosophical consideration, and in which neither art nor the power of nature is rooted."[43] Moreover, "there is no need for us to aspire to magic, because art and nature are sufficient" in order to effect the greatest prodigies ("non est necesse nobis aspirare ad magicam cum ars et natura sufficiant").[44]

Bacon remains faithful to his teacher Guillaume's manner of expression and relegates magic to a negative semantic level, but then allows it to reemerge under a different name. Giovanni Pico praises magic and turns it into the dynamic center of his world view. Thus, a terminological turnabout has happened between the two men. However, is this a real or only a verbal revolution? An enlightening indication that speaks for a close relationship—though not exactly for continuity—which is stronger and of greater import than the lexical variants can be found in this distinction between art and nature; it reemerges in Pico and Ficino's works.[45] Even if this distinction can be traced back to Plotinus, the enunciation that it undergoes in Florence is closer to that of Bacon where the formulas show a clearer and more articulate structure.

Trithemius, Agrippa, and many others will quote him while considering his magic unjustifiedly much less natural than their own. The dichotomous definition of magic that is clearly recognizable in Albertus Magnus's writings[45] was launched again by Pico and soon found its way to France and Germany where it was repeated. In 1493, shortly after he had met Pico in Florence, Lefèvre wrote the book *De magia naturali*,[47] and covered it with a tight network of classical quotations emphasizing the elementary aspects of magic while suppressing all others. The book starts with some of Ficino's well-known topics. But even before 1504 the author had decided not to publish his work—something unusual for him—and declared, in public and in private, that no magic was good and that it was a mere figment to assume the existence of a natural kind of magic.[48] Champier made use of Ficino's topoi in many of his compilations, but in the *Dialogus in magicarum artium destructionem* (1500?) he had already made depreciatory allusions to witches.[49] In any case, both edit and write commentaries on *Pimander* and the *Definitiones Asclepii*. Even more complex are the circumstances under which Hermeticism and the definition of natural magic reach Germany, where they are of even greater importance for the development of intellectual, religious, and social history. Johann Reuchlin's *De verbo mirifico* was saturated with Ficino's Hermeticism, natural magic, and Pico's cabala. However, all this is not under discussion here, since his orignality lies especially in the last component.[50] The great Hebrew scholar who became himself the victim of a witch-hunt, even though he never expressed himself in regard to the problem of witchcraft, represents the most important link between Pico and Agrippa (who in his encyclopedic *De occulta philosophia* made sure that these ideas were adequately known up to the late sixteenth and seventeenth centuries, when the works of Pico and Reuchlin were published less and were less remembered).

Along the same thought pattern was the Benedictine abbot Trithemius, who wanted to end his philosophical and occult work with the nondecipherable seal of an initiate. To his own contemporaries—less so to historians—it was quite obvious that he was a disciple of the Florentines. Among others there is his confrere Johannes Butzbach who used the *Macrostroma de laudibus trithemianis*, preserved in a Bonn palimpsest,[51] to defend Trithemius against the charges of necromancy proferred by Charles de Bouelles. In connection with other complaints (which his confreres interposed because they were tired of having to copy manuscripts in the time of Gutenberg), he was finally deposed in 1505 as abbot of Sponheim.[52] His faithful friend Butzbach, who must have had on his desk at Maria Laach a copy of Pico's *Apologia* (it was banned and for half a century out of print, but widely circulated in Germany) used some of its main arguments against Trithemius's critics,

who do not understand, or do not wish to, that in this book he deals with natural magic; he teaches with extreme elegance with the strongest arguments and a multitude of testimonies, as did recently the erudite Pico: that this [magic] is different and has to be distinguished from the magic which is impious and criminal. Indeed, no person who has read Pico's *Apologia* could be in doubt that "magic is twofold"; as the author says, the one of the two is concerned with the entire work and authority of the demons, a practice most certainly abominable and unnatural. The other is, when correctly examined, nothing but the absolute perfection of natural philosophy.[53]

Thus, the existence of two forums of magic became a topos; however, that cannot be considered a new discovery. As D. P. Walker has so keenly shown in his standard work, *Spiritual and Demonic Magic,* it is impossible to separate the one from the other entirely.[54] Given the fact that Ficino's *De vita coelitus comparanda* and Pico's magical cabalistic theses did not exclude instances of spiritual magic (Hermetic characters, talismans, seals, Orphic hymns, fumigations) such a definition is in reality more than a dichotomy; it can be misunderstood, it is ambiguous, and in those dark years when demonology was codified and the witch-hunts had their beginnings, this ambiguity afforded some aid and relief.[55] John of Salisbury[56], Guillaume d'Auvergne, Roger Bacon, Arnau de Villanueva,[57] Thomas Aquinas,[58] and even Erasmus[59] were very different from the two elitist Florentines who would not discuss witches expressly; and yet it is the very existence of witches—even within the reach of their favorite academic walks (like the one at Fontelucente that Poliziano mentioned with some irony)[60]—that provides the indispensable prerequisite to a proper understanding of their insisting on this difference. If I may make this somewhat irreverent and paradoxical comparison, that distinction has essentially the same purpose as Albertus and Thomas Aquinas's distinction in regard to the *duae viae* of theology and philosophy, namely to legitimize and render practicable the second way, the *via naturalis.* Giovanni Pico, who had received Scholastic training (at Padua and Paris) more comprehensive and deeper than that of Ficino and of other magicians, had managed to find some formulations that would eventually become classic definitions and (like that on magic as "naturalis *philosophiae absoluta consummatio,*" taken from Psellus) would be repeated systematically as late as Agrippa and Della Porta.[61] And Butzbach makes use of them when he defends Trithemius:

> As the Greeks do mention both, they do not think that one deserves the name of magic, thus they call it γοητεἰαν, whereas they use as a specific and proper name μαγεἰα to denote the other which they consider the perfect and highest science. Equally, according to Porphyrios, the word "magician" in the Persian language denotes those we call interpreters and worshippers of divine things. Great and indeed enormous are the difference and dissimilitude between the two arts. The one is condemned and loathed not only by the Christian religion, but by all religions and every orderly state; the other is approved of and cherished by wise people and nations who love the knowledge of divine and celestial things. The one is a most fraudulent art, the other is the highest and holiest philosophy. The one is false and useless; the other is reliable, enduring and solid. Those who cultivate the first always keep it secret, because it causes shame and offence to its practitioners from the other and that from the earliest times and almost always since men have sought the greatest literary glory.[62]

Butzbach, being rather naive, seems to be in the dark about Trithemius's demeanor as an initiate—unless he himself was an initiate and wanted to misuse Pico's fine rhetorical tirade in order to dispel any suspicion on his teacher in the order and in the art itself. Ambiguity, by the way, was already inherent in the formulations of Pico, an honest man, who never acted as an initiate. In Persian, *magic* is synonymous with *wisdom* (as everyone would from now on repeat, while constantly adding to a long list of equivalent roles such as magicians, sages, priests, and druids).[63] Magic was also the favorite of those persons and communities who were "coelestium ac divinarum rerum studiosae," such as astrologers, speculative theologians, and at times even priests. In fact Pico, the natural magician,[64] did not limit himself to combining occult (less well known) properties of elementary substances *(elementata)* on all levels of the scale of existence and thus to having "the world wedded"; the most objectionable of his theses even maintained that such magic combined with the cabala was useful for the certification of miracles wrought by Christ,[65] whereas another thesis, the final one, maintained that "sicut vera astrologia docet nos legere in libro Dei, ita Cabala docet nos legere in libro Legis,"[66] and other theses again talked of "voces et verba in opere magico"[67] and even indicated that "plus posse caracteres et figuras in opere magico, quam possit quecunque qualitas materialis."[68]

It is probably no coincidence that almost all of the Renaissance theoreticians of magic had probed deeply into religious meditation (often verging on heterodoxy) including Lefèvre, Zorzi, Postel, Servetus, Paracelsus, Bruno, and Campanella.[69] It is thus understandable that at least some of them were doubly motivated to take a stand on the phenomenon of witchcraft that has also been interpreted as a phenomenon of alternative religion.[70] Even today there are heated disputes among historians in regard to the nature of witchcraft, but at that time such an issue was even less painless and safe. And yet, more than one Hermetic philosopher felt obliged to express his opinion on witchcraft, perhaps because of his own conscience and sensitivity to either religious or magic problems, or perhaps in response to the need of those turbulent times. This is common knowledge, so far as the time span during and after the Council of Trent is concerned. The Agrippa disciple and Erasmus admirer Johannes Weyer, the encyclopedist and natural magician Giambattista Della Porta, Montaigne, Reginald Scot, Friedrich von Spee, Christian Thomasius, and others spoke out in defense of witchcraft. Meanwhile, on the other side of the barrier, a dramatic contradiction is shown within the works of a great intellectual such as Jean Bodin *(Universae naturae Theatrum* and *Heptaplomeres* versus *Démonomanie des sorciers,* 1581).[71] This contradiction can be understood when one takes into consideration, as Lucien Febvre has taught the common mentality prevailing at that time, without defining it as pure "sottise."[72]

But even before the reformed Johannes Weyer, a follower of Erasmus, had started this well-known debate, not everyone had observed the elitist silence that was somewhat opportunistic as practiced by Pico and Ficino. There is Champier, who as early as 1500 spoke out against the witches. There is Pico's nephew, Gianfrancesco, who continued to move away from the "vanity of pagan doctrines" (the Hermetic and Neoplatonic ones included). At the request of a Dominican Inquisitor who was battling, between Padua and Bologna, some radical Aristotelians (Achillini, Pomponazzi, and Tiberio Russiliano), Gianfranceso even wrote a dialogue, *Strix* (The Witch). These Aristotelians were spreading doubts about the existence of demons, even though the Hermetic tradition was not unknown to Nifo, to Pomponazzi, and to Russiliano.[72] But the most noteworthy case is the one that involved the Germans, already mentioned. Trithemius and Agrippa, who cooperated in the elaboration of the Hermeticism and natural magic of the Florentines in Germany, both participated in the debate on witchcraft, but on opposite sides.

Agrippa, then in his early twenties and after a discussion that must have been an eye-opener in regard to a good many secrets and to the two ways of magic, showed in 1510 the first manuscript draft of his *De occulta philosophia* to Trithemius. The abbot urged him not to stop at the mere natural magic as required by the "ox" Bouelles who would "take an oath only on a single discipline" ("in unius duntaxat facultatis rudimentum iuravit"), but to probe under the veil of initiation into the prodigies of magical practice. Trithemius makes it incumbent on Agrippa to keep the occult a secret: "ut vulgaria vulgaribus, altiora vero et arcana altioribus atque secretis tantum communices amicis."[74]) The pique that finds its echo here on having been denounced by the traitor Charles de Bovelles shows clearly that Trithemius's instigation is an obvious case of double-dealing that he revealed only to the few disciples who had arrived at the final initiation. And also Trithemius's game with magic and witchcraft amounts to double-dealing. In his form of magic, the aspect of ceremonial magic is present, indeed it is prevalent. In the *Steganographia* denounced by Bouelles there is to be found, apart from a strange cryptograph, spiritual magic of the cabalistic type.[74] His letters to Joachim von Brandenburg,[75] beside the one to Agrippa mentioned earlier, leave little room for doubt; and yet Trithemius wrote three works against witches who engage in the same practices. The preface of one of these works, *De daemonibus* (dated about 1507 or shortly after) has recently been published. There is also a detailed survey of all twelve books that were probably never completed;[77] however, their contents are very similar to an unpublished pseudepigraphical appendix to *Antipalus maleficorum* written in 1508 for the Elector of Brandenburg, but published posthumously and censored. This censored section, titled *Synusiastes Melanii Triandrici ad Iaymielem,* about *maleficium impotentiae* and other thorny problem is, however, considered authentic by Klaus Arnold, the specialist for Trithemian manuscripts.[78] A few months prior to that, also in 1508, Trithemius had answered in writing eight topical questions Emperor Maximilian had intended to put him at the Diet of Cologne and at the castle of Boppard.[79] Half of the questions (3, 5, 6, 7) were concerned with witchcraft. While he did not publish the other works, Trithemius had this one published in 1515. But—and this is indeed rare—two manuscripts written by the author or by Trithemius's usual copyist have been preserved. The Viennese manuscript corresponds to the printed version and was probably written around 1515;[80] the second manuscript, on the other hand, preserved at Uppsala, is shorter, but at times more explicit, and one is inclined to date it at 1508, soon after the meeting with the emperor. The pertinent correspondence indicates that the variants were agreed upon with Maximilian or even urged upon Trithemius by the emperor.[81] Question 3, "On the miracles of the heathen,"[82] states in one of the first sentences that "indeed, magicians having made implicit or explicit pacts with demons are capable of performing miracles,"[83] whereas the published edition deals generically with "heathen," not magicians; in this context the discussion frequently involves demonic magic because beside God and the angels, the Devil also with "monkeylike curiosity"[84] "qui quasi simia imitari gliscit quodcumque viderit"[85] performs miracles on the natural level "cum [daemones] naturas optime noverunt herbarum omnium,"[86] as well as in his answers to inquiries that in the eyes of Trithemius do not constitute merely astrological practices, but are real vaticinations by the Devil. At times demons enjoy practical jokes:

> They behave like children who sometimes put on masks and hide, only to jump out and when they succeed in terrifying their shocked friends they enjoy themselves enormously, as if they had achieved some great honor.[87]

Some of their jokes are really in bad taste, but once again one is dealing here with delusions according to the *Canon Episcopi,*

> as when they force their way into corpses and are reputed to restore them to life for a short time, or having thrown them in some remote place, they exhibit somehow the image of the dead.[88]

The misdeeds of witches, however, are anything but jokes.

> Those who appeal to demons are capable of marvels; like witches who having submitted to the power of evil spirits renounced the Catholic faith, and turned toward damnation by paying demons the basest homage of loyalty. With God's permission, demons always take part in evil when appealed to; sometimes they appear in visible form, at other times they are invisible; they upset the atmosphere, cause storms, hail and lightning, they ruin crops and ravage with their spells whatever is produced by the earth. They cause illness in man and beast, and use every skill to carry out whatever plan they can think of to ruin man.[89]

The hymns and sacrifices, so dear to Ficino, the Orphic priest, and to other highly sophisticated humanists, together with the very formulas that Trithemius in his *Steganographia* directs to the planetary spirits, are seen here at the zenith in the list of witches' crimes. In this quaestio Trithemius talks, as in other places, of an explicit pact; and though it is true that he does not advocate the stake, he does insist on exorcism and ecclesiastical purification as they were in use before the *Malleus,*[90] and his indictment is illustrated with the most atrocious and gruesome details.[91] In regard to the other quaestiones (which I intend to analyze in their handwritten version and publish elsewhere, since that almost constitutes an entire book), only quaestio 5: "De reprobis et malificis," and 7: "De permissione Dei" should be taken up here. These questions correspond to the usual themes of the literature on witchcraft. Like all other Trithemius texts on demonology, they are studded with quotations from Augustine (whose theology of providence spread the idea that demons and witches perform evil according to a divine plan that allows them to do so, but does not remove their subjective guilt from them). Quaestio 6 on the other hand, entitled "On the power of witches" (De potestate maleficarum") appears to be a new, reworked, version of the treatise *De daemonibus,* attributed to a Byzantine scholar of the eleventh century, Michael Psellus, and translated by Ficino. The quaestio contains a classification of the types of demons and adds to those which correspond to the four elements two further categories, the "subterranean" and "lucifugous." Of all Trithemius's demonological texts, this is by far the most Florentine-Hermetic in character, even more so than the bibliographical section of the *Antipalus maleficiorum* which obviously also lists pseudo-Hermetic writings in great number.

In fact, this classification of demons is then greatly expanded in Trithemius's *De daemonibus* and assumes here in question 6 that only two out of six demons—the terrestrial and aerial ones—have dealings or intercourse with witches in some unusual cases. All this has been taken literally, even if tacitly, from the excerpts of Michael Psellus's work on demons, translated by Marsilio Ficino soon after he had finished his book *De vita coelitus* in 1488.[92] This translation was perhaps the most specific, or rather the only, contribution Marsilio has made to the debate on witchcraft; for the small treatise dwells in detail on the individual and collective practices ascribed to witches at the end of the Middle Ages, both in the Byzantine and Latin world. Not only poisoning and evil charms are mentioned, but also ointments causing demoniacal apparitions and nocturnal flights onto bewitched trees, and real orgies and sabbaths with the sacrifice of the children such promiscuous unions between demons and human beings. Nevertheless, Trithemius introduces a classification acknowledging the Byzantine-Florentine source ("sicut Michael Psellus dicit"),[93] but he does not include these pages on witchcraft in his quaestiones. One must, however, admit that even though Trithemius places the demonologists Johannes Nider and Jacob Sprenger among the "Illustrious Men of Germany"[94] and has certainly read Sprenger's *Malleus* (its first edition is preserved in the Würzburg library),[95] one cannot read anywhere in his writings about instigations to the burning of witches—apart from the quote from Exodus 22:18: "Maleficos non patieris vivere," which he repeats as a topos.[96] As Arnold points out, Trithemius recommends only ecclesiastical means employed in less difficult times, such as exorcisms and purifications.[97] I should like to add here that Trithemius does not include the Sabbath in his list, that characteristic element which since the appearance of the *Malleus* or a few decades earlier begins to change the intellectual and judicial attitude in regard to witchcraft. In my view, the Sabbath is not dealt with in the *Octo quaestiones* and in the *Antipalus*, while only 4 out of 343 chapters of the envisaged book *De daemonibus* announce remarks concerning that particular theme. Namely, "liber X, caput 18: Quomodo per aera vehantur a daemonibus"; ch. 19: "Qualia convivia et chorizaciones cum daemonibus habent"; ch. 20: "Qualia maleficae offerunt sacrificia"; ch. 22: "Quis modus sit daemonum coeundi cum maleficis." But the bare scheme of an unfinished text does not permit any conjecture as to the probable development of this qualifying point nor of the other that is connected with the maintenance of the *Canon Episcopi* "liber X, ch. 26: An maleficarum delacionibus contra alias sit credendum").[98]

It seems, therefore, that in selecting from Psellus's sources the most truculent pages have been omitted deliberately, maybe just because Trithemius wanted to be moderate in his intervention against witches. In the first writing of the quaestio 6 there are furthermore various other quotes drawn on the heritage of Florentine magic—to corroborate Psellus's definitions on the first two types of demons, and only in this case does Trithemius quote Ficino, as well as Orpheus, Porphyrius, and Apuleius.[99] In a passage that was added on, he solemnly reminds us that "before that time Mercury, the Thrice Great, had said: 'Surely no part of the world is free of the presence of demons.' "[100] But the most revealing is a long passage absent in the edition and in the Viennese manuscript; that passage defines demons not in the manner of an inquisitor, but in that of Porphyrius and Plato, whose dialogue *Ion,* very often used in this context by Ficino as well as by Pomponazzi, had already been quoted at the beginning in a passage that remained in the 1515 text.[101]

All this leads me to believe that in his maturity Trithemius had not forsworn that "Reformatio hermetica" which Noel L. Brann,[102] his recent biographer, had read into his letter of 1499 to Arnold Bost, in which the abbot of Sponheim solemnly professes an exclusively natural magic introducing the *Steganographia,* full of names of every kind of demons.

I cannot, therefore, trace a change in Trithemius's attitude toward the Hermetic conception, as well as toward spiritual and demonic magic, toward witchcraft. On the other hand, I see a clearer evolution in his disciple, Cornelius Agrippa. In order to explain the contradictions within his two major works, *De occulta philosophia* and *De vanitate scientiarum et artium,* various hypotheses have been put forward by many scholars and also by me.[102] I have tried to show the existence of a coherent line of thought, even if complex and uneven. Considering just the magician Agrippa's attitude vis-à-vis witchcraft, here I shall only recall his two most famous polemic documents, some letters in which he describes his own defense of a peasant woman charged with having inherited witchcraft from her mother in Voippy, a village near Metz in 1519 and his better-known, vehement chapter 96 against the Inquisitors in *De vanitate.*[104] It is not so well known that this author (who provides a historical concrete link between Trithemius, his model and master, and Johann Weyer, his disciple and defender) wrote *Adversus Lamiarum inquisitores* probably a little earlier than 1533 (two years before his death). This work was still quoted with horror in 1566 by a Dominican Inquisitor, Sisto da Siena.

> Cornelius Agrippa, a follower of the Lutheran heresy, in his book which he published under the title of *Adversus Lamiarum inquisitores* [Against the Inquisitors of Witches], turns this sentence by John [Galatians 3:1] against those who prosecute and punish women for witchcraft, when it is proved they had sexual intercourse with demons; he mocks the thing as a tale born of the imagination and the dreams of old delirious women, since often asleep, they are deceived by dreams, and at times, even when they are wronged by the thought of vehement libido, and even think that acts which are only formed in imagination, really occurred to them.[105]

From the quotes of the Dominican, who probably saw in Agrippa a radical reformer, it appears in the first place that Agrippa mocks the belief in intercourse between witches and demons, interpreting them—along the lines that will be developed by Weyer and Della Porta—as delusions due not to the presence of demons, but to dreams and hysteria, and so described by the *Canon Episcopi.* Sisto da Siena, moreover, does not seem to know the *De praestigiis daemonum* by Weyer, published three years previously, and therefore cannot make the comparison, which would have been enlightening, between the famous work by the disciple and the lost work by the master. From data given by Sisto's *Bibliotheca sancta* it appears certain that, in order to strengthen the thesis of delusion, Agrippa quoted the *Canon Episcopi* extensively to show that this document (superseded by the *Malleus*) proved the impossibility of flight of witches "corporaliter" to the sabbath and considered those "vectationes et translationes" always only imaginary ("semper sola imaginatione fieri").[106] Among the faculties attributable to imagination, Agrippa, however, did not include the evil eye (*fascinatio* of witches on children).

> Cornelius Agrippa, a heretic, in the book *Adversus Lamiarum inquisitores* published by him, takes the occasion offered by this sentence [by John Chrysostom] to stigmatize inquisitors as heretics and charges them, among other things, of having invented this last kind of slander against those simple and innocuous women, called witches, namely that they fascinate children showing their faces and corrupt them by the fixed gaze of their eyes.[107]

Agrippa was indeed courageous; primarily because of his intellectual honesty he was anxious not to legitimize the misdeeds attributed to peasant witches with the refined magic of imagination, which, from Avicenna to Ficino and later, had been the principal and favorite resource for natural magicians and also for himself. He in fact was rethinking it in those same years while preparing the *De occulta philosophia* for print (1533), including in it various heretical motives such as psychopannychism and Nicodemism[108] (this resulting from a more serious and deeper understanding of that Pythagorean Hermetical silence, so forcefully recommended to him by Trithemius and so sought after in his earlier works).

Hermetic positions could at times take on progressive roles in social, intellectual, and religious conflicts. But certainly through these circumstances in Germany, Hermes Trismegistus had lost that marvelous peaceful impassiveness which at the beginning he expressed in *pia philosophia, docta religio,* and the general concordia according to the Florentines. In the wooden choir chairs of Ulm cathedral Jörg Syrlin in 1474 had sculpted in a most accomplished manner the sibyls escorted by the prophet Micah, and also by Terence, Cicero, Quintilianus, Seneca, Pythagoras, and by a rather egg-headed Ptolomeus. But the German artist had no space left for Hermes, who instead dominates the physical and ideal space of the floor mosaic in the cathedral of Siens, where the sibyls and Hermes himself with the scrolls are clearly connected to the Florentine rebirth of ancient magic and theology. The Sienese cycle was accomplished about fifteen years after the one in Ulm (1481–98?) and in both it is possible to recognize the local peculiarities of two traditions already firmly rooted in humanism. If the stalls of Ulm had been built somewhat later, one might have been able to admire the wooden carved figure of a German Hermes Trismegistus, but just a few decades later, when the conflicts of ideas that I have tried to outline in the field of Hermeticism were better defined—I wonder if the canons of the cathedral of Ulm would have wanted and been able to have their sibyls keep such bad company with a Hermes by then so irredeemably compromised. These ladies themselves would have appeared, so says Johannes Weyer, "Sibyllae a daemone conductae."[109]

Notes

A shortened German translation of this paper has been published in *Archiv für Kulturgeschichte* 67 (1985): 41–79.

1. *Divinae Institutiones*, 1.6 [Hermes] "maiestatem summi et singularis Dei asserit, iisdemque nominibus appellat, quibus nos, Deum et Patrem" and other quotations of a theological character from *Asclepius* about "God, son of God" and his incarnation as divined by Hermes in 4.6 and 11; 7.18; while in 2.15 to differentiate two types of demons is used the Hermetic pejorative definition "immundum, malum, terrenum." Cf. *De ira Dei*, which, like the preceding text, follows Cicero's *De natura Deorum* by presenting Hermes as "longe antiquior" than Pythagoras and the seven Wise Men.

2. *De civitate Dei*, 7.23–24, passim. Augustine and Thomas Aquinas are considered the two principal founders of demonology; this traditional conception is summarized in H. Trevor-Roper, *The European Witch-Craze of the 16th and 17th Century, and Other Essays* (New York, 1969). Cf. *Corpus iuris canonici I. Decretum Gratiani*, ed. E. Friedberg (Leipzig, 1879) cols. 1019-ff.: pt. 1, chap. 26 ("Sacerdos sortilegus"); pt. 2, chaps. 5, 7, 8, 10; pt. 3, chap. 1–2; pt. 5, chap. 13. Augustine is cited on account of this and other works of his, but particularly through Hrabanus Maurus's *De magicis artibus*.

3. M.-T. d'Alverny, "Le cosmos symbolique du XIIe siècle," *Archives d'histoire doctrinale et littéraire du Moyen Age* 20 (1953): 38–81; idem, "La survivance de la magie antique," in *Miscellanea mediaevalia* I: *Antike und Orient im Mittelalter*, ed. P. Wilpert (Berlin, 1962), pp. 154–78; E. Garin, "Un dialogo sull'immortalità dell'anima: il *Liber Alcidi*" [1940] in *Studi sul platonismo medievale* (Florence, 1958), pp. 89–151; idem, "Nota sull'ermetismo" [1955] in *La cultura filosofica del Rinascimento italiano* (Florence, 1961), pp. 142–54, and the studies by Liebeschütz, Silverstein, Woolsey, Delhaye, Chenu there quoted at p. 150n. In addition, the substantial introductions to both the English and French translations of *Hermetica*, ed. W. Scott and A. S. Ferguson (Oxford, 1924–36), 4: XLIV–XLVI; *Corpus Hermeticum*, ed. A. D. Nock and A.-J. Festugière (Paris, 1945), 2: 264–75. (From now on abbreviated as *CH* + vol. + page.) Among the recent special studies, cf. T. Gregory, *Anima mundi* (Florence, 1958), p. 105n, on the influence of the *Asclepius* (6.301–2) on the development of the idea of microcosm in the twelfth century, and pp. 152–53 on Hermann of Carinthia and the *De sex principiis*, attributed to Hermes; pp. 134n, 183n on Thierry de Chartres and the *Asclepius*; pp. 98 and 199 on the *Asclepius* in Bernard Silvestris's *De mundi universitate;* idem, "L'idea di natura nella filosofia medievale prima dell'ingresso della *Fisica* di Aristotele" in *La filosofia della natura nel Medioevo* in *Atti del terzo Congresso Internazionale di filosofia medievale 1964* (Milan, 1966), pp. 61–65. In the Hermetic or pseudo-Hermetic literature current in the twelfth century it is observed "in the background of the play between sympathy and antipathy, of magic rituals and of witchcraft, where they appeal to a god in whom it is difficult to recognize the Christian god, a new desire is afoot to know nature and its most hidden secrets." In the following Bernard Silvester's and Pico's notions of microcosm according to the *Asclepius* are collected; idem, "La nouvelle idèe de nature et de savoir scientifique au XII siècle" in *The Cultural Context of Medieval Learning* (Dordrecht, 1975), pp. 193–218; B. Stock, *Myth and Science in the Twelfth Century: A Study of Bernard Silvester* (Princeton, 1972), pp. 150-ff. (on *Asclepius* interpreted as source, particularly in the Stoic sense), pp. 170-ff. (on Apuleius demonology, *De Deo Socratis*). It is still fundamental L. Thorndike, *A History of Magic and Experimental Science*, 8 vols. (New York, 1923–58), which in its volumes 1 and 2 treats of these and many other medieval authors. In the successive volumes all those of the Renaissance dealt with here are mentioned.

4. Cf. below note 14.

5. Thorndike, *History*, 2: 339; cf. p. 355 and all of chap. 52.

6. *Guilelmi Alverni Opera omnia* (1673; reprint, Frankfurt, 1963), 1. 953, col. 1C (= *De universo*, 2.2.100).

7. Ibid., 1. 881, col. 2A (= *De universo*, 2.2.37).

8. *CH*, 2.325-ff. (pars. 23–24). It should be noted that in connection with this action harshly condemned by medieval and Renaissance demonologists, those Hermetic terms reemerge which will appear again in Pico's central section of the *Oratio de dignitate hominis* (ed. E. Garin in *Scritti*, Florence, 1942, p. 102) introductory to his *Conclusiones*: "felicissimum hominem iudico . . . Nec immerito miraculo dignus est." Mentioned several times is the section on the creation of the gods: E. Garin, "Nota sull'ermetismo," in: *La cultura filosofica del Rinascimento italiano* (Florence, 1961), pp. 143-ff., and even more so in F. A. Yates, *Giordano Bruno and the Hermetic Tradition* (London, 1964), pp. 36–37.

9. *Guilermi Alverni Opera*, (1.66, col. 2GH (= *De legibus*, chap. 2): "Ita homo effector est Deorum, qui in templo sunt, humana proximitate contenti." Having quoted extensively from the Hermetic text, Guillaume criticized it in the same chapter: "Nullatenus dubitandum est quin virtutem

divinam et naturam attribuerit huiusmodi erroneis statuis seu imaginibus" and then compiles his classification of ten kinds of idolatry among which there is "prima et radicalis" the cult of demons incarnate and evoked by other means. Guillaume mentions the same means ("imagines . . . figuras quasdam, quarum alias sigilla planetarum, alias annulos, alias characteres eorum, alias imagines vocant"), which will be still used by Ficino (*De vita* bk. 3), Agrippa, and Trithemius. Guillaume's discussion of *Asclepius*'s theurgy is extended; here only a brief criticism of his will be quoted: "quantum erravit Mercurius, qui eas [imagines] deos factitios mentitus est" (ibid., 1.83, col. 2B [= *De legibus*, chap. 26]).

10. Ibid., 1.85, col. 1A (= *De legibus*, chap. 26) where he continues "Humana natura est magis dea et maiori divinitate naturaliter erit quam huiusmodi statuae" (an observation that must have pleased Giovanni Pico). He then cites again the magic treatment with officinal herbs and the fumigations in the Hermetic tradition: "Quod si dixerit, quia virtus ista causa est humanae naturae herbarum et aromatum, dixit enim Mercurius quia usi sunt maiores nostri ad hoc herbis et aromatibus, vim divinitatis in se habentibus (1.85, col. 1C) and concludes: "Huiusmodi substantias vocat ipsemet Mercurius animas daemonum et dicit quia maiores nostri animas daemonum statuis indiderunt, quae locutio non potest habere intentionem nisi erroneam." Chap. 27, pp. 86–ff. says: "Confutat alium errorem veteris idolatriae, sc. de statuis quae stultis visae sunt esse dii factitii."

11. Ibid., p. 77, col. 2, D (Chap. 25) "destruit cultum stellarum et corporum caelestium" and in this context Guillaume discusses at the very outset the definitions of the world soul in *Timaeus*, those of Aristotle (as interpreted by Avicenna), and of Hermes and Boethius.

12. Ibid., p. 78, col. 1, EF in the same chapter (followed by chap. 26 on idolatry of the four elements) Guillaume summarizes the harmony of the stars in the world regions, in the body limbs, and in the "elementata," which is not very different from the net of correspondences to be used two centuries later by natural magic: "Solem et lunam rectores orbis terrarum deos putaverunt, et ipsis planetis atque signis duodecim orbem inferiorem terrarum totum partiti sunt, [. . .] ut Marti Germaniam, Saturno Italiam, Cyprum Veneri. *Sectas* etiam et *leges* et artificia, virtutesque at vitia eisdem distribuerunt; eidem modo ornamenta et instrumenta, colores, odores et sapores per singulos diviserunt necnon et animalis, etiam furnos, molendina et quidquid etiam de locis et habitudinibus hominum: animalia quando eisdem partiti sunt, ut animali gypsei coloris attribuerunt Veneri et aves ruffi coloris Marti et corvinum genus Phaebo sive Apollini; litteras et numeros similiter eisdem partiti sunt, et ad ultimum ipsum corpus humanum per partes et membra distribuerunt eisdem; et haec omnia in libris iudiciorum astronomiae et in libris magorum atque maleficorum tempore adolescentiae nostrae nos meminimus inspexisse."

13. Ibid. vol. 2,796–1G (= *De universo* 2.2.27) where he construes an unusual connection between *fatum* (fate) and the fairy of the folktale: "Nomen autem fati vel fatae vel fatationis apud utramque gentem [hebraicam et christianam], sicut praedixi tibi, horrificum est et abominabile . . . quoniam utraque lege antiquior est mentio culturae deorum atque dearum et idolatria; velut reliquia quaedam ex sequela aliqua huiusmodi culturae remansit opinio fatationis, potissimum autem circa anus seu vetulas, quae vel curiositate faciente muliebrique levitate vel quaestuatione, pre qua mentiri non verentur, nondum recesserunt ab eis."

14. Albertus Magnus, *Sententiarum* [1.3.18] in *Opera*, 21 vols., ed. Pierre Jammy (Lyon, 1652) 16:68–69, quoted and commented on by L. Sturlese, "Saints et magiciens: Albert le Grand en face d'Hermès Trismégiste," *Archives de philosophie* 43 (1980): 620–21. The following hypothesis ("omnia enim que dicitur dixisse Trismegistus [in libro XXIV philosophorum, quem credo confictum], inveni in quodam libro magistri Alani") does not, it would seem to me, present any proof that young Albertus was little familiar with Hermetic writings nor does it constitute a *comparaison ambiguë*. In Alanus there is found a kind of theological Hermeticism that is closely related to that of Lactance in *Contra Haereticos* [1 chap. 30; 3, chaps. 2–4] *PL* 210: 223, 276, where Asclepius is cited among other "auctoritates gentilium philosophorum," not only to prove "quod anima humana sit immortalis" but also "quod tres sunt personae divinae et una est eorum natura." If Alanus represents a middle course here between Lactance and Ficino, he is by no means a stranger to the medieval Hermeticists he quotes (ibid. 405). The *Liber XXIV Philosophorum* with its famous "Monas gignit monadem et in se suum reposat ardorem" is taken up by Albertus in the same context as in *Sententiarun* 11.1 (*Opera*, ed. Jammy, 14:206). However, the background, only theological and not at all historico-philological, of the doubt must be stressed which arose in Albertus as to the author of *Liber XXIV Philosophorum*. (A doubt not at all occasioned by the very old age which is assigned to Hermes by *Asclepius* and other noncontroversial texts, as becomes evident of Albertus's earlier and later writings): "Si tamen philosophus fuit ante incarnationem, et non didicit in libris Veteris Testamenti, nec per revelationem, tunc dico quod loquitur de uno Deo generante, id est producente suum intellectum in mundo et omnia quae fecit diligenter propter seipsum" (*Opera*, ed. Jammy, 14:69).

15. *IV Sententiarum* 34.9 (*Opera*, ed. Jammy, 16:710) as quoted by L. Sturlese, p. 621.

16. *De somniis* 3:1.5; *Opera,* ed. Jammy, 5:97; quoted by Sturlese, p. 627.

17. *De mineralibus* 3:1.8; 1.1.1; 2.2.4; 2.3.3; quoted by Sturlese, pp. 618–19. Cf. also 2.2.10 [in D. Wyckoff's excellent English translation (Oxford, 1967), p. 103 and ibid. 273–74 compilation of quotations from *Asclepius* in this work in "De animalibus," 22.1.5 and "De natura loci," 1.5; see notes 19 and 20 below.]

18. *De vegetabilibus* 4.4.2; 5.2.6 and 6.1.32; *Opera,* ed. Jammy, 5:414, 429, 455; cf. Sturlese 629 note 41.

19. *De natura loci* 1.5; *Opera,* ed. Jammy, 5:268: "Egregie dicit Hermes in libro de virtutibus universalibus, quod constellatio est causans virtutem qualitatum eorum quae infunduntur in inferioribus et est formativa ipsorum per qualitates elementorum, quae sunt sicut instrumenta virtutum caelestium."

20. Cf. Sturlese, p. 27. Those expressions which would indicate this text to have been a source of Pico's *Oratio* are e.g., "sicut testatur Hermes, si aliquando aliquis hominum per electionem se mundo inferiorem fecerit, iam quasi honore humanitatis exutus, proprietatem accipit bestiae." As to the technical aspects of magic practices, this typical Pico text stresses the foundation—in regard to the relationship between Man and World—of the "fascinatio qua anima unius agit ad alterius impedimentum vel expeditionem per visum vel alium sensum." See ed. Stadler, *Beiträge Bäumker* 15–16:1353 [bk. 22, chap. 1. sec. 5].

21. Ibid.

22. Cf. *De intellectu et intelligibili* 3.6 (*Opera,* ed. Jammy, 5:268): "Antiquissimos idiotas Hermes increpans dixit tales nulli humanorum in vita opera dedisse, sed more porcorum vitam expendisse"; in the same work, 3:9 (5:260): the Hermetic topos "homo nexus est Dei et mundi" is repeated twice, as Sturlese points out appropriately, without however, explaining the dynamic interpretation by which Albertus seems to have anticipated Pico.

23. Albertus's comments on themes closest to witchcraft and demonology are found in the theological works, e.g., *IV Sententiarum,* 34:8–9 (*Opera,* ed. Jammy, 16:709–10): Art. VIII; An malefici impedimento aliquis potest impediri a potentia coeundi; Art. IX: An maleficium sit excludendum per maleficium. *Summa theologiae* 2.8.30 (*Opera,* ed. Jammy, 18:176–ff.): "Si praestigia magorum facta sint miracula vel non"; compare note 25 below. See also *II Sententiarum,* the *Distinctiones,* which discuss the angels' fall together with some articles regarding characteristics of demons and their *praestigia: Dist.* VI, Art. V: Utrum aer caliginosus sit proprius locus daemonum? (*Opera,* ed. Jammy, 16:73–74); *Dist.* VII, Art. IV: "Utrum daemones triplicem habeant scientiam?" (particularly "de his quae sunt contingentia de futuro, de quibus praecedit signum in natura, ut in motu caeli vel dispositione elementorum"); Art. V: "Utrum daemones possunt futura praedicere?" ("daemones futura scire possunt corporalia aliquo modo ad cursum naturae ordinata tribus modis, scil. per cursum siderum et per dispositiones rerum naturalium et per revelationem sibi factam"); Art. VII: "Quomodo et qualiter daemones transmutant corpora, utrum scil. corpore assumpto vel alio modo?" (all in *Opera,* ed. Jammy, 16:81–85); Art. IX: "An daemones in suis operibus constellationibus iuventur an non? Et utrum scienta imaginum fiat operatione daemonum an non? (*Opera,* ed. Jammy, 16:87–88); and, last but not least, *Dist.* VIII, Art. V: "Queritur de actibus Angelorum: an boni possunt comedere et mali generare? et unde mali habeant semine suae generationis?" (*Opera,* ed. Jammy, 16:97–98). Among the arguments *quod sic,* Albertus concedes: "Verissime legitur de incubis et succubis daemonibus, et vidimus personas cognitas ab eis et loca in quibus vix unquam per noctem potest dormire vir, quin veniat ad eum daemon succubus. Item, rumor publicus de Merlino filio incubi testatur hoc, ut videtur." Among the arguments *contra* the basic question is whether the semen that permits such a demonic procreation amounts to a real secretion of these spiritual beings or whether the semen can be provided by other means: "Sicut videtur dicere Augustinus, quod accipit semen a pollutis et transfundit, vel facit se succubum uni incubum alteri, et ita transfundit." But in this, physiological problems ensue ("propter longitudinem genitalium vel ineptitudinem evaporat semen in egressu et expirat ab se spiritus, ita quod non sit aptum generationi"); in addition, the thesis that the coitus is necessary in order to cause the female semen to come to the fore is not correct—according to Avicenna. He ascribes such a secretion only to the "motum matricis," therefore in the case of the demon "cum possit matricem movere, videtur quod sit superfluum coire"). As to the *solutio,* Albertus appears to be extraordinarily irresolute: "Nescio secundum veritatem quid dicam, sed hoc videtur probabilius quod succubi sint ad unun et incubi ad alium; tamen verissime ab eo nuper, qui adhuc vivit intellexi, quod dum mollitei vitio subiaceret quodam tempore, infiniti catti circa eum pollutum apparuerunt, maximo ejulatu et strepitu semen lingentes et deportantes." If, therefore, Albertus hesitates to assume bisexuality in the case of the demons, he considers it logical that the wicked fruit excreted in the course of male masturbation provides these demoniacal procreations with the indispensable matter that can be conserved "in vasis seminariis ad tempus" when namely the devils "circumponunt illud seminibus similibus calore naturali" (*Opera,* ed. Jammy, 15:97–98).

24. Note, however, that even an author like Thomas Aquinas (*Summa theologiae*, 1.32), who was to become the model for the most famous and most cruel demonologists of the Renaissance, does not refer directly to the fourth dialogue of *CH*, but to the *Liber XXIV Philosophorum* ("Monas gignit monadem"). This point is stressed by E. Garin, "Ludovico Lazzarelli," *Giornale critico della filosofia italiana* 42 (1963): 280.

25. Cf. Albertus, *II Sententiarum, Dist.* VII, Art. VII; to be specially noted is the reference to this theory that is supposed to explain the bodily changes ascribed to demons: "Quidam philosophi sicut Avicenna in *Libro VI de naturalibus* et Algasel in *Physica* sua, ponunt fascinationes, ita quod anima unius hominis per adspectum vel propinquitatem impediat processus operum alterius hominis virtue spiritualiter egrediente de una anima et operante super alia." Albertus acknowledges only one reservation that can be held against this theory (to which he refers in many other writings)—namely, that the firm belief in God makes the faithful immune: that in fact (to him) "non nocet fascinatio, nec nocere potest ars magica, nec facit aliquid ex his quae de talibus timentur." Since the completion of this paper (1982) I have examined other medieval texts on "fascinatio" in my paper "L'immaginazione e il suo potere. Da al-Kindi, al-Fārābi e Avicenna al Medioevo latino e al Rinascimento," in *Miscellanea Mediaevalia 17: Orientalische Kultur and Europäische Mittelalter* (Berlin and New York; 1985), pp. 188–206.

26. E. Garin, "Ermetismo e antica teologia," *Rivista critica di storia della filosofia*, 28 (1973): 332, insists on the central role of Hermeticism in *De verbo Dei* by Bradwardine; L. Sturlese, "Proclo ed Ermete in Germania da Alberto Magno a Bertoldo di Mosburg," *Von Meister Dietrich zu Meister Eckhart*, ed. K. Flasch (Hamburg, 1984), pp. 22–33. Already Ferguson (*Hermetica* 4.46) stressed that *Asclepius* and another Hermetic text (which could not be located under the title "De mundo et caelo") were used by Bradwardine (who considered the text just mentioned as the source of "De mundo" ascribed to Aristotle), as well as by Bernard Silvester in his "De mundo universitate."

27. Details about these cultural goings-on are well known: suffice it to mention here P. O. Kristeller, *Supplementum Ficinianum*, 2 vols. (Florence, 1937) 1.95,–ff.; idem, "M. Ficino e L. Lazzarelli," *Annali della R. Scuola Normale Superiore di Pisa*, 2d ser., 7 (1938): 243; D. P. Walker, *Spiritual and Demonic Magic: From Ficino to Campanella* (London, 1972), pp. 1–113; E. Garin, "Immagini e simboli in M. Ficino," in *Medioevo e Rinascimento* (Bari, 1954), p. 288; idem, "Nota sull'ermetismo"; Frances Yates, "G. Bruno"; Kristeller, "La diffusione europea del platonismo fiorentino," in *Il pensiero italiano del Rinascimento e il tempo nostro* (Florence, 1971) p. 27. Kristeller concludes that Ficino's translation of Plato and Hermes Trismegistus, as well as his books *De vita* were the most read of his works.

28. *Christianismi restitutio* (1553; reprint, Frankfurt, 1971), pp. 212–13: "Videtur daemon ille Pimander vere docere voluisse, sed Christum ignorasse," quoted by C. Manzoni, *Umanesimo e eresia: Michele Serveto* (Naples, 1974) pp. 104–5; Manzoni then (p. 113, but cf. passim) observes that Servetus criticizes Hermes Trismegistus on account of his insufficient glorification of man.

29. This name given him by the editor Johann Huser in the first corpus of Paracelsian and pseudo-Paracelsian works (Basel, 1583–91) was already noted by A. Rotondò, *Studi e ricerche di storia ereticale italiana del Cinquecento* (Turin, 1974), p. 363 n. 280; as to the existence of "cultured" Hermetical elements passed on by German and Italian humanists, there are conflicting evaluations in regard to their presence in Paracelsus's writings. W. Pagel, *Paracelsus* (Basel, 1956), p. 296, concurs with Peuckert's old monograph and also with Walker (cf. note 27 above), see p. 85. C. Webster, "Paracelsus and Demons: Science as a Synthesis of Popular Belief," in *Scienze, credenze occulte, livelli di cultura* (Florence, 1982), pp. 3–4; idem, *From Paracelsus to Newton: Magic and the Making of Modern Science* (Cambridge, 1983), chap. 4. For later Paracelsism, apart from Rotondò quoted above, see C. Gilly, "Zwischen Erfahrung und Spekulation: Theodor Zwinger und die religiöse und kulturelle Krise seiner Zeit," *Basler Zeitschrift für Geschichte und Altertumskunde* 77 (1977): 57–123; 79 (1979):125–233. Of great interest for Hermeticism at the end of the sixteenth century, see F. Purnell, "F. Patrizi and the Critics of Hermes Trismegistus," *Journal of Medieval and Renaissance Studies* 6 (1976):155–78; idem, "An Addition to F. Patrizi's Correspondence," *Rinascimento*, 2d ser., 18 (1978):135–50; idem, "Hermes and the Sybil: A Note on Ficino's Pimander," *Renaissance Quarterly* 30 (1977):305–10.

30. I have tried to investigate these correspondences, also comparing similar cases in the Aristotelian school (mainly for Pomponazzi). See "Il problema della magia naturale nel Rinascimento," *Rivista critica di storia della filosofia* 28 (1973): 271–ff.; also in French translation with an appendix of documents in "Magia astrologia e religione nel Rinascimento," in *Convegno polacco-italiano* (Wrocław, 1974) [= Accademia Polacca delle Scienze in Roma, Conferenze, 65], pp. 48–82.

31. R. M. Volterrano, *Commentariorum urbanorum libri XXXVIII* (Lyon, 1552), col. 680.

32. Walker, *Spiritual and Demonic Magic*, pp. 60–ff.

33. "Neoplatonism and Active Principles: Newton and the Corpus Hermeticum", in *Hermeticism and the Scientific Revolution*, ed. R. S. Westman and J. E. McQuire, papers read at a Clark Library

Seminar, 9 March 1974. (Los Angeles, 1977), pp. 126–27. Cf. review by B. P. Copenhaver in *Annals of Science* 35 (1978): 527–31.

34. "Reappraisals in Renaissance Science," *History of Science* 16 (1978): 201: "The relation of Bruno to the history of Science plays a relatively small role in Yates's book and the attentive reader will find that she focuses rather upon other issues, e.g., symbolic, occult, political and religious ones, and touches upon Bruno's role in science only in passing." Cf. ibid., p. 203: "While symbols may well play a role in scientific discovery from time to time, they have little to do with finished formulations of science . . . The real difficulty dealing with symbols is that their use goes specifically against the ideal precision which has always been one of the chief criteria of any valid science"; p. 208: "In my view it still remains to be shown that hermeticism ever functioned as an important, independent world-view in the Renaissance"; and finally, p. 206, where Schmitt takes up and emphasizes McGuire's theory concerning the dependent relationship between Hermeticism and Neoplatonism. Schmitt's survey of the preceding discussions is very thorough and useful.

35. P. Zambelli, "Platone, Ficino e la magia," in *Studia humanitatis: Ernesto Grassi zum 70. Geburtstag* (Munich, 1973), pp. 121–42.

36. E. Peters, *The Magician, the Witch and the Law* (Hassocks/Sussex, 1978), p. 90. According to Guillaume d'Auvergne, "the Advent of Christianity condemns all magic except natural magic to the status of maleficia."

37. *De legibus,* chap. 24; 67–69: While he treats of "corruptio humanae naturae" from which emerges "prostitutio curiositatis," he dwells on "idolatria naturalis . . . sicut curiositas quae est fornicatio prostitutae virtutis nostrae et voluptuositas sive luxuria, fornicatio virtutis concupiscibilis nostrae . . . quia igitur fornicationes duarum aliarum virium [animae], quas novimus, naturales sunt, hoc est ex nativa seu innata nobis corruptione procedentes." Having enumerated various forms of such prophetic idolatry, he proposes his definition: "Et de operibus huiusmodi est *magia naturalis* quam necromantiam seu philosophicam philosophi vocant, licet multum improprie, et est totius licentiae naturalis pars undecima" (69-2D).

38. *Epistola de secretis operibus artis et naturae* in Bacon, *Opera quaedam hactenus inedita,* ed. by J. S. Brewer (Wiesbaden, 1965), p. 523.

39. R. Carton, *L'expérience physique de Roger Bacon* (Paris, 1921), p. 177; also cf. pp. 168, 178, in regard to the distinctive terms Bacon uses for these secret sciences, in "Metaphysica," in his "Opus maius," "Opus Tertium." See also T. Gregory, "Il Duecento," in *Storia della Filosofia diretta da M. Dal Pra,* 10 vols. (Milan, 1976), 6:185–94.

40. *De legibus* chap. 26; 85-1AB.

41. *Epistola,* p. 523: "Humana natura est magis Dea et maioris divinitate naturaliter erit, quam huiusmodi statuae [. . .], non solum erit Dea humana natura, sed etiam deifica." This position of Bacon, more so than that of Guillaume d'Auvergne, is close to a text of the unpublished "Polychronicon" by Ralph Ridge, a Benedictine from Chester monastery who lived about 1340: "sensus naturae, quae est una de radicibus magiae naturalis." This would constitute an alternative to God's miraculous powers. See Owst, "Sortilegium in English Homiletic Literature of the Fourteenth Century," in *Studies Presented to Sir Hilary Jenkinson,* ed. J. Conway Davies (London, 1957), p. 287.

42. *Epistola,* p. 538; cf. pp. 535, 532–33: "Narrabo igitur nunc primo opera artis et naturae miranda, ut postea et modum eorum assignem, in quibus nihil magicum est; ut videatur quod omnis magica potestas sit inferior his operibus et indigna." This methodological explanation introduces some technological miracles "per figuram et rationem solius artis," i.e., plans for navigation and aeronautics that are to replace human propulsion. But this explanation is immediately preceded by an attack against books on necromancy: "Qui nec artis, nec naturae continent potestatem, sed figmenta magicorum . . . Nam si quis in aliquo illorum opus naturae vel artis inveniat, illud accipiat; si non, relinquat velut suspectum et sicut indignum est sapienti et illicitum magica pertractare, sic superfluum est, nec est necessarium." Bacon continues the subject when he comments on the "Secretum secretorum," in *Opera hactenus inedita,* 16 vols., ed. Robert Steele (Oxford, 1920), 5:6–7, and controverts witchcraft in a harder than usual form of expression. Witchcraft is transferred from the parents to their children: "Ulterius procedit demencia mathematicorum falsorum sine apparicione daemonum *nec est ars, nec natura* . . . errores vetularum sortilegarum et virorum similiter. Nam edocti fuerunt primitus a magicis et matres docent filias et patres docent filios."

43. *Epistola,* p. 524: "In his vero omnibus nec philosophica consideratio considerat, nec ars, nec potestas naturae consistit. Sed praeter haec est nequior occupatio, quando homines contra leges philosophiae et contra omnem rationem spiritus invocant nefarios, ut per eos suam compleant voluntatem. Et in hoc est error, quod credunt sibi subjici spiritus, ut ipsi cogant humana virtute; hoc enim est impossibile, quia vis humana longe inferior est quam spirituum. Atque in hoc magis oberrant huiusmodi homines, quod per aliquas res naturales quibus utuntur, credunt vel advocare vel fugare spiritus. Et adhuc erratur, quando per invocationes et deprecationes et sacrificia nituntur homines eos

placere, et adducere pro utilitate vocantium." Ibid., 531: "Multi igitur libri cavendi sunt propter carmina et characteres et orationes et coniurationes et sacrificia et huiusmodi quia pure magici sunt."

44. Ibid., pp. 542–43 (where directly following, the *Secretum secretorum* is cited); ibid., p. 530, a particularly lucid example showing that Bacon agreed with the imagination theory of Avicenna: "Natura enim corporis (ut Avicenna docet . . .) obedit cogitationibus et vehementibus desideriis animae; immo nulla operatio hominis fit, nisi per hoc quod virtus naturalis in membris obedit cogitationibus et desideriis animae. Nam (sicut Avicenna docet tertio Metaphysicae) primum movens est cogitatio, deinde desiderium conformatum cogitationi, postea virtus naturalis in membris, quae obedit cogitationi et desiderio; et hoc in malo (ut dictum est) et in bono similiter."

45. Compare Ficino, *Commentaire sur le Banquet de Platon*, ed. R. Marcel (Paris, 1956), p. 220 (6.10); Pico, "Conclusiones magicae," in: *Opera*, Basileae, 1575, conclusio 10, and *Oratio de dignitate hominis*, p. 152, cf. also my commentary in "Platone, Ficino e la magia," pp. 130–ff.

46. *Metaphysica* 9.3.2; *Opera*, ed. Jammy, 3:405, col. 2: In a context, in which the movement of the heavens is defined as being natural and not artificial ("artificialis"), Albert observes that the latter "non est a natura, sed a principio naturae minister artifex, sicut est medicus et alchimicus aliquando." Cf. *Summa theologiae* 2.8.30; ed. Jammy cit. 18.176, 180 defends in the same *quaestio* 30 the "magia naturalis," which is founded on the Augustinian "rationes seminales." ("Adhuc Augustinus in Glossa magna: 'Insunt rebus corporeis elementa mundi per omnia quaedam occultae seminariae rationes' . . . Si ergo per incantationes magorum, per semina indita virgis, virgae proruperunt in serpentes modis et finibus illorum debitis et tale opus verum est et naturale, etiam vera et naturalia fuerunt opera magorum, et propter modum quia subito fecerunt, vera miracula sunt dicenda") and in his detailed description of witchcraft based on the interpretation of Canon Episcopi: "Daemones quaedam futura praedicunt et quaedam mira faciunt, quibus homines alliciunt et seducunt. Unde quaedam mulierculae post Satanam conversae, daemonum illusionibus et phantasmatibus seductae, credunt se et profitentur nocturnis horis cum Diana Paganorum dea, vel Herodiade, vel Minerva et innumera mulierum multitudine equitare. Ipse namque Satanas, qui transfigurat se in Angelum lucis, cum mentem cuiusque mulierculae ceperit, et hanc sibi per infidelitatem subiugaverit, illico transformat se in diversarum personarum species ac similitudines: et mentem quam captivam tenet in somnio deludens, modo laeta, modo tristia, modo cognitas, modo incognitas personas ostendens, per devia quaeque deducit. Et cum solus hoc patitur spiritus infidelis, non in animo tantum, sed et in corpore evenire opinatur. Idcirco nimis stultus et hebes est, qui haec omnia qua in spiritu fiunt, etiam accidere in corpora arbitratur." Like prophets and apostles, witches only "in spiritu, non in corpore tales visiones viderunt" (p. 18.1).

47. E. Rice (who continues to work on his research) reported on this still unpublished work, handed down in two manuscripts and a short fragment, in *The Prefatory Epistles of Jacques Lefèvre d'Etaples* (New York, 1976), p. 118 n. 7; and in the article "The 'De magia naturali' of Jacques Lefèvre d'Etaples," in *Philosophy and Humanism: Renaissance Essays in Honor of P. O. Kristeller*, ed. E. P. Mahoney (New York, 1976), pp. 19–29. The date of origin of this work, as well as the date of the visit to Pico in the spring of 1492 have been established by A. Renaudet, *Préréforme et humanisme* (Paris, 1953), pp. 142, 153 n. 6, 668. It is probable that during the course of such a visit to Florence, Lefèvre learned nothing about the criticism of astrology and other such heathenlike "vanities," which was being worked out by Giovanni Pico at that time (the only surviving documents thereof are the *Disputationes adversus astrologiam,* which were first published by Gianfrancesco Pico in 1496, namely after the completion of *De magia naturali*). The "Disputationes" of Pico was soon to cause different reactions in France, starting with the long epistle of Robert Gaguin to Wilhelmus Hermannus, an Augustinian canon, of 16 September 1496, against the astrologers, "saepenumero ad magiam se convertentes" (*Epistolae et orationes*, 2 vols., ed. Louis Thuasne [Paris, 1904], 1:26–35) and continuing up to the contemporary document, which Thuasne refers to in a note, i.e., the "Invectiva contra astrologos" by Thomas Murner, published in 1499 in Strasbourg. Concerning an older document written against the astrologers (Jean de Bruges, 1484; Paris, bibl. Mazarine, MS 3893) ibid. cit., I, 39; cf. H. de Lubac, *Jean Pic de la Mirandole: Etudes et discussions* (Paris, 1974), chaps. 4 and 5, pp. 307–32. However, Lefèvre expresses a strong belief in astrology also in his edition of the "Pseudo-Dionysius" in 1499. Therefore, it cannot be traced back to his reading of Pico's "Disputationes" alone, if he rethinks the question of the occult sciences, but that is still to be explained.

48. A. Horowitz, *Michael Hummelberger* (Berlin, 1875), pp. 39–40, quotes a letter from Hummelberger to Christophorus Sertorius, which, in the year 1512, makes a reference to that judgment "a praeceptore meo Jacobo Fabro Stapulensi olim accepi nullam scilicet magiam esse bonam, figmentum etiam ullam esse naturalem," cited by Rice, *Prefatory Epistles,* p. 120.

49. Recently, two editions of this dialogue have been published, along with the corresponding translations into English and French by A. Rijper in *Anagrom* 5/6 (1974): 1–54; and in the monograph of B. P. Copenhaver, *S. Champier and the Reception of the Occultist Tradition in Renaissance France* (The Hague, 1978), pp. 243–330. In regard to Champier's Hermetic edition, see C. Vasoli, "Temi e fonti

della tradizione ermetica in uno scritto di S. Champier," in *Umanesimo e esoterismo,* ed. E. Castelli (Padua, 1960).

50. Cf. F. Secret, *Les Kabbalistes chrétiens de la Renaissance* (Paris, 1964), chap. 4 and passim; L. Spitz, *The Christian Reformation of the German Humanists* (Cambridge, Mass., 1963), chap. 4; idem, "The 'Theologia platonica' in the Religious Thought of the German Humanists," in *Middle Ages-Renaissance-Volkskunde: Feschrift J. G. Kunstmann,* University of North Carolina Studies in the Germanic Languages, no. 26 (Chapel Hill, 1959), pp. 118–33. In the expectation of the critical edition of *De occulta philosophia* by Agrippa (on which Vittoria Perrone Compagni is working, continuing a project that I outlined in my dissertation about Agrippa, discussed with Professor Eugenio Garin of the University of Florence in 1958), I quote a few examples from this dissertation to show the influence on the first edition (Würzburg, Universitätsbibliothek, cod. M.ch.q.50, henceforth cited as W) of Agrippa by *De verbo mirifico* and on the final version published in 1553 in Cologne, also by *De arte Kabbalistica,* writings of Reuchlin that contain not only cabalistic matters but also numerous classical and Platonic-Florentine quotes. *De verbo mirifico* (Lyon, 1551), p. 213 (2:21) resumes the Hermetic "magnum miraculum est homo," cited passim in *De occulta philosophia; De verbo mirifico,* 218–19 (2:21) quotes Vergil's verse "Igneus est ollis vigor," also cited in *De occulta philosophia,* 1.7, in Agrippa, *Opera* (Lyon, 1600), (Ferguson, edition IV), 1.13, where the Zoroastrian rule is taken up again; "barbara et antiqua verba" not translated in the magical ritual other Zoroastrian quotes are to be found in Reuchlin as well as in the first version W of Agrippa: W III, 4 = *De verbo mirifico,* III, 7; W III, 42 = III, 55; W.III, 45 = iii, 58. The most exemplary case is the one in which those ancient wise men are enumerated who used natural magic, the list starting with Plinius, 31.1–6, to Ficinus and Picus, (*Oratio,* note 8, 150) from which Agrippa derives material (*De occulta philosophia,* 3; I, 2 = W.I, 2) especially in *De verbo mirifico* 92, where also the names of the younger and more dubious magicians are listed (Robert of Sareshel, Roger Bacon, Pietro d'Abano and *Picatrix*), added by Agrippa in the second version (Epistle to Trithemius).

51. H. Fertig, *Neues aus dem literarischen Nachlasse des Humanisten Johannes Butzbach (Piemontanus),* (Würzburg, Programm d. k. Neuen Gymnasiums, 1906–7), which gives a detailed description of the handwritten works (pp. 25–ff.) as well as a correct biography of this Benedictine who started as a tailor and then became a student of Trithemius's literary history, later carrying on this work himself (cf. K. Rühl, *Das "Aktuarium de scriptoribus ecclesiasticis" des J. Butzbach,* Bonn, 1937). In the quoted *Macrostroma,* in *Microstroma,* in which Butzbach sings Trithemius in verses (fol. 54r: "doctrina exundans ut Trismegistus erat"), and finally in the section of his "Apologia ad Johannem Trithemium" which refers to this work (ed. by H. Fertig, cited above, pp. 76–78, from Bonn UB, Cod. S 358), Butzbach proves himself to be a valuable source for the ideas and fate of Trithemius in the years that directly follow the crisis at Sponheim. The three works—of which the *Macrostroma* is the first and by far the most interesting—were actually written in short succession during the year 1508. Fertig (p. 70), had already emphasized that certain sections of the "Apologia" were literally dependent on the letters of Giovanni Pico to Poliziano and to Paolo Cortesi, in Pico, *Opera,* 2 vols. (Basel, 1557), 1:364–65. See also the "Epistola sive tractatus de differentia sive qualitate stili" (Cologne, Historisches Archiv, MS W 8°, 352, fol. 166v–166r), where both Picos as well as Ermolao Barbaro and Lefèvre "in triplici lingua orator doctissimus/philosophus diviniloquus qui plurima culto/ edidit in sacros libros commenta stilo" appeared. In addition, Erasmus, philosopher, orator and author without comparison, neither in Italy nor in France, and among the frequently quoted Germans, Trithemius, Reuchlin "triplici sermone politus" and Cardinal Cusanus, mentioned for his Vulgar and Latin works; also: Murmelius, Hermann van den Busch, Ortwin Gratius (still among the famous men "clari"), Peutinger, Alexander Hegius, Rudolphus Agricola, Bebel and—despite an only recently past polemic with his friend and master, Trithemius—Jacob Wimpfeling. See also P. Richter, "Die Schriftsteller der Benediktinerabtei Maria-Laach," *Westdeutsche Zeitschrift für Geschichte und Kunst* 17 (1898): 314–31, on Butzbach.

52. The episode is discussed by F. W. Roth, "Studien zum J. Trithemius—Jubeljahr (1516)," *Studien und Mitteilungen zur Geschichte des Benediktiner ordens* 37 (1916): 267–73; by K. Arnold, *J. Trithemius (1462–1516), (Quellen und Forschungen zur Geschichte des Bistums u. Hochstifts Würzburg,* 23 = Würzburg, 1971), pp. 203–8. [This is an excellent biography and an important work on the MSS, not to be overlooked in any future research dealing with this author, as recently happened in a work by N. L. Brann, *The Abbott Trithemius (1462–1516): The Renaissance of Monastic Humanism* (Leiden, 1981), pp. 31–53.] It is difficult to assess the gravity of the plot organized by the prior of Sponheim, Nicholaus von Remich, who is mentioned by Trithemius and Butzbach; Nicholaus exploited the scandal caused by a letter written in 1499 by Trithemius to Arnold de Bost, a Carmelite in Gand: this letter summarized and announced the first occult work just written by Trithemius, the *Steganografia.* The letter, upon the death of its recipient, made its way to the Gand monastery, only to be intercepted by the abbot; it most certainly enjoyed wide circulation, a fact documented in a number

of manuscripts. One of these originated from the hand of J. Reuchlin (London, British Library, Add. MS 11416, fols. 200v–202r), together with an unknown and unpublished letter about Johannes Mercurius from Correggio, which prompted an extremely harsh judgment from Trithemius. It is taken up in his *Chronicon Hirsaugiense*, in *Opera historica* 2 vols. (St. Gallen, 1690), 2:584. In this document there is a parallel to his famous letter to J. Virdung of Haßfurt, in which he severely attacks the historical Faust and emphasizes his intolerance of these prophets and popular seers.

53. *Macrostroma* (Bonn UB, cod. S 357, fol. 92r): "non intelligentes, nec intelligere volentes eum de naturali magia ibi agere, quam non parvo intersticio sicut et doctissimus ille Picus dudum ab impia et scelesta differre [et] separari fortissimis rationibus et multorum testimonio elegantissime edocet. Nam 'duplicem esse magiam' nemo, qui ipsius Pici 'Apologiam' legerit: 'inficiabitur,' quarum altera inquit— demonum toto opere et auctoritate constat, res medius fidius execranda et portentosa; altera nichil est aliud cum bene exploratur quam naturalis philosophiae absoluta consummatio" the section quoted from "Apologia" corresponds to Pico, *Opera*, 1:80. Butzbach also adopts Pico's topical enumeration of the magi and wise men of antiquity (Pythagoras, Empedocles, Democritos, Plato "who went on journeys in order to learn magic," Zalmoxides, Abbaris Yperboreus, Oromasis's son Zoroaster, Karondas, Damigeron, Apollonius Tyanaeus, Osthanes, Dardanus, Homer, Eudoxus, Hermippus) and of some "iunores" who had only a limited knowledge ("olfecerint") like al-Kindi, Roger Bacon, Guillaume d'Auvergne; in addition, Antonio Vinciguerra alias Chronicus, a Venetian diplomat, probably mentioned in such august company by Pico in order to gain support from the Roman court. Shortly after that (fol. 92v) Butzbach adopts from Pico's "Apologia" (pp. 81, 112) the definition of natural magic that is ascribed to Guillaume somewhat par force ("Guilhelmus Parisiensis episcopus, coetaneus Roberti Linconiensis qui dicit quod magi prohibiti dicuntur magi quasi mali, quare mala faciunt; magi autem naturales dicuntur magi quasi magni, quia magna faciunt.") He cites Guillaume's "De universo" to relegate in Egypt the prohibited magic "quia ibi vigebat cultus daemonum," the good one in Ethiopia and India, where there exists an abundance of herbs and other substances effective in natural magic. He assigns Pico's thesis that magic is "pars scientiae naturalis" to Guillaume's other work, "De legibus." Then Butzbach refers to an extraordinarily distinguished personality in the Germanic church tradition, Albertus Magnus, who is, however, considered by many to have been in error in regard to magic to the same extent as Trithemius: "Hanc naturalem magiam vir catholicus et sanctus Albertus Magnus se dicit esse secutum et experientiis in ea multa comperisse, quamobrem apud vulgus iners, quod omnia in sinistrum facilius interpretatur, nicromanticus dicitur fuisse. Quod et Trithemius iste noster . . . sibi quandoque perspicuum habuit evenire. Sic enim ad Bostium scribens sit: "Hec ideo dixerim, ut si forte aliquando ad te rumor aliquis pervenerit, me scilicet impossibilia posse, non me magum [*supple: malum*], sed philosophum existimes. Nam quod Alberto Magno, profundissimo naturalium rerum scrutatori contingit, ut propter miranda quae occulte virtute naturae operatus est, magus a vulgo sit habitus, michi similiter contingere posse certum sum." The comparison between Trithemius and Albertus Magnus is again continued in fol. 94r: "Similiter cum legant Albertum inter experimenta magiae multum temporis consumpsisse, de magia naturali hoc intelligant, non de prohibita, ne exemplo tanti viri illi [magiae experimento] se dedant, quo illi licuit, sibi quoque licere praesumentes. Cum itaque Trithemium nostrum, quem in manibus habemus, mirabilia exercere vel scire scimus, audimus et legimus, non ea *per magiam* nicromanciam, sed per naturalem fieri credamus." The same comparison in Wolfgang Treffler, "Epistola D.no Wolfgango de Solms," 21 July 1508; ed. Ziegelbauer-Legipontanus in *Historia litteraria O.S.B.* (Augsburg-Würzburg, 1754), 1:493: "Sed ut Trithemius licentius excusare possis, magnus ille Albertus tibi prima fronte occurrat, cui non nihil superstitiositatis quoque ascribitur, quod ipse etiam vel nunc vita functus suum esse negabat." About Treffler, see Pertz's Archiv, 2 (1820), 239–44; Catalogus librorum MSS Bibliothecae Bodleianae D.Thomae Phillipps, A.D. 1837, 8 Nr. 705 (see now Berlin, Staatsbibliothek Preussischer Kulturbesitz, cod. Lat. fol. 666); AN., "Aus dem Gelehrten Freundeskreis des Abts Trithemius," in *Historisch-politische Blätter* 77:923–ff.; D. König, "Mainzer Chronisten: W. Treffler" (Göttingen, 1880) (*Histor. Kommission bei d. K. Akademie d. Wissenschaften/Forschungen z. Dt. Geschichte*, 20) 40–ff.

54. Quoted above, note 27. The great merit of this book is to have pursued, in a pioneering way, the entire discussion on magic even in the demonological writings of Wier, Erastus, Bodin, Del Rio, and particularly in the Aristotelian theories. It deals with Trithemius (pp. 86–90), and considers it highly probable that Trithemius carried out magic feats "with the help of planetary angels." Starting with the "Steganographia" and the paper "De septem secundeis" (both considered "dangerous demonic Magic" by Bouelles, Wier, and Del Rio), Walker distinguishes the first two cryptographic books from book 3 (ed. Heidel, Nurnberg 1721, p. 310), which prescribes "fac imaginem ex cera vel pinge in chartam novam figuram Orifielis in modum viri barbati et nudi; stantis super taurum varii coloris, habentis in dextra librum et in sinistram calamum," in order to address, at an astrologically propitious time, a magic prayer to them. Walker's interpretation was reviewed by E. Garin, "La magia da Ficino a Campanella," *Giornale critico della filosofia italiana* 39 (1960): 156–57; cf. K. A. Nowotny, ed., *H. C.*

Agrippa de occulta philosophia (Graz, 1967), p. 429. Of different opinion is W. Shumaker, *Renaissance Curiosa* (Binghamton, N.Y., 1982) pp. 91ff.

55. It is noteworthy that the *topos* ascribed to Plotinus is taken up again by Butzbach, but is not emphasized, "ubi naturae ministrum et non arteficem magum demonstrat" (*Macrostroma*, see note 52, fol. 92*r;* Pico, *Opera*, 1:81). Also he reverts time and time again to the theme of sympathy developed already in Ficinus's "De amore." It is on this basis that the magician makes full use of the peculiarities that are hidden in nature by means of certain enticements ("illecebrae") "in mundi recessibus, in naturae gremio, in promptuariis Dei latitantia miracula, quasi ipsa [Natura] sit artifex, promit in publicum. Et sicut agricola ulives vitibus, ita magus terram caelo, id est inferiora superiorum dotibus virtutibusque maritat . . . Neque enim ad religionem, ad Dei cultum quidquam promovet magis quam assidua contemplatio mirabilium Dei, que ut per hanc de quo agimus *naturalem magiam* bene exploraverimus in Opificis cultum amoremque ardentius animati illud canere compellemur" (*Macrostroma*, fol. 92*r*).

56. *Polycraticus*, 2 vols., ed. C. C. J. Webb (London, 1909), 1:9–10, 14; 2:26–28. *Materials towards a History of Witchcraft*, 2d ed., ed. A. C. Howland (New York, 1957), pp. 127–28; cf. E. Peters, *The Magician*, pp. 46–50, passim. See also Heinrich von Langenstein, *Unterscheidung der Geister*, ed. by Th. Hohmann (Munich, 1977).

57. P. Diepgen, "Arnaldus de Villanova: De improbatione maleficorum," *Archiv für Kulturgeschichte* 9 (1911): 385–403; Arnaldus, *Opera* (Lyon, 1532), fols. 123*r*–130*r* ("De parte operativa"), fols. 215*v*, 290*r*–292*v*, 295*v*.

58. Cf. note 24 above.

59. *Opus epistolarum Erasmi*, 12 vols., ed. P. S. Allen (Oxford, 1906), 1:336–40. Letter no. 143 to Antonius de Bergen (Paris, 14 January 1501) reports in great detail on a case about which he had learned in the previous year at Meugn-sur-Loire: A necromant about to die entrusted to his wife forbidden books he had in his house. She was to give them to a priest and accomplice at Orléans who held ceremonies "non insciente uxore, filia quoque virgine etiam adiutante." Erasmus provides, though secondhand, one of the most precise reports on the ceremonies ascribed to witch masters in which Church rites were used.

60. *La Strega: Prelezione alle "Priora" di Aristotele*, ed. Isidoro Del Lungo (Florence, 1864), p. 184: "Vicinus quoque adhuc faesulano rusculo meo Lucens Fonticulus est . . . ubi sedem esse nunc quoque Lamiarum narrant mulierculae, quaecumque aquarum ventitant . . . Sed enim Lamia heec quoties domo egreditur, oculos sibi suos affigit vagaturque per fora, per plateas, per quadrivia, per angiportus, per delubra, per thermas, per ganeas, per conciliabula omnia; circumspectatque singula, scrutatur, indagat, nihil tam bene texeris ut eam lateat. . . . Semper domi caeca, semper foris oculata. Quaeras forsitan, domi quid agitet? sessitat lanam faciens atque interim cantillat. Vidistine, obsecro, unquam, Lamias ista, viri florentini, quae se et sua nesciunt, alios et aliena speculantur?" The ironic image that has its origin in Plutarch's saying that witches have artificial eyes concludes with facetious polemics against those who do not believe in the philosophical vocation germinating in the poet Poliziano.

61. Cf. Zambelli (note 35), p. 136 n. 23.

62. *Macrostroma* (Bonn, U.B., cod. p. 357), fols. 90*v*–91*r:* "Utriusque [magiae] cum greci meminerint, illam magiae nullo modo [ms: minus] nomine dignantes, γoητείαν nuncupant, hanc propria peculiarique nuncupatione μαγείαν, quasi perfectam summamque scientiam vocant. Idem enim, ut ait Porphirius, Persarum lingua magus sonat apud nos divinorum interpres et cultor: magna aut immo maxima inter has artes disparilitas [ms: disparitas] et dissimilitudo. Illam non modo christiana religio, sed omnes leges, omnis bene instituta respublica damnat et execrat. Hanc omnes sapientes, caelestium et divinarum rerum studiosae nationes approbant et amplectuntur. Illa arcium fraudulentissima, haec altior sanctiorque philosophia; illa irrita et vana, haec firma, fidelis et solida; illam quisquis coluit semper dissimulavit, quia in auctores esset ignominiam et contumeliam; ex hac summa literarum claritas et gloria antiquitus et pene semper petita." Cf. Pico, (n. 45). An indication as to the disquieting presence of the scandal initiated by the "Steganographia," as well as by the letter cited above, through which Arnold de Bost was notified in advance, can be recognized in Butzbach's mention of this; namely, the course of events that forced Trithemius to abdicate as abbot of Sponheim. On fol. 89*r*, after having given a brief summary of the work still in the process of writing, Butzbach criticizes his contemporaries: They may be noble and well educated, but there are many "qui existimant ista impossibilia et supernaturalia exclamant. His ipse et omnibus nobis multa naturaliter esse possibilia, quae vires nescientibus impossibilia et supernaturalia videntur." As Trithemius wrote to Bost, "Sunt omnia pure naturalia sine deceptione aliqua, sine suspicione, sine magica, sine invocatione aut mysterio spirituum quarumcumque. Haec ideo [Trithemius] dixit, ut si forte aliquando ad eum rumor perveniret eum scire impossibilia, non eum magum, sed philosophum existimaret. Quod equidem et nos idem de se sentire voluit. Nam quod Alberto Magno profundissimo naturalium rerum scrutator contingit, ut propter miranda quae occulta virtute operatus est magus a vulgo sit habitus." Apart from

the famous letter (published in *Polygraphia* as early as 1518 in Basel, pp 240ff.), Trithemius developed the idea that Albertus Magnus was his famous and saintly precursor in the natural magic in *De septem secundeis* (Cologne, 1567), pp. 89–ff.

63. Cf. note 54 above; see also D. P. Walker, *The Ancient Theology*, pp. 80–ff.

64. It is to be noted that Butzbach knows about Pico's change of opinion in regard to astrology; however, he does not attach the right value to it: "Sic Picus contra astrologos probe insurgens, iam vita functus a quodam astrologiae professore [Lucio Bellanti] carpitur."

65. Pico, "Conclusiones," in *Opera*, 10, p. 79 (no. 7).

66. Ibid., p. 90 (no. 72).

67. Ibid., p. 79 (no. 19).

68. Ibid., p. 80 (no. 24).

69. Cf. notes 47–48 for Lefèvre. For Francesco Giorgio Veneto, cf. V. Perrone Compagni, "Una fonte di C. Agrippa: Il 'De Harmonia Mundi' di F. Zorzi," *Annali dell' Instituto di Filosofia* 4 (1982):45–74, with extensive bibliography. For Postel, see F. Secret, *Bibliographie des Mss. de G. Postel* (Geneva, 1970); and M. Leathers Kuntz, *G. Postel, Prophet of the Restitution of All Things: His Life and Thought* (The Hague, 1981). For Michael Servetus and Paracelsus, see note 28 above; and K. Goldammer, *Paracelsus Studies* (Klagenfurt, 1954), pp. 42–66; idem, ed., *Paracelsus, Theologische u. religionsphilosophische Schriften* (Wiesbaden, 1955–73). For Bruno; cf. Yates,; and A. Mercati, *Il sommario del processo di G. Bruno* (Vatican City, 1942); cf. L. Firpo, "Il processo di G. Bruno," *Rivista storica italiana* 60 (1958); 61 (1959). For Campanella, see idem, *Ricerche campanelliane* (Florence, 1947), pp. 137–ff.; idem and N. Badaloni's papers in *L'opera e il pensiero di Giovanni Pico della Mirandola*, 2 vols. (Florence, 1965), 2:363–ff., and 373–ff. Still valid is L. Blanchet, *Tommaso Campanella* (Paris, 1920), pp. 193–225.

70. I prefer not to join the intense discussions as to the reality of the so-called Sabbath meetings. But even if those were different from the fantasies of collective unconsciousness—cf. N. Cohn, *Europe's Inner Demons* (London, 1975), pp. 223–ff. and 258–63—involved here are always phenomena difficult to grasp. They originate just as much in the religious sphere as they do in the sexual and depth-psychological spheres.

71. S. P. Burke, "G. F. Pico and His Strix," in *The Damned Art*, ed. S. Anglo (London, 1977), pp. 32–ff. Ibid., pp. 53–ff. and 76–ff. C. Baxter's papers on Weyer and Bodin.

72. "Sorcellerie, sottise ou révolution mentale?" [1948], in Febvre, *Au coeur religieux du XVIe siècle* (Paris, 1957), pp. 301–9.

73. For G. F. Pico, see Burke, for the Aristotelian Nifo, see P. Zambelli, "I problemi filosofici del necromante A. Nifo," *Medioevo* 1 (1975): 129–17; idem., "Une réincarnation de Jean Pic à l'époque de Pomponazzi," *Abhandlungen der Akad. der Wiss. u. Lit. in Mainz*, Geistes-und Sozialwissenshe Freiche Klesse, Jahrgeng 10 (1977); idem, "Una disputa filosofica ereticale proposta nelle Università Padane," *Il Rinascimento nelle corti padane* (Bari, 1977), pp. 499–528; idem, "Aut Diabolus aut Achillinus," *Rinascimento*, 3d ser., 18 (1978): 59–86.

74. *De occulta Philosophia* ([Cologne,] 1533), fol. a6r: "ut vulgaria vulgaribus, altiora vero et arcana altioribus atque secretis tantum communices amicis." Charles de Bouelles, who in 1504 had visited Trithemius at Sponheim, will charge him on account of the necromantic content of his "Steganographia" only several years later ("Ep. Germano Ganaio, ex S. Quintino, 8 Martii 1509," in C. Bovillus, *Opera* [Amboise, 1510], fols. 172v–73r). Trithemius admired Cusanus and his follower and had voluntarily submitted the work to Bouelles. Cf. Trithemius, "Epistolae familiares," 1:39, in idem, *Opera historica*, 1:476. On 22 August 1505 (at the height of the abbot's crisis) Trithemius writes on his own initiative to Bouelles, reminds him of the two weeks he had spent as guest, and praises his style of thought: "Quoniam veterum more doctorum solidus es et veritatis enucleator lucidus, neque verborum multiplicatione superfluus, neque deficientia in his quae fuerint necessaria recisus. Ea quae De intellectu scripsisti et mihi complacuerunt et multis. Continent enim vera Christianorum theologiam, puram et absolutam, quae menti cognitionem et affectui confert summi boni desiderium, consistens in se pura, integra et candida . . . sapientiam praestans parvulis." Bouelles, on his part, takes up Trithemius's magic numerology and his theory concerning the seven "Secundeis" or planetary angels in two letters of 1508 addressed to Ganay (*Opera*, fols. 171v–72r). But Bouelles betrayed his host's trust and denounced him in March 1509, thus even before the letter quoted wherein Trithemius, on 8 April 1510, accepts the dedication of Agrippa's "De occulta philosophia" (cf. CLM 4392, fol. 5r–v). Not to mention the letter of 20 June 1515 to Germain de Genay—recently published by K. Arnold, "Ergänzungen zum Briefwechsel des J. Trithemius" in *Studien und Mitteilungen zur Geschichte des Benediktiner Ordens* 83 (1972):185, 203–4—there the dedication of the *Polygraphia* (printed with the exact intention to produce a cryptography, this time without necromantic appendixes) is combined, in a polemical manner, with the criticisms broadcast in France by Bouelles. "Verum ne quis Bovillo similis

artis huius archana, quae leges naturae christianaeque fidei normas nec excedunt, nec offendunt, in aliquo non intelligens, propterea quod enigmatibus involuta cernuntur, aut pravis demonum artibus aut supersticiosis ascriberet vanitatibus . . . conscripsi, quod Clavem Polygraphiae praenotavi . . . nihil peto abs te, nihil requiro a Bovillo, nisi quod iustum est, decens et honestum. Non sum inimicus hominis, neque iniurias mihi factas in eum contumeliose retorquere, ut possem, disposui, sed innocentiam meam plano atque veraci demonstrare sermonem. Steganographiam vero meam, de qua non recte intellecta Bovillus omnem de me male ac false suspicionis materiam sumpsit." Unfortunately he cannot send it to Ganay because he does not have a scribe at his disposal. Trithemius protested publicly, particularly in the prefatory remarks of the *Polygraphia* and that with clear allusions to the "Bovillina societas." According to K. Arnold's data, (pp. 183–84), Trithemius wrote a real "Apologeticus in Bovillum" in two books: the first was to refute Bouelles's letter to Ganay (cf. Bovillus, *Opera*, p. 172 n. 75); the second one for discussion and in order to convince those who might have given credence to his lies, was put by Trithemius on the last list, prepared in 1514, of his own works. (In the prefatory to the *Polygraphia* of 1516 he mentions, however, only one book.) Arnold observes that Bouelles may have been stirred into action by Trithemius's letter to Bost, which deals with the *Steganographia,* and which in the previous years had been widely circulated and had had an aura of scandal about it. See also Braun, *The Abbot Trithemius,* pp. 29–31, 44–45, 266–67.

75. Yates, *G. Bruno,* pp. 145–ff.

76. After the unhappy episode of the *Steganographia* and of the corresponding letter to Bost in 1499, there is a series of letters in which Trithemius begins to present his magic convictions by means of frequently repeated numerological concepts. It is appropriate to mention Libanius Gallus's works and the correspondence addressed to him; he is supposed to have been a disciple of the hermit Pelagius of Mallorca, i.e., perhaps of Joan Llobet, or, according to Trithemius's *Chronicon Hirsaugiense* (note 53), 585 f. of Fernandus of Cordoba (+ 1480) who had in the nineties [?!] withdrawn to the island of Lull in order to devote himself to magic. See J. N. Hillgarth, "Some Notes on Lullian Hermits in Majorca saec. XIII–XVII" in *Studia monastica* 6 (1964): 310 f. (about J. Llobet + 1460); J. Gayà, "Algunos temas lulianos en los escritos de Charles de Bouelles" in: *Estudios lulianos* 24 (1980): 53–55. For years now, F. Secret has been promising to publish the magic works attributed to Libanius. Several of his manuscripts exist in French and German collections; in addition, there is a codex in private hands and accessible to Secret who published "Qui etait Libanius Gallus, le maître de Jean Trithème?" in: *Estudios Lulianos* 6 (1962): 127–37; *id.,* "Histoire de l'ésotérisme chrétien" in *Annuaire de la 5e Section EPHE* 86 (1977–78), 411–15. While awaiting such material I prefer not to present my hypotheses in regard to these "teachers" of Trithemius, who on their part were in contact with the circles around Bouelles, Germain de Ganay, Wolfgang Hopilius and Narcissus Brunus. But there are, in many places, brief treatises on ritual and numerological magic; e.g., in the 1503 letter to Johannes von Westerburg (*De septem secundeis,* pp. 81–ff.). See also the numerous letters to Joachim von Brandenburg who will be his benefactor and disciple in this domain: 26 June 1503 (in *De septem secundeis,* pp. 48–57); 11 and 20 June 1505, 10 June 1506, 14 October 1506, 25 November 1506, 17 January 1507, 9 April 1507, 29 May 1507, and 16 October 1507 (*Opera historica,* 2: 441, 490, 519–ff., 526, 531–32, 571)— some of them also mentioned in *De septem secundeis,* in letters addressed to his French correspondents, Germain de Ganay, Johannes Capellarius, and Wolfgang Hopilius (from 1505 onward, all in *Opera historica,* 2: 453–ff., 471–72, 473, 555–ff.). A dozen letters (partially taken from the collection of the *Epistolae familiares* [Hagunau, 1536], then partially unpublished) constitute an appendix to *De septem secundeis* of 1567, particularly on account of their occultist character. Already in the oldest letter addressed to Westerburg (10 May 1503), Trithemius defends his innocence in regard to the accusations brought against him as a consequence of the Bost episode. But he admits: "Magiam me penitus ignorare naturalem dicere non possum, per quam quae miranda fiunt naturaliter fiunt." Also here he cites Albertus Magnus's influential precedent and says that he (Trithemius) followed in his footsteps when investigating natural phenomena as well as in regard to mysticism: "Scientia autem mali non est malum, sed usus . . . Multa fateor magorum volumina legi, praestigiorumque non pauca synthemata perlustravi. Nec ea volumina, quae ligamenta spirituum docent, et eis consimilia penitus a lectione nostra reieci, et in his omnibus firmior semper fateor in sancta fide christianorum evasi, quia divino munere quae legeram, intellexi, ut plurimum." In order to refute every error and invention of these books ("abominanda quae occultantur in libris magiae supersticiosae et in illis quae de coniurationibus daemonum conscribuntur"), a learned Christian is necessary who would know how to understand them. "Magia naturalis, quae aliquando principiis naturae innixa in sua simplicitate pura constabat, tot mendacibus, tot impuritatibus, tot deceptionibus confusa est, ut nemo nisi in utraque doctissimus sit, qui alteram ab altera discernere possit." In the following he criticizes those who "tempus et substantiam Alchymiae impendentes perdunt" and lists "tria principia in magia ista naturali occulta" all of a numerological character, as well as those contained in Bouelles's letters and from book

2 of Agrippa's *De occulta philosophia.* Here, however, Trithemius fails to notice that "opus in magia naturali et supernaturali" is being realized thanks to these numerical secrets. "Fugiunt daemones acceduntque vocati secundum dispositionem quaternarii."

77. K. Arnold, "Additamenta Trithemiana. Nachträge zu Leben u. Werke des J. Trithemius, insbes. zur Schrift "De daemonibus,'" *Würzburger Diozesan Geschichtsblätter* 37/38 (1975): 239–67, where Arnold makes reference to many codices, among them also those which deal with the *Steganographia* (pp. 245-ff., nn. 32–36), a work that really ought to be philologically analyzed. This introduction to the "proemium" and the synopsis—i.e., the only known parts of *De daemonibus,* ibid., pp. 254-ff.—as well as Arnold's *J. Trithemius,* pp. 199-ff., show that he knows the letter of 31 August 1507 to Rutger Sicamber in which Trithemius announces his intention to write this treatise "in posterum . . . quod libris duodecim foret distinguendum," but then also remarks that he would have "ad tempum differre intentionem meam hanc." See also the other letter of 16 July 1507, which mentions it to Nikolaus Gerbelius (both letters in *Opera historica,* 2:545, 565); however, he does not appear to be informed about Butzbach's quotation of the *De daemonibus* in *Macrostroma,* which come into being at about the same time these two letters were written, but Butzbach refers to it as if it constituted already a finished work (see fol. 94r): "Nullo ergo modo debuit cuique esse suspectus Trithemius de magia nicromantica, cum enim refellere sciamus omnem magiam prohibitam ab ecclesia, illam damnans et detestans. Scripsit namque super hoc opus pergrande contra omnes artes ab ecclesia prohibitas in XII libros distinctos et *De daemonibus* praenotatum. Quod si etiam quaedam similia callere cognoscitur, quam diu ad malum usum non verterit ipsam, redarguendus est minime. Malum quippe scire non est malum reputandum, sed malum malo operari. Sunt qui eum artem Lulli, alii notoriam, alii scientiam cabalisticam, quam nos mosaycam dicere possumus, callere ex individia dicunt." Butzbach's testimony in regard to the existence of a completed *De daemonibus* seems to be consonant with that of the autographical list written by Trithemius in 1514. There the introductory words of *De daemonibus* are "Multi vigiliis et" instead of "Maximis et vigiliis et," the same as in MS Würzburg, Stadtarchiv, Biographische Abteilung s.v. "Trithemius;" Arnold, *J. Trithemius,* p. 256. Inexplicably, he considers them as being identical (ibid., p. 254). The 1515 list was published in P. Lehmann, "Merkwürdigkeiten des Abtes J. Trithemius" (Munich, 1961) [*Sitzungsber. d. Bayer. Akademie der Wissenschaften/Phil.-hist.-Kl.-H.2],* p. 74. I am, of course, aware that the initial words may be a stylistic variant or a slip of the pen, and as happens in many cases, a badly informed correspondent could have thought the work had already been completed. I thank R. Wolfe, Rare Books Librarian in the F. A. Countway Library of Medicine, for having sent me photocopies of their MS 8 so quickly. I collated Lehmann's edition with it. That which must be particularly emphasized in this section on Butzbach is by no means an accidental connection of the accusations of necromancy with this work's project. It had, as did later on the *VIII quaestiones* and the *Antipalus,* the function of exculpating him. Böcking, the editor of *Hutteni Operum supplementum* (Leipzig, 1870), 2:478–90, published a bibliography of Trithemius taken from the actuary of Butzbach. It contains the title *De daemonibus* in 1508, without its incipit.

78. Arnold, *J. Trithemius,* p. 199, observes correctly that the Pseudepigraph makes use of the pseudonyms Trithemius (Melanius Triandricus) and Joachim (Iaymiel Megalopius) have adopted in the letter to Libanius Gallus (6 October 1507). This equation is confirmed by the dedicatory letter. Cf. *Opera historica,* 2:570. For this part of the *Antipalus* (not to be found in all MSS) see Staats- und Stadtbiblisthak Stuttgart, 2° cod. 212 (Trithemius's friend, Konrad Peutinger, owned it), fols. 118r–30v, 236r–45r: Cornell University Library, cod. M61 (folios not numbered). This miscellany at the beginning of the seventeenth century in the possession of Heinrich Khunrath seems to have been copied, in the library of the Elector of Brandenburg (see its first part, fol. 1r: "Liber Abdelachi vatis Arabi de sortilegis ad Delium regem Persarum") considering the fact that a preface dated 1510 refers to Joachim and his angel Iaymiel; the second part of the MS, fol. 1r says that the *Antipalus* originates "ex manuscriptis Serenissimi Electoris Joachimi." For the authenticity of the books named here speaks the fact that book 5 (here in part 2, fol. 5r dated Würzburg, 20 October 1508) and also several recipes at the end of book 4 are found in a manuscript of proven authority. I did not investigate a late fragmentary MS that according to Arnold, is found in Liège; but the authenticity of these recipes in book 5 seems to me indubitable. The editor, J. Busaeus, of the *Paralipomena opusculorum P. Blesensis et J. Trithemii* (Mainz, 1605), p. 426, declares categorically that the recipes must be considered as "remedia super-stitiosa."

79. Thanks to the *Epistolae familiares* of this time Trithemius's experiences and travels in the era between Sponheim and Würzburg are well known. They were collected by him and then published in 1536 at Hagenau. After his stay in Speyer, Trithemius (who had become acquainted with the Elector Joachim, margrave of Brandenburg, at the Imperial Diet at Frankfurt as early as 1503) accepted the Elector's invitation to meet him at the Imperial Diet in Cologne, at the end of June 1505. There and at the castle of Boppard, he also met Emperor Maximilian who, according to the dedication letter, put to

him the famous "eight questions"—which were in reality pure topoi. When the Imperial Diet ended, Trithemius accepted, in spite of several other invitations (among them one from Bishop Germain de Ganay) Joachim's offer to come to his court at Berlin and Ursel. Trithemius stayed in Brandenburg from 11 September 1505 until Easter 1506. In October of the same year, he withdrew to the very modest abbey of Würzburg ("Schottenkloster") where only three monks lived. He preferred the abbot's life to that of a courtier, in spite of many tempting offers. The three works on demonology and witchcraft can be traced back to this interim period, which was also filled with worries such as being accused of necromancy. The *Polygraphia* also belongs in this era. Cf. Arnold, *J. Trithemius,* pp. 204–8; Brann, *The Abbot Trithemius,* pp. 31–55.

80. Vienna, Österreichische National Bibliothek, cod. 11716, fols. 4r–112v, indicated as autograph by Arnold who, however, did not notice the difference between the two versions.

81. *Annales hirsaugienses,* in *Opera historica,* 2:670–72: In his reply of 25 August 1511 from Würzburg addressed to Maximilian who had asked for advice in view of his pending participation in the schismatic council of Pisa, Trithemius advises the emperor not only to distrust "levitas Gallorum" and to make his peace with Pope Julius III; he also remarked on the work that is of interest here: "De octo quaestionum serenitatis tuae libello, quem te imperante conscripsi, faciam quod iubes." This sentence may refer to the revision in the Viennese MS, as well as to the Oppenheim edition of 1515, or even to both.

82. Uppsala University Library, cod. C IV, fols. 125r–56r.

83. Ibid., fol. 131v: "magi quidem per privatos cum demonibus contractus implicitos sive explicitos miranda faciunt."

84. Ibid., fol. 134v.

85. *Liber octo quaestionum* (Oppenheim, 1515), reprinted by Busaeus, *Paralipomena,* p. 459; see also Vienna, cod. 11716.

86. Uppsala, cod. C IV, fol. 134r. = ed. cit: "quemadmodum pueri faciunt, qui larvati quandodque latitantes erumpunt ac territis ex inopinato coevis mirum gaudent in modum quasi magnum ex hoc videantur assecuti honorem."

87. Ibid., fol. 133v.

88. Ibid., fols. 134r–v: "quandoquidem aut ipsi mortuorum ingressi cadavera ad tempus illa vivificare putantur, aut illis in locum aliquem remotiorem proiectis, aliquod in forma defunctorum simulachrum exhibent."

89. Ibid., fols. 135r–v: "Miranda faciunt homines invocatione daemonum manifesta, sicut mulieres maleficae, quae, malignorum se spirituum potestati submiserunt, fidemque abnegates catholicam homagium fidelitatis in reprobum sensum averse daemonibus praestiterunt. His permittente deo semper in malum rogati daemones cooperantur aliquando visibiliter, aliquando invisibiliter apparentes, aerem turbant, suscitant tempestates, choruscaciones et grandines inducunt, ledunt fruges, et queque nascencia terrae suis maleficiis devastant. Denique homines infirmant et bestias, et quicquid in perniciem excogitare generis humani possint summo studio exequuntur"; cf. Busaeus, *op. cit.,* p. 465, where the definitive text skips the central sentence about the demoniacal pact (as it does in the Vienna MS): "Necromantici daemonum invocatione mirandos producunt effectus. Maleficae quodam professionis genere subiiciuntur daemonibus, quorum ministerio aerem turbant, tempestates suscitant, fruges devastant, homines et iumenta infirmant, agunt cum daemonibus spurcissimae voluptatis foeda commercia, et eos perniciosis carminibus, quos voluerint, ab inferis revocant in aspectum."

90. Arnold, *J. Trithemius,* p. 199, in translation: "He never occupied himself with the worldly persecution of witches: his remedies are the old exorcisms of the Church, and whatever he found in the medical literature of his library." But in addition to Albertus Magnus, Arnau de Villanueva, Petrus Hispanus named by Arnold, there must also be mentioned the Trotula Gynacology, the Korannides (from *Antipalus* cited in Cornell MS, part 2, fol. 5v), his most beloved hermit Pelagius (*Antipalus,* p. 395); Arnold, "Additamenta," pp. 254, 256 n. 77, stresses that the *VIII quaestiones* enjoyed a wide circulation (since they were printed). He lists thirteen complete editions; particularly emphasized are the edition of *quaestiones* 5, 6, and 7 (N. Jacquier, *Flagellum haereticorum fascinariorum* [Frankfurt, 1581], pp. 452–94, as well as the incomplete German translation in *Theatrum de veneficiis,* "Von Teuffelsgespenst" [Frankfurt, 1586]). Though these questions were to contribute to the persecution of witches, Arnold avows that when Trithemius composed his writings on this particular subject he certainly could not foresee this development of persecution. Yet these witch-hunts were very noticeable in Germany—twenty years after the appearance of the *Malleus.* It is true that Trithemius abstains from issuing any directions in regard to persecution measures and he does not prescribe exorcisms. But from the historical point of view, it is not unimportant that he copies chapters 5 through 11 of book 1 and chapters 3, 5 through 9, 12, 14, and 15 of book 2 (cf. Arnold, "Additamenta" p. 256 n. 77) from the *Malleus Maleficarum* (a copy of which he had in the Würzburg abbey) and uses them verbatim in his *De daemonibus* and *Antipalus.* A. Ruland had pronounced a much more severe judgment upon

Trithemius's responsibility in a review of J. Silbernagl's *J. Trithemius,* in which Trithemius is portrayed as having completely adopted the point of view of the *Malleus Maleficarum* (see *Theologisches Lite-raturblatt* 3 [1868]: 734–, 765–ff.). J. Hansen, *Quellen und Untersuchungen zur Geschichte des Hexen-wahns und der Hexenverfolgung* (Bonn, 1901), p. 379n, 291–97, quotes his most concrete passages and many details given by Trithemius in regard to the activity of witches. H. C. Lea, *Materials towards a History of Witchcraft,* 2d ed. (New York, 1957), pp. 369–70, is of the opinion that Trithemius "makes full use of the *Malleus* and is fully persuaded of the truth of all the absurdities attributed to witchcraft." Such an opinion is perhaps unjustified considering the unpleasant, unfree circumstances when Trithemius wrote these demonological treatises. Hansen as well as Lea (who relied heavily on the former) stress the sentence expressly.

91. The great interest in blessings and exorcisms is verified by descriptions of Abbot Adam's activities. In charge of the Saint Martin monastery in Cologne and a famous exorcist, he healed numerous nuns possessed in monasteries of various regions. Cf. *Chronicon Hirsaugiense,* pp. 576–79.

92. Ficino's translation did not get much attention from the critics. Kristeller, *Supplementum,* p. 135 n. 27, lists only a few pages from Corsi, Galeotti, Della Torre, and Saitta. Psellos's short treatise was also investigated in the light of his hagiographic writing. Cf. Zervos, *Un philosophe néoplatonicien du XIe siècle* (Paris, 1920), chap. 5, pp. 135–ff., 162–91; K. Svoboda, *La demonologie de M. Psellos* (Brno, 1927), pp. 11–18; P. P. Joannou, *Démonologie populaire—Démonologie critique au XIe siècle: La vie inedite de S. Auxence par M. Psellos* (Wiesbaden, 1971), pp. 11–42. More recently the authenticity and the date itself (corrected to the end of thirteenth century) have been questioned by P. Gautier, "Le *De Daemonibus* du pseudo-Psellos," *Revue des études byzantines* 38 (1980): 105–94.

93. Uppsala, cod. C IV, fol. 145v.

94. *Catalogus illustrium virorum Germaniam . . . exornantium* in, *Opera historica* (note 53), 1 : 154 no. 53, about Joannes Nider "studiosus eruditus et in philosophia scholastica probe instructus . . . muliercularum quas maleficas vulgus appellat acerrimus persecutor" (about Nider, cf. also *De scriptoribus ecclesiasticis,* ibid., p. 354); *Catalogus,* p. 177 no. 45, about Jacobus Sprenger "divinarum scripturarum professor et interpres eruditus, atque in philosophia aristotelica egregie doctus, ingenio clarus, sermone scholasticus, cum olim ab Innocentio VIII una cum Henrico Institoris eiusdem ordinis theologo inquisitor haereticae pravitatis esset constitutus scripsit pro cautela et instructione simplicium contra mulierculas maleficas, instrumenta diaboli, volumen non abiciendum, quod praenotavit Malleus Maleficarum 1. I, si quid amplius scripserit, ad notitiam meam non pervenit."

95. Arnold, "Additaments," p. 254, n. 71.

96. Ibid., p. 253.

97. Ibid., pp. 253–54.

98. Ibid., pp. 265–66.

99. Uppsala, C IV, fol. 145v; missing words taken from Busaeus, *Paralipomena,* p. 501, in square brackets; "Primum genus sicut grecus [Michael Psellus tradit] igneum nuncupatur . . . Et [Marsilius Ficinus] Apuleium daemonia quaedam ignea esse animalia dicentem introducit . . . [hos Orpheus igneos sive celestes appellat, propter eo ut opinor quod eorum corpus est ignis]" (fols. 147v–148r; not in Busaeus ed.). "Sicut Porphirius asserit . . . ut inquit Plato." Complete passus to be found in the following note there: 102.

100. Uppsala, cod. C IV, fol. 145v; passage also in Busaeus ed., p. 502.

101. Uppsala, cod. C IV, fols. 147r–48r (at end of *quaestio* 6; not in Busaeus edition): "Omnia haec daemonum genera sic affecta sunt, ut Deum aversentur et angelos bonos, odientque homines et insidiis persequantur, licet aliud alio peius. Aereum et terrestre maleficis invocatum obsequitur, quibus non uniformiter se consueverunt exhibere, sed pro varietate affectionum, ut vel actio requirit, vel materia, unde formam accipiunt visibile, permittit. Nihil ergo mirandum quod maleficae tanta possunt mortalibus inferre maleficia, quando sua sponte daemones in pernicie humani generis unanimiter omnes conspirant. Quae autem causa inimicitiarum nisi invidia, sicut in libro *Sapienciae* scribitur: 'quoniam invidia diaboli mors introivit in orbem terrarum?' Invidie autem causa beatitudo hominis in paradyso posito fuit. Constat igitur nunc manifeste quod maleficarum potestas tota cooperatione stat daemonum, qui omnes semper inquieti et perturbati ubicunque fuerint suis passionibus agitantur prava habitudine acquisitis, et quantum in eis est quiescere neminem permittunt. Nam et inter se compugnant adinvicem saepius concitati rabie furoris. Sunt enim superbia pleni et superbioribus agitantur, usque adeo sicut Porphirius asserit, ut nihil vehementius optent quam dii a nobis estimari supremi et pro illis maxime coli atque timeri, quorum princeps, quem Luciferum Scriptura vocat, id potissimum contendit, ut deus primus omnium habeatur. Incitant nos ad corporis huius oblectamenta quibus ipsi in nobis ferme similiter oblectamur. Incendunt nos ad contenciones et praelia, at assiduo gaudent mendacio. Est enim diabolus ut inquit Plato, animal humectum immortale, passibile, plenum nequicia, odio et invidia, bonis hominibus torquetur, malis laetatur. Libenter itaque daemones utuntur voluntate maleficarum de-

pravata in odium et perniciem generis humani, et tota eis virtute quantum deus permittit cooperaturi occurrunt."

102. Brann, *The Abbot Trithemius* (note 53), p. 117.

103. C. J. Nauert, *Agrippa and the Crisis of Renaissance Thought* (Urbana, Ill., 1965); P. Zambelli, "A proposito del 'De vanitate' di C. Agrippa," *Rivista critica di storia della filosofia* 15 (1960): 47–71; idem, "Agrippa von Nettesheim in den neueren kritischen Studien und in den Handschriften," *Archiv für Kulturgeschichte* 51 (1969): 264–95.

104. These and the following segments are cited more completely and in greater detail in P. Zambelli, "C. Agrippa, Sisto da Siena e gli inquisitori," *Memorie domenicane*, n.s., 3 (1972): 146–64. See also W. Ziegeler, *Möglichkeiten der Kritik am Hexen- und Zauberwesen* (Cologne, 1973), pp. 137–99.

105. Sisto da Siena, *Bibliotheca sancta* (Venice, 1566), pp. 556, 558 (cf. 1574 ed., 2:52–53).

106. Ibid.

107. *Bibliotheca sancta,* (1566), pp. 869–70 (cf. 1574 ed., 2:428).

108. P. Zambelli, "Magic and Radical Reformation in Agrippa of Nettesheim," *Journal of the Warburg and Courtauld Institutes* 39 (1976): 69–103.

109. J. Weyer, *De praestigiis daemonum* (Basel, 1660), pp. 18–19 (book 1, chap. 8).

7

Good Witches, Wise Men, Astrologers, and Scientists: William Perkins and the Limits of the European Witch-Hunts

LELAND L. ESTES

Most nineteenth-century historians believed that one important effect of the witch-hunts of the sixteenth and seventeenth centuries was the intimidation of those who wished to challenge the medieval physical cosmology. This historiographical tradition assumed that witch-hunters were attempting to reimpose a rigid order on an intellectual and social world whose coherence had been shattered by the Renaissance, the Reformation, and the scientific revolution. The "witch-craze," as H. R. Trevor-Roper has called it, was seen as an attack on the cultural and intellectual diversity that characterized the early modern period, and one of the chief glories of the age was the destruction of the root "superstitions" that supported this hunt for witches.[1] Recent research, however, has failed to uncover any detailed or sustained opposition to contemporary scientific innovations in the records of witch trials despite the recent highlighting by historians of science of the Hermetic and Neoplatonic roots of the scientific enterprise of this period and the frankly magical pursuits of some of even the greatest of the early modern scientists.[2] In fact, not a single major figure of the scientific revolution was executed as a witch, and only a handful were even seriously inconvenienced.

Where then did earlier scholars get the idea that the witch-craze was a threat to the scientific community? They got it from reading learned demonologies. For while the new science was rarely attacked in an actual witch trial, various aspects of the scientific endeavor of these centuries were savaged in print by those who wrote against the supposed malice of witches and the evil of witchcraft. One such demonology was the *Discourse of the Damned Art of Witchcraft* by William Perkins.[3] The author was one of the most important English Puritan theologians of the sixteenth century, and his treatise on witchcraft one of the most thoroughgoing and lucid expositions of the subject penned by an Englishman. Using this work, I

154

would like to suggest some reasons that the courts and the general population were seldom willing to pursue a course of action advocated by most demonologists; why a major program of many of the writers of demonological tracts, the extirpation of good as well as bad witches, went almost entirely unheeded. It was this failure on the part of men like Perkins to turn the witch-hunts against the good witch, and against all of his or her magical techniques and paraphernalia, that accounts for the quite limited appearance of scientists and protoscientists as defendants in witchcraft trials.

At the root of most of the various conceptions of witchcraft that have flourished in Western society over the last 1,500 years lie three fundamental ideas: divine permission, satanic power, and human agency in the witch. One finds these basic elements of the Christian witchcraft complex in Augustine, in Aquinas, in the *Malleus Maleficarum,* and, of course, in the *Damned Art.*[4] What is a witch in this tradition? "A witch is a magician who either by open or secret league, wittingly and willingly, consenteth to use the aid and assistance of the devil in the working of wonders."[5] Perkins suggested two reasons that God might permit such a league: "to punish the ingratitude of men" and "to prove whether his children will steadfastly believe in him, and seek unto his word, or cleave unto the devil."[6] Satan was granted wide powers to implement this scheme, but he "cannot go a whit further than God gives him leave and liberty to go."[7] Yet almost all theologians agreed that he could be a formidable opponent.

The Devil's need for a human agent proved a much more intractable problem than either divine permission or satanic power. It was never made entirely clear why the Devil needed human help. This was probably the result of the ambiguity or even nonexistence of biblical evidence on this point.[8] Nevertheless, a limited consensus did develop. Satan sought to gain human adherents to his cause because he wanted

to imitate God, and to counterfeit his dealings with his Church. As God therefore hath made a covenant with his people so Satan joins in league with the world, laboring to bind some men unto him, that if it were profitable, he might draw them from the covenant of God, and therefore disgrace the same.

Through these close adherents, he hoped more easily to ensnare and harm others. Oddly enough, it was also widely believed that "if the devil were not stirred up, and provoked by the Witch, he would never do so much hurt as he doth."[9]

These three fundamental propositions received "the uniform consent of all ages."[10] But on this rather broad base a whole host of particular witch traditions could be constructed or supported. One of the oldest and most widespread of these traditions has been discussed by Edward Peters, who argues that the "professional magician" was "the object of most theological, moral, and legal condemnation from the fifth to the fifteenth centuries."[11] The "small practitioners of the art" were especially vulnerable to prosecution, although the learned sorcerer actually generated the most hostility.[12] The animus of the medieval clerical writer was not directed against the "ugly old hag, living alone, and known for her eccentricities"—the principle victim of the witch-craze—but toward the astrologer, necromancer, diviner, charmer, and wise man.[13] It was also directed, although somewhat more obliquely, toward what were perceived as the many magical aspects of the scientific enterprise of this period, especially its demonstrably Hermetic, Neoplatonic, astrological, or alchemical roots. Many of the most important natural philosophers of the Middle Ages—including Albertus Magnus, Roger Bacon, Pietro d'Abano, and Robert Grosseteste—were attacked for their allegedly magical practices.[14]

It is still commonly accepted that Perkins and other sixteenth- and seventeenth-century theologians wrote on the subject of witchcraft because of their desire to vindicate the Bible by unequivocally establishing the existence of witches.[15] Undoubtedly such a motive did play some role in his selection of this subject. Yet the *Damned Art* is not so much a plea for a belief in witches as an attempt to explain something that was already taken for granted. When Perkins wrote that "witchcraft is a rife and common sin in these our days," he was doing more than merely bandying about stock invectives borrowed from the Bible and the church fathers; he was noting a hard reality.[16] The decade in which he wrote his demonology—the 1590s—was a period of intense witch-hunting in England, including areas near his home in Cambridge.[17] And, despite the existence of a skeptical countercurrent, few doubted that witchcraft existed and that witches were really doing harm; "the man that calls it into question, may as well doubt of the Sun shining at noonday."[18] Though it was widely believed that witches posed some kind of threat, there was little agreement on the exact source of this threat, on how it might manifest itself, and on how it might be counteracted. To answer these questions Perkins and his clerical colleagues turned quite naturally to the ancient, mostly clerical traditions later described by Peters. Perkins wrote his treatise to try to explain the witch-hunting of his own time, but the actual content of his response to these contemporary hunts was controlled by intellectual traditions that long antedated the witch-craze.

In order to understand what witchcraft was and how it worked, Perkins and his intellectual progenitors first asked themselves why men became witches. They argued that the chief motivation was "curiosity,"

> when a man resteth not satisfied with the measure of inward gifts received, as of knowledge, wit, understanding, memory, and such like, but aspires to search out such things as God would have kept secret: and hence he is moved to attempt the cursed art of magic and witchcraft, as a way to get further knowledge in matters secret and not revealed.[19]

Witchcraft was then, at least in part, the attempt to exceed the normal bounds of human knowledge. What gave this definition teeth—a hard cutting edge—was that these bounds were immediately obvious. "The rules and conclusions of all good and lawful arts," are "so generally and undoubtedly true that they cannot deceive." They "have their ground in experience, and are framed by observation."[20] They require no deep searching. And because "the world so runs . . . in a circle . . . if a man should but ordinarily observe the cause of things either in the weather, or in the bodies of men, or otherwise, he might easily foretell beforehand what would come after."[21] Predictions of this sort are made every day "by Physicians, Mariners, and Husbandmen."[22]

There is a clear bias in Perkins's formulation of the problem of witchcraft and curiosity in favor of the scientific status quo. It is much too easy to equate the "generally and undoubtedly true" with what is merely hallowed by long tradition. Perkins falls into this trap on numerous occasions. There was little room in his thought for the sophisticated experiments and the counterintuitive hypotheses that powered the scientific revolution. But if all attempts to explain or manipulate nature in ways other than those supported by the reigning scientific orthodoxy were theoretically suspect, in fact Perkins singled out only a few for condemnation as demonic. These he divided into two broad classes: the "divining" type and the "working" type.[23] Divination for Perkins was that "part of witchcraft, whereby men reveal strange things, either past, present, or to come, by the assistance of the devil."[24] He attacked divination using the flights of birds, the entrails of animals, dreams, lots, dead bodies, and the observation of days.[25]

Perkins particularly loathed the practice of astrology. His antagonism in this regard is especially interesting, since many of the best scientific thinkers of his day were engaged in the reformation and extension of astrological thought. Much of the best astronomical work of the scientific revolution was motivated by a desire to make predictions by the stars more accurate. But like most Protestant and even Catholic thinkers, Perkins believed that astrology "can be done by none but such as are in league with Satan."[26] It was a diabolical art whose efficacy depended on secret knowledge gained from the Devil. But why, a contemporary scientist might have asked, could this knowledge not have been gained from a direct inspection of the heavens? The answers that Perkins provided underline his commitment to an epistemology that saw man as limited to the immediate and direct apprehension of only a small number of natural laws and the comprehension of only some of the simpler physical processes. Successful astrological predictions were to be viewed with suspicion because those who "would make sound rules of art by observation, must know the particular estate of all things he observeth: But . . . no man knoweth the particular estate of all the stars."[27] What is more, the stars' "virtues being all mixed together in the subject whereon they work, can no more be known distinctly than the virtue of a mass of herbs of infinite sorts beaten together."[28] Finally, because "a general and common cause" cannot "immediately produce a particular effect, but only moveth and helpeth the particular, immediate, and subordinate causes," astrologers cannot possibly reason directly from a certain configuration of the sky to some specific prediction of a future event.[29] These objections emphasize that some natural processes are so complex that the human mind cannot really understand them. For this reason, sure knowledge cannot be derived from the study of such things. Only spiritual beings like the Devil, "an ancient spirit, whose skill hath been confirmed by experience of the course of nature, for the space [of] almost six thousand years" and who understood "the hidden causes in nature," had the wherewithal to predict the future based on the position of the stars.[30]

Satan not only helps his servants to divine the future, but also to work wonders in the present. Of the many ways of working such wonders that Perkins discussed, none was more widespread than charming. He argued against the natural efficacy of charms because all words made and uttered by men are in their nature but sounds framed by the tongue, of the breath that cometh from the lungs, and that which is only a bare sound, in all reason can have no virtue in it to cause a real work.

Perkins also rejected charms because he believed it to be "a granted rule in nature, that every agent worketh upon the patient by touching." A thing must touch that "which it hurteth or affecteth." But the words used in charms commonly referred to persons or things that were not even present.[31] As with astrological predictions, the efficacy of a particular charm was attributed by Perkins to the machinations of the Devil. "A charm is a spell or verse, consisting of strange words, used as a sign or watchword to the devil, to cause him to work wonders."[32] The power of images can be traced to a similar source, "for the bare picture hath no more power of itself to hurt the body represented, than bare words."[33]

The ability of the Devil to operate in the physical world in ways that were fundamentally alien and incomprehensible to human beings is at the very center of Perkins's conception of witchcraft. This alienness or incomprehensibility was the defining characteristic of those particular activities or events deemed to be of demonic origin. Such activities or events were "extraordinary works in regard to man, because they proceed not from the usual and ordinary course of nature." Yet the Devil could not perform miracles. His works were "done by virtue of nature, and not above and against the ordinary course thereof."[34] It is difficult to tell how cogent and convincing people found this distinction, even in theory; in practice it was almost useless. How was one to distinguish between the transformation of "the substance of a rod into the substance of a serpent," which is a true miracle, and "an illusion of the outward senses . . . whereby [the Devil] makes a man think that he heareth, seeth, feeleth or toucheth such things as indeed he doth not?"[35] Perkins cut this Gordian knot by restricting true miracles to the first two hundred years of the Christian Era, while most other Protestent and even Catholic thinkers greatly reduced the number of contemporary events that they were willing to accept as miraculous.[36]

Theoretical and practical attacks on the attribution of "extraordinary works" to God probably meant that they could be more easily and readily attributed to the Devil. The virtual elimination of the possibility that the preternatural event could be a godly miracle also probably made it easier for Perkins to argue against the activities of the good witch, the wise man, and the wise woman, whom he thought to be just as calpable as the bad witch who did only harm.[37] In fact, he argued that "if death be due to any then a thousand deaths of right belong to the good witch."[38] The crime of the good witch is the pact that he or she has made with the Devil in order "to heal and cure the hurts inflicted upon men or cattle by bad witches."[39] And the fact that he or she has done only good actually makes the matter worse, because

men do commonly hate and spit at the damnifying Sorcerer, as unworthy to live among them; whereas the other is so dear unto them, that they hold themselves and their country blessed that have him among them, they fly unto him in necessity, they depend upon him as their god, and by this means, thousands are carried away to their final confusion.[40]

Perkins did leave an escape hatch. Not everyone who uses charms and performs "extraordinary works" is to be accounted a witch. "A man who uses spells etc. knowing they are useless in themselves is making a pact with the devil. But one who uses spells etc. thinking they are efficacy in themselves is not." Yet "they are on the high way thereunto."[41]

In attacking the good witch, Perkins drifted so far from the common conception of witchcraft, as it emerges from the trial records, that it is hard to believe that he is talking about the same thing. Of course, it must be pointed out that neither he nor most of the other clerical demonologists in northern Europe during the period of the witch-craze actually participated in the hunts. These were mostly secular affairs. Yet distance from the event cannot, by itself, really explain why Perkins concerned himself so obsessively with an issue that was decidedly peripheral for most people. Many others who wrote on the crime of witchcraft during the craze also had few connections with the actual prosecution of witches, but nevertheless directed their attentions to evil witchcraft rather than toward the activities of the good witch.[42] Why then were theologians and clerics like Perkins so interested, even obsessed, with the problem of beneficent witchcraft?

It seems unlikely that this tradition would have so thoroughly controlled Perkins's response to witchcraft if it had not been an integral part of some larger intellectual program. As Peters has demonstrated, the Church had always opposed the arts of the good witch and the learned magician. But it had lived with popular "superstitions" for centuries without having been seriously threatened by their existence. In fact, for most clerics compromise with such superstitions was not only possible, it was welcomed, and on the fringes it had always been difficult to tell where Christianity ended and magic began. But for those of a dogmatic and zealous bent, like Perkins and his fellow Puritans, this coexistence had always loomed as a festering sore, a rent in the seamless garment of Christ. Many of these groups, the Puritans included, attacked anything they believed substituted the dead for the living Word, the outward symbol for the inward spirit. This meant that no mere set prayer or sacramental sign had the power of aiding in a material or spiritual care. Their use could even be counterproductive, because they might anger God by suggesting that he could somehow be coerced. Only a person who truly believed in the goodness and mercy of the Creator could hope to have his prayers answered and his suffering reduced. Puritans believed that the formation of such a belief was seriously hampered by the resort of the established Church to the rote recital of prayers and an overreliance on uninspired dogma.[43] Perkins went so far as to urge his readers to "reckon for Charms . . . whatsoever actions, gestures, signs, and ceremonies are used by men or women to work wonders, having no power to effect the same, either by creation and nature, or by special appointment from God."[44] In this passage Perkins explicitly draws the connection between "magic" within the Church and that outside of it, and condemns both. The Puritans hostility toward the merely external in contemporary religious practice led them to view the spells of the typical village folk healer in a more critical light than their Anglican counterparts. Such charms were thought to be at best attempts to coerce good spirits or even God himself. At worst, they were seen as the outward signs of an inward pact with the devil.

There can be little doubt that the Puritan attack on the folk healer, magician, astrologer, and charmer was partly ideological in character, based on a certain broad conception of the Christian religion. But it is impossible to ignore the various social and economic interests that were also involved. The typical clergyman had to compete vigorously with such people for the material and spiritual allegiance of his parishioners because, for a great variety of physical and mental afflictions, the priest or minister was seen as only one of many possible sources of comfort, support, and aid. In order to get the better of their competitors, clergymen often adopted some of the very techniques that had made the competition so successful. As in the Middle Ages, the resort of clergymen to high and low magic was widely remarked upon, and clerical charmers were widespread.[45] But for many like the Puritans such a strategy would have been an anathema. What alternatives were available? The Puritan clergy discovered early in their competition with the local folk healer that no weapon proved more serviceable than the charge that the opposition was in league with the Devil. They argued that where a cure had been effected by such means, the patient was merely exchanging a present good of minor proportions for a greater evil in the future. "He who will be beholden unto the devil, for his life or health, then choose to die in the gracious and merciful hand of the creator, can never expect to participate [in] any portion of salvation in him."[46]

Interestingly enough, the attempt by Perkins and several other Puritan writers to extend the witch-craze by turning it against the wise man and the wise woman may actually have helped in bringing about the craze's demise. When it became clear in the 1580s and 1590s that Puritanism was no longer merely a "hotter" variety of the established faith, but was becoming an organized and militant movement both inside and outside of the Church, certain Anglican divines, especially the powerful bishop of London, Richard Bancroft, and his chaplain, Samuel Harsnet, turned against witch-hunting.[47] It became a partisan issue; an attack on the popular belief in the existence of witches served as an indirect thrust at the principles near the foundation of the Puritan threat.

Even though, as he supposed, he had the plain word of God on his side, Perkins realized that he was probably fighting a losing battle. He knew that "charming [was] in as great request as physic, and charmers more sought unto than physicians in time of need," and that "there be charms for all conditions and ages of men, for diverse kinds of creatures, yea for every disease."[48] He also knew what the surviving records of witch trials clearly demonstrate; that folk healers were rarely executed as witches in England. The usual response to the presense of a wise man or wise woman in a village was, in Perkins's own words, "oh happy is the day, that ever I met with such a man or woman to help me."[49] Why did the folk healer remain unmolested despite the eloquent pleas of many demonologists? Again, Perkins himself provides some of the best testimony on this point.

They [who go to wiseman] allege, we go to the physician for counsel; we take his *Recipe,* but we know not what it meaneth; yet we use it and find benefits; if this be lawful, why may we not as well take benefit by the Wiseman whose course we be ignorant of?[50]

Perkins's answer to this query is straightforward and predictable. The wise man uses Devilish charms, while the physician uses "a composition and mixture of natural things," which is acceptable to God. For Perkins, "there is not the same reason of physic and charms."[51] Yet clearly for most people there was no fundamental difference between the cures effected by learned physicians and those of the village folk healer.

Most people probably found Perkins's views on the good witch to be counterintuitive and even nonsensical. He went wrong on this point because he was reasoning in the wrong direction. Perhaps because he was a theologian, Perkins believed that the crux or starting point of the witch-craze was the Devil and his human allies.[52] But this was not generally the way that most people then thought of the matter. Keith Thomas has demonstrated that for England at least, witch-hunting mostly got along without the demonic pact, the witches' sabbath, and even without the Devil.[53] None of these ideas was much developed in English witch trials during the heyday of the hunts in the second half of the sixteenth century. These aspects of the witch-craze were secondary and derived. The driving force behind witch-hunting, and the necessary starting point for any useful consideration of witchcraft, was *maleficia,* the harm that the witch was supposed to have done. People were responding not to "extraordinary works" generally, but only to "strange passions and torments in men's bodies."[54] They were not really interested in the unnatural quality of the witchcraft act, whether it be a charm, an image, or a nativity, but only in a few very particular results of that act. They reasoned from the illness to the Devil and the witch, and not the other way around. It was generally thought quite ludicrous to suppose that there might be a causal link, however indirect, between some evil act and the unalloyed good of the wise man. In such a scheme it was easier, more natural, and more direct to assume that the wise man was provided by God to counter the machinations of the bad witch than to argue that the good and bad witch were fundamentally the same. Perkins and other demonologists were not successful in equating the two, at least not in the popular mind.

The charms and rituals of white witchcraft were not created during the witch-craze. They had always been the people's first line of defense against witches. If a man found himself bewitched and desired to be cured, he

> sendeth for the suspected witch; being come, he offers to scratch him or her, thinking by this means to be cured of witchcraft. His reason is no other, than a strong persuasion, that there is simply virtue in his scratching to cure him, and discover the witch.[55]

Perkins knew differently, for the afflicted man did not suspect "that the help cometh by the devil," and though "he may be healed . . . the truth is, he sinneth and breaks God's commandment. For the using of these means is plain witchcraft."[56] But what did Perkins offer as an alternative? In truth, very little. He even argued that "the gift of casting out Devils, and curing Witchcraft be ordinarily ceased, since the Apostles times."[57] He is willing to grant that "to be within the covenant of grace . . . and not outwardly in profession only . . . but truly and indeed as all the elect are" is a "sovereign preservative."[58] But who really knew that he or she had been elected and was thus safe? It was widely believed that even outwardly upright men were occasionally attacked by witches. In fact, few seemed immune from their molestations. It is easy to see why few people supported Perkins in his campaign against folk healers and their techniques. To have given up recourse to scratching and the other similar methods of fighting witches that Perkins abominated left one with only a single practical method of defense—the law. "The discovery of a witch is a matter judicial," he insisted, that should "be done judicially by the Magistrate, according to the form and order of the law."[59] But the law was both slow and extremely expensive, and for these and other reasons it was only used where the suspect had a longstanding reputation for witchcraft. The daily struggle against witches required cheaper and quicker techniques.

There can be little doubt that Perkins and other clerics who thought as he did about folk healing, magic, astrology, and divining were successful in turning at least a portion of the population against those who practiced these arts. Resort to them, after all, "hath not been universal."[60] But I must agree here with E. P. Thompson, as against Thomas, that among the peasantry, and perhaps elsewhere, belief in and practice of such arts remained as strong as ever.[61] In fact, it could be argued that recourse to all of the various types of magic that Perkins condemned actually might have been increasing just at the time that he was writing. Perkins certainly thought so!

> Let a man's child, friend, or cattle be taken with some sore sickness, or
> strangely tormented with some rare or unknown disease, the first thing he doth,
> is to bethink himself and inquire after some wiseman or wise-woman, and
> thither he sends and goes for help.[62]

And why not? As Perkins also clearly recognized, maleficent witchcraft was also on the rise. It was quite natural for people to press all available antiwitchcraft techniques into service. Since so many theologians opposed the use of the Church's traditional methods for finding and punishing witches, the peasantry had to fall back on devices of their own creation. Perkins failed in his campaign to extend witch-hunting to the good witch and all of her various spiritual and intellectual cousins not only because his image of the witch was peripheral to the concerns of the vast majority of his contemporaries, but also because his program would have stripped them of their main defenses against supernatural attack.

The witch-craze was not then a simple extension of the ideas about witches, sorcerers, and magicians held by medieval demonologists. Thus attempts by men like William Perkins to use the medieval witch paradigm to understand and control its direction were mostly failures. This was not the case everywhere, however. In Spain and in many parts of Italy the clergy remained in firm legal control of magical activities of all sorts, and in these lands the older ideas of witchcraft continued to dominate thinking.[63] In many ways this conservative attitude was a blessing. In both Italy and Spain the pattern of few prosecutions and light sentences that had characterized most of the Middle Ages persisted throughout the sixteenth and seventeenth centuries. But a more pernicious aspect of the older witch paradigm was also carried forward into the early modern period: the often openly hostile attitude of the authorities toward the Hermetic, the Neoplatonic, the astrological, and the alchemical aspects of the scientific enterprise. And while this attitude did not choke off scientific advance altogether, it did limit it to a rather narrow path.[64]

The paradigm that guided witch-hunting north of the Alps and the Pyrenees, while it quite seriously disrupted the fabric of society, never threatened the flexibility of science in these areas. Paracelsus and Paracelsianism, for example, flourished in just those regions where witch-hunting was fiercest.[65] And while Johannes Kepler's mother was pursued by the authorities as a witch, Kepler himself, despite the many mystical, spiritual, magical, and even heretical parts of his scientific work, was never seriously threatened.[66] In England, while Perkins was railing futilely against the inequity of allowing wise men and magicians to go unpunished, John Dee was openly promoting many of the Hermetic and Neo-platonic aspects of the "new science" at Court, and even attempted to conjure spirits and communicate with the dead.[67]

Dee and Kepler simply could not be assimilated to the stereotypical image of the witch that guided the craze. Where the medieval view of the activities of witches and sorcerers still held sway, they might have been prosecuted for their activities, but this was not the case in northern Europe in the sixteenth and seventeenth centuries. Perkins knew this and, I suspect, so did most of the other clerical writers who argued that the major supernatural threat to European civilization was the "professional magician." The witch-hunters were looking for something quite different. The chief victims of the witch-craze were not scientific heretics, charmers, astrologers, wise men, folk healers, or even those magicians who openly and explicitly worshiped the Devil, but wizened and eccentric old crones whose only real crime seems to have been their foul tempers and loose morals.[68] Medieval theologians and many of their early modern clerical successors hardly spoke of this problem at all.

Notes

1. W. E. H. Lecky, *History of the Rise and Influence of the Spirit of Rationalism in Europe*, 2 vols. (London, 1865), 1:90; Andrew Dickson White, *A History of the Warfare of Science with Theology in Christiendom*, 2 vols. (New York, 1896), 1:351; Preserved Smith, *A History of Modern Culture*, 2 vols. (New York, 1930), 1:434–58; H. R. Trevor-Roper, *The European Witch-Craze of the Sixteenth and Seventeenth Centuries and Other Essays* (New York, 1969), pp. 186–ff; George Sarton, *Six Wings: Men of Silence in the Renaissance* (Bloomington, Ind., 1957), pp. 212–18.

2. Frances A. Yates has been especially influential in exposing the "occult" roots of the scientific revolution. See her *Giordano Bruno and the Hermetic Tradition* (Chicago, 1964). Yates explicitly supported the idea that the witch-craze was a response to occult aspects of sixteenth- and seventeenth-century science: *The Occult Philosophy in the Elizabethan Age* (1979; reprint, London, 1983), pp. 61–74.

3. William Perkins, *A Discourse of the Damned Art of Witchcraft* (Cambridge, 1608). This work circulated in manuscript before Perkins's death in 1602. Perkins is one of the most important but least studied of the Puritan theologians. No single monograph or article has been devoted exclusively to his demonology.

4. On the attitude of the church fathers and Scholastics toward the possibility of witchcraft, see

Jeffrey Burton Russell, *Witchcraft in the Middle Ages* (Secaucus, N. J., 1972). For selections from some of these authors, see Alan Kors and Edward Peters, *Witchcraft in Europe, 1100–1700: A Documentary History* (Philadelphia, 1972).

5. Perkins, *Damned Art,* p. 167. See also pp. 3–4, 41–42.

6. Ibid., p. 38.

7. Ibid., pp. 39–40.

8. See Norman Cohn, *Europe's Inner Demons: An Enquiry Inspired by the Great Witch-Hunt* (New York, 1975), pp. 60–65; Henry Ansgar Kelly, *The Devil, Demonology and Witchcraft: The Development of Christian Beliefs in Evil Spirits* (Garden City, N. Y., 1968), chap. 1.

9. Perkins, *Damned Art,* p. 253.

10. Ibid., p. 128.

11. Edward Peters, *The Magician, the Witch, and the Law* (Philadelphia, 1978), pp. xiii, 133.

12. Ibid., p. 133.

13. H. C. Erik Midelfort, *Witch Hunting in Southwestern Germany, 1562–1684: The Social and Intellectual Foundations* (Stanford, 1972), p. 1; Alan D. J. Macfarlane, *Witchcraft in Tudor and Stuart England: A Regional and Comparative Study* (New York, 1970), pp. 158–64.

14. See Lynn Thorndike, *A History of Magic and Experimental Science,* 8 vols. (New York, 1923–58), vols. 3–4.

15. Wallace Notestein argued that this was Perkins's motivation and guide; see *A History of Witchcraft in England from 1558 to 1718* (1911; reprint, New York, 1968), p. 228. John L. Teall thought the *Damned Art* needed "no extensive analysis" because it was "based almost exclusively upon Scripture"; see "Witchcraft and Calvinism in Elizabethan England: Divine Power and Human Agency," *Journal of the History of Ideas* 23 (1962): 29.

16. Perkins, *Damned Art,* p. 1.

17. See Cecil L'Estrange Ewen, *Witch Hunting and Witch Trials* (London, 1929), p. 101; Macfarlane, *Witchcraft,* pp. 26–27.

18. Perkins, *Damned Art,* p. 128.

19. Ibid., p. 11. See also Thomas Pickering's introduction to *Damned Art,* sig. 5f. On the medieval view of *curiositas,* see Peters, *Magician,* pp. xiv, 2, 16, 90; G. R. Owst, "Sortilegium in English Homiletic Literature of the Fourteenth Century," in *Studies Presented to Sir Hilary Jenkinson,* ed. J. Conway Davies (London, 1957), pp. 272–303.

20. Perkins, *Damned Art,* p. 78.

21. Ibid., p. 64.

22. Ibid., p. 71. The unproblematic character of knowledge for most early modern thinkers, and some of its ramifications, is well discussed by M. M. Slaughter, *Universal Languages and Scientific Taxonomy in the Seventeenth Century* (Cambridge, 1982).

23. Perkins, *Damned Art,* p. 55.

24. Ibid.

25. Ibid., pp. 91–115.

26. Ibid. pp. 75, 79–80. For the Renaissance debate on astrology, see Wayne Shumaker, *The Occult Sciences in the Renaissance: A Study in Intellectual Patterns* (Berkeley, 1972), chap. 1. On the attitude of medieval clerics toward astrology, see Theodore O. Wedel, *The Mediaeval Attitude towards Astrology* (New Haven, 1920); Max L. W. Laistner, "The Western Church and Astrology during the Early Middle Ages," *Harvard Theological Review* 34(1941): 251–75; Richard C. Dales, "Robert Grosseteste's View on Astrology," *Medieval Studies* 29 (1967): 357–63.

27. Perkins, *Damned Art,* pp. 78–79.

28. Ibid., pp. 84–85.

29. Ibid., p. 77.

30. Ibid., p. 19. See also Pickering's introduction, sig. 6f.

31. Ibid., pp. 134–35.

32. Ibid., p. 130. See also pp. 132, 144–47.

33. Ibid., p. 149. See also p. 140. The natural efficacy of images and charms was widely supported in the Renaissance. See D. P. Walker, *Spiritual and Demonic Magic: From Ficino to Campanella* (London, 1958).

34. Perkins, *Damned Art,* p. 18.

35. Ibid., pp. 13–14, 22–23.

36. Ibid., p. 238. Interestingly enough, Perkins held this view in common with the archenemy of the witch-hunts in England. See my article, "Reginald Scot and His *Discoverie of Witchcraft:* Religion and Science in the Opposition to the European Witch Craze," *Church History* 52 (1983); 444–56. On Catholic attitudes toward miracles in the sixteenth century, see A. N. Galpern, *The Religions of the People in Sixteenth-Century Champagne* (Cambridge, Mass., 1976), pp. 53, 92–93, 159–60; William A.

Christian, *Local Religion in Sixteenth-Century Spain* (Princeton, 1981), pp. 102–5, 148. For a fascinating study of a world and age more open to the miraculous, see Howard Clarke Kee, *Miracle in the Early Christian World: A Study in Sociohistorical Method* (New Haven, 1983).

37. Perkins, *Damned Art,* p. 177.

38. Ibid., p. 178.

39. Ibid., p. 174.

40. Ibid., pp. 256–57. See also p. 184.

41. Ibid., pp. 53–54.

42. See, for instance, the English physician John Cotta. He vigorously attacked medical empirics, but does not accuse them of making pacts with the Devil: *A Short Discoverie of the Unobserved Dangers of Severall Sorts of Ignorant and Unconsiderate Practisers of Physicke* (London, 1612). Yet he wrote at length against the crimes of the bad witch: *A Triall of Witch-craft* (London, 1616).

43. See M. M. Knappen, *Tudor Puritanism: A Chapter in the History of Idealism* (1939; reprint, Chicago, 1970), chaps. 10, 17.

44. Perkins, *Damned Art,* pp. 152–53.

45. See Michael MacDonald, *Mystical Bedlam: Madness, Anxiety, and Healing in Seventeenth-Century England* (Cambridge, 1981), pp. 176, 214.

46. Cotta, *Triall,* p. 78.

47. See D. P. Walker, *Unclean Spirits: Possession and Exorcism in France and England in the Late Sixteenth and Early Seventeenth Centuries* (Philadelphia, 1981), chap. 4.

48. Perkins, *Damned Art,* p. 153.

49. Ibid., pp. 175–76.

50. Ibid., p. 155.

51. Ibid.

52. This was the starting point of the medieval tradition.

53. Keith Thomas, *Religion and the Decline of Magic* (New York, 1971), pp. 444–45.

54. Perkins, *Damned Art,* p. 128.

55. Ibid., pp. 54–55. See also p. 152.

56. Ibid.

57. Ibid., p. 229.

58. Ibid., p. 220. See also pp. 221, 224, 227–28.

59. Ibid., p. 200.

60. Ibid., p. 153.

61. E. P. Thompson, "Anthropology and the Discipline of Historical Context [Review of *Religion and the Decline of Magic*]," *Midland History* 1 (1972): 53–55.

62. Perkins, *Damned Art,* p. 175. See also pp. 1, 253.

63. On the dominant role of the Inquisition in witchcraft cases in Spain and Italy, see Carlo Ginzburg, *The Night Battles: Witchcraft and Agrarian Cults in the Sixteenth and Seventeenth Centuries,* trans. John Tedeschi and Anne Tedeschi (Baltimore, 1983): Gustav Henningsen, *The Witches' Advocate: Basque Witchcraft and the Spanish Inquisition (1609–1614)* (Reno, Nev., 1980).

64. This attitude probably explains why Paracelsianism failed to thrive in Spain or Italy and perhaps why Galileo had so little sympathy for the work of Kepler.

65. See Allen G. Debus, *The Chemical Philosophy: Paracelsian Science and Medicine in the Sixteenth and Seventeenth Centuries,* 2 vols. (New York, 1977). This was mostly a northern European phenomenon.

66. Edward Rosen, "Kepler and Witchcraft Trials," *Historian* 28 (1966): 447–50.

67. On the mixture of Dee's "sciences," see Nicholas Clulee, "Astrology, Magic, and Optics: Facets of John Dee's Early Natural Philosophy," *Renaissance Quarterly* 30 (1977): 632–80.

68. For one interpretation of the origin or source of the witch-hunts, see my "The Medical Origins of the European Witch Craze," *Journal of Social History* 17 (1983): 271–84.

8

Bruno's "French Connection": A Historiographical Debate

EDWARD A. GOSSELIN

> It is therefore possible that it was Henri III who, by sending Bruno into England . . . changed the course of his life from that of a wandering magician into that of a very strange kind of missionary indeed.
>
> Frances Yates

Introduction

The main events of Giordano Bruno's life are well known. Born in 1548 in Nola near Naples, he entered the Dominican monastery, San Domenico, in 1565, eventually left it and the Kingdom (1576), wandered up through Italy into Switzerland and France, obtained a doctorate in theology at the University of Toulouse, proceeded on to Paris (1581), went to England in 1583, returned to Paris in 1585, journeyed to Germany, thence to Prague, eventually to Frankfurt, and then to Venice. In Venice he was betrayed by his host, Zuan Mocenigo, and was turned over to the Venetian Inquisition on 23 May 1592. The following year, the Republic of Saint Mark was persuaded to turn Bruno over to the Roman Inquisition into whose dungeons he entered on 27 February 1593. He languished in his Roman prison for seven more years until he was convicted of heresy, "relaxed" to the secular arm, and on 17 February 1600 escorted to the Campo dei Fiori by the Brothers of Saint John the Beheaded. There, stripped naked, tongue staked so he could utter no blasphemies, he—unlike most other heretics who were executed by strangulation in prison before being burned in effigy on the Campo—was burned alive.

It is also known that Bruno adopted the Copernican theory, became an apostle of the concept of an infinite universe, and preached the existence of innumerable worlds. Those who have followed the writings of the late Dame Frances Yates also realize that Bruno was a Hermetist, a latter-day follower of the putative author of the *Corpus Hermeticum,* Hermes Trismegistus. Those who have read Yates's books are also aware that Bruno was an adept of the art of memory and was deeply influenced by the late medieval Spanish mystic, Raymond Lull.

Given all this, there are still two outstanding issues that cloud one's understanding of Giordano Bruno, even though that knowledge is today far deeper than it was thirty or forty years ago. The first problem is that historians always seem to treat Bruno as if his thought system had been born all of a piece, as if from Zeus's head. To be sure, such Bruno scholars as Dorothea Singer and Frances Yates[1] recognized Bruno's intellectual lineage: Aristotle, Plato, Plotinus, Lucretius, Lull, Cusanus, and Copernicus. However, they and other Bruno scholars have made few efforts to understand when or why Bruno adopted or adapted the ideas of these thinkers. The second and collateral issue, insufficiently dealt with thus far, is that of ascertaining where Bruno adopted these idea systems. If one can conjecture the latter, then one may better understand the larger intellectual and perhaps even political wrapping that came with his adoption of these thinkers' ideas. In this paper, I wish to deal with Giordano Bruno's acquisition of Lullism and Copernicanism, the two most important elements in his intellectual makeup.

Frances Yates wrote a magisterial study of the Hermetic tradition and of Bruno's participation in that tradition. In *Giordano Bruno and the Hermetic Tradition,* she points to the importance of both Raymond Lull (1232–1316) and Nicholas Copernicus (1473–1543) to Bruno's thought, seeing each of them as intimately related to Bruno's Hermetic synthesis. Concerning Lull, she wrote in her preface that "there is a great omission in this book, namely the influence on Bruno of Raymond Lull which I have hardly mentioned."[2] Yates in part rectified this omission in her stunning book, *The Art of Memory.*[3] There she showed how the Nolan's mnemonic writings were influenced by Lull's *Ars magna.* Lull's mnemonic Art taught that the divine attributes were creative forces. Bruno, in true Renaissance fashion, "magicized" this teaching, in the belief that the Art could be used operationally in the three worlds: the elemental world, the celestial world, and the intellectual world.[4] The "artificial Art" became a persistent topic in Bruno's literary production, at least after 1582. Yet nowhere, so far as I know, did Yates speculate as to exactly when or where Bruno adopted the ideas of Doctor Illuminatus. Yates has also been extremely helpful in deepening the understanding of Bruno's Copernicanism, but again, the question of when, where, or why Bruno became a Copernican was not really addressed by her. Indeed, implicit in the otherwise perceptive remark that prefaces this paper is Yates's notion that Bruno had been fully formed before the "wandering magician" left Italy.

I hope in this paper to give a tentative answer to the questions of when, where, and why, and to draw therefrom some new understanding of Bruno's self-described messianic mission. The hypothesis I will be elaborating is incapable of certain proof, but I think the argument has a great deal of circumstantial probity. Simply put, I argue that it was Giordano Bruno's "French connection" that lured him into his post-1582 Lullian mnemonics and Copernicanism.

There are, alas, few records of Bruno's activities and life. What is known are the bits he chose to allude to in his published works as well as scanty records of his activities as a young monk and as a visitor to Geneva, Paris, London, and other cities. The most complete are the records of his responses to his religious superiors and examiners, especially in Venice in 1592. However, his published comments about his youth are literary and unverifiable, and his conversations in prison are sometimes self-serving, even if revealing.[5] These bits and pieces of information leave unresolved not only questions of Bruno's personal life but also of his intellectual life and growth. Accordingly, it has been easy for Bruno's biographers to treat his thought system as a static whole, as if, in other words, he had not developed new insights or approaches and preferences at certain times and in certain places.

The Literature

There has been considerable debate in the Bruno literature about the very content and meaning of Bruno's thought.[6] Frances Yates's interpretation of Bruno as a Hermetic magus has been severely criticized by Hélène Védrine. Védrine also disagrees with the older interpretations of Tocco, Olschki, Gentile, Mondolfo, and Corsano.[7] She is correct, in my view, in criticizing these latter historians for either finding Bruno's thought incapable of being seen as a coherent whole or placing undue importance on particular philosophers whom Bruno quotes at various times (in the case of Tocco, for instance, Bruno's changing emphasis on Plotinus, Parmenides, Heraclitus, and Democritus).[8] It is clear, for example, that in a relatively early work such as *La Cena de le Ceneri* (1584), Bruno draws from a spectrum of sources, especially from Plotinus and Lucretius.[9]

In place of these various interpretations all striving to fit sometimes quite divergent philosophical approaches into Bruno's intellectual outlook—and being able to do so only by tracing a misleading chronological adoption and rejection of ancient thinkers—Védrine argues that

> il nous semble que la diversité des oeuvres, la place qu'elles tiennent dans les intérêts théoriques et pratiques du Nolain, interdisent d'attendre trop d'une simple étude chronologique. On ne peut mettre sur le même plan les ouvrages mnémotechniques destinés à un grand publique et les recherches fondamentales sur l'être et les mondes infinis.[10]

Instead, then, of providing a general interpretation of Bruno's thought, as did Yates, or an interpretation based either on ineptitude (Olschki) or on change over time (Tocco, Corsano), Védrine advances the view that Bruno's writings can be divided into two basic categories: those which were aimed at a credulous audience and those which were serious interpretations of nature. Hers is basically a Marxist approach, and it assumes that Bruno's writings, divided into these two categories, were governed by his precarious social and economic situation—the problem, perhaps, of being an "academician of no academy."[11] Indeed, it is Bruno's Lullist writings that force Védrine to this interpretation, as she, like Dorothea Singer before her, finds them an embarrassment:

Comment expliquer, dès lors, qu'il ait écrit tant d'oeuvres mnémotechniques? Nous pencherions vers une hypothèse que n'étaye sans doute aucune confidence, aucune lettre, mais qui au moins a le mérite d'être plausible. En tant qu'intellectuel sans attaches sociales précises, Bruno est dans une situation précaire: il lui faut donc flatter les grands et se livrèr plus que tout au jeu des modes et des préjugés. Or, les procédés mnémotechniques ont toujours la faveur de ceux qui veulent apprendre rapidement et sans douleur.[12]

This argument is curiously parallel to a statement made by Emile Namer, another noted French Bruno scholar:

Sans doute, est-il facile de constater que la plupart des ouvrages de Bruno cèdent à la mode du temps, parce qu'alors, comme aujourd'hui, la magie se vend mieux que la philosophie rigoureuse et la science. Mais si Bruno n'était que cela, il ne mériterait pas d'être étudié comme penseur original et moderne. . . . On a parfaitement le droit de s'interesser à l'hermétisme à la mode au XVIe siècle, mais non d'y ramener la grande pensée de Giordano Bruno.[13]

For both these historians there were two Brunos: one sincere, in those rare moments when his "true" beliefs on nature were made known; and the other cynically cunning, pandering to the superstitious follies of his contemporaries. Interestingly enough, Namer is the French translator of *La Cena de le Ceneri,* a translation that not surprisingly expurgates those sections which do not relate to a "scientific" reading of the dialogue.[14] Singer, Védrine, and Namer all suffer from an inability to reconcile Bruno's mnemonic and Copernican works. Their solutions to this "problem" are no better than the solutions based on chronological adoption and rejection or on Bruno's ineptitude. Neither Védrine nor Namer gives any evidentiary justification for distinguishing between "true" and "false" *verba et opera.* They create an unnatural division between works that in fact are not totally dissimilar.[15]

Frances Yates's study of Bruno's thought, therefore, remains more compelling than the preceding, as it brings together the various facets of Bruno's mind into a coherent whole, neither denying some facets nor trying to explain them away. She simply notes two major categories of Bruno's works ("natural" and "mnemonic"), but finds them synergistically related.[16] The one failing, if it be that, of her Bruno book is that it does not attempt to trace a development—geographically, temporally, and causatively—in Bruno's thought. One is left with the impression, as is also the case from reading his other biographers, that Bruno's cognitive habits remained unchanged, at least from 1576 on. Yet, one of Antonio Corsano's most intriguing and valuable comments on Bruno is his suggestion that there may have been different intellectual episodes to his life. He further suggests that the first one was marked by a reformist bent, probably adopted from his reading of Erasmus. It was this ecclesiastical reformism, Corsano avers, that was behind Bruno's difficulties with his superiors in 1576.[17]

Corsano's intuition seems sound. Why should Bruno not have developed intellectually as he moved northward to Paris? It is my view, in fact, that Giordano Bruno's journey to Paris was probably as much an educational experience as was his time in the monastery. For one thing, he would have been more thoroughly introduced, especially after he reached France, to the realities of confessional strife. This would have been particularly the case in Toulouse. It had been a Huguenot stronghold. Only around the time of Bruno's arrival there (1580–81) did the situation ease, so much so that the requirement that a university professor must participate in the Calvinist Eucharist was not enforced.[18] Indeed, in 1579 before arriving in Toulouse, Bruno had been in Geneva where it seems he may have participated in the Reformed Sacrament and professed the Reformed confession.[19]

One finds then, that by the time Bruno reached Paris late in 1581, he had come to know the Reformation controversy at the point where it was in some ways most acute—that is, over the acceptance of the "right" definition of the Sacrament. It is difficult to believe that Bruno would have had this awareness in his Neapolitan monastery, and it is known (as shall be seen below) that in the early and mid 1580s Bruno was very concerned with finding a way out of the impasse over the Eucharistic controversy.

Consequently, Bruno entered Paris a seasoned participant in the turmoil over the Sacrament. He was a man, it would seem, of intense religious sensibilities.[20] However, it can be reasonably argued that it was in Paris that Giordano Bruno, if not introduced for the first time to the ideas of Lull and Copernicus—although this may have been the case—at least found his views on and insights into these writers deepened and even transformed.[21] The few works arguably written by Bruno before 1582 are no longer extant, and whatever little one surmises of their contents comes from remarks Bruno made, later, in other works or to the Venetian Inquisitors in 1592. Such evidence is not necessarily reliable for the putative works' contents.[22] One cannot, therefore, be certain that Bruno was not first introduced to Lull and Copernicus after he arrived in Paris in 1581. More to the point, one can marshal persuasive circumstantial evidence to suggest that Bruno's understanding of these authors would, at the very least, have been transformed by his Paris experience.

Bruno's Lullism

Bruno could have arrived at no better place than Paris to be introduced to the works of Raymond Lull as well as to an understanding of them that was particularly well suited both to his own religious sensibilities and to the experiences he had had with confessional strife since his arrival in Geneva and France in 1579.

Although Paris had experienced an anti-Lull period in the fifteenth century, it had, from the time of Lull's visit there in 1287, been a "fruitful" center of Lullist studies.[23] Paris's importance for Lullian studies was due to the fact that the Catalan master had left collections of his works at the Sorbonne and at the Chartreuse de Vauvert.[24] Another important repository of Lull's manuscripts was the library of the Abbey of Saint Victor. Lull's mystical mnemonic and cosmological ideas were attacked by the Parisian nominalists Pierre d'Ailly and Jean Gerson, who excoriated the Spanish system builder for his lack of university preparation and standing and for the absence of scholastic terminology from his writings. However, in the late fifteenth and early sixteenth centuries, Lullist studies once again became prominent in Paris, thanks especially to the scholarly efforts of Jacques Lefèvre d'Etaples and Charles de Bovelles.[25]

Lefèvre d'Etaples (1460–1536) was a humanist scholar, best known today perhaps for his edition of the *Quincuplex Psalterium* and for his reformist activities under Guillaume Briçonnet, first at the Abbey of Saint-Germain-des-Prés and then in Meaux. Lefèvre was an Aristotelian humanist who edited many Aristotelian texts between 1492 and 1515. His interests also extended to medieval mystics such as Dionysius the Areopagite and Richard of Saint Victor, as well as to Ficino's *De triplici vita* and the writings of Nicholas of Cusa. Not only did Lefèvre publish Lull's works but he also venerated him as a saint because of his simple life and viewed him as a "champion of Christian truth" against Averroës and the Averroists.[26] He respected Lull for the very reasons that the Parisian Schoolmen of the fifteenth century had attacked him. Lefèvre used the Lullian collections at the Chartreuse de Vauvert and at the Abbey of Saint Victor.[27] Accordingly, before Lefèvre turned his attention primarily to sacred Scripture and diocesan reform, he was very much influenced by the medieval mystics.[28] I would argue, moreover, based on Lefèvre's use and understanding of the prophetic voice of David in the Psalms,[29] that the impulses that led him to the medieval mystic tradition also governed his understanding of the Psalms. As he "totalized" David into Christ in his comments on the Psalter,[30] Lefèvre made the spiritual meaning of the Psalter into the literal meaning of the Gospels. This totalization of meaning led, thereby, to a kind of pansophism, as when Lefèvre wrote: "Extra evangelium nihil scire est omnia scire."[31] This pansophism became typical of much of sixteenth- and seventeenth-century thought, from Lefèvre to Bruno to Leibniz.[32]

While Lefèvre d'Etaples was "perhaps more responsible than any other man for the divulgation of Lullism outside Spain in the early sixteenth century,"[33] his colleague Charles de Bovelles also contributed to the Lullist publishing program in Paris during the first two decades of the sixteenth century.[34] Charles de Bovelles (1479–1553), as did Lefèvre, incorporated Lull's ideas—for example, that of *concordia*—into his thought system. He, too, saw Lull as a saint or near saint.[35] His *Life* of Lull, based on a copy of the fourteenth-century *Vita* in the Abbey of Saint Victor, adopted the view that Doctor Illuminatus had suffered martyrdom. Bovelles was profoundly influenced by Lull's Art,[36] and saw it as a "transcendent discipline of unity."[37] By 1514, Lefèvre and Bovelles had attained such international fame as Lullist scholars that in May of that year the Spanish Lullist Nicolas de Pax wrote to Bovelles seeking his opinion on abstruse points in the Lullian text. That a Lullist from Lull's homeland would request help on Lull's teachings from this Parisian scholar "is an indication of the growth and prestige of Parisian Lullism . . . unthinkable in 1500."[38]

How far Lullism had indeed progressed in Paris from the days when it had been attacked there by Pierre d'Ailly and Jean Gerson is indicated by the fact that a course in the Art of Lull was established at the Sorbonne in 1515. The man selected to profess Lullism at the university was Bernardo de Lavinheta, Spaniard by birth, Franciscan by vocation, and Scotist by training.[39] In addition to his teaching in Paris, he oversaw the publication of Lullian works between 1514 and

1517 in Lyons, Paris, and Cologne.[40] Unlike Lefèvre and Bovelles who approached Lull as, respectively, a spiritual and a rational guide[41]—and for both a foil to Averroist Aristotelianism and sterile nominalism—Lavinheta viewed Lull's Art as both a logic and mnemonic device, an *ars combinatoria* that, he believed, could lead to a method for universal truth.[42] It was he, too, who endeavored to unite Lull's letter-coded *quaestiones,* referring to the divine attributes, with the classical Ciceronian, or "Tullian," *memoria localis,* a union that would nourish the encyclopedism of the magical art of memory in the later sixteenth century.[43]

By the end of the second decade of the sixteenth century, Paris had achieved a paramount role in the propagation and teaching of Lullian doctrine. More than this, as I have shown, this preeminence was attained within an ambience of totalizing pansophism and reformist and mystical impulses, and because of Paris's three important repositories of Lullian manuscripts, many of which had been left there by the master himself.

Why should one not think that Bruno's serious interest in Lull was born in Paris? The general assumption in the literature is that Bruno's intellectual formation occurred during his schooling and novitiate in the Kingdom. Spampanato and Tocco[44] carefully surveyed Neapolitan culture in the mid-sixteenth century, but as Corsano admits,

> Sui successivi studi . . . non abbiamo documenti diretti. . . .Il Tocco e lo Spampanato . . .cercarono stabilirli . . . ma sono metodi purtroppo entrambi necessariamente estrinseci.[45]

There is no convincing evidence that Bruno had ever dabbled in artificial memory before his arrival in Paris. And even if he had, it most likely would have been in the mnemonic art as it was practiced by the Dominicans: the classical art, without the combinatory method of Raymond Lull so much advanced by Bernardo de Lavinheta.[46]

There is, on the other hand, circumstantial evidence that allows one to infer that Bruno either picked up his knowledge of Lull in Paris or, at least, transformed his understanding of the Tullian art of memory as a result of his being there.[47] First, Bruno explicitly mentions both Lefèvre d'Etaples and Charles de Bovelles in the introduction to his *Lampas combinatoria lulliana.*[48] He praises Lefèvre's work as a "glory to France"; and he lauds Bovelles in the context of his Lullist interests. It is thus known that Bruno was familiar with the work of these two famous early-sixteenth-century Lullists. Moreover, Bruno's *Medicina lulliana* (1590)[49] is little more than a copy of Lavinheta's *Explanatio compendiosaque applicatio artis . . . Lulli* (1523).[50] Once more Bruno is involved with Lullist doctrine in the context of the Parisian school of Lullism. Finally, it would seem that Paris had a synergetic influence on Bruno, for it was only after his arrival in Paris that he began a series of works dealing with the Lullian art of memory: *De umbris idearum, Ars memoriae, Cantus Circaeus, De compendiosa architectura,* and *Complemento artis Lullii,* all of which were published in 1582. These were followed by five mnemonic works published in 1583 and 1584 in London.[51] This spate of publications, totally unlike Bruno's practice before his arrival in Paris, indicates that

Paris's preeminence in Lullist studies and Bruno's ability to use the great Lullian manuscript repositories in that city had made of him a zealous convert to Lullism.[52] Certainly he had been in Geneva and Toulouse long enough to have allowed him to see some works through the press. He seems not to have, and the reason seems evident.

The question also arises as to why Bruno finally did devote his energies to the Lullian art of memory. If Hélène Védrine were correct, Bruno expended these efforts in order to write self-enriching, popular books. The same point of view, without the underlying Marxist explanatory agency, is perhaps implicit when Dorothea Singer asks:

> Why should this man, occupied with the formulation of a lofty philosophy, have turned aside and spent so much time on the idle elaborations of logic and mnemonics devised by Raymond Lull?[53]

Both these attitudes reflect an imperfect understanding of Bruno's mind and of the qualities that made Lull such a fascinating thinker for Bruno as well as for such earlier scholars as Lefèvre d'Etaples, Charles de Bovelles, and Bernardo de Lavinheta.

If one recalls that Bruno's first run-ins with his Dominican superiors seem to have involved reformist tendencies on his part, activated by his reading of Erasmus,[54] it may be concluded that these tendencies found nourishing ground and a sympathetic chord in the reformist and anti-Averroist inclinations of Lefèvre and Bovelles, and that Lavinheta's combination of Lullism with the classical art of memory may have opened new vistas for Bruno, new approaches to the use of artificial memory. Indeed, I shall soon show that Lullian reformist interests, inherited from Lefèvre, Bovelles, and Lavinheta, accorded well with the liberal, reunionist reformism Bruno met with among Henry III's court circle. As Lull had wanted to use his Art to unite Muslims, Jews, and Christians, this court circle and Bruno would want to reunite the European Christian community. Thus, I shall show that *pace* Védrine, Singer, et alia, Bruno's Lullian works were no more frivolous than his Copernican works. They complemented one another. Both Lull and Copernicus were to be used by Bruno for the curing of social ills. In this respect, his Copernicanism was an aspect of his Lullian medicine.

Bruno's Copernicanism

These social ills were the same as those Bruno encountered as he journeyed from Italy to Geneva, and through the Midi from Lyons to Toulouse and then to Paris. He had found at the center of the Reformation controversies the debates over the Eucharist. In Paris, he came across a community of men—former Pléiadeistes, now Palace Academicians—who were discussing issues that gave Bruno that other key to what he called the "troubles in religion": Copernicus.[55]

One must not insist that all the Academicians in Henry III's circle were ardent Copernicans. Indeed, it is known that Ronsard, conservative in his cosmological views as in his poetry,[56] opposed the Copernican doctrine. Jean-Antoine de Baïf, on the other hand, left open the possibility that Copernicus was correct. The Huguenot-born, Roman Catholic convert, and bishop of Evreux and cardinal, Jacques Davy Du Perron, was both a Lullist and a defender of Copernicus. Finally, Pontus de Tyard, bishop of Chalon-sur-Saône and author of the *Premier Curieux* and of *Mantice*, was favorable to Copernicus's teachings.[57]

At first glance one might think that not too much should be made of the fact that members of Henry III's court circle disputed and discussed the Copernican theory. To put it another way, perhaps Frances Yates's comment is the most extreme position that (perhaps) merely coincidental interests should allow:

> It is remarkable how many of the ingredients of Giordano Bruno's mind we meet with in the French academic philosophers. Both his philosophical opinions and his Lullism would not have seemed out of place in this atmosphere. It is not surprising, therefore, to find that Bruno was a philosopher who found favour in the eyes of Henri III.[58]

But these "ingredients" seem to be more than merely coincidental. They are of such a sort that two conclusions may be inferred: that Bruno learned his Copernicus in Paris, and that he did indeed have a politico-religious "mission" to England from the French king.

The most striking feature of Bruno's Copernicanism was his insistence upon both the infinity of the universe and the plurality of inhabited worlds. While one could ascribe these teachings to a philosophical doctrine of Plenitude,[59] they are as easily seen as having been learned from conversations in which Bruno joined after his arrival in Paris. Pontus de Tyard was clearly interested in the Copernican theory, even if not an out-and-out follower of that teaching. In *Mantice*, he entertains the idea that the stars are other inhabited worlds.[60] Jean-Antoine de Baïf assumed that Copernicus had taught the infinity of the universe.[61] The likelihood that Bruno picked up these notions in Paris is evidenced by a critical passage in *La Cena de le Ceneri (The Ash Wednesday Supper)*, when, Bruno tells us, Copernicus's *De revolutionibus* is brought out to settle a point in contention between Doctor Torquato and the Nolan. The issue at hand concerns whether the earth and moon are "contained in the same epicycle."[62] Torquato, the Aristotelian anti-Copernican, correctly argues that the earth and moon do not follow each other on the same epicycle, while the Nolan, the self-professed Copernican (who a few lines before had said, "I care little about Copernicus")[63] incorrectly argues the contrary. The telling point here is that Bruno's error seems to have resulted from the fact that he follows Pontus de Tyard's muddled translation of Copernicus. Copernicus's text unambiguously states that the moon lies as if on an epicycle about the earth.[64] Pontus de Tyard less carefully writes that the earth and the entire sublunar region, with the globe of moon, are contained as if within an epicycle.[65] The Nolan says that the earth and the moon are as if contained in the same epicycle.[66] That Bruno's understanding of Copernicus devolved from Pontus de Tyard seems clear, especially since if Bruno had cared to notice, he would have read on that same diagram of the Copernican model to which he called his auditors' and readers' attention the very unambiguous words that label the orbit of the earth: "Telluris cum orbe lunari annua revolutio."[67] It is not coincidental, I think, that when Bruno lectured at Oxford in 1583, supposedly on Copernicus, he was caught quoting from Ficino's *De vita coelitus comparanda* rather than from *De revolutionibus;*[68] and that on the page of *De revolutionibus* to which the Nolan would have his audience in *La Cena de le Ceneri* turn, there is a quotation from Hermes Trismegistus calling the sun "a visible god." Bruno certainly did "care little" about Copernicus the astronomer and about the Copernican system as an astronomical reality, but he did care deeply about the Copernican model and its diagram as an occult, Hermetic sign, a "secret."[69]

What was this secret? It had to do with the healing powers of the sun, which on one level, renews the earth as they revolve about each other. On another level, it had to do with the Supper, the Eucharist. The Supper was, as Bruno had learned, the *pons asinorum* for those not able to transcend religious quibbles. How this point must have struck home to Bruno when, at last in Paris, he discovered that ever since the Colloquy of Poissy in 1560 there had been a royalist policy of attempting to compose the confessional differences over the Lord's Supper—in part by making concessions in liturgical practice and fasting discipline.[70] Among those with whom Bruno would have come into contact at Henry III's court was Jacques Davy Du Perron, who was a Lullist and a Copernican. It was Du Perron whose plans for "reuniting religions" included presenting the Sacrament to Protestants as "the Supper disguised." His plans also included revisions of the fasting rules.[71]

After Bruno had been betrayed to the Venetian Inquisition by Zuan Mocenigo in May 1592, the Inquisitors asked him a critical question—

> if in his writings he had made any mention of the Ash Wednesday Supper, and what was his intention.[72]

Bruno clearly shifted gears and replied:

> I wrote a *book* [italics added] titled *La Cena de le Ceneri,* which is divided into five dialogues that deal with the motion of the earth; and because I had this discussion in England during a supper that took place on Ash Wednesday in the French ambassador's residence where I was staying, I titled these dialogues *La Cena de le Ceneri* and dedicated them to the ambassador.[73]

Bruno then claimed to be willing to admit any error he might have made on this topic. The Inquisitors did not raise the issue of the book; rather, they raised that of theological or liturgical concession. Bruno shifted discussion to the book and to Copernicus because he must have felt that Copernicanism was a safer topic.

It was. Bruno's interrogators ignored his response about earth movement and returned to another aspect of the point they had originally raised. Had he ever praised any heretics or heresiarchs (Elizabeth I or Henry of Navarre, for example)?[74] The pressing of their point shows that the Inquisitors recognized the connotations of *La Cena de le Ceneri* and thought of them in connection with

Bruno's relations with the circle of Academic philosophers in Paris who were the instigators of "la cène desguisée."

Even though Bruno feigned innocence when questioned in 1592, his remarks in 1585 to Guillaume Cotin, the librarian of the Abbey of Saint Victor, give an entirely different impression. On 7 December Cotin reported that Bruno

> condemned the subtleties of the scholastics and of the sacraments as well as of the Eucharist; subtleties of which he said Saints Peter and Paul had known nothing, for they only knew that *hoc est corpus meum*. He says that the troubles in religion will evaporate when these subtle questions disappear, and he says that he hopes it will be the end of them very soon.[75]

Well could Bruno hope that the "troubles in religion" would soon end. He had recently returned from London where he had lived with King Henry's ambassador, the marquis de Mauvissière, and he had labored there under the impression that he was on a clandestine mission from the French king.[76] This may well not have been a foolish conceit on Bruno's part for, if my reading of his Paris "education" is correct, it would not at all be farfetched to think that Bruno had been almost specially prepared—in Lullism and Copernicanism—for his English sojourn.

As I have shown, this preparation could have been in the use of Lullism and Copernicanism as part of the French Valois policy of "the Supper disguised," a kind of Eucharistic secret. In the prefatory epistle to *La Cena de le Ceneri,* Bruno wrote the following about the subsequent dialogues:

> Then, if on occasion you see lighter subjects presented herein which might raise fears of being subjected to the haughty censorship of Cato, do not worry, since such Catos would be blind and mad indeed if they could not discover what is hidden under these *Sileni.*[77]

Blindness and madness are diseases that Bruno reports as being endemic in England in *La Cena de le Ceneri.* The Nolan's opponents in the debate, doctors Nundinio and Torquato, are blind precisely because they could not perceive the *Sileni* hidden in the Nolan's Copernican teachings; they insisted he should at least read his Copernicus accurately. Thus, when he did not, they reproached him as would have Cato of old.[78] Bruno's Venetian interrogators, on the other hand, were not blind, although Bruno certainly tried to cloud the issue.

The conviction that Bruno was on a mission from Henry III is strengthened by his description in *Lo spaccio della bestia trionfante* (The expulsion of the triumphant beast), also published in England, of Henry III's device of the three crowns, into which description Bruno placed a plea for English support of France against Spain and the French Catholic League.[79] It is no wonder that when Bruno embarked for England in 1582, the English ambassador to France wrote to Francis Walsingham, "Doctor Jordano Bruno Nolano, a professor of philosophy, intends to pass into England, whose religion I cannot commend."[80] England, ever watchful against expensive foreign entanglements and alliances, needed to be warned against Bruno and "the Supper disguised."

When Giordano Bruno returned to France with Mauvissière in 1585, he probably expected once again to be welcomed as a royal Reader into the company of Henry III's intellectual circle, that same circle which had introduced him to Parisian-style Lullism and Copernicanism. It must, therefore, have come as something of a shock when in late May 1586, Bruno and his disciple Jehan Hennequin were opposed, in their attack on Aristotle at the Collège de Cambrai, by Rudolphus Calerius, a young lawyer in the employ of Jacques Davy Du Perron. Calerius humiliated the Nolan and his follower, forcing them unceremoniously to depart the debate and Paris.[81] Henry III had been under vitriolic attack by the Guisards (who had recently gained the upper hand in France). The humiliation of Bruno by an agent of the king's orator and chronicler way well have been a way of ridding the king of the embarassment of Bruno and his secret mission to England. Frances Yates intuited the importance of this event:

> The fact that it was the . . . friend of Du Perron who intervened against Bruno at the Cambrai debate, shows that the intervention was inspired, not by the Guise or the Leaguers, but by the King's own group.[82]

Bruno's role in the Valois policy of "the Supper disguised" had to be quickly terminated. My evidence and arguments support and clarify Yates's intuition. Giordano Bruno was "left out in the cold," the victim of raisons d'état.

Conclusion

I have, in this paper, reprised aspects of the Bruno literature on his Lullism and Copernicanism. I have found that the common opinion—that his Lullism was the result of adolescent and novitiate readings and study (at best a foolish pastime) and that his Copernicanism represented his maturer thought—simply does not ring true. It is probably correct to say that he had been a student of the art of memory in Italy, but Naples was no center of Lullian studies. As a Dominican, Fra Giordano Bruno would have followed the classical or Tullian art, as it was understood and practiced by such Dominican mnemonic masters as Peter of Ravenna and Thomas Aquinas (the latter had likewise been an inmate in San Domenico). Nor, for that matter, is there any special reason to think that Bruno at that time viewed Hermes Trismegistus as the first *priscus theologus,* antedating Moses. Neither is the fact that Bruno lectured on Sacrobosco's *Sphere* in Noli, before leaving Italy, sufficient evidence to prove either that he was adept in astronomy or that he was a Copernican. After all, Lefèvre d'Etaples had published the *Sphere* and his own commentary on it, and no one has ever suggested that he was an astronomer.[83] The beliefs that Bruno was a Lullist, a Copernican, even a Hermetist, before he broke loose from San Domenico in the Kingdom, are not based on hard evidence.

The evidence of Bruno's surroundings and connections after he left Italy strongly suggests that Paris was the most likely place for him to have absorbed and embraced these teachings. His reformist inclinations and his medieval Dominican mnemonics would have prepared him for the mystical inclinations of Lefèvre and Bovelles, and for their understandings of Lull. It is known that Bruno made Lullism into a healing art as a result of reading Lavinheta's rendition of Lull's Art.

It is known, too, that Lavinheta's pansophist version of Lullism influenced late-sixteenth-century Parisian Lullists' understanding of Lull and of the encyclopedia, an understanding very close to Bruno's mnemonic encyclopedism.

However, what seems to tie the argument together is the realization that Giordano Bruno's Copernicanism was intimately linked with a kind of religious reformism and reunionism. One can recognize that Bruno's *Cena de le Ceneri* was part of his royal mission to England, and that Valois policy between 1560 and 1584 involved trying to reach new, transcendent understandings of the Supper and fasting rules. Bruno's activity in England and France strongly suggests that he was "on a mission," that he was an active agent of the French king, and that he had been introduced to the policy of "the Supper disguised" for this very purpose. Such seems to have been the assessment of the Catholic Inquisitors in 1592 and probably of the English ambassador at the French court in 1583. One wonders if that mission might not have been more successful—the English ambassador's warning and the political volte-face in Paris notwithstanding—had Henry III's agent been someone less grating and more endearing than Giordano Bruno.

Even after his return to France and the turn in Henry's fortunes, Bruno continued to publish—works dedicated now to Piero del Bene, agent of the king of Navarre (to whom Catherine de Medici and Henry III were sending secret emissaries).[84] It was after Henry III's death and the growing certainty of Navarre's victory over the Guisards and Leaguers that Bruno elected to return to Italy, there to put his mystical program of universal reform and reunion before the pope. His betrayer, Mocenigo, told the Venetian Inquisitors that Bruno held out great hopes for Henry of Navarre and for himself.[85] It may just be that, in 1591, Giordano Bruno still saw himself on a mission from France, preaching "the Supper disguised," and curing the "troubles in religion" via the mystical Lullism and Copernicanism he had learned years before in Paris from Lullian texts, humanist editors, and royal Academicians.

Notes

1. Dorothea W. Singer, *Giordano Bruno: His Life and Thought* (New York, 1950); Frances Yates, *Giordano Bruno and the Hermetic Tradition* (Chicago, 1964).

2. Yates, *Bruno,* p. x.

3. Frances A. Yates, *The Art of Memory* (London, 1966).

4. For a survey of Lull scholarship as well as for a study of Lull's works and thought, see J. N. Hillgarth, *Ramon Lull and Lullism in Fourteenth-Century France* (Oxford, 1971). See also Frances A. Yates, *Lull and Bruno: Collected Essays* (London, 1982), pp. 3–125.

5. For the surviving records of Bruno's remarks and conversations, see Vincenzo Spampanato, *Documenti della vita di Giordano Bruno* (Florence, 1933).

6. A succinct survey of this debate can be found in Hélène Védrine, *La conception de la nature chez Giordano Bruno* (Paris, 1967), pp. 103–7.

7. *Le opere latine di Giordano Bruno* ed. F. Tocco, (Florence, 1889); F. Tocco, "Le fonti più recenti della filosofia del Bruno," *Rendiconti della Reale Accademia dei Lincei,* 5th ser. (Rome, 1892), 1 : 503–38, 585–622; Leo Olschki, *Giordano Bruno* (Bari, 1927); Giovanni Gentile, *Giordano Bruno e il pensiero del Rinascimento* (Florence, 1920–25); R. Mondolfo, "La filosofia di Giordano Bruno e l'interpretazione di F. Tocco," in *La cultura filosofica* (Florence, 1912); Antonio Corsano, *Il pensiero di Giordano Bruno nel suo svolgimento storico* (Florence, 1940–48).

8. Védrine, *Conception de la nature,* pp. 104–5.

9. Giordano Bruno, *The Ash Wednesday Supper,* trans. and ed. E. A. Gosselin and L. S. Lerner (Hamden, Conn., 1977). See especially the introduction, pp. 11–60. This translation is based on the

Gentile/Aquilecchia edition of Giordano Bruno, *La Cena de le Ceneri*, in *Dialoghi italiani* (Florence, 1972), pp. 5–171.

10. Védrine, *Conception de la nature*, p. 105.

11. Bruno calls himself "l'Academico di nulla academia" in his comedy, *Il Candelaio* (Paris, 1582), recently edited by Giorgio Squarotti (Turin, 1969), 1.2 (p. 38).

12. Védrine, *Conception de la nature*, pp. 107–8.

13. Emile Namer, review in *Revue d'histoire des sciences et de leurs applications* 29 (1976): 274–76.

14. Giordano Bruno, *Le banquet des cendres*, trans. Emile Namer (Paris, 1955). For example, Namer excluded the second dialogue of the *Cena*, which recounts the Nolan's journey from the French embassy to Sir Fulke Greville's home.

15. I am embarking upon a comparative study of Bruno's *Cena de le Ceneri* and his *De umbris idearum* (Paris, 1582).

16. Yates, *Bruno*, p. x: "The three strands of the Hermetism, the mnemonics, and the Lullism are all interwoven in Bruno's complex personality."

17. Corsano, *Il pensiero*, p. 51; Védrine, *Conception de la nature*, p. 33.

18. Singer, *Bruno*, p. 16.

19. Ibid., p. 15. Singer thinks that Bruno did not accept membership in the Calvinist communion. However, at the end of May 1579, he petitioned the Consistory for a reversal of the ban on participating in the Lord's Supper.

20. Bruno had been censured and brought before his superiors in the Dominican order in Naples and Rome in 1576 for, among other things, having used and sequestered in his privy forbidden works of Erasmus. Bruno also removed pictures of the saints from his monastic cell, allowing only a crucifix to remain. See *Documenti*, pp. 124–26; and P.-H. Michel, *La cosmologie de Giordano Bruno* (Paris, 1962), p. 6.

21. Singer, *Bruno*, p. 11, opines that Bruno read Aristotle; his Arabic and Hebrew commentators (in translation); the pre-Socratics (at second hand); classical writers such as Cicero, Vergil, Lucian, Seneca, and Ovid; and the works of Raymond Lull. However, it would seem that it is certain only that Bruno had read Aquinas and Peter Lombard's *Sentences* (and perhaps some Aristotle) in school and the monastery. The other writers cited by Singer are conjectured, as may be ascertained by her use of subjunctives; besides, Bruno explicitly mentioned in Venice that he had read Aquinas and Lombard. Singer's argument is based on the fact that Bruno cites the other names in his works. However, such citations are in works written several years after he had left the monastery, during which time he might have read them; or, he might have picked up smatterings of Cicero, Ovid, etc., from using the florilegia that were common at the time.

22. See Singer, *Bruno*, pp. 204–13, for a listing of Bruno's lost and published works. This listing essentially duplicates that found in V. Salvestrini, *Bibliografia di Giordano Bruno (1582–1950)*, 2d ed., ed. Luigi Firpo (Florence, 1958).

23. Hillgarth, *Lull and Lullism*, p. 317.

24. Ibid. Lull himself had tried to establish centers of Lullist study. Late in his life, he saw to it that there would be three principal collections of his works. According to the anonymous author of the contemporary *Vita* (Paris, 1311), "his books are dispersed through the world, but he made three special collections; that is, in the monastery of Carthusians at Paris, and in the house of a certain noble of the city of Genoa [Perceval Spinola], and in the house of a certain noble of the city of Majorca [probably the house of Lull's son-in-law, Pere de Sentemenat]." The concentration of manuscripts is confirmed by Lull's will, dated 26 April 1313. Lull's wishes were not immediately fulfilled: Majorca became a center of Lullism only after about 1450, when scholars from western Europe began going there to study. Genoa also proved to be disappointing as an active center of Lullist studies. Only Paris (and derivatively, Valencia) became an immediate center of Lullism—although Lullist activity there was interrupted by the nominalists' attack on Lullism in the fifteenth century. (See Hillgarth, *Lull and Lullism*, pp. 142–43, 148–49, for a fuller discussion of these matters.)

25. On Lefèvre and Bovelles, see Augustin Renaudet, *Préréforme et humanisme à Paris pendant les premières guerres d'Italie* (Paris, 1916–53), pp. 671–73 and passim; Eugene F. Rice, Jr., "The Humanist Idea of Christian Antiquity: Jacques Lefèvre d'Etaples and His Circle," *Studies in the Renaissance* 9 (1962): 126–60; Joseph M. Victor, "The Revival of Lullism at Paris, 1499–1516," *Renaissance Quarterly* 28, no. 4 (1975): 504–34; José Tarré, "Los códices Lullianos de la Biblioteca Nacional de Paris," *Analecta Sacra Tarraconensia* 14 (1941): 171, 173; and Miquel Batllori, "El lulismo en Italia," *Revista de Filosofía* 2 (1943): 507–10.

26. Hillgarth, *Lull and Lullism*, pp. 286–87.

27. Ibid., p. 288.

28. See Eugene F. Rice, Jr., "Jacques Lefèvre d'Etaples and the Medieval Christian Mystics," in *Florilegium Historiale: Essays Presented to Wallace K. Ferguson*, ed. R. G. Rowe and W. H. Stockdale (Toronto, 1971), pp. 95, 97, 99–100.

29. See Edward A. Gosselin, "Two Views of the Evangelical David: Lefèvre d'Etaples and Theodore Beza," in *The David Myth in Western Literature*, ed. R.-J. Frontain and J. Wojcik (West Lafayette, Ind., 1980), pp. 57–62, 66–67; see also idem, *The King's Progress to Jerusalem*, Humana Civiltas, vol. 2 (Malibu, Calif., 1976), pp. 49–63.

30. Gosselin, "Evangelical David," p. 66.

31. Quoted by Eugene F. Rice, Jr., in *The Pursuit of Holiness*, ed. C. Trinkhaus and H. A. Oberman (Leiden, 1974), p. 473.

32. I borrow the concept of "pansophism" from Paolo Rossi, "The Legacy of Ramon Lull in Sixteenth-Century Thought," *Mediaeval and Renaissance Studies* (Warburg Institute) 5 (1961): 211.

33. Hillgarth, *Lull and Lullism*, p. 283.

34. On Lefèvre's circle, see Rice, "Humanist Idea of Christian Antiquity," pp. 126–41.

35. Lull was never canonized, although he was beatified and his cultus was formally established by Pope Pius IX in 1858. It was the Franciscans who revered him as "Doctor Illuminatus," and his feast day is celebrated in that order on 3 July. Although attracted to both the Franciscans and the Dominicans, Lull never took holy orders.

36. On Lull's Art, see Yates, *Lull and Bruno*, pp. 9–77; idem, *Memory*, pp. 178–94; *New Catholic Encyclopedia*, s.v. "Lull, Raymond, Bl."; and R. D. F. Pring-Mill, "The Trinitarian World Picture of Ramon Lull," *Romanistisches Jahrbuch* 7 (1956): 229–56.

37. Victor, "Revival," p. 523.

38. Ibid., p. 530. See n. 24 above on Paris as a Lullist center.

39. On Lavinheta, see Hillgarth, *Lull and Lullism*, pp. 288–89; Victor, "Revival," pp. 533–334; Rossi, "Legacy," pp. 208–10; Yates, *Memory*, p. 194; Paolo Rossi, *Clavis Universalis* (Milan, 1960), pp. 74–78; and Michela Pereira, "Le opere mediche di Lullo in rapporto con la sua filosofa naturale e con la medicina de XIII secolo," *Estudios Lulanos* 23 (1979): 6–7.

40. Hillgarth, *Lull and Lullism*, p. 288.

41. Coming to Lull from Cusanus, Lefèvre saw him as a mystical guide; for Bovelles, approaching Lull from Cusanus and from Raymon de Sebond's *Theologia naturalis*, Lull's *Ars* was a rational tool for inquiry. See Victor, "Revival," p. 519.

42. Cf. Rossi, "Legacy," p. 210; and Victor, "Revival," p. 533.

43. Cf. Yates, *Memory*, pp. 194–98; and Rossi, "Legacy," pp. 208–10.

44. See notes 5 and 7 above. (For Tocco, the reference is to "Le fonti più ricenti.")

45. Corsano, *Il pensiero*, p. 44.

46. On the Dominicans' practice of mnemonics, see Yates, *Memory*, chap. 8. Bruno claimed to have read Peter of Ravenna's *Phoenix, sive artificiosa memoria* (1st ed., Venice, 1491), the most widely known late medieval memory treatise. Cf. William Boulting, *Giordano Bruno: His Life, Thought, and Martyrdom* (1914; reprint, Freeport, N.Y., 1972), p. 8. On Peter of Ravenna, see Yates, *Memory*, pp. 112–15.

47. Transformed, that is, from the Tullian method used by the Dominicans into the combinatory encyclopedism used by Lull and Lavinheta.

48. Giordano Bruno, *Opere latine*, 2.2.235: "Mitto quantum Lullio tribuat mille in propositis Stapulensis ille Faber, in cuius unica philosophia iuxta Peripateticorum dogmata Gallia gloriatur; mitto Carolum Bovillum, non tam (si Aristarchorum ferulae subiiciantur) orationis stilo Fabro ipso humilior, quam (si e cathedra philosophiae examinentur) ingenio illustrior iudicioque in multiplici disciplinarum genere maturior et excultior, qui de Lullii vita scripsit, Lullianae doctrinae edit ubique specimen et ubique pro summo habet honore, ut Lullianus appareat."

49. Bruno, *Opere latine*, 3:569–633.

50. Pereira, "Opere mediche," p. 7.

51. Cf. Singer, *Bruno*, pp. 205–6.

52. Bruno is known to have visited the library of the Abbey of Saint Victor in 1585 and 1586 (*Documenti*, pp. 39–45). However, he may have used this and/or one of the other libraries that had Lullian collections between the time of his arrival in Paris and his departure for London.

53. Singer, *Bruno*, p. 151.

54. Cf. Corsano, *Il pensiero*, pp. 47, 51; and above, p. 168.

55. *Documenti*, p. 40.

56. A. Kibedi Varga, "Poésie et cosmologie au XVIe siècle," in *Lumières de la Pléiade* (Paris, 1966), p. 137 n. 6.

57. Frances A. Yates, *The French Academies of the Sixteenth Century* (London, 1947), pp. 96–97, 99–100. For a somewhat different assessment of Henry III and of his Palace Academy, see Robert J. Sealy, *The Palace Academy of Henry III* (Geneva, 1981), pp. 167–73.

58. Yates, *French Academies*, p. 101. See also idem, *Bruno*, p. 202: "Bruno was a magician who was sympathetically receptive to the influences of the [Parisian] milieu in which he found himself."

59. A. O. Lovejoy, *The Great Chain of Being* (Cambridge, Mass., 1936), pp. 116–21.

60. Yates, *French Academies,* p. 97.

61. Ibid., p. 96. F. R. Johnson, *Astronomical Thought in Renaissance England* (Baltimore, 1937), pp. 106–7, discusses the existence of some confusion on this point. Thomas Digges, the English Copernican in whose circle Bruno traveled when he was in London, also subscribed to the infinity of the universe. Copernicus had refused to "commit himself definitely on the question of the infinity of the universe" (p. 107).

62. Bruno, *Ash Wednesday Supper,* p. 193.

63. Ibid., p. 192.

64. Nicholas Copernicus, *De revolutionibus* (Nürnberg, 1543), p. 9: "Quartum in ordine annua revolutio locum obtinet, *in quo terram cum orbe lunari tanquam epicyclo contineri diximus*" (italics added).

65. Pontus de Tyard, *Discours philosophiques* (before 1584, there were two editions: *L'univers, ou discours des parties de la nature du monde* [1552], p. 99; and *Deux discours de la nature du monde et de ses parties* [1578], p. 70): "Au quatrieme lieu est logee la sphere qui se tourne en un an: *en laquelle comme dans un Epicycle, la Terre* et toute la region Elementaire, *avec la globe de la Lune est contenue*" (italics added). On Pontus de Tyard and science, see John C. Lapp, "Pontus de Tyard and the Science of His Age," *Romanic Review* 38 (1947): 16–22.

66. Bruno, *La Cena,* p. 141, says, correspondingly to Tyard, *"dicea la terra e la luna essere contenuto come da medesmo epiciclo"* (italics added).

67. Copernicus, *De revolutionibus,* p. 102.

68. Robert McNulty, "Bruno at Oxford," *Renaissance News* 13 (1960): 300–305.

69. In his dedicatory epistle to *De umbris idearum* (*Opere latine,* 2.1.3), Bruno tells Henry III that he is going to reveal a Hermetic "secret." That secret was mnemonic and Lullist. The *Cena* also reveals a secret, as shall be seen, this time in occult, Copernican guise. On the *Cena,* see Edward A. Gosselin, "'Doctor' Bruno's Solar Medicine," *The Sixteenth Century Journal* 15, no. 2 (1984): 209–24.

70. Yates, *French Academies,* p. 215; H. O. Evennet, *The Cardinal of Lorraine and the Council of Trent* (Cambridge, 1930), pp. 244–253, 264–76, and chapter 9.

71. Yates, *French Academies,* pp. 228–29. One should not necessarily conclude that such attempted rapprochements with Protestants meant that either the Valois king and Academicians or Bruno foresaw a genuine tolerance as the end result. Bruno's comments on the Protestants and their "dead" Sacrament (see, e.g., *Ash Wednesday Supper,* pp. 126–27) clearly show that he viewed Protestantism with aesthetic loathing. Henry III and his politique Academicians most likely viewed such concessionary policies as that of "the Supper disguised" as ways of smoothing over differences so that Protestants could be brought back into the "one true fold." This is an interpretation that needs more research and refinement. (I am indebted to Professor Jeanne Harrie for her thoughts on this matter.)

72. *Documenti,* p. 121.

73. Ibid.

74. Ibid., pp. 121–23, for their question and Bruno's response.

75. Ibid., p. 40.

76. See ibid., p. 85, where Bruno tells the Inquisitors that he went to England with letters of introduction from Henry III.

77. Bruno, *Ash Wednesday Supper,* p. 72. This hinting at deep, Silenus-like meanings is repeated throughout the dedicatory epistle to Mauvissière.

78. On disease as a major thematic in *The Ash Wednesday Supper,* see Gosselin, "Solar Medicine."

79. Giordano Bruno, *The Expulsion of the Triumphant Beast,* ed. A. D. Imerti (New Brunswick, N.J., 1964), pp. 270–71 (*Dialoghi italiani,* pp. 286–87). Cf. Yates, *French Academies,* p. 227.

80. *Calendar of State Papers, Foreign,* January–June 1583, p. 214.

81. *Documenti,* pp. 44–46, for Cotin's account of the debate. Bruno (*Documenti,* p. 85) gives a much less dramatic account to his Venetian interrogators: "E partito de Paris per causa di tumulti, me ne andai in Germania."

82. Yates, *Bruno,* p. 301. Yates, *French Academies,* pp. 230–31, has suggested that Bruno may have been thus discredited in order to prevent the king from being attacked by the Guisards. However, she did not see this humiliation of Bruno as a way of ending his "mission."

83. D. P. Walker, *The Ancient Theology: Studies in Christian Platonism from the Fifteenth to Eighteenth Century* (Ithaca, 1972), remarks (p. 69) that both Pontus de Tyard and François de Foix de Candale opined that Hermes Trismegistus antedated Moses. It has been shown, in the context of this paper, that Bruno may have gotten the idea that Hermes lived before Moses from one or both of them. On Lefèvre d'Etaples and Sacrobosco's *Sphere,* see Eugene F. Rice, Jr., *The Prefatory Epistles of Jacques Lefèvre d'Etaples and Related Texts* (New York, 1972), p. 26.

84. Yates, *Bruno,* p. 303.

85. On Bruno's return to Italy, see Yates, *Bruno,* chap. 19.

9

Newton's *Commentary* on the *Emerald Tablet* of Hermes Trismegistus: Its Scientific and Theological Significance

B. J. T. DOBBS

The focal point of this paper is a unique document, a *Commentary* on the *Emerald Tablet* of Hermes Trismegistus written by none other than Isaac Newton, the fountainhead of modern science, and preserved among his alchemical papers at King's College, Cambridge.[1] Few scholars are even aware that Newton composed this commentary on Hermetic materials; thus a part of my purpose should perhaps be characterized as archaeological—simply to bring the document once more into the light of day. The larger part of my purpose, however, is to examine its significance in both the scientific and theological realms.

The basic fact of Newton's heavy commitment to the alchemical enterprise is now widely known.[2] Studies of Newton that attempt to ignore or explain away his intense interest in alchemy may have provided only a gross misinterpretation of Newton's career. The *Principia*, so often seen as the central monument to Newton's life, may have seemed to him "more like an interruption of his primary labor."[3] The large volume of surviving alchemical papers and the cryptic but meticulously kept record of his alchemical experiments bear silent witness that such may indeed have been the case.

Newton's study of Hermes Trismegistus, with which I am here concerned, falls within that general alchemical context and extended over a period of at least twenty years. The principle evidence for Newton's interest in Hermes is comprised of two manuscripts, Keynes MSS 27 and 28, now held by King's College, Cambridge. These manuscripts, though one should not suppose that they represent the entirety of Newton's exploration of Hermetic materials, do show that he knew well the two primary alchemical tracts attributed to Hermes, the *Emerald Tablet* and the so-called *Seven Chapters* (or the *Golden Work*, the *Tractatus aureus de Lapidis Physici Secreto in Cap. 7 divisus*).[4] These two Newton manuscripts, which ink stains indicate once formed a single unit, contain two title pages (each bearing the single word *Hermes*), two versions of the *Emerald Tablet* (one Latin and one English), and an English version of the *Seven Chapters,* apparently translated by Newton himself from the French published in 1678.[5] Deletions, interlineations, corrections, annotations, and changes in ink and handwriting show Newton working through the materials many times and thus enable scholars to build up a plausible reconstruction of his activities with these pieces of paper.

First, in the early 1680s, he copied a version of the *Emerald Tablet,*[6] wrote a commentary on it, and, putting a cover with the title "Hermes" around the pages, laid them aside for other work (perhaps the *Principia*). Then, a decade later, in the early 1690s, "ye French Bibliotheque" having fallen into his hands, he made translations of the Hermetic material he found there and put a similarly titled cover around those sheets. His translations produced the English version of the *Emerald Tablet* now in Keynes MS 28 and the English version of the *Seven Chapters* now in Keynes MS 27. Later still—after perhaps another decade or so—he reorganized the two sets, putting both versions of the *Emerald Tablet* with the commentary, adding a few annotations to the latter, and giving the *Seven Chapters* a new cover and an analytical table of contents. By that time, judging by the handwriting, Newton had become Master of the Mint and had given up active laboratory work in alchemy, though he still continued to revise his alchemical papers (as notes on mint business on some of them indicate).

Of these two Hermetic tracts with which Newton worked, the *Emerald Tablet* is by far the better known. It is, in fact, one of the best-known tracts in all of alchemy. Of indeterminate but great antiquity, it was long supposed to encapsulate in its mysterious phrases all the occult wisdom of the ancients regarding divine actions in the creation of the world and regarding the alchemist's actions in the great work of alchemy, which was of course widely considered to be a little replication of divine creativity.

Since it is short and so pithily arcane, I include here the entire text, utilizing Newton's English from the 1690s.

Tabula Smaragdina

Tis true without lying, certain & most true.

That wch is below is like that wch is above & that wch is above is like y^t wch is below to do ye miracles of one only thing

And as all things have been & arose from one by ye mediation of one: so all things have their birth from this one thing by adaptation.

The Sun is its father, the moon its mother, the wind hath carried it in its belly, the earth is its nourse. The father of all perfection in ye whole world is here. Its force or power is entire if it be converted into earth.

Separate thou ye earth from ye fire, ye subtile from the gross sweetly wth great indoustry. It ascends from ye earth to ye heaven & again it descends to ye earth & receives ye force of things superior & inferior.

By this means you shall have ye glory of ye whole world & thereby all obscurity shall fly from you.

Its force is above all force. ffor it vanquishes every subtile thing & penetrates every solid thing.

So was ye world created.

From this are & do come admirable adaptations whereof ye means ⚹ (Or process) ⚹ is here in this.

Hence I am called Hermes Trismegist, having the three parts of ye philosophy of ye whole world

That wch I have said of ye operation of ye Sun is accomplished & ended.[7]

Even though this compressed and cryptic composition is world famous, it remains virtually incomprehensible; although tantalizing, it still is essentially occult. From Newton's comments upon it, however, one may glean something of what it meant to him—and for historians of Renaissance Hermeticism, that is perhaps the more exciting prospect. In his *Commentary* on the *Emerald Tablet* of Hermes Trismegistus, written probably in the early 1680s, Newton left hints of scientific and theological views directly related to specific Hermetic passages, and it is to the scientific and theological significance of his *Commentary* that I now turn.

Scientific Significance

On the scientific side, the *Emerald Tablet* appears to have had significance for Newton primarily in the area of matter theory. This discovery is not surprising, of course, since alchemy concerned itself with the various manifestations and transformations of matter, and the *Emerald Tablet* was no exception to that rule despite its obscurity. One will not find in it the particles associated with modern matter theory, but even a casual reading of the *Emerald Tablet* will reveal several pairs of related material opposites: sun/moon, father/mother, earth/fire, subtle/gross, things superior/things inferior. To Newton, pairs of that sort, and their unions, represented the most fundamental, the most basic, relationships of matter as it arose in organized forms from a primitive chaos. He commented on and explained the pairs from the *Emerald Tablet* as follows:

> Inferior and superior, fixed and volatile, sulfur and quicksilver have a similar nature and are one thing, like man and wife. For they differ one from another only by the degree of digestion and maturity. Sulfur is mature quicksilver, and quicksilver is immature sulfur; and on account of this affinity they unite like male and female, and they act on each other, and through that action they are mutually transmuted into each other and procreate a more noble offspring to accomplish the miracles of this one thing.[8]

Newton might have used a large variety of paired symbols to name the two materials, for similar duos are frequently encountered in the alchemical literature. It is possible to give a psychological explanation of their prevalence,[9] yet there is no real evidence that Newton was engaging himself in the psychic progression of mystical alchemy or "spiritual chemistry." He was interested in the structure of matter and in what alchemy could teach him about its forms and changes and about the universal spirit that animated the changes and molded the forms. I will return to the subject of the animating spirit; here let it suffice to say that Newton continued for many years to argue for a matched pair of opposites as basic constituents of matter. He spoke of them in many of his alchemical papers[10] and in his small tract, *On the Nature of Acids,* he observed "that what is said by chemists, that everything is made from sulphur and mercury, is true, because by sulphur they mean acid, and by mercury they mean earth."[11]

Of even greater interest than the pairs themselves is the marriage between them that produces "a more noble offspring," for it is in the begetting of the offspring that the activating spirit comes into play. The activating spirit was in some sense divine, and Newton presented the alchemical process as quite explicitly parallel to God's creative activity at the beginning of time.

> And just as all things were created from one Chaos by the design of one God, so in our art all things . . . are born from this one thing which is our Chaos, by the design of the Artificer and the skilful adaptation of things. And the generation of this is similar to the human, truly from a father and mother.[12]

It is impossible to mistake the vitalistic—indeed the organic—nature of the process as Newton describes it. One must realize, however, that Newton did not assume that two related forms of matter came together and generated "a more noble offspring" by the volition and powers of matter itself. Newton was quite clear that matter itself was passive and that only the spiritual realm could initiate activity. In this he stood within the general Neoplatonic tradition, but given his belief that "all matter duly formed is attended with signes of life,"[13] that position led Newton into an interminable search for the spiritual agent that acted on matter to give it life as organized forms arose from chaos.

The persistent theme of the activating spirit runs through Newton's alchemical papers, and he follows up the hints given about it in the alchemical literature with the greatest diligence. Knowledge about this occult spirit was one of the most carefully cloaked secrets of alchemy, however, and it was hidden under various names. It was probably what the alchemists meant by "the mercury of the philosophers," "our gold," "the salt of nature," "the blood of nature," "a moist fire," and other ambiguous terms. Newton himself called it "a fermental virtue," "the vegetable spirit," and later "the force of fermentation."[14] In his commentary on the *Emerald Tablet,* interestingly enough, he has concluded that Hermes himself symbolizes the activating spirit, for he says:

> On account of this art [alchemy] Mercurius [Hermes] is called thrice greatest, having three parts of the philosophy of the whole world, since he signifies the Mercury of the philosophers . . . and has dominion in the mineral kingdom, the vegetable kingdom, and the animal kingdom.[15]

The activating spirit "signified" by Hermes is thus universal in scope and operation, having "dominion" in all three kingdoms, where "all matter duly formed is attended with signes of life."

It is difficult to place Newton's system as it is thus revealed in his Hermetic commentary within the context of the mechanism-vitalism controversy.[16] He was

of course a part of the community of seventeenth-century mechanical philosophers, but he was not an orthodox one. His force of gravity did not operate by
mechanical means, and contemporary critics were quick to argue that he had
reintroduced an occult quality into philosophy with it. In light of the analysis of his
alchemical compositions, one must also recognize that he was not an orthodox
mechanical philosopher in matter theory either. Mechanists usually want to explain biology in terms of physics, as did Descartes and the iatromechanists of the
later seventeenth century.[17] Newton by contrast seems to want to explain all
organized matter in terms of biology, and this not only for the obviously living
forms of the vegetable and animal kingdoms but for the very lowest forms of the
mineral kingdom as well. With the passivity of his matter and his insistence upon
the spiritual origin of activity and organization, Newton created a dualistic system
that is reminiscent of extreme forms of vitalism, yet one finds him elsewhere
making explicit allowance for "mechanical" operations in chemistry. Once a
certain (fairly high) level of organization had been reached in substances, the vital
processes associated with the lowest forms of matter passed into quiescence, and
the operations in common or "vulgar" chemistry took place mechanically, he
said.[18] As a result of statements like that, even Newton's vitalism, though certainly
strong, does not appear to have been entirely consistent. In fact, Newton had
loaded his system with a heavy burden of theological concerns, which perhaps
precluded a successful search for consistency, and to these concerns I now turn.

Theological Significance

The theological significance of Newton's commentary on the *Emerald Tablet* lies
with his speculations about the activating spirit. For Newton, as I have shown, it
was theologically unacceptable for the forces that generated activity in nature to be
designated as intrinsic components of matter. Activity—the generation of activity—had to reside in the realm of the spirit. The generation of activity was the
province of divinity. To attribute to "brute matter" the capacity for initiating
motion would give it an independence of the divine that could lead to atheism.
Newton was always aware of the dangerous potentiality of attributing activity to
matter, and he always insisted that his forces acted only between particles. They
were not really a part of matter itself, but were manifestations of God's activity in
nature, a position that was soon emphatically rejected by subsequent philosophers.[19]

Even when matter was in his judgment properly passive, Newton was still
concerned that it not be left unattended by divine influences in a closed mechanical system. Like his older contemporaries Isaac Barrow and Henry More (and
many others), he was alarmed at the atheistic implications of the revived cor-
puscularianism of their century, particularly of Cartesianism.[20] Although the ancient atomists had not really been atheists in any precise sense, they had
frequently been so labeled because their atoms in random mechanical motion
received no guidance from the gods. Descartes, Gassendi, and Charleton had been
at pains to allay the fear that the stigma of atheism adhering to ancient atomism

would be carried forward with the revived corpuscular philosophy. They had solved the problem, they thought, by the simple expedient of having God endow the particles of matter with motion at the moment of creation. All that resulted then was due not to random corpuscular action but to the initial intention of the Deity.[21]

Later writers, going further, had carefully instated a Christian Providence among the atoms, where the ancients, of course, had never had it. Only Providence could account for the obviously designed concatenations of the particles, especially in living forms. This development was all to the good in the eyes of most Christian philosophers: Atomism now supported religion, because without the providential action of God the atoms could never have assumed the lovely forms of plants and animals so perfectly fitted to their habitats. Though present in Christianity from a very early period, this "argument from design" assumed unparalleled importance in the seventeenth century, and if the new astronomy had raised doubts about the focus of Providence upon such an obscure corner of the cosmos, the new atomism seemed to relieve them.[22]

The difficulty came when one began to wonder how the operations of Providence were effected in the law-bound universe that was emerging from the new science, and that difficulty was especially severe in the Cartesian system, where only matter and motion were acceptable explanations. Even though Descartes had argued that God constantly and actively supported the universe with his will, in fact it seemed to Henry More and others that Descartes's God was in danger of becoming an absentee landlord, one who had set matter in motion in the beginning but who then had no way of exercising his providential care.

It was this theological problem that Newton faced and that drove him into his interminable search for an activating spirit that could act upon the primordial particles of matter and shape them into the diverse forms of the natural world. The alchemical active principle, the vital spirit that he pursued so diligently, was no more and no less than the agent by which God exercised his providential care among the atoms. Newton understood alchemy to be one of the most, if not the most, important of his many studies, for if all went well it would enable him to demonstrate God's action in the world in an absolutely irrefutable fashion, through demonstrations of the operations of the nonmechanical vegetable spirit, and thus lay the specter of atheism to rest forever more. With some appreciation of the momentous issues at stake from Newton's point of view, let me return now to the statements he made about that spirit in his commentary on the *Emerald Tablet*.

One will recall that Newton said there that the activating spirit symbolized by Hermes "has dominion in the mineral kingdom, the vegetable kingdom, and the animal kingdom." The use of the word "dominion" is striking, for it is a word Newton used in a familiar passage of the General Scholium to the *Principia* with reference to the Deity:

> This most beautiful system of the sun, planets, and comets, could only proceed from the counsel and dominion of an intelligent and powerful Being. . . .
> This Being governs all things, not as the soul of the world, but as Lord over all; and on account of his dominion he is wont to be called *Lord God*. . . . It is the dominion of a spiritual being which constitutes a God.[23]

Dominion thus seems to Newton to be an important attribute of God himself, and it is curious to find him using the word in connection with an alchemical spirit.

Perhaps Newton meant nothing more in his Hermetic commentary than to indicate the divine nature of the alchemical spirit. At that one need not be surprised, since the spirit was deemed capable of generating life and activity and so was necessarily divine in Newton's system. But was the spirit a *direct* manifestation of God himself acting in nature, exercising his dominion in an intimate and immediate fashion? Perhaps that is what Newton meant, but then again perhaps it was not, for some recently published theological papers of Newton's suggest that it may, in Newton's estimation, have been the Second Person of the Trinity—Christ—who acted as God's viceroy in these matters.

Taking literally the beginning passages of the Gospel of John, Newton identified Christ with the Word and argued that he was with God before his incarnation, "even in the beginning," and that he was God's active agent throughout time, speaking to Adam in Paradise and appearing to the patriarchs and Moses "by the name of God": "For the father is the invisible God whom no eye hath seen nor can see." Christ wrestled with Jacob and gave the law on Mount Sinai; after his resurrection his testimony was "the spirit of prophecy."

> He [Christ] is said to have been <wth God, *deleted*> in the beginning ✓ with God ✓ & that *all things were made by him* to signify that as he is now gone to prepare a place for the blessed so <he, *deleted* > in the beginning he prepared & formed this place in wch we <live. ffor God Almighty, *deleted*> ✓ live, & thenceforward governed it. ffor the supreme God ✓ doth nothing by himself wch he can do by others.[24]

These views on the nature of Christ are related to Newton's Arianism,[25] for he goes on to argue that "God & his son cannot be called one God upon account of their being consubstantial," but that they may and should be called one God through a "unity of Dominion,"

> the Son <being subject to ye father, *deleted*> receiving all things from the father, being subject to him, <&, *deleted*> executing his will, <&, *deleted*> sitting in his throne & calling him his God, <ffor, *deleted*> & so is but one God wth the ffather as a king & his viceroy are but one king. ffor the word God relates not to the metaphysical nature of God but to his dominion. . . . And therefore as a father & his son cannot be called one King upon account of their being consubstantial but may be called one King by unity of dominion if the Son be Viceroy under the father: So God & his son cannot be called one God upon account of their being consubstantial. <Nothing can make them one God, *deleted*> ✓ The heathens made all their Gods of one substance & sometimes called them one god & yet were polytheistic. Nothing can make two persons one God but ✓ but <*sic*> unity of dominion. And if <they, *deleted*> the ✓ Father & Son ✓ be united in dominion, the son being subordinate to the father ✓ & sitting in his throne ✓ they can no more be called two Gods then a King & his viceroy can be called two kings.[26]

That curious word *dominion* occurs again, this time to unite the Son with the Father, and so Christ becomes the viceroy, the spiritual being that acts as God's agent in the world. He is a very unorthodox Christ indeed, but one whose many duties keep him engaged with the world throughout time. A part of his function is to insure God's continued relationship with his creation; Newton's God is in no danger of becoming an absentee landlord, for he always has Christ transmitting his will into action in the world.

Newton apparently thought that in the beginning Christ, as God's executive, directed the vital, generative processes between the most minute primordials as organized matter first arose from chaos ("in the beginning he prepared & formed this place in which we live") as he continued to direct the vegetative operations of nature ("& thenceforward governed it"). It was Christ, united with God in a "unity of Dominion" though not of substance, who put God's ideas into effect. Once the alchemical significance of Christ's cosmological function appears, and it becomes apparent that the most intimate operations of Providence may be studied in nonmechanical, "vegetable" chemistry, then, to return to my former point, one can better appreciate the momentous issues at stake in the alchemical enterprise from Newton's point of view.

Conclusion

In conclusion, one may say that Newton made his Hermetic commentary a vehicle for his curiosity about matter, its changes, and its organization. He also made it a vehicle for his concern with the relationships between matter and spirit. The Hermetic materials thus seem to have provided for a natural conjunction of Newton's alchemical and theological studies, for his scientific and religious interests.

One lesson that should be drawn from this brief encounter with his *Commentary* on the *Emerald Tablet* is that there was a basic unity to Newton's work. When one divides his genius into the segments that will coincide with modern academic departments, one runs the risk of missing the powerful motivations that fueled all his work—a search for the truth about God as well as about the world. Whether he really thought that the Second Person of the Trinity was equivalent to, or was in direct control of, the activating spirit of alchemy is a question that only future investigations will be able to answer decisively. I have shown some evidence here that he did identify the two—and also some of his reasons for belaboring the question—though the evidence is not totally conclusive. I can say with certainty, however, that in his comments on the Hermetic material I find the intersection of some of Newton's deepest concerns.

Notes

1. Isaac Newton, Keynes MS.28, King's College, Cambridge, fols. 6r–7r. Quotations from this, and the other Keynes MSS used in the present study, are made by permission of the Provost and Fellows of King's College, Cambridge.

2. See, for example, P. M. Rattansi, "Some Evaluations of Reason in Sixteenth- and Seventeenth-Century Natural Philosophy," in *Changing Perspectives in the History of Science: Essays in Honour of Joseph Needham,* ed. Mikuláš Teich and Robert Young (London, 1973), pp. 148–66; Richard S. Westfall, "The Role of Alchemy in Newton's Career," in *Reason, Experiment and Mysticism in the Scientific Revolution,* ed. M. L. Righini Bonelli and William R. Shea (New York, 1975), pp. 189–232; B. J. T. Dobbs, *The Foundations of Newton's Alchemy; or, "The Hunting of the Greene Lyon"* (Cambridge, 1975).

3. Westfall, "Alchemy in Newton's Career," p. 196. For the most recent statement of the opposite point of view, which sees Newton's alchemy as entirely peripheral, cf. I. Bernard Cohen, *The Newtonian Revolution: With Illustrations of the Transformation of Scientific Ideas* (Cambridge, 1980).

4. John Ferguson, *Bibliotheca Chemica: A Catalogue of the Alchemical, Chemical and Pharmaceutical Books in the Collection of the Late James Young of Kelly and Durris, Esq., LL.D., F.R.S., F.R.S.E.,* 2 vols. (1906; reprint, London, 1954), 1 : 389–94.

5. *Bibliotheque des philosophes [chymiques,] ou recueil des oeuvres des auteurs les plus approuvey qui ont e'crit de la pierre philosophale,* 2 vols. (Paris, 1672–78).

6. Though I have not traced the exact source of this version of the *Emerald Tablet,* Newton had long had access to very similar versions in his copy of the massive *Theatrum chemicum.* Cf. *Theatrum chemicum, praecipuous selectorum auctorum tractatus de chemiae et lapidis philosophici antiquitate, veritate, jure, praestantia, & operationibus, continens: In gratiam Verae Chemiae, & medicinae Chemicae studiosorum (ut qui uberriman inde optimorum remediorum messem facere poterunt) congestum, & in Sex partes seu volumina digestum; singulis voluminibus, suo auctorum et librorum catalogo primis pagellis: rerum verò & verborum Indice postremis annexo,* 6 vols. Strasbourg, 1659–61), 1 : 8, 6 : 715.

7. Newton, Keynes MS. 28, fol. 2r, v. In this and subsequent quotations from Newton's manuscripts, his minor deletions have been omitted; arrows up and down indicate his interlineations.

8. Ibid., fol. 6r, v: "Inferius et superius, fixum et volatile, sulphur et argentum vivum similem habent naturam et sunt una res ut vir et uxor. Nam solo digestionis et maturitatis gradu differunt ab invicem. Sulphur est argentum vivum maturum, et argentum vivum est sulphur immaturum; ↗ et propter hanc affinitatem ↙ coeunt ut mas & fœmina et agunt in se invicem ↗ et per actionem illam transmutantur in se mutuo & prolem nobiliorem generant ↙ ad perpetranda miracula hujus rei unius." The word *generat* spills over from fol. 6v to fol. 9r.

9. Cf. Dobbs, *Foundations of Newton's Alchemy,* pp. 26–35, and the literature cited there.

10. Some of these papers have been examined in B. J. T.Dobbs, "Newton's Copy of *Secrets Reveal'd* and the Regimens of the Work," *Ambix* 26 (1979): 145–69.

11. Isaac Newton, *The Correspondence of Isaac Newton,* ed. H. W. Turnbull, J. P. Scott, A. R. Hall, and Laura Tilling, 7 vols. (Cambridge, 1959–78), 3 : 206, 210.

12. Newton, Keynes MS. 28, fol. 6v: "Et sicut res omnes ex uno Chao per consilium Dei unius creatæ sunt, sic in arte nostra res omnes id est elementa quatuor ex una hac re quæ nostrum Chaos est per consilium Artificis & prudentem rerum adaptionem nascuntur. Est et ejus generatio humanæ similis, nimirum ex patre et matre qui sunt Sol et Luna."

13. Isaac Newton, draft query for the *Opticks,* quoted by J. E. McGuire and P. M. Rattansi, "Newton and the 'Pipes of Pan,'" *Notes and Records of the Royal Society* 21 (1966): 108–43, esp. 118. See also Ernan McMullin, *Newton on Matter and Activity* (Notre Dame, Ind., 1978), and the literature cited there.

14. Cf. Dobbs, "Newton's Copy of *Secrets Reveal'd*"; and B. J. T. Dobbs, "Newton's Alchemy and His Theory of Matter," *Isis* 73 (1982): 511–28.

15. Newton, Keynes MS. 28, fol. 7r: "Ob hanc artem vocor Mercurius ter maximus habens tres partes philosophiæ totius mundi, ut significetur Mercurius philosophorum qui ex substantijs tribus fortissimis componitur habetque corpus animam et spiritum & est mineralis vegetabilis et animalis & in regno minerali vegetabili et animali dominatur." The abbreviation of *que* in *habetque* has been expanded.

16. Although concerned primarily with the post-Newtonian period, the following article provides an excellent historical and analytical framework: Hilde Hein, "The Endurance of the Mechanism-Vitalism Controversy," *Journal of the History of Biology* 5 (1972): 159–88.

17. See, for example, François Duchesneau, "Malpighi, Descartes, and the Epistemological Problems of Iatromechanism," in *Reason, Experiment and Mysticism,* pp. 111–30.

18. Newton treated the distinction between "vegetable" and "mechanical" chemistry at some length in his "Of Natures obvious laws & processes in vegetation," Dibner Collection MSS. 1031 B, Dibner Library of the History of Science and Technology of the Smithsonian Institution Libraries, Washington, D.C. This manuscript was formerly Burndy MS. 16. Cf. *Manuscripts of the Dibner Collection in the Dibner Library of the History of Science and Technology of the Smithsonian Institution Libraries*

(Smithsonian Institution Libraries, Research Guide no. 5; Washington, D.C.: Smithsonian Institution Libraries, 1985), p. 7 (no. 80) and Plate 7 (facing p. 46); B. J. T. Dobbs, "Newton Manuscripts at the Smithsonian Institution," *Isis* 68 (1977): 105–7; idem, "Newton's Copy of *Secrets Reveal'd*"; idem, "Newton's Alchemy."

19. McMullin, *Newton on Matter and Activity;* J. E. McGuire and P. M. Heimann, "The Rejection of Newton's Concept of Matter in the Eighteenth Century," in *The Concept of Matter in Modern Philosophy,* rev. ed., ed Ernan McMullin (Notre Dame, Ind., 1978), pp. 104–18; P. M. Heimann and J. E. McGuire, "Newtonian Forces and Lockean Powers: Concepts of Matter in Eighteenth-Century Thought," *Historical Studies in the Physical Sciences* 3 (1971): 233–306.

20. Dobbs, *Foundations of Newton's Alchemy,* esp. pp. 100–105.

21. Robert Kargon, *Atomism in England from Hariot to Newton* (Oxford, 1966), pp. 64–68, 87–89; Margaret J. Osler, "Descartes and Charleton on Nature and God," *Journal of the History of Ideas* 40 (1979): 445–56.

22. Jacob Viner, *The Role of Providence in the Social Order: An Essay in Intellectual History,* Jayne Lectures for 1966, foreword by Joseph R. Strayer (Philadelphia, 1972), pp. 8–9.

23. Isaac Newton, *Sir Isaac Newton's Mathematical Principles of Natural Philosophy and His System of the World. Translated into English by Andrew Mott in 1729. The translations revised, and supplied with an historical and explanatory appendix, by Florian Cajori,* 2 vols. (Berkeley and Los Angeles, 1966), 2:544.

24. Isaac Newton, Yahuda MS. Var. 1, Newton MS. 15.5, Jewish National and University Library, Jerusalem, fols. 96r–97r. Italics in original. Cf. David Castillejo, *The Expanding Force in Newton's Cosmos as shown in his unpublished papers* (Madrid, 1981), pp. 61–62.

25. Richard S. Westfall, *Never at Rest: A Biography of Isaac Newton* (Cambridge, 1980), pp. 311–19.

26. Newton, Yahuda MS. Var. 1, Newton MS. 15.7, fol. 154r. Cf. Castillejo, *Expanding Force,* p. 74.

10

Mysticism and Millenarianism: "Immortal Dr. Cheyne"

G. S. ROUSSEAU

> *If* there might not, I say, be higher, more noble, and more enlightening
> *Principles* revealed to Mankind *somewhere.*
>
> This material *Metaphysicks* of a *Regimen.*
>
> George Cheyne

"Immortal Doctor Cheyne," to echo the *aperçu* of the circle of Pope,[1] can no longer be viewed merely as a failed Newtonian, or Newtonian *manqué,* but instead should be considered a particular type of physician who coped with the obliquities of his own life—especially anomalies in health, weight, and physical constitution—by turning early disappointment to eventual advantage, as well as by ministering to the dozens, even hundreds, of fashionable patients he treated. Elsewhere I have suggested that Cheyne was among the first—perhaps *the* first—of the great English "nerve doctors":[2] those shrewd physicians of the eighteenth century who erected a myth about the magisterial role of wealthy man's nervous constitution in relation to the health he could expect to enjoy and the degree of high living his body could withstand. In this essay, I consider the shape of Cheyne's life in relation to his diverse millenarian and mystical activities, a discussion that would have been of particular interest to the author of *Giordano Bruno and the Hermetic Tradition* and *The Rosicrucian Enlightenment* had she lived long enough to read it.

It is usually an error to dwell on one's own methodology, but the matter here is that the task I have set myself cannot be accomplished without laying out—however briefly—a map of how these millenarian activities could fit into the larger picture of Cheyne's biography.[3] For my thesis is that his so-called failed Newtonianism played only a small, if emotionally painful, role in his life; and that this admittedly shattering disappointment of early manhood eventually served him well.[4] If Cheyne had succeeded in rapidly winning Newton's favor, in joining the ranks of the Gregories and Pembertons, he probably would have made fewer original, if no less controversial, contributions to his culture than he did. And

PORTRAIT OF DOCTOR GEORGE CHEYNE, F.R.S. *(Courtesy of the British Library, Department of Prints and Drawings.)*

although Cheyne was a capable enough young mathematician, he nevertheless possessed a more unique ability to cash in on England's remarkable economic prosperity in the aftermath of the South Sea Bubble by cultivating some of the nation's richest patients through a then new type of medical practice—one that required two extraordinary, and specific talents in which "Immortal Doctor Cheyne" eventually proved himself to be masterful: flattery and an ability to anchor his nervous mythology in medical or pseudomedical language. If the former is straightforward, the latter—especially its linguistic dimensions—is not, and a portion of this discussion is devoted to Cheyne's use of language. In brief then, Dr. Cheyne recognized what any competent twentieth-century psychiatrist, or other health-care professional, specializing in the problems of the wealthy necessarily would: first and foremost, that the rich must be assured of their fundamental difference from all other social classes, all other groups; and that unction alone, no matter how enthusiastic, or how subtly coated with veneer, would not persuade his clients. It was an unusual combination of skills in the manipulation of unctuous behavior and flair for a type of language about which I say more below.

Therefore, when Dr. Cheyne treated illustrious patients of such delicate nervous constitutions as the notorious Lord Hervey—the "vile Antithesis" and "Amphibious Thing" of Pope's stinging lines (325–26) in the *Epistle to Dr. Arbuthnot*—or when Cheyne wrote to the less controversial but much more pietistic Countess of Huntingdon, an ardent devotee of Wesley, about her chronic illnesses—a lingering depression brought on by ardent religious melancholy—his language was always cast into a bed of flattery;[5] repeating, however unctuously as accepted fact, and as if with the stamp and seal of authority, that the rich lived better, and enjoyed themselves much more so, than the poor. It was an ingenious tactic. Yet Cheyne soon realized that if he hoped to prosper financially in treating the wealthy and the famous, the aristocratic and the great, even the notorious and the controversial, he would also have to explain their illnesses to them *in concrete terms* that made sense to educated persons: he would need to explain why the rich were so often indisposed, as well as interpret the nature of the high living that had precipitated their bodily discomfort in the first place. It was not sufficient merely to flatter them with the assurance, for example, that high living and luxury were preferable to the dull tedium of the lives of laborers. For Cheyne's wealthy patients paid for their fashionable excesses by sustaining a torrent of complaints of a bodily—usually of an intestinal—nature, as well as through mental exhaustion and depression. And Dr. Cheyne needed a ready explanation of why these fashionable valetudinarians—as they were then called—were burdened with these specific aches and incessant pains, the inevitable consequences of abundant rich food, excessive drink, and late nights, while the poor remained much less indisposed in this way. Brilliantly and inventively, then, he conjured new explanations grounded in— indeed almost entirely based on—what he called the uniquely delicate nervous constitutions of the wealthy classes who—he perceptively reasoned—were actually endowed from birth to death with a *different* anatomy and a *different* physiology from the poor. His rationale was a blend of the then-accepted facts of anatomy with the fabrications of his own considerable imaginative powers. The description of this idiosyncratic combination of unction and pseudomedical language must await another essay. Nevertheless, its outline is fundamental to the story I want to tell here about the evolution of Cheyne's life. For unless we gain a securer sense of Cheyne's life than we have entertained in the past, it will be difficult to explain why he succeded so well in treating the rich, and, even more significantly, why, of all the large tribe of English physicians then practicing, he was by far the most beloved by his affluent, famous, and aristocratic patients—in brief, how he rose to become England's leading "nerve doctor."

The Literary Response

Cheyne's weight was legendary in his own time. He swelled to 448 pounds—"32 stone"—and whereas no handy eighteenth-century *Guinness Book of Records* is extant to report whether he was the fattest man of the eighteenth century, he certainly must rank among the heaviest.[6] Literary evidence demonstrates the attitude of his contemporaries better than any other source. For example, Pope knew Cheyne well and relished his Falstaffian benevolence, as well as his eccentric blend of reason and madness: "So very a child in true Simplicity of Heart, that I love him; as He loves Don Quixote, for the Most Moral and Reasoning Madman in the world."[7] This reference caresses Cheyne and is one of many vignettes of the doctor that abounds in Pope's correspondence. "He is," Pope later affirmed, echoing the book of St. John, "a kind of living parson Adams, in the Scripture language, an *Israelite in whom there is no Guile,* or in Shakespeare's, *as foolish a good kind of Christian Creature as one shall meet with."* All Pope's estimates of the childlike Cheyne portray the doctor as a fundamentally good man; deluded, eccentric, even quixotic, confusing windmills and giants, but nevertheless a fine man who was as good as the salt of the earth. Fielding's patron, Lord Lyttelton, agreed with Pope but was more melodramatic in his assessment: ". . . Immortal Doctor Cheyne . . . The Doctor is the greatest Singularity, and the most Delightful I ever met with."[8] Every Scriblerian, even Swift, adored Cheyne, the only famous physician in England other than Dr. Arbuthnot who escaped their ridicule and venomous collective pen.[9] And as one reads between the lines of chapter 2, book 4, of *Gulliver's Travels,* Swift's famous "Voyage to the Houyhnhyms" containing extensive descriptions of the "very insipid diet" of these rational, equestrian-like creatures and Gulliver's perfect health while surviving on it ("I never had one hour's sickness, while I stayed on this island"), one wonders to what degree Dr. Cheyne's diets—which Swift knew well—lurk behind these pages, even if Cheyne's name is nowhere mentioned. John Gay continued to be overwhelmed by "Cheyne huge of size" whom he greets in *Mr. Pope's Welcome from Greece;*[10] and Edward Young, the poet and himself no stranger to melancholy, nostalgically immortalized Cheyne in a key passage in the *Epistle II. To Mr. Pope* when imprecating for "three ells round huge Cheyne."[11] Fielding was much too robust to consider adopting Cheyne's lettuce and milk diet, but even he nodded approvingly at "the learned Dr. Cheyne" in *Tom Jones.*[12] Richardson the novelist was much more devoted, perhaps because he needed Cheyne's counsel in so many different areas. He and Cheyne were in constant correspondence for many years—certainly throughout the composition of *Pamela*—indeed for such a long time that Richardson may not have enjoyed the necessary perspective to determine precisely who or what Cheyne represented to the rest of England. And Richardson relied monolithically on Cheyne for professional medical advice, as well as for literary guidance in the composition of *Pamela*. He told Stephen Duck, the "thresher poet," that Cheyne "was so good as to give me a Plan [in *Pamela*] to break Legs and Arms and to fire Mansion Houses to create Distresses."[13] Toward the goal of improving Richardson's health by exercise Cheyne also prescribed "a chamber horse"—a primitive version of our contemporary exercise bike; and Richardson discovered such novelty in the idea, as did the valetudinarian novelist, Laurence Sterne, a decade later, that one wonders if Cheyne's "chamber horse" could have played any role in the formation of Sterne's less literal "hobby horse" in *Tristram Shandy*. Few patients who were also novelists ever trusted their doctor to this degree of compliance.

The catalog of contemporary comments is seemingly endless. In January 1742 Thomas Gray concocted an "Imaginary Conversation" between ancient and modern geniuses, including Aristotle, Virgil, Locke, Swift, and Cheyne, wherein Cheyne is made to recite his own aphorism: "Every Man after forty is either a fool or a Physician."[14] The young Hume turned to Cheyne, among all the English physicians, for medical advice about his mysterious illness in 1734, entreating Cheyne as if he were Galen or Hippocrates.[15] Lord Chesterfield intensely disliked metaphysics but he valiantly wrote to Cheyne to say that, if ever he were compelled to choose "a system," he would select Cheyne's medical cosmology as the most probable.[16] Lord Hervey, already mentioned as Cheyne's patient and Pope's rival in politics and love, considered Cheyne the most eminent physician in England; he was not abashed to say so in public. He sang praises of Cheyne at Court and complimented him in a long document entitled "An Account of My Own Constitution and Illness . . . For the Use of My Children," which he wrote in 1730.[17] Proclaiming himself a loyal disciple, Hervey continued to defend Cheyne's therapies even when they were ridiculed by those who claimed to understand the human body better than Cheyne had. "I have not bragged," Hervey wrote to Cheyne in 1732, "of the persecutions I suffer in this [your] cause; but the attacks made upon me by ignorance, impertinence, and gluttony are innumerable and incredible." Incredible they must have appeared in an age of rampant gluttony, when the upper classes were practically eating themselves into the grave, but they continued to win adherents from diverse quarters among both sexes. The wealthy and lovely Countess of Huntingdon, also mentioned, became Cheyne's patron, the only man in the Realm—except for the Methodist preacher George Whitefield— fortunate enough to have captured her attention and her purse.[18] Wesley himself, the great reformer, converted to Cheyne's diet and advocated it in his popular handbook of medicine, *Primitive Physick;* and Charles Delafaye, the radical English freemason and amateur Newtonian, permitted no other doctor to treat him for gout than "the good Doctor Cheyne."[19] William Somerville, the now little read poet, versified Cheyne's best-selling book *The English Malady* in his poem "The Hip." Sir John Hill, a notorious enfant terrible of his epoch, extolled Cheyne in *The*

Construction of the Nerves (1768) and praised his theories of nervous physiology. The medical writings of the too little known ophthalmologist William Porterfield are permeated with approving glances at the authoritative Cheyne.[20] Porterfield was the first secretary of the Edinburgh Literary and Philosophical Society; from him many who were later to become lights in the Scottish Enlightenment first heard about "immortal Doctor Cheyne." The Great Cham, Samuel Johnson, paternally advised the lecherous Boswell to read Dr. Cheyne's books on temperance and health, advice that Boswell probably never heeded but counsel which adumbrates Johnson's very high esteem.[21] Thomas Tyers, the miscellaneous writer who was one of Johnson's favorite people, wrote the first biographical sketch of Johnson a day after he died on 13 December 1784; while Tyers mourned the dead, he composed a "Set of Resolutions" for himself founded on Cheyne's principles: "especially to make exercise a part of one's Religion," and "to be religiously observed."[22] This material represents just the tip of an unsurveyed iceberg that constitutes the literary evidence.

> Not all the Gemmy Treasures of the East,
> Nor yet the Spicy Odours of the West;
> Not all the Glorious Trophies of the Great,
> Would please so much, or form one joy compleat,
> Like that I feel, great wond'rous Genius, when
> I scan th' amazing Beauties of thy Pen.

Thus an anonymous poet rhapsodized Cheyne in 1733 on reading his works.[23] Lyrical though the mode is, the praise is specific:

> Long did the Sacred Art in Bondage mourn,
> Become the Jest of Fools, or else their Scorn;
> 'Till Heav'n, to set the fetter'd Science free,
> And pit'ing abject Man, created Thee.
> Made Thee to act of Gods the healing Part
> And live a Pillar to the Noble Art,
> To be the only shining acting Sage,
> Not giv'n, but lent from them to heal this Age.
> Great Wonder from above, thou Boast of Men,
> Accept these Offerings from a Namesake's Pen.

The fact that this catalog of response can be extended considerably is only the first of my points about Cheyne's life, as is the repeated strain about Cheyne's corpulence and medical eminence, although it is intriguing to notice how often in history physical size is equated with heroic greatness.

Cheyne's contemporaries were no doubt amazed by his weight reduction from 448 pounds to 130.[24] The further fact that he practiced what he preached about the relation of weight and diet also lent him credibility lacked by many eighteenth-century physicians. But the public's image of Cheyne in the eighteenth century was nevertheless jaded and distorted—was not at all the sense he had of himself. Obesity vanquished; a long life of seventy-two years in an epoch when so many

died in youth or early adulthood; national fame as a writer; a close friend of so
many famous and influential Britons: these unassailable facts were important to
Cheyne, but they were distant from the center of his intellectual and private
emotional life. Cheyne's idea of selfhood and the niche he had carved depended to
a certain extent on these incontrovertible facts, but rested equally, if not more so,
on other private beliefs that can only be understood in the light of his chronological biography. Without this crucial background, the flow of his ideas over the first
five decades of the eighteenth century remains a muddle and a mystery.

Chronological Biography and Intellectual Development

Cheyne was born in Aberdeen in 1671 in a Scottish Episcopalian family that
intended him, like his father and both grandfathers, for the Church. His early
education was classical, as were his university studies in Edinburgh where he read
mathematics. One teacher alone, Archibald Pitcairne, the illustrious mathematician and physician, enjoyed remarkable sway over him. Both had an Episcopalian
religion in common, and Pitcairne urged Cheyne to follow in his iatromathematical
footsteps: to apply mathematics in the service of medicine.[25] Cheyne ardently
followed the advice, obtained a medical degree (at Aberdeen), and even became
Dr. Pitcairne's staunchest defender in fierce paper wars about iatromathematics.
Yet Pitcairne's impact on Cheyne extended beyond this sphere. As Boerhaave's
most important teacher at Leiden, Pitcairne had attracted the best minds there and
was known throughout Europe as a towering intellect, as the most distinguished
iatromathematician of the seventeenth-century fin de siècle.[26] His protégés rapidly
became fervid Newtonians—especially Freind, Mead, and James Keill—and built
a kind of "school of iatromathematics" around him in which Newtonian calculus,
or fluxions, was applied to medical theory. But Pitcairne was also an enthusiast in
religion, and generated his medical theory with the zeal of an apostle, a characteristic of personality Cheyne discovered to be temperamentally compatible with
his own.[27] Calculus, geometry, and medicine filled only part of Cheyne's imagination during his twenties[28]—intellectually his most formative period—the rest of
his energy occupied by a deep-seated religious mysticism. He joined a group of
Scottish mystics in the 1690s centered around George Garden, the Quietist.
Through them he obtained a post as tutor to the young Earl of Roxburgh; but more
importantly, he made friends who remained loyal to him for the rest of his life and
who joined him later on in his endeavor to become one of Britain's main dis-
tributors of Quietist literature.

Why then did the young Cheyne have such conflicting aspirations:
iatromathematics on the one hand, and mystical religion on the other? The 1690s
was understandably the great decade of chiliasm and millenarianism in western
Europe,[29] and although Cheyne was too young personally to have witnessed the
events of the 1650s, he was attentive to those of the 1690s. He heard much
millenarian talk at Roxburgh House, the Scottish country estate where he lived in
comfortable circumstances during those years. He had also heard millenarian talk
at home and in Aberdeen.[30] He knew about Jane Lead and the English Phila-

delphians, and about her prediction of an imminent millennium commencing in 1700. At Roxburgh he had read about the chiliastic interpretations of the year 1697: that the Treaty of Ryswick which finally brought peace to Europe was evidence—"public testimony"—of the Deity's intention to commence the millennium. And he certainly read John Craig's *Theologiæ Christianae Principia Mathematica* (1699), which applied Newton's inverse-square law to derive the precise year of the Second Coming, for Cheyne continued to refer to it and quote from it.[31] Cheyne was also related to Thomas Burnet, the author of the *Sacred Theory of the Earth*, and knew Burnet's descriptions of millennial life. Although Burnet had not dated his predictions, he implied they were soon to occur. Furthermore, through Pitcairne Cheyne had been introduced to the most devoted young Newtonians—especially to David Gregory and the Keill brothers—and discovered, if he had not already realized it, that iatromathematics could be compatible with mystical religion. This discovery cannot be precisely dated, but it must have occurred sometime around 1699 or 1700, a crucial millenarian moment. Finally, there was the example of Pitcairne himself. Pitcairne was not a hardened mystic, but he showed mystical tendencies. He was anything but a solid member of the Scottish church ("the Kirk"), a fact that hindered his academic career after he returned to Scotland from Leiden,[32] and precipitated various attacks by his medical brethren.

Cheyne's career drastically changed after he migrated to London in the winter of 1701/2.[33] Now, daily, he saw before his own eyes the millenarian fervor about which he had read so much in Scotland. If there were relatively few Philadelphians or Quietists in Roxburgh, or even in the more urban Edinburgh, there were plenty in London. Here was millenarianism of another magnitude. Medical degree in hand, and letters of introduction, too, Cheyne arrived in a city riven by diverse opinion about the politico-religious development at the turn of the century. This was especially true among the Fellows of the Royal Society, with whom Cheyne was closely associated when he arrived. He had been resident in London only a few weeks when the War of the Spanish Succession broke out. To some mystics this gruesome event signified that the Deity had interrupted his millenarian intentions, and demonstrated his dissatisfaction with English national behavior. Cheyne had not yet arrived in London when the Philadelphians read in public their famous Proclamation on Easter Day 1699,[34] but he certainly heard accounts of their radical prophecies. During his first spring and autumn in London—1702—he focused his energy, as he recounts in his autobiography, on establishing a successful medical practice. He pursued this goal by appearing in the "right" coffeehouses, and by cultivating the wealthy and the great in their private salons and drawing rooms.[35] Years later, Cheyne described this period of his life as one of immense "luxury, gluttony, and upper-class vice without exercise," and typified it in his memoirs by the act of forever "taking snuff out of a ponderous gold box."[36] (An essay is not the place to discuss the sociology of medicine in the eighteenth century, but it should be noted that while Cheyne's method of gaining patients was common, his degree of application was not.) During these years he also frequented Batson's and Child's, and the townhouses of dukes and duchesses; and he wrecked his health through drink and gluttony. The talk Cheyne heard in these places must be of as much concern as his dissipation. Here he was apprised of the aspiring

physician's need for written credentials and the value of word-of-mouth recom-
mendation. But he also heard about the mounting war on the Continent, and the
radical prophecies interpreting it. On streetcorners he saw freethinkers and mystics chanting about the millennium come or interrupted, and he heard tales about
the hysterical uprising of the Camisards in the Cévennes Mountains.[37] Cheyne's
urban hedonism was excessive and extravagant, but apparently not so extreme as
to prevent him from writing a mathematical treatise in 1703,[38] which so annoyed
Newton that he dropped Cheyne from the circle of young disciples to whom his
bounty was given. Cheyne suffered the Newtonian fall miserably, as I suggested
above, but eventually used it to his benefit. He repressed it and never again
commented on it in any of his autobiographical memoirs.

Newton's dispraise, however, did not prevent Cheyne from setting to work
shortly thereafter—probably in 1703—on another book that proved far more
theological than the previous two. Two years earlier, late in 1701, Cheyne proclaimed the need for a *Principia Medicinae Theologiae Mathematica* based on
Newton's *Principia*—one that would integrate medicine and mathematics.
Cheyne's idea derived, in part, from John Craig's 1699 *Theologia . . . Mathematica,* which Cheyne read and acknowledged in the preface of the new book. But
Cheyne's desideratum is not what he eventually produced. Hoping to reingratiate
himself with the Newtonians—by 1703–5 the most powerful scientific coterie
within the Royal Society—Cheyne abandoned mathematical medicine and composed a type of "Boyle-lecture," which he called *Philosophical Principles of
Natural Religion* (1705), modeling the title, as well as the book, on Newton's
Mathematical Principles. Not surprisingly, *Philosophical Principles* was greeted
by the Newtonians with more hostility than Cheyne's previous book.[39] Dislike was
based—it was alleged—on two grotesque and unpardonable errors: first, that
Cheyne had misunderstood the essence of Newtonian gravity, and, then, that his
analogical method of reasoning was altogether unsatisfactory and unscientific.
Cheyne replied to the first charge that Newton had "stolen" certain points in the
Queries appended to the Latin *Opticks* from him "in private conversation,"[40] an
argument no one then seems to have construed seriously. At least it did not
persuade the Newtonians, old or young, that Cheyne understood anything about
gravity, or that he ought to be readmitted to the clique. The second charge—
unscientific analogy—appeared to be less critical in 1705, but this is, of course, the
aspect of Cheyne's writing that renders him such a unique figure in the phys-
icotheological world of the early eighteenth century. It is also the aspect, however
linguistically perverse, of his thinking that leads directly to his curious doctrines of
early eighteenth-century millenarianism.

Cheyne's analogies derive from a "Universal Law of Attraction, whereby all the
parts of Matter endeavour to embrace one another."[41] From this quasi-Platonic,
given "Law" he reasons that a "Divine Providence permeates" both the natural
and supraterrestrial universe. Yet almost every conclusion he draws from this
point forward remains at odds with the basic assumptions of Newtonian thinking.
Moreover, Cheyne's inability to grasp the inconsistencies and obliquities of his
own principles in relation to those of Newton constitutes the best comment on his
scientific abilities. Such defect of grasp certainly did not go unnoticed by the

English Newtonians, within and without the Royal Society, who now began to wonder if Cheyne was a mathematician at all; the mere fact of an earned medical degree counted for nothing—especially inasmuch as it was granted in far away Aberdeen—in an epoch when medicine was commonly anything *but* scientific. Geoffrey Bowles has argued that Cheyne's discussion of short-range attraction is the most interesting feature of *Philosophical Principles,* observing as well that Newton had not pronounced publicly on this matter until 1706.[42] Bowles's contention is that Cheyne's method of analogical reasoning permitted him to make an intuitive leap: reasoning from long-range to short-range attraction. This may be true, but the English Newtonians hardly saw the matter in this light. They grasped on to Cheyne's mathematical errors, and were troubled by the Stoic undertones of his concept of Providence. Only Jean Le Clerc, the erudite head of the Remonstrant-Arminian Seminary in Amsterdam and himself an ardent if controversial theologian, reviewed Cheyne's book.[43] Otherwise, the *Philosophical Principles* went unnoticed and bitterly disappointed Cheyne. In this capacity, it did not matter whether his medical practice was a success, or even whether his urban hedonism had wrecked his physical health.[44] He had lost the support of the Newtonians and other Fellows of the Royal Society whose approval he direly sought. A second attempt to reenlist himself proved futile. Now he had elicited their fury twice. At the very least, he was *persona non grata.*

Collapse and Crisis

The result was breakdown and collapse in 1706. It may never be known whether this condition was primarily physical or mental. But Cheyne's account of the collapse is so detailed that he must be believed when commenting that at this time (1706) he "went about like a *Malefactor* condemn'd, or one who expected every Moment to be crushed by a *ponderous* Instrument of Death."[45] However, Cheyne's attribution of the collapse to his London hedonism, and to the defects of his physiological constitution, is probably inchoate, although not inaccurate. More than 440 pounds of human flesh will afford even the soberest human being with a perfect rationalization for anything that ever happens, or happened, to him! What counts far more is the curious way that Cheyne permitted his breakdown to determine the course of his whole future career.

He swiftly departed from London—from the hub of luxury and glut—and fled to the country, hoping to die in pastoral simplicity. He was uncertain about many things; but he was sure, at thirty-five, that death could not be far away. He also "fix'd on one, a worthy and learned *Clergyman* of the *Church of England,* sufficiently known and distinguished in the *Philosophical* and *Theological* World (whom I dare not name, because he is still living, tho' now extreamly old)."[46] This may have been William Whiston, whose Arianism and disavowal of the coeternity of the Father and Son were notorious by late 1706. Ill and despondent, Cheyne, following Whiston's example, "resolved to purchase, study, and examine carefully such *Spiritual and Dogmatic Authors,* as I knew this *venerable Man did* most approve and delight in."[47] These were works of primitive Christianity, "a *Set of religious Books and Writers,* of most of the *first Ages* since *Christianity.*" They confirmed Cheyne's developing sense that the material world was proximate to dissolution and the New Jerusalem imminent. They encompassed the writers of the first four centuries who had not been contaminated by the Council of Nicaea and the apostolic succession. Cheyne and Whiston probably did not meet: Cheyne was in Bath, Whiston in Cambridge. Neither is known to have traveled to the other place. But there is a good deal of circumstantial evidence to suggest that Whiston is the "now extremely old"—"now" as Cheyne writes in 1733, not 1706—mathematician and philosopher whose "primitive Christianity" subdued Cheyne's misery during this illness.

But Cheyne did not remain in "the country" (wherever that may have been) throughout 1706, the year of collapse. He very often returned to London, and may have been there when the first French prophets arrived that autumn.[48] Fatio, Newton's disciple, quickly enlisted himself in the service of Elie Marion, their leader, and introduced David Gregory, Newton's follower, and possibly Cheyne, to the prophets. But whereas Gregory was resistant to their cause, Cheyne was sympathetic. By Christmas 1706, the prophets predicted that the millennium had arrived and that the "hidden keys of Divine Wisdom" were daily being revealed to women, children, and common folk. During these months at the end of 1706, Cheyne—ill, despairing, craven, believing he was near death—began to connect the apocalypse with medicine, and started to suspect that his life could serve a higher purpose than he had ever dreamed.

Strangely, he soon began to improve, this after six or seven months. His near-fatal illness, he concluded, was lucid revelation: not only that he should instantly mend his hedonistic ways—his whole style of life then—but also that he should serve his Maker by delivering "a message" to mankind. When Cheyne reflected (in 1733, thinking about the curve of his whole life) on the validity of the cosmological picture he had painted in *Philosophical Principles,* he was altogether dissatisfied. "I found," he writes, "that *these* [*Philosophical Principles*] alone were not sufficient to *quiet* my Mind at that Juncture."[49] Then he describes the new vision acquired since his illness:

> Especially when I began to reflect and consider seriously, whether I might not (through Carelessness and Self-Sufficiency, Voluptuousness and Love of Sensuality, which might have impaired my Spiritual Nature) have neglected to examine with sufficient Care: If there might not be more required of those, who had had proper *Opportunities* and *Leisure;* if there might not, I say, be higher, more noble, and more enlightening *Principles*[50] revealed to Mankind *somewhere* . . . and lastly, if there were not likewise some clearer Accounts discoverable of that State I was then (I thought) apparently going into, than could be obtained from the mere Light of *Nature* and *Philosophy.*

This "mere Light of *Nature* and *Philosophy*"—especially Cheyne's new perception of the limits of empirical science—constitutes the source and background of his mental frame during the next decade. Now, more than before, he believed that religion itself was nothing but revelation; and that the body of man—symmetrical and asymmetrical by a principle of *concordia discors*—had been the most sorely neglected source within the book of nature.

Healing and Rebirth

Still believing himself close to death in 1707, Cheyne heard the voices of another type of natural revelation than those he had heard on London street corners or read about in books. Medicine, like mathematics, had been part of the Deity's grand plan from the start;[51] but now Cheyne understood how the Deity would reveal his wisdom and might through suffering and healing. The body of man, like the Book of Nature, was a major seat of revelation; and anatomy and physiology its correlatives within "natural philosophy." Cheyne's illness—his "crisis of 1706"—was then a part of a larger providential plan. Had there not been evidence of revelation through the body of man in recent social events as well? Sudden healing of the sick poor; the unprecedented establishment of almshouses; other medical services that rescued men and women who would have been given over for dead only a few years before?[52] It seemed to Dr. Cheyne that the millennium had commenced or soon would, and that he had been chosen to be instrumental in the establishment of the New Jerusalem in England. This was a far more important calling, he reasoned, than the previous Newtonian one.

Now persuaded that the human form—especially his own body—could not be overlooked, Cheyne turned elsewhere in the apocalypse than to mathematics or iatromathematics. His primary task, as he recounts in his "case history," was to recover. He persuaded himself that only by practicing the most vigilant temperance he could avert further collapse. He increasingly renounced London, the Old Jerusalem, returned there less frequently, and abjured its indolence and luxury. Precisely why he did not join Fatio and the other prophets remains unknown,[53] unless his decision owed something, now lost to time, to the personal or public intervention of his mentor Whiston. By the autumn of 1706 Whiston's *Essay on the Revelation of Saint John* had appeared, announcing that certain of his earlier prophecies had been fulfilled and that others were yet to come. Cheyne may not have read this work, but he probably heard or read Whiston's Boyle lectures delivered in the next winter (1707–8) and printed the following summer (1708). Here Whiston argued that scriptural prophecy is capable of one, and only one, interpretation; he also fixed the precise date of the millennium as 1736, which he later updated to 1766. More urgently for Cheyne, Whiston warned against the placing of trust in the messages of the French prophets,[54] a position that may have weighed somewhat in Cheyne's decision not to join them. One further consequence of possible Whistonian influence was Cheyne's apparent realization that he (Cheyne) had been wrong about the source of the "Universal Attraction" discussed in *Philosophical Principles*. At least, this line of argument—that Cheyne revised his theory as a consequence of Whistonian influence—is more likely than the arcane explanation that for a third time he tried to regain the bounty of the Newtonians.

Alone then in the country, ailing but improving, and no longer near death,

Cheyne set about to revise his "philosophical principles" in a calm manner that would take account of his "great crisis" of 1706. "If my Life was to be sav'd," he comments in his memoirs looking back at these years between 1706 and 1709, "it was only by this [temperate] *Regimen.*" Cheyne's solace in his illness was that he had learned to understand Grace in a new light: "If my Time of *Dissolution* was come, I knew I should die under Misery . . . [rather] than by an other Means."[55] By 1709 he settled in Bath, close to the mineral waters in case further personal crises of health should arise. Here he could practice medicine, if and when he recovered, but the main attraction was the pure quality of the air and the proximity of the medicinal spa.

He arose early and retired early; his diet consisted exclusively of vegetables, milk, and seeds; he sought out new patients and lived frugally, almost monastically. In the terms of modern psychoanalysis, his ego underwent radical redefinition. If a patient visited him, he would treat him, but he no longer craved to be a fashionable London physician. James Cuninghame (1665–?), one of the four main French prophets, sought him out while recuperating from his own mysterious illness in Bath early in the spring of 1709, and filled Cheyne's ears with talk about the prophets' activities and the imminence of apocalypse.[56] Cuninghame read Augustine Baker's *Sancta Sophia* during recuperation, while Cheyne still scanned the works of the early Christian fathers, and possibly of Böhme.[57] It must have occurred to both of them how remarkably parallel their lives were: both men were Scots who craved worldly recognition in England; both had been introduced to mystical religion by the Aberdeen-Garden group; both had recently been afflicted with a near-fatal illness; the recovery of each coincided with new insight into the nature of Providence and resulted in a major conversion of his style of life. Immediately thereafter, in 1709, Cuninghame, now converted, joined the French prophets, whereas Cheyne renounced his previous life. Cuninghame resolved to work for the prophets in Scotland,[58] while Cheyne aimed to convert Englishmen to the New Jerusalem by the same doctrines of abstemiousness in diet he himself was rigidly following. By 1709 or 1710 Cheyne may not have considered himself a quietist per se, but an observer of his daily life in Bath would have concluded that he was one. Well-read in the works of Madame Guyon, Bourbignon, and other Continental female and male pietists, and possibly by now in the writings of Böhme, Cheyne believed that the millennium had begun, that recent political and social events were sufficient proof, and that he bore a special mission in its commencement and eventual fulfillment. It is not known whether he agreed with Whiston that the millennium would not begin until 1736 or 1766,[59] but Cheyne was confident that the important day could not be very far away. Besides, Cheyne's conversion had occurred unequivocally in 1706, during the very same months when the French prophets landed in England and when many were prophesying that doomsday was close at hand. What evidence, all seeming to convene, could be more explicit from Cheyne's point of view?

During the next five years (1709–14) Cheyne revised *Philosophical Principles* and practiced his body in rigid diet, regular exercise, plenty of sleep, pure air— nonnaturals, as the eighteenth century called them, the abuse of which had been a primary cause of his collapse. In 1711 the French prophets began to roam the west country and to proselytize more fervidly than they had in London. Cheyne probably heard them in Bath or Bristol, even if he resisted them. During these years he also associated with Richard Roach (1662–1730), their foremost apostle who, like Cheyne and Cuninghame, had experienced a pattern of illness, healing, conversion, and redemption through new works.[60] Roach also published a diary that would have aroused Cheyne's sympathy if Cheyne could have read it. "Divines and Physicians, Literal and Mystical," Roach cryptically wrote, "There is a world of Science, Soul of the Science unknown to the former."[61] Roach also scrutinized the Cabala, and may have introduced Cheyne to the interpretations he—Roach—would publicize before his death in 1730 in *The Imperial Standard of Messiah Triumphant* and *The Great Crisis*. For all three men, millenarianism and medicine were interrelated, and even if no one of the three was consciously searching for a universal panacea[62]—as Fatio was—each had learned that extreme illness followed by bodily healing was itself the highest form of revelation: the basis for a philosophical natural religion based on, and grounded in, the body of man.

Then, in 1713, the German baron Metternich published an explication of Böhme under the guise of an attack on John Locke, entitled *Fides et Ratio—Faith and Reason*. Cheyne acquired it and sent it to William Law, the author of the popular *Serious Call to a Devout and Holy Life* (1728), which implored mankind to renounce the hustle and bustle of material life in preference for a quiet world of constant religious devotion.[63] By 1715 the second edition of Cheyne's *Philosophical Principles* appeared, resorting to fanciful linguistic analogies between the body of man and the body of the universe, and reasoning again "by way of Analogy" but now espousing a more mystical, if indeed somewhat more emphatically Neoplatonist, theory of attraction than before. Creatures of the world were now direct reflections, or embodiments, of the Creator. Because of this similitude, Cheyne purported one could reason *exclusively* by analogy and without hesitation from the material to the spiritual realm.[64] He placed everything in the service of analogical reason.

Yet Cheyne's argument is not at all Shaftesburian. Attractions between living creatures are merely a different manifestation of that which is between the Deity and his material creation, but are no less valid or real. Therefore, spiritual love between man and fellow man is attraction of as noble a type as that between man and God. The 1715 revised edition also contained reflections on God and the "Divine Essence." Here Cheyne argued that forms of "divine things" exist as well as of material things, the material ones having been "Copied out" in the process of original genesis.[65] God's creatures, man included, become "Images, *Emanations, Effluxes,* and *Streams* out of his own *Abyss* of Being,"[66] a position that appears closer to the *Book of Urizen*—as we shall also see later—than to the *Principia* or *Opticks*. By 1720 Cheyne prepared another book championing Stoic abstemiousness entitled *Observations concerning the Gout*. This was a book less about gout than about the healthful effects of a diet composed of lettuce, milk, and seed, one promoting plenty of sleep, good air, and complete avoidance of luxury in diet.[67] It was well received by the medical community, which was so obsessed with gout in the 1720s that almost any book by a medical doctor would have been construed seriously. But since the book proclaimed nothing about cosmology or physicotheology, the Anglican Newtonians overlooked it or shunned it altogether. What Cheyne did, or said, in his medico-mystical moods was of no concern to them.

The Second Revelation

But Cheyne relapsed. In 1723, now over fifty, Cheyne again swelled to enormous size—"I exceeded 32 Stone," about 450 pounds—and grew so ill that "if I had but an Hundred Paces to walk, [I] was oblig'd to have a Servant following me with a Stool to rest on."[68] This time Cheyne was better prepared for dire calamity than he had been in 1706, and could rely more on the resources of his acquired mystical millenarianism. Certain that misery is the mother of salvation, he bore up to his "perpetual *Sickness, Reaching, Lowness, Watchfulness, Eructation,* and *Melancholy*"[69] for almost two years, and diagnosed gout as the source of these melancholic conditions. Returning to a diet of "lettuce, little wine, and water best," this second protracted illness caused him to grow increasingly Hermetic and herbalistic in his theory of diet. Unlike Bernard Mandeville and Nicholas Barbon before him, Cheyne argued against the virtues of luxury; yet like them, he considered luxury to be a psychological state as well as a physical reality (that is, sugar was uncommon among the poor in the eighteenth century). And he linked himself with others who related psychic health to daily diet. He would surely have encountered a kindred spirit if he had then read the works of Thomas Tryon, the author of the tome on the mystical divination of dreams.[70] But if Tryon advocated a similar rigid vegetarianism, he possessed little of Cheyne's mystical faith— "naked faith," as John Byrom later referred to it—nor was Tryon medically trained. Yet both men, to be sure, were of the Hermetic tradition of Böhme: a lineage descended from Paracelsus and van Helmont to Böhme, and from Böhme to the Baptists, Pentecostalists, and other versions of English pietism that flourished in Cheyne's most formative years. Actually, Cheyne would probably have found himself in greater spiritual agreement with Thomas Byfield, the Anglican physician who turned prophet in 1707 after the arrival of the Camisards in England.[71] Byfield, too, came to Bath in search of health, where he may have sought out Cheyne to diagnose his case. While there, Byfield joined forces with those of the French prophets based in Bath-Bristol, and converted the vicinity into a stronghold of radical millenarianism.

In the midst of all this religious tumult, Cheyne was following his old pattern of publication accompanied by illness. Late in 1723 or early in 1724 James Leake, the novelist Samuel Richardson's brother-in-law whom the Earl of Orrery described as "the Prince of all the Fraternity of Booksellers" in Bath, opened a business on one of the parades, a few yards from Cheyne's house, and printed as his first book Cheyne's *Essay on Health and Long Life*—yet another Cheyne treatise advocating abstemious diet, this time referring historically to the writings of Cornaro, Lessius, and other early vegetarians. It is impossible to know—at least Cheyne's memoirs offer no clue—whether this publication bolstered Cheyne's spirits sufficiently to cure him. But by December 1725 he was well enough to travel to London to consult with the most "distinguished physicians" then alive about his ailments.[72] Cheyne's habit, then, of growing seriously ill just before and shortly after the publication of his books seems by now to have hardened into a predictable pattern. (It was a pattern similar to that of Dr. Alfred Kinsey, the American zoologist who also grew ill shortly before and after the publication of each of his books, and who actually died shortly after the negative reception of his study of sexual behavior in the human female.)

Geoffrey Bowles has perceptively called attention in the essay already cited to a correlation between Cheyne's theory of "attraction" and his attitude to the medical profession.[73] It is equally plausible that a correlation exists between the reception of Cheyne's books and his health, that is, a kind of therapy by reception. If this approach is valid, it would have to include Cheyne's anticipation of the reception he would receive. Every time the Newtonians had criticized him, his health declined. When no one took notice of *Philosophical Principles* in 1705, he again grew dangerously ill. Now, in 1723, he again blistered into mania and broke out with raging fever while writing the *Essay on Health and Long Life*, only to be cured by the eventually favorable reception of the book. The *Essay* of 1723 received more attention than any previous work by Cheyne, and within eighteen months was translated into several languages.[74] Gilbert Nelson, then an authority on gout, wrote approvingly of Cheyne, claiming that he was the only physician in England who could rank with Sydenham on the subject.[75] The great Arbuthnot himself, the Queen's physician, was willing to be deflected from other pressing professional work to study Cheyne's theories about vegetarian diet, on which he commented in *An Essay concerning the Nature of Ailments* (1731). As these and many other medical estimates and literary appraisals appeared, Cheyne improved; by 1729 he claimed "compleat Recovery."[76]

Yet it falsifies the known facts to sketch a picture of praise without blame for Cheyne's reception. As the negative criticism mounted and continued to surpass the positive,[77] he began to see medicine and millenarianism—together and apart—in a different light from the view he held during his first collapse. In 1729—his second medical *annus mirabilis*—Cheyne was fifty-eight, no longer young. According to Whiston, the millennium was now only seven years distant (1729–36), or if Whiston had altered his view by then, thirty-seven years (1729–66). Unfortunately, no evidence exists to learn whether Cheyne still extolled Whiston as he had in 1706—as a beacon of primitive Christianity—and the lack of any reference to Cheyne in Whiston's *Memoirs* complicates the matter further. But whether Cheyne was still reading authors of primitive Christianity, by 1730 he was certainly grieving over the death of Richard Roach, perhaps the most inspired of the English prophets who had converted to the cause of the French.

As Cheyne's books continued to be reprinted and as the negative record began to accumulate,[78] his evangelical mission to connect medicine and millenarianism increasingly obsessed him. Doubt crept in too: Perhaps he had not accomplished enough in the conventional medical spheres of diagnosing symptoms and treating patients. Furthermore, as social and economic conditions changed for the better in England after the disastrous South Sea Bubble, and as the tide of luxury dramatically increased, Cheyne believed that his energy was urgently needed to combat this appallingly widespread condition of opulence. Accordingly, sometime around 1730 he set about to write a treatise on scurvy, the only major disease he had not written about before. He noticed that it had peaked during the last two centuries, concomitant with melancholia. He also observed that there had been a drastic upsurge of dyspepsia in England—the main symptom of "flatulent melancholy"— during the decade of the 1720s, as well as an increase in suicide. By the mid-1720s the medical profession was calling suicide, even more so than gin, "the English vice." Cheyne imaginatively combined all these currents of ideas into a single work, and in the same year (1733) in which Pope published *An Essay on Man,* he brought out *The English Malady,* no doubt his best-known book today.

Medicine and Millenarianism

Cheyne made clear in his preface to *The English Malady,* first of all, that he was writing for a particular audience. "Such a *Diet,*" he insists at once, "is only proper for the *thinking, speculative* and *sedentary* Part of Mankind, and not for the *active, laborious* and *mechanical,*"[79] Yet this "thinking Part"—clergymen, scholars, writers, artists, the whole intellectual establishment—constituted practically the whole group that was committing suicide with such astonishing frequency. What had these types in common? A weak constitution, Cheyne concluded; one whose blood and, more significantly, whose nervous system, was either congenitally defective or imperiled through abuse. His own condition had been a case in point: From youth onward he had observed a weak physiological constitution composed of "feeble Solids" and "excessive Juices."[80] Yet the nervous system—the constellation of nerves, spirits, and fibers—was the ultimate culprit; and Cheyne concluded that the only remedy, given that "none can choose his own Degree of *Sensibility,*"—the all-important sensibility—was the spartan life-style he had been recommending since his visionary experience in 1706. The assiduous reader who was willing to peruse all three hundred pages of *The English Malady* could discover how the nerves and fibers actually produced the melancholy about which so many Britons (including Hume, Smart, and others) complained to their physicians and which actually drove many of them to suicide. Theoretically and methodologically viewed, *The English Malady* by no means endorsed "the mechanical philosophy," but it infused Newtonian and mathematical learning to a degree Cheyne had not used since 1715. Only a novice reader then, who had not followed Cheyne's bizarre scientific and personal career, could reasonably have concluded in 1733 that Cheyne was still the dyed-in-the-wool iatromathematician he had once been. But he was not. If anything, his preface anticipates precisely the opposite allegation: that he has now "turn'd mere *Enthusiast,* and resolv'd all Things into *Allegory* and *Analogy,* advis'd people to turn *Monks,* to run into *Desarts,* and to live on *Roots, Herbs,* and *wild Fruits.*"[81]

The English Malady was an instant success, a bestseller almost overnight. Within fifteen months it went into six editions. Cecil Moore, the American literary historian, was so awed by its reception that solely on the basis of it he wrote of the mid-eighteenth century: It "deserves to be called," not the Age of Reason, Enlightenment, or Exuberance, but "the Age of Melancholy."[82] It is something to ponder. An element of Moore's attitude was influenced by Cheyne's own explanation of the title: "The title I have chosen for this treatise is a reproach universally thrown down on this island by foreigners, and all our neighbours on the Continent, by whom spleen, vapours, and lowness of spirits are in derision the English Malady."[83] But *The English Malady,* as its title suggests, is not an apology for eccentricity or a justification of a dangerously high rate of English suicide. It is an explanation to the rich of their own condition: their high living, their nervous constitutions, their nervous ailments. It is also a cultural treatise embodying many of the unwritten assumptions of the age, and it synthesizes a whole range of current medical topoi (melancholy, spleen, vapours—the whole repertoire of then current psychosomatic illnesses) and controversial physiological assumptions (the nervous system in relation to the rest of the body and its behavior), as well as fundamental laws about the nature of man.[84] In view of Cheyne's ingrained iatromechanical and Newtonian beliefs, it is not surprising that many of the explanations in the book are mechanical and mathematical. But it would be a serious error to interpret *The English Malady* merely within the development of English mechanistic theory, especially because the deepest explanations—answers to the question, What is life?—are remarkably nonmechanistic. *The English Malady* also has historical value because it assembles so many prevalent mid-eighteenth-century biases and discusses them within a social and topographical context, an instance of which is the effect of English climate on human health. And—more than anything—it flatters the rich, the fashionable, by setting them apart; by explaining why those of only the "most delicate nervous constitutions" were privileged to come down with "the English Malady," the most "nervous" disease known to civilized urban man. The poor were too rough, too crude, their nerves not subtle enough.

Viewed, however, from the perspective of millenarianism, *The English Malady* is less significant than the revelatory treatise appended to it: "The Case of the Author," a fifty-page memoir delineating Cheyne's life, his various crises, and his conversion to "more enlightening *Principles.*"[85] Ten years later, in 1742, Cheyne told Samuel Richardson, his constant correspondent, that he wrote this work to prevent his patients from believing he was "really mad." But this was recollection in hindsight, and it may be that Cheyne himself did not fully realize how well his "Case" formed a companion piece to *The English Malady.* Cheyne's memoir of his spiritual life provides a context for *The English Malady* and demonstrates how "nervous physiology"—one of his favorite scientific subjects—lies directly in the service of these "more enlightened principles." Here Cheyne suggests, however vulgarly, that we *are* our physiology, we *are* our nerves, and that our constitution will predetermine most aspects of our behavior; yet he does so as justification of his own "naked faith." For more than anything else he wants to remind his imagined readers—especially those fashionable patients he treated—that they possess nerves: the nerves of the rich. But he also hopes to impress upon them the larger claim that health depends upon "Simplicity," and that every physiological type—whether a robust Fielding or a willowy Richardson—can improve his bodily condition by adopting a spare diet.[86] "*Simplicity* is the greatest Contradiction to

Laziness, Foreign Studies, Negligence, Incuriosity and *Ignorance* in the Profession; but such a *Simplicity* . . . is worth a *Million* of these *false* and *foreign Arts* sometimes us'd to rise in it; for it [Simplicity] is, in Truth and Reality, an *Eminence of Light* and *Tranquillity*."[87] Cheyne's final trope is characteristically mystical; it is the clue to his medical symptomology as well as his whole physicotheology. If others looked at the stars and heavens to discover "the Book of Revelation," he gazed inwardly at the body. There only lay the way to the New Jerusalem, to the *"Eminence of Light* and *Tranquillity"* toward which he was striving.

Yet a deep-seated need to confess—to lay one's heart bare—is as crucial to the intentions of the author narrating his "case history" as are my observations about temperance and abstinence. This is why Cheyne locates abstinence within the Stoic or quietist life as subservient to the "universal attraction" he thought he now (1733) understood better than ever. "For the Means us'd by *infinite Wisdom* and *Goodness* towards reclaiming his *wandering Creatures,* seem only to be either *Love* or *Punishment:* that those whom *Love* will not draw and allure, *Punishment* may drive and force."[88] Both types of revealed "attraction"—love and punishment—have strayed from any philosophical model: Newtonian or otherwise. Now Cheyne belittles the march of empirical science and the revolutionary value of the Newtonianism he had formerly championed, postulating that the "body physics" (medicine) of the early Christian fathers had achieved equally good results, "tho' not quite so soon perhaps as we by all our *Mathematicks, Natural Philosophy, Chymistry,* . . . *Animal Oeconomy.*"[89] His tropes are consequently those of the antiempiricist who discovers who he "really is" by deconstructing his former empirical life; and there is something very nearly Sartrean and Barthean about Cheyne's concept of autobiography. Yet Cheyne proclaims himself to be an open enemy of "those *Divine Sciences,*" and explains that luxury is the ultimate culprit of man. Luxury has outpaced empiricism, as it were, and rendered its wisdom ineffectual in England. He concedes that Cornaro and Lessius, earlier diet theorists discussed in *The English Malady,* lived in simpler times, when science and theology were not so intertwined. But they wrote long before the onset of the apocalypse. Their ideas of health, Cheyne reasons, were not colored by the approach of the millennium. As a consequence, they could not perceive man's ultimate needs so clearly as he could. Nor did physiological necessity— there, again, was Cheyne's law of physiological determinism—cause them, as it compelled him, to remain apart from society while contributing to it.[90]

Cheyne was now (1733) growing old, in his mid-sixties. He professes not to worry if death be close; all his goals have been accomplished and his mood is irenic. He has become, he thinks, the most dedicated spokesman of the age for the medicomillenarian analogy. Of this he seems practically certain.

Fame and Mysticism

Cheyne's remaining years (1733–43) displayed no evidence of mental decline but a rather marked intensity of belief in mystical religion. Amazingly, he had lost two-thirds of his weight, and remained thin and relatively well (relative to what his health had been) until his dying day. This last decade, the 1730s, was the period, ironically, when his fashionable medical practice soared. Fashionable ladies of every variety—dowagers, duchesses, princesses, young misses—and from everywhere sought him out in Bath where he was now a legendary figure. By 1734 he was treating the wealthy Countess of Huntingdon, already mentioned, and continued in constant correspondence—"pious conversation"—with her.[91] Her confessional letters to Cheyne portray her attitude as that of a worshiper in a temple. In Cheyne's inimitable brand of mystical millenarianism she discovered, she claimed, the reflection of her own ideas; simultaneously, as she obeyed him, her own health mended. The pattern was as predictable as Cheyne's had been.

By 1738 Cheyne was also in constant correspondence with Richardson—his "literary patient"—and trying to persuade Richardson that extreme abstinence was the only salvation for someone physiologically as "nervous" and "delicate" as he was.[92] The source, Cheyne patiently explained, lay in Richardson's "defective nerves." But Richardson's "nervous paroxysms" and "paralytic tremors," Cheyne pleaded, were those of a creative artist; therefore, they could not be treated, Cheyne cautioned, as if Richardson were merely a brutish Fielding or another, untalented aristocratic lady in Bath. The masculine-feminine implications were too obvious to belabor. Cheyne expended much energy and more ink to persuade Richardson in dozens of extant, and remarkably long, letters that his malady could be constructive—no less productive than Cheyne's illnesses had been for him. Cheyne, as we shall now see, had something specific in mind, though it did not surface for three or four years.

While corresponding with Richardson, Cheyne published another book, *An Essay on Regimen* (1740), attempting to delineate "the principles and theory of philosophic medicin [*sic*] and point out some of its moral consequences." This was the medicomoral analogy Cheyne had established long ago; only now it was extended more explicitly into a medical arena. A year before his death in 1743, he produced another long essay arguing that "disorders of the mind" depend "upon the body," and that care should be taken to keep the body healthy.[93] This position was the reverse of the psychosomatic one gaining ground at mid-century: namely, the notion that diseases of the body were owing to mental distress. Yet, however receptive to psychosomatic theories of illness Cheyne may have been, by the end of his life he was more ardent than ever about the body as an instrument of divine revelation and as the primary source of the truest revealed religion. If there were such an ideological state as "Enlightenment" in the England of the 1740s, this religion of the body and its nervous states was Cheyne's most enlightened credo. Cheyne grew so fanatic about the matter that he could not imagine any revelation at all that circumvented the body—an intellectual stance that ought to cause scholars of Romantic literature, especially Blake, to be much more interested in him than they have been.

Of course Richardson knew his constant correspondent well and was aware of his bent. As late as August 1742—eight months before Cheyne's death—Richardson continued to "bribe" Cheyne with gifts of "Boehme bound."[94] A few volumes would elicit the free medical advice Richardson direly needed. Sometimes, it was Cheyne, rather than Richardson, who drove the bargain. By September 1742 Cheyne was imploring Richardson to print a "Catalogue of Books for the Devout . . . and Nervous."[95] Actually persuaded that it "would be of greater Use in England than any Book," Cheyne advised Richardson that he hoped to model it on "the Catalogue of the mystic Writers published by Mr. Poiret."[96] Richardson was not altogether unreceptive to the idea, but Cheyne could not have known he would be dead within a few months. When Richardson niggled and coyly procrastinated, Cheyne conceived yet another "project in mystical religion." "Pray be so good," he begged his constant correspondent, "to inform me if you know any Person having a Taste of Spiritual Religion that could translate a little French Book into clean English, entitled 'L'Essence de la Extract de Religion Chretiene.' "[97] Richardson had apparently found a translator of whom Cheyne did not approve and whose identity today remains obscure. So this ultimate dream, like some of its awe-inspired predecessors, went the way of all flesh.

During this period at the end of his life Cheyne also corresponded with his old friend William Law, although many of their letters have disappeared, as Stephen Hobhouse, Law's recent knowledgeable student, has discovered. The subject they entertained most was religion and science: especially the diffusion of "mystical religion" among the growing numbers of naturalists. Cheyne was amazed at the number of young Newtonians who continued to carry on the work of their real and symbolic "father"; Law was intent, for obvious reasons, to prove that Newton himself had been a mystic of profound dimensions, and there is, of course, something in Law's position. Yet Cheyne wondered why Law claimed that Böhme *in particular* had been the source of much of Newton's science. On 31 March 1742 Cheyne put the question to Law in a letter, asking him to substantiate what Law had just claimed in his recently published *Appeal to All That Doubt* (1742): "that [Newton] had been a *diligent Reader* of that wonderful Author [Böhme], that he made large extracts out of him." Law replied by repeating his claim in the *Appeal,* and assured Cheyne that these "large extracts" had been among Newton's papers at the time of his death. Law's reply to Cheyne was not published in the lifetime of either man—Law died in 1761—but appeared in the September issue of the *Gentleman's Magazine* (p. 329), and was later republished by Christopher Walton, Law's Victorian biographer, in *Notes and Materials for an Adequate Biography of . . . William Law* (1954). Cheyne may have been satisfied by Law's letter; at least he had no reason to deny what had been included among Newton's manuscripts at the time of his death in 1727. But it is also possible that Cheyne was too preoccupied with Richardson and his fashionable invalids and neurotics at Bath, whom he continued assiduously to treat, to pursue the intriguing question about Böhme and Newton.[98]

Throughout that summer of 1742—Cheyne's last—and during the next autumn he continued to search for a translator. The search became compulsive. Precisely why he relied so preponderantly on Richardson, and why he could not locate a translator by himself, must be something to preoccupy Cheyne's future biographers. Of greater concern here is the situation of the septuagenarian millenarian-dreamer knocking at death's door in this precise stance; still diffusing mystical but "more *enlightening* Principles" by scattering books throughout the British Isles, still compulsively imposing on Law, still enticing Richardson. According to so many commentators in his own day, Cheyne had been a brilliant medical mind, a caring doctor, a personality totally worthy of the notice he would no doubt receive in future ages. Yet time's winged chariot has somehow managed to obscure the very aspect that his contemporaries deemed to have been so original to the Bath physician: his unique blend of medicine and mysticism, as even his bodily corpulence and exiguity demonstrated. It is one matter, then, to depict Cheyne in his own milieu and against the backdrop of his own times, and quite another to rescue him now. If greater emphasis is placed on the second concern, then a different question ought perhaps to be put to the modern student. In this case the absolute historical portrait loses some of its thunder as one wonders—today—if Cheyne's career does not pose some major paradoxes for the intellectual historian of today who happens to be interested in the eighteenth-century Enlightenment. Cheyne, Richardson, Newton, Law, Böhme, Pope, Poiret: what a strange lot of bedfellows it seems. Surely, one wonders whether this is a jumble worthy of commemoration in a polished neoclassical English couplet. But the confusion of diverse names may reflect our own sense of "jumble" according to rigid principles of "Enlightenment" we have inherited rather than historical truth warrants. Perhaps our sense of *the* Enlightenment and its attributes requires some radical adjustment, especially in the domains of religion and science. This is the issue I want to discuss in conclusion, isolating it in relation to Cheyne's demise.

Death in the Apocalypse

Cheyne died in April 1743, naturally having failed to convince the English upper classes about a balanced diet, and valetudinarians like himself about the terrific value of abstinence. His program for scurvy—*the* disease of the seas at the time— had to await the late eighteenth century before gaining public recognition; and his plan for a balanced diet containing plenty of vegetables and nuts rather than meat and potatoes has lingered into the twentieth century before partial adoption. His attack on luxury, it is true, impressed many of his patients (though not all), but "Estimate" Brown, Smollett, Goldsmith and others in the 1750s and 1760s were needed before the war against luxury could be formulated, let alone combated.[99] When Goldsmith earnestly reported that Beau Nash "would swear, that [Cheyne's] design was to send half the world grazing like *Nebuchadnezzar,*"[100] one views the comic strain of Cheyne's program. Indeed, there is a sense in which he must have appeared to many of his contemporaries as if he had been—or *ought* to have been—a Hogarthian caricature in a Smollettian novel. Viewed solely as a type, or a stereotype, he was a celebrated but decidedly eccentric physician who had become a best-selling author. But his contemporaries could not view him merely from within. If they had been able, they would have found a complex man who firmly believed that he had resolved intellectual dilemmas through a doctrine of "Universal Attraction" based on analogy, and furthermore, viewed from within, that he had faithfully served his Maker by carrying forward the supreme message about man's nervous body. And, despite the weight of a quarter of a ton, he had managed to live to seventy-two! As he told Richardson near the end of his life:

I [who] have gone the whole Road had one of the most cadaverous and putrefied
Constitutions ever was known, and I thank God am returned safe and sound at
70 every way well . . . and surely he knows the Road better who has gone to and
come from the Cape of Good Hope, all the Surroundings, Rocks, Shelves, and
Winds, than they who have only seen them in a Map.[101]

In other words, he had been a good physician but a better Christian, and by
ranking the two in this way he had practiced what he preached: "Medicine begins
where philosophy ends." Despite his unorthodox Christianity it would be wrong to
see Cheyne—whether from without or within—as a hermit, even though he had
retreated from city life to encourage the apocalypse. In my view it is equally
incorrect to portray him merely as an energumen who repressed his earthly needs
by rationalizing them in the name of millenarian enthusiasm,[102] or as a type of
eighteenth-century democrat, socialist, or leveller, whose medical therapy was but
a dimension of a larger political program. Although Cheyne's politics have received no attention, it is palpable that more often than not his medical-religious
mission compelled him to bend to the views of his affluent patients whose politics
ran the gamut from the most retrograde Tory beliefs to progressive Whig views.
Even so, and even when Cheyne's politics are construed within the political milieu
of his times, he was no political revolutionary, as were the French prophets, or—in
an altogether different context and manner—William Blake the poet (see page 219
below). However odd Cheyne's politics appeared to his contemporaries as a consequence of his bizarre regimens and abstemious diets, he was never bent on the
destruction of existing hierarchy, order, ranks, and property. The meat-loving
gluttons and duck-hungry sensualists who viewed him as a threat to their epi-
cureanism understandably ridiculed him and his followers and disciples in any way
they could; and the opprobrious tags of political radical or social leveller were then
sufficiently volatile to raise the ire or hackles of those who heard him denounced in
this way. But Cheyne neither deserved these political labels, nor had any consistent political program worthy of them. If he was a political creature at all, it was as a
type of Arcadian or Pythagorean elitist: a believer in the simple, pastoral life whose
charisma permitted him to become the darling of the wealthy and the famous.
Temperamentally, Cheyne was as social as he was given to retiring. Socially, he was
not so recalcitrant as his memoirs suggest; this is known from his medical activities in Bath. His personality was outgoing, permeated with a constant sunny
cheerfulness he never abandoned. But he had been born with chronic obesity that
played havoc with his physiological constitution, to such a degree that he never
expected to live to more than twenty or thirty. From youth onward his religious
tendencies had been mystical, but when the crisis of 1706 broke, followed by the
subsequent conversion experience, something new in his apocalyptic and millenarian imagination jelled. Mentally and emotionally he was never again the same.
The Cheyne who wrote to the ailing Richardson, "It is true you are not a Physician, but I hope you are a Christian,"[103] was the mature, final Cheyne—anything
but a Hogarthian or Smollettian caricature—who was persuaded he had found the
way to Grace and eternal redemption:

Our Saviour bids us fast and pray and deny ourselves without Exception, but for
this there is no need for Revelation Advice. If you read but what I have written in

this last in the Essay on Regimen in long Life and Health or Cornaro's or Lessius' little Treatise your own good sense would readily assure you; but you puzzle yourself with Friends, Relations, Doctors, and Apothecaries, who either know Nothing of the Matter, or whose Interest it is, or at least that of the Craft to keep you always ailing.

Medicine and millenarianism, at least for Cheyne could not impinge more on each other if they tried.

Cheyne and the Cultural Map of His Times

These conclusions about Cheyne's temperament and career may be valid, but they are incomplete in themselves unless Cheyne is properly related to the temper of his times. In this sense, it is irrelevant whether he was a major or minor figure. His activities as a representative man of the Enlightenment are far more crucial, and not merely his intellectual thought but his frenetic energy in dispersing quietist literature from the Continent. It is necessary, then, to ask two or three large questions in order to understand precisely how he is a representative man and how he relates to the map of his times. Prominent among these topics is his relation to the overall science—especially to the natural philosophy—of the enlightenment. The question is precisely how does Cheyne relate to eighteenth-century science?

Clearly, he was one of the more interesting early Newtonians—not only because he was, Arbuthnot notwithstanding, the physician closest to "the Wits"—Cheyne himself was something of a "scientific wit" whose numerous best-sellers made his name a household word among the very "Hackney Scribblers" he described in the preface of *The English Malady*—but also as a result of his Hermetical way of reasoning. Cheyne may not appear to be a "scientist" when viewed from a modern perspective or when judged by modern criteria of the impartial observer; but he was certainly considered a mathematician and fine physician (whether medicine is a science is another matter) in his own time, although—as I have shown—a poor one by the Newtonians. The foundations of his system thrive on a Hermetical concept of analogy that is neither logical nor accessible.[104] Rather than attempts at mathematical logic or secular accessibility, Cheyne's analogies were exercises to derive the love of God in a hostile, yet hardly void, universe. Yet Cheyne's life and works display no contradiction, no tension, between science and theology, although it is patent that more historians of science would be less uncomfortable with his career if it had evolved in the early seventeenth, rather than the early eighteenth century. If it is true that in the seventeenth century a good scientist also had to be a good theologian, this law applies integrally for Cheyne, although he lived a century later. In this sense, though, the relation of his science and theology may compel contemporary students of Enlightenment culture to ask some hard-nosed questions about the so-called rational century or Age of Reason. It is true that Cheyne stands apart from many of his medical brethren—the Arbuthnots, Cheseldens, and Olivers—who were less interested in mystical theology than he was, and that he was a harbinger of Hartley and Priestley.[105] But the larger point is not that Cheyne was born too early or too late; but rather that he, like Fatio, was immensely taken with the French and English prophets, and that this near seizure impelled him to integrate "mathematics" and "naked faith" in a way that scholars have yet to describe. Perhaps there is an even larger point to be gathered: Cheyne was not solitary in his mystical millenarianism; he had his brand, just as Pitcairne, Fatio, Byfield, and many others had theirs. Yet Enlightenment scholars have remained largely uninterested in this huge underbelly of their so-called Age of Reason, or Age of Passion.

Moreover in the relation of science and theology, Newton was not a messiah for Cheyne, and Cheyne would have agreed with those in the 1730s who interpreted Pope's famous couplet in the *Essay on Man*—about "showing Newton as we show an Ape"—as a satiric barb. And he probably would have reasoned that the censure was directed specifically at those of his empirical and medical brethren who gadded about, within and without the Royal Society, portending that the messiah had arrived in the form of Sir Isaac Newton. As Cheyne gradually retreated throughout his lifelong pilgrimage from a system that may crudely be called Newtonian metaphysics, he substituted a set of poetic analogies derivative from Platonic, Hermetic, and other forms of spiritual love. At least nothing in the empirical universe could even begin to corroborate these similitudes which formed the basis of a metaphysics that increasingly denied the bases of physics. But this is precisely why Cheyne is so interesting, and why the literati were so attracted to him. In this sense his career violates the paradigm crudely referred to earlier about a good scientist also having to be a good theologian, yet it shows a man continually striving to wed science and theology.

In this evolving drama Newton is represented as an antihero who continues to lose ground to the more potent tradition of Böhme. Even Pitcairne recedes, although Cheyne could never reject his symbolic father. Newton had been a pillar of Cheyne's early intellectual life—but not because he was any type of saviour. Furthermore, there is no evidence whatever that Cheyne read Newton's posthumously published prophecies, neither the *Observations upon the Prophecies of Daniel and the Apocalypse of St. John* nor the unpublished manuscript about the conversion of the Jews,[106] nor is there any evidence that Cheyne was curious about this aspect of Newton's thought. Besides, even if Cheyne had read these works, it is doubtful that his quasi-Behmenistic attitude to the laws of universal attraction would have changed. Newton, for Cheyne, had been too whimsical in his wedding of science and religion, perhaps as a consequence of the way he was lionized by the whole intellectual establishment of England. The obese Cheyne had enjoyed no such instant success; he believed that the millennium was here, that there could be no doubt it had started in his lifetime. He had been old enough in the 1690s to witness, and then to remember, its first appearances. He had personally watched the events of 1706 and reasoned that they coincided with unprecedented brilliance in the mathematical sciences. Newton's appearance as the most perfect mathematician the world had ever known seemed to be evidence of the Deity's providential intentions, even though Cheyne was personally (and obviously) less awed by Newton's achievement than were most Englishmen; and he viewed the rapid succession of several mathematical geniuses—Pitcairne, Newton, the Bernoullis—as an important millenarian clue.

What remained, Cheyne believed, was to integrate medicine—"queen of the sciences"—into this state of mathematical perfection.[107] Finally in the scientific sphere, Cheyne's role in the development of medicine is clearer than is his precise millenarian niche. I would even venture to suggest that it is perilous to omit him from any so-called Whig history of eighteenth-century medicine, to echo the late Sir Herbert Butterfield, for this is one category in which he shines constantly. In what is today approvingly called holistic medicine, he may be the most important spokesman of the previous century. He not only developed a theory but advocated a therapy as well.[108]

We must also enquire into what Cheyne's career reveals about the orthodox theology of the period. This is a far less equivocal issue than the scientific matter because recent eighteenth-century studies have been demonstrating the century's ever-increasing secularism. Historians have been willing to concede to the occasional appearance of quietism, chiliasm, and millenarianism as a backdrop on the stage of ordinary life in the period, but few historians other than historians of religion have acknowledged these appearances as the period's underbelly. Yet Cheyne's career demonstrates that more radical enthusiasm existed—even among "the wealthy and the great," as Pope might have said—than has been thought. The important question, then, about Cheyne's theology is not precisely of what blend or version it was, but rather how it related to that of his contemporaries, and how it grew hand-in-hand with his scientific and medical hypotheses. Clues must be drawn from his lifelong attachment to the Aberdeen quietist group centered around George Garden and James Keith, as well as from Cheyne's highly unique linguistic tropes (even their grammar and syntax is unusual) which thrive on a principle of analogy and which suggest a symbolic rather than empirical imagination.[109]

Yet Cheyne does not fit the labels currently invoked by historians; Platonist, quietist, chiliast, Philadelphian, Behmenist, French prophet, English prophet. In a sense he was all, yet paradoxically none of these; his personal theology, to the degree that it can be isolated and defined, was a blend of these. But he cannot be cavalierly labeled by any of these tags without some analysis of his life and his particular constellation of beliefs. For example, if one must label, then it is equally accurate to consider him a neo-Pythagorean or neo-Stoic, for Cheyne certainly practiced aspects of Pythagorean and Stoic religion in his daily life. Perhaps the point to be gathered without belaboring it is that scholars have been coerced into dividing the religious sensibility of the early eighteenth-century into opposed camps of traditional versus dissenting religions, while neglecting what I am calling the underbelly of religion: the great *diversity* of types of radical enthusiasm. Moreover, one is willing to acknowledge the terrific influence of Shaftesbury as a Platonist and Stoic, especially on diverse English writers, but not of a Cheyne, altogether different though his influence was, this even though Cheyne's books appear in the libraries of writers at least as frequently as Shaftesbury's. A new sense of the widespread activities of the French prophets in England will eventually change this bipolar thinking, but it may be a decade or two before this recent research is assimilated into eighteenth-century studies.[110]

The final matter pertains to Cheyne's peculiar brand of millenarianism in relation to his sense of life in the apocalypse, as well as to Christ's role in man's eventual redemption. But only his remarkable life, with its startle of ups and downs, can begin to account for the contours of his piety. At the moment of greatest crisis in his life, he turned to the early Christian fathers and to Madame Guyon and her followers rather than to the traditional Church. Like the quietists with whom Cheyne associated, he extolled natural and revealed religion in place of the teachings of Jesus, attitudes that earned him the reputation of enthusiasm, and even of Arian heresy. This is why he was "indicted for heresy" shortly before his death in *The Arraignment of George Cheyne . . . for . . . Logical heresies.*[111] But Cheyne was not an Arian, despite his one-time worship of Whiston. He was a millenarian fanatic, or more accurately, a medicomystical millenarian. His portrayal as such has not been made, preeminently because his early students (Marx, Greenhill, G. D. Henderson) knew little about his medical career, and conversely, because his close ties to all types of enthusiasts have been overlooked by those scholars (H. R. Viets, C. A. Moore, R. Schofield, G. Bowles) who have studied only his empirical career. Cheyne, of course, has been connected to William Law, then the leading British exponent of Böhme, but not to the quietists, chiliasts, and millenarians from the Cévennes Mountains, or to their numerous English converts whose influence on British soil was far more extensive than has been thought. Cheyne's life demonstrates the trend I am attempting to delineate: An effect of radical millenarianism on early eighteenth-century England has been neglected to such a degree that most scholars write and think as if it never occurred.[112] Our Newtonians, for instance, explicate much about Fatio, but say little about his role in the radical millenarianism I have been describing.[113] Yet, this quietist-mystical context is the one in which Cheyne belongs, with one important exception: the neo-Stoical cults of the period.

Elsewhere I have suggested that neo-Stoicism is the least understood intellectual development of the Restoration and early eighteenth century.[114] Amos Funkenstein has described with what consequences the Cambridge stoics (Stoa) have been inaccurately labeled Cambridge Platonists. For Cheyne, aspects of his radical theory of abstinence derive from Stoic and sometimes neo-Pythagorean attitudes, rather than from neo-Platonic beliefs. But Cheyne usually does not name his sources, as a consequence of which his commentators have overlooked his relation to the Stoic and Pythagorean cults of the time.[115] I do not want to engage in unnecessary Hermetical classification; I see no reason to typify Cheyne as a "Stoic medico-millenarian." But I do believe it is important to stress the affinities he has with neo-Stoic thinking, and I would want to add, moreover, that he came by his Stoicism through reading of the early Christian fathers and the quietists, and when prompted by near-fatal illness and chronic suffering, rather than by reading of the Cambridge Platonists or Cambridge stoics.

In conclusion, Cheyne's radical millenarianism is ultimately paradoxical, a veritable aporia. On the one hand he advocates extreme abstinence in diet; on the other, he tries to convert a nervously depressed Richardson with all the ardor of a Christian missionary in China: His approach is anything but Stoic or passionless. Every restraint Cheyne espouses in diet is contradicted by apparent excess in mystical proclivity. His career is replete with other paradoxes as well: he begins to write, as I have shown, as an avowed mechanist (iatromechanist) and ends as an animist, although this shift, too, has not been studied in the light of his religious beliefs. All the Stoic fervor about relinquishing the needs of the self are contradicted, it would seem, by his intense search for a professional identity in an epoch when the physician could appear in almost any typology; for surely his blend of personal interests and misfortunes would not readily fit any profession. An example of these paradoxes is found in his unrelenting need to take stock and confess: Whenever he studied himself he uncovered layer upon layer of Providence tending to favor him.

I agree with Robert Schofield that Cheyne's "progress from kinematic mechanism toward vitalistic materialism, by way of Newtonian dynamic corpuscularity, was . . . occasioned by religious considerations."[116] But this explanation does not extend far enough. It omits consideration of these all-important religious contexts in relation to his personal and professional life. Moreover, Cheyne's death in the early 1740s has been said to make of him a transitional figure: his career—the argument goes—lies on the boundary of a vast continental shift between apparently opposed sets of values.[117] But these are not merely the differences of neoclassicism and romanticism, mechanism and vitalism (animism), or mechanism and organicism. Cheyne's mysticism deserves to be studied precisely because of the way in which it accommodates iatromechanism, Newtonianism, and animism, and especially for its blend of mechanism and vitalism. A close look at his theology demonstrates its affinities not only with animism, but with a pantheism of the type developed by the romantics, especially the pantheistic Coleridge. The Cheyne who at the end of his life espouses a pantheism in which every living creature embodies the specific attributes of the Godhead is hardly the same thinker who at the beginning wrote mechanistically about fevers or analogically about "philosophical principles." Inconsistency is a minor, venial sin for a mystic; intellectual growth is not. But Cheyne's was intellectual growth incapable of adequate explanation unless his millenarianism is also consulted.

Ultimately, the Cheyne who wrote just before his death that "Man is a diminutive *Angel,* shut up in a Flesh Prison or Vehicle,"[118] has more in common with Blake's visionary physics and Coleridge's pantheism than with his own early thought. Does this alteration make of him a Romantic thinker? I think not. The Cheyne who argues as he approaches his Maker that man's creative powers are somewhat analogous to God's—are "Something *analogous* to Creative Fecundity"[119]—sounds more like Wordsworth on the creative imagination than the mechanistic Pitcairne or the mathematical Newton he served at the start of his career. Does this Hermetic reasoning of Cheyne's render him a transitional figure in the shift from pre-Romanticism to romanticism? Again I think not: the flaw lies in these *isms* rather than in Cheyne's development. The Cheyne who laboriously anatomizes the mystical revelations he has experienced surely deserves to be considered as more than merely "one of the early Newtonians." Yet he has consistently been described as nothing more than another early Newtonian. The Cheyne who was anonymously extolled by a rhyming scribbler in the 1730s as having tamed "the Sacred Art . . . the Fetter'd Science,"[120] was someone far more prone to romantic agony and temperamental pantheism than any labels such as Neoplatonist or early Newtonian can suggest. Again, paradoxically, the same

Cheyne who finally claimed to have understood himself so well seems never to have comprehended to what an extent he had been one of England's staunchest antiluxury campaigners—perhaps the fiercest opponent of luxury anywhere.[121] Yet the most recent scholarly survey of luxury never—not even once—mentions Cheyne's name.[122] Finally, the Cheyne who wrote so prolifically about nervous diseases seems never to have realized to what an extent the very diet of abstemiousness he was advocating would induce nervous tension.[123] An epoch whose wealthy members practically ate themselves into the grave would certainly not have been capable of going on if nine-tenths of its daily diet is suddenly removed by the rabbit-likes of a Cheyne.

Perhaps my subtitle—"Immortal Doctor Cheyne"—indicates the ultimate aporia: Immortal he has hardly been, for most scholars today do not know who he was, do not recognize the name. Yet in his own day one could have flirted with the idea that history would keep his name alive because he managed, despite his colossal corpulence, to live on for so long. A type of myopic immortality, then, was granted to him by his contemporaries, but for the wrong reasons.

BIOGRAPHICAL AND ICONOGRAPHICAL NOTE ON THE PORTRAIT OF GEORGE CHEYNE

This portrait is the only one known to have been painted of George Cheyne. Sometime ca. 1735 Cheyne sat for Johan Van Diest (ca. 1680–1760), son of the Dutch landscape painter Adrien Van Diest (1656–1704). The resulting portrait was later engraved by the prolific engraver John Faber the Younger (1695?–1756). Van Diest resided in the vicinity of Bristol-Bath during the period 1730–50 where he was employed for a while by Ralph Allen; he was known to practically all the members of the circle that gathered around Allen at Prior Park and included Pope, Bolingbroke, Fielding, John Wood (the author of an *Essay on Bath*), lords Burlington and Bathurst, Bishop Warburton, painters and landscape architects, and Drs. Oliver, Pierce, and Cheyne (see B. Boyce, *The Benevolent Man: A Life of Ralph Allen of Bath* [Cambridge, Mass., 1967], pp. 38–39). Together with Pope, Van Diest advised Allen on the statues to be be built in the library at Prior Park, and he may have painted them. Pope also seems to have hired Van Diest to paint in his grotto, but the work was never completed, nor was the portrait of Pope by Van Diest to which the poet himself alludes in his correspondence: "Vandiest has made an Excellent Picture of Mr. [Nathaniel] Hook, which I hope will fall to your [Allen's] Lott. I will sit to him too, when we meet at your house" (*Correspondence of Pope,* ed. Sherburn, 4:239). Nathaniel Hooke (d. 1763) was a lifelong friend of Pope and a very close associate of Dr. Cheyne. According to Warburton, Hooke was also "a mystic and Quietist, and a warm follower of Fenelon and Mme. Guyon." In the latter capacity Hooke undertook an English translation of Michael Ramsay's *Cyrus,* and employed Dr. Cheyne's half-brother William Cheyne (1704–67), vicar of Weston-near-Bath, as his amanuensis (see *Spence's Anecdotes,* ed. J. M. Osborn, 2 vols. [Oxford, 1966] 1:455–56). Cheyne, who had been a boyhood friend of Ramsay while both men were youthful members of the mystical circle rallied around George Garden in Aberdeen, was sympathetic to the translation. He permitted Hooke to live in his house in Bath while translating, as Pope acknowledged several times in his correspondence and as was widely known by Allen's circle in Prior Park: "This elegant translation was made at Dr. Cheyne's house at Bath" (Joseph Warton, *An Essay on the Genius and Writings of Pope,* 4th ed., 2 vols. [London, 1782], 2:129); and also according to Spence: "Mr. Hooke was then at Bath for his health, and Dr. Cheyne's brother was so good as to write for him. Hooke walked about [Cheyne's] chamber and dictated to him, so that it was a sort of [Cheynean] exercise as well as study" (*Spence's Anecdotes,* 1:455). The mezzotint version of Cheyne's portrait is lettered "sold at the Great Toy Shop at Bath," at a location close to Cheyne's house. There is also a later copy (in reverse) of the print by J. M. Berngroth.

Notes

1. George Sherburn, ed., *The Correspondence of Alexander Pope,* 5 vols. (Oxford, 1956), 4:46. I am grateful to Professors Richard Popkin, M. E. Novak, James Force, and Donald Greene who commented on several versions of this essay, although my gratitude to them should not imply that they agree with my conclusions about Cheyne's niche.

2. See G. S. Rousseau, "Nerves, Spirits and Fibres: Towards Defining the Origins of Sensibility," in *Studies in the Eighteenth Century III: Papers Presented at the Third David Nichol Smith Memorial Seminar, Canberra 1973,* ed. R. F. Brissenden and J. C. Eade (Canberra, 1976), pp. 151–56; "Psychology," in G. S. Rousseau and Roy Porter, *The Ferment of Knowledge: Studies in the Historiography of Eighteenth-Century Science* (Cambridge, 1980), pp. 172–75, 207–8; and *England and the 'Nerve Doctors,'* a book-length manuscript currently in preparation.

3. There is no twentieth-century biography in any language, although several short articles exist. The fullest of these is H. R. Viets, "George Cheyne," *Bulletin of the History of Medicine* 23 (1949): 435–54. The only lengthy account is W. A. Greenhill's *Life of George Cheyne, M.D.* (Oxford, 1846), but it is anecdotal, based on secondary sources, and often unreliable. An estimate of Cheyne as an "eccentric genius" is found in J. H. Burton, *History of the Reign of Queen Anne,* 3 vols. (Edinburgh, 1880), 3:429. Though it is limited in its explanations about Cheyne, W. G. Hiscock, ed., *David Gregory, Isaac Newton and Their Circle: Extracts from David Gregory's Memoranda 1677–1708* (Oxford, 1937), is far more useful. Valuable information is also found in G. D. Henderson, *Mystics of the North-East* (Aberdeen, 1934), still the best source on Cheyne's relation to the circle of George Garden; M. D. Altschule, *Origins of Concepts in Human Behaviour* (Washington, 1977), pp. 53–74; and in L. S. King, "George Cheyne: Mirror of Eighteenth-Century Medicine," *Bulletin of the History of Medicine* 48 (1974): 517–39. Need exists for a detailed modern scholarly biography.

4. It is best to state—at the start—that I consider Cheyne's, "The Case of the Author," *The English Malady* (London, 1733), a reliable source for the shape of Cheyne's life, and my references to it below are taken from Strahan's and Leake's first London edition, not from the 1733 Dublin edition printed by G. Risk. Given the romantic excesses and mystical turns of Cheyne's temperament, it is possible that he exaggerated the pain he suffered during the various crises he endured. It is also probable that during the composition of these memoirs in the early 1730s, his memory distorted or confused events that had occurred three decades ago. But no reason exists to believe that Cheyne intentionally distorted the facts of his past life, or fabricated others, in order to endow posterity with a better image of himself, or that the agony and anguish of repeated breakdowns and collapses had put him out of touch with a minimal reality. The failure of scholars who have not relied on these memoirs must be attributed to their lack of interest in Cheyne's life, or to their sheer neglect and ignorance of this book.

Furthermore, if twentieth-century anthropologists and sociologists are correct in believing that cult figures in every age are trusted by their devotees while viewed suspiciously by the rest of the world, then George Cheyne deserves to be categorized as a cult figure. For almost everyone who knew him well trusted him and liked him, whereas those who did not either disliked or despised him, or disparaged him as a socialist or leveller of sorts. And most fashionable people of the eighteenth century knew who he was and were aware of his reputation as a celebrated physician and author. But here agreement about Cheyne ended; the only other consensus was about his colossal weight.

5. See C. F. Mullett, ed., *The Letters of Dr. George Cheyne to the Countess of Huntingdon* (San Marino, Calif., 1940).

6. The anonymous author of *A Treatise on Corpulency and Matter in Fat Persons* (1754), thought so (p. 23).

7. Sherburn, *The Correspondence of Alexander Pope,* 4:208.

8. Ibid, 4:46.

9. Cheyne is nowhere mentioned in *The Memoirs of Martinus Scriblerus* (London, 1714), a natural locus in view of the satires of science and the lampoons of doctors and their hypotheses found in this collaborative work, but he is discussed as a "mathematical authority" in William Wotton's *Defence of the Reflections upon Ancient and Modern Learning* (London, 1705), p. 10. The reference in Wotton makes it clear that by 1705 Cheyne was well known to Bentley and to others whom Swift attacked in *A Tale of a Tub* (London, 1704).

10. John Gay, *Mr. Pope's Welcome from Greece* (London, 1725), line 33.

11. Edward Young, *Epistle to Pope* (London, 1757), pt. 1, line 199. Young read at least one of Cheyne's books. In February 1746 he visited Richardson and "inadvertently stole one of [his] books." A few days later he wrote to Richardson: "On turning over my cargo, I find Dr. Cheyne among my other books." See H. Pettit, ed., *The Correspondence of Edward Young, 1683–1765* (Oxford, 1971), p. 231. It is impossible to know which book of Cheyne's this is, but Young apparently knew of Cheyne's *Philosophical Principles* (1705 edition) in *The Force of Religion* (London, 1714).

12. M. Battestin, ed., *Henry Fielding: The History of Tom Jones, a Foundling,* 2 vols. (Oxford, 1975). 2:605; and n. 73 below.

13. See J. Carroll, ed., *Selected Letters of Samuel Richardson* (Oxford, 1964), p. 52; and C. F. Mullett, ed., *The Letters of Doctor George Cheyne to Samuel Richardson (1733–1743)* (Columbia, Mo., 1943).

14. See P. Toynbee, ed., *The Correspondence of Gray, Walpole, et al;* 2 vols. (Oxford, 1915), 2:19.

15. J. Y. T. Greig, ed., *The Correspondence of David Hume,* 2 vols. (Oxford, 1932), 1:12. Ernest Mossner attributes this letter to Dr. Arbuthnot rather than to Cheyne, but his reasons, as given in *The Life of David Hume* (Oxford, 1980), p. 84, are unconvincing. Hume's self-diagnosis was "melancholic mania," the eighteenth-century term for manic depression, and he wrote to Cheyne as the leading authority on melancholy.

16. Cheyne dedicated his last book—*The Natural Method of Cureing the Diseases of the Body and the Disorders of the Mind depending on the Body* (London, 1742)—to Chesterfield.

17. This document is printed as Appendix 2 of R. Sedgwick, ed., *Some Materials towards Memoirs of the Reign of George II,* 3 vols. (London, 1931), 3:961–87. Hervey's letter to Cheyne, quoted here, is found in the Holland House MS in the British Library but has not been cataloged as yet. Numerous references to Cheyne made by the Hervey family are found in S. H. A. Hervey, ed., *Letter-Books of the Earl of Bristol,* 3 vols. (London, 1894).

18. See C. F. Mullett, ed., *The Letters of Dr. George Cheyne to the Countess of Huntingdon* (San Marino, Calif., 1940). On p. 17 of *Letters to Richardson,* Mullett notes: "There is no reason to suppose that the letters printed by me constituted the entire correspondence of Cheyne with her ladyship." A limited search has failed, however, to produce further letters.

19. *The Works of John Wesley,* 15 vols. (London, 1856), 11:493, entry for 12 March 1742. For Cheyne and Delafaye, see British Library MSS ADD, 32689, fols. 373 and 464; Delafaye's career, as well as his relation to the Newtonians, is discussed in M. C. Jacob, *The Radical Enlightenment: Pantheists, Freemasons and Republicans* (London, 1981), pp. 133–35.

20. See the many references, for example, in W. Porterfield, *A Treatise on the Eye, the Manner . . . of Vision,* 2 vols. (Edinburgh, 1759).

21. G. B. Hill, ed., *Boswell's Life of Johnson,* rev. L. F. Powell, 6 vols. (Oxford, 1934–50), 3:26–27; see also H. R. Viets, "Johnson and Cheyne," *Times Literary Supplement,* 5 February 1954, p. 89. Johnson admired Cheyne's *English Malady; or, A Treatise of Nervous Diseases of All Kinds* (London, 1733) as the best account of modern melancholia, frequently cited it, and owned a copy. See D. J. Greene, *Samuel Johnson's Library: An Annotated Guide* (Victoria, B.C., 1975), p. 48.

22. John Nichols, *Literary Anecdotes of the Eighteeenth Century,* 8 vols. (London, 1812), 8:82.

23. "To Dr. Cheyne of Bath: On Reading his Works," *Gentleman's Magazine* 3 (1733): 205. For other similar poems, see *Letters to Richardson,* pp. 126–37.

24. Cheyne himself is probably the best source for this figure; see "The Case of the Author," p. 342.

25. Cheyne describes this influence in ibid., and in *The English Malady* (1733), but there is no mention of Cheyne in Pitcairne's correspondence; see W. T. Johnston, ed., *The Best of Our Owne: Letters of Archibald Pitcairne* (Edinburgh, 1979). See also Hiscock, *David Gregory,* pp. 23–26.

26. For example, when someone calling himself Sir Edward Ezat attacked Pitcairne as "Apollo Mathematicus" in *The Art of Curing Diseases by the Mathematicks, according to the Principles of*

Archibald Pitcairne (London, 1695), Cheyne counterattacked brilliantly in several pamphlets and showed how effectively he could demolish the enemy. Cheyne's first book, *A New Theory of Fevers* (London, 1701), which originally appeared as a Latin dissertation, was an attempt to combine Newtonian mathematics with Pitcairnean mechanics, but the Newtonians disapproved of it, and their dispraise in the years 1702–6 eliminates Cheyne from consideration as a future Boyle lecturer.

27. In precisely which year in the period from 1695 to 1706 Cheyne absorbed, rather than paid lip service to, Pitcairne's influence, it is difficult to say.

28. According to Cheyne, *Essay on Health and Long Life* (London, 1724), p. 47 during the 1690s he had read the works of: Sir William Temple, Willis, Glisson, and Borelli. In *The English Malady,* pp. 78–80, he claims also to have read Glisson, Bernoulli, Molieres, Sydenham, and, of course, Newton and Pitcairne; see *The English Malady,* pp. 77–78.

29. See D. P. Walker, *The Decline of Hell* (London, 1964); E. Tuveson, *Millennium and Utopia* (Berkeley and Los Angeles, 1949); K. Thomas, *Religion and the Decline of Magic* (London, 1971); R. T. Vann, *The Social Development of English Quakerism, 1655–1755* (Cambridge, Mass., 1969); M.C. Jacob, *The Newtonians and the English Revolution, 1689–1720* (Ithaca, 1976), chap. 3.; P. Toon, ed., *Puritans, the Millennium and the Future of Israel* (Cambridge, 1970); Desiree Hirst, *Hidden Riches: Traditional Symbolism from the Renaissance to Blake* (London 1964); and still a standard work for the radical millenarian sects of the 1690s, Nils Thune, *The Behmenists and the Philadelphians* (Uppsala, 1948). Craig believed that the millennium would commence when faith left the earth; by applying the law of the inverse square he calculated the rate at which faith was disappearing.

30. Religious talk abounded in his house, especially on his paternal side; yet there were clergymen on both sides of the family, and Cheyne's mother was Thomas Burnet's second cousin.

31. See the prefaces of both versions of Cheyne's *Philosophical Principles* (London, 1705; rev. 1715). Hiscock (n. 3) briefly discusses the reception of this work by the Newtonians and shows how they laughed it straight out of court.

32. See Johnston, ed., *Letters of Pitcairne,* p. 42.

33. Edinburgh University MS. 38,305 (anonymous) describes reasons for his departure from Scotland, as well as the basis for his medical degree: "He's not only our owne countryman, and at present not rich, but is recommended by the ablest and most learned Physicians in Edinburgh as one of the best mathematicians in Europe; and for his skill in medicine he hath given a sufficient indication of that by his learned Tractat *De Febribus* [see n. 26 above], which hath made him famous abroad as well as at home; and he being just now goeing to England upon invitation of some of the members of the Royal Society." The invitation may have come from Arbuthnot, whom Cheyne met upon arrival and with whom he quickly became closely associated. The two Scots remained associates for three decades.

34. *A Declaration of the Philadelphian Society of England* (London, 1699), which is discussed by Cheyne's friend Richard Roach in *The Great Crisis* (1725–27), a mystical work containing a description of millennial life. Roach's description on pp. 181–85 also bears similarities with Thomas Burnet's position in *De Statu Mortuorum & Resurgentium* (Of the state of the dead and of those that are to rise). But few copies of Burnet's book were printed before 1727, as Frances Wilkinson, Burnet's literary executor, explains. It would be interesting to know whether Cheyne had seen a copy before 1727.

35. Dr. Richard Mead's medical career had rocketed to fame in just this way, and may have been held up as a paragon to Cheyne by his friends in the Royal Society. In any case, Cheyne and Mead were friends by 1703.

36. *Letters to Richardson,* p. 73.

37. A picture of religious street life at the time is found in Walker, *Decline of Hell,* pp. 245–52.; and in Hillel Schwartz, *The French Prophets: The History of a Millenarian Group in Eighteenth-Century England* (Berkeley and Los Angeles, 1980), pp. 37–45.

38. *Fluxionum methodus inversa* (London, 1703). For the response of the Newtonians, see Hiscock, *David Gregory,* p. 15; and R. Schofield, *Mechanism and Materialism: British Natural Philosophy in an Age of Reason* (Princeton, 1970), p. 59, who comments: "Scorned by Gregory and attacked by deMoivre, it provoked Newton into publishing his *Tractatus de Quadratura Curvarum* as an appendix to the 1704 *Opticks.* This was its only virtue and it was quickly forgotten."

39. For the reception, see Hiscock, *David Gregory,* pp. 24–25.

40. Ibid., p. 35. In fairness to Cheyne, it must be noted that the extant evidence comes primarily from Gregory, who was no friend of Cheyne. Gregory also persuaded Arbuthnot that Cheyne was a poor scientist, and attempted to intercept their association.

41. *Philosophical Principles* (1705 ed.), p. 104.

42. See G. Bowles, "Physical, Human and Divine Attraction in the Life and Thought of George Cheyne," *Annals of Science* 31 (1974): 473–88, especially the discussion on p. 481. Other commentators have been less sympathetic to Cheyne. H. Metzger discovered little of scientific value in

Philosophical Principles and categorized the book, disparagingly, as "Neo-Platonist" in *Attraction universelle et religion naturelle chez quelques commentateurs anglais de Newton* (Paris, 1938), pp. 139–53. D. Kubrin is more sympathetic, but has discovered little that is original in Cheyne's 1705 *Principles;* see "Newton and the Cyclical Cosmos: Providence and the Mechanical Philosophy," *Journal of the History of Ideas* 28 (1967): 325–46. Cheyne's skepticism about "the mechanical philosophy" is as pervasive in these 1705 *Principles* as his Hermetic notion of analogy. See, for example, *Philosophical Principles* (1705 ed.), p. 12: "But if any one can tell by what Laws of Mechanism, any one animal or Vegetable was produc'd, or from what Mechanick Principles the Planets describe Elliptick Orbits, I shall for the sake of these allow their [i.e., the mechanists'] whole Scheme to be true."

43. J. Le Clerc, *Bibliothèque ancienne et moderne: Pour servir de suite aux bibliothèques universelle et choisi,* 27 vols. (Amsterdam, 1715), 3 : 41–157. Although Le Clerc waited ten years to publish the review, he reviewed the 1705 first edition of *Philosophical Principles.*

44. Years later, Cheyne confided to Richardson a progression throughout his life of composition and publication, followed by illness. See *Letters to Richardson,* p. 69: "I never wrote a Book in my Life but I had a Fit of Illness after." There are many other versions of this self-confession in the Cheyne-Richardson correspondence.

45. "The Case of the Author," p. 327.

46. Ibid., p. 332. George Garden (1649–1733), the religious figurehead of the Aberdeen mystical group with which Cheyne had been involved in the 1690s, was also "now extream'ly old," but had not been scientifically or philosophically distinguished. Besides, Cheyne would not have described the mystical Garden in this way. Other possibilities—Samuel Clarke, John Craig, Newton himself—were either dead or incapable of fitting this description in 1733. Andrew Michael Ramsay (1686–1743), the direct link between Madame Guyon and George Garden's mystical group in Scotland, was hardly "old" in 1733; see D.P. Walker, *The Ancient Theology* (Ithaca, 1972), p. 232. Five or six others may be possible candidates, but no one then on the horizon fits the whole description and context of the allusion so well as Whiston.

47. "The Case of the Author," p. 332. By this time—1706–7—Cheyne probably read much that Whiston had written, and may have heard about or read Whiston's theory of attraction. But Whiston's Boyle Lectures, *The Accomplishment of Scripture Prophecies,* were not delivered until the following year—1707—and were not published until 1708. Useful information on Whiston's Boyle Lectures is found in M. Farrell, *The Life and Work of William Whiston* (New York, 1981), pp. 262–66, and in James Force, *William Whiston* (Cambridge, 1984), 71–84.

48. The most authoritative study to date is Schwartz, *The French Prophets,* from which I have learned much. See also M. C. Jacob, "Newton and the French Prophets," *History of Science* 6 (1978): 134–42, who concludes on the basis of manuscript evidence that Newton was not altogether hostile to the prophets during the first few years of their residence in Britain.

49. "The Case of the Author," p. 331, i.e., narrating the events of the summer and autumn of 1706.

50. I.e., than those "principles" Cheyne had studied in his last book, *Philosophical Principles* (1705 ed).

51. Suffering and healing had, of course, entered everywhere into millenarian discussion, especially in sermons, but medicotheologies had not been delivered in the Boyle Lecture series. There are many reasons for this absence, not least the fact that iatromathematics was unpopular with the Newtonians. It may be, then, that Cheyne now (1706–9) returned to an old project, one whose idea had germinated ca. 1699–1700, at the turn of the century, when talk of the millennium peaked and shortly after Cheyne read and discussed John Craig's *Theologiae Christianae Principia Mathematica* with the author. The profuse acknowledgments to Craig in the preface of *Philosophical Principles* suggest this chronology and development. It is also possible that John Freind of Christ Church, Oxford, with whom Cheyne had been in correspondence before 1704, played some role in the genesis of *Philosophical Principles.* Whatever the case actually was, Cheyne's statement in the preface that he composed the work "to record his dialogues in the 1690s, with his former pupil, the Earl of Roxburgh," is inadequate as explanation. The likelier reason is that Cheyne wrote the book to win back the support of the Newtonians.

52. Schwartz, *The French Prophets,* is right to remind historians of science (on p. 250) that many scientists in the apocalypse "sought a tincture that would cure every disease because it was in essence a microcosm of the soul's union to the body and of God's relationship to Christians. The panacea was the apex of medicine just as the perpetual motion machine was the apex of physics. Universal perfect health, like universal perfect motion, was as close as the apocalypse." See also such works as *Universal Health . . . Made Possible for the Poor* (1697), a rare and anonymous treatise in the Wellcome Institute Library for the History of Medicine, London.

53. While Fatio was swiftly converted, Gregory was hostile and skeptical of the new prophets;

Cheyne's role in the early days (1706–9) is unclear, as is that of Dr. James Keith and several other members of the Aberdeen-Garden mystical group who had by now migrated to London. By 1709, however, Cheyne had befriended a number of the prophets' leaders, especially Cuninghame (a friend of the Garden group) and Roach, and was engrossed in reading mystical literature (see no. 63 below).

54. In his *Boyle Lectures,* 2 vols. (London, 1739): 2:329, Whiston warned his countrymen to beware of the "dangerous and false" prophets: "If any person in this age, who pretend to a prophetic spirit do foretell events, whether of mercy or of judgment, which do not come to pass according, we have the warrant of God himself for their rejection."

55. "The Case of the Author," p. 349.

56. On 21 May 1709 Cuninghame wrote from Bath that he "had recovered to a miracle," and did not recognize himself "to be the same man I was some weeks ago"; see National Library of Scotland MS. 493,73; and Henderson, *Mystics of the North-East,* p. 192.

57. It is impossible, on the basis of extant material, to determine with accuracy when Cheyne first read Böhme, but he certainly knew his works by 1714–15; I suspect, on the basis of Cheyne's friendships and associations in Bath in 1709, that he knew Böhme's works by 1709. Cuninghame may have introduced Cheyne to Böhme's works when they met during that spring. For the dissemination of Böhme in England during this time, see S. Hutin, *Les disciples anglais de Jacob Boehme aux XVIIᵉ et XVIIIᵉ siècles* (Paris, 1960), chap. 2.

58. See Schwartz, *The French Prophets,* pp. 157–58.

59. The date had been announced in Whiston's 1707 Boyle Lectures, publicized in 1708 in his *Account of Scripture Prophecies,* and repeated as an accurate calculation in his *Literal Accomplishment of Scripture Prophecies* (London, 1724).

60. Roach, like Cheyne and Cuninghame, suffered a major illness in his early adulthood that he interpreted as providential, as "an Internal Call to a more silent Attendance on the Powers of the Work of the Kingdom to come"; see the unpublished Roach Diaries, 6 vols., Bodleian Library, Oxford, Rawlinson MSS D. 1152–57 (dated 8 December 1706 to 8 June 1730), esp. vols. 2–4; and Schwartz, *The French Prophets,* pp. 195–98, where they are discussed. Cheyne and Roach may have been brought together by Cuninghame sometime in 1709; some of their correspondence, still unpublished, is at Culladen, Scotland, in the Garden archives.

61. Roach Diaries, vol. 2, fol. 304v.

62. A salt compound based on sal ammoniac.

63. Cheyne probably obtained the book from his old friend Dr. James Keith in London, the main link between Pierre Poiret in Leiden and Cheyne in Bath. The typical route for Cheyne's dissemination of quietist literature throughout Britain was this: Pierre Poiret (Madame Guyon's secretary and disciple who now wrote prolifically in semiseclusion in Leiden) → the firm of J. H. Wetstein (the originally Swiss Protestant printer and bookseller now entrenched in Amsterdam—Cheyne could not pronounce or write his name and continued to refer to him as "Western") → Paul Vaillant (the immigrant French Hugenot printer and bookseller in London) → Dr. James Keith (the Scot and London friend of Cheyne) → Cheyne (Bath). Cheyne then circulated these books throughout England, as is known from the correspondence of James Keith and Lord Deskford. In his diary for 28 May 1743 John Byrom, Law's loyal disciple, commented on this fascinating Anglo-Dutch network in his journal: "Dr. George Cheyne . . . was always talking about naked faith, pure love," and Byrom explained that Cheyne had been "the providential occasion of [Law's] meeting or knowing Jacob Behmen, by a book" that Cheyne had sent to Law; see H. Talon, ed., *Selections from Byrom's Journals and Papers* (London, 1950), p. 221. The "book," Metternich's *Fides et Ratio collatae, ac suo utraque loco redditae, adversus J. Lockii* (Amsterdam, 1708), was translated into English in 1713 as *Faith and Reason Compared: Shewing That Divine Faith and Natural Reason Proceed from Two Different and Distinct Principles in Man.* See also S. Hobhouse, " 'Fides et Ratio': The Book Which Introduced Jacob Boehme to William Law," *Journal of Theological Studies* 37 (1936): 350–68, where Cheyne's role is acknowledged. Cheyne's enormous activity as a transmitter of quietist mystical literature from Holland to England, and from Jews to Christians, has been overlooked, even by the most erudite recent scholar of the Dutch book trade; see I. H. van Eeghen, *De Amsterdamse Boekhandel 1572–1795,* 6 vols. (Amsterdam, 1960–78). In fact he, together with Dr. Keith, was actually the main disseminator in the early eighteenth century, as Samuel Richardson, the printer and novelist well knew.

64. But it is important to ask whether this assumption in itself, and without further consideration of the contexts and facts of Cheyne's life, renders Cheyne a Platonist or Neoplatonist. Cheyne did, of course, write a short poem in rhymed pentameters, "On Platonism," which deals with conventional Platonic love, but it refers to neither analogies nor causes nor a Platonic cosmology. See the manuscript collection of poems collected by Charles Parr Burney in the British Library, Burney MS. 390, fol. 8b.

65. *Philosophical Principles* (1715 ed.), pt. 2, p. 46.

66. Ibid., pt. 1, p. 47.

67. The book was in part autobiographical, as Cheyne was now "in a regular Fit of the *Gout*" ("The Case of the Author," p. 346). Perhaps the stinging criticism of the Newtonians in 1705–6 had not yet been forgotten, for Cheyne avoided all metaphysical claims here.

68. "The Case of the Author," p. 343.

69. Ibid., p. 346.

70. See *Pythagoras His Mystick Philosophy Reviv'd; or, The Mystery of Dreams Unfolded* (London, 1691). Tryon, a constant reader of Böhme, sustained a "crisis of the spirit" in 1657 partly as a result of his reading of Böhme, after which time he recommended vegetarian diets similar to those later advocated by Cheyne. In the 1690s Tryon joined up with some of the London Philadelphians; a splinter group formed calling itself Tryonists, reading the works of Madame Guyon, and practicing abstinence in diet; see *Memoirs of the Life of Mr. Thomas Tryon, Late of London, Merchant* (London, 1705), which appeared a few weeks after the publication of Cheyne's *Philosophical Principles* (1705 ed.) and on the advent of Cheyne's "great crisis." Cheyne refers to several Pythagorean cults ("The Case of the Author," p. 368), but I have found no evidence to suggest that he had heard of Tryon or the Tryonists or had read their works. Benjamin Franklin recounts in his *Autobiography* how he became "a Tryonist" during his youth. Presumably, Franklin absorbed the vegetarian aspect and neglected the Behmenistic-quietist strain of Tryon's thought.

71. In old age Byfield published *Directions tending to Health and Long Life* (London, 1717), a book advocating a modicum of the abstemiousness Cheyne insisted upon. Byfield was also the author of a number of medicomillenarian works such as *The Christian Examiner* (London, 1720).

72. See "The Case of the Author," p. 349. These included the luminaries one would expect: Arbuthnot, Noel Broxholme (Pope's physician in London), James Douglas, Richard Mead, and John Freind (Cheyne's old friend at Christ Church in Oxford who had been one of the first Pitcairnean protégés and whom Cheyne mentions with gratitude in the preface of *Philosophical Principles*). But Cheyne apparently did not consult John Freke, by 1723 Richardson's physician and a great friend of Dr. James Keith, Cheyne's main supplier in London of quietist literature arriving from Wetstein's firm in Amsterdam. I have searched in vain for manuscript notes these physicians may have scribbled while treating Cheyne, on the grounds that such materials could illuminate the specific nature of Cheyne's ailment. My own diagnosis is that Cheyne suffered primarily from what we would call manic-depression, but that as he aged this psychiatric condition was aggravated by chronic cardiac arrest. I date the onset of cardiac-pulmonary arrest ca. 1722–24, around the time of his second "crisis," when Cheyne was in his early-mid-fifties.

73. See n. 42 above.

74. Clifton Wintringham translated it into Latin with extensive commentary. It also appeared in French and German. Seven years after Cheyne's death in April 1743, Edmond Litton, a self-styled disciple of Cheyne's, synthesized its argument in *Philosophical Conjectures on Aereal Influences, the Probable Origin of Diseases* (London, 1750).

75. See G. Nelson, *The Nature, Cause and Symptoms of the Gout: As Stated by Dr. Sydenham, Cheyne . . .* (London, 1728).

76. "The Case of the Author," p. 352: "Upon the Whole, as in my *Nervous* and *Scorbutical* Disorder, I had continued my Milk, Seed, and Vegetable Diet, with proper Evacuations, for above two Years [1727–29], before I obtain'd a compleat Recovery, so in this last Illness, I had observ'd the same Regimen near twice as long, before my Health was perfectly established."

77. It had been accumulating for four years. In 1724 two anonymous books hostile to Cheyne appeared: *Remarks on Dr. Cheyne's Essay on Health and Long Life: By a Fellow of the Royal Society* and *A Letter to G.C., M.D., Occasion'd by his Essay on Health.* In 1725 Edward Strother, M.D., vigorously attacked Cheyne in *An Essay on Sickness and Health in which Dr. Cheyne's Mistaken Opinions in His Late Essay Are . . . Taken Notice Of,* and someone merely calling himself "Pillow-Tisanus" published *An Epistle to Ge——ge Ch——ne, M.D., F.R.S. upon His Essay on Health,* which ridicules every aspect of Cheyne's writings, especially his "stilted style." Also in 1724 John Wynter, a somewhat jealous Bath rival, published a tepid appraisal of Cheyne's milk and seed diet in *Cyclus Metasyncriticus,* which Richardson's brother-in-law, James Leake, printed. Other works discussing Cheyne during the late 1720s are listed by F. Shum in *A Catalogue of Bath Books* (London, 1913), pp. 5–9. Negative criticism of this type continued to be published to the end of Cheyne's life. In three separate numbers of the *Champion* (15 November 1739, 17 May and 12 June 1740), Fielding ridiculed Cheyne's ungrammatical style, although he dropped the charge when referring to Cheyne fifteen years later in *The Journal of a Voyage to Lisbon* (London, 1755), "Sunday, July [14]." Such harsh criticism extended into the 1760s and 1770s, especially in unpublished correspondences and after Cheyne had long since been dead. For example, John Rutty, the Quaker physician, condemned Cheyne's diet to William Clark, the Wiltshire physician and author of an interesting treatise on psychosomatic illness; see Rutty's letter to Clark dated 8 August 1773 in Rutty MSS, Case 32, Friends House, London.

78. Four years later, in 1733, he wrote in the preface of *The English Malady,* p. iv: "I have been slain again and again, both in verse and prose."

79. Ibid.

80. "The Case of the Author," p. 325.

81. *The English Malady,* p. ii.

82. C. A. Moore, *Backgrounds of English Literature, 1700–1760* (Minneapolis, 1953), p. 179.

83. *The English Malady,* p. i.

84. Although a best-seller, *The English Malady* was apparently unknown in certain quarters for over a decade. For example, John Morris wrote in his *Observations on the Past and Present State of the City of London* (London, 1751) that "hypochondriasis" and the "hysterical passion" were clearly the two main "forms of lethargy," then known, but he wrote entirely unaware of Cheyne's analysis in *The English Malady.*

85. This work is not the posthumously published compilation entitled *Dr. Cheyne's Own Account of Himself . . . His Remarks upon Pythagoras, Cornaro, Sir Isaac Newton, the famous Mr. [William] Law . . .* (London, 1743), which was edited by John Campbell (1708–75). Cheyne had read Campbell's *Voyage to the Levant . . . and the Abyssinian Empire* (London, 1739) as a consequence of his belief that "our [best] diet is *Eastern*" (*Letters to Richardson,* p. 121). Early in 1743 Campbell had finished a translation of Johann Heinrich Cohausen (1665–1750), *Hermippus Redivivus; or, The Sage's Triumph over Old Age and the Grave: Wherein, a Method Is Laid Down for Prolonging the Life and Vigour of Man,* and wished to publish extracts before his complete translation appeared in 1744. Cohausen may have used Cheyne's death in the spring of 1743 as the rationale for a brief compilation that he called *Dr. Cheyne's Account,* which concludes with a sample of his forthcoming translation.

86. Although Cheyne and Fielding never met, so far as is known, Cheyne took every type of personal liberty with Richardson, even reassuring him that he was physiologically *beyond* madness (*Letters to Richardson,* p. 94), and contending that Richardson's physiology and physique had predetermined his literary destiny and medical condition: "Your constitution is not like Dr. [Stephen] Hales's: you are short, round, and plump; he is taller, and very thin and uses a good deal of Exercise" (ibid., p. 70). In *The English Malady* (pp. 366–67), Cheyne generalizes a monolithic law of physiological determinism: "None have it in their *Option* to choose for themselves their own particular *Frame* of Mind, nor *Constitution* of Body; so none can choose his own Degree of *Sensibility.* That is given him by the *Author* of his *Nature,* and is already determined." The consequences of this "law" have yet to be absorbed by students of the cults of eighteenth-century sensibility, but see, for a preliminary outline, G. S. Rousseau, "The Debate about Historical Culture and the Status of the History of Science," *Literature and History* 11 (1985): 159–75 and idem, "England and the Great Nerve Doctors," in Sydney J. Conger, ed., *The Sensibility Movement: A Reconsideration* (forthcoming 1988).

87. "The Case of the Author," p. 370.

88. Ibid., p. 367.

89. Ibid., p. 369.

90. Schwartz, *The French Prophets,* perceptively inquires if "one might, applying Erik Erikson's developmental schema, associate kinds of millenarian ethos with stages of psychological development. For example, the ethos of judgment might be attractive to those who wish to resolve the issue of trust vs. mistrust, the ethos of cataclysm might appeal to those who must resolve the issue of initiative vs. guilt, the ethos of pentecost might be advocated by those resolving the issues of identity vs. identity confusion, and the methods of the New Jerusalem might be taken up by those perplexed by the issue of intimacy vs. isolation" (pp. 261–62). Such a suggestion, no doubt, is fraught with peril, but it is interesting to notice how well Cheyne's career fits the schema of the last category. Intimacy vs. isolation continued to be the major dynamic issues of his adult life, even at the geographical level: whether to live in Scotland or England; whether to live in Bath far away from the booksellers and printers; or to expose himself to the excesses, luxury, and illness-producing conditions of London, etc. The only caveat is economic dislocation. In the Middle Ages and Renaissance, millenarian fervor, especially in its hysteric versions, was often the result of severe and sudden economic deprivation, even within one generation. Cheyne had certainly been "dislocated" in this sense: moving from his parents of middle income to the estate of the fabulously wealthy earls of Roxburgh, and then on to the Newtonians in London and to poverty in Bath where his finances fluctuated as much as his health. Only in the last two decades of his life—from about 1730 onward—did economic stability manifest itself.

91. See n. 18 above. In the winter of 1741–42, the Countess of Huntingdon wrote to her husband from Bath that she had been engaged "in most pious and religious conversation" with Cheyne, who had been "talking like an old apostle. He really has the most refined notions of the true spiritual religion I ever met with"; see Hastings MS, 3 fol. 32. Cheyne sent her many of Poiret's quietist books.

92. *Letters to Richardson,* p. 104. At this time Cheyne was also being praised in magazines and newspapers, especially by the clergy, for his regimen of diet and exercise; see, for example, "extract of

a Letter written some Years ago by the Rev, Mr. H——e, concerning Dr Cheyne and Temperance," *Gentleman's Magazine* 8 (1738): 362–63.

93. *The Natural Method of Cureing the Diseases of the Body.* As one way of keeping his own problematic body healthy, Cheyne continued at this period of his life to praise the pious, particularly the pious dead who had followed his prescriptions and potions for health; see, for example, Cheyne's "Historical Character of the Honourable George Bailie, Esq," in *Gentleman's Magazine* 8 (1738): 467, an obituary dated from "Bath, August 12, 1738," and a eulogy that elicited a poem addressed "To Dr. Cheyne," which was published on the same page.

94. *Letters to Richardson,* p. 107.

95. Ibid., p. 111.

96. I.e., Poiret's *Bibliotheca Mysticorum* (Amsterdam, 1708), which had been translated into French and which printed excerpts from the Baron de Metternich, the German adherent of Madame Guyon who has already been mentioned. Later in the letter Cheyne states that he owns Poiret's "Catalogue of Mystic Writers," which he describes as "finely and elegantly painted on a small Octavo in Latin" (*Letters to Richardson,* p. 111). Cheyne then explains to Richardson where Poiret's book can be obtained, pointing to the specific network described in n. 63 above. The significant matter here is not the specific work by Poiret, but rather Cheyne's intentions in the project. For many years now, Cheyne had dreamed of continuing in the footsteps of Garden and Ramsey by disseminating quietist literature throughout England. Now he hoped to obtain Richardson's assistance—it must not be forgotten that Richardson was first and foremost a prolific printer—in the somewhat underground Anglo-Dutch network already delineated. For Cheyne and Richardson and their contacts in the Netherlands, see - W. C. Slattery, ed., *The Richardson-Stinstra Correspondence and Stinstra's Prefaces to Clarissa* (Carbondale, Ill., 1969). Cheyne's intention was not merely reaching such converted readers as William Law to whom he had already sent many quietist books; now, in 1742, he also hoped to convert to quietism naturalists such as the young Richard Symes, eventually the author of *Fire Analysed* (Bristol, 1771), and a large group of scientific disciples in the Bath-Bristol area. Thus, when Law published an *Appeal to All That Doubt* in 1742, the stage was set for Cheyne. Law's book introduced Behmenism unequivocally into natural philosophy. What remained was Cheyne's persuasion of Richardson to print an English translation of Poiret in a cheap single volume that could conveniently be sent through the post. As Cheyne was dying in March–April 1743, he continued to dream of the fulfillment of his plan. It was his last project, his private version of "rational Enlightenment," or as proximate to Enlightenment as he would come while on earth.

97. *Letters to Richardson,* p. 124. This work is another of Poiret's Bourignonist compilations; it describes the life and works of Madame Guyon and was printed by Wetstein in Amsterdam.

98. The state of Newton's papers at the time of his death, and the precise number of manuscripts left, remains mysterious although his relation to Böhme has now been admirably studied by Betty J. T. Dobbs in *The Foundations of Newton's Alchemy* (Cambridge, 1975), pp. 9–12. Also important is Stephen Hobhouse's discussion of Cheyne as the link between Newton and Law in *Selected Mystical Writings of William Law . . . and an Enquiry into the Influence of Jacob Boehme on Isaac Newton,* with a foreword by Aldous Huxley, (2d ed., rev. (New York, 1948), pp. 397–422. Walton's manuscript copy of his *Notes and Materials* is found in Dr. Williams' Library, London; for Cheyne see Walton MSS, book 1118 (1.1.38).

99. As J. Sekora has demonstrated in *Luxury: The Concept in Western Thought, Eden to Smollett* (Baltimore, 1978), although he omits medical literature, the all-important messianic and millenarian tradition of luxury, and, perhaps more consequentially, neo-Stoic and neo-Pythagorean attacks on luxury by Cornaro, Lessius, Tryon, Byfield, and—of course—Cheyne. Sekora does not acknowledge to what an extreme degree luxury is a psychological rather than a physical state, and therefore why its religious strains and conponents are of crucial concern to the historian of luxury.

100. A. Friedman, ed., *The Life of Richard Nash,* in *Collected Works of Oliver Goldsmith,* 5 vols. (Oxford, 1966), 3:364. For Cheyne in *The Bee,* see ibid., 1:400.

101. *Letters to Richardson,* p. 81.

102. Karl Marx (not the political philosopher but the illustrious nineteenth-century professor of medicine at the University of Göttingen and the prolific commentator on Blumenbach) wrote a Lucianic "Letter to the Dead Dr. CHEYNE," which James Mackness translated into English and published in *The Moral Aspects of Medical Life: Consisting of the "Akesios" of Professor Karl Marx* (London, 1846), pp. 34–46. Here Marx incorrectly addresses Cheyne as a fanatic "Quaker, who belonged to that respectable body of Quakers." Marx claims to have been profoundly moved by Cheyne's two most outstanding qualities: his "Quietist aversion to all personal strife" (p. 36) and his "peace-loving disposition" (p. 38). Neither quality perfectly tallies with the facts of Cheyne's diversified career, but the notion of an irenic personality at the root of his temperament is worthy of consideration.

103. *Letters to Richardson,* p. 81.

104. I use the vexed term *Hermetical* as it has recently been developed by B. J. T. Dobbs in *Newton and the Tradition in Alchemy* (Baltimore, 1978) and F. Yates in *The Rosicrucian Enlightenment* (London, 1972). Unfortunately, there is no book such as Thomas's *Religion and the Decline of Magic,* which deals primarily with England in the period of Cheyne's adult life (1695–1743), nor is R. S. Neale's *Bath: A Social History, 1680–1850* (London, 1981) of any help in these matters.

105. Cheyne was in fact more self-reflective about his use of analogy than any other millenarian thinker I have encountered in the early eighteenth century. His writings abound with comments about his self-consciousness in the use of analogy, and even his rhetorical tropes are worthy of scrutiny when he is in this reflective mood. See, for example, *The English Malady,* p. ii.

106. See F. E. Manuel, *The Religion of Isaac Newton* (Oxford, 1974), pp. 99–104. Manuel comments (p. 35) that Cheyne's "new-found principle of Reunion with God, analogous in the system of intelligent beings to the principle of attraction in the material universe, was too saturated with religious Neo-platonism for [Newton's] taste." True, but Manuel seems unaware that Cheyne's pietism led him to far more byzantine beliefs than mere Neoplatonism.

107. The idea that mathematics and medicine, in the Greek sense both Apollonian activities, represented the pinnacle of the sciences was a commonplace of seventeenth- and eighteenth-century thought. See Gideon Harvey, *The Vanities of Philosophy and Physick* (London, 1699).

108. Cheyne continued to argue that *both* body and mind—in this priority—had to be sound for health to obtain. In the *Essay on Health and Long Life* he comments: "When I see a gloomy, melancholy, heavy, stupid, thoughtless, joyless creature, much more a whimsical, anomalous or libertine . . . I conclude him in a bad state of health, under a dangerous bodily disease, or under a perpetual mal-regimen, which will soon terminate in one, whatever appearances be to the contrary, and, sooner or later, I have been always confirmed in the justness of this opinion . . . For I am convinced that calmness, serenity, cheerfulness, and common-sense . . . are the constant attendants and only infallible symptoms of perfect bodily and intellectual (or of *sana mens* in *corpore sano*) health."

109. The analogical frame of mind and the type of imagination stimulating it has been ignored for scientific thinkers in the period from 1680 to 1780. Here Cheyne is a natural candidate who ought to be included in the continuum of thinkers pronouncing about the natural world from Newton and Whiston to Priestley and Erasmus Darwin.

110. See G. S. Rousseau, "Science Books and Their Readers in the Eighteenth Century," in *Books and Their Readers in Eighteenth-Century England,* ed. Isabel Rivers (Leicester, 1982), pp. 237–38 for the locations of Cheyne's books; this situation vis-à-vis Cheyne may change when the work of Hillel Schwartz (n. 37) is assimilated. Schwartz's monograph, *Knaves, Fools, Madmen, and that Subtle Effluvium* (Gainesville, Fla., 1978) is also important in this context, but it does not exhaust this response, pro and con, to the French prophets. Much more work remains to be done.

111. The work is pseudonymously signed by "T. Johnson," and is ultimately disappointing, despite its title, because the "heresy" focuses on Cheyne's grammar rather than his mysticism: "The English language has had more Violence done it by a very great and eminent Physician, George Cheyne . . . [who] hath so mangled and mauled it, than when I came to examine the Body, as it lay in Sheets in a Bookseller's Shop, I found it an expiring heavy Lump, without the least Appearance of Sense" (p. 34).

112. Yet another example is found in the commentators on *A Tale of a Tub,* who discuss this complex satire as if it had been written in a religious milieu that consisted only of Anglicans and Puritan Dissenters, without appreciating the cults of mysticism and millenarianism that flourished while Swift was writing (1696–1704). Another instance is found in secondary writing about Swift's published predictions (e.g., *Predictions for the Year 1708: A Famous Prediction of Merlin* [London, 1709], which fails to understand the millenarian context of these prophecies. Swift's adult life from 1690 to 1710 needs to be reconsidered against this background.

113. See F. E. Manuel, *A Portrait of Isaac Newton* (Cambridge, Mass., 1968), p. 274, who merely notes this about Fatio: "By the time Newton became President of the Royal Society, Fatio had fallen into disfavor, though he lingered on the sidelines for a few years."

114. See G. S. Rousseau, "Science," in *The Context of English Literature: The Eighteenth Century,* ed. Pat Rogers (London, 1978), p. 192.

115. Scholars such as Metzger *(Attraction universelle et religion naturelle)* and F. Manuel *(Religion of Newton)* considered Cheyne a Neoplatonist for four main reasons: (1) They were unaware of his central role in the Anglo-Dutch dissemination of quietist literature. (2) They were apparently unaware of his involvement with the leaders of the French prophets. (3) They overlooked or were unaware of his ties to the mystical Garden-Ramsey group and to the type of millenarianism it fostered. And (4) they wrote with little appreciation of Cheyne's health and bizarre personal life. In bewilderment, then, they grasped at the label Neoplatonist in the hope that this catchall would sum up the many conflicting tendencies they despised. All they knew for certain was that Cheyne had fallen out of favor with the Anglican Newtonians.

116. R. Schofield, *Mechanism and Materialism: British Natural Philosophy in an Age of Reason* (Princeton, 1970), p. 62.

117. Ibid., pp. 61–63.

118. *The Natural Method of Cureing the Diseases of the Body*, p. 79.

Despite a whole library of Blake scholarship accumulated in the last decade, Blake's reading of Cheyne has not been discussed. Nelson Hilton comments on Cheyne's works in relation to Blake's imagery of the body in a perceptive chapter of *Literal Imagination: Blake's Vision of Words* (Berkeley and Los Angeles, 1983), entitled "Fibres of Being," pp. 91, 93, 97, but does not discuss Blake's reading in, or knowledge of, Cheyne's medico-mystical works. Yet Cheyne and Blake held remarkably similar views of the anatomical nerves and fibres, and even more proximate ideas of the aesthetic beauty of the human form as a perfectly created symmetry organized into an even higher, more perfectly asymmetrical, organicism. Even in the single comparison of Cheyne and Blake it makes sense therefore to contemplate a medico-mystical analogy; indeed Blake's possible reading of medical authors like Cheyne represents a new avenue of scholarship for critics interested in the near-contemporary sources, rather than the more remote neo-Platonic sources (Kathleen Raine), of his mysticism. For the internalization of these matters in Blake, especially ideas of selfhood in relation to human psychology, see chapter 8 of Stephen D. Cox's lucid study of *"The Stranger within Thee": Concepts of the Self in Late-Eighteenth-Century Literature* (Pittsburgh, 1980), pp. 127–56.

119. *Essay on Regimen* (London, 1740), p. 270.

120. *Gentleman's Magazine* 8 (1738): 136, anonymous poem.

121. Vicesimus Knox, the physician and commentator who wrote at the end of the eighteenth century, seems to have comprehended Cheyne's extraordinary contribution to counter the immense gluttony of the epoch, as well as the degree of hostility shown him by his contemporaries; see *Personal Nobility* (1793), p. 90.

122. See Sekora, *Luxury.*

123. The lingering question is why did so many nervous diseases proliferate after mid-century? The situation vis-à-vis nervous ailments grew so seriously by the 1780s that James Makittrick Adair, the physician with whom the poet Robert Burns took walking tours, replaced Cheyne at Bath as its leading "nervous doctor" and wrote book after book about the reduction of food intake as a direct cause of depression and anxiety.

11

Alchemy in an Age of Reason: The Chemical Philosophers in Early Eighteenth-Century France

Readers of the *Mémoires* of the Académie Royale des Sciences of Paris may have been more than a little surprised to find a paper in the 1722 volume on the deceits practiced by alchemists.[1] The author was Etienne François Geoffroy (1672–1731), one of the earliest of the French Newtonians and the author of the first table of affinity (1718). His name is usually included with a few others in a select pantheon of eighteenth-century chemists whose work forms the background of the Chemical Revolution.[2]

This paper by Geoffroy is seldom referred to as it reflects a literature that stems back to the Middle Ages rather than the Enlightenment. Here Geoffroy warned those who sought quick wealth not to be duped by alchemists. They were ready prey for those who claimed to have made the elixir of life or the philosophers' stone.[3] He felt a need to write because of the widespread belief in this art. He described the many tricks of these charlatans: their double-bottomed cupels and hollow stirring rods, their amalgams with concealed precious metals, their acids with dissolved gold and silver—and even filtration papers prepared with minute amounts of gold that could be recovered on combustion.[4] They were a clever lot, and their ingredients and equipment had to be carefully checked because they had frequently deceived skilled chemists. Geoffroy himself had been part of a committee named by the Academy to investigate a process of the abbé Bignon that supposedly destroyed gold. This, too, had proved to be a clever trick.[5]

Bernard Fontenelle (1657–1757), Perpetual Secretary to the Academy from 1697 to 1739, gave prominent attention to Geoffroy's paper in the *Histoire*.[6] He declined to take a firm stand on the theoretical possibility of transmutation, but he did warn his readers against the pretended "adepts, Infants in the Art, Hermetic Philosophers, Cosmopolites, Rosicrucians, and others, people whose mysterious language, fanatic conduct, and exorbitant promises must render them highly suspect." They speak of a powder of projection of which a few atoms may produce great masses of gold, but what rational system of physics could possibly accommodate such a concept?

Geoffroy's attack on alchemy is indeed a very late example of a genre that may be traced back in European literature at least to Chaucer's "Canon's Yeoman's Tale." But more important is the fact that here is clear evidence of the concern felt by members of the academy over the widespread contemporary interest in alchemy and transmutation.

To find a serious attack on alchemy by one of the major figures of eighteenth-century chemistry may seem inexplicable—most studies of this period emphasize its rationality compared to the past. But what of figures such as Swedenborg, Cagliostro, or Saint-Germain? Over the years, some intellectual historians have pointed to the prevalence of magic, alchemy, and other occult arts in the eighteenth century.[7] Still, such studies remain relatively uncommon and the subjects are too frequently relegated to popular superstition.

For the most part historians of science have paid little attention to the continued interest in mystical systems of natural philosophy in this period that derived from the Renaissance. Few would argue with this neglect if the answers sought centered on the so-called progressive elements of science. But if one is interested in a broader view of nature, one need not go far to meet the proponents of natural magic and the occult. The fact that alchemists, magicians, and astrologers flourished in the eighteenth century along with the Bernoullis, Laplace, and Lavoisier should be of real interest for a fuller understanding of the Enlightenment as well as an understanding of the later romantic reaction to the mechanistic views of the philosophes.

One might approach this literature from a number of paths. My approach is predetermined by my past research, which has concentrated on alchemy and the Paracelsian iatrochemistry of the sixteenth and seventeenth centuries. If one approaches the period from this vantage point rather than that of traditional history of science, one may come away with a sense of continuity—of the old coexisting with the new.

Alchemy and the Chemical Philosophy

The French literary works of the early eighteenth century leave little doubt that alchemy and the supernatural attracted widespread interest. This is seen in works as well known as Montesquieu's *Lettres persanes* (1721)[8] and Bordelon's *Histoire de M. Oufle* (1710).[9] And in his *Voyages* (1712), Paul Lucas described a visit to Central Asia where he learned that the fourteenth-century French alchemist, Nicholas Flamel, was still alive and at work on the secrets of the world,[10] a story that excited numerous other authors throughout the century who had an interest in alchemy and the prolongation of life.

If I turn from literary to occultist texts, it would be difficult to ignore the many editions of the *Secrets* of Albertus Magnus that appeared throughout the century,[11] the new French translation of Agrippa's *De occulta philosophia* (1727),[12] or the Abbé Villars de Montfaucon's best-seller, the *Comte de Gabalis,* which appeared first in 1670 and frequently thereafter.[13] Indeed, booksellers supplied their clientele with a broad spectrum of titles on both black and white magic, the divining rod, witchcraft, astrology, and all forms of occultism.

But Geoffroy was not concerned with witchcraft and magic. He was concerned about the alchemists of his day. And, had he wished, he could have pointed to a seemingly unending publication of alchemical texts. Still popular were such traditional texts dating from the past century or earlier as Jean Colleson's *L'idée parfaite de la philosophie hermétique* (1630[14] and Limojon de Saint Didier's *Le triomphe hermétique* (1689).[15] The seventeenth-century classic by Michael Sendivogius, the *Novum lumen chymicum,* was translated into French in 1723, and this became an edition highly sought after by alchemists and chemists alike.[16] The copy at the Cornell University Library bears the bookplate of Antoine Lavoisier.

But there were new works as well. A *Traité de la poudre de projection* (1707) by one D.L.B. sought a new key to alchemy through a novel interpretation of the story of Abraham, Sarah, and Lot in Genesis.[17] In 1719 an anonymous *Lettre à un ami* deplored current attacks on alchemists when one should honor them because of the wonderful metallic remedies they have discovered.[18] How productive this is compared to the useless work done by the members of the Royal Academy![19] In truth, one should return to the problems posed by the alchemists. One should recognize that the search for the determination of longitudes among mathematicians is no less important than the search for a potable gold among chemists and physicians.[20]

So well known was this literature that it resulted in several warnings in the decades immediately prior to Geoffroy's 1722 paper. An anonymous *Explication de quelques doutes touchant la médecine* (1700) turned specifically to the alchemical claims of the wonders of potable gold and the conviction that there is a universal remedy for illnesses. The reader was told that the hope of a soluble gold is only an illusion. False chemists had adopted astrology, and they were little more than charlatans who hid their shame and ignorance in an enigmatic language and allegorical emblems.[21] In 1711 François Pousse produced a stinging *Examen des principes des alchymistes sur la pierre philosophale* in which the possibility of the multiplication of the metals was flatly denied. The long search for the elixir of life had been a waste of time. Gold and silver are practically useless as metals. Rather, it is the lowly iron that is used to make the instruments that are necessary for life. Why, then, is there no learned attack on alchemy—especially in France, where it is most needed?

> Les Allemans & les Anglois s'y appliquent. Les Hollandois n'en sont pas si curieux. (On dira que le commerce les retire des Sciences.) Mais de toutes les Nations, les François sont les plus ardens, & les plua entêtez: C'est donc pour cette raison que j'ai ce petit Examen en Français, pour être lui-même examiné de tout le monde.[22]

However, the scope of alchemy was not limited to transmutation alone. Over the centuries many alchemists had adopted a far-reaching philosophy of nature that served as a basis for the explanation of a broad spectrum of natural phenomena.

These authors argued for a vitalistic universe, one in which all parts of the macrocosm and the microcosm were interconnected. Confirmation of these concepts was avidly sought through laboratory observations. One example is the "Tree of Diana." The method of production was simple. An ounce of silver was dissolved in a few ounces of nitric acid and then evaporated to half its volume. The remainder was then poured into a container with twenty ounces of water and allowed to stand for forty days. At the end of that time the silver "will have formed a sort of Tree, with Branches and little Balls at the end of them, which represent the Fruit." Well known by the mid-seventeenth century, this demonstration was used by Chemical Philosophers to show that "Art mimicks what Nature does, when she produces Silver in the Mines; and some have pretended that this Artificial Vegetation is like the Vegetation of Plants."[23]

Nicholas Lemery had described the process in his popular *Cours de chymie* (1677) and had then proceeded to draw "a great Analogy between this Operation, and what passes in the Earth in order to the Generation and Growth of Plants."[24] In short, the Tree of Diana seemed to offer Chemical Philosophers proof of life in the mineral kingdom. Here, too, was experimental evidence of metallic growth that confirmed the belief that ores would replenish themselves in mines if allowed to stand fallow—a belief that persisted into the twentieth century in certain parts of Europe. This was an important discovery for chemical philosophers, for it upheld a significant part of their world view.

The Tree of Diana was also of interest to chemists of the Royal Academy. Guillaume Homberg (1652–1715) examined this experiment in detail in 1693, but he rejected the vitalist explanation and argued that the formation was simply a case of crystallization.[25] Nevertheless, papers on this observation and similar metallic formations were to be described in the pages of the *Mémoires* for the next forty years.

For Pierre Le Lorrain, the Abbé de Vallemont (1649–1721), the Tree of Diana was an important subject for discussion in his *Curiositez de la nature et de l'art sur la vegetation. . .* , which went through at least eight editions between 1705 and 1715. In this instance the abbé sided with Homberg in his belief that the formation was due to crystallization. But on other matters Vallemont reflects his alchemical heritage. He wrote another popular monograph on the divining rod—and he closed his *Curiosities* with a forty-page discussion of one of the greatest miracles of the age, palingenesis. From the late sixteenth century, it was widely believed among chemists that if plants were calcined to ashes, and these ashes then heated in an hermetically sealed flask, the appearance of the original plant would reappear in the flask.[26] Vallemont cited accounts by Paracelsus, Joseph Duchesne, Sir Kenelm Digby, Athanasius Kircher, and other prominent authors to prove that "there is no longer room for incredulity."[27] However he added, even greater wonders are possible than the resuscitation of plants since

I am assured that this Reproduction has been effected, not only upon Plants, but also upon Animals. Particularly they speak of a little Sparrow, that was made appear in that manner, in a Vial where its Ashes were kept. . . . Thus we have a Sparrow rais'd to Life, like a Phoenix, from the midst of its Ashes. . . . *Digby* has done more than this. From Animals that were dead, and pounded to Dust, he has drawn living Animals of the same Kind.[28]

In this observation is to be found experimental evidence of divine truth. "There is not in the World a more faithful Image of the Resurrection of the Dead, and I am persuaded that Nature and Art can never offer to our Eyes a More divine Spectacle."[29]

Vallemont's interest in alchemy and traditional Chemical Philosophy reappear in another text, Harcouet de Longeville's monograph on the lives of those who had lived for many centuries.[30] Here the author drew heavily on the alchemical dream of the prolongation of human life, and he referred to a newly discovered manuscript of Arnaud de Villeneuve in the possession of the Abbé de Vallemont. This text seemed to be an important key to rejuvenation, and he asked for financial support to make it available in print.

De Longeville's work underscores the close connection between medicine and alchemy that had existed in western Europe since the thirteenth century. This traditional alchemical medicine was still current in early eighteenth-century France. Books on the universal remedy and chemical elixirs were common,[31] but the complex interrelation of alchemy and medicine in this period may best be illustrated by the three small books published by Charles Le Breton, Médecin de la Faculté de Paris. His first publication (1716) was a very general collection of herbal and chemical preparations.[32] Six years later, one finds him preparing a French translation of the *De statica medicina* (1614) of Sanctorius (1561–1636), a landmark work that introduced quantification to medicine through a study of variation of weight due to ingestion and excretion.[33] But Le Breton had other interests as well. In the same year he published a work on *Les clefs de la philosophie spagyrique*.[34] Here are to be found a series of alchemical aphorisms. The first part concentrates on chemical operations, the second on the preparation of the mineral elixir for transmutation. In short, here is member of the medical establishment who was aware of the significance of the work of Sanctorius, but who could at the same time see fundamental truths in the mystical texts of the alchemists.

Although evidence of medical alchemy is easy to find in the early eighteenth-century literature, there is no doubt that the main thrust of the sixteenth- and seventeenth-century Chemical Philosophy was to be found in the often mystical medical chemistry and cosmology of the followers of Paracelsus (1493–1541) and Jan Baptista van Helmont (1580–1644).[35] They had formulated an anti-Aristotelian and anti-Galenic world view that had been based on a firm conviction that chemistry was the key to nature and especially to medicine. The cosmology of Paracelsus—and to a limited extent that of Helmont as well—was based on the interrelation of the macrocosm and the microcosm. The system had strong appeal to nonestablishment types of all kinds. Until late in the seventeenth century this Chemical Philosophy appeared to be a viable alternative to the Mechanical Philosophy.

Nowhere had the followers of Paracelsus caused more debate than in France.[36] It began as early as 1566 with the condemnation of the internal use of antimony by the Faculty of Paris and it grew in intensity over the next century. In time it was to create serious tension between the medical schools of Paris and Montpellier, and it certainly raised problems as to the use of remedies derived from mineral substances. Since the macrocosm/microcosm cosmology of the Paracelsians retained sympathetic action, astral influences, and a fair amount of Aristotelian physics to boot, it was all anathema to the Mechanical Philosophers even though the chemists opposed the ancient authorities.

With this background one need not be too surprised to learn that the familiar late-seventeenth-century battle of the ancients and the moderns is much more than simply a struggle between Aristotelians and mechanists. Evidence for this in France may be found in an anonymous text of 1697, *Le Parnasse assiegé; ou, La guerre declarée entre les philosophes anciens & modernes*. In the preface, the reader is told that the plan is to "demonstrate the reality of the Hermetic science and the truth of the Medicine of Paracelsus."[37]

The plot is simple. Apollo, god of the sun and of the healing arts, has died on Mount Parnassus. Each philosopher takes this as an opportunity to assert his primacy over all others.[38] The mountain need only be climbed and the throne seized. But lack of success on the part of any one of them to dominate the others leads to the abandonment of this civil war, and the philosophers join together to assault the mountain in unison. There follows a list of the various philosophers and their place in this unusual army. At one side are the academicians commanded by Plato and his disciples. Closer to the mountain are to be found the followers of Gassendi and Descartes who discover roads that lead to the top. Even Confucius and other Chinese philosophers are present and demand a proper place for the attack.[39]

Dissension arises when Aristotle is appointed the Prince of Philosophers, but this does not delay the continuing preparations for the assault.[40] Galileo is placed in charge of the cavalry; Cardan and Porta are to lead the artillery; while Parmenides, Heraclitus, and Democritus are given command of the infantry.[41] Descartes commands the dragoons, and his lieutenants include a group of his disciples and other seventeenth-century corpuscularians. Surprisingly, one finds that the chemical physicians Daniel Sennert and van Helmont have been placed in charge of the baggage.[42]

But now four spies—all important alchemists—inform the assembled army that the mountain is nearly inaccessible and open only to philosophers of the school of Hermes. The officers of Hermes carry a standard marked *FRC* (Fraternity of the Rosy Cross). After a lengthy discussion, these spies disappear.[43]

In a new stratagem various groups try unsuccessfully to penetrate the mists leading to the summit. Notably, a group of chemists including Libavius and Glauber lose their way and are forced to return to camp.[44] Then another spy is caught, the alchemist Geber. He informs the besiegers that the mountain is defended by many philosophers who are guided by reason and truth, men who have been taught by Hermes, the father of all knowledge.[45] Galen explodes in rage,[46] but he is stilled by the announcement that an important prisoner has been captured. This is no less than Paracelsus who had already injured the members of his escort and was using such strong language that some were calling for his death.

But Aristotle called for his interrogation and permitted Paracelsus to defend himself.[47]

It was from the prisoner that the leaders of the attacking army were to learn the names of the principal defenders of the summit: Moses, Solomon, Roger Bacon, Nicholas Flamel, Hippocrates, Basil Valentine, Raymond Lull, Arnaud de Villeneuve in the first rank with others behind them including Joseph Duchesne, Gerhard Dorn, Roch le Baillif, Agrippa von Nettescheim, Oswald Crollius, Robert Fludd, Heinrich Khunrath, and Michael Maier.[48]

Unexpectedly a copy of Paracelsus's *Archidoxes magica* is found and condemned to the fire. Paracelsus is given a reprieve from his fate only if he agrees to show the philosopher-warriors the road by which they might avoid the mists and clouds that shield the summit from those below. He agrees to this and begins to lead a physician up the slope by hand. But the latter is not worthy of his charge, and he falls to the ground in the darkness, an event that symbolizes his ignorance. Paracelsus, the true champion of truth, continues on to join his comrades at the top leaving behind the bickering philosophers who represent every modern and ancient philosophical sect except the true one.[49]

The view of Paracelsus as the ultimate alchemist that is seen in the *Le Parnasse* is even more explicit in the work of François Pompée Colonne (ca. 1649–1726), an author who published very little until late in life. But beginning in 1718 and continuing past his death, there appeared a number of alchemical texts under his name or pseudonyms.[50]

These works clearly establish Colonne as a man interested in the more mystical interpretations of nature. He was interested in geomancy, astrology, and above all, in alchemy. He taught the theory of metallic growth, the means of extracting quintessences, and the secrets of transmutation.

But it would be wrong to dismiss Colonne simply as a popularizer of the occult. He was well aware of the work of Boyle and Descartes,[51] and his understanding of generation was based largely on his reading of Harvey and Malpighi, both of whom he quoted at length.[52] Although Colonne had read widely, it is clear from his *Abrégé de la doctrine de la Paracelse et de ses Archidoxes* (1724) that there is one author to consult above all others. In this substantial volume of five hundred pages he is unequivocal in his praise: "Among the moderns Paracelsus seems to have surpassed all of his predecessors and for this reason he has been given the title, the Monarch of Arcana."[53] Paracelsus had established his doctrine on physical reasons rather than on unintelligible enigmas.[54] And Paracelsus was a true physician who presented to his readers the rules for the preparation of all sorts of remedies for the cure of mankind and for the perfection of metals.[55]

This work began with a primer of theoretical chemistry in which Colonne discussed the elements, the principles, and the qualities. The true principles are those of the chemists because they are based on experience, and therefore they differ from the speculative elements of the Aristotelians and the principles of the Cartesians.[56] Still, Colonne was a corpuscularian, and he believed that matter could be described in terms of the size, the shape, and the motion of its particles.

Having prepared the reader, he then went on to discuss the *Archidoxes*. The text was presented in the form of a "commentary-abridgment" with the addition of two works on alchemy. For Colonne, as for earlier alchemists, the true chemist should be able to apply his knowledge not only to the imperfect metals, but also to the ills of man. The macrocosm/microcosm universe assured the operator that a cure for the one would succeed also for the other. Colonne also discussed at great length the growth process of metals from the seed,[57] and he was clearly convinced of the possibility of transmutation in the laboratory.

Colonne's interest in Paracelsus was associated primarily with his belief in transmutational alchemy. But authors whose concerns were mainly medical referred more often to the great Flemish iatrochemist, van Helmont, whose *Opera* had been printed in 1648 and had ushered in a new enthusiasm for chemical explanations of nature and man. His work on fevers had been translated into French as early as 1652,[58] and this had led to an early debate over the value of his theories, even before the French translation of his works in 1670.

As in the case of Paracelsus, interest in van Helmont continued well into the new century. There are several reasons for this, one of them surely being his stirring call for a new understanding of the great world and man based upon chemistry. Another reason, not to be overlooked, is the fact that van Helmont believed in the transmutation of the base metals into gold and in a universal medicine. His alkahest was a universal solvent sought by generations of chemists and alchemists. So here, too, one finds a number of eighteenth-century Helmontian texts reflecting alchemical themes. It is interesting, for instance, to note that Joachim Polemann's Helmontian *Novum lumen medicum* (1647) was translated into French in 1719.[59] For Polemann the attraction of Helmont was to be found less in his medicine than in his alchemical mysteries. The same interest is to be found in Jean Le Pelletier's *L'alkaest; ou, Le dissolvant universal de Van-Helment* (1704; reprint, 1706),[60] where the entire alchemical corpus is reviewed in a search for references to the alkahest.

More ambitious was a work titled *Le chimiste physicien* (1704). Here, J. Mongin, Docteur en Médecin, lauded the modern discoveries that had overturned the sterile ancient philosophy.[61] Chief among the moderns were van Helmont "who dared to cry out against the errors of the ancient School, and M. Descartes to whom the learned have a special obligation for having struck out on a new path."[62] The discoveries of these two pathfinders have excited others and deeply influenced them. Indeed, the scholars of the Royal Academy have recently uncovered so much new material that the concept of nature is now very different from that of the ancients. In the shade for so many centuries, the sciences have finally blossomed in the reign of Louis the Great.[63]

Mongin agreed with van Helmont that the greatest hope for advance was through chemistry.[64] This was a field in which there had been a special interest in France. French chemists had done much to overturn the elements of the ancients, but this research had not been sufficiently utilized. Both the nature and the uses of the bodily fluids must be examined chemically in order to determine how the functions of the body are sustained. This work will be in the tradition of other discoveries that have already offered a clear and distinct idea of the dissolution of foods, of the change in the chyle and the blood, of the nourishment and growth of the bodily parts, and of the different filtrations that occur in the body.

After these wonderful discoveries it may seem that there is nothing more left to uncover. But, Mongin insists, there still remains an infinity of wonders to be found. The more one learns, the more one stands in awe and adoration of the first cause, God.[65] It is, then, Mongin's intent to address himself to the most fundamental subject of all, the true elements of nature.

Mongin's book is less a chemical investigation of physiology than it is a comparison of the rival schemes of the elements in the tradition of Boyle's *Sceptical Chymist*. It is not enough for chemist to know his way aobut the laboratory, he must also be an expert analyst able to separate the principles of bodies, know their nature, be able to distinguish one from another, and—as a physician—know how to prescribe them.[66] Like Boyle, he rejected the Paracelsian principles and the Aristotelian elements before going on to discuss van Helmont's single-element theory. He devoted the third section of his book to van Helmont's tree experiment and concluded that salt, sulfur, and earth are not produced by water.[67] Thus, although van Helmont was one of the two chief founders of the new science, he had erred in his concept of the primal nature of water.

The Paracelsian and Helmontian medical influence is best seen in the lengthy texts of Joseph Chambon (16 October 1656–2 October 1732).[68] Here one may clearly see a continuation of the chemical philosophy into the mid-eighteenth century. Born at Grignon, Chambon studied medicine at Aix where he received his doctorate. He began practice at Marseilles, but a quarrel forced him to leave the city, and he traveled to Italy, Germany, and Poland where he became the physician to the king, John III Sobieski. At the siege of Vienna (1683), Chambon left the royal service to confer with Paracelsian and Helmontian physicians in the Low Countries. From there he traveled to Paris where he was well received by Fagon, physician to Louis XIV, but not by the Faculty of Medicine, whose members continued to oppose chemical physicians. Hoping to bypass the medical establishment, Chambon sought a special sanction and managed to continue his practice until his involvement in politics resulted in imprisonment in the Bastille for two years. After his release he returned to Grignon for the remainder of a long life.

Chambon's reputation ultimately rested on two publications, his *Principes de physique* (1st ed.?; reprint, 1711, 1714, 1750) and his *Traité des metaux* (1st ed., 1697?; 1714, 1750). In them he pointed to the relatively slow progress of medicine compared to other sciences—all the more evident in a period when astronomy and mathematics were rapidly changing.[69] Why, even the basic principles of medicine had not yet been discovered!

The rules of mathematics are infallible, and those of medicine should be no less so.[70] But how should one proceed? The ancients said that one must travel in order to learn, and Chambon agreed. He had no desire to rest on book learning alone, so for "eight years I went to study medicine in foreign countries."[71] The result was his belief that the advance of medicine was dependent upon chemistry and that Paracelsus was the greatest of all men.[72] True religion, a knowledge of nature, and the healing art are all interrelated, but this truth is unknown to the academic physicians who follow the books of Galen and Hippocrates or their commentators. These books must be renounced; in their place one should learn by direct observation in nature.[73] And here the key to understanding was to be found in chemistry.[74]

Even van Helmont would have applauded Chambon's insistence that properly "pénétrer dans les véritables connoissances de la nature, le Philosophe & le bon Médecin n'ont besoin que du feu; ils naissent du feu, ils se perfectionent avec le feu, & pratiquent le feu: *In igne, cum igne & per ignem.*"[75]

Chambon's deep convictions led him to open his *Principes de physique* with a chemical catechism—so essential that no student should proceed in his medical studies without having mastered it. Above all Chambon insisted on the essential nature of the three Paracelsian principles: salt, sulfur, and mercury.[76] The physician must know that since there are only three principles, there can only be three categories of illness, each related to one of them.[77]

On a more fundamental level, Chambon believed in a single *prima materia,* and like van Helmont he thought this was water.[78] There was an essential unity to be found in nature. One of the problems of the medical schools is that they taught anatomy through the dissection of cadavers—the separation and division of lifeless matter—when one should be studying the human body as a living whole.[79] Indeed, all nature—heaven, earth, and man—is one.[80]

The books of Chambon are lengthy, and he digressed on many topics. He discussed the work of Descartes unfavorably;[81] he compared the growth of metals in the earth with the progress of the tartaric diseases in the body;[82] and he noted the similarity between the calcination of the metals and their subsequent recovery through reduction with the death and resurrection of Jesus Christ.[83] But above all, Joseph Chambon was presenting to a new century an approach to chemical medicine that differed little from that proposed by the medical chemists of the mid-seventeenth century. The fact that his books were to go through a number of editions down to 1750 attests to their interest in the midst of the Enlightenment.

Alchemy and the Royal Academy of Sciences

To this point I have discussed authors outside of the scientific and medical mainstream. What does one find turning to the Royal Academy, the medical schools, and the learned journals? In fact, one finds some of the same issues being debated. In medicine the University of Montpellier continued to be identified with chemical medicine. The Paracelsian influence there may be traced back to the sixteenth century, and throughout the seventeenth century one sees evidence of an interest in chemistry at Montpellier. The chemical—and many of the medical—texts printed there in the first half of the eighteenth century clearly show this influence.

And what of the Royal Academy of Sciences? If one looks at the activities of the academicians in the first decades of the century, one does find that the members were keenly aware of problems relating to their alchemical heritage. True, they were opposed to alchemy, but the subject remained current and it was frequently brought to the fore.

The *Histoire* and *Mémoires* of the Academy—beginning in 1699—seem at first glance to reflect a world far removed from that of the authors I have been discussing. The prefatory essay to the first volume is a hymn of praise to mathematics and the physical sciences.[84] Among the biological sciences only anatomy equals astronomy for the person who seeks his Creator through nature.[85] And what of chemistry? This subject leads to a knowledge of mineral remedies valuable for the physician, but the mystical concepts of traditional alchemy are to be avoided.

This theme reappears frequently in the early volumes of the *Mémoires*. The chemical observations of alchemists were to be reported, but not their theories.[86] Committees were also formed to investigate possible fraud. I have already noted the investigation of Abbé Bignon. Another committee was delegated to examine a "potable gold" that was being hawked on the streets of Paris. The conclusion? This was another deceit by a charlatan rather than the much-vaunted universal solvent of van Helmont.[87]

One senses a conscious attempt to renew chemistry as an acceptable part of the new philosophy by stripping away the mysticism of the past. Fontenelle reported hopefully that chemistry had at last left behind the mysteries and shades of the false philosophers.[88] But Guillaume Homberg was not so sure. His chemical essays, which appeared in the *Mémoires* from 1702 to 1709, were written to serve as a new foundation for chemistry.

> Les anciens Chimistes dont la plus grande partie ont été pour le moins un peu visionnaires, ont enveloppé cette Science d'une obscurité affectée, &, pour ainsi dire, d'une sainte horreur; le temps est venu que des Chimistes plus sensés & de meilleure foi ont dissipé ces ténèbres artificielles: mais l'obscurité naturelle est demeurée du moins en partie, & c'est la plus difficile à dissiper.[89]

In traditional fashion Homberg began with a discussion of the elements and the principles. However, as a mechanist he argued that the chemical principles must be those of physics because chemistry is but part of physics.[90] This was far from the approach of Colonne or Chambon.

Homberg was concerned about the lingering influence of alchemy, but it is interesting that the academy had one member who was bitterly opposed to the mechanists. Martino Poli (1662–1714)[91] was an Italian chemist who chanced to discover a secret of chemical warfare, which he offered to Louis XIV. The king declined this offer because of its destructive potential, but he conferred a pension on Poli with the title of Engineer to the King. He was also made an extra foreign associate of the academy in 1702.

Four years later Poli published *Il trionfo degli acidi vendicati dalle calunnie di molti moderni . . .*[92] Here he strongly defended the Paracelsian tradition. Like other chemists Poli laid stress on the elements. The four elements of the Aristotelians, the acid-base system of Tachenius, and the five principles of Thomas Willis were all dismissed. Far better are the three principles of the Paracelsians who are the true Hermetic chemists. Salt, sulfur, and mercury are confirmed by experience; the others are not.[93]

The second part of the book contained his refutation of the mechanists. The hope of the Cartesians that all could be explained in terms of the motion, rest, shape, and place of the particles that composed bodies was rejected as a hopeless dream.[94] More specifically, Poli argued that living bodies cannot be discussed in terms of inert ones. Why, then, do the mechanists continue to use gross mechanics and analogies taken from machines when these are meaningless. They speak of filters transmitting some liquors to the exclusion of others. But neither the passage of the chyle in the lacteal veins, the separation of urine in the reins, nor the bile in the liver is the result of filtration or any purely mechanical cause. Rather, it is due to fermentation, dissolution, sublimation, "and other similar operations that occur in the body of an animal as in the laboratory of a chemist."[95]

In short, Poli bitterly opposed the medicine and physiology of contemporary iatrophysicists such as Baglivi.[96] In a large sense, his views express the doubts of a number of physicians who questioned the attempt to reduce life processes to mechanical analogies. Still, Fontenelle was not pleased, and in his eloge of Poli he noted that this man had attacked the corpuscular philosophy. But, he added, "one need not be surprised at this mode of thought in an Italian since this is a country in which the ancient philosophy still dominates."[97]

One last example from the pages of the *Mémoires:* In 1704 Geoffroy noted that on combustion a mixture of a sulfur (here an inflammable oil of vegetable origin), a vitriolic salt, and an earth always result in an ash containing iron. This seemed to be a synthesis of a metal. One could go further: Iron particles are always to be found in the ashes of plants, and these may be detected with a magnet. He questioned in print whether there was any plant ash devoid of iron.[98]

Louis Lemery (1677–1743) replied to Geoffroy in a denial that iron could be synthesized as he claimed.[99] The iron to be found in plants is there because of the growth process. It is drawn into the roots and then elevated through the vessels of the plant by its life force. It is similar to what is seen in the Tree of Diana, and, indeed, he had discovered a "Tree of Mars," its iron analog.[100] Over the next four years a series of attacks and counterattacks were printed. The final paper in this exchange was by Lemery.[101] Not only was Geoffroy wrong, he was not even original. His method and conclusions were to be found in J. J. Becher's *Actorum laboratorii chemici monacensis* (1671). And who was Becher? "Nothing but a medical chemist, known as such by his many writings given to the public, a man who wished to revive the spirits of those who sought transmutation, and who hoped to defend alchemy."[102] Truly guilt by association, since the purpose of Becher's work had been to prove that it was easier to make metals than most authors would admit. At the very least Geoffroy was being tagged a fellow traveler of the alchemists. Harsh words, indeed, for the man who was to condemn the deceits of the alchemists not too many years later.

The Journal des Sçavans

These notes on the *Mémoires* can be balanced with reference to a second periodical: the *Journal des Sçavans,* which had been published since 1665 and had a regular policy of including scientific and medical reviews. The *Journal* is important also because it covered works published in all major European languages and because it did not reflect the bias of any one special school.

Surely the most recent publications on alchemy were well covered in the pages of the *Journal.* Manget's massive folio compilation of alchemical texts appeared in 1702 and was discussed in an eight-page review the following year.[103] A review of this scholarly work may have been expected, but texts of lesser importance were reviewed as well. New editions of alchemical classics as well as publications by living alchemists were all given serious attention. Playing no favorites, the editors also reviewed works attacking alchemy, such as the *Examen des principes des alchymistes,* which were discussed earlier.[104]

Other volumes reviewed were devoted to topics closely associated with alchemy. The reviewer of Jonas Schramm's *Introductio in dialecticam cabbalaeorum* (1703) noted that this subject was far removed from the spirit of the times.[105] He was astonished to find scholars still devoting themselves to the cabala, but explained it by the fact that such authors all seemed to be German and Aristotelians. After all, the Peripatetics accommodate themselves well to the obscure sciences. A Cartesian needs light to understand, while the Aristotelian sees light in the shades of darkness. But this anonymous reviewer could not have been the one who soberly discussed the content of Cohausen's *Ossilegium historico-physicum* (1714), in which the concept of palingenesis was extended to man.[106] Do sparks of life and seeds of immortality remain in the ashes after death? Cohausen offered many accounts by chemists to indicate that this was so. One of the most convincing was by Robert Fludd who had calcined the skull of an executed criminal and then dissolved the ashes in water. Within the solution was seen the figure of the hanged criminal!

The disciple of antimechanistic medical systems was even better served than the devotee of alchemy. The reviews clearly illustrate the rivalry of the various medical sects of the period. A good example is the review of a work in Spanish by Miguel Boix, *Hippocrates defendido* (1711), a work of such interest to the reviewer that his review ran to thirty-six pages in two consecutive issues of the *Journal* in 1712.[107] Here the author painted a scene in which physicians of each major medical sect sought to cure a patient. The Galenist suggested frequent bleedings, while the followers of Paracelsus and van Helmont "spoke only of elixirs, quintessences, and other mysterious remedies." A disciple of Willis suggested a variety of medicines and bleeding as did a follower of Sylvius. The Cartesian suggested nothing specific, but rambled on about the proportions of the particles in the blood. The follower of Baglivi spoke rather of the equilibrium of solids and fluids, the correction of contractions, and of the wrinkling and shriveling of the bodily fibers. Having thus established the foolishness of current medical theory, Boix allowed Hippocrates to lead these doctors to truth.[108]

It is clear from this review—and from a number of others from the same period—that chemical medicine remained influential in the early decades of the eighteenth century. It is surely for this reason that so much space was devoted to new works on Paracelsian and Helmontian medicine. Among authors I have mentioned earlier, it is interesting that Poli's *Trionfo degli acidi vendicati* was given a twenty-page lead review in the November 1707 issue.[109] Here his objections to the mechanical philosophy were presented in great detail. And four years later there was an account of Chambon's *Principes de physique* that showed the reiewer's considerable understanding of the chemical and alchemical bases of the author's medical system.[110] The final collected edition of van Helmont's *Opera omnia* (1707), edited by Michael Valentini, was reviewed in 1708.[111] The prefatory material was singled out for comment, noting that Valentini compared the persecution of Helmont in his lifetime with that of Bacon and Descartes. Indeed, his reforms in medicine were as important as those of Luther and Zwingli in religion.

Many monographic studies related to chemical philosophy were also reviewed in the pages of the *Journal des Sçavans*. I have already noted a number of divergent views on the elements expressed by chemists. This debate was also reflected in reviews. In 1704 there was a review of Mongin's *Chemical Physician* detailing this author's theory of four elements and his rejection of van Helmont's primal water.[112] But the same volume contained a review of a book by David Van der Becke suporting the Helmontian view that water is the material principle of all things.[113] There is also a review of Le Pelletier's book on the alkahest, which was discussed in its alchemical context[114]—and a number of books on the Helmotian archeus and fermentation.[115]

Other aspects of nonmechanistic medicine were also reflected in the pages of the *Journal*. The early years of the new century witnessed a running debate over digestion. Iatrophysicists argued for a mechanical cause—trituration—while chemical physicians were certain that the result was due to fermentation.[116] No less controversial was the acid-base theory that had been developed late in the seventeenth century by chemists.[117] Rejected by mechanists as insufficient for the explanation of bodily processes, others found it essential for medical theory and practice. These debates had their roots in the seventeenth-century conflict between the chemists and the mechanists, and they were well covered in reviews appearing in the *Journal*.

Conclusion

I began by referring to Geoffrroy's 1722 attack on the frauds of the alchemists. I believe that the appearance of such a paper at this late date is rather surprising—especially for those accustomed to the better-known accounts of Enlightenment science. Even readers of the recent *Ferment of Knowledge,* a collection of essays by authorities in various areas of eighteenth-century science and medicine, would have little reason to believe that there was such a large quantity of alchemical literature in this period. Of course, the fierce debate between the mechanical and the chemical philosophers in the seventeenth century did result in a scientific establishment that favored mechanistic explanations in both science and medicine. But does this mean that the mystical world view of the Renaissance alchemist was overwhelmed in a violent Kuhnian paradigm shift? Far from it! Alchemy remained a subject of great interest, and the search for the philosophers' stone and the elixir of life was pursued by many scholars and true believers.

All of this was intertwined with the tradition of the Chemical Philosophy of the physicians. The medicochemical world view of Paracelsus and Helmont was meaningless without an understanding of macrocosmic influences and chemical analogies as they related to man. They had believed in alchemy, and alchemical concepts played a crucial role in their views of nature. Their French disciples of the eighteenth century did as well. Colonne's Paracelsian text of 1724 was an alchemical work, while Chambon's treatises on medicine and metallic remedies clearly reflect their Paracelsian and alchemical origins.

Even in the Academy of Sciences alchemy was not entirely a thing of the past. To many it seemed so widespread that it simply could not be ignored—so much so that Homberg wrote his chemical essays as a replacement for the outmoded mysticism of the alchemists and the Paracelsians. It must have distressed him sorely to have as a foreign associate Martino Poli, one of the most prominent opponents of the mechanical philosophy, a man who sought to establish the Paracelsian principles as the basis of physics and medicine. Even debates within the academy were occasionally found to have alchemical overtones. I have remarked on Geoffroy's belief that artificial iron could be produced from plant substances, and that he was attacked for reviving an alchemical view originally proposed by Becher.

But most interesting is the broad coverage of alchemical and antimechanical science and medicine in the *Journal des Sçavans*. From this source one can see that alchemy remained a subject of considerable interest to French scholars. As for the chemically oriented Paracelo-Helmontians, it is obvious that they were still treated as members of a major medical sect in this period.

One may conclude that early-eighteenth-century French science and medicine is far more complex than it is sometimes presented. There is no doubt that the overwhelming majority of the academicians believed in a new science dominated by mechanistic principles. But outside of this group, one finds a far broader spectrum of scientific and medical views being discussed: not only alchemy, but also many other Renaissance natural philosophies that are normally heard little of in the Enlightenment. In short, Geoffroy had good reason to be concerned about the activities of the alchemists when he presented his paper in 1722.

Let me pose a final question. Did Geoffroy's paper have any real influence? It was certainly well known. Lenglet du Fresnoy reprinted it with a commentary in his *Histoire de la philosophie hermétique* (1742, 1744),[118] and it formed part of the article on alchemy in the *Encyclopédie méthodique*.[119] But the eighteenth century was to be the high-water mark of French alchemy. Lenglet du Fresnoy's *Histoire* remains an important source today, while the four-volume *Bibliothèque des philosophes chimiques* (1740–54)[120] is still the most extensive collection of alchemical texts ever printed in French. Antoine-Joseph Pernety's massive Hermetic interpretation of ancient mythology appeared in three editions (1758, 1786, 1795)[121] and his alchemical dictionary (1758, 1787) was also to become a classic.[122]

Nor were Paracelsus and van Helmont forgotten. In the pages of Diderot's *Encyclopédie* a professor of Montpellier, Gabriel François Venel, called for a new Paracelsus to reform that science.[123] And at the end of the century, Dr. Joyand, a physician of Brest, planned an enormous work, *Précis du siècle de Paracelse,* in which he reviewed the state of physics and then proceeded to try to prove that the wonders of animal magnetism had first been described in the work of Paracelsus.[124] These are not scattered instances. Throughout the eighteenth century there was a steady stream of alchemical and iatrochemical publications.

One could present a history of eighteenth-century French science (or European science as a whole) emphasizing continuity rather than change. Historians of science have been interested in progress, and they have concentrated on the Chemical Revolution, electrical theory, the triumph of Newtonianism, specific medical discoveries, and any number of other topics that have helped to explain the great contributions of the eighteenth to the following century. Here I have been concerned with something quite different, the persistent interest in alchemy and the chemical medicine of an earlier period. It has been my purpose to give some indication of the extent of this literature in France. But what I have described is at best a beginning. Most of the research remains to be done in regard to the seventeenth-century background of this literature, and its relationship to other developments in the sciences and medicine—as well as other areas of thought. Even the identification and description of the texts must be completed. In short, there is much work ahead for many scholars. I believe that it is an important field—one that will contribute much to the understanding of the period.

Notes

The author wishes to thank the National Science Foundation for partial support of this research (Research Grant SES-8008919 AO1).

1. "Des supercheries concernant la pierre philosophale," *Histoire de l'Academie royale des sciences, année MDCCXXII: Avec les Mémoires de mathématique & de physique, pour la même année; Mémoires* (1722): 61–70.
2. On Geoffroy's life and work, see *Dictionary of Scientific Biography*, 1972, s.v. "Geoffroy, Etienne François"; and J. R. Partington, *A History of Chemistry*, 4 vols. (London, 1962), 3:49–52.
3. Geoffroy, *Mémoires* (1722): 61–62.
4. Ibid., pp. 62–63.
5. Ibid., pp. 68–69.
6. Fontenelle, *Histoire* (1722): 37–39.
7. A short, but useful, survey of this literature is to be found in Constantin Bila, *La croyance à la magie au XVIIIe siècle en France dans les contes, romans & traités* (Paris, 1925). A far more exhaustive account of the end of the century will be found in August Viatte, *Les sources occultes du Romanticisme, Illuminisme, Théosophie, 1770–1820*, 2d ed., 2 vols. (Paris, 1969).
8. Charles Louis de Secondat Montesquieu, *The Persian Letters . . . Now First Completely Translated into English with Notes and Memoirs by John Davidson . . .* , 2 vols. (Philadelphia, n.d.), see letter 58 (1:151–52).
9. Laurent Bordelon, *A History of the Ridiculous Extravagancies of Monsieur Oufle; Occasion'd by His Reading Books Treating of Magick, the Black-Art, Daemoniacks, Conjurers, Witches, Hobgoblins . . . , and other Superstitious Practices. With Notes Containing a Multitude of Quotations out of Those Books, Which Have Either Caused Such Extravagant Imaginations, or May seeme to Cure Them* (London, 1711), pp. 223–25.
10. See the long account by Claude Chevalier and Sabine Stuart Chevalier in *L'existence de la pierre merveilleuse des philosophes, prouvée par des faits incontestables: Dédiré aux adeptes par un amateur de la sagesse* (En France, 1765), pp. 84–89. The Chevaliers cite Paul Lucas, *Voyages* (1712), p. 102.
11. Editions referred to in the course of this research include the *Secrets merveilleux de la magic naturelle & cabalistique du Petit Albert . . .* (Lyons, 1743); and *Les admirables secrets d'Albert le Grand, contenant plusieurs traités sur la conception des femmes, des vertus des herbes, des pierres précieuse, & des animaux . . .* (Lyons, 1758).

12. Henri Cornelius Agrippa, *La philosophie occulte de H.C.A. . . . Davisée en trois livres, et traduite den Latin* (The Hague, 1727).

13. Nicolas Pierre Henri de Montfaucon Villars, *Le comte de Gabalis: ou, Entretiens sur les sciences secretes: Nouvelle edition, augmentés des genies assistans & des gnomes irreconciliables* (London, 1742). There are at least three eighteenth-century editions (1700, 1715, 1718) prior to the publication of Geoffroy's paper.

14. Jean Colleson, *L'idée parfaicte de la philosophie hermétique; ou, L'abrégé de la théorie & practique de la pierre des philosophes* (1630; reprint, Paris, 1719).

15. [Limojon de Saint Didier], *Le triomphe hermétique; ou, La pierre philosophale victorieuse: Traitté plus complet & plus intelligible, qu'il y en ait eû jusques ici, touchant le magistère hermétique* (Amsterdam; 1699). This work was translated into German and English.

16. *Cosmopolite on Nouvelle Lumière Chymique, pour servir d'éclairissement aux trois principes de la nature, exactement décrits dans les trois traitez suivans: Le Ier. De la nature en général, où il est parlé du mercure; Le II. Du soufre; Le III. Du vray sel des philosophes; Dernière édition, revûë & augmentée de la lettre philosophique d'Antoine Duval et de l'extrait d'une autre lettre assez curieuse* (Paris; 1723).

17. D.L.B., *Traité de la poudre de projection, divisé en deux lettres: Analyse tirée de l'Ecriture Sainte. Moriens pour parvenu à la poudre de projection par l'humide substantial premier principe* (Brussels, 1707).

18. Lettre à un ami, touchant la dissolution radicale & philosophicale de l'or, & de l'argent, sans corrosifs. Avec des remarques sur l'opinion général, qu'il ne faut point chercher de remède à la goutte (London, 1719), pp. 3–4.

19. Fontenelle is characterized as the author of dialogues of the dead (ibid., p. 8).

20. Ibid., sig. A2r.

21. *Explication de quelques doutes touchant la médecine* (ca. 1700), p. 64.

22. [François Pousse], *Examen des principes des alchymistes sur la pierre philosophale* (Paris, 1711), sig. a viii.

23. Pierre Le Lorrain, abbé de Vallemont, *Curiosities of Nature and Art in Husbandry and Gardening* (London, 1707; originally published as *Curiositez de la nature et de l'art sur la vegetation; ou, L'agriculture, et le jardinage dans leur perfection* [1705], pp. 302–7.

24. Ibid., p. 304.

25. Ibid., pp. 305–6.

26. Recent papers on palingenesis include Jacques Marx, "Alchimie et palingénésie," *Isis* 62 (1971): 274–89; Allen G. Debus, "A Further Note on Palingenesis: The Account of Ebenezer Sibly in the *Illustration of Astrology*," *Isis* 64 (1973): 226–30; and François Secret, "Palingenesis, Alchemy and Metempsychosis in Renaissance Medicine," *Ambis* 26 (1979): 81–99.

27. Vallemont, p. 327.

28. Ibid, pp. 348–49.

29. Ibid., pp. 327–28.

30. Harcouet de Longeville, *Histoire des personnes qui ont vecu plusieurs siècles et qui ont Rajeuni avec le secret da rajeunissement, tiré d'Arnauld de Villeneuve* (Paris, 1715).

31. As examples, see Domenico Auda (ca. 1656), *Les admirables secrets de la médecine chimique du Sr. Joseph Quinti, docteur venetien. Qu'il a recueillis avec beaucoup de soin & de travail: lesquels ont été plus d'une fois experimentez par lui-même en plusieurs infirmitez, & maladies dangereuses,* trans. from the Italian (Liège, 1711); and D.J.B.D.F.Y.C., *La messager de la vertié traité. Contenant la composition & proprieté d'un remède spécifique pour toutes sortes de maux; la manière de s'en servir avec le régime de vivre, nourritures & boissons; . . . l'explication de la figure philosophique & du globe céleste . . .* (Paris; 1722).

32. Charles Le Breton, *Remèdes choisis et éprouvés tant de médecine, que de chyrurgie, pour les maladies du corps humain, dont un grand nombre n'ont pas encore esté imprimés* (Paris, 1716).

33. Sanctorius Sanctorius, *La médecine statique de Sanctorius; ou, L'art de se conserver la santé par la transpiration,* trans. Charles Le Breton (Paris, 1722).

34. Charles Le Breton, *Les clefs de la philosophie spagyrique, qui donnent la connoissance des principes & véritables operations de cet art dans les mixtes des trois genres* (Paris, 1722).

35. For a general account, see Allen G. Debus, *Man and Nature in the Renaissance* (Cambridge, 1978); and more specifically, idem, *The Chemical Philosophy: Paracelsian Science and Medicine in the Sixteenth and Seventeenth Centuries,* 2 vols. (New York, 1977).

36. For a general account of the early history of French Paracelsism, see Debus, *Chemical Philosophy,* 1:145–73. Howard W. Solomon has discussed a specific case of the relation of French Paracelsian thought to seventeenth-century politics in his *Public Welfare, Science, and Propaganda in Seventeenth-Century France: The Innovations of Théophraste Renaudot* (Princeton, 1972).

37. Anon., *Le Parnasse assiegé; ou, La guerre declarée entre les philosophes anciens & modernes* (Lyons, 1697), sig. Aiiv.

38. Ibid., p. 1.

39. Ibid., pp. 4–6.

40. Ibid., p. 11.

41. Ibid., p. 12.

42. Ibid., p. 13.

43. Ibid., pp. 14–15.

44. Ibid., p. 103.

45. Ibid., pp. 109–10.

46. Ibid., p. 115.

47. Ibid., p. 116.

48. Ibid., pp. 127–28.

49. Ibid., pp. 136–38.

50. Little is known of the life of this author beyond the fact that he died in the flames of his house, and that a student (Gosmond) prepared several of his manuscripts for the press and answered one of his master's critics, the Reverend Father Castel. His first publication is *Introduction à la philosophie des anciens, par un amateur de la verité,* which appeared in 1698, but then there was complete silence for a quarter century. His *Les secrets les plus cachés* (1722; reprint, 1762); *Les principes de la nature* (1725); *Suite des expériences utiles* (1725), a work on geomancy (1726), and possible a few additional texts appearing under the name of Le Crom were published shortly prior to his death. There appeared posthumously his *Principles de la nature ou de la génération* (1732) and a multivolume *Historie naturelle de l'univers* (1734).

51. François Marie Pompée Colonne, *Abrégé de la doctrine de la Paracelse, et de ses archidoxes. Avec une explication de la nature des principes de chymie. Pour servir d'éclairessement aux traitez de cet auteur & des autres philosophes. Suivi d'un traité pratique de differentes manières d'operer, soit par la voye séche, ou par la voye humide* (Paris, 1724), pp. vii–viii.

52. François Marie Pompée Colonne, *Les principes de la nature, ou de la génération de choses* (Paris, 1731), pp. 70–200.

53. Colonne, *Abrégé de la doctrine de la Paracelse,* pp. iiiv–iiiir.

54. Ibid., sig. iiiir.

55. Ibid., sig. iiiiv.

56. Ibid., sigs. i–v.

57. Crosset de la Haumerie [F. M. P. Colonne], *Les secrets des plus cachés de la philosophie des anciens découverts et expliqués, à la suite d'une histoire des plus curieuses* (Paris, 1722).

58. Jan Baptista van Helmont, *Doctrine nouvelle de Iean Baptiste de Helmont, Seigneur de Royenborch, Pellines, & c. natif de Bruxelles: Touchant les fièvres,* trans. Abraham Bauda (Sedan, [1652])

59. Joachim Polemann, *Nouvelle lumière de médecine, du mistère ou souffre des philosophes* (Rouen, 1721).

60. Jean Le Pelletier, *L'alkaest; ou, Le dissolvant universel de Van-Helmont, revelé dans plusieurs traitez qui en découvrent le secret.* (Rouen, 1704).

61. J. Mongin, *Le chimiste physicien; ou, l'on montre que les principes naturels de tons les corps sont vertiablement ceux que l'on découvre par la chimie. Et où par des experiences & des raisons fondée sur les loix des méchaniques, aprés avoir donné des moyens faciles pour les separer des mixtes, on explique leurs proprietez, leurs usages & less principaux phénomènes qu'on observe es travaillant en chimie* (Paris, 1704), sig. ãiiiv.

62. Ibid., sig. ã iiiiv.

63. Ibid.

64. Ibid., sigs. ã iiiiv–ã vr.

65. Ibid., sigs. ãvv–ã vir.

66. Ibid., p. 5.

67. Ibid., pp. 195–223.

68. On Chambon's life, I have followed the accounts in the *Nouvelle biographie général* and the *Dictionnaire de biographie française.* His earliest work (which I have not seen) is Cl Guiron and Joseph Chambon, *E. sanitas a calidi, frigidi, humidi & sicci moderatione* (Paris, 1696).

69. Joseph Chambon, *Principes de physique: Rapportes à la médecine pratique, & autres traitez sur cet art,* rev. ed. (Paris, 1711), preface, pp. a vv–a viv.

70. Joseph Chambon, *Traité des métaux, et des minéraux, et des remèdes qu'on en peut tirer; avec des dissertations sur le sel & le soulphre des philosophes, & sur la goutte, la gravelle, la petite vérole, la rougeole & autres maladies; avec un grand nombre de remèdes choisis* (Paris, 1714), pp. á ivv–á vv.

71. Chambon, *Principes de physique* (1711), p. ë ivv.

72. Chambon, *Traité des métaux*, p. 321.

73. Ibid., pp. 459–60.

74. Chambon, *Principes de physique*, p. ī iir.

75. Joseph Chambon, *Principes de physique: Rapportes à la médecine-pratique*, rev. ed. (Paris, 1750), p. 478.

76. Ibid., pp. 4–6.

77. Chambon, *Traité des métaux*, p. ë ivv.

78. Chambon, *Principes de physique* (1711), p. 23.

79. Ibid., p. a viir.

80. Chambon, *Traité des métaux*, p. 390.

81. Chambon, *Principes de physique* (1750), pp. 492–ff.

82. Chambon, *Traité des métaux*, pp. 210–16.

83. Ibid., pp. 367–70.

84. *Histoire de l'Académie royale des sciences, année MDCXCIX: Avec les Mémoires de mathematique & de physique, pour la même Année. Tirées des registres de cette académie*, 2d ed. (Amsterdam, 1734), preface: xvii.

85. Ibid., p. xxi.

86. *Histoire* (1699): 71.

87. See the discussion of the investigation of De Fronville's potable gold by Homberg and Lemery, *Mémoires* (1701): 95–96.

88. *Histoire* (1701), 2d ed. (Amsterdam, 1735): 86.

89. *Histoire* (1702), 2d ed. (Amsterdam, 1737): 60.

90. Guillaume Homberg, "Essais de Chimie," *Mémoires* (1702): 44.

91. On the life of Martino Poli, see Fontenelle's eloge in *Histoire* (1714): 165–72.

92. Martino Poli, *Il trionfo degli acidi vendicati dalle calunnie di molti moderni: Opera filosofica e medica fondata sopra de principii chemici & adornata di varij esperimenti; contro il sistema, e prattica delli moderni Democritici & Epicurei reformati* (Rome, 1706). I have not been able to examine the book in detail (there is a copy at Cornell University), and the present account is based primarily on the long review in the *Journal des Sçavans* 38 (1707): 328–47.

93. Ibid., p. 333.

94. Ibid., p. 335.

95. Ibid., pp. 336–38.

96. Ibid., pp. 338–39.

97. *Histoire* (1714): 165–72, esp. 169.

98. E. F. Geoffroy, "Probleme de chimie: Trouver des cendres qui ne contiennent ancunes parcelles de fer," *Mémoires* (1705), 2d ed. (Amsterdam, 1746): 478–80.

99. L. Lemery, "Que les plantes contiennent réelement du fer, & que ce métal entre nécessairement dans leur composition naturelle," *Mémoires* (1706), 2d ed., 2 vols. (Amsterdam, 1747): 529–38.

100. L. Lemery, "Sur une vegetation chimique du fer," *Mémoires* (1707), 2d ed., 2 vols. (Amsterdam, 1747): 388–425.

101. L. Lemery, "Nouvel éclairicissement sur la prétendue production artificielle du fer, publiée par Becher & sontenne par Mr. Geoffroy," *Mémoires* (1708), 2d ed., 2 vols. (Amsterdam, 1750): 482–515.

102. Ibid., p. 484.

103. *Journal des Sçavans* 31 (1703): 834–41.

104. *Journal des Sçavans* 49 (1711): 179–86.

105. *Journal des Sçavans* 33 (1705): 167–69.

106. *Journal des Sçavans* 59 (1716): 71–79.

107. *Journal des Sçavans* 52 (1712): 212–28, 264–84.

108. Ibid., pp. 276–83.

109. *Journal des Sçavans* 38 (1707): 328–47.

110. *Journal des Sçavans* 50 (1711): 132–36.

111. *Journal des Sçavans* 41 (1708): 123–29.

112. *Journal des Sçavans* 32 (1704): 476–79.

113. Ibid., pp. 174–89.

114. *Journal des Sçavans* 34 (1706): 831–38.

115. As examples, see the review of Mart. Heer Lusati, *Introductio in archei vitale & fermentale viri magnifici Joannis Baptistae Van-Helmont, philosophi per ignem* (1703), in *Journal des Sçavans* 32 (1704): 47–49; and Henri Louis de Rouvière, *Reflexions sur la fermentation et sur la nature du feu* (1708), in *Journal des Sçavans* 39 (1708): 317–23.

116. As an example, both sides of the debate are discussed in the review of Jean Baptist Gastaldi,

Quaestio proposita . . . An alimentorum coctio seu digestio à fermentatione vel à tritu fiat (1713), in *Journal des Sçavans* 55 (1714): 24–32.

117. Here see the review of Gastaldi's *Institutiones medicae . . .* (1712), in *Journal des Sçavans* 54 (1713): 200–206, in which the reviews concentrated on the author's views on acid-base theory.

118. Nicolas Lenglet-Dufresnoy, *Histoire de la philosophie hermétique,* 3 vols. (Paris, 1742), 2:104–17, with Lenglet-Dufresnoy's "Observation" continuing on pp. 117–20.

119. See the article on alchemy, *Encyclopedie méthodique* 66 (1792), pt. 1, pp. 30–60. A long extract from the Geoffroy article (1722) is combined with a chronology borrowed from Lenglet-Dufresnoy's *Histoire*.

120. Jean Maugin de Richebourg, comp., *Bibliothèque des philosophes chimiques,* rev. ed., 4 vols. (Paris, 1741–54).

121. Antoine-Joseph Pernety, *Les fables égyptiennes et grecques dévoilées & reduites au même principe, avec une explication des hieroglyphes, et de la Guerre de Troye,* 2d ed., 2 vols. (Paris, 1786).

122. Antoine-Joseph Pernety, *Dictionnaire mytho-hermétique, dans lequel on trouve les allégories fabuleuses des poetes, les métaphores, les enigmes et les termes barbares des philosophes herméti-ques expliqués* (Paris, 1758).

123. G. F. Venel, "Chymie," in Diderot and D'Alembert, eds., *Encyclopédie; ou, Dictionnaire raisonné des sciences, des arts et des métiers,* (Paris, 1753), 3:408. Diderot's antimechanistic views have been noted by Charles Coulston Gillispie in "The *Encyclopédie* and the Jacobin Philosophy of Science," in *Critical Problems in the History of Science,* ed. Marshall Clagett (Madison, Wis., 1962), pp. 255–89; and idem, *The Edge of Objectivity* (Princeton, 1960), pp. 184–87.

124. M. Joyand, *Précis du siècle de Paracelse* (Paris, 1787).

12

Magic, Science, and Institutionalization in the Seventeenth and Eighteenth Centuries

KARIN JOHANNISSON

Magic and mysticism have long been excluded from the history of science as being irrelevant to the development of modern science. But Frances Yates and others in a series of brilliant studies in recent decades have shown that science and mysticism are not antipodes. Rationality cannot unequivocally be placed in opposition to irrationality, nor progress to superstition. On the contrary—mysticism within the framework of the Hermetic tradition played a decisive role in the conception of modern science as a social activity and institution.[1]

The Hermetic tradition had its starting point in the translation of the Neoplatonic writings that was carried out in the fifteenth century within the Florentine circle of Marsilio Ficino and that included the so-called *Corpus Hermeticum*, a collection of texts attributed to the mythic Hermes Trismegistus. Here the proud notion of a pristine knowledge was depicted, a gift from God to Adam and an exhortation to Man to complete the work of creation by unlocking it and decoding its underlying structure. (This Hermetic Adam should be compared with the Mosaic Adam: When he attempts to become initiated into the divine wisdom and eats from the Tree of Knowledge, he is punished—he is not God's equal.) Nature had its own language, and the means of interpreting it was a secret alphabet, derived from Greek number mysticism and the cabala, accessible only to the chosen. This Hermetic tradition with its specific natural philosophy was carried further by Paracelsianism and other magical systems, transmitted by Cornelius Agrippa, John Dee, and Robert Fludd, and merged in a utopian vision of a deeper insight that would initiate man's return to an earthly paradise.

In the two renowned Rosicrucian manifestos—*Fama fraternitatis* (1614) and *Confessio fraternitatis* (1615)—these traditions were transformed into a concrete program, and this is where I will start.[2] I shall attempt to show that the scientific ambitions proclaimed in the manifestos and carried out within the fertile Rosicrucian movement, rather than being regressive were progressive. They maintained the idea that knowledge cannot be limited by given methods, and that against rationality, objectivity, and critical doubt as the cardinal virtues of science must be placed proud hope that the boundaries of science can always be transcended, the dream of a perfectible science directly in the service of mankind. I shall bring this account to the end of the eighteenth century, to the years around the French Revolution, when the concepts of magic and science once again seem to merge in the intense mystical activity of the orders, and when the scientific academy and the secret society fulfill similar functions as platforms for scientific activity and propaganda.

Let me first set out the basic outlines of magical science, comparing and contrasting it with the science that was to come. It is important to remember that the magus of the sixteenth and seventeenth centuries considered himself a natural philosopher in the same way as the scientist who gained his professional status during the following centuries.

Most important here is the different approach to nature. Whereas the magus understands nature as an animate and active network of ultimately spiritual forces, the scientist sees it as a "machine," a manifestation of the universal laws of nature. The magus believes that because nature is animate—not completed and finished— he can enter into it, operate on it, and manipulate it. Magic means using nature instrumentally, becoming more powerful. *Magic is art, having the power to change and to transmute.* The scientist on the other hand would not attempt to exceed nature; his task is to understand and to describe it, to come as close as possible to its unassailable mechanism; for him the laws of nature are inexorable and un-breakable, absolute criteria for what is natural and supernatural. For the magus, the supernatural simply coincides with the unusual, the marvelous, the artificial; the laws of nature are not regarded as absolute and can be exceeded by art. It should be kept in mind that this outlook was present both in the Aristotelian tradition and in Bacon's writings.

Magic and science also work with different methods. Whereas science is based on the conviction that experience and reason are valid instruments of knowledge, magic is based on the conviction that such values cannot be fixed, and the aim is continually set far beyond the boundaries of what is empirically and rationally verifiable. The theories of science are dictated by logic, those of magic by analogy. In opposition to rationality and understanding (episteme) stand irrational hope and use (techne). At its most general, then, magic can be characterized as the utiliza-tion of art in order to attain specific desired ends, not in order to attain knowledge and understanding per se.[3]

The concrete content of magical science issued from the emphasis in the Hermetic writings on alchemy, geometry, physics, astrology, and medicine set in a mathematical system derived from number mysticism and the cabala. Experimen-tation was central—experiments, it is true, biased toward hoped-for results.

Cornelius Agrippa's *De occulta philosophia* (1533), based on among others Ficino's and Pico della Mirandola's works, can be seen as a practical handbook for this type of magical activity. Agrippa distinguishes among three different types of magic. First, *natural magic,* the manipulation of forces in the world of elements, mostly based on notions about so-called sympathies; here are also included the many magical and illusionist tricks that were eventually to become established as legitimate parlor entertainment.[4] Second, *mathematical magic,* operations performed on the basis of insights into mathematics and its subdivisions (arithmetic, geometry, music, astronomy, and mechanics). Especially interesting in this context is magical mechanics, demonstrated in the art of creating different mechanical marvels and lifelike automatons. Third, *religious magic,* rituals of magic intended to establish contact with inhabitants of supercelestial worlds—that is, spiritism. This magical approach to the cosmos thus contains a combination of practical and theoretical elements, an operative use of number, and an understanding of mechanics as an application of mathematics; here clearly appears one way in which magic can be joined together with the science that was to triumph during the seventeenth century.

To summarize, magic as a scientific activity builds on a defined conception of knowledge—derived from the Hermetic tradition—stressing experiments and rationality in a mathematical sense, together with a visionary utopianism aiming at practical results.

I would like to assert from this starting point that the ambitions of magical science coincided at several points with the science that was to become institutionalized during the seventeenth century, and that it to a certain degree supplied basic ideological elements in the development and establishment of modern science. "The Renaissance magus," Frances Yates says, "was the immediate ancestor of the seventeenth-century scientist."[5]

Among these ideological elements several could be mentioned; for example, utilitarianism, utopianism, and the complex concept of progress. But I will here concentrate on what is the most central point in this context: the concept of institutionalization.

Here the idea can be traced directly back to the Hermetic belief in a select group—the *prisci theologi,* those possessing the highest knowledge. It is reasonable to assume that this belief was eventually combined with the practically gained insight that magical practice pursued by the individual could be regarded as dilettantish, obscure magic for the sake of personal power and gain. Only when incorporated into the activities of the group could it be connected to utopian, humanitarian ambitions beyond individual interests. When Agrippa, in *De occulta philosophia,* developed the theoretical basis and practical operations of magic, he created at the same time the necessary conditions for this magic to be systematized and institutionalized; the idea of secret magic societies seems also to have existed already in sixteenth-century Europe. But it was primarily the Rosicrucian movement that would convey the idea that science could only in an organized and institutionalized form be made a force of change. And such a change was urgently needed at a time when Europe was plagued by wars, epidemics, famine, and misery, and confused by the destruction of Christian unity brought about by the Reformation.

The Rosicrucians—whether existing as an actual society or not—integrated in their program an open view of the world and a rejection of the Church's authority together with a passionate belief in science as the way to progress, thus combining a longing for religious and scientific unity and the demand for a radical reformation of the world. I focus my interest on two main points in their manifestos: first, their emphasis on science as an instrument for the great transformation; and second, that this science must be pursued and propagated through institutionalization.

The definition of science, as presented in the manifestos, issued from Hermeticism and Paracelsianism, and signified by *science* the threefold system magia, cabala, and alchymia combined with mathematics, physics, cosmology, and a medicine that stressed humanitarian ends. The concept of institutionalization was formulated in the idea of an invisible Collegium Magiae, a center for practical experimentation and collective, transnational exchange of experience.

The Rosicrucian manifestos spread throughout Europe with extraordinary speed and effectiveness during the second decade of the seventeenth century. It is evident that the program was actually regarded as the beginning of a worldwide reformation.[6] Its main points are to be found in all the utopians of the time: Johann Valentin Andreä, Johann Amos Comenius, and Francis Bacon. These all stress the main role played by the scientist in the creation of the future realm, even if he is a scientist who gradually shifts from supreme magus to a more mundane type of observer and rationalist; they all emphasize the necessity for a "house of science" from which science shall be directed and carried on in the name of humanity, "for the benefit and use of life," in the words of Bacon.

What happened, then, to this proud dream when science actually became institutionalized with the establishment of the Royal Society? The history of the Society shows that it was conceived from two different directions and two different scientific ideals. On the one hand, there was a practical, technological ideal issuing from those societies which had been built around the great trading companies, stressing practical questions concerning communications, transport, navigational problems, and so forth. On the other hand, there was a more visionary ideal, which through such societies as the Invisible College stemmed directly from the Hermetic vision of a science heading to the deepest mysteries of nature. It is well known that the first outlook came to dominate the activities of the Society during its first period of establishment. But the price that science had to pay for this establishment was high: limited practical application instead of visions of revolutionary results (gold, elixir of life, panacea); gradual and humbly gained knowledge instead of exclusive insight; critical doubt instead of proud hope; and neutrality of values instead of science as a political-utopian means of struggle. It was perhaps this neutralization of values that hit magic hardest. It led to science being harmoniously incorporated into established society, and all normative elements being rejected as unscientific and socially dangerous. At that very moment, politically charged magic was relegated to the background.

With the formation of the Royal Society a new science thus arose, which triumphed through clarity, critical analysis, and the capability of social adjustment; magical science was forced to retreat, banished as obscure and illicit. But it is important to establish that it did not die. And by this I mean, in contrast to Frances Yates, that it lived on not only as a series of impulses within the new science but also as concrete action and program. Expelled, it came to develop radical and contradictory institutional models within the framework of the secret societies, principally Freemasonary. Here the expectations for science could still be kept boundless, a future Paradise could still be assured with the help of science. Throughout the eighteenth century, there was continous magical activity within Freemasonry that maintained the loftiest ambitions in the Hermetic tradition: to guarantee progress, utility, and perfection. These scientific ideals intensified toward the end of the century and appeared for a moment even to triumph over established science. Interestingly enough this tendency was especially noticeable in those political milieus which seethed with a desire for social change. Here the expectations for science increased in consequence. The border line with magic became more and more blurred, and the political and scientific ambitions fused in an atmosphere of change, transformation and unlimited possibilities. The Rosicrucian vision seemed once again to apply at all points. As examples of such a development, I shall consider Sweden and France.

But first, something about Freemasonry. To trace its roots is complicated.[7] One must first of all distinguish between its legendary and its actual history. According to legend, Freemasonry goes back to Solomon and Hiram's building of the temple in Jerusalem—the wonderful secret that Adam had inherited from God himself lay enclosed in the architecture or geometry of the temple. "Adam, our first parent, created after the Image of God, the great Architect of the Universe, must have had the Liberal Sciences, particularly Geometry, written on his Heart."[8] The legend was thereby tied to Hebraic and Egyptian antiquity and fused with the Hermetic notion of the *prisci theologi*. The connection of Freemasonry with the Rosicrucian movement is evident: Both are characterized by a deeper striving for knowledge combined with a programmatic humanitarianism and the dream of a worldwide reformation.[9]

Freemasonry appeared as an organized institution at the beginning of the seventeenth century in England, Germany, and France. During its first period, it sems to have led a rather withdrawn existence but blossomed in the second part of the eighteenth century with intense activities, then in the strangely dual position of both secret society and established social institution. At the same time, a border line became clearly perceptible between two types of Freemasonry, differing both in recruitment and in ambitions. On the one hand, there was a bourgeois Freemasonry with philanthropy and pedagogical reforms as its main programs, described both as a bourgeois attempt to hold its own against the aristocratic salons, through fixed ritual patterns of social intercourse, and as ideological cells of propaganda for enlightenment. The history of the German *Illuminatenorden* shows that this type of Freemasonry could appear socially dangerous indeed.[10]

But on the other hand, there was another type, which was mixed with medieval chivalrous romanticism and tied directly to the Hermetic-Rosicrucian tradition. Toward the end of the century, a new set of rituals or grades, the Rose Cross grades, was introduced in France and Germany, where the innermost knowledge of nature's mysteries was said to be handed down through historic succession. Here the experimental elements of Hermeticism in the form of magical activities lived on.

This so-called high-grade Freemasonry is interesting because of its mainly aristocratic makeup—it is evident that it channeled political opposition against either bourgeois or monarchist camps. Here the aristocracy could find its time-honored claims to privilege legitimized through the conception that it alone possessed the key to nature's secrets, to progress, and to world reformation. Here resided the notion of a select group that by virtue of deeper insight had the power to manipulate nature's most fundamental forces and thereby power to transform totally the conditions of human life. That such goals could lead far beyond the boundary of scientific activity in any sense is clear from the German *Gold- und Rosenkreuzorden,* of interest since it counted remarkably many scientists among its members.[11] Calling themselves Rosicrucians, the members of this society still stressed science as the transformative weapon, but—and this must be underlined—by stressing at the same time secrecy together with claims to supernatural powers, they were moving very far from the original Rosicrucian ambitions. To quote their secret *Kontitution der Magie:* "Wir besitzen die wahre göttliche Magie . . . Wir besitzen die zwei Hauptwissenschaften Jehovahs: Das ist die Gebährung und die Zerstörung aller natürlichen Dinge. Wir können wie Josuah ganze Städte durch den Schall der Instrumente in Schutt verwandeln. Wir können der Sonne, dem Mond und den Sternen und den Winden gebieten, wir können wie die Propheten die Sterne verwandeln und an verschiedene Orte versetzen."[12]

Sweden provides a good example of this form of high-grade Freemansonry, where magical activities of a profoundly secret character were central. Freemasonry reached Sweden during the 1730s, but it was not until the 1780s—and associated with the political aims of the aristocracy—that a branch with a pronounced Hermetic direction developed. Here political ambitions blended with magical experiments of a very spectacular kind.[13]

Partly, these activities proceeded from the more undisguised forms of alchemy, mesmerism, divination, and spiritism that were being carried on at the same time in Sweden. These were mainly tied to bourgeois groups centered around Swedenborgianism and not without utopian revolutionary features. But it was only within Freemasonry, with its aristocratic composition, that the magical activities received the dignity of a higher kind of science, aiming at the recreation of a Paradise on earth, but still restricted to the select few—the wise.

The experiments performed were all in the outlying areas of science and consciously strove to transcend established borders. But in the knowledge of alchemy, physics, astrology, and medicine promised in the initiation rites were incorporated scientific discoveries that could be molded into an effective experimental form. Simpler chemical and physical experiments, performed in separate sanctuaries where the atmosphere was heightened with smoke and flickering candlelight, appeared as important interventions into nature. Medical drugs based on ancient magic recipes were prepared in a ritual manner; alchemical experiments were performed around speculations on the *prima materia,* and around the old dreams of gold, elixirs, and cure-alls. Animal magnetism was taken as the starting point for a special series of experiments that were said to show "a supernatural degree of physics, what we used to call magic."[14]

Experiments taken from the new sciences, spectacular pseudosciences, and old magical traditions were thus merged in a complicated manner, where the boundary between magic and science became more and more indistinct. Without a doubt, the Freemasons themselves regarded their experiments as precisely scientific, separated from magic in the "black" sense: They built more on insight than on sorcery, and reason and observation were the instruments directing the extraction of nature's mysteries. A series of statements by the leaders of Freemasonry can be adduced in this context; thus it was asserted that "the sciences of hidden natural knowledge are at least as exact as the empirical sciences."[15] The image was built up methodically of a select group involved in scientific activities that ultimately aimed toward a total transformation of society. Against this background it is hardly unexpected that the magical activities ceased at the same moment that the aristocracy's political hopes were dashed in connection with the Swedish Diet of 1789. Freemasonry's function as a stronghold for political conspiracy was no longer relevant; the innermost secrets were made public; the previously mysterious experiments were made shallow parlor entertainment.

France during the years before the Revolution presents another example of the complex relationship among magic, science, and utopianism tied to the secret societies. Robert Darnton has, in a most interesting study of mesmerism, analyzed the scientific climate in prerevolutionary France and shown how the heated political atmosphere was combined with an almost apocalyptic faith in the possibilities of science.[16] It was a time when everything seemed possible. Benjamin Franklin demonstrated in a grand manner atmospheric electricity; Mesmer introduced the sensational animal magnetism; Lavoisier was still fighting to refute the enigmatic phlogiston—everything seemed to be a question of miraculous forces, elements, and forms of energy that man had discovered and decoded by virtue of his reason. The belief in science intensified more and more; the experiments arranged by the scientific academies grew to become popular entertainment; and amateur science became a fashion. To quote a contemporary reporter, "Everywhere—in parlors, at evening suppers, even in the ladies' room—do people speak of nothing else but experiments."[17] Particularly around experimental physics and chemistry, a whole genre of science as entertainment developed with special encyclopedias, manuals for do-it-yourself experiments, and academies that devoted themselves to science solely as entertainment and game.[18] At the same time, enthusiasm for the technical applications of science increased. The first balloon flights over Paris and Nantes attracted tens of thousands of spectators, and the balloon travelers were honored as heroes of science. The press launched one sensational invention after the other: shoes to walk on water with, eyeglasses for use in the dark, and so on. Man had learned to conquer the air, why not water or darkness as well? Or as the author of an article in the *Journal de Bruxelles* put it: "Who knows how far we can go? What mortal dare set limits to the human mind?"[19]

The Hermetic, magical view of science is evident here. Magic strove to transcend the laws of nature, science to decode them, but also to accept subordination to them. Pride stood in contrast to humility. In France during the 1780s the concepts of transformation and transcendency were once again in the center. Scientific pride emerges once again, striving to demonstrate that the borders between what is natural and what is supernatural, what is possible and what is impossible, can continually be shifted.

This feverish belief in science could be channeled in several different ways. First, it could be incorporated into established science within the framework of the academies and used as an effective means of propaganda for science. But this was hardly what happened. The Academie des sciences and many scientific commissions of inquiry came to appear more as prestigious social institutions, anxiously guarding authority and already secured results, than as bold instruments in the service of human progress. Perhaps this was not so strange. Charles Gillispie has pointed out that hostility toward all that can be labeled charlatanism expresses a collective feeling of professional identity; it creates an opportunity for scientists to gather around fixed values and can be used as a weapon in order to further strengthen the group's own professionalism.[20]

Second, it could indeed be turned into charlatanism and pseudoscience. The market for charlatans in France during the 1780s was splendid; the most sensational discoveries and inventions were announced, given prominence by the press, and enthusiastically received by the public, but the results were in general to be seen only in the innovator's own purse. The traditional tricks of natural and mathematical magic, however, were also transformed into fully legitimate parlor entertainment. Here, too, a market was created in the form of traveling showmen and lucrative publications of practical handbooks in magic, mostly translations of sixteenth-century originals—and who did not want to be entertained by mechanical marvels, to be tickled by the startling effects of illusionism?[21]

Third, this belief in science could be channeled within the secret societies and Freemasonry, where established scientific criteria could be left behind and where the very essence lay in a transcending view of science. At this time and within the framework of mystical Freemasonry, the concept of *haute science* was created to denote the chemical, physical, and medical activity which, raised above academic trivialities, strove to penetrate nature's most fundamental mechanisms. It is clear that the border separating magic and science did not exist in this context. Magic was in general considered to be the natural extension of science, a science freed from faith in authority and rigid rules, fueled only by the dream of the perfectibility of knowledge. "Above science is magic, because magic follows it, not as an effect, but its perfection."[22]

But this form of science must be carried on in organized groups as well, that is to say, in the academy or the order. The fact that France teemed with secret societies during the years before the Revolution is quite fascinating. Many of these societies concerned themselves with scientific activities more or less directly tied to political demands for reform. Sometimes science was more a veil than the principal purpose. As was said in one of the society programs, "It is necessary to unite men under the pretext of experiments in physics, but in reality, for the overthrow of despotism."[23]

In this context, mesmerism is a good example. Expelled by academic science, it retired into Freemasonry under the name of the Ordre de l'harmonie universelle. Here it was tied directly to the utilitarian and humanitarian program of the Rosicrucian movement. The members of the order claimed to recreate the immediate contact between science and its practical application, which academic science had failed to do, and in contrast to the academies' inflated but empty goals, to represent the true interests of mankind—indeed a marketable theme in prerevolutionary France![24] At the same time, their activities were stressed as being precisely scientific. In the secret manifesto of the order the elements of magic and the cabala are presented typically side by side with the definition of the order's main purpose: to activate reason and to study nature on a scientific basis—a goal that might have been formulated by any scientific academy.[25]

Set within the mysticism of the orders, natural science returned to the scheme of magic-science-utopianism that originated from the Hermetic tradition. Here, the proudest dreams of science hibernated. Here, too, the institutionalized forms for a science in the service of progress and social transformation, which had been drawn up by the Rosicrucians, were propagated. A comparison between the structural and the ideological forms of the secret societies and the scientific academies displays striking similarities. They are exemplified by their organization, with classes, ranks, and set meetings according to ritual schemes; likewise by their closeness of principle and their claims for control of definitions and methodologies in their own sciences. Did the mysticism that had been rejected by the academic institutions strive to assert itself with the same academic language or did it propagate patterns that had been its own all the time? Obviously, a complex relationship prevailed here. Thus, for example, the awareness of the status that academic honors gave a scientific activity was one element that the secret societies took over from the academies. The expelled science must acquire its own, better, less prejudicial courts where it could choose and reward its own heroes. This was a theme also emphasized by such a scientific outsider as Jean-Paul Marat.[26]

In the extensive literature on Freemasonry, there has been a tendency to indicate a sharp boundary between a bourgeois, humanitarian Freemasonry and an occult, spectacular one; the former is consistent with such concepts as enlightenment and radical pedagogical and political demands for reform, the latter with regressiveness in both the political and the scientific sense.[27] I do not agree with this categorization. The scientific activity that was carried out in the secret societies was—in spite of secrecy and elitism—progressively directed and deeply attached to the idea of a radical transformation of society. Clearly, it is not by chance that the magical activities of Freemasonry accelerated during the years just before the French Revolution in such countries as France, Germany, and Sweden. Time and time again, it was asserted that science must serve human progress, was and must be a means of struggle. These were the same demands that had been made in the Rosicrucian manifestos. Magical science, imbued with alchemical symbols and the concept of transmutation, once again powerfully expressed the dream of transformation, not only of matter, but of man, society, the world, and ultimately the dream of a Paradise regained on earth. Along these lines, magic in a very fundamental way could be united with the visions of freedom of the Enlightenment and of later revolutionary ideologies.

Let me summarize. The philosophy and the sociology of science show that the development of modern science has proceeded through the processes of institutionalization, visible and invisible. In this context, the important role played by the secret societies has landed in the background. During the seventeenth and eighteenth centuries, it was repeatedly emphasized that science must be carried on and directed from a defined, institutional platform. These demands were made for the first time in the Rosicrucian manifestos, and at that time they were political demands.

My intention has been, first of all, to show that magic is not regressive, but rather progressive; not in a quantitative and accumulative sense, but in a qualitative sense, when judged by its own presumptions and always stressing science as a force of change.[28] Second, that magic is built on values and the conviction that science can never be disconnected from certain purposes—an important reminder in a time when the possibility of an objective, value-free science is more and more being questioned. Third, that magic as expelled science on the one hand strives to accept the forms of established science, but on the other hand to break these forms up, presenting them as bound to convention.

The relation between magic and science must thus be seen as reciprocal. Basic ideological elements—that science must be carried out collectively, communicated transnationally, and connected to utilitarian purposes—were indeed of crucial importance in the magic tradition of the seventeenth and eighteenth centuries. Perhaps we are not so remote from the visions of the old magus as we tend to believe.

Notes

1. Frances Yates, *Giordano Bruno and the Hermetic Tradition* (London, 1964); idem, *The Rosicrucian Enlightenment* (1972; reprint, Saint Albans, 1975); idem, "The Hermetic Tradition in Renaissance Science," in *Art, Science and History in the Renaissance,* ed. C. S. Singleton (Baltimore, 1968); Paolo Rossi, *Francis Bacon: From Magic to Science* (1957; reprint, London, 1968); M. L. Righini Bonelli and W. R. Shea, eds., *Reason, Experiment and Mysticism in the scientific Revolution* (London, 1975); also C. Webster, *The Great Instauration: Science, Medicine and Reform, 1626–1660* (London, 1975).

2. *Fama fraternitatis* (Ger. original); *Confessio fraternitatis* (Lat. original; Ger. trans.), in M. W. Fischer, *Die Aufklärung und ihr Gegenteil: Die Rolle der Geheimbünde in Wissenschaft und Politik* (Berlin, 1982); Eng. trans. in Yates, *Rosicrucian Enlightenment,* pp. 279–306.

3. The classical study on magic and science up to 1700 is L. Thorndike's comprehensive *History of Magic and Experimental Science,* 8 vols. (New York, 1923–58). Renaissance magic is treated in D. P. Walker, *Spiritual and Demonic Magic: From Ficino to Campanella* (London, 1958). See also Keith Thomas, *Religion and the Decline of Magic* (New York, 1971). A useful short introduction is B. Hansen, "Science and Magic," in *Science in the Middle Ages,* ed. D. C. Lindberg (London, 1978).

4. Cf. below, p. 257.

5. Yates, "Hermetic Tradition," p. 258.

6. Fischer, *Die Aufklärung und ihr Gegenteil,* pp. 54 ff., 82 ff.; Yates, *Rosicrucian Enlightenment,* pp. 126–54.

7. Generally on the secret societies see K. R. H. Frick, *Die Erleuchteten.* Volume 1, *Gnostisch-teosophische und alchemistisch-rosenkreuzerische Geheimgesellschaften bis zum Ende des 18. Jahrhunderts;* volume 2, *Licht und Finsternis: Gnostisch-teosophische und freimaurerisch-okkulte Geheimgesellschaften bis an die Wende zum 20. Jahruhundert* (Graz, 1973–78); P. C. Ludz, ed., *Geheime Gesellschaften* (Heidelberg, 1979); C. W. Heckethorn, *The Secret Societies of All Ages and Countries,* 2 vols. (New York, 1965). The literature on Freemasonry is vast; a useful guide is E. Lennhoff and O. Posner, *Internationales Freimaurer-Lexikon* (1932; reprint, Vienna, 1975).

8. Quoted in Yates, *Rosicrucian Enlightenment,* p. 256.

9. Fischer, *Die Aufklärung und ihr Gegenteil,* pp. 95 ff; Yates, *Rosicrucian Enlightenment,* pp. 249–63.

10. See R. von Dülmen, *Der Geheimbund der Illuminaten* (Stuttgart, 1975); N. Schindler, "Aufklärung und Geheimnis im Illuminatenorden," and E. O. Fehn, "Zur Wiederentdeckung des Illuminatenordens," in *Geheime Gesellschaften;* Fischer, *Die Aufklärung und ihr Gegenteil,* pp. 213 ff.

11. See A. Marx, *Die Gold- und Rosenkreuzer: Ein Mysterienbund des ausgehenden 18. Jahrhun-*

derts in Deutschland (Zeulenroda, 1930); H. Möller, "Die Gold- und Rosenkreuzer," in *Geheime Gesellschaften;* Fischer, *Die Aufklärung und ihr Gegenteil,* pp. 242ff.

12. Quoted in Marx, *Die Gold- und Rosenkreuzer,* p. 106.

13. Karin Johannisson, *Magnetisörernas tid: Den animala magnetismen i Sverige,* with an English summary, *Mesmerism in Sweden* (Uppsala, 1974), pp. 102–10; idem, "Naturvetenskap pá reträtt: En diskussion om naturvetenskapens status under svenskt 1700-tal" (with an English summary, "Natural Science in Retreat: A Discussion on the Status of Science in Sweden during the Eighteenth Century"), *Lychnos* (1979/80): 143–53.

14. Quoted in Johannisson, *Magnetisörernas tid,* p. 103.

15. Martin Lamm, *Johan Gabriel Oxenstierna* (Stockholm, 1911), p. 265.

16. R. Darnton, *Mesmerism and the End of the Enlightenment in France* (Cambridge, Mass., 1968).

17. Quoted in Darnton, *Mesmerism,* p. 24.

18. See, e.g., *Dictionnaire encyclopédique des amusements des sciences mathematiques et physiques* (Paris, 1792).

19. *Journal de Bruxelles,* 29 May 1784, pp. 226–27, as quoted in Darnton, *Mesmerism,* p. 23.

20. Charles C. Gillispie, *Science and Polity in France at the End of the Old Regime* (Princeton, 1980), p. 257.

21. See, e.g., H. Decremps, *La magie blanche devoilé* (Paris, 1784).

22. Quoted in Darnton, *Mesmerism,* p. 38.

23. Ibid., p. 79.

24. F. A. Mesmer, *Le magnétisme animal: Oeuvres publiées par R. Amadou* (Paris, 1971), pp. 110–15.

25. Ibid., p. 377.

26. Gillispie, *Science and Polity,* p. 307.

27. Cf. Fischer, *Die Aufklärung und ihr Gegenteil,* pp. 132ff., 213ff.

28. By the distinction between a quantitative and a qualitative kind of progress I am quoting Paul Feyerabend, "Progress and Reality in the Arts and in the Sciences," in *Progress in Science and Its Social Conditions,* Proceedings of a Nobel Symposium, ed. Tord Ganelius (Oxford, 1986).

PART 3
Literature and Art

13

On the Function of Analogy in the Occult

BRIAN VICKERS

There are sufficient internal resemblances among astrology, alchemy, numerology, iatromathematics, and natural magic for one to be able to describe the occult sciences as forming a unified system. They all invoke a distinction between the visible and invisible worlds; they all depend on the designation of symbols relating to this dichotomy; they all make great use of analogies, correspondences, and relations among apparently discrete elements in man and the universe. As a system the occult sciences were imported into Greece from various oriental cultures, and were systematically codified in the Hellenistic period, following the death of Alexander in 323 B.C. Once codified they retained their essential assumptions and methodology through the Middle Ages, into the Renaissance, and beyond—indeed, one of the most remarkable features of the occult tradition is its static nature, its resistance to change.[1] If I may designate, for purposes of simple contrast, an experimental scientific tradition, then a study of scientists at various points along it—for instance, the Ptolemy of the *Almagest,* Archimedes, Robert Grosseteste, Bradwardine, Galileo, Boyle—will reveal a wide range of methods, assumptions, and goals. But if one juxtaposes the Ptolemy of the *Tetrabiblos* with Cornelius Agrippa, or Hildegard of Bingen with Robert Fludd, or the Arabic Brethren of Sincerity with Athanasius Kircher, one finds a fundamental homogeneity and continuity.

As a unified tradition the occult showed a remarkable ability to absorb many diverse traditions of thought. The Hellenistic period itself was, of course, marked by a striking proliferation of thought systems, as in such figures as Philo, who harmonized Greek philosophy and Hebrew religion, or in such schools as Neoplatonism, which reconciled Aristotle, Plato, and much else. Alexandria, the most fertile meetingpoint for Eastern and Western traditions, also saw the rise of neo-Pythagoreanism, with its important influence on numerology, astrology, alchemy, and medicine. "By as early as 300 or 400 A.D., alchemy had become 'a bewildering confusion of Egyptian magic, Greek philosophy, Gnosticism, Neo-Platonism,

Babylonian astrology, Christian theology and pagan mythology.' "[2] When the occult sciences were rediscovered in the Middle Ages, as again in the Renaissance, still more schools of thought were integrated with them, so that in studying the most prolific syncretists of the period—Ficino, Agrippa, Fludd, and Kircher—one is confronted with a tradition in which nothing has been abandoned, all ideas have been absorbed into ever more comprehensive syntheses.[3] It is no accident that the period in which the occult sciences were finally discredited—the seventeenth century—saw the emergence of autonomous, nonsyncretist systems; scientists were no longer content to amalgamate two thousand years of written tradition.

The mental habits of the occult sciences, especially the use of analogies and correspondences, help to give them their internal consistency. Yet these habits are not exclusive to the occult, being found in ancient Greece, China, Africa, and in many other mainstream cultures.[4] What is unusual is that in the Western occult tradition these thought patterns became the basis of sciences that professed to interpret, control, and even transform reality. Yet, instead of deriving their methods from the physical world by processes of observation, experiment, quantification, theory, and so forth, the occult imposed traditional thought categories onto the world and "read" nature in the light of them. Obviously some of the occult sciences—alchemy and astrology, for example—made a partial use of observational techniques, but the results were then subordinated to some preformed interpretative model, often magical or mystical, which was neither derived from reality nor testable by it.

1

In evaluating the role and function of analogy in the occult, I will attempt to define occult methodology overall, a topic that has not been much discussed. In brief, I shall argue that the occult sciences evolved a self-contained system in which one can distinguish a triple process of attribution, distribution, and assimilation. Many of the basic operations of occult science take the form of grading reality in terms of a limited number of categories, and then maneuvring or interrelating these categories. These are mental categories, self-generated to create a system, not derived by observation from reality. Occult science first constitutes a matrix, then assimilates experience to this matrix. I shall try to separate these processes for clarity of definition, but in practice they often occur simultaneously.

By *attribution* I mean the ascribing of a symbolic or metaphysical dimension to such things as inanimate objects, numbers, or planets. This "descriptive symbolism," as it has been called,[5] is usually anthropomorphic or animistic, and reproduces human categories that are themselves hierarchical and evaluative, social and ethical. Here again one is dealing with recurring constants in human thought—animism, for instance—deriving from such impeccable authorities as Plato in the *Timaeus* (35A, 36D–E), who described the universe as being composed of a world soul and a world body, or Aristotle, in *De caelo* who ascribed "life, and action like that of plants and animals, to stars," and conceived of the earth's interior as "growing and decaying like the body of a plant or animal."[6] Such ideas were extremely widely diffused, especially through Neoplatonism: "Both Ficino and Agrippa write . . . as though nothing in the entire universe lacked soul";[7] and in Diacceto, a disciple of Ficino, one finds a fully concrete version, with "the world as one animal, whose soul, by means of the stars, imprints forms on the sub-lunar world."[8]

D. P. Walker, in his valuable "General Theory of Natural Magic,"[9] outlines the belief in "planetary influences" on man using a model of intermediate stages, through the *vis imaginativa* down through four categories:

VIS IMAGINATIVA

Vis Imaginum	*Vis Verborum*	*Vis Musices*	*Vis Rerum*
A. Meaning & Beauty (visual Arts)	A. Meaning & Beauty (oratory, poetry)	A. Meaning & Beauty (music & song)	A. Elemental Qualities
B. Figures & Characters (talismans, etc.)	B. Words as Essences of Things (incantations)	B. Proportion & Number (Harmony of spheres; sympathetic magic)	B. Occult Qualities

In each category he distinguishes two levels: A, the primary, natural level of operation; and B, which represents the superadded symbolic or metaphysical dimension, and in which is found the characteristic preoccupations of the occult sciences. Whereas the experimental scientist deals directly with nature in both theoretical and practical terms, the occult scientist lays more stress on the manipulation of preformed categories—such as letters, numbers, and symbols—to produce significant combinations. Walker's subsequent analysis shows very clearly how the proponents of the occult depended on the attributed symbolic level, while their opponents denied its existence or reality.

The same process of symbolic attribution can be seen very clearly in arithmology, or numerology, where certain numbers had metaphysical qualities assigned to them. The monad symbolized creative unity; the dyad, doubleness and discord; three meant unity or perfection; four symbolized justice; six, perfection; seven, opportunity, isolation, virginity, expiation and sacrifice, or trial and punishment.[10]

The amount of variation and contradiction in the numerological tradition is symptomatic of the personal, subjective, and arbitrary nature of symbolism in general.[11] True, some of the symbols did become widely accepted, but others vacillated constantly, such as alchemical symbols, which themselves had something of the quality of mercury.[12]

The other main category used in this initial process of attribution is hierarchical or evaluative, expressing a preference of the almost universal kind in traditional societies, putting right above left, male above female, odd above even, and so on. Whereas the experimental sciences evolved, in the course of the sixteenth century, a series of neutral categories—space, mass, time, and velocity—a process well analyzed by E. A. Burtt,[13] categories that are no longer anthropomorphic, where bigger is merely bigger, not better, where the "slowness" of a planet is not a sign of age or lethargy, the occult tradition has always stuck to evaluative or hierarchical categories. In numerology, odd numbers are male, and better; even are female and worse. The perfect shape is a sphere; all other shapes are imperfect. Even triangles can be classified, some being superior, others inferior. Planets are good or evil; the universe has a right and a left side. In various systems all the superior categories could be interequated, so that even = female = left-handed = evil or inferior.[14] In other words, the symbolism is at the service of a constant classification of reality on scales running from better to worse, good to evil. Nothing is neutral.

After—sometimes together with—attribution comes the second stage that I distinguish in the occult methodology, that of *distribution,* in which larger, self-contained categories are established; and the third stage, of *assimilation,* in which categories are linked or correlated with one another. Such a correlation depends, in theory at least, on the existence of a common property, a similarity of class or an identity of medium. In the macrocosm/microcosm analogy, man is related to the universe by some common elements, as in the early parallel made by Anaximenes: "Just as our soul which is air holds us together, so it is breath and air that encompasses the whole world."[15]

For Hermes Trismegistus, "what is below is like that which is above" and vice versa.[16] For Plotinus, "the parts of the universe are sympathetic, like the parts of a living being"; to Proclus, "man is a microcosm, and all the things which the world contains are . . . contained partially in him"; to Paracelsus "man contains everything found in either sidereal or elemental regions," indeed "man contains more than a thousand species of minerals, manna, and metals, and has the qualities of all animals"; to Pico della Mirandola, "celestial or even earthly names are often given to divine things," and vice versa, for, "bound by the chains of concord, all these worlds exchange natures as well as names with mutual liberality."[17]

The discovery of the identical "principle of order" running through creation, which Rudolf Allers saw as fundamental to microcosm theories,[18] often moved from a distribution of parts to their reconnection through an intermediate, such as the intelligences in Neoplatonism, "spiritual beings intermediate between God and men," or for Ficino "the rays of a star associated with a co-operating daemon."[19] For Ficino, the stars' rays "confer astral qualities" on the *spiritus mundanus,* which transmits them to the *spiritus humanus,* into body and soul. "These now in their turn—according to the principle of structural 'concinnitas' which was the central tenet not only of primitive magic but also of any cosmology based on something other than mechanical causality—were determined by astral qualities," to which body and soul either already corresponded or had attuned themselves.[20] The movement exists in two directions along the path emanating from the matrix.

The process of analogy also depended on similarity or identity at less abstract, more easily graspable levels, notably that of categories containing the same number of items. In numerology, astrology, alchemy, and all occult sciences, it is an unquestioned principle that any category of four can be related to any other category of four; any seven to any other seven. In the famous *Encyclopaedia* produced by the Arabic Brethren of Sincerity (ca. A.D. 950), the seven planets correspond to seven creative powers, seven spiritual powers (the five senses, together with thinking and reasoning), the seven bodily organs, the seven bodily orifices, the seven geographical regions on earth, the seven races inhabiting those regions, the seven classes of angels, the seven months in the life of a human embryo, the seven periods of man's life, the seven human characteristics, and the seven colors.[21] This technique might be called the principle of equipollence; as a principle it is never questioned. Any set containing the same number of items must have a significant relationship with any other matching set.

Although such correlations of number categories always look impressively scientific and systematic—Cornelius Agrippa fills pages of his *De occulta philosophia* with them—as instruments for scientific exploration or discovery they have several failings. They are in fact extremely plastic; the categories could be abridged or expanded at will, juggled to produce the desired numbers. Their fixed nature, once established, could limit developments. Alchemists impressed by the correspondence between the seven planets and the seven metals refused to recognize further metals when these were identified. Similarly, in the *cabala*, the "relations between successive emanations" are "expressed by means of the relations between numbers, in a decimal notation," with the result that "the world can consist of only nine stages."[22] And since these categories derive from a system of hierarchies and evaluations, involving symbols and other arbitrary ascriptions, they, too, can be arbitrary. To take a familiar example, the planet-god Saturn originally received a very negative series of associations due to the time it took to complete its revolution. It was called slow, heavy, leadenish, cold, and aged. When the seven ages of man were correlated with the seven planets, Saturn "was allotted the last and saddest phase of human existence."[23] Yet, when the Neoplatonists identified Saturn with Cronus, symbolized him as intellect or nous, he became a newly positive figure. In the Gnostic world journeys correlation of the seven planets with human failings (which, as Morton Bloomfield has shown, provided the basis for the classification of the seven deadly sins), Saturn signified lethargy; in the Neoplatonist system (as in Macrobius), he now represents "reasoned thought and understanding."[24] It is due to this dual inheritance that Saturn in the Renaissance could symbolize slowness and stupidity to some, but intelligence and contemplation to others. The point I wish to underline is that within the apparently fixed and complete grid, positions or attributes could be freely interchanged.

The third stage (assimilation) raises the major problem with correspondences— that is, their mode of existence in the horizontal plane. I would like to distinguish here between primary or formative assimilation (the establishing of a dominant matrix) and secondary or duplicatory assimilation (the linking up of matrices). As an example of the first, I take one of the most influential books in the history of the occult sciences, Ptolemy's *Tetrabiblos,* the four books expounding astrology.[25] As Bouché-Leclercq showed in a classic study,[26] Ptolemy, writing in a period when astrology was almost universally accepted, devoted much care to censoring the astrological tradition, removing many bizarre and extravagant points. Yet his own system, although more coherent and less fanciful than his predecessors, is shot through with the habits of hierarchical, analogical thinking, and a priori category formation, that characterize occult science. Ptolemy begins with the Aristotelian principles of hot, cold, wet, and dry, classifying the planets by a combination of two qualities—the sun is hot and dry, the moon hot and moist, and so on—an arbitrary but seemingly neutral classification (1.4). Yet these combinations are used to establish a hierarchical, anthropomorphic category, in that qualities of good or evil are then ascribed to the planets. Since the hot and the moist are fertile and active, the dry and the cold destructive and passive, then the moon, Jupiter, and Venus are said to be beneficent; Saturn and Mars maleficent; while the sun and Mercury (being hot and dry) share both powers of creation and destruction (1.5). This type of binary classification into good and evil is repeated in his next chapter, where the planets to whom the moist quality has been ascribed are said to be feminine, the dry are masculine, and Mercury is "common to both genders" (1.6). The sun, it is noted, has been removed from the company of Mercury, and Jupiter—although moist—has been segregated from the feminine planets because masculinity had been given to him by his initial personification. In other words, the factors governing these classifications are sexual and social, reproducing the common Greek belief of the superiority of the male. That is shown in his further dichotomy, according to the planets' aspects to the sun: "When they are morning stars and precede the sun they become masculine, and feminine when they are evening stars and follow the sun" (1.6; Loeb ed., p. 41). The woman walks behind the man, we may infer, because she is inferior.

The male/female dichotomy is one of the basic blocks used in building Ptolemy's astrology. When in the eastern quadrant, stars are masculine; when in the western, feminine (1.6). Masculine stars are associated with the day, because of its "heat and active force"; feminine with the night, "because of its moisture and its gift of rest" (1.7; Loeb ed., p. 43). As he comes to a new topic Ptolemy classifies it according to the categories already established. The result is systematic and coherent, but it has the paradoxical attributes of what one might call an expanding closed system. New elements are allowed in but are formed to the existing matrix, the system builder not questioning or revising the original model, or relating it to observable reality. I shall call this process *assimilation,* in the sense used by C. R. Hallpike.[27] When Ptolemy discusses the zodiacal and other fixed stars, this category—call it *Y*—is interpreted in terms of the prior category, *X,* the planets. Beginning with Aries, Ptolemy assigns to the stars in each part of the zodiacal figure qualities that they derive from the various planets. Those in the head of Aries have an effect like the power of Mars and Saturn; those in the mouth have an effect like Mercury and Saturn; the hind foot corresponds to Mars; the tail to Venus (1.9). Category *Y* is correlated with, or fitted to, category *X.* The process is one of attribution and distribution. If one takes the Aristotelian qualities, again, they can be correlated with the four seasons. Spring exceeds in moisture, summer in heat, autumn in dryness, winter in cold. Here is a neat example of category fit, four to four. But when it comes to relating that correlation to the zodiac, which is a circular or cyclic system for the year's progress, Ptolemy is aware that the correlation made by his predecessors was arbitrary, a matter of choice.

For this reason, although there is no natural beginning of the zodiac, since it is a circle, they assume that the sign which begins with the vernal equinox, that of Aries, is the starting-point of them all, making the excessive moisture of the spring the first part of the zodiac as though it were a living creature, and taking next in order the remaining seasons, because in all creatures the earliest ages, like the spring, have a larger share of moisture and are tender and still delicate. (1.10; Loeb ed., p. 61)

Ptolemy goes on to enumerate the four ages of man, correlating them with the four qualities and the four seasons, then using the matrix of four to classify the winds that blow from the cardinal points: east is dry, south is hot, west is moist, north is cold. As his editor points out, Ptolemy here follows in the tradition of the Pythagorizing arithmologists, as he will do again when he correlates the seven planets with—now, of course—the *seven* ages of man (4.10). One reason that numerology is found in all the occult sciences is that it is the system par excellence of correlating preformed categories.

In the remainder of book 1, Ptolemy assimilates the B category (the zodiac) to the A category (the planets), first in terms of gender, a relatively easy operation, since twelve divides equally into six of each sex. But not into two groups of six: "An alternating order was assigned to them because day is always yoked to night and close to it, and female to male." Equally anthropomorphic and hierarchical is the reason for starting from Aries: "As the male likewise rules and holds first place, since also the active is always superior to the passive in power, the signs of Aries and Libra were thought to be masculine and diurnal" (1.12; Loeb ed., p. 69). The social and sexual attitudes so prominent in Greek thought govern the division of the "aspects" of the signs into familiar and opposed, with harmony being ascribed to affinity between signs of the same sex, and opposition or discord to those of different sex (1.13; Loeb ed., p. 75). The planets' houses, too, are connected to the zodiac by a sequence of distribution, correlating Leo (masculine) with the sun, and Cancer (feminine) with the moon, thus allowing the remaining five planets to be fitted to the ten zodiacal signs (1.18). If a certain amount of number juggling was necessary there, the designaton of triangles is easier, the twelve zodiacal signs neatly yielding four groups of three, correlated with the four points of the compass, a distribution into equilateral triangles that has the added virtue to the neo-Pythagorean "inasmuch as the triangular and equilateral form is most harmonious with itself" (1.18: Loeb ed., p. 83).

The system of classification used in the first of Ptolemy's four books is hierarchical, using categories of superior and inferior (male/female, east/west), and assimilative, classifying new elements in terms of the original matrix. Ptolemy, who is highy conscious of this process of classification or "tabular exposition"[28] moves on, in book 2, to consider national and climatic characteristics in terms of the astrological system so far established, assimilating the new category C to categories A and B. That this is a self-contained system, an autoperpetuating classification process, is revealed by the fact that—as Franz Boll first pointed out[29]—in order to retain internal coherence Ptolemy follows the astrology of Posidonius and diverges in many details from the system developed in his own *Geography*. The result is an "astrological ethnography" that includes some empirical observation (those who live at the equator "have black skins and thick, woolly hair" [Loeb ed., p. 123]), but is in the main another instance of assimilation. Instead of deriving observation from nature, a mental set or matrix is applied to nature and yields data in terms of that construct. Attributes are assigned to inhabitants of various parts of the world, not by observation but by extension of the extant hierarchical categories. Inhabitants of the region between the summer tropic and the Bears may be divided into dwellers in the west and those in the east:

> Of them . . . the eastern group are more masculine, vigorous of soul, and frank in all things, because one would reasonably assume that the orient partakes of the nature of the sun [which is masculine]. This region therefore is diurnal, masculine, and right-handed, even as we observe that among the animals too their right-hand parts are better fitted for strength and vigour.
>
> Those to the west are more feminine, softer of soul, and secretive, because this region, again, is lunar, for it is always in the west that the moon emerges and makes its appearance after conjunction. For this reason it appears to be a nocturnal clime, and, in contrast with the orient, left-handed. (2.2; Loeb ed., pp. 125–27)

Armchair anthropology used to be a term of scorn used by field-workers for those of their colleagues who stayed at home and theorized without visiting primitive tribes. This may be called armchair geography, since to describe the inhabitants of the world it is not necessary to leave one's room; all that is needed is a scheme. The result here is wholly theoretical—*abstract,* one might be tempted to say, were it not for the concrete details of right-handedness being ascribed to males *and* animals.

The system is ethnocentric and anthropocentric, and its slightly comic application to the animal world reveals the astrologer's transparent unawareness of having imposed his own categories onto reality.

Ptolemy's system is perfectly coherent, but it is closed. The qualities or attributes of the matrix categories are used to classify each part of the subordinate category. Since the area of northern Europe including Britain, Gaul, Germany, Italy, and Spain falls under "the occidental aspect of Jupiter and Mars," and since, furthermore, "the first parts of the aforesaid triangle are masculine and the latter parts feminine," it follows that the men inhabiting this region must reflect these characteristics; hence "they are without passion for women, and look down upon the pleasures of love," preferring the company of men (2.3; Loeb ed., p. 135).[30] Those who live in southeastern Asia fall under the triangle of Taurus, Virgo, and Capricorn, and "are governed by Venus and Saturn is oriental aspects," whose nature is of course "generative." One is not surprised to discover, then, that they practice "consecrating the genital organs," are "concupiscent," and "carry out their relations with women openly"; but one may be amazed that "most of them beget children by their own mothers" (p. 141). Again, an ancient ethnic prejudice, against the supposed immorality of these countries, has been presented as the effect of astral influence. While the correlation of categories in the occult tradition appears to produce automatic results, there is in fact much room for maneuvre.

The process of assimilation of new data to the original matrix is able to explain the nature of eclipses in terms of the planets' characters (2.8: from 1.5), and also the eclipses' colors (2.9: black = Saturn; white = Jupiter; red = Mars; yellow = Venus; variegated = Mercury). The most remarkable demonstration of assimilation, however, occurs in book 3, which classifies human temperaments in terms of planetary movement. Ever aware of the classification system he is using, Ptolemy reminds the reader of the distinction between male and female planets "set forth by us in the tabular series in the beginning of this compilation" (1.6). He notes that the signs and the planets have gender associations, and that their geographical position (east is masculine) and relation to the sun (rising in the morning is masculine; in the evening, feminine) all constitute criteria for evaluating planetary control over the sex (3.6; Loeb ed., p. 257). Then, since each planet rises and sets, there are fourteen groups into which human physiology may be divided. If Saturn is orient, for instance, he "makes his subjects in appearance dark-skinned, robust, black-haired," with curly hair and hairy chests; if he is setting they will be "straight-haired, with little hair on the body" (3.11; Loeb ed., p. 309). If Jupiter is rising they will have "moderately curling hair," if setting "lank hair, or even bald in front and on the crown." This binary correlation between curly hair and a rising planet, straight hair and a setting one, as if follicular vitality waxed and waned with the planets, is repeated with Jupiter and Mars (Loeb ed., pp. 309–11), to go no further. The same methods are applied to correlate parts of the body with the planets, a process known as *melothesia*. Saturn is the lord of the right ear, the spleen, the bladder, the phlegm, and the bones; Mars is lord of the left ear, kidneys, veins, and genital (3.12; Loeb ed., pp. 317–19). And he correlates social occupations with the planetary and zodiacal matrices (4.4; Loeb ed., pp. 385–91), a virtuoso exercise of a wholly abstract nature. A textbook of astrology, Ptolemy's *Tetrabiblos* is also a triumphant demonstration of the human capacity for classification. Self-generating, it is also self-referring.

In all the operations by which Ptolemy forms his system, the movement is not from the observation of nature, or man, or climate, or geography, to the forming of general classes, but the extension of a few basic matrices to cover a wealth of diverse material. I am not proposing a distinction between inductive and deductive reasoning as differentiating the experimental from the occult sciences. The occult is neither inductive nor deductive, but paratactic: that is, categories are joined up to each other laterally, added on like building-blocks. The typical method of astrology, as also alchemy and numerology, is the use of hierarchical categories derived from human gender to generate related categories of superior and inferior (right/left, east/west, rising/falling, preceding/following), and the classification of reality in these terms. The method underlying the whole system is the correlation of preexisting categories, with all the evaluations already attached to them.

2

In primary assimilation (such as this of Ptolemy; or that traced by Klibansky, Saxl, and Panofsky of how Saturn came to acquire its various characteristics), an original matrix is extended out into interrelated categories and assimilates them to it. Their account of the process by which evermore human types were assimilated to the dominion of Saturn describes, in fact, a universal process in occult science. By the time of Vettius Valens, in the second century, Saturn "governs a vast number of different types of men, and in fact not only governs them but even generates them: to him are subordinated also a series of substances (like lead, wood and stone), parts of the body, diseases . . . and manners of death."[31] The operative word there is "generates"; in other words, the matrix reproduces itself, not quite by cloning, but by forming subsequent categories in its own image. In primary assimilation, then, there is a single coherent process, which fixes a correlation; in time it is forgotten that such a process ever took place. In secondary assimilation, however, heterogeneous categories, formed on other principles, and often having nothing in common with one another, are juxtaposed and interrelated. Both systems represent an imposition of a priori categories onto reality, but the first type has at least the possibility of being coherent in its own terms. With secondary assimilation the problem of horizontal reading becomes critical.

A fairly typical example of late-Renaissance category fitting, or secondary assimilation, is this table from Athanasius Kircher, *Mursurgia universalis* (The Universal Work of the Muses), which is headed "The sympathetic harmony of the world, demonstrating the symphony of all nature in ten enneachords." I take the illustration and description from S. K. Heninger.[32] Kircher sets out in this grid a "9-fold correspondence between ten distinct categories of existence: angels, heavenly spheres, metals, stones, plants, trees, water creatures, winged creatures, four-legged animals, and colors." S. K. Heninger writes that "when read up-and-down" the diagram "designates the hierarchical stratification within any given category," such as the nine orders of angels in column 1. He continues:

> When read across, the diagram designates the items which are correspondent in each of the ten categories. For example, cherubim are correspondent to lead, the topaz, the hellebore, the cypress, the tunny-fish, the bittern, the ass and the bear, and black. Kircher sees the whole as a unified, harmonious system which reconciles opposites in musical terms of the diapason.[33]

Yet, the critical reader must ask, what do those items have in common? If one were given them outside this grid, how could they be connected? Do they have any real correspondence, either of structure or of function? Apart from providing ten categories (arbitrarily), and arranging the items in each, does the grid, in fact, connect anything?

Heninger believes that it does. He claims to find a "coadunating tendency," in which "each level directly and immediately relates to *all* other levels because of the common pattern. The result is symphysis." The common factor, he claims, unifies, provides a "common denominator" that "allows the several levels in the hierarchy to be organized into a homogeneous system."[34] Well, according to the *OED*, the term *symphysis*, in anatomy and zoology, refers to "the union of two bones or skeletal elements originally separate, either by fusion of the bony substance *(synostosis)* or by intervening cartilage *(synchondiosis)*." That sounds rather like something one would suffer from, not aspire to! Heninger claims that in "Pythagorean cosmology"—a label that he uses deplorably loosely—"since the universe is a system of metaphors such as the microcosm-macrocosm analogy, the method of knowledge consists in the straightforward process of translating mean-

Harmonia Mundi Sympathica, 10 Enneachordis totius naturæ Symphoniam exhibens. Ddd

Diapaſon Ditonus; Diapaſon cum Tono; Diapaſon; Heptachordon; Hexachordon; Diapente; Diateſſaron; Ditonus; Tonus

Enneachordon I	Enneach. II	Enneach. III	Enneach. IV	Enneach. V	Enneach. VI	Enneach. VII	Enneach. VIII	Enneach. IX	Enneach. X
Mundus Archetyp. DEVS	*Mundus Sidereus* Cœl.Emp.	*Mundus Mineralis*	*Lapides*	*Plantæ*	*Arbores*	*Aquatilia*	*Volucria*	*Quadrupedia*	*Colores varij*
Seraphim	Firmamentum	Salia,ſtellę Minerales.	Aſtrites	Herbæ & Flor.ſtell.	Frutices Bacciferę	Piſces ſtellares	Gallina Pharaonis	Pardus	Diuerſi Colores
Cherubim	♄ Nete	Plumbum	Topazius	Helleborus	Cypreſſus	Tynnus	Bubo	Aſinus, Vrſus	Fuſcus
Troni	♃Paranete	Æs	Amethiſtus	Betonica	Citrus	Acipenſer	Aquila	Elephas	Roſeus
Dominationes	♂Parameſ.	Ferrum	Adamas	Abſynthiũ	Quercus	Pſyphias	Falco Accipiter	Lupus	Flammeus
Virtutes	☼ Meſe	Aurum	Pyropus	Heliotropium	Lotus, Laurus	Delphinus	Gallus	Leo	Aureus
Poteſtates	♀Lichanos	Stannum	Beryllus	Satyrium	Myrtus	Truta	Cygnus Columba	Ceruus	Viridis
Principatus	☿ Parhypa.	Argentum Viuum	Achates laspis	Pæonia	Maluſpunica	Caſtor	Pſittacus	Canis	Cæruleus
Archangeli	☽ Hypate	Argentum	Selenites Cryſtallus	Lunaria	Colutea	Oſtrea	Anates Anſeres	Ælurus	Candidus
Angeli	Ter.cũEle. Proslamb.	Sulphur	Magnes	Gramina	Frutices	Anguilla	Struthio camelus	Inſecta	Niger

SOURCE: Athanasius Kircher, *Musurgia universalis*, 2 vols. (Rome, 1650), 2:393.

ing from one level of being to another by use of these metaphors."[35] Yet correlating metaphors does not constitute a method of knowledge, but only a rearrangement of the known. A page or two later, Heninger himself comes to see that the correspondence process is not one of discovery, as with the normal experience of metaphor, for in such a cross-reference system the metaphors lie ready.

> The job of "making" then becomes not so much a creation of something new, but rather a discovering of something already prescribed in God's book of nature. The creative act rests more in selecting the prefabricated metaphor which is most expressive. . . . For the poet, therefore, the framing of metaphors is an act of discovery and choice more than of creating *ex nihilo.*[36]

To me this is a far from adequate account of the creation of metaphor. It describes, rather, some kind of linkage process, like a telephone operator pushing plugs into sockets, linking up subscribers, bringing together preexisting units. In such a conception the world is a vast but static series of items, arranged into neat but finite categories, like Berlitz school vocabulary, tables of words with no grammar or syntax. The occult scientist—a Kircher, an Agrippa, a Fludd—is engaged in a game of cosmic dominoes, putting all the double-sided sevens together, doctoring an eight occasionally by blacking out a dot (in Agrippa, the seven planets figure, with discreet adjustments, in the table of fours, fives, sixes, and sevens), or upgrading a six with a dot of white paint. Here is neither creation nor discovery, since the form is predetermined and self-duplicating. Heninger claims that the juxtaposition creates a "transfer of information from one level to another," by which "the poet explains the unknown by means of the known and fulfils the purpose of metaphor."[37] Yet, since all is known, how can information be transferred, and how can the unknown be known?

The more fundamental criticism of Heninger is that the items in the correspondence grid are not metaphors at all. Whereas metaphors suggest resemblances between two discrete entities or levels of existence—resemblances that are perceived by the imagination, and assented to or not—the correspondences are claimed to be not just resemblances but actual identities, in the realm of objects or essences. They are not perceived by the imagination but by the rational mind, and *must* be assented to—otherwise the whole system risks being abandoned. Again, where metaphors and models, in indicating similarities, also insist on differences—my love is like a red, red rose only in some respects, thank goodness!—correspondences assert similarity or identity and are not interested in differences. The properties of the solarian object, for instance, are held to be identical and interchangeable. And metaphors allow for development, correction and refinement in a reciprocal relationship with the reality that they illuminate; correspondences are made once and for all, by a kind of collective fiat of the occult tradition. The ingredients of the correspondence grid, then, are not metaphors but things, which, it is claimed, represent patterns of connection within reality. But can one connect them horizontally?

A more critical scholar than Heninger, D. P. Walker, has also noted what I call the problem of horizontal reading. Commenting on Ficino's magic, which is based on correspondences between the seven planets and their associated categories—the appropriate animals, metals, parts of the body—he allows that the system has two defects:

First, this way of controlling effective states is rigid and over-simplified; there is no good reason for cramming our whole emotional life into seven immutable categories. Secondly, the system of ordering all mental contents under these seven headings is obviously in some measure arbitrary; there is always *some* reason why any given thing is, say, solarian, but the kinds of reason differ wildly and meaninglessly—lion, because of kingship and yellowness; honey, just because of yellowness; heart, because it is the source of life and spirits; cock, because it sings to the rising sun, etc.

These are objections with which many would agree. But, Walker goes on, the arbitrariness

does not in itself matter, provided the system is widely and firmly established— any more than it matters that our words have no real likeness to what they designate. The system of correspondences was in fact like a language, in that it was understood and worked only as long as people went on learning and speaking it. The error lay in supposing that it was not largely founded on convention and tradition, but that it had an objective reality; it was therefore at the mercy of anyone who exposed its arbitrariness and conventionality.[38]

The conclusion is absolutely just, but it seems to me that in describing the correspondence system as a language, Walker is giving just as misleading a judgment of language as Heninger did of metaphor. The correspondence system is based on resemblances, similarities, often heterogeneous and superficial, yet it claims to represent real, purposeful connections. The linguistic sign, as defined by Saussure, is known to be arbitrary and is based not on likeness but on difference, the crucial element being the line that separates the sign and the concept signified:

$$\frac{\text{Signified}}{\text{Signifier}} \quad = \quad \frac{}{\text{Tree}}$$

This line shows that the word and the concept to which it refers exist on different levels and cannot be fused or conflated. The relationship of signified to signifier may be arbitrary, but it is known to all speakers of that language and provides a system that can comprehend or interpret reality in all its forms. The planetary correspondences can only comprehend limited areas of reality, and can only do that by reducing those areas to the forms of its own matrix. Lastly, and the point that most needs to be asserted against claims that this system constitutes a language—whereas the planetary correspondences can only reduplicate themselves and can never get on to a higher level of thought or expression, language is creative, flexible, Protean, and thus capable of fulfilling any demands one makes on it.

The correspondences in fact constitute a classification system, not a mode of discovery. This position leads to a further point: that there are fundamental differences in the way that the occult sciences and the experimental sciences use analogy. In the experimental tradition, metaphors are used as models that attempt to describe some observable process or relationship in the physical world, the body, or the brain. One fundamental criterion for the model is that it be based on similarity, but also on difference, in the sense that the model must be different from the reality it is used to describe. If the two are fused, the operative distinction collapses. In the experimental tradition, analogies are used to comprehend parts of reality; in the occult tradition, reality can only be understood by being turned into analogy. In the experimental tradition, metaphors are used once only, as it were, used for specific instances. In the occult tradition, analogy becomes structured as a matrix to which is ascribed universal generalizing power: All phenomena can be comprehended in the terms of the matrix. Experimentalists use analogies only so long as they function, discarding them without compunction if they do not; occultists cling, have clung, to their analogies, which never change.

All these are obvious differences. A more specific way of differentiating what I see as two opposed and incompatible attitudes toward metaphor is provided by Mary Hesse's book, *Models and Analogies in Science*.[39] Hesse argues that the use of models and metaphors is essential to scientific theories, which themselves "bring something *new* into our description of events."[40] A scientific model "is any system . . . which has the characteristic of making a theory *predictive*."[41] Models are predictive when they lead to "new and obvious interpretations of some theoretical terms which may then be used to derive new relationships between observables."[42] Hesse distinguishes two modes of operation within analogies: horizontal and vertical. The common properties of the two analogues are related horizontally, in a "one-to-one relation of identity or difference between a property of one of the analogues and a corresponding property of the other." The vertical relationship is a relation vertically between properties of the same analogue such that they are "properties of the same object," but may, in addition, stand in a causal relationship to each other.[43]

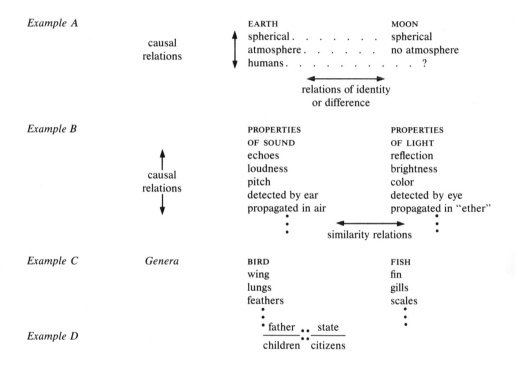

In Hesse's example A, which might be used to inquire whether human beings can exist on the moon, there are horizontal relations of identity or difference, and vertical relations of causality, since human life depends on the presence of atmosphere. In example B, comparing the properties of sound and light, the vertical relations are again causal, all the properties being mutually interdependent, but the horizontal relations are weaker, "since the pairs of corresponding terms are never identical but only *similar*."[44] In example C, "an analogy in a classification system," the horizontal relations "may be one or more . . . similarities of structure or of function, and each list may contain some items which have no, or no obvious correspondent in the other list."[45] As for the vertical relations, these "may be conceived as no more than that of whole to its parts, or they may be regarded as causal relations depending on some theory . . ." of evolution or adaptation.[46]

The important distinction for my argument about occult analogy lies not in the similarities or differences among these first three models, but in their radical difference from the fourth model, which, I argue, is the basic form of correspondence. Here, Hesse writes, the analogy is being used to assert that "the relation between father and child is the same in many respects as that between state and citizens, for example, in that the father is responsible for the maintenance, welfare, and defense of the child"—so that "the citizen owes respect and obedience to the state."[47] There are three main differences between this example and the others: First, "its purpose is persuasive rather than predictive. It is not arguing from three known terms to one unknown," as they do, but claiming that certain consequences "of a moral or normative character" should or must follow "from the relations of four terms already known." It resembles the occult use of correspondences, then, in that the constituent terms are all known; it differs from them in that it points on to action, where the occult correspondences seem to invite mere mental recognition or agreement. Second, in this model "the vertical relation is not specifically causal. There are in fact several vertical relations, provider-for, protector of," and so on, all insinuating a desired further relation: respect and obedience.[48] While this is again dynamic, the static model of the correspondence system shares the lack of causality in vertical relations. The seven planets, metals, beatitudes, gifts of the Holy Ghost, orifices in the body, or whatever else have no causal relationship; they are merely the seven members of a class, and not even a fixed class at that.

Third and crucially, in Hesse's example D "there does not seem to be any horizontal relation of similarity between the two terms, except in virtue of the fact that the two pairs are related by the same vertical relation. That is to say, there is no horizontal relation *independent* of the vertical relations, and here this example differs from all the other three types, where the horizontal relations of similarity were independent of the vertical and could be recognized before the vertical analogies were known."[49] Such analogies are "useless for prediction precisely because there is no similarity between corresponding terms."[50] This example seems to me to describe perfectly the situation of the reader confronted with Kircher's row 2 out of context, wondering what possible connection there could be between cherubim, Saturn, lead, the topaz, the hellebore, the cypress, the tunny-fish, the bittern, the ass and the bear, and black. One can now say that the vertical relation is merely that of being members of the same class, such as *colores varii*, of which nine representatives have been arbitrarily chosen for insertion into this grid. As for the horizontal relationship, there is no identity, and no similarity, other than that of being the second, or fourth, number in each list. There is no innate or causal link.

Many of the mental maneuvres of the occult sciences fall under the same verdict. In astrology, the process of *melothesia,* which is a distribution of the parts of the body to correspond to the signs of the zodiac, is just such a correspondence fit. If one imagines a left-hand table with the zodiacal signs, and a right-hand table with the parts of the body, it is obvious that both lists cohere vertically, each consisting of a whole or class divided into its parts, but that the two cannot cohere horizontally. Any survey of the history of *melothesia* will show how often the parts of the body have been shifted around according to the ideas of the person adapting the system.[51] Or consider the widespread attempt to correlate macrocosm and microcosm in detail, the left-hand table consisting of the earth and its component parts (mountains, seas, rivers, trees); the right-hand consisting of the parts of the human body (bones, head, eyes, veins, and so on). Again both lists cohere vertically but not horizontally; there is a faint sense in which *rivers* corresponds to *intestines,* sufficiently strong for one to be able to say, "I see what you mean." But a moment's thought shows how noncongruent the two categories are, in structure as in function.

My analysis of the treatment of analogy in the Western occult tradition receives support from a recent study of magic in primitive societies by a distinguished anthropologist, S. J. Tambiah. In an essay on "magical acts,"[52] Tambiah starts from the fieldwork of Sir Edward Evans-Pritchard on the Zande of the Upper Sudan, and from his observation that much of Zande magic was based on analogical thought and action. The Azande used material substances in their rites according to the principles of an "imitative symbolism," homoeopathic or simile magic, as it might be called, in which certain woods or roots "were chosen to represent specialized ideas," and were accompanied by spells and utterances that reveal "which feature of an object-symbol is the focus of attention on an analogical basis" (p. 205). The problem is to define the axis on which these analogies work. Drawing, as I also have, on the work of G. E. R. Lloyd and Mary Hesse, Tambiah compares the analogies used in Zande magical rituals with those used in Greek and later science, and concludes that the magical analogies do not resemble Hesse's first three types of scientific analogy, and do not meet her criteria for theoretical and predictive models, where vertical relations are interrelated, usually causally, and where horizontal relations exist independently of the vertical. But he finds, as I also have, that they do resemble Hesse's fourth model, the "persuasive" or propagandist one, in that in many primitive societies the magic action "rests on the explicit recognition of *both similarity* (positive analogy) *and difference* (negative analogy) *between the vertical relations of the paired terms.* And the rite consists in persuasively transferring the properties of the desired and desirable vertical relation to the other which is in an undesirable condition, or in attemting to convert a potential not-yet-achieved state into an actualized one" (p. 212). As with the occult, it is on the horizontal plane that the relationship breaks down.

In the Zande practices, the transfer (recall the root meaning of *metaphor,* transfer or removal) is made not only by word but also "by bringing a material piece of the object in the desirable/desired analogy into contact with the object in need of the transfer" (p. 212). In a case of leprosy, for instance, an analogy is drawn with the *araka* creeper, which loses its leaves at one point in its growth cycle, to be replaced by a double row of bands which, in their turn, dry out and split up into small pieces, just as the extremities of the hands and feet disappear in leprosy. The Zande's use of this creeper in a magical rite to expel leprosy rests on the acknowledgment of both similarities and differences in the vertical relations of the two terms, in that the shedding of its extremities is part of the plant's growth cycle, while the same phenomenon in the human being leads to degeneration and death.

> Thus this comparison proceeds to use the *araka* creeper in the rite as a vehicle or agent of life, the message being: may the leprosy disappear and health appear,

just as the shedding process in the creeper stimulates growth. The rite expresses the wish that one "vertical" relation that is undesired be replaced by another desired one; it itself represents symbolic not causal action. (P. 215)

The Trobrianders, similarly, "having postulated an analogy (or homology) between the yam house with yams stored in it and the human belly with food inside it, act upon the former in order to influence the latter" (p. 217). They have wrongly seen causal links *across* the analogy, moving from a common factor to an implied equivalence. In much the same way, the magical practices recommended by Ficino, Agrippa, and others, using simile magic—contact accompanied by words and sometimes music—was supposed to effect a transfer of a "vertical" relation from one object or person to another. It lacked, that is, a horizontal relationship to substantiate the metaphor, or metonymy, of transfer. Like the Zande's magic, it represented "symbolic not causal action," a point that must cast further doubt on the thesis espoused by Frances Yates and others, whereby the experimental sciences in the Renaissance were supposedly much influenced by the occult magus "acting on the world." The magus thought, and claimed, that he was acting on the world, but he was acting only within a symbol system that could confirm itself but not change anything. The correspondences are mental constructs, not facts of life, or nature.

3

If my criticism of the occult correspondence tables seems anachronistic, let me give some historical examples of the kinds of objections frequently made against the horizontal relationships posited by the correspondence system. As has been seen, correlation works by translating attributes from the main category to subsequent categories, or by assimilating them to the original matrix. In Dürer's painting of the four Apostles (in the Alte Pinakothek, Munich), the Apostles are highly differentiated in terms of physiognomy and personality. Klibansky, Panofsky, and Saxl reconstructed the genesis of this category fit, which was made by assimilating the Apostles to the system of temperaments or complexions, so that John became sanguine, Mark choleric, Peter phlegmatic, and Paul melancholic (pp. 366–69). This is a relatively trivial example, not involving, for instance, the falsification of history, but there is no innate reason that each of the Apostles should have this quality rather than another, or indeed that they should be in any way different. This example does show how categories reproduce themselves, and how the matter of the subordinate categories is sufficiently plastic to be reshaped to the matrix. With other examples of category fit, however, more serious objections must be made. Augustine used several parallelisms, including the famous one between the "seven periods of human (Old and New Testament) history and the ages of man—given variously as six, or seven. Augustine sees a defect in the scheme, for it makes Christ come in a period of history which corresponds to old age in the life of an individual, instead of that which corresponds to youth."[53] But of course, being Augustine, he was able to deal with that.

The first systematic objections to the microcosmic theory were made by Maimonides, who reviewed the traditional parallels and concluded that "none of the foregoing analogies justifies the calling of man a microcosm, any more than of a horse. It is the intellectual faculty . . . which raises man to that dignity."[54] Maimonides objected to the parallels between the human body and the Ptolemaic universe, invoking both of the criteria (later posited by Hesse) of similarity and function. "Whereas in man the benefits of organs subordinate to the heart also benefit the heart, in the universe that outer sphere which bestows authority and distributes power does not receive any benefit, but merely imitates the Most High. In man . . . the heart is internal, and in the universe its analogue is the outmost sphere. Moreover, the faculty of thinking is inherent in man's body, and inseparable from it, while God is not inherent in the universe and may exist apart from it."[55] These are serious-minded objections, rather pedantic it might seem, but that is the occupational hazard for anyone who sets out to criticize or refute the occult. Suggesting invisible connections within the universe is an exciting activity; doubting or denying them, however useful a service to the cause of truth, cannot but appear less exciting.

For a second example of objections to the horizontal reading of the correspondences, I shall draw on Wayne Shumaker's account of Pico della Mirandola's refutation of astrology. Pico rejected the correlation between the twelve signs and the twelve houses since it made the subordinate category simply reflect the dominant one. Because Jupiter is "the second of the planets, after Saturn, and has to do with riches, the second house is the place of wealth," and is said to follow directly on the first, or nativity, " 'because [the astrologers] say, nothing is nearer to a man than riches.' " In fact, Pico replies, "many things are nearer: the gifts of mind and body, wisdom and health (though these are assigned to the ninth and sixth houses), parents, wife, friends, sons, and glory."[56] Working from an ethical standpoint here, Pico elsewhere attacks the logical contradictions within the parallelisms. "Saturn is the first of the planets and fire the first of the elements, yet Saturn is cold"; in other words, no horizontal relationship of similarity exists, the terms "correspond" only by virtue of holding the first place in their respective lists. Blood, "the swiftest of the four bodily humours, is assigned to Jupiter, the next-to-slowest of the planets"; choler, similarly, "is related to Mars, which has a relatively short cycle, although it is slower than black bile, which is assigned to Saturn."[57] As well as showing the internal inconsistencies of horizontal correlation, Pico rejects the process of correspondence itself; of Ptolemy's correlation "between the four seasons and the moon's quarters Pico remarks, 'This is rather very pretty than natural and true.' " Savonarola, who popularized Pico's rejection of astrology, also rejected the symbolism of the zodiacal signs, and objected to the identification of Mercury with Christianity because "its movements are hard to understand, as Christian dogmas are difficult."[59] This was not true of Christianity.

The process of denying that correspondences can be read horizontally has led some critics of the occult to reject the whole principle of analogy on which it is based. Pico said of the complicated system of analogies between the houses and kinship categories that " 'in this way anything can easily be proved, since nothing exists which it is impossible to imagine by an argument of this kind to have some similarity and dissimilarity with something else.' "[60] Pico is of course a special case: he rejected astrology, but in the *Heptaplus* and elsewhere he was a prolific exponent of correspondences, signatures, and all forms of Neoplatonist magic. Yet attacks on the occult tradition do become more frequent, and more articulate, in the period between 1580 and 1680, and one can trace—although one cannot yet wholly account for it—a rejection of the symbolism basic to the occult. It is as if the B, or symbolic, level distinguished by D. P. Walker simply gets detached from the empirical level, and fades away. It does not merely dwindle through lack of use; one finds a number of perfectly coherent attacks, quite conscious of the issues involved, on the macrocosm/microcosm analogy. One constant feature of the occult is its tendency to turn concepts into essences, abstract into concrete, to reify and hypostatize metaphors or ideas. In Saussurian terms, the line separating signified and signifier is removed, and the two concepts fuse as one. Some modern historians of literature have found Renaissance writers attractive for their ability to "think in images." Where this phrase describes the fluent use of metaphor to illuminate judgments, states of mind or feeling, I, too, find it attractive. But where it implies reducing abstract thought to concrete symbols, maneuvring symbols as if they were objects in order to influence other objects, then the result is not attractive but limiting and confusing, especially in the discourse of science.

A good example of the limitations of this form of thinking in images is Paracelsus, who is notorious for his tendency to operate via analogy. Several commentators have noted independently of one another how analogies become, in his work, concrete objects; abstraction is rejected; any attempt to synthesize his ideas onto some higher plane faces the irreducible thing-ness of his object-ideas. Owsei Temkin commented on this rejection of rational discourse in favor of intuitive particularism:

> With Paracelsus the analogy almost takes the place of the parable in the New Testament. To make his reader see the truth of his interpretation, Paracelsus has no other means but to lead him as near as possible through examples. Hence the style of Paracelsus is marked by a series of statements connected by analogies or by open or hidden biblical references. It fits none of the great scientific methods, be they scholastic, mathematical, classificatory, purely descriptive, or even experimental in the modern sense. And these pictures, these visions are offered as interpretations of what is otherwise hidden and obscure in its causes.[61]

Alexandre Koyré put the same point more concisely:

> Paracelse ne peut penser autrement que par des analogies psychologiques ou organiques.[62]

In effect, Paracelsus pushes the correspondence between macrocosm and microcosm to the point where they become interchangeable, identical, as if fused with each other.

Yet Paracelsus's contemporaries saw the point equally clearly. Jan Baptista van Helmont, a disciple of Paracelsus, criticized his master on many grounds of doctrine: for misunderstanding the natural world, for imposing his own ideas or categories on experience, for contradicting himself, for being tyrannical, and much else.[63] The particularly relevant criticicms are directed against Paracelsus for taking the macrocosm/microcosm analogy too literally, so that the model fuses with the phenomenon it supposedly represents. Helmont frequently asserts the need for scientists to keep metaphoric and literal language clearly distinct. "Surely I have hated Metaphorical Speeches in serious matters";[64] "I shun proportionable resemblance [analogy], as also metaphorical speeches as much as I can."[65] Helmont's critique is representative of the shift in attitudes toward the use of analogy in science that can be traced to around the turn of the sixteenth century. He is perfectly clear where the source of Paracelsus's confusion lies; as a chapter title puts it, "*He was deceived by the* Metaphor *of a* Microcosme *or little World.*"

> To wit, he translated the Metaphor of a *Microcosme* into the truth it self; Willing, that we should express every way and fully, the whole Universe exactly . . . to contain in it all the differences of Earths, Mountains, Fountains, Stones, Mines, Plants, Fishes, Birds, four-footed Beasts, creeping things, also of the Stars, with all the properties, motions, Tempests, Diseases, Defects, and interchangeable courses of the same.[66]

Helmont rejects the parallel, first on Christian grounds: Man is made in the image of God, not in that of the universe.[67] On scientific grounds, he mocks it because, if literally understood, it would mean that man should be "made stony, that we may represent Stones and Rocks," and that in fact "we ought to fly; seeing it is more rational, for us sooner to shew our selves Birds, than great Stones, or storms of the Air, or water."[68] More seriously, since Paracelsus's use of the analogy implies a correspondence fit of part to part, Helmont rejects point by point the claim that "all Salts, Stones, Minerals, Herbs, &c. should lurk in man, as it were in their own Seminaries or Seed-plots":

> Away with thy trifles: For we have no fountains of Salt, no reducements of venal bloud into feigned and lurking metals. Neither are there minerals in us. . . . Neither also are there microcosmical Lawes in us, any more than the humors of four Elements mutually agreeing in us, and the fights or grudges of these.[69]

Paracelsus's theory is as defective as Galen's, for it, too, imposes an a priori model onto experience, passing up the direct observation of man and nature for allegory. His use of the microcosm analogy is not only reductive and opportunistic, but forces the human organism to conform to some preformed model derived from the macrocosm. In a typical occult maneuvre, Paracelsus correlates two preexisting categories; thus he "divides the wringings of the bowels into four parts, according unto the four accustomed hinges of the Winds." But this category fit involves him in such absurdities as placing the north wind "in the loyns, whose wind in its colick should blow against the Navil. But in the Navil he placeth the Southern one." Hence the correlation is inconsistent on its own terms, a curious mixture of system and antisystem. Paracelsus follows through the practice of correspondence, correlating the two categories point by point, until he at length ascribes to every wind their proper Remedies, involved under Hieroglyphicks, as yet to him unknown. Alas! with how sorrowful a pledge are all these things, and by how sporting a means hath that man invaded the principality of healing? to wit, that we are all little Worlds! for at how dear a rate doth he sell us this Idea or Image of the Macrocosme! and by what a scanty argument doth he found his dreams! when as, in very deed, there are no winds, nor matter of winds in us which we do not breath in and breath out, . . . unless in one way . . . To wit, from the stomack, through the bowels, even into the fundament.[70]

With this brief refutation, based on the appeal to empirical medical evidence, Helmont shows that he is near enough to the mental world of Paracelsus to understand the extent to which it was based on analogical reasoning, yet far enough away from it to abandon correspondences and metaphors, all the old paraphernalia of astrological medicine.

In a section called "A Modern Pharmacopolium and Dispensatory," Helmont attacks the belief that provided the foundation of astrological medicine, the doctrine of signatures:

I believe that God doth give the knowledge of Simples, to whom he will, from a supernatural grace: but not by the signes of nature! For what Palmestrical affinity hath the Boars tooth, the Goats blood, the peisle of a Bull, the dung of a Horse, or the Herbe Daysie, with a Pleurisie? or what signature have those Simples with each other?[71]

It is for this reason, Helmont writes, that "I have laughed at *Paracelsus*, because he hath erected serious trifles into the principles of healing." Other theorists have tried to correlate disease and astrology. But the only result has been that the variety and specific nature of human disease has been limited and distorted by being forced to correspond to the much simpler system of the zodiac. Such thinkers

have brought the huge Catalogue of Diseases into the signes of the Zodiack: whose number, seeing it was too narrow, they have enlarged every one of the signes into a threefold Section: To wit, that they might divide all the virtue of Herbes into 36, and gather them into a narrow fold. (p. 458)

One sees here the plastic nature of the grid in such category correlation, that can be expanded or contracted to provide the requisite number of slots. In this case the available categories will never be sufficient. However many artificial classes the occultist should distinguish in the matrix category—that of the zodiac—he is still merely performing a manipulation or redistribution of given categories until they match. In fact, given that the number of herbs is greater, he is having to adapt his matrix category in order to fit it to his subordinate category. In this way he inverts the normal process and shows that instead of working with one fixed point and one variable, he has two variables. The zodiac, too, is a closed, finite system, known and fixed; the extent of human disease is unknown, open, and if not—one hopes—infinite, at any rate neither constant nor fixed.

In any case, Helmont continues, the whole system is founded on a mistaken idea:

> The earth hath of itself a seminal virtue of producing Herbes, the which, therefore, it doth not beg from the Heavens. For the whole property of Herbes is from their Seed, and the seminative power is drawn from the earth, according to the holy Scriptures: but not from the faces of the lights of Heaven. (p. 458)

In effect, Helmont denies the whole basis of astrology; once that step has been made, the rest of the occult system collapses. The concept of astral influence determining the nature of herbs being itself wrong, it is futile to build a classification system on correspondences, which are limited in number and express an outmoded set of beliefs. One can juggle with twelve or thirty units,

> But in what sort could so few Stars contain the essences, seeds, faces, and properties perhaps of five hundred plants, differing in their species and internal properties? Moreover, besides a thousand vain attributions of so many things, as well humane as politick? Away with these trifles! The properties of Herbes are in the Seeds, but not in the Heaven or Stars. The powers of the Stars are grown out of date, the which by an old Fable have stood feigned unto heats, colds, and complexions. For the Stars, in whatsoever manner they are taken, do differ from Plants, much more than Herbs do from mists and frosts, or fishes from precious stones. Let it therefore be a faulty argument, to have attributed effects to causes which do contain nothing at all like a cause in them. (p. 458)

In exchange for this old-fashioned reasoning from analogies Helmont calls for empirical research:

> Therefore let allegorical and moral senses depart out of nature. Nature throughly handles Beings as they do in very deed and act . . . neither doth it admit of any other interpretation than by being made, and being in essence, from ordained causes.[72]

Like other scientists in this transitional period, Helmont can glimpse what a rigorous experimental science needs without being in any position to fulfill those needs consistently, and in much of his work he relies on mystical or magical ideas. Yet his objection to the occult use of analogy as if it provided experimental data is formulated perfectly coherently and was part of a wider sense of dissatisfaction with macrocosm/microcosm analogies.

Francis Bacon's first reference to the analogy comes in the *Advancement of Learning* (1605), in the discussion of medicine, where he write:

> The ancient opinion that man was Microcosmus, an abstract or model of the world, hath been fantastically strained by Paracelsus and the alchemists, as if there were to be found in man's body certain correspondences and parallels, which should have respect to all varieties of things, as stars, planets, minerals, which are extant in the great world.

Certainly the human body has the most varied diet of all, since it needs "the flesh of beasts, birds, fishes, herbs, grains, fruits, water,"[73] but this is very different from asserting that it contains in itself all the components of the universe, or has any identity with them. In the *Wisdom of the Ancients* (1609), discussing the fable of Prometheus, Bacon repeats his criticism:

> The Alchemists, when they maintain that there is to be found in man every mineral, every vegetable, &c., or something corresponding to them, take the word *microcosm* in a sense too gross and literal, and have so spoiled the elegance and distorted the meaning of it.[74]

It remains true, despite their excesses, that "the body of man is of all existing things both the most mixed and the most organic," and in that sense man may be called a little world. But the tolerance shown here evaporates in the *Sylva Sylvarum* or *Natural History* (1627), where, beginning his discussion of imagination, Bacon is at pains to refute the superstitious philosophy of Pythagoras, which planted the "monstrous imagination"—subsequently "watered and nourished" by Platonism—that "the world was one entire perfect living creature," which breathed, had a soul, and constituted an organic unity such that "no distance of place" within the world "could hinder magical operations," but that these would be instantly perceived anywhere within this unity, due to "the unity and harmony of nature." Not content with this belief, Bacon writes, there were some that

> went further, and held that if the spirit of man (whom they call the microcosm) do give a fit touch to the spirit of the world by strong imaginations and beliefs, it might command nature; for Paracelsus, and some darksome authors of magic, do ascribe to imagination exalted, the power of miracle-working faith. With these vast and bottomless follies men have been (in part) entertained.[75]

Bacon again is far from having liberated himself from the occult tradition, yet his criticism is cogent and coherent.

Another transitional figure, Andreas Libavius, attacked the Paracelsian alchemist Oswald Croll for allowing the macrocosm/microcosm analogy to blur essential differences between heaven and earth: "Their very acceptance of the macrocosm-microcosm analogy invalidates their work. No one with any wisdom can agree that celestial substances will be found in man. Furthermore, there can be no mixture of the celestial and terrestrial worlds."[76] A contemporary of Libavius, Daniel Sennert, who attacked some aspects of occult science yet retained a belief in signatures, complained that while the Paracelsians have revived the ancient doctrine of macrocosm and microcosm, the concept "is extended too large by the Chymists, because they make not an Analogie, but an identity, or the same thing."[77] It is absurd to argue that the existence of a thing in one world necessitates its existence in the other. Some chemists have actually claimed "that there can be no humours because they have not been found in the macrocosm, but such proof by analogy cannot be accepted seriously." Similar objections were made by Erastus, Charleton, Boyle, Mersenne, and others. The practice of linking disparate categories by a horizontal grid, in which the component elements were supposed to be interconvertible, was not taken over by the new science of the seventeenth century.

4

If this analysis has been sound, two conclusions can be drawn. One concerns the applicability of models to science. Whatever one's estimate of the debt of experimental science to occult science—on this count I cannot see that any constructive borrowing took place. Mary Hesse wrote of analogies that have a vertical coherence but no horizontal one that they are "useless for prediction"—and therefore useless for science—"because there is no similarity between corresponding terms."[78] Whereas in the models of experimental science, analogies are chosen to illuminate an observed phenomenon in reality, the items placed side by side in a correspondence grid have been put in position by some predetermined scheme. They owe their place not to an innate, freshly perceived functional relationship, but to a preexisting design, a plan to which they are assimilated.[79] In the experimental tradition analogies function as intermediaries between theory and observation, in a process that constantly evolves, and uses computational and verificational procedures. In the occult, by contrast, there seems to be no dialectical interplay between theory and observation, and no interest in computation and falsification. Observation is not an open-ended inquiry but a form of classification that is used to support theory in an unquestioning manner. In the occult, the distinction between theory and practice is never coherently for formulated, as it comes to be in the experimental tradition. Perhaps the occult correspondence represents in itself a fusion of theory and practice. It is both the theory governing the processing of material and the material itself—a circular, self-justifying process.

My second conclusion concerns the relation between these two forms of analogical thinking and man's general conception of the universe. The positive aspect of the occult's use of hierarchical and evaluative categories is that in grading and discriminating reality in animistic and socioreligious terms, they gave a comforting sense of the universe as having been constructed in man's image and likeness. In the course of the sixteenth century men no longer needed to see the universe in such homocentric terms, and granted inanimate nature its own purely neutral categories of space, volume, density, and velocity. It is not the case that they abandoned the need to understand the universe as a system, but that they stopped constructing a system out of human, social, sexual, and religious categories. This was certainly a major change, and to some eloquent modern students, such as E. A. Burtt and Marjorie Hope Nicolson,[80] the change was lamentable, potentially tragic. According to them man felt less at home in this dehumanized cosmos, where matter obeys its laws, not man's.

If this change had really been so tragic, one might expect to find a widespread contemporary recognition of it. But apart from a few phrases by John Donne, in poems written on commission to lament the death of a young girl—phrases taken out of context and linked with a wholly different debate concerning antiquity and modernity, the age of the earth, and whether nature was exhausted[81]—I find no such widespread lament for the passing of the analogical mentality, or the rejection of microcosms and macrocosms. To understand the seventeenth century in truly historical terms is to note there a sense that the gains involved in this shift of attitude far outweigh the losses. The nostalgia for a humanized universe is the nostalgia of some modern historians of ideas, who are themselves thinking in the old hierarchical and evaluative categories when they lament "the breaking of the circle," as if perfection had somehow been sullied or shattered. All scholars have been trained to be scrupulously neutral in analyzing the past. I believe that it is impossible to be totally neutral, and that the best thing is to become aware of one's prejudices, and to try to correct them. I also believe that critical detachment needs to be supplemented, at the right time, by evaluation. Looking at the genesis and operation of the correspondences, then, I see this reaction against the occult not so much as the destruction of analogy but as the reassertion of its true function. What the critics of the occult did was to assert, or rediscover, the difference between using analogy as a descriptive or heuristic tool and using it as a matrix into which reality has to be assimilated. For all its attractiveness the occult's use of analogy in fact constituted a closed system, which constantly reduplicated its very limited understanding of the universe. The fusion of tenor and vehicle, while seemingly favorable to metaphor, actually destroyed the flexibility and creativity of metaphor, and its proper functioning in an open-ended system. In the occult, metaphor tends to become coagulated, rigidified. Instead of lamenting the breaking of the circle, one should celebrate that the seventeenth century finally dissolved the tyranny of the grid.[82]

Notes

1. On the continuities within the occult tradition, see Rudolf Allers, "Microcosmos: From Anaximander to Paracelsus," *Traditio* 2 (1944): 319–407, see esp. pp. 391, 399n; Raymond Klibansky, Erwin Panofsky, and Fritz Saxl, *Saturn and Melancholy: Studies in the History of Natural Philosophy, Religion and Art* (London, 1964), pp. 188–89; Wayne SHumaker, *The Occult Sciences in the Renaissance: A Study in Intellectual Patterns* (Berkeley, 1972), pp. 2, 73–75, 111, 168–69, 185, 205, 224, 239, 246–47, 257, 258; Karl Preisendanz, "Zur Überlieferungsgeschichte der spätantiken Magie," *Zentralblatt für Bibliothekswesen* 75–77 (1951): 223–40.

2. Shumaker, *Occult Sciences*, p. 169, citing E. J. Holmyard, *Alchemy* (Harmondsworth, 1957), p. 25.

3. On syncretism in the occult tradition, see R. Reitzenstein and H. H. Schaeder, *Studien zum antiken Synkretismus aus Iran und Griechenland* (Berlin, 1926); George P. Conger, *Theories of Macrocosms and Microcosms in the History of Philosophy* (New York, 1922), pp. 16, 20, 53; Klibansky et al., *Saturn and Melancholy*, pp. 95, 189, 263; Morton W. Bloomfield, *The Seven Deadly Sins*, 2d ed. (East Lansing, Mich., 1967); D. P. Walker, *Spiritual and Demonic Magic: From Ficino to Campanella* (London, 1958), pp. 93, 126–27. On syncretism in Renaissance philosophy, see e.g. Charles Trinkaus, *In Our Image and Likeness: Humanity and Divinity in Italian Humanist Thought*, 2 vols. (London, 1970), esp. pp. 503–4 (Ficino), 507–8, 520 (Pico).

4. See G. E. R. Lloyd, *Polarity and Analogy: Two Types of Argumentation in Early Greek Thought* (Cambridge, 1966); Bloomfield, *Seven Deadly Sins*, with remarkably rich documentation; Joseph Needham, *Science and Civilisation in China*, vol. 2: *History of Scientific Thought*, (Cambridge, 1956), pp. 232–303; Derk Bodde, "Types of Chinese Categorical Thinking," *Journal of the American Oriental Society* 59 (1939): 200–219; Germaine Dieterlen, "Les correspondances cosmo-biologiques chez les Soudains," *Journal de Psychologie Normale et Pathologique* 43 (1950): 350–66, and "Classification des végétaux chez les Dogon," *Journal de la Société des Africanistes* 22 (1952): 115–58; C. R. Hallpike, *The Foundations of Primitive Thought* (Oxford, 1979); Rodney Needham, *Reconnaissances* (Toronto, 1980), chap. 2, "Analogical Classification," pp. 41–62.

5. Allers, "Microcosmos," p. 328.

6. Conger, *Theories of Macrocosms,* pp. 8–11.

7. Shumaker, *Occult Sciences,* p. 157.

8. Walker, *Spiritual and Demonic Magic,* p. 32.

9. Ibid., pp. 75–84 and table, p. 77.

10. On numerology, see Walter Burkert, *Lore and Science in Ancient Pythagoreanism,* trans. E. Minar (Cambridge, Mass., 1972), which displaces all previous studies of Pythagoras; Christopher Butler, *Number Symbolism* (London, 1970), a useful and reliable introduction to the history and theory of numerology, but oddly uncritical when it comes to detecting numerological patterns in Renaissance poetry; Vincent F. Hopper, *Medieval Number Symbolism* (1938; reprint, New York, 1969); and Edward W. Strong, *Procedures and Metaphysics: A Study in the Philosophy of Mathematical-Physical Science in the Sixteenth and Seventeenth Centuries* (Berkeley, 1936; Hildesheim, 1966), an admirable study of the rejection of neo-Pythagorean numerology by the Renaissance scientific-mathematical tradition.

11. The study by Hallpike, *Foundations of Primitive Thought,* is illuminating on the arbitrariness of symbolism.

12. See the outstanding work of Maurice P. Crosland, *Historical Studies in the Language of Chemistry* (London, 1962).

13. E. A. Burtt, *The Metaphysical Foundations of Modern Physical Science,* 2d ed. (London, 1932), pp. 32–33, 35, 37, 46–47, 67, 75, 81, 84–85, 89, 92–93, 97, 102, 107–8, 113, 152, 159–60, 172–73, 210–12, 220–22, 240–53, 303.

14. See Rodney Needham, ed., *Right and Left: Essays on Dual Symbolic Classification* (Chicago, 1973).

15. Conger, *Theories of Macrocosms,* p. 2, citing Stobaeus, *Eclogae,* 1.10.12.

16. Shumaker, *Occult Sciences,* p. 179.

17. Conger, *Theories of Macrocosms,* pp. 23, 24, 56; Pico, *Heptaplus,* 2d proem, trans. D. Carmichael, in *On the Dignity of Man and Other Treatises,* ed. Paul J. W. Miller (Indianapolis, 1965), p. 78.

18. Allers, "Microcosmos," p. 403.

19. Shumaker, *Occult Sciences,* pp. 113, 123.

20. Klibansky, et al., *Saturn and Melancholy,* p. 265.

21. Conger, *Theories of Macrocosms,* pp. 48–49.

22. Ibid., p. 47.

23. Klibansky et al., *Saturn and Melancholy,* p. 149.

24. Ibid., pp. 155–59.

25. Ptolemy, *Tetrabiblos,* Loeb Library ed., trans. F. E. Robbins (London, 1940).

26. A Bouché-Leclercq, *L'astrologie grecque* (Paris, 1899), pp. 188–91, 211, 215, 243–45, 296, 324–25, 339–40, 398 (the sole exception to Ptolemy's normal rejection of mythological and fantastic associations), 410–11, 428, 497–98, 500, 565.

27. Hallpike, *Foundations of Primitive Thought,* pp. 136–39, 141–45, 196, 198, 202–3, 232–33, 496.

28. For Ptolemy's comments on the classification process, see *Tetrabiblos* (Loeb ed.), pp. 25, 65–66, 69, 91–95, 99, 101–2, 117, 221, 235, 257, 437–38.

29. Robbins (ibid., p. 121) cites Boll's *Studien über Claudius Ptolemäus: Jahrbuch für Classische Philologie,* supp. vol. 21 (1894), pp. 181–238.

30. As his editors point out, Ptolemy draws here on a Greek tradition designating northern Europeans as homosexual (the insult seems to have been returned with interest during the Renaissance). What is significant is that Ptolemy is able to integrate it into his system.

31. Klibansky et al., *Saturn and Melancholy,* pp. 142–43.

32. S. K. Heninger, Jr., *Touches of Sweet Harmony: Pythagorean Cosmology and Renaissance Poetics* (San Marino, Calif., 1974), pp. 330–31. See also his richly illustrated survey, *The Cosmographical Glass: Renaissance Diagrams of the Universe* (San Marino, Calif. 1977).

33. Heninger, *Sweet Harmony,* p. 331.

34. Ibid., p. 329.

35. Ibid., p. 335.

36. Ibid., p. 338.

37. Ibid., p. 341.

38. Walker, *Spiritual and Demonic Magic,* pp. 143–44.

39. Mary Hesse, *Models and Analogies in Science* (Notre Dame, Ind., 1966).

40. Ibid., p. 15.

41. Ibid., p. 19.

42. Ibid., p. 35.

43. Ibid.

44. Ibid., p. 60.

45. Ibid., pp. 61–62.

46. Iid., p. 62.

47. Ibid., pp. 62–63.

48. Ibid., p. 63.

49. Ibid.

50. Ibid., p. 69.

51. See Bouché-Leclercq, *L'astrologie grecque;* and Wilhelm Gundel, *Dekanen und De-kansternbilder* (Hamburg, 1936).

52. S. J. Tambiah, "Form and Meaning of Magical Acts: A Point of View," in *Modes of Thought: Essays on Thinking in Western and Non-Western Societies,* ed. Robin Horton and Ruth Finnegan (London, 1973), pp. 199–229. For further suggestions on how anthropological studies can illuminate the occult sciences, see my introduction to *Occult and Scientific Mentalities in the Renaissance,* ed. Brian Vickers (Cambridge, 1984), pp. 32–44. For a useful survey of "simile-magic" in medicine, see Karl E. Rothschuh, *Konzepte der Medizin in Vergangenheit und Gegenwart* (Stuttgart, 1978), esp. "Iatromagie," pp. 106–57.

53. Conger, *Theories of Macrocosms,* p. 35.

54. Ibid., p. 44.

55. Ibid., pp. 44–45.

56. Shumaker, *Occult Sciences,* pp. 21–22.

57. Ibid., p. 22.

58. Ibid.

59. Ibid., pp. 43–44.

60. Ibid., p. 22.

61. Owsei Temkin, "The Elusiveness of Paracelsus," *Bulletin of the History of Medicine* 26 (1952): 201–17, at p. 211.

62. Alexandre Koyré, *Mystiques, spirituels, alchimistes du XVIe siècle allemand* (Paris, 1966), p. 61.

63. For an account of Helmont's criticisms of Paracelsus, see Allen Debus, *The Chemical Philosophy: Paracelsian Science and Medicine in the Sixteenth and Seventeenth Centuries,* 2 vols. (New York, 1977), pp. 314–15, repeating the substance of an earlier essay in *Ambix* 15 (1968): 22.

64. All quotations from Helmont are taken from *Oriatrike; or, Physick Refined,* trans. J[ohn] C[handler] (London, 1662); this is an English version of Helmont's *Ortus medicinae* (Amsterdam, 1648); this reference on p. 719.

65. Ibid., p. 112.

66. Ibid., pp. 235, 237.

67. Ibid., pp. 237, 322–23.

68. Ibid., pp. 237–38.

69. Ibid., pp. 322–23.

70. Ibid., p. 418.

71. Ibid., p. 458.

72. Ibid., pp. 237–38.

73. Francis Bacon, *Works,* 14 vols., ed. J. Spedding et al. (London, 1857–74), 3:370–71.

74. Ibid., 6:747.

75. Ibid., 2:640–41.

76. Libavius, *Commentatorium Alchymiae* (1606), sig. Aa3v, cited and trans. A. Debus, "Guintherius, Libavius and Sennert: The Chemical Compromise in Early Modern Medicine," in *Science, Medicine and Society in the Renaissance,* 2 vols., ed. A. Debus (New York, 1972), 1:151–65, at p. 157. See also Owen Hannaway, *The Chemists and the Word: The Didactic Origins of Chemistry* (Baltimore, 1975).

77. Daniel Sennert, *De Chymicorum cum Aristotelicis et Galenics Consensu ac Dissensu* (1619), partial English translation by Nicholas Culpeper and Abdiah Cole, *Chymistry Made Easie and Useful; or, The Agreement and Disagreement of the Chymists and Galenists* (London, 1662), pp. 25–26, 96; cited by Debus, ibid., pp. 158–59.

78. Hesse, *Models and Analogies,* p. 69.

79. I am glad to discover that sinologists have made similar judgments about analogical category fits in Chinese thought. Derk Bodde writes of the Chinese attempt "to reduce all phenomena under sets of orderly, all-inclusive schemata"—such as the three rituals/sacrificial animals; four seas/cardinal points; five colors/sounds/smells, and so on—that such attempts "failed to produce a true physical science, because, being based upon false, man-made analogies, they disregarded the use of the empirical method of direct observation of nature, and thus distorted and forced natural phenomena into an artificial pattern. Indeed, their uncritical acceptance in later times has even tended to discourage the development of a true scientific method" ("Chinese Categorical Thinking," pp. 200–203). See also Joseh

Needham, *Science and Civilisation in China,* pp. 261, 266–68, 271–72, 280–81, 287–88, 293–94, 298, 304, 310, 325–28, 335–40, 368–82. While arguing that the "correlative thinking" of the Chinese had some positive effects on science, Needham is particularly scathing on the empty and arbitrary manipulation of categories performed by numerology.

80. Burtt, *Metaphysical Foundations,* pp. 104, 238–39, 301; Marjorie Hope Nicolson, *The Breaking of the Circle: Studies in the Effect of the "New Science" upon Seventeenth-Century Poetry* (Evanston, Ill., 1950), pp. xxi, 16, 104, 146–47.

81. Victor Harris's development of these topics, *All Coherence Gone* (Chicago, 1949), seems to me a fundamentally misleading account of the temper of seventeenth-century thought. In his examination of this problem Paul Kocher concluded that "decay was not one of the ruling ideas of the Elizabethan period; that it was shallow-rooted by comparison with such other pessimistic ideas as that of original sin, or the mutability of fortune, or the inflictions of God's providence; that it was rather a rationalization than a cause of despondency": *Science and Religion in Elizabethan England* (San Marino, Calif., 1953), p. 87.

82. I would like to thank Professor John North, of the Rijksuniversiteit Groningen, for some helpful comments on this essay.

14

Literary Hermeticism: Some Test Cases

WAYNE SHUMAKER

The topic I shall discuss here is similar to, but in focus different from, one I addressed in chapter 5 of a book called *The Occult Sciences in the Renaissance* (Berkeley, 1972). Continental writers mentioned in that survey numbered thirteen; English writers also thirteen. Although the gist of my comment was often that persuasive evidence of Hermetic influence was lacking, I did not then, and do not now, deny that Hermetism—or Hermeticism, to be defined in a moment—had considerable impact upon Renaissance thought. In order not to be led into the analysis of foreign words and idioms and of hidden allusions that require specialized knowledge to interpret, I shall limit myself to English. Further, because prose is usually more explicit than poetry and makes less use of fictions and metaphorical language, all my examples will be taken from verse. I undertake the study partly to combat extreme claims that have been made recently for Hermeticism: specifically, that it was the dominant philosophy of the Renaissance itself and, in fact, constituted the background of that period. Also, articles and books have advanced what appear to me to be untenable theories about specific authors: for example, that Marlowe's Tamburlaine, besides being morally perfect— an arresting thesis—was a magician (see J. R. Howe, *Marlowe, Tamburlaine and Magic* [Athens, Ohio, 1976]). It is, therefore, appropriate that the entire subject should be reopened in the present collection; but before addressing it, I must clear the ground both by defining what is to be meant by *Hermeticism* and by speaking generally of the difficulties of assessing occultism in creative works that do not always assert as true what they appear to say.

Between *Hermeticism* and *Hermetism* I make a perhaps idiosyncratic but nevertheless convenient distinction. *Hermetism* is the mystical philosophy of Hermes Trismegistus, modified of course by varying interpretations offered at different times. *Hermeticism* is a more amorphous body of notions and attitudes deriving not merely from Hermes but also from the mystical side of Plato and his Neoplatonic successors and from such other esoteric systems as the numerology of Pythagoras and the Jewish cabala. As such, Hermeticism includes all the varieties of magic except natural magic, not excepting the daemonic magic of which D. P. Walker has written. Thus Cornelius Agrippa, John Dee, and Thomas Vaughan, who are not consistently Hermetists, are indisputably Hermeticists. The distinction is similar to that between Southern and Northern Buddhism. Astrology and alchemy fall into this purview not only because Hermes was the reputed patron of both but also because they had traditionally been discussed only in the learned languages or in veiled writings intended to be comprehensible only to especially fit readers. The distinction was that between exoteric and esoteric knowledge. One link between Hermetism and Hermeticism was the tendency of both to be called simply Platonism in the Renaissance. Another was a common belief that the esoteric philosophy was unitary and had descended from Trismegistus in a direct line through Orpheus, Aglaophemus, Pythagoras, and Philolaus to Plato, both Pythagoras and Plato having spent years studying the Hermetic tradition in Egypt. Even biblical mysticism could be assimilated, as by the identification of Hermes with Moses, who lived near the same time and by birth and upbringing was Egyptian, and of the entire Hermetic philosophy with an esoteric revelation made to Moses on Sinai along with the exoteric doctrine accessible in Scripture. All this is well known and need not be insisted on. The tendency of Renaissance thinkers to meld ideas from different sources was very strong, syncretism being as characteristic of much Renaissance reflection as discrimination is of modern. For all these reasons, I shall give my attention not to Hermetism but to Hermeticism.

How influence will be recognized is harder to describe. Milton's *Il Penseroso* offers an illustration of the difficulties. When, in it, the poet expresses a wish to "out-watch the *Bear*, / With thrice-great *Hermes*" (lines 87–88), a connection with Hermetism is explicit. Because the allusion is not to the author of the *Corpus Hermeticum,* however, but to the Hermes who was patron of astrology, it is not immediately clear that Milton had read either the long document then known as the *Poimandres* or the Latin *Asclepius.* The reference might easily have been drawn from allusions or from hearsay. Platonism is evident in immediately following lines when the spirit of Plato is called on "to unfold / What Worlds, or what vast Regions hold / The immortal mind that hath forsook / Her mansion in this fleshly nook" (lines 89–92). Herbert Agar and Irene Samuel have written books on Plato and Milton, and Sears Jayne has argued that the entire framework of *Comus* is Neoplatonic. What, however, is to made of "Those *Daemons* that are found / In fire, air, flood, or underground" (lines 93–94)? Is the poet drawing upon the daemonic lore of ancients like Trismegistus and Dionysius, who by distributing spirits liberally throughout the universe encouraged the ascription of them to the four elements? Or are the daemons merely sylphs, gnomes, salamanders, and water creatures taken, like the Puck mentioned in *L'Allegro,* from popular tradition? If the former, does mention of the daemons imply belief, or is acquaintance with them a poetic metaphor of solid knowledge obtained by long study of the hidden causes of phenomena? Since the daemons "are" in the four elements, not merely "said to be" there, mention of them may seem to be accompanied by commitment. One must remember, however, that according to Sidney's *Apologie* the poet "never affirmeth" and that "therefore, though he recount things not true, yet because he telleth them not for true, he lieth not." I should be hesitant, on the basis of these excerpts, to assert that as a young man Milton took Hermeticism seriously; and when he was older, I am relatively sure he did not. Yet in ten lines of a short poem I have found references to Hermes, to Plato, and to the daemons that in both the Hermetic and the Hermetistic world view permeated the universe.

In view of the existence of such problems, which vary from text to text, it is impossible to prescribe either an invariable mode of investigation or a set of criteria for the judgment of evidence. The most that can be done is to suggest a set of flexible guidelines. First, and perhaps most important, it is essential not to begin with a determination either to assert influence or to deny it. Scholarship has passed the stage at which it was necessary to find Hermeticism everywhere in the Renaissance in order to justify the study of it. That it existed, and had considerable importance, is recognized—for instance—by the publication of this volume. Second, I urge the danger of claiming specific sources of notions that were "in the air" simply because they had been expressed many times by persons of some repute. Not every mention of a World Soul implies direct, or perhaps even indirect, acquaintance with Ficino, nor does every allusion to the Ladder of Love derive certainly from a reading either of Castiglione's *Cortegiano* or of Plato's *Symposium*. After 1596, Spenser's *Hymne in Honovr of Beavtie* is a possible source, and other sources can be found both earlier and later.

This proposal militates against a common scholarly methodology, that of reading intensively in a single Hermeticist and then trying to make him important by finding his influence everywhere. In theory, a better procedure is to search not for influences *from* but for influences *on*—in other words, to speculate where a given writer's ideas came from, not what effect his ideas produced on others. The *parti pris* is less damaging because there is less danger of coming up with no results; but here, too, there is no protection against unconscious bias. The only suggestion I can offer is that all such researches should be preceded by the widest possible reading outside the scholar's specialty as well as inside it. For example, students of literature may be skimpily read in philosophy, so that they impute every apparent allusion to archetypal ideas to Platonic influence, not realizing that these are not easily distinguished from the Aristotelian universals taught in the Schools. Conversely, students of philosophy may misread belles lettres because of discomfort with figurative language and unfamiliarity with literary traditions and conventions. To make matters even worse, not every modern scholar is sufficiently at home in Latin to pick up cheerfully not only folio volumes written in that language but also sets of volumes and perhaps whole shelves of collected opera. My advice is therefore perfectionist, not realistic, and throws doubt not only upon what others have written but also upon what I write here. One can, however, perhaps benefit from an awareness of hazards if doing so helps somewhat to modify the desire to prove too much and encourages recognition of a certain contingency in the findings.

Against this background I proceed at once to my first test case, that of Shakespeare. I do not wish to search merely in nooks and corners; but in any event Shakespeare deserves notice, for his plays (I shall not consider the poems) contain obvious traces of Hermeticism.

No reader of *The Tempest* can avoid recognizing that Prospero is a magician. He raises a fearful storm that drives a chosen ship to his island and causes passengers to go over the side but permits them to be washed ashore without injury. Indeed, he prevents even damage to their garments, which after a dunking in the sea appear "fresher than before" (act 1, sc. 1); and the ship itself is safely harbored, with the crew—who are not needed in the later action—"under hatches stow'd" (ibid.) and asleep. This is accomplished with the aid of Ariel, an aerial spirit or sylph, whom Prospero has freed from a cloven pine in which he had been imprisoned by Sycorax, a witch and the mother of an earth spirit, or gnome, who had been fathered by a devil. Prospero's control over the sylph is magical, and the sylph himself is a magician, if only because he can make himself invisible. While performing his major feats Prospero wears a mantle, which he lays aside when he is to perform lesser marvels. He puts a spell upon his daughter Miranda, and when she awakens causes her and Ferdinand, whom he intends to become her husband, to fall instantly in love. He has also acquired power over Caliban, the gnome, and can make him suffer from cramps and side stitches when he is disobedient. When Ferdinand refuses to follow directions, Prospero causes his nerves or muscles to be "in their infancy again, / And have no vigour in them" (ibid.). All this magic is assisted by the fact that Prospero had discerned "a most auspicious star" to be favorably situated in the heavens.

The details I have mentioned are drawn only from the first act. In the fourth, a masque evoked by "Some vanity" of Prospero's art—that is, chiefly for fun— includes appearances of Iris, Ceres, Juno, and "certain nymphs," who speak and sing (act 4, sc. 1). Since Miranda is the only woman on the island, these are evidently either the personages themselves—three of them pagan goddesses—or, more probably, spirits who impersonate them. At the end, as everybody knows, Prospero breaks his staff and abjures magic forever, intending to devote much of his remaining life to prayer. In the meantime he has exercised power like that sought by John Dee and taught by Cornelius Agrippa, whose *De occulta philosophia libri tres* may well have been among the books Prospero was allowed to carry into exile.

Elsewhere in the plays occultism is occasionally present. Owen Glendower, in *Henry IV, Part 1,* was born to the accompaniment of prodigies and summons spirits from a thousand-leagues' distance to provide music (act 3, sc. 1). Lorenzo, in *The Merchant of Venice,* knows that the heavens are filled with music; to Jessica he says, "There's not the smallest orb that thou behold'st / But in his motion like an angel sings" (act 5, sc. 1). Joan of Arc is portrayed as a witch in *Henry VI.* The Weird Sisters, in *Macbeth,* whatever their ancestry in Norse mythology, are presented as witches who can afflict cattle, cause storms, change themselves into rats, and use loathsome objects in their rites. One boasts of her intention to become succubus to a sailor (act 1, sc. 3). *A Midsummer Night's Dream* includes fairies and a goblin who are capable of affecting perceptions by the application of magical juices to the eyes and of giving Bottom an ass's head. Pagan deities appear:

Hecate twice in *Macbeth,* where she once says that he will make artificial spirits out of a drop distilled by the moon (act 2, sc. 5), and Diana (though, to be sure, in a dream sequence) in *Pericles.* Portents are described frequently; not only in *Julius Caesar,* where most were borrowed from tradition, but in such a passage as one in *Richard II,* where the king's fall is predicted by a withered bay tree, meteors, and a red moon. Astrology is often alluded to, sometimes skeptically but sometimes not: Romeo and Juliet were "star-crossed."

The catalog could be extended for some time. Obviously, Shakespeare underwent an influence from Hermeticism in the sense that he introduced occultist notions into his plays. When, however, one asks, Was he himself an occultist? the answer comes hard. It is a question that perplexes the entire subject with which I am dealing. One wants to know the answer because it matters, but the way to obtain it is uncertain. Do such contemporary writers as Tolkien, Mary Stewart, Mary Renault, Charles Williams, C. S. Lewis, and Madeleine L'Engle believe in the literal possibility of the marvels they have introduced into their fictions? Sometimes, as with Williams and Lewis, one can infer an answer from nonfictive writings. Theoretically, inquiries can be addressed to fictionists who are still alive. But what is one to do with men like Shakespeare, who are beyond the reach of spoken and written queries and lived at a time when preassumptions differed from modern ones? Are the wonders they describe merely probable impossibilities? The most impressive evidence I have offered is from *The Tempest;* but a common, and very plausible, interpretation of that play is that the magic is a metaphor for the power of the aesthetic imagination to produce a fictive cosmos in which truths are projected figuratively.

It is tempting to reply that the question is irrelevant: The proper concern is not with convictions but with uses. In my opinion the retort will not do because, I say again, one wants to know (or at least I want to know) whether Frances Yates and others who accept her guidance are right in believing that, among persons who mattered, Hermeticism was the dominant philosophy of the Elizabethan age. And this problem cannot be resolved without speculating about credence. Sometimes a probable answer can be ventured, though often not a simple yes or no. Shakespeare, in my opinion, no doubt believed, like virtually everybody in his time, in the existence of witches. As Kittredge said in a class lecture, he must often have had premonitions, some of which (I hypothesize) may have been generated by observations that impressed his conscious or subconscious mind as portents. As for astrology, he probably granted the likelihood of some planetary and stellar influence on nature and man while remaining skeptical about horoscopal predictions. On the other side, apart from his acceptance of Christianity, he had no driving transcendental bent; also, unlike such authentic philosophers as Bruno and Campanella, he felt no strong urge to fit into a coherent system every idea he entertained. Although obviously acute and possibly wise, he was basically not a systematic thinker but a *poiētēs* or "maker." His plays accordingly testify to the currency of occultist ideas but not necessarily to his acceptance of them as true. It is so also with many other writers of belles lettres, judgments of whom may have greater or lesser credibility but can rarely be altogether certain, one sobering consideration being the realization that the better authors make all their fictive universes so self-subsistent that while an empathizing reader is inside them no question of disbelief arises.

What has just been said about authors and whole works does not always relate to passages, which are sometimes unambiguous. I shall illustrate, very briefly, from George Herbert and John Donne. In Herbert's *Elixir* the final stanza begins, "This is the famous stone / That turneth all to gold." The allusion is to alchemy, which the arch-Hermeticist John Dee practiced off and on in England and during his Continental journey in the 1580s. "This," however, refers to a principle stated a few lines earlier, where the poet says to his God and King, "All may of thee partake: Nothing can be so mean, / Which with his tincture (for thy sake) / Will not grow bright and clean." A servant who sweeps a room in this spirit will dignify both the room and the sweeping. Alchemy is a metaphor—nothing more. In *Loves Alchymie,* by Donne, transmutation is mentioned only to be rejected: "no chymique yet th'Elixar got, / But glorifies his pregnant pot, / If by the way to him befall/ Some odoriferous thing, or medicinall." The true use of alchemy is to produce perfumes and medicaments by accident. Dozens, perhaps scores, of such allusions might be collected to prove that Hermetic ideas evoked scorn. These, however, are cheap victories, which I now abandon in favor of an effort to consider whether a case can be made for actual Hermeticism in an especially promising candidate, Henry Vaughan.

Vaughan not only has the reputation of a mystic but had a brother, Thomas, who wrote occultist treatises that in scope invite comparison with Agrippa's *De occulta philosophia.* I do not have space to examine the whole body of Henry Vaughan's poetry but must confine my attention to a selection of his best known and most frequently anthologized pieces.

The general opinion of Vaughan is that he was in some degree a Hermeticist. Helen C. White, Ruth C. Wallerstein, and Ricardo Quintana say in their anthology of seventeenth-century verse and prose that he accepted "Hermetic-Christian ideas of the relations of the microcosm and the macrocosm, with the resulting correspondences and sympathies" (*Seventeenth-Century Verse and Prose* [New York, 1951], 1:472). Another anthology, edited by Alexander M. Witherspoon and Frank J. Warnke, remarks of Vaughan that he frequently used as a frame of reference "the kind of recondite learning cultivated by his brother Thomas, who was famous as an alchemist and mystical philosopher" (*Seventeenth-Century Prose and Poetry* [New York, 1963]). The *Dictionary of National Biography* notes Vaughan's translation of a volume of excerpts called *Hermetick Physic* and calls him a pantheist. Of the microcosm/macrocosm parallels I will not speak beyond saying that in my limited survey I found no clear indications of them, and that Leonard Barkan does not mention Vaughan in the exhaustive survey called *Nature's Work of Art;* but I will consider briefly passages that appear to merit special attention.

I begin with the final lines of *The Retreate:*

> Some men a forward motion love,
> But I by backward steps would move,
> And when this dust falls to the urn
> In that state I came, return.

If after death the poet returns to the state he had experienced before birth, his soul must have preexisted earthly embodiment: a Platonic idea. The atheistic reading—that as he was nothing before birth so he will be nothing after death—is unacceptable.

This interpretation is supported by the beginning of *Corruption:*

> Sure, it was so. Man in those early days
>   Was not all stone, and Earth.
> He shin'd a little, and by those weak Rays
>   Had some glimpse of his birth.
> He saw Heaven o'r his head, and knew from whence
>   He cam (condemned,) hither.

Before the Fall, man was exceptionally intelligent, and when he looked at the sky he could remember (or less probably, guess) that his original home had been there. Later, after he had sinned, he could remember only the bliss of the lost earthly paradise: "He sigh'd for *Eden,* and would often say / *Ah!* what *bright days were those?*"

So far the evidence has been positive; what remains is less so. In *The Constellation* he denies the Pythagorean music of the spheres by assigning to the heavens a "motion without noise." One can understand this to mean "a motion without audible noise" only by ignoring what the line says in favor of something one would prefer it to have said. According to the White, Wallerstein, and Quintano volume something said in the first stanza of *Cock-Crowing* had a Hermetic source:

> Father of lights! what Sunnie seed,
> What glance of day hast thou confin'd
> Into this bird? To all the breed
> This busie Ray thou hast assign'd:
>   Their magnetisme works all night,
>   And dreams of Paradise and light.

The comment is that "According to Hermetic theory things terrestrial can exert magnetic attraction on things spiritual." Perhaps so, but I cannot verify the assertion either from my study of the Hermetic documents and commentaries on them or from my readings in Renaissance discussions of magnetism. Such claims cannot always be accepted at face value but must be considered as hypotheses to be confirmed or refuted, just as I should wish my ideas here to be received by my readers.

I take a final passage from *The Bird:*

> So murthered man, when lovely life is done,
> And his blood freez'd, keeps in the Center still
> Some secret sense, which makes the dead blood run
> At his approach, that did the body kill.

In other words, the blood of a murdered man boils in the presence of his murderer, a belief now sufficiently unfamiliar to the general reader to seem occultist. On this topic I can speak with more than usual confidence, having recently completed a manuscript on natural magic. The predominant opinion at the time Vaughan wrote was that reported by Gaspar Schott in his four-volume *Magia universalis* of 1657–59, namely, that "spirits" which lingered in the body after death became inflamed with enmity at the approach of the murderer and consequently liquified the curdled blood. Schott cites twenty-four writers on the subject and acknowledges the happening itself as fact. The cause was "natural," and the effect was not produced by the special skill of a magician, "spirits" playing an important role in the science and philosophy of the time.

If there were space, I should like to speak in detail about another major poet, Edmund Spenser, whose uses of occultism I recently studied for several months in preparing an article for a forthcoming Spenser encyclopedia. Of all Spenser's poems, *An Hymne in Honovr of Beavtie* is perhaps the most basically Platonic because the whole argues a thesis presented in the *Symposium* of Plato and popularized by Castiglione's *Il Cortegiano,* that of the Ladder of Love. The numerological stanza in the description of the House of Temperance (2.9.22) is notoriously and indisputably Hermeticist. The making, by the magician Archimago, of a false Una in book 1 is described in sufficient detail to reveal some acquaintance with magical rituals and procedures. (Elsewhere the magic is simply the usual magic of epic, a part of the tradition from Homer and Vergil onward and especially dense in the Italian epics that served as Spenser's model.) The Garden of Adonis in book 3 embodies the notion that souls preexisted human birth. Belphoebe's horoscope is suggested in 3.6: Jupiter, in his daytime house, was in friendly aspect with Venus, and so, too, was the sun. Canto 7 of book 5 presents an Egyptian temple, and though it contains no Hermetic doctrines, it suggests an awareness that the vogue of Hermeticism had made Egyptian religion prestigious.

A few other passages and phrases may also have Platonic overtones. All this does not, however, in my opinion, justify a conviction that Spenser was a convinced and consistent Hermeticist or that he necessarily had a detailed firsthand knowledge of Plato, Ficino, and the disciples of both. Bryskett's reported assertion that the poet was "very well read in Philosophie" (*The Poetical Works of Edmund Spenser,* ed. J. C. Smith and E. de Selincourt [Oxford, 1932], p. xxvi), Digby's that he was "thoroughly verst in the Mathematicall Sciences, in Philosophy, and in Divinity" (*The Works of Edmund Spenser: A Variorum Edition,* ed. Edwin Greenlaw et al. [Baltimore, 1961], 4:472), and de Selincourt's that "his early hymns to Love and Beauty, are the completest expression in our literature of the doctrines of Bembo and Ficino" (*Poetical Works,* p. xlvi) seem to me at least slightly overenthusiastic.

The results of this brief survey have been partly negative. I have no conscious wish to minimize the influence of Hermetism; doing so would lessen the importance of my own researches. I once again suggest, however, that scholarship is ill served by a strong desire to widen the relevance of its findings through a demonstration that whatever may have been found was central, and determinant, for its age. Sometimes it may have been; but one may, I think, usefully proceed with caution, trying rather to add a little to knowledge than to foment an immediate revolution. If it is needed, the revolution will come all the more forcefully, in due time, as the result of a gradual accumulation of details. I have intended no reproach to scholarship as a whole, thinking its predominant learning impressive and its temper usually admirable. It is only to the rare excess that my strictures are intended to apply—and perhaps, at times, to myself.

15

Aurora; or, The Rising Sun of Allegory: Hermetic Imagery in the Work of Jakob Böhme

INGRID MERKEL

How does Jakob Böhme—one might ask—figure in the circle of learned *umanisti* and Hermetists, of brilliant and public personnages? He was a quiet and humble man, from an obscure part of the world and a shoemaker for all his life. To the *philosophi* and *physici* among his friends and followers he would protest, "Neither can I say anything of myself, nor boast or write of anything, save this: that I am a simple man" (p. 33).[1] Pious and fastidious, he would take offense at being counted among doctors who "always played upon the fiddle of pride" (p. 471) and had yielded "to the spell of Heathenish wisdom" (p. 66), or being held in the company of the "blind and proud necromancers, jugglers and sorcerers" who "suffer the devil to play ape" with them (pp. 423–24). It is with caution and reservation that I introduce Jakob Böhme into the circle of Hermetists.

Within that circle and despite his protestations, he nevertheless deserves the title of "prince de l'ésotérisme occidentale" that Antoine Faivre accords him.[2] He disliked pagan ancestry, to be sure, and was decidedly no child of Hermes. Still, I propose that he belonged to Hermes' extended Renaissance family. While in his time much of the early Renaissance enthusiasm had already worn thin, he transformed some of the still vital impulses into a philosophy that survived into the eighteenth and nineteenth centuries and was able to kindle the interest of men who in turn molded what would become twentieth-century thought. I mention in passing the influence of Böhme on romantic writers and on German idealism, notably on Franz von Bader, on Schelling and Hegel.[3]

Böhme was both a shoemaker and a philosopher. The English, who were among his earliest and most ardent disciples, proudly called him *philosophus teutonicus.* A contemporary of Robert Fludd, he was born in 1575 in Altseidenberg, Silesia, and he died in 1624 in Görlitz. As a young journeyman he had traveled on the Continent, but rarely did he leave Görlitz after he had set up business and had gotten married. He had read the Bible and, it seems, books of a mystical and alchemical nature, foremost the works of Paracelsus, since these were available in German and Böhme did not know Latin. There were some stirrings of humanism in Görlitz while Scultetus (a friend of Johannes Kepler and of Tycho Brahe and himself a mathematician) was mayor of the town. But stark and oppressive orthodoxy also reigned, through the town's pastor Georg Richter, a zealot who had Böhme silenced on accounty of heresy. Later in his life and through discourse with his disciples, most of whom were Silesian nobles and Paracelsian physicians, Böhme grew in learning. Still, no reference to the philosophy of his time fully explains the originality of Böhme's *philosophia* and its power, by which he set out "to treat very plainly and comprehensively of the being of God, and of angels, by similitudes, that the reader may from one step to another, at last come to the deep sense and true ground" (p. 37).

This was, however, a gigantic task. While Böhme struggled in "the deepest births of God in their being," in order "to comprehend them in my reason" (p. 488), he wrought a profoundly new vision of the Deity. Böhme's urgent question—whether informed by Gnosticism or Neoplatonism—struck right at the center of Renaissance philosophy. Ficino and Pico had celebrated the notion of a beautiful and harmonious universe, in which a multitude of forces strove in diversity to be reconciled by eros *(philia)* to the great One and All ($\dot{\eta}\nu$ και $\bar{\pi}\alpha\nu$): Böhme, on the contrary, experienced a radical alienation. "I fell into a very deep melancholy," he professed, "when I beheld and contemplated the great deep of this world, also the sun and stars, the clouds, rain and snow, and considered in my spirit the whole creation of this world. Wherein then I found to be in all things evil and good, love and anger, in the inanimate creatures, viz. in wood and stones, earth and the elements, as also in men and beasts" (p. 486). In this melancholy recognition of the fundamental conflict in the world, even if Böhme had found it through the reading of Paracelsus, he certainly drew exorbitant conclusions that went far beyond the mind-set of his master. There is a Heraclitean radicalism in Böhme's perception of an objective dialectic, and it was this notion that reshaped the elements of Renaissance Platonism and prepared this philosophy for adoption by later generations who would recognize and identify with Böhme's alienation.

Whatever the sources for Böhme's experience might have been, they have forever attracted and frustrated the curiosity of Böhme enthusiasts and scholars. Little is known about his formal education or about his autodidactic readings. Abraham von Franckenberg, a devoted disciple and Böhme's first biographer, was not an unbiased historian, and what little is known is known through his *De vita*. He reports that in conversations with learned friends Böhme acquired the contemporary knowledge of science and Gnostic and Neoplatonic concepts, along with an alchemical vocabulary.

Yet by any measure, and in spite of his modesty, Böhme had an extraordinary mind. His *Philosophia* unfolds, book by book, in ever-growing circles, to tell the story of light and darkness in God and in his creation. This being a difficult task for anyone—mystic, poet, or philosopher—Böhme labored painfully but with determination to forge into discourse his vision of the "deep ground" of God. He remained suspended, as it were, between the immediacy of his vision and its conceptualization. His writings, therefore, strain between myth and philosophy.

One can admire his courage, nevertheless, and enjoy his gift of mythopoeia. For he was a man whose spirit, much like Jacob struggling with the angel, wrestled with God, and who after much "storm upon God," broke through "the gates of hell, even into the innermost birth . . . of the Deity." His subsequent joy could not "be compared to anything, but to that wherein the life is generated in the midst of death." "In this light," he said, "my spirit suddenly saw through all, and in all and by all creatures, even in herbs and grass it knew God, and who he is, and how he is, and what his will is." This he followed with the extraordinary profession that "suddenly in that light my will was set on by a mighty impulse, to describe the being of God" (p. 488).

What ultimately emerged from this mighty impulse was a cosmogony and cosmology of archaic power, the ancient drama of the birth of God, of eternal nature, of Lucifer's hubris, and of the creation of the world. This myth unfolded within twelve years that Böhme spent in silence, tending to his business and to the raising of his children. In 1612 a sudden "rain," as he described it, "burst down and where it hits it hits."[4] He composed *Aurora, That Is, . . . Morning Redness in the Rising of the Sun* in five months, in a storm of inspiration, laboring in an unruly and untamed language, but keenly aware that he stood at the threshold of divine knowledge "which had not been revealed ever to such extent in any man's heart."[5]

The *Aurora* was the mythical and mystical revelation of a dramatic rebirth. It touched at the very heart of a generation of discontented Protestants who were saddened by the decline of Luther's Reformation into a new orthodoxy. The *Aurora* spread like bushfire among the intellectuals of Silesia, while Böhme became the immediate victim of bigotry. Pastor Richter, alarmed by Böhme's revolutionary dreams, reported to the city council that Böhme's god was made of sulfur and mercury. Böhme did not write for seven years, then yielded to requests of disciples and produced twenty more treatises, harassed though he remained to the end of his life by the authorities. In his important writings—*Forty Questions of the Soul* (1620), *Six Theosophical Points* (1620), *The Signature of Things* (1622), and *Mysterium Magnum* (1623)—he rewrote with an ever-sharper focus, with greater mastery of the material, and with clearer concepts the original vision of the *Aurora,* which he later retracted.

2

When I turn to the Hermetic imagery in Böhme's works, I use the term *Hermetic* in an ambiguous way. As there is little factual knowledge of influences on Böhme except for that of Paracelsus, one may assume that elements of the Hermetic tradition had come down to Böhme through him.[6] Böhme would have used them with the reservation of the mystic who is well aware of their inadequacy. And in fact they do reflect more of his millenarian enthusiasm than of their traditional meaning. Böhme's *Aurora* shared with the Hermetic tradition, nevertheless, the fundamental belief in the living forces of the Neoplatonic universe. He called those forces "Qualitäten," retracing their ethymology to "quellen," to well up, to be born, and to "Qual," torment and torture. The Platonic *catena aurea* was consequently called "Band der Qualitäten." In Böhme's cosmos the supracelestial and pregnant Nous gives birth to Logos, the son, very much like in the *Corpus Hermeticum* and the paraphernalia of the heavens: angels and demons, planets and fixed stars, turn around *mundus,* the world of man, just the same.[7] This world of man is the pivotal point of the universe, because it is here that the story of God evolves into the history of the world, becomes "Weltgeschichte," an idea that was not lost on Hegel. At the same time, the world of man is not a subject of gnosis, as in the Hermetic vision, but a very real experience. The *Aurora* abounds with common-life metaphors of trees and green meadows, of children and lovers at play. In terms of philosophical discourse, the realism of this language is crude. Hegel, who otherwise admired Böhme for his "profundity of mind,"[8] objected that this mind "is confined in the hardy knotty oak of the senses—in the gnarled concretion of the ordinary conception—and is not able to arrive at a free presentation of the Idea."[9]

Palingenesis was yet another fundamental notion that the *Aurora* shared with the Hermetic tradition. When Tat, the son of Hermes, had been invaded by the ten powers and had been cleansed, he was endowed with the vision of τὸ πᾶν, the All.[10] He then rose through the seven spheres, leaving his old body and the world behind, to become a god himself. This regeneration was achieved through the suspension of the senses and by rejection of the sensory world: "τὸ αἰσθητὸν τῆς φύσεως σῶμα πόρρωθέν ἐστι τῆς οὐσιωδοῦς γενέσεως"[11] Böhme, on the contrary, experienced his regeneration, not after intellectual concentration, but upon the sight of a material thing. One day in 1600 he saw, according to Franckenberg, a tin plate on the wall of his shop glow "mit lieblich jovialem Schein" (with a lovely, jovial glow). The radiance of the tin opened his eyes to the comprehension of the primordial relation of "Lichtwelt" and "Finsterwelt," the light and darkness, or "the yes and no in all things."[12] His senses were thus not suspended but restored to their original faculty to perceive of the root of all things in the *deus absconditus.* Tat transcended the world of things, but Böhme took on the responsibility to help bring forth *sophia*—the wisdom that will restore nature. Man's regeneration, therefore, is the eschatological promise of the regeneration of all creation. The *Aurora* was the morning redness of its palingenesis.

The notion of a holistic universe, whose structure could ultimately be reduced to the circle and whose center lay *ubique et nusquam* in the heart of man, informed both the Hermetic and Böhme's philosophies. It was, however, Böhme's resolution to face the tragic conflict in the world and to understand the history of man on earth as the battleground of good and evil on which the fate of God would evolve as "Natur- und Weltgeschichte." His acute awareness of history was Christian, to be sure, but in its voluntarism was also decidedly modern. This ethos broke the Hermetic circle and released the dynamics of world history in a spiral—that is, in a circle that pushes upward—through the driving force of the dialectics of "yes and no in all things."

3

Hegel, a rational reader with a Hermetic language of his own, to be sure, criticized Böhme for his lack of lucid concepts:

The forms that he employs are really no longer determinations of the Notion at all. They are on the one hand sensuous, chemical determinations, such qualities as acid, sweet, sour, fierce; and, on the other, emotions such as wrath and love . . . For him these sensuous forms do not, however, possess the sensuous significance which belongs to them, but he uses them in order to find expression for his Thought. . . . However rude and barbarous this may on the one hand be, and however impossible it is to read Böhme continuously, or to take a firm grasp of his thoughts (for all these qualities, spirits and angels make one's head swim), we must on the other hand recognize that he speaks of everything as it is in its actuality.[13]

Böhme himself begs his reader's patience with his awkwardness and simplicity, yet there is more to his barbarous language than a simple man's lack of eloquence. "I must indeed use this earthly tongue, yet there is a true heavenly understanding couched under it, which in my outermost birth I am not able to express either in writing or in speaking . . . and though I should write mere spirit . . . yet the heart understandeth only flesh" (p. 500). The reader's dilemma emerges clearly when Böhme admonishes him to" get into thy spirit the Holy Ghost . . . and he will lead the . . . Then thou wilt . . . understand those things which are written hereafter following" (p. 66).The reader's state in the flesh blinds him to the meaning of the text: "For without the illumination . . . you will not understand this Mystery; for there is a strong lock and bar before it" (p. 315). Unless the reader himself is reborn, the *Aurora* remains concealed.

Böhme shared with many of his contemporaries—millenarians, Pentecostals, and linguists—a speculative cabalistic passion for the *lingua adamica*,[14] the language of Adam before the Fall, when he named things and when a name *was* the idea of its object, a perfect symbol inasmuch as signifier and signified corresponded in actuality. When the gates of Paradise closed, creation turned mute. But Böhme did not see, as structural linguists do today, a complete rupture between word and object. All objects still retain, as he explained in *The Signature of Things*, their idea in themselves, but hidden as if in a "Kasten" (box). If Böhme "speaks of everything as it is in its actuality," to quote Hegel again, it is because actuality is the box from which the ideas have to be unlocked by a regenerated mind that can read as well as write "mere spirit."

Another connotation of Böhme's Platonic notion of language, which Hegel did not touch upon explicitly, involves what might be called the principle of allegory. I do not suggest that Böhme was familiar with the intricacies of baroque rhetoric or that he knew the technique of mythological or biblical *allegorese*. He arrived at his concept of figurative speech naively through the frustrated awareness of mystics that all language is inadequate in the communication of mystical truth. The alchemist, on the contrary, used allegory on purpose in order to preserve the secrecy of the chemical process, ἵνα μὴ ὦμεν διάβολοι τοῦ παντὸς εἰς τοὺς πολλούς,[15] just as the baroque poet deliberately heaped metaphor upon metaphor to achieve a hyperbolic éclat of wit. Böhme, on the other hand, suffered from the deficiency of language, because its allegorical function is an alienation from the Divine truth. He describes how the sweet qualities in God love warmth, similar to young lovers who "creep into the body and heart of one another." But this simile is corrupted, because "this earthly love is only cold water, and is not true fire. A man cannot find any full similitude of it in this half-dead world" (p. 198). Thus, as Hegel observed, the sweet qualities of God are not metaphors in any traditional sense; they are as they are in their actuality. They are neither notion nor objects. Language, however, is unredeemed actuality. Böhme struggled with such half-dead matter consistently in order to not write "silently, from sheer vision." If he achieved greater clarity and some form of system in his later works, the *Aurora* remains his most mysterious, most beautiful work for its very chaos of concealed imagery.

Böhme's use of allegory, unmediated by rhetoric and informed only by his mystical alienation from language, adds a new, deeper, and even tragic dimension to the iconography of his time: "A man cannot find any full similitude in this half-dead world." There is a self-consciousness, a Saturnian *acedia* in the allegorical compilations of half-dead things in baroque poetry and art, an unredeemed distrust of their substance, an anguished *horror vacui,* as though the divine life, which the early Renaissance had kindled, had frozen in them. Walter Benjamin was one of the first in the twentieth century to recognize the hidden allegiance to guilt in baroque allegory and to understand its motivating power.[16] The futility, the muteness—muteness of fallen nature—the sheer "Stofflichkeit" (materiality) of allegory reminded him of the "fragmented, disordered, cluttered laboratories of alchemists"[17] and, I might add, of their precarious hope for miraculous transmutation. For in their sullen muteness, in their half-dead state, all things beg for redemption, for deciphering, for the unlocking of their concealed meaning: "God is in the center of the innermost birth . . . hiddenly, but it is not known, except in the spirit of man alone" (p. 504). For Böhme, whom Benjamin called one of the "greatest allegorists,"[18] creation was an allegory of the *deus absconditus.* The *Aurora,* however, was the new life in the rising sun of allegory, its redemption, and the beginning of a true hermeneutics.

This tragic notion of allegory, as a fragmented cipher that conceals the Hermetic God, obviously contrasts with a more current, albeit more innocent, understanding of allegory: as of a sign that, within a referential frame, corresponds to a pregiven universal (as a rose can refer to the ideal of beauty). It is also at odds with the holistic symbol, so much preferred by such classicists as Goethe or Hegel: that sign which presumably *is* the universal and thus, by an act of ultimate hubris, pretends to restore the innocence of Paradise.

4

The true nature of the *Aurora* is myth. It tells the story of God allegorically in the sense of the romantics, who had a great proclivity both for allegory and for Böhme. "Allegory," explained Friedrich Creuzer, "is progress in a sequence of moments; allegory therefore subsumes myth, whose perfect representation is the epopee."[19] In terms appropriate to the *Aurora,* allegory "is a dramatically moving and flowing image of ideas. It is their succession and progress in time." If one reads the *Aurora* with greater patience than Hegel had for its "rude method of presentation,"[20] if one understands it as the half-dead concealment of eternity in time, one might still learn to appreciate the redeeming function of myth.

Böhme has long had eminent status in the history of philosophy. He worked out a rudimentary dialectic, after all, and he recovered reason and consciousness of self from the philosophy of nature, in whose confinements he labored much like the pre-Socratic philosophers before him. He is also read for the archaic beauty of his mythical lore, because there is beauty in his tales of the innermost birth of God. However, to read the *Aurora* allegorically and properly as myth, one must read it in the light of its cosmic origin: the fall of Lucifer.

Böhme's account of Lucifer's rebellion lacks the heroic pathos of Milton's epic and the somber beauty of the latter's archangel:

> as when the sun new-risen
> Looks through the horizontal misty air
> Shorn of his beams, or from behind the moon
> In dim eclipse, disastrous twilight sheds
> On half the nations, and with fear of change
> Perplexes monarchs. Darkened so, yet shone
> Above them all th'archangel.[21]

Still, there is sufficient drama in Böhme's story: "When king Lucifer was so gloriously, beautifully and divinely created . . . as a king in God, then he suffered his bright, beauteous form to befool him that he saw how noble, glorious and fair a spirit rose up in him. Then his seven qualifying spirits . . . thought they would elevate and kindle themselves . . . as a new god" (p. 420). Böhme emphasized again and again the mystery that was the fall of this king of light, who was born from the center of God as an image of God the Son and who resided in the core of eternal nature. The mystery lies in the fact that Lucifer, who sprang from God's love, became by hubris the wrath of God: "The gracious and amiable blessed light was extinguished . . . And there was nothing but an astringent, bitter, fiery burning, tearing and raging" (p. 427). Böhme touched here on his most profound and most perplexing question about good and evil in God. Wrestling with the "love and mercy" of God he came to understand that Lucifer "had kindled the wrath of God, which indeed, had otherwise rested eternally in secret, and so he hath made the Salitter [sal niter] of God to be a murderous den." God has not turned into the Devil, for "the wrath-fire of God doth not reach in nature into the innermost kernel of the heart, which is the Son of God" (p. 428). Lucifer's hubris only spoiled his own realm, for "all became very dark, perished and spoiled; the water became very cold and thick." Thus nature was corrupted, but "only in the outermost birth . . . but the innermost . . . retained its own right to itself" (p. 430). Böhme concluded that Lucifer "must now lie captivated and imprisoned in the outermost birth . . . till the Last Judgement Day, which is at hand" (p. 431).

To have resolved the conflict of good and evil in God by the theodicy of Lucifer's fall has not satisfied enlightened and critical readers, because stories do not do so. For myths, to quote Sir Thomas Browne, are "frivolous, obscure, fabulous, un-couth, magical and superstitious" stories that "might humour our fancy where we cannot satisfy our reason."[22] Browne spoke of the "Egyptians' lore," the Hermetic tradition. But, of course, nothing is easier than the debunking of myth. If myth had any function as a pseudo, or prescientific science, real science would have had to supersede it until all storytelling would have been replaced by science.[23] Unexpectedly and fortunately, though, myth has prevailed, because it is not prescientific science and therefore infantile or corrupt, but an essential alternative to science in dealing with reality. The telling of stories—supect as it has been for spreading lies, frivolous, fanciful, and magical nonsense—conquers the fear of the unknown. It gives man a small freedom and some confidence in the world. Rational science has labored hard to transmute the base matter of myth into the gold of logos, but it has not yet produced the philosopher's stone. Instead it has produced its own myths. It is important to remember that Hegel retold Böhme's story as his own mythology of reason, the "Phänomenologie des Geistes," but God has remained concealed. One may have to study the *Aurora* for a long while for release from fear and for the sake of confidence. That is why I find myself speaking, not in defense, but in praise of Hermeticism.

Notes

1. All quotations in English, except where indicated otherwise, are from Jacob Boehme, *The Aurora,* trans. John Sparrow (London, 1960). Quotations are followed in text by page number from the Sparrow translation.

2. A. Faivre, "La critique Boehmienne de Franz von Baader," in *Jacob Boehme, ou l'obscure lumière de la connaissance mystique. (Paris, 1979), p. 137.*

3. There is an extensive literature on the subject. Some titles may serve as an initial guide: E. Ederheimer, *Jakob Böhme und die Romantiker* (diss., Universität Heidelberg, 1914); K. Lese, *Von Jakob Böhme zu Schelling* (Erfurt, 1927); R. F. Brown, *The Later Philosophy of Schelling: The Influence of Böhme on the Works of 1809–1815* (Lewisburg, Penn., 1977). Much of Faivre's scholarship deals with the subject of Böhme's influence on romanticism and idealism.

4. "Was er trifft, das trifft er," from the letter to H. S. Schweinichen, 3 June 1621, in *Sendbriefe,* ed. W. E. Peuckert, (Stuttgart, 1955); my own translation.

5. "In keines Menschen Herze also ganz und gar offenbar worden," Jakob Boehme, *Aurora, oder Morgenröthe im Aufgang,* in *Sämtliche Schriften,* 11 vols. (Stuttgart, 1955–61), 1:195; my own translation.

6. For recent scholarship on the subject, see R. H. Hvolbek, "Was Jacob Boehme a Paracelsian?" *Hermetic Journal* 19 (Spring 1983): 6–17.

7. There are indications in Böhme's work that he became aware of the new astronomy of Copernicus before 1600. Quite possibly it was this recognition that led to the radical change in his religious experience. See H. Grunsky, *Jacob Böhme* (Stuttgart, 1956), pp. 19–20.

8. G.W.F. Hegel, *Lectures on the History of Philosophy,* 3 vols., trans. E. S. Haldane and F. H. Simson (New York, 1955), 3:191.

9. Ibid., p. 195.

10. *Asclepius,* in *Corpus Hermeticum,* ed. and trans. A. D. Nock and A.-J. Festugière, 4 vols. (Paris, 1946–54), 2:206.

11. Ibid.: "le corps visible de la nature est bien éloigné de la generation."

12. Jakob Böhme, *Betrachtung göttlicher Offenbarung: Questiones theosophicae,* in *Sämtliche Schriften,* 9:12.

13. Hegel, *History of Philosophy,* 3:193.

14. See the paper by H. Ormsby-Lennon in this volume. Also, K.R. Popp, *Böhme and Newton* (Leipzig, 1935); E. Benz, "Die metaphysische Begründung der Sprache bei Jakob Böhme," in *Euphorion: Dichtung and Volkstum* 37 (1936); and by the same author *Adam: Der Mythus des Menschen* (Munich, 1955).

15. *Asclepius,* 2:206: "Afin que nous ne divulguions pas le Tout à la foule."

16. W. Benjamin, *Ursprung des deutschen Trauerspiels,* ed. Rolf Tiedemann (Frankfurt, 1978).

17. Ibid., p. 165.

18. Ibid., p. 179.

19. F. Creuzer, *Symbolik und Mythologie der alten Völker, besonders der Griechen*, pt. 1, para. 2 (Leipzig, 1819), pp. 70–71.

20. Hegel, *History of Philosophy*, 3:189.

21. John Milton, *Paradise Lost*, book 1, lines 594–600 (*The Norton Anthology of English Literature* [New York, 1974], p. 1377). For influences of Böhme on Milton, see M. Lewis Bailey, *Milton and Jakob Boehme: A Study of German Mysticism in Seventeenth-Century England* (New York, 1914).

22. Quoted from W. Shumaker, *The Occult Sciences in the Renaissance: A Study in Intellectual Patterns* (Berkeley, 1972), p. 241.

23. See the study on the topic by H. Blumenberg, *Arbeit am Mythos* (Frankfurt, 1979).

16

Rosicrucian Linguistics: Twilight of a Renaissance Tradition

HUGH ORMSBY-LENNON

1

In an appendix to *The Rosicrucian Enlightenment*—if not her best book, one redolent, nonetheless, of a first-rate whodunit—Dame Frances Yates reprints the first English translations of the *Fama* and *Confessio . . . dess Löblichens Ordens des Rozenkreutzes*.[1] Originally published in Kassel "durch Wilhelm Wessell" in 1614 and 1615, the Rosicrucian manifestos appeared in English in 1652, ostensibly the handiwork of Thomas Vaughan but actually the fruit of a manuscript tree that antedated by some twenty years the "translation" of this feisty Welsh alchemist.[2] Whether one sees the *Fama* and *Confessio* as an irenic program for reform tragically wrecked on the battlefields of Europe, as the *ludibria* of an imaginary band of merry pranksters, or as spectacular scum on the mainstream of seventeenth-century history, the manifestos have still not received, particularly in English translation, the philosophical and linguistic analysis they deserve. Their occult, theological, and scientific contexts have been variously studied by A. E. Waite, John Warwick Montgomery, and Frances Yates,[3] but no one has examined the *Fama* and the *Confessio* for their late and peculiarly rich flowering of Renaissance book mysticism. And even if one skims the manifestos as examples of that intellectual dross which, so Bacon averred, should sink rather than float, one must still acknowledge the role, particularly in mid-seventeenth-century England, of Rosicrucian linguistics within a tradition of thinking about language that Sir Ernst Gombrich has denominated Platonic.[4]

What I shall explore in this essay is the twilight (or apparent twilight) of linguistic Platonism during the Puritan revolution. I shall also examine the growing conviction that this twilight heralded a new dawn of rational thought about language and signification. Whether the Royal Society and its latitudinarian allies were right or whether their own program for semiological reform betrayed ines-

311

capable affinities with Rosicrucian book mysticism are questions that will function as the matrix of my inquiry. The Brotherhood of the Rosy Cross may never have existed—no one disclosed his membership; its defenders emphasized that they were not initiates—but its ethos and mythos pervaded England during the Interregnum and early Restoration. And Rosicrucian linguistics provided Englishmen with a theory of signification that, by turns, captivated, perplexed, and infuriated them.

2

In *Icones Symbolicae,* Gombrich contrasts linguistic Platonism with its Renaissance rival, Aristotelian linguistics, observing that each remains a dialectical antagonist in that larger drama of signification which continues to unfold. For if the Aristotelians use language as "a tool, an 'organon' developed by mankind under the evolutionary pressures which favoured collaboration and communication between members of a clan or tribe"—as an organon, that is, "adapted to the intrasubjective worlds of facts and of arguments"—then the Platonists, Gombrich explains,

> made man feel the inadequacy of "discursive speech" for conveying the experience of a direct apprehension of truth and the "ineffable" intensity of the mystic vision. It was they, also, who encouraged a search for alternatives to language in symbols of sight and sound which could at least offer a simile for that immediacy of experience which language could never offer.[5]

Within Gombrich's Platonic tradition, one discovers the dramatis personae of Yates's many books: Renaissance cabalists, Hermetists, occultists of every stripe, including the Brotherhood of the Rosy Cross. For such Platonic linguists, there was a necessary or "motivated" (usually magical) connection between words and the things they signified. "The world of things and the world of names form a single undifferentiated chain of causality," Ernst Cassirer remarks of such a "pre-philosophical" vision of language: "the same form of substantiality and the same form of causality prevail in both, linking them into one self-enclosed whole."[6] For the Aristotelian, by contrast, language was a distinctively social creation that found no correspondent echo in the world of things; human speech was a conventional and arbitrary construct, differentiated by an unbridgeable gulf from the world it represented. For the Platonist, however, the immediacy of experience *was* linguistic (here I want to qualify Gombrich), an experience afforded via a privileged lexicon of names understood mystically rather than rationally.

Thus it was that the Rosicrucians perceived in "some new stars which do appear and are seen in the Firmament in *Serpentario* and *Cygno* . . . powerful *Signacula* of great weighty matters."[7] To other sky watchers, exhausted by their daily business of living with mundane words, the stars were visible as phenomena but indecipherable as *numina*—or so the Rosicrucians liked to believe. "Although that great Book of *Nature* stand open to all Men," they declared, "yet there are but few who can read and understand the same."[8] Both the *Fama* and the *Confessio* teem with metaphors for and from this great book to which the brotherhood claimed privileged access: "*Librum Naturae* or a perfect Method of all the Arts" and "the Magical Language and writing, with a large Dictionary"; "our Philosophical *Bibliotheca*"; Christian Rosenkreutz's "parchment book, called I. the which next unto the Bible, is our greatest treasure"; "those great Letters and Characters which the Lord God hath written and imprinted in Heaven and Earths edifice."[9] These are linguistic metaphors that turn normal speech inside out, proclaiming, as they do, not the intrasubjective world of facts and arguments but the ineffability (to all but a coterie) of the *liber naturae*. To be sure, the fraternity also espoused an Aristotelian view of language insofar as its members were obliged to communicate among themselves. Even so, the Fratres R. C. declared that the codes and ciphers they used to maintain contact with their brethren were derived from a primal insight into the *liber naturae*, "from the which Characters or Letters we have borrowed our *Magick* writing, and have found out, and made a new Language for our selves in the which withall is expressed and declared the Nature of all Things."[10]

More discernibly Aristotelian was the Rosicrucians' promise to "offer our Treasures freely, and without any difference to all men."[11] This promise of communication and collaboration notwithstanding, the brotherhood's vision of plenitude and pansophia was so chiliastic that the linguistic apocalypse upon which it depended erodes Gombrich's contrast between Platonic and Aristotelian. "Our Trumpet shall publiquely sound with a loud sound, and great noise," declared the Fratres R. C.,

> when namely the same (which at this present is shown by few and is secretly, as a thing to come, declared in Figures and Pictures) shall be free, and publiquely proclamed, and the whole World be filled withal.[12]

The Rosicrucians' apparent eagerness to communicate their arcana—spiritual, medical, epistemological—to the entire world was, however, belied by a secrecy so stringent that the brotherhood's very existence was often doubted. With their esoteric paraphernalia—CR's "Seal, Mark, and Character," "dark and hidden words," "the solemn oath of fidelity and secrecy"[13]—the brethren celebrated not social cooperation but the exclusivity of a secret society in which initiates could experience the truth of symbols directly and without the trifling mediation of everyday speech.

From such highly illuminated readers the *liber naturae* demanded not rational comprehension but mystical apprehension. "We must quit the dark Lanthorne of Reason," wrote Walter Charleton in 1650, capturing the antirationalistic spirit of his age.[14] Against "the unconstant, variable, and seductive imposture" of rational comprehension, Charleton opposed a Platonic epistemology of mystical apprehension. Fortified by the latter, he explained,

> the mind shall have all her knowledge full, entire, abstracted, in one single act; not successive, not extorted by the oblique violence of premises, not erroneous, controvertible, or dubious; she shall no longer groan under the perplexity of

framing Demonstrations, by wresting, deducing, inferring one proposition from another.[15]

The mood of Interregnum England was propitious for the book mysticism of the Fratres R. C.

In the next section I shall reopen the brotherhood's "great book of Nature" and show how its members apprehended what Michel Foucault has recently called "la prose du monde" and Jakob Böhme before him "signatura rerum" and "the language of nature."[16] I shall not, however, examine the brethren's origins in Germany, but concentrate instead upon their manifestos' impact upon England during the Puritan revolution and early Restoration. I shall show how Rosicrucian book mysticism both complemented and intensified the anti-intellectualism of radical sectaries like John Webster, the theorizing of alchemists like Thomas Vaughan, the Edenic raptures and folk medicine of visionaries like George Fox, and the millennial spirituality of the English Behmenists, translators and devotees of Böhme whose own book mysticism emerged from the same German crucible as the brotherhood's. In short, mid-seventeenth-century England swarmed with linguistic Platonists—my list is far from exhaustive—who can aptly be described as "Rosicrucian linguists."

Clearly my application of *Rosicrucian* can be construed as dangerously ecumenical. "Wider application of the term 'Rosicrucian' is undesirable," Charles Webster has cautioned in a critique of the Yates thesis:

It would tend to attach undue importance to one of a number of seventeenth-century hermeticist myths. Rosicrucianism is best thought of as a peripheral and extreme expression of hermeticism, which never appealed to more than a small group of devotees of the esoteric.[17]

When I use the term *Rosicrucian,* I shall not use it like Humpty Dumpty to mean anything I choose it to mean. For it seems to me that the notion of a "Rosicrucian linguistics" has great utility once one sets about describing that "Platonic" complex of beliefs about language which prevailed in revolutionary England, a complex which was, by turns, Adamic, Hermetic, magical, incarnational, Johannine, Pentecostal, and millenarian. Not surprisingly, *Rosicrucian* became a byword, among critics of linguistic Platonism, for a meretricious attitude toward *res et verba.* In the fourth section of my essay I shall analyze what can usefully be described as the "Aristotelian" critique of the brotherhood's book mysticism, a critique provoked not simply by the chicanery of quacks like Heydon but also by the semiological assumptions underpinning the *Fama* and *Confessio.* The Fratres R. C. may just have been a small and peripheral group of Hermetists (assuming they existed) but for their adversaries, many of whom hailed from the Royal Society, the brotherhood's esotericism provided an indispensable target for abuse and polemic.

Indeed, the new organon for language that latitudinarian divines and new scientists began to shape during the Interregnum was meant to serve as an antidote, explicitly administered, to Rosicrucian excess. Men like Seth Ward and John Wilkins worked diligently on the creation of a "real character and philosophical language," a rational and Aristotelian construct in which magicomystical assumptions about semiology could be exploded. "Such a language as this (where every word were a definition and contain'd the nature of the thing)," Ward and Wilkins explained,

> might not unjustly be termed a naturall Language, and would afford that which the *Cabalists* and *Rosycrucians* have vainly sought in the *Hebrew,* and in the names of things assigned by *Adam.*[18]

Ward and Wilkins fueled their search for a "naturall Language" with rationalist theology and modern science, and in each of the ensuing sections I shall show why the Edenic signatures deciphered by Adam from the *liber naturae* threatened that divorce of nature from a mystical reading of Scripture upon which Bacon (usually), Galileo (always), and their beneficiaries in the Royal Society (variously) believed that both scientific progress and a sound theology necessarily depended. Almost every Fellow of the Royal Society thus damned, as epistemologically dangerous and religiously intolerable, what Wilkins called "a kinde of *Cabalistical* or *Chymical, Rosicrucian* Theology."[19]

Most of the imaginative links that Yates has forged between the brotherhood and the Royal Society disintegrate when put to the test.[20] Certainly Wilkins was a member of the Palatinate circle—during the 1640s he served as chaplain to the elector—which Yates claims was responsible for the dissemination of Rosicrucian ideology in revolutionary England; and his *Mathematical Magick* (1649) owes something, as she shows, to the esoteric traditions of John Dee and Robert Fludd, the first a putative source of Rosicrucian doctrine, the second the brotherhood's most distinguished English spokesman.[21] But Wilkins's scorn for the Rosy Cross is a matter of public record, and unless one casts him as an implausible double agent, the future secretary of the Royal Society and bishop of Chester cannot be numbered among the Fratres R. C. or their supporters. More interesting is the case of Elias Ashmole, a cofounder with Wilkins of the Royal Society. Like Thomas Vaughan (or rather, Vaughan's anonymous predecessor), Ashmole translated the *Fama* and *Confessio,* adding an elaborate letter in which he petitioned for membership, and in his *Theatrum Chemicum Britannicum* he celebrated their skill as iatrochemists.[22] But Ashmole's interests were more far-flung (or farfetched) than those of the typical virtuoso, and he did not contribute to Royal Society propaganda.

What Ashmole's presence in the Royal Society helps to show, however, is the intellectual complexity of that institution, a complexity too often oversimplified by Whig historians. For if Gresham College, where the Fellows met, was the nursery of Boyle's Law and Newton's *Principia Mathematica,* it also witnessed experiments on unicorns' horn (from circles of which spiders were said to escape with difficulty) and passionate defenses of witchcraft by Joseph Glanvill, another critic of Rosicrucian linguistics.[23] Charleton's own conversion from a mystical epistemology (and its attendant rhetorical excesses) to the mechanical philosophy (and a plainer style) represents another twist of the Society's ideological kaleidoscope.[24] In short, Ashmole's contradictory allegiances do not prove, as Yates suggests, that the Royal Society was an outgrowth of the brotherhood but merely corroborate the continuing, if paradoxical, interaction of occultism and the new science in Restoration England. Most Fellows, moreover, self-consciously envisioned the Society's scientific and linguistic program as an exoteric alternative to the secretive organization and "Chymical Theology" of groups like the brethren. Only by default, then, do most historians of modern sciences see the Fratres R. C. as contributors to its triumphant ethos. But if the Yates thesis remains unproven (at best), one still finds all kinds of Rosicrucian echoes, however inadvertent, within Royal Society polemic. Even Thomas Sprat, the Society's historian, did not always seem capable of saying what he thought he meant: Upon examination, his famous canons of style disclose a cabalistical subtext!

Where intuition surely served Yates best (in *The Art of Memory* no less than *The Rosicrucian Enlightenment*) is in her sense of the mid-seventeenth century, both in England and in Europe, as a period of intellectual crisis, during which the Renaissance "light *Mosaick*" of linguistic Platonism faded, gradually to be replaced by the sharper edges of Enlightenment logic.[25] "The seventeenth-century universal language enthusiasts," Yates writes of Wilkins and his associates,

> are translating into rational terms efforts such as those of Giordano Bruno to found universal memory systems on magic images which he thought of as directly in contact with reality . . . the search for "real characters" comes out of the memory tradition on its occult side.[26]

Here one can glimpse that odd transformation of Platonic into Aristotelian assumptions about *res et verba,* a transformation illustrated when Ward and Wilkins reflect, somewhat complacently, about the superiority of their schemes for "naturall Language" over those of the cabalists and Rosicrucians. Nor is it surprising, at the end of the century, to find Leibniz returning both to Wilkins's *Essay towards a Real Character and Philosophical Language* and to Rosicrucian linguistics when he fashioned his own *characteristica universalis*.[27] In consequence, those who worked with language theory during the revolution and early Restoration as well as their later beneficiaries saw in those decades a critical juncture for speculation about the *liber naturae* and its semiology. With characteristic brio, Yates has dramatized the accompanying debates, but they have been most brilliantly illuminated by a philosopher–turned–historian of science, Ian Hacking.

In *The Emergence of Probability,* Hacking discriminates sharply between the "low science" of Paracelsus and his fellow doctors and alchemystics—inferential, uncertain, parabolic, and posited upon a signaturist apprehension of the *liber naturae*—and the "high science" of Galileo and his fellow astronomers and physicists—precise, predictive, mechanical, and posited upon a mathematical comprehension of the "libro della natura."[28] What made possible the discovery of statistical inference—"a quite specific event that occurred around 1660"[29]—was, Hacking maintains, the book mysticism of Paracelsus rather than Galileo's precise quantification. The scrupulous calibration demanded by Galilean experiment could not provide the conceptual space needed for probability; that space was defined instead by the inevitable ambiguities of interpreting signs from the great book of nature.[30] To illustrate his argument (too intricate for summary here),

Hacking quotes not from the Fratres R. C.—as one might expect, given his perception of the 1650s as the critical decade—but from their vaunted predecessor, Theophrastus Bombastus von Hohenheim: Paracelsus. "The first and highest book of medicine is called *Sapientia,*" Paracelsus explains.

> Without this book no one will achieve anything fruitful . . . for this book is God himself . . . The second book of medicine is the firmament . . . for it is possible to write down all medicine in the letters of one book . . . and the firmament is such a book containing all virtues and all propositions . . . the stars in heaven must be taken together in order that we may read the sentence in the firmament . . . Signatures are ultimately derived from the sentences in the stars, but a bountiful God has made them legible on earth.[31]

Paracelsus deciphers a sample sentence for us: "pictures, stones, herbs, words . . . comets, similitudes, halos and other unnatural products of the heavens."[32] In it he nicely confirms Ernst Cassirer's sketch of linguistic Platonism as a single undifferentiated chain of causality, as a "pre-philosophical" system that eliminates the normal distinctions between words and things. During the 1650s Englishmen like Ward and Wilkins reasserted the normality of those distinctions, unaware of the benefits modern science had accrued from Rosicrucian linguistics.

3

In their *Confessio,* the Rosicrucians embarked upon the longest and most sustained defense of their book mysticism. "These Characters and Letters," they announced,

> as God hath here and there incorporated them in the Holy Scriptures the *Bible,* so hath he imprinted them most apparently into the wonderful Creation of Heaven and Earth, yea in all Beasts. So that like as the *Mathematician* or the *Astronomer* can long before see and know the eclipses which are to come, so we may verily fore-know and fore-see the darkness of Obscurations of the Church, and how long they shall last. From the which Characters or Letters we have borrowed our *Magick* writing, and found out, and made a new language for ourselves, in the which withall is expressed and declared the Nature of all Things: So that it is no wonder that we are not so eloquent in other Languages, the which we know that they are altogether disagreeing to the Languages of our forefathers, *Adam* and *Enoch,* and were through the Babylonical Confusion wholly hidden.[33]

This celebration of the "two-book" theory of knowledge and of its constituent *Ursprache* was far from unique, either in post-Paracelsian Germany or in revolutionary England. But what gave the *Fama* and the *Confessio* their recurrent appeal was the brethren's astute combination of esoteric commonplace with the romance of their imaginary founder, Christian Rosenkreutz. In the mythology that they wove around Rosenkreutz's life, death, suspended animation, and eventual resurrection, the Fratres R. C. reallegorized biblical and folkloristic accounts of Adam and Christ: of Adam's loss of the *prisca sapientia* and its recovery after the

Expulsion, of Christ's First and Second Coming and the attendant signs and miracles. Trumpeting a "new language" not subject to the "Babylonical Confusion," the Rosicrucians proclaimed their fluency both in the *lingua adamica* and in the "new song" or "pure language" that the truly illuminated would, as prophesied, speak during the Last Days.[34]

Elsewhere I have discussed the "millenarian linguists" of the Puritan revolution.[35] In this section of the present essay I shall show how the Rosicrucians and their German precursors contributed to the "millenarian linguistics" of these English antinomians. And in so doing, I shall employ that temporal double vision which is indispensable if one wishes to understand the debate over signification that racked revolutionary England as it had already racked post-Paracelsian Germany. That one can conveniently use English translations, made during the 1650s and 1660s, to study the Renaissance debate between Platonists (like Paracelsus, Croll, and the Rosicrucians) and Aristotelians (like Libavius) exemplifies the German impact upon radical Puritan speculation about language.

"The Art of Signing," Paracelsus wrote in his treatise on signatures, "doth teach how true and sutable names are to bee put on all things, all which *Adam* truly knew."[36] To a man, Paracelsians hunted for the true names of things, whether, like Oswald Croll, as practicing alchemists, or as theosophists like Jakob Böhme. For the godly initiate, Croll argues, naming day in Eden became a present reality, conferring an Adamic pharmacopoeia and Apostolic gifts of healing. "All Herbs, Flowers, Trees, and other things which proceede out of the Earth," Croll explained,

> are Books, and Magick Signes, communicated to us, by the immense Mercy of God, which Signes are our Medicine . . . For Plants do as it were in occult words, manifest their excellency, and open the Treasures of hidden things to sickly Mortalls . . . *Stars,* according to *Paracelsus,* are the Forms and Matrices of all Herbs; and every Star in the Heavens, is no other, but a Herb prefigured in a spiritual and Catholick manner, representing the like of every Vegetable in the Earth. . . . For the Characters of Nature, and these Natural Signatures, which from the Creation, not with Inke, but with the very finger of GOD are imprinted in all Creatures (indeed every creature is a book of GOD), are the better part of true Literature, by which all occult things are read and understood.[37]

Like Paracelsus and Croll, the Rosicrucians were also stargazers, iatrochemical bookmen who promised "to cure the sick and that *gratis.*"[38] Their "Universal medicine for all diseases," commented Thomas Vaughan, English popularizer of the manifestos, "is that great character of the book of nature out of which her whole alphabet doth arise . . . existing from the foundation of the world . . . a knowledge which God almighty by his word breathed into nature."[39] Originally this alphabet was composed of pristine Jewish letters, a "sermo purus, incorruptus, sanctus, brevis et constans" as Reuchlin termed it,[40] which survived the Fall and Babel only among cabalists and Hermetists. In the Garden, added Cornelius Agrippa, Adam had deciphered its letters from the heavenly bodies that were perfectly spaced above him.[41]

Frances Yates was not the first to posit a direct Behmenist influence upon the

Fama and *Confession,* but the evidence, although highly suggestive, still remains sketchy.[42] What cannot be doubted is Böhme's impact upon the Rosicrucian linguistics of mid-seventeenth-century England, for "the Teutonick's" language of nature was quickly assimilated into book-mysticism of the Brotherhood.[43] "I cannot passe over in silence," wrote John Webster, "that signal and wonderful secret (so often mentioned by the mysterious and divinely inspired *Teutonick* and in some manner acknowledged and owned by the highly illuminated fraternity of the *Rosie Crosse*) of the language of nature."[44] In the first Behmenist tract to appear in English translation—*The Life of One Jacob Boehmen* (1644)—Abraham von Franckenberg, himself a Rosicrucian, tells how the Silesian cobbler gained his primordial insight into the *liber naturae.*[45] In 1600 Böhme was dazzled by sunlight glancing off a pewter dish in Görlitz and immediately "went forth into the open fields, and there perceived the wonderful or wonderworks of the Creator in the signatures, shapes, figures, and qualities of all created things, very clearly and plainly laid open."[46] Bohme complemented this "primordial revelation" with etymological and cabalistic analysis—of the vocalic meaning of IEOVA, for example[47]—which drove more than one English sectary to dismember his own alphabet, limb by symbolic limb.[48] What concerns me more directly is Böhme's polemic against the *confusio linguarum* at Babel and his proposed remedy, the restitution of the *lingua adamica* by "openings" that were at once Edenic and Pentecostal.

"Now it plainely appeares," Böhme wrote of man before the two general curses of the Fall and of Babel,

> he stood in the *Divine* Image and not the *beastiall* for he knew the properties of all creatures, *and gave names to all Creatures* from their essence, forme and property; He understood the language of nature, *viz.* the manifested and formed Word in every ones Essence, for thence the *Name of every Creature* is arisen.[49]

If Croll emphasized the medicinal utility of this language of nature, Böhme celebrated its symbolism, a theosophical matrix in which he reconciled the three Paracelsian principles of salt, sulfur, and mercury with his own lucubrations upon vowel sounds.[50] Both Germans, moreover, were convinced that their alchemystical grasp of the *signatura rerum* was Pentecostal no less than Paradisial. Croll numbered himself among "the Intellectual school of *Pentecost* in which the *Prophets* and *Apostles,* all truly learned men walking in the life and steps of *Christ* have been taught and learned without labor and toyle."[51] And Böhme gave a new twist to the orthodox typology of Whitsun, providing a radically different gloss of Acts 2. "This compacted formed tongue," Böhme wrote of the *Ursprache,*

> the Holy Ghost did *open* on the *day of Pentecost* in St. Peter's Sermon, where *Peter* from the opened sensuall tongue spake *in one Language all Languages;* and this was also *Adams Language whence he gave Names to all creatures.*[52]

Like Croll, Böhme was confident that he, too, had joined this spiritual aristocracy that stretched from Adam to the Apostles and beyond. For the Rosicrucians, as for Croll and Böhme, it was the Tower of Babel that prevented the restitution of the language of nature to all mankind. Only when Pentecost was understood as present reality—not as a long-gone rationale for Aristotelian communication but as a gift perennially renewed—could the second general curse finally be lifted. "We are not so eloquent in other Languages," the brotherhood explained, because those were "disagreeing to the language of our forefathers *Adam* and *Enoch* which were through the Babylonical confusion wholly hidden."[53] Like Böhme, the Roiscrucians could not respect what passed for linguistic scholarship in the universities of Europe, manned as those were by latter-day "builders of the Towre."[54]

"Let not your thoughts feed now on the phlegmatic, indigested vomits of Aristotle," Thomas Vaughan told the aspiring alchemist: "Run over the Alphabet of Nature, examine every letter, every particular creature in her booke."[55] Fortunately, Aristotle had not infiltrated Eden to ruin the linguistic Platonism of its naming day. From Paradise Vaughan derived "the books which God ordained for Adam, and for us his posterity," dismissing "the quintessence of Aristotle" and "the temperament of Galen the Antichrist."[56] Clearly the heathens were part of Revelation's "Babylonical confusion," and the appropriate antidote was to be found in the *lingua adamica.*

Webster's onslaught upon the Schoolmen's Babel—"the dead paper idolls of creaturely-invented letters"[57]—was more strident than either the Germans' or Vaughan's. For Webster, like his fellow sectaries, was militantly antiprofessional as well as anti-intellectual; he resented the social and pecuniary benefits conferred by Oxford and Cambridge, by the Inns of Court and the College of Physicians, as much as he loathed their *confusio linguarum.*[58] He provided a program of educational reform in his *Academiarum Examen,* asking

> that youth may not be idly trained up in notions, speculations, and verbal disputes, but may learn to inure their hands to labour, and put their fingers to the furnaces, that the mysteries discovered by *Pyrotechny,* and the wonders brought to light by *Chymistry,* may be rendered familiar unto them. . . . so that they may be true Natural Magicians, that walk in the center of nature's hidden secrets, which shall never come to pass, unless they have Laboratories as well as Libraries.[59]

In the university as reformed by Webster, the library and the laboratory are almost indistinguishable. In the library, the Rosicrucian linguist worked on the construction of a universal language, "a potent means (in some measure) to have repaired the ruines of Babel . . . almost a Catholick cure for the confusion of tongues"; in the laboratory, he toiled over "the recovery and restauration of the Catholique language in which lies hid all the rich treasury of nature's admirable and excellent secrets."[60] What unites these two fields of endeavor is the "living book," the signatures of which brought *res et verba* into a single undifferentiated chain of causality.

Not all Rosicrucian linguists, however, subscribed to Webster's program of institutional reform. Like George Fox, many sectaries saw signs of Babel in every human institution, even new ones proposed by their fellow Puritans. "So that he might see the many languages began at Babel," Fox explained to an Interregnum functionary dispatched from London to set up a new University in Durham, they set them atop of Christ the Word when they crucified him. And John the Divine, who preached the Word that was in the beginning said that the beast and the whore have power over tongues and languages, and they were as waters . . . natural, confused languages, at Babel and in Babylon, set a-top of Christ and life, by a persecutor.[61]

Here Fox extends earlier sectarian attacks upon "the language of the Beast"— Greek, Latin, and debased Hebrew—to all human languages, each of which had stemmed not from Eden's "pure language of the Spirit of Truth" but from Babel's *confusio linguarum*."[62] "All languages are to me no more than dust," Fox declared, "who was before languages were, and am come'd before languages into the power where all man shall agree."[63] I have already suggested that the *Ursprache*— what Webster calls "the pure language of nature"[64]—constituted a semiology that can only be conceptualized during an Edenic trance like Böhme's outside Görlitz. And I shall shortly show that Pentecostalism also provides a glossolalic strategy for dispensing with linguistic convention, as that was reflected in the Aristotelian organon of language. In practice however, the Quakers devised a pure language for their quotidian use, a sanitized version of the English vernacular.[65] Of such a tongue—at once vernacular and transcendental—Böhme explained that "every nation builds it out of its own materials for in the Right universall Sensuall tongue (if it be manifest in one) we are altogether but one only *people* and *Nation* even from *Adam*."[66] Quaker plain style was far more commonsensical than such theosophical commentary might suggest but behind it, nonetheless, lurked Böhme's Pentecostal dream of Adam's *signatura rerum* and of its universal restitution.

Before the outbreak of hostilities in 1642 Behmenist and Rosicrucian tracts circulated only in Continental editions or manuscript translations, their audience limited thereby to a select and educated group of Englishmen.[67] But once Böhme had appeared in print during the 1640s, his philosophy of language gained an immediate currency, providing sectaries with a theological (if heterodox) matrix for notions of word magic and logotherapy then popular among the common people.[68] "Paradise is in the world," Böhme maintained, adding that "if our eyes were opened, we should see it."[69] Adam's "living library" was still available for consultation, if one joined the intellectual school of Pentecost. Regrettably, the Tower of Babel stood between most readers and their repossession of the *signatura rerum*. "Let everyone prove himselfe," Böhme counseled: "He shall indeed find the Great Mystery of the babilonicall Towre in himselfe; and also the *Number* of *the* false *Beast*."[70] Fortunately, devout believers, once they had been initiated into Böhme's cabala, could shake off Antichrist, and join the intellectual school of Pentecost, rediscovering within themselves the divine image, both of Adam and of the resurrected Christ.

Similar to Böhme's revelation was George Fox's "opening" of 1648:

Now was I come up in spirit through the flaming sword into the paradise of God. All things were new, and all the creation gave another smell unto me than before, beyond what words can utter. I knew nothing but pureness, and innocency, and righteousness, being renewed up into the image of God by Christ Jesus, so that I can say I was come up to the state of Adam which he was in before he fell. The creation was opened to me, and it was showed me how all things had their names given them according to their nature and virtue. And I was at a stand in my mind whether I should practise physic for the good of mankind, seeing the nature and virtues of the creatures were so opened to me by the Lord . . . And the Lord showed me that such as were faithful to him in the power and light of Christ, should come up into the state which Adam was in before he fell, in which the admirable works of the creation, and the virtues thereof, may be known, through the openings of that divine Word of wisdom and power by which they were made.[71]

The medical arcana for which Webster labored manually in the laboratory, Fox gained instantly through mystical illumination, regaining, in the words of the brotherhood, "such a Truth, Light, Life and Glory, as the first man *Adam* had."[72]

Rarely remarked today is Fox's subsequent career as a folkdoctor—a career unique among the sectaries only for its length and for the surviving documentation.[73] For Fox was not alone in claiming intimacy with the botanical signatures of Eden (although he did not mention the astral influences that, according to Paracelsus and Croll, suffused them). Laurence Clarkson, for example, narrates how he "attempted the art of Astrology and Physick, which in a short time I gained and therewith travelled up and down Cambridgeshire and *Essex*."[74]

What differentiates Fox from the shaman, but not from a spiritual alchemist like Böhme, is his Paradisial (and apocalyptic) recreation in the divine image, not simply of Adam but of Christ.[75] "I was immediately taken up in spirit," Fox felt, "to see into another or more steadfast state than Adam's in innocency, even into a state in Christ Jesus, that should never fall."[76] Being "Godded with God" in a *vergeistigter Chiliasmus* was the ultimate goal of those Rosicrucian linguists who set individual perfection above social revolution.[77] "They boast that *Christ* is come to *them,* neither look they for any other coming," a Baptist complained of the Quakers, "that the world is ended with *them,* neither look they for any other end."[78] Many Englishmen went beyond what words could utter to achieve reabsorption into the Word itself; a mysterious humming presaged James Nayler's Christic descent upon Bristol.[79] In the face of such ineffability, Aristotelian analysis like mine will always falter. And quotidian modes of expression must also suffice for my analysis of "the language of the birds," that most enigmatic manifestation of the "secret language" shared by shamans and Rosicrucians, by Fox and Böhme, by Elias Ashmole and John Webster, and by Jonathan Swift.[80]

In 1656 the alchemist Edward Bourne accompanied Fox from Worcester to Tewkesbury, later recording in his journal that the Quaker spoke "of the Glory of the first body, and of the Egiptian Learning, & of the Language of the birds, & of wt was wonnderful to mee to heare."[81] Bourne did not elaborate upon Fox's dazzling, if enigmatic, choice of topics, but their relevance to the *liber naturae* is clear. Illuminated by Eden, Adam had conversed with (as well as named) "the fowl of the air and every beast of the field" (Genesis 2:20). After the Fall, the language of the birds was again revealed to the intellectual school of Pentecost into whose "Egiptian Learning" Moses had initiated Hermes Trismegistus. Subsequent beneficiaries included Solomon, who had communicated with the Queen of Sheba via the birds, and Apollonius of Tyana, a contemporary of Christ, who enjoyed the gift of tongues, and was, like Jesus, fluent in the "birds most learned Original."[82] From Apollonius, wrote Samuel Butler, mocking Vaughan's edition of the manifestos, "the *Rosie-cross Philosophers* / . . . do confess they owe, / All that they do, and all they know."[83] Within the shrine of their founder, Butler added, in yet another burlesque of Vaughan's Rosicrucianism, "they found a World of most precious Secrets and Mysteries, with a deal of Treasure, and a Dictionary of all those Names, that *Adam* gave the Creatures, and these they have since given one another: for they profess to understand the Language of Beasts and Birds, as they say Solomon did."[84]

As graduates of the Pentecostal School, Rosicrucian linguists were necessarily fluent in mystical birdsong because, as M. Bastiaensen has shown, the language of the birds was intrinsic to the gift of tongues conferred by the Dove at Whitsun.[85] Nongraduates, by contrast, still labored under the second general curse, being, as Böhme lamented, "more foolish than the Birds in the Air which doe all praise and honour God in *one* tongue and understanding."[86]

In mystical birdsong Böhme's *signatura rerum* were thus translated into his "opened sensuall tongue" of Whitsun, a language of pure connotation, tongues of men and angels, in which sounds were liberated from postlapsarian constraints of reason and discursive meaning.[87] Paradisial union with what Henry Vaughan called "The great *Chime* / And *Symphony* of nature" could be regained through this linguistic Platonism which promised through its "symbols of sight and sound," as Gombrich notes, an "immediacy of experience that [quotidian] language could never offer."[88] When visually apprehended, the signatures disclosed an ideal language "where every word were a definition and contain'd the nature of the thing." In this purity of denotation, the *confusio linguarum*—which had unleashed polysemy, ambiguity, equivocation, and logomachy—was paradisially and pentecostally transcended. Hence Thomas Vaughan prayed for "an art that is a perfect entire map of the creation, that can lead me directly to the knowledge of God . . . the Art wherein the physics of Adam and the patriarchs consisted."[89] We recall Marvell's conversion of Fairfax's estate into *"Heaven's Center, Nature's Lap / And Paradice's only Map"* as well as the Edenic openings of George Fox, whom Marvell met at Appleton House.[90] But the "map" of Thomas Vaughan and Marvell defies logical conciliation with Henry's "symphony," for the semiology of the first is visual and denotative, that of the second auditory and connotative. Only by accepting the ineffability of Rosicrucian linguistics can such contradictions be satisfactorily resolved. Not everyone, however, treated the *liber naturae* as a *Gesamtkunstwerk* of unutterable (if imaginable) complexity. In Galileo and the Royal Society, Rosicrucian linguists met their hermeneutic match.

4

"The pervasive book of nature metaphor is highly ambiguous," William R. Shea explains.

While it was at the tip of everyone's pen, it did not carry the same meaning for every writer. Galileo and Kepler believed that God wrote the book of nature in mathematical characters but Bruno and Campanella interpreted it as the work of the Arch-magician. It is true that mathematics can work wonders and that magicians juggle with numbers but the methodological programmes of the two schools are profoundly at variance. The "book of nature" metaphor used by all parties serves to conceal the differences.[91]

Unlike the Rosicrucian linguists who juggled cabalistically with numbers, Galileo and his fellow "high" scientists (to use Hacking's terminology) discerned in nature a mathematical language. "Philosophy is written in this grand book, the universe, which stands continually open to our gaze," Galileo maintained in 1623, not long after the *Fama* and *Confessio* had appeared.

But it cannot be understood unless one first learns to comprehend the characters in which it is written. It is written in the language of mathematics, and its characters are triangles, circles, and other geometrical figures without which it is humanly impossible to understand a single word of it; without these, one is wandering in a dark labyrinth.[92]

Galileo thus forced a sharp distinction between what scientists could humanly read in the *liber naturae* and the occult characters of the signaturists. Despite some rhetorical flourishes about the "great book of nature" as "the creation of the omnipotent craftsman," Galileo vehemently rejected any conflation of nature and Scripture.[93] "The intention of the Holy Spirit is to teach us how one goes to heaven," he quipped, "not how heaven goes."[94]

Francis Bacon agreed. In *The Advancement of Learning* he, too, attacked esoteric readings of the stars, hammering at the misappropriation of Psalm 19 by occultists like Dee, although he himself never appreciated the importance of the mathematical alternative.[95] "We conclude that sacred theology," Bacon insisted, "is grounded only upon the word and oracle of God, and not upon the light of nature: for it is written *Coeli enarrant gloriam Dei;* but it is not written *Coeli enarrant voluntatem Dei* (Psalms 19:1)."[96]

As is known from hindsight, Galileo's version of the *liber naturae* triumphed over rival methodologies; during the Puritan revolution, however, its final victory seemed by no means certain. Some scientists like Sir Thomas Browne shared Bacon's contempt for pure mathematics but still discerned (or seemed to discern) the will of God in nature. "There arc two bookes from whence I collect my Divinity," Browne explained in *Religio Medici,* "besides that written one of God, another of his servant nature, that universall and publik Manuscript that lies expans'd unto the eyes of all."[97] Yet although Browne soared into an "altitudo" over the world's "stenography and short Characters," he conceded that there were, in his treatise, "many things delivered Rhetorically, many expressions therein meerely tropicall . . . to be taken in a soft and flexible sense and not to be called to the strict test of reason."[98] Browne did not subscribe to Galileo's strict test of mathematical reason, hymning instead the omnipotent craftsman's skill with "reall and mysticall letters."[99] Yet Browne was not a Rosicrucian linguist, his

Hermetic choice of vocabulary notwithstanding. For Browne's "tropicall" expressions were far closer to medieval commonplace and Renaissance *concetto predicabile*—an Aristotelian tradition of thought about the *liber naturae* fully documented by E. R. Curtius among others—than they were to an uninhibited linguistic Platonism.[100] For Rosicrucian linguists this "soft and flexible" reading of the *liber naturae* posed as great a threat as Galileo's discovery that nature proved to be written in mathematical language: If the latter demanded formal expertise—logical, mechanical, academic—quite foreign to the intellectual school of Pentecost, then the former threatened their literal (and apocalyptic) reading of nature's language.

"Many readers will suppose that Paracelsus speaks metaphorically of books, sentences, letters, alphabets, and reading," Hacking remarks, emphasizing, however, that "the sense of his words is essential to the sense of his system."[101] It was this inflexible sense of the *liber naturae* that Webster passionately reasserted in 1654. "Many do superficially and by way of *Analogy* (as they term it)," he complained,

> acknowledge the Macrocosm to be the great unsealed book of God, and every creature as a Capital letter or character, and all put together make up one word or sentence of his immense wisdom, glory and power; but alas! who spells them aright, or conjoyns them so together that they may perfectly read all that is therein contained? Alas! we all study and read too much upon the dead paper idolls of creaturely-invented letters, but do not, nor cannot read the legible characters that are only written and impressed by the finger of the Almighty . . . not as mute statues but as living and speaking pictures, not as dead letters, but as preaching *Symbols*. And the not understanding and right reading of these starry Characters, therein to behold the light of *Abyssal* glory and immortality, is the condemnation of the sons of lost *Adam*.[102]

Contradicting Bacon, Webster affirmed both God's glory and His power as manifested in the heavens. And even if his complaint about the spiritual "illiteracy" of modern Englishmen seems to echo Browne's—"surely the Heathen knew better how to joyne and read these mysticall letters, than wee Christians who cast a more carelesse eye on these common Hieroglyphicks, and disdaine to suck Divinity from the flowers of Nature"[103]—Webster would have insisted that *nothing* was delivered rhetorically in the *Academiarum Examen;* the literal sense of Webster's words (whatever that was!) remained essential to the referential force of Rosicrucian linguistics.

"There is a Harmonie between nature and the Gospel," Thomas Vaughan asserted, summoning intellectual assistance from Fox's "Egiptian Learning."

> Thus we see the Incarnation and the birth of Christ Jesus (which to the common philosopher are fables and impossibilities, but in the booke of Nature plaine evident truth) were proved, and demonstrated by the primitive Apostles and teachers out of the creation of the World . . . I will first speake of the Aegyptian theologie, that you may see how far they have advanc'd, having no leader but the light of Nature. Trismegistus is so orthodox and plaine in the Mysterie of the Trinity, the Scripture it self exceeds it not.[104]

With such dark and labyrinthine logic, Galileo had no truck; as a common philosopher he was committed to the scientific possibilities of human comprehension, not to impossibilities afforded by an apprehensive divination. By contrast, Bacon's putative response to Vaughan and Webster would be much harder to predict. For although Bacon was determined to replace the Aristotelian organon with his own, he remained mired in linguistic Platonism. Indeed, Webster and his fellow sectaries actually celebrated Bacon as a Rosicrucian linguist, conveniently overlooking Aristotelian elements in his theory of language and focusing instead upon those which bolstered their own book mysticism and millenarian linguistics.

Despite his violent rejection of Paracelsus and other Renaissance alchemists, Bacon often succumbed to their Paradisial vision of the *liber naturae*. In the commentary upon Psalm 19 that he offered in the "Historia Naturalis et Experimentalis," Bacon directly contradicts his own "Galilean" observations in *The Advancement of Learning*. Like John Dee or any Rosicrucian linguist of the Interregnum, Bacon reconstructs the unbroken chain of causality that links the language of the creatures to God's astral handiwork. Thus Bacon exhorts scientists

> to approach with humility and veneration to unroll the volume of Creation, to meditate and linger therein, and with minds washed clean from opinions to study it in purity and integrity. For this is that sound and language which went forth into all lands and did not incur the confusion of Babel; this should men study to be perfect in; and becoming again as little children condescend to take the alphabet of it into their hands, and spare no pains to search and unravel the interpretation thereof.[105]

This is a passage that might have come directly from the Rosicrucian manifestos or from Webster's *Academiarum Examen*, and indeed Webster frequently enlists the aid of Bacon, alongside that of Böhme and the brotherhood, for his onslaught upon the "high-towring Babell" of Aristotle and the Schoolmen. But it was John Heydon who paid Bacon the ultimate (if backhanded) Rosicrucian compliment when he plagiarized the *New Atlantis* as *A Voyage to the Land of the Rosicrucians*.[106]

Such misreadings of their "Moses" the founders of the Royal Society found insupportable.[107] "There are not two waies in the whole World more opposite then those of the L. *Verulam* and D. *Fludd*," Ward and Wilkins observed sourly,

> The one founded upon experiment, the other upon mystical Ideall reasons . . . even now Webster was for the way of strict and accurate induction, but is fallen into the mysticall way of the Cabala and numbers formall.[108]

Some modern historians concur; others emphasize the "semi-Paracelsian" cosmology from which Bacon's book mysticism sprang. What cannot be disputed is the fervor mid-seventeenth-century Englishmen brought to the debate over the meaning of "Baconianism." Webster read Verulam through the Rosicrucian spectacles of Fludd, passionately defending, as did other sectaries, the Baconian contribution to magical tradition and to Puritan millenarianism. Ward and Wilkins, by contrast, appear to have read Bacon through the experimental spectacles of

Galileo, the scientist whose redefinition of the *liber naturae* helped shape the Royal Society's conception of the high sciences.

"Galileo remains the dominant intellectual light of the period," Barbara Shapiro maintains, labeling Wilkins *his* follower rather than Bacon's.[109] For the Royal Society, she argues, Bacon was a patriotic figurehead not a methodological pilot; his role as their Moses was purely honorary. "Nature proved to be written in mathematical language," adds René Taton, and for accuracy of induction Galileo proved a stricter reader than Bacon.[110]

Certainly Wilkins was no Rosicrucian linguist, but one should not underestimate his tenacious biblicism, issuing, as it did, in the taxonomic digression on Noah's Ark in his *Essay*.[111] Wilkins's colleague Ashmole succumbed to Rosicrucian influences, but his career can hardly be construed as that of an experimental scientist. Nevertheless, one of the mid-century's leading experimentalists, Robert Boyle, also fell under the spell of astrology, alchemy, and the cabala during the Civil Wars and Interregnum. When discussing the "coveted Elixir," he noted in signaturist vein that "there are certain Hints . . . which to discerning Eyes (as Plants do to Physicians reveal their Properties) disclose much of what they conceale."[112] And from an unpublished manuscript, "Of the Study of the Booke of Nature," it is clear that Boyle, like Vaughan, believed that scriptural revelation was corroborated by the *liber naturae*.[113] After the Restoration, "the Christian virtuoso" reconsidered his youthful interests, moderating his enthusiasm for the occult.[114]

In *The History of the Royal Society,* Thomas Sprat compares the Fellows' scrutiny of "the large Volume of the Creatures" with their scriptural hermeneutics; indeed, the *History* is markedly (if rhetorically) chiliastic, and in it, as shall be seen shortly, Sprat popularized the Society's blueprint (appropriately qualified) for millenarian linguistics.[115] "The *Subject* of their *Studies* is as large as the *Universe,*" he concludes, reminding one of the Rosicrucians' worldbook.[116] Sprat's use of the book metaphor has recently been described as "exceptionally interesting,"[117] but more remarkable by far was Robert Hooke's paean to the language of nature. For, unlike Sprat, Hooke was not a belle-lettrist—prone to commonplaces about God's script—but a "high" scientist famous for the mathematical precision of his work on horology, chronometry, and mechanics. Hooke, however, was also an ardent Baconian and drew upon the "low" sciences for this *Discourse on Earthquakes* in which he bids the scientific observer

> peruse, and turn over, and spell, and Read the Book of Nature, and observe the *Orthography, Etymologie, Syntaxis,* and *Prosodia* of Nature's Grammar, and by which as with a *Dictionary,* he might readily turn to and find the true figures, Composition, Derivation, and Use of the characters, Words, Phrases and Sentences of Nature written with indelible, and most exact, and most expressive Letters, without which Books it will be very difficult to be thoroughly a Literatus in the Language and Sense of Nature.[118]

Here Hooke's scientific lexicon seems distinctly Rosicrucian in tone. But Hooke's vision of the *liber naturae* remains metaphorical rather than referential, the con-

ventional exuberance of a parson's son rather than a set of Paracelsian correspondences. What we witness is the subtle metamorphosis of Renaissance book
mysticism into the Augustan argument from design.

These were shifts also registered in the social organization of science, as esoteric
coteries gave way during the Interregnum to exoteric institutions. Rationalization
and institutionalization were, however, accompanied by a wild outburst of occultism. "It was the bond of secrecy," Charles Webster explains, "which stimulated the proliferation of secret societies, ranging from the groups of disciples
around particular chemists, such as Glauber, to more underground movements like
the Rosicrucians."[119] Yet it is also from the 1650s, when Ward and Wilkins wrested
Bacon from the Rosicrucian linguists, that Joseph Ben-David dates the modern
ideal of "an ever expanding and changing yet regularly functioning scientific
community."[120] "For those who adopted it," argues Ben-David,

> experimental doctrine became a medium of unequivocal communication, a way
> of reasoning and refutation in limited fields of common interest. By sticking to
> empirically verified facts (preferably by controlled experiment) the method
> enabled its practitioners to feel like members of the same "community," even in
> the absence of a commonly accepted theory.[121]

Crucial to the early stages of this development, Ben-David and B. J. T. Dobbs
agree, was the scientific circle of Samuel Hartlib.[122] Yet in that circle Rosicrucian
linguists mingled comfortably with experimentalists like Robert Boyle. Indeed,
Hartlib supervised Boyle's first (anonymous) publication—"An Invitation to All
True Lovers of Vertue and Mankind to a Free and Generous Communication of
Their Secrets and Receits in Physick"—but pride of place in his collection of
Chymical, Medicinal, and Chyrurgical Addresses (1655) Hartlib gave to a loose
commentary on alchemy and millenarian linguistics, "A Short Discourse Proving
Urim and Thummim to Be Perfected by Art, and to Be of Like Pure Substance
with the White and Red Elixirs."[123]

During the 1650s, then, secret societies and scientific communities did not
evolve along the distinctly separate paths that some historians of science have
imagined. Nor did their respective versions of the *liber naturae* or the theories of
language sustaining them. For the same occultists who strenuously preserved their
bonds of linguistic secrecy—"hard words" as Charles Webster calls them, drawing
upon Böhme's theosophy[124]—also championed (as did the Fratres R. C.) unequivocal communication and free access to "secrets and Receits in Physick."[125]
These were also ideals that stimulated the language planner, and from Hartlib's
circle—the meeting place of esotericists and exotericists—emerged the earliest
published scheme for a real character, one that nicely confirms the ideal of a
linguaggio commune that Garin sees emerging: Francis Lodwick's *A Common
Writing, Whereby Two, although Not Understanding One the Others Language,
Yet by the Helpe Thereof, May Communicate Their Minds to One Another.*[126]
Frances Yates has been reproved for scrambling together esotericists like the
brethren and exotericists like the Fellows of the Royal Society, but intuition serves
her well when she juxtaposes Rosicrucian linguistics with the Society's reform of
language. Wilkins was, to be sure, opposed to the "naturall language . . . which the

Cabalists and *Rosycrucians* have vainely sought for in the Hebrew, and in the names of things assigned by *Adam*," and he resolved to stand the *Ursprache* on its head.[127] But tumbling down from his *Essay towards a Real Character and Philosophical Language* one can catch, as Yates predicts, unassimilated fragments of Adamicism, pansophia, and the "new language" of the apocalypse.

Like the Edenic dictionary rediscovered by the Fratres R. C., Wilkins's *Essay* constituted a perfect map of the entire creation, an encyclopedia taxonomized, like the reality it reflected, into forty categories. Instead of returning *in illo tempore,* Wilkins (and his botanical advisor, John Ray) started from externalist scratch, inventing a set of arbitrary rather than motivated (or internal) correspondences between *res et verba.* Unlike Croll's intellectual school of Pentecost, Wilkins knew that no substitute for the first Whitsun, magicomystical or otherwise, could completely eliminate the "labour and toyle" entailed by the acquisition of every language, including his own philosophical language. Hence the *Essay* is a streamlined Aristotelian organon—indeed, a substitute for everyday language—rather than some Platonic shortcut to a set of *res et verba* causally self-enclosed. Wilkins's coadjutor in language planning, George Dalgarno, reemphasized the instrumentality of words, since the internal efficiency, as a mechanism of real character and universal language, was essential if those were to fulfill their referential function. His own *Ars Signorum* Dalgarno offered as a toolbox of "more wieldy and manageable instruments of operation for defining, dividing, demonstrating &c."[128]

Most Aristotelians view language, not as an ideal taxonomy of the world (though categorization is essential), but as a machinery conducive to social collaboration and the organization of facts and arguments that such collaboration requires. To these Aristotelian desiderata of linguistic convention Wilkins and Dalgarno still brought Platonic preconceptions, but for them correspondence was unthinkable (as it was not for Rosicrucian linguists) unless it was strengthened by a semiological system that functioned with algebraic efficiency. Hence Dalgarno promised that his *Ars Signorum* would show

> a way to remedy the difficulties and absurdities which all languages are clogged with ever since the Confusion or rather since the fall, by cutting off all redundancy, rectifying all anomaly, taking away all ambiguity and aequivocation, contracting the primitives to a few number, and even those not to be of arbitrary but of rational institution . . . In a word, designing not only to remedie the confusion of languages by giving a much more easie medium of communication than any yet known, but also to cure even Philosophy itself of the disease of Sophisms and Logomachies.[129]

Wilkins and Dalgarno shared with the Rosicrucians a vision of a semiology "where every word were a definition and contain'd the nature of the thing," but neither pretended that he had, in his remedy for the confusion, cracked the primordial codes of Eden. To be sure, Wilkins promised that his *Essay* would, like the linguistic schemes of Comenius and the Rosicrucians, "tend to the universal good of mankind" because it afforded "a remedy against the Curse of the Confusion," a remedy comparable to "the gift of Miracles, and particularly that of Tongues poured out upon the Apostles in the first planting of Christianity."[130] Thereby the "time and pains Men are content to bestow in the Study of language" would be significantly reduced, and scientists could turn, without more ado, to the *liber naturae,* confident that Wilkins's new order of language had given them privileged access to the old order of things.[131] In short, language planners were determined to construct novel mechanisms of denotation and communication, whereas the Rosicrucian linguists refused to accept that "confusion is the precondition for communication,"[132] searching instead for a *lingua adamica* in which the post-Babylonian exigencies of cooperation would be mystically (even telepathically) transcended.

Thus Wilkins's "shortest and plainest way for the attainment of real Knowledge that hath yet been offered to the World" demanded not secrecy or solitary trances but laborious public cooperation among England's many scientists and language planners.[133] What bedeviled both the *Ars Signorum* and the *Essay,* however, was the inability of either Dalgarno or Wilkins to prove that his medium of unequivocal communication was more than just another convention that an ever-expanding and changing community of scientists would discard as the scope of empirical investigation inexorably broadened. For once the language planner has eliminated recourse (however specious) to the *Ursprache* (or rather, to its *possibility*), he becomes another Canute menaced by tides of linguistic and scientific change.

If Wilkins was committed in his *Essay* to building an *alphabetum naturae* that was, simultaneously, all correspondence and all convention, then Thomas Sprat reapplied that commitment, in *The History of the Royal Society,* to the more mundane business of scientific communication, namely the Fellows' *"manner of Discourse."* But like Wilkins, Sprat also lacked the courage of his conventional convictions and attempted to sanitize their language from any Hobbesian (or Saussurean) imputations of sheer arbitrariness. Characteristically fulsome, Sprat strove to bring the world of words into correspondence with the world of things, praising the Fellows for their determination

> to reject all amplifications, digressions, and swellings of style, to return back to the primitive purity and shortness, when men deliver'd so many *things* almost in an equal number of *words* . . . a close, naked, natural way of speaking, positive expressions, clear senses, a native easiness, bringing all things as near the Mathematical plainness as they can.[134]

This passage has been quoted ad nauseam—often to prove that Sprat and his colleagues were logical positivists before their time!—but almost no one has caught its odd echoes of Rosicrucian linguistics: of Reuchlin's *sermo purus;* of the Quakers' "pure language of the Spirit of Truth"; and of "the naturall language . . . which the *Cabalists* and *Rosycrucians* have vainly sought in the Hebrew, and in the names of things assigned by *Adam.*"

In his determination to help create a "new language" for the "new philosophy," Sprat thus retrod the brotherhood's linguistic path back to Eden, distrusting "the language of Wits and Scholars." The brethren, it will be recalled, had also boasted that they had "made a new language for ourselves, in which the withall is expressed and declared the nature of all things." And lest one dismiss Sprat's description of the Society's linguistic ideals as an altogether accidental echo of the manifestos, one should consult the anonymous Fellow who contributed a preface to volume 6 of the *Philosophical Transactions*. "The new philosophy," this Fellow declared,

> is so old as to have been the discipline in paradise; and from the first of mankind (who from observing the kinds and differences of animals gave them their names) to have been practiced and countenanced by the best of men; patriarchs and prophets; oft times with divine assistance and inspirations; giving them, that were successful therein, very eminent attributes of glory, as in Noah, Moses, Solomon, Daniel, and others.[135]

Here, quite unexpectedly, one has rejoined the Adamic namegiver of Paracelsus and Croll's intellectual school of Pentecost. And when one recalls the chiliastic aura surrounding Zephaniah's "pure language"—disclosed again at Whitsun—one can see how Sprat's canons of style support the millenarian structure of his *History*. But whether Sprat meant what he said about "primitive purity and shortness" (or knew what he meant) remains problematic.

The founders and Fellows of the Royal Society, however, shared with the Rosicrucian linguists a neurotic distrust not only of eloquence but of everyday language. All were "logophobes" obsessed with the "Babylonical Confusion," both as the source and as the terminus ad quem of the second general curse afflicting their own era.[136] Wilkins and his associates were too well educated to emulate Fox in dismissing all languages as "no more than dust," but in their cogitations one can discern a common flight from postlapsarian words to a prelapsarian (or potentially prelapsarian) order of things; at times John Webster's diatribe against sophism and logomachy is well-nigh indistinguishable from George Dalgarno's. But conservatives and radicals vilified one another as "Babelbuilders" precisely because the definition of the *liber naturae* was under dispute. The language planners and their allies blamed magicomystical speculation about "the language of nature" for the culmination, in mid-seventeenth-century England, of the *confusio linguarum,* thereby overlooking the beneficial consequences of book mysticism for the new science. Yet the "Restoration revolt against enthusiasm" and the Royal Society "reform of prose"—spearheaded by Wilkins, Sprat, Glanvill, and Parker—were sociocultural phenomena that did not adequately reflect the empirical research and methodologies of practicing scientists like Boyle, Hooke, and Newton.[137] But the language planners' distrust of everyday usage is itself contradicted by the almost Orwellian norms of clarity advocated by Glanvill and Parker.

"Every sect was for setting up its own *Frame* and every one had a different *Model* from every other," complained Glanvill in "Anti-Fanatical Religion and Free Philosophy."[138] So far from restoring the *lingua adamica,* sectaries like Fox, Nayler, and Webster had exacerbated the confusion of tongues with their "*Metaphors,* vulgar *Similitudes, Fanatick* Phrases, and *Fanciful* schemes of speech."[139] Glanvill's canons of theological style closely parallel Sprat's canons of scientific style (although they are devoid of Rosicrucian echoes), which should not be surprising given the Royal Society's rapproachment between nature and Scripture. After an attack upon the alchemists' "*boasts, vanity,* and *canting*" in *Plus Ultra,* Glanvill praised the Royal Society for "laying aside the *Chrysopoietick,* the *delusory Designs* and *vain Transmutations,* the *Rosie-Crucian Vapours, Magical Charms,* and *superstitious Suggestions,*" and turning instead to "the *Glory* of the Almighty discovered in his *Creatures* . . . Gods GREAT BOOK, UNIVERSAL NATURE."[140] Thus the *liber naturae* makes its reappearance—but duly purged of magicomystical signatures.

Far more vituperative in his critique of sectarian and Rosicrucian language was Glanvill's colleague Samuel Parker, so rebarbative in his opinions that it is only with difficulty that one can group him with the latitudinarians. "We express the Precepts and Duties of the Gospel in plain and intelligible terms," Parker maintained, while the sects

> trifle them away by childish Metaphors and Allegories and will not talk of Religion but in barbarous and uncouth similitudes.[141]

Confusion was worse confounded by what Sprat called the "many outlandish phrases which several *Writers* and *Translators* in that great hurry brought in and made free as they pleased."[142] Here Sprat condemns, among others, those who had Englished the Rosicrucian, Behmenist, and other alchemystical texts from Germany. Of such works, he concluded, "their Writers involve them in such Darkness; that I scarce know, which was the greatest Task, to understand their Meaning, or to effect it."[143] Needless to say, Rosicrucian linguists conceived differently of their incomprehensible enterprise. In the preface to his translation of Böhme's *Signatura Rerum,* for example, John Ellistone justified as a Pentecostal antidote to Babel those very features of style to which Parker, Glanvill, and Sprat objected. "For we must know," Ellistone explained, finding in Böhme not a confusion but the gift of tongues,

> that the Sons of *Hermes* who have commenced in the Highschool of true Magick and Theosophy, have always spake their hidden Wisdome in a Mystery, and have so couch it under Shadows and Figures, Parables, and Similies, that none can understand their obscurely-clear writings, but those that have had admittance into the same School and have tasted of the Feast of Pentecost . . . a parabolical or Magical Phrase, or Dialect, is the best, and plainest habit, and dress that Mysteries can have to travell up and down the wicked world.[144]

Rosicrucian linguistics cannot, in short, be brought to the strict and comprehensive tests of reason—as administered by language planners and their supporters—because it is accessible solely to those who eschew demonstration and propositions, accepting instead an Adamic or Pentecostal epistemology by which truth is apprehended in one single act. In accordance with the alchemist's principle of the double audience, only Rosicrucian linguists can understand Rosicrucian linguistics!

But even allowing for the paradoxes that abounded in England's twilight of linguistic Platonism, it is hard to square this "new language" of figure and simile with Webster's (and Paracelsus's) objections to a metaphorical reading of the *liber naturae* or with Vaughan's "perfect map of the entire creation" in which "every word were a definition and contain'd the nature of the thing." Nor did the Rosicrucian linguists make any real effort to square connotation with denotation. "That the same thing should have a thousand names is no news to such as have studied the philosopher's stone," Vaughan declared with a blithe disregard for consistency.[145] In William Gratacolle's *Names of the Philosopher's Stone* (1652), one can find 170 of these synonyms—ranging from "the spittle of lune" and "most vild black, blacker than black, Virgins milke" to "Auripigment, a body cynaper, and almost other infinite names of pleasure"—which Vaughan did not pause to enumerate.[146] For a skeptic like Parker there was only nonsense and blasphemy beneath such diversity of phrases. And Walter Charleton dismissed this "dialect of *Hermeticall Mineralogists*" as no more than "the *Babel* of *Paracelsus*."[147]

Among adversaries of the Rosicrucian linguists this flight from and recourse to metaphor provoked both intellectual objection and abuse. In his *Essay,* Wilkins soberly marshaled the case against metaphor, whereas Parker wildly castigated, in *A Free and Impartial Censure of the Platonick Philosophie* (1666), the brethren's "Rampant Metaphors and Pompous Allegories" as well as the key doctrine of their linguistic Platonism: that "names have in them a natural resemblance and sutableness to things and are peculiarly expressive of their several natures."[148] Parker lacked the philosophical acuity to note how richness of connotation ("Rampant Metaphors") contradicted purity of denotation ("natural resemblance"); nor did he acknowledge that his Hobbist conventionalism—thinly disguised but a necessary by-product of the age's paradigm shift as outlined by Hacking—made nonsense of the language planner's determination to fix unique singular characteristics of things in a correspondent semiology not of arbitrary but of rational institution.[149] What Parker does provide, however, is the Royal Society's most scathing indictment of Rosicrucian linguistics. "From the beginning of time to this day," Parker wrote of the brotherhood, "there has not been so great a Conjunction of Ignorance with confidence, as in these Fellows which certainly of all other Aspects, is the most contrary and malignant to true knowledge." As bogus decrypters of the *liber naturae,* Parker complained, the Rosicrucians

> pretend to be Natures Secretaries, & to understand all her Intrigues, or to be Heavens Privadoes, talking of the Transactions there, like men lately drop'd thence encircled with *Glories,* and cloathed with the Garments of *Moses* and *Elias,* and yet put off with nothing but Rampant Metaphors, and Pompous Allegories, and other splendid but empty Schemes of Speech, I must crave leave to account them (to say no worse) Poets and Romancers, true Philosophie is too sober to descend to these wildnesses of Imagination, and too rational to be cheated by them . . . Her Game is things not words.[150]

Of all verbal games played by linguistic Platonists, metaphor was the worst—mere semantic legerdemain—and Parker spelled out the rationale behind Sprat's suave indictment of their countrymen's propensity for being gulled by "this Trick of *Metaphor*."[151] "Now to discourse of the Natures of Things in Metaphors and Allegories," Parker charged,

is nothing else but to sport and trifle with empty words, because these Schems
do not express the Natures of Things but only their Similitudes and Resemblances, for Metaphors are only Words, which properly signifying one thing,
are apply'd to signifie another by reason of some Resemblance between them.
When therefore any thing is express'd by a Metaphor or Allegory, the thing it self
is not expressed, but only some similitude observ'd or made by Fancy. So that
Metaphors being only the sporting of Fancy comparing things with things, and
not marks nor signes of Things. All those Theories in Philosophie which are
expressed only in metaphorical Termes, are not real Truths, but the meer
Products of Imagination, dress'd up (like Childrens *babies*) or a few spangled
empty words . . . Thus their wanton & luxuriant fancies climbing up into the
Bed of Reason do not only defile it by unchast and illegitimate Embraces, but
instead of real conceptions and notices of Things, impregnate the mind with
nothing but Ayerie and Subventaneous Phantasmes.[152]

Parker's is an argument that demonstrates the author's salty skills as a controver-
sialist rather than a genuine flair for linguistic philosophy: His account of verbal
representation of how the *liber naturae* is registered in language is altogether
jejeune. Nor was the bawdry with which Parker mounted his attack upon metaphor
unique, particularly during the 1650s.

What united both Rosicrucian linguists and language planners was their failure
to accept the ineluctable march of science and its *mathesis universalis.* "As
distinguished from scripture," Frank Manuel explains, "science was composed in
a special arcane language that was differentiated from the superficial language of
the senses used in everyday speech and the Bible."[153] This was the colorful and
multiform language of Koyré's pre-Cartesian world, a language appropriate, as
Galileo noted of Moses' auditory, for "a rather boorish and unruly people."[154]
Such was the audience—"young Apprentices, old women, and wenches"—at
which Heydon pitched his Rosicrucian *nugae.*[155] Wilkins addressed the better
educated, but animating his *Essay* was a conviction that fluency—which, he
promised, would come rapidly—did not require any specialized knowledge of
Galileo's "triangles, circles, and other geometrical figures." In effect, Galileo's
language was more "arcane" than Ellistone's "Shadows and Figures, Parables and
Similies." Certainly Galileo's world picture contained no esoterica—"no secret
books, no temples, no mystical conventions or ciphers for the initiate"[156]—but to
master it one needed a highly technical education, an education available only to
few and unintelligible to most of those. So far from instituting a *linguaggio
commune,* Galileo had actually redefined the occultist's "double audience." No
longer did that comprise a spiritual aristocracy and an unilluminated laity; like the
mobile vulgus, language planners were denied automatic fluency in the new codes
of mathematics, their vaunted universalism notwithstanding. Indeed, if Newton's
Principia and *Mathematical Papers* constitute the arcane terminus ad quem of the
scientific revolution, then Rosicrucian linguists and language planners were both
stranded down the same cul-de-sac. Neither the primordial revelations of the
former not the "labour and toyle" of the latter would bring one much closer to the
liber naturae. "It is impossible that we should alienate our speech from the sense
of our eyes," Kepler had remarked.[157] Even in an international auxiliary like

Esperanto, the sun will always rise and set. Whether legislated exoterically by language planner or esoterically by the intellectual school of Pentecost, human speech cannot reflect very much scientific reality.

Paradoxes abound, however hard one strives to illuminate the Rosicrucian twilight with the cold dawn of rationality. For example, Manuel has attempted to distinguish the modern scientist's *liber naturae* from the pansophist's. The scientist, Manuel argues, discovered in both "the Book of Nature and the Book of Scripture . . . equal sources of Christian knowledge, both leading to truth but remaining separate with distinct languages, modes of expression, institutional arrangements, and areas of specialization."[158] By contrast, the pansophist sought "a virtual integration of the two spiritual corps, the scientists and the ministers of religion, into a single body."[150] Yet the pansophist's ideal seems a perfect description of the Royal Society, whatever deference its Fellows showed to the new institutional and linguistic criteria outlined by Joseph Ben-David. Moreover, the society's most distinguished Fellow, Sir Isaac Newton, shuttled between the high sciences of astronomy and mathematics and the low science of alchemy. Converging upon Newton's physics and his alchemy was, as B. J. T. Dobbs shows, his fascination both with the *prisca theologia* and with eschatology.[160] First and last things mingle in the mind of the period's greatest scientist just as they had mingled in the minds of Rosicrucian linguists. Publicly respected for his *Principia,* Newton believed in private that "Pythagoras's music of the spheres was intended to typify gravity"; the Book of Revelation complemented his work with the *liber naturae.*[161] Indeed, the universal laws of gravitation represent pansophia in its purest form, at least until the advent of Einstein. And Newton's interest in "ye voyce of birds" had, as I have shown, ample precedent in England's Rosicrucian twilight.[162] To be sure, Newton scribbled in his copy of Vaughan's *Fame and Confession of the Fraternity R. C.* "this was a history of that imposture."[163] But after hearing McGuire and Rattansi deliver "Newton and the 'Pipes of Pan' " Yates remarked, with a grandiloquent gesture, "Newton was one of us."[164]

Notes

Much of the research for this essay was completed in the Rare Book Room of the Newberry Library where I held an NEH Fellowship 1979–80. My thanks go to all the Newberry's staff but particularly to the directors of the Center of Renaissance Studies, John Tedeschi and Mary Beth Rose. I would also like to thank Jean Dietz Moss (Catholic University) who so kindly helped me edit a longer version of the present essay (now the basis of *Nature's Mystick Book: Magical Linguistics, Modern Science and English Poetry from Spenser to Coleridge*). I am also grateful to the late D. P. Walker for his encouragement and to Christopher Hill, who has waited patiently for published word on "Marvell's language of the birds" and other manifestations of Rosicrucian and millenarian linguistics.

1. Frances Yates, *The Rosicrucian Enlightenment* (1972; reprint, Saint Albans, 1975), pp. 282–306.

2. Eugenius Philalethes [Thomas Vaughan], *The Fame and Confession of the Fraternity of R. C. Commonly of the Rosie Cross: With a Praeface Annexed Thereto, and a Short Declaration of Their Physicall Work* (London, 1652). For details of the manuscript tree and of publication, see F. N. Pryce, introduction to the facsimile edition of ibid. (Margate, 1923); and Thomas Willard's excellent survey, "The Rosicrucian Manifestos in Britain," *Papers of the Bibliographical Society of America* 77 (1983): 489–95.

3. A. E. Waite, *The Real History of the Rosicrucians* (London, 1887); idem, *The Brotherhood of the Rosy Cross* (London, 1924). John Warwick Montgomery, *Cross and Crucible: Johann Valentin Andreae (1586–1654), Phoenix of the Theologians,* 2 vols. (The Hague, 1973).

4. Ernst Gombrich, *"Icones Symbolicae:* Philosophies of Symbolism and Their Bearing upon Art," *Symbolic Images: Studies in the Art of the Renaissance 2* (Oxford, 1972), p. 190.

5. Ibid.

6. Ernst Cassirer, *The Philosophy of Symbolic Forms,* trans. Ralph Manheim (New Haven, 1955), 1:118.

7. *Confessio,* p. 47. All quotations from the Rosicrucian manifestos are taken from the English translations published in 1652.

8. Ibid.

9. *Fama,* pp. 2, 12, 18, 24. (The original text refers to the "parchment book" with the letter *M* that Bernard Gorceix rightly suggests is the *liber mundi,* although he interprets this not as the world itself but as an Arabic commentary on it: see *La bible des rose-croix: traduction et commentaire des trois premiers écrits rosicruciens* [Paris, 1970], p. 5n.). *Confessio,* p. 44.

10. *Confessio,* p. 42.

11. Ibid., p. 41.

12. Ibid., pp. 42–43.

13. *Fama,* pp. 15, 18, 19.

14. J. B. van Helmont, *A Ternary of Paradoxes,* trans. Walter Charleton (London, 1650), "Epistle Dedicatory," sig. f2*v.* As shall be seen, Charleton quickly changed his Platonic tune. It is interesting to note, nonetheless, that the translation is dedicated to Viscount Brouncker, later so active in the affairs of the Royal Society.

15. "Epistle Dedicatory," sig. f3*r.*

16. Michel Foucault, *Les mots et les choses: Une archéologie des sciences humaines* (Paris, 1966), pp. 32–59. Foucault's highly stimulating survey of book mysticism is, however, quite unreliable as an account of Renaissance linguistics in its totality. For a withering critique, see George Huppert, *"Divinatio et Eruditio:* Thoughts on Foucault," *History and Theory* 13 (1974): 191–207. Jakob Böhme, *Signatura Rerum; or, The Signature of All Things Shewing the Sign, and Signification of the Severall Forms and Shapes in the Creation,* trans. John Ellistone (London, 1651).

17. Charles Webster, *The Great Instauration: Science, Medicine and Reform, 1626–1660* (London, 1975), p. 516. See further idem, "Macaria: Samuel Hartlib and the Great Reformation," *Acta Comeniana* 26 (1970): 147–64.

18. Seth Ward and John Wilkins, *Vindiciae Academiarum containing, Some Briefe Animadversions upon Mr. Websters Book, Stiled, The Examination of Academies* (Oxford, 1654), p. 22. I have used the facsimile provided by Allen Debus, *Science and Education in the Seventeenth Century: The Webster-Ward Debate* (New York, 1970). Authorship of the treatise is uncertain, but I have attributed it jointly to Ward and Wilkins.

19. John Wilkins, *Ecclesiastes; or, A Discourse concerning the Gift of Preaching,* 5th ed. (London, 1656), p. 71.

20. For a vigorous critique of Yates's methodology, see Brian Vickers, "Frances Yates and the Writing of History," *Journal of Modern History* 51 (1979): 287–316.

21. Frances Yates, *Theatre of the World* (Chicago, 1969), p. 1.

22. Bodleian Library, Ashmole MS 1459, fols. 280–331; see Yates's discussion, *Rosicrucian Enlightenment,* pp. 236–37. Ashmole, *Theatrum Chemicum Britannicum* (London, 1652), "Preface."

23. For a gallimaufry of gullibility, see Lawrence Stone, "The Disenchantment of the World," *New York Review of Books,* 2 December 1971, pp. 17–25.

24. Charleton was an intellectual chameleon, particularly during the 1650s and 1660s. After flirting with linguistic Platonism and van Helmont, he was, inter alia, instrumental in England's acceptance of atomism. See Robert Hugh Kargon, *Atomism in England from Hariot to Newton* (Oxford, 1966), pp. 77–91. Charleton's shifts in scientific methodology suggest how difficult it is to catch the quiddity of the new philosophy and how easy it would be to exaggerate the occult components of that philosophy. Indeed, van Helmont himself vigorously criticized Paracelsus, a thinker with whom he is often bracketed.

25. For the "light *Mosaick*" of Renaissance syncretism, see Andrew Marvell, "Upon Appleton House," stanza 73. In *Nature's Mystick Book: Magical Linguistics, Modern Science, and English Poetry from Spenser to Coleridge,* I shall explore the impact of Rosicrucian book mysticism upon literature in mid-seventeenth-century England.

26. Frances Yates, *The Art of Memory* (Harmondsworth, 1969), p. 364.

27. For Leibniz's response to the manifestos, see *Opuscules et fragments inedits de Leibniz,* ed. Louis Couturat (Paris, 1903), p. 562. For the general context see Couturat, *La logique de Leibniz* (Paris, 1901), chaps. 2–4, notes 3, 4; Paolo Rossi, *Clavis Universalis: Arti Mnemoniche e logica combinatoria de Lullo a Leibniz* (Milan, 1960), esp. chap. 8; Hans Aarsleff, "The Study and Use of Etymology in

Leibniz," *Studia Leibnitiana Supplementa* 3 (1969): 173–89; D. P. Walker, "Leibniz and Language," *Journal of the Warburg and Courtauld Institutes* 35 (1972): 294–307.

28. Ian Hacking, *The Emergence of Probability: A Philosophical Study of Early Ideas about Probability, Induction and Statistical Inference* (Cambridge, 1975), esp. pp. 39–54. See also Barbara Shapiro, *Probability and Certainty in Seventeenth-Century England* (Princeton, 1982).

29. Hacking, *Emergence of Probability*, p. 9.

30. Linguistic Platonists would not, as I shall demonstrate, agree with Hacking that their scrutiny of the *liber naturae* yielded ambiguous data. Since they believed themselves restored to the state of Adam, the first name giver, how could this be the case?

31. Hacking, *Emergence of Probability*, pp. 41–42 The last sentence is Hacking's own gloss.

32. Ibid., pp. 39–40.

33. *Confessio*, p. 48.

34. Psalms 40:3: "And he hath put a new song in my mouth." Cf. John Boys, *An Exposition of Al the Principall Scriptures* (London, 1610), p. 674: "He speaketh with a new tongue and walkes in newe wayes: and therefore doth new things, and sings new songs: his language is not of *Babylon*, or *Egypt*, but of *Canaan*." Zephaniah 3:9: "For then will I turn to the people a pure language, that they may all call upon the name of the LORD, to serve him with one consent." See further: notes 40, 65, and 105.

35. See Hugh Ormsby-Lennon, " 'Babylonish Dialects?': Sectarian Linguistics during the Puritan Revolution," in *La politica linguistica delle chiese*, ed. Lia Formigari (Florence, forthcoming).

36. "Of the Signature of Naturall Things," in *A New Light of Alchymie . . . Also Nine Books of the Nature of Things, Written by Paracelsus*, by Michael Sendivogius (London, 1650), p. 137.

37. "A Treatise of Oswaldus Crollius of Signatures of Internal Things; or, A True and Lively Anatomy of the Greater and Lesser World," in *Bazilica Chymica & Praxis Chymiatrice or Royal and Practical Chymistry* (London, 1670), sigs. A3r, B1r, B4v.

38. *Fama*, p. 14.

39. Eugenius Philalethes [Thomas Vaughan], *A Perfect and True Discoverie of the True Coelum Terrae; or, The Magician's Heavenly Chaos* (London, 1650), in *The Magical Writings of Thomas Vaughan*, ed. A. E. Waite (London, 1888), p. 136. All quotations from Vaughan's magical works are from Waite's 1888 edition. Waite's two editions (1888, 1919) have not, as Vaughan scholars had hoped, been fully superseded by *The Works of Thomas Vaughan*, ed. Alan Rudrum (Oxford, 1984): see my review, *ISIS* 77 (1986): 195–96. The best study of Vaughan, Thomas Willard's, remains unpublished.

40. Johannes Reuchlin, *Liber de verbo mirifico* (1494; reprint, Leiden, 1533), p. 124. This was the language "quo Deum cum homine, et homine cum angelis locuti perhibenter coram et non per interpretem, facie ad faciem . . . sicut solet amicus loqui cum amico" (ibid.). Cf. Exodus 33:11 (for Moses on Sinai where the cabala was received) and 1 Corinthians 13:12 (where the Parousia is adumbrated). These texts (among others) helped constitute the Quakers' "pure language of the Spirit of Truth"; see Richard Farnsworth, *The Pure Language of the Spirit of Truth* (London, 1655), and note 65.

41. Cornelius Agrippa, *De occulta philosophia libri tres* (n.p., 1533), bk. 1, cap. 74: "De proportione, correspondentia, reductione literarum ad signa coelestia et planetas"; cf. idem, *Three Books of the Occult Philosophy*, trans. John French (London, 1651), pp. 160–62. This is the language termed by John Dee that "which *Adam verily spake in innocency, and was never uttered nor disclosed to man since, till now*"; see Meric Casaubon, *A True and Faithful Relation of What Passed for Many Years between Dr. John Dee . . . and Some Spirits* (London, 1659), p. 92.

42. Yates, *Rosicrucian Enlightenment*, p. 135: "A new approach to Boehme could be opened up through the new historical approach to the Rosicrucian movement." It still remains easier to document the later interaction of Behmenism and Rosicrucianism than to demonstrate their earliest relationships. For some speculations on the earlier affinities see Montgomery, *Cross and Crucible*, 1:154–56.

43. Serge Hutin, *Les disciples anglais de Jacob Boehme* (Paris, 1960), pp. 77, 238–42.

44. John Webster, *Academiarum Examen; or, The Examination of Academies* (London, 1654), p. 26. I have used the facsimile in Debus, *Science and Education*. Like the *Fama* and *Confessio*, Webster's book emerged "from Lame *Giles Calvers* [*sic*] shop, that forge of the Devil, from whence so many lying scandalous Pamphlets, for many years past, have spread over the Land" (Thomas Hall, *Histrio-Mastix: A Whip for Webster* [London, 1654], p. 215; facsimile in Debus).

45. Abraham von Franckenberg, *The Life of One Jacob Boehmen* (London, 1644). On Franckenberg's Rosicrucianism, see Paul M. Allen, ed., *A Christian Rosenkreutz Anthology* (Blauvelt, N.Y., 1968), p. 490.

46. Franckenberg, *Life*, sig. A2r.

47. *Mysterium Magnum; or, An Exposition of the First Book of Moses Called Genesis*, trans. John Elliston and John Sparrow (London, 1654) pp. 227–29. Such analyses can be found throughout the Böhme corpus. For a microscopically close reading of the original German, see Steven a. Konopacki,

The Descent into Words: Jakob Böhme's Transcendental Linguistics (Ann Arbor, Mich., 1979), pp. 141–52.

48. Abiezer Coppe, "An Additional and Preambular Hint as General Epistle Written by ABC," to Richard Coppin, *Divine Teachings* (London, 1649); Thomas Tany, *Theauraujohn His Aurora in Tranlagorum in Salem Gloria* (London, 1655), two more works of language mysticism from Giles Calvert's print shop.

49. Böhme, *Mysterium Magnum*, p. 86.

50. Böhme takes this interpretive strategy still further in his reading of the Crucifixion as an alchemical work; see *Signatura Rerum*, pp. 118–21. but as Coleridge remarked in the marginalia to his copy of Böhme's *Aurora* (BL shelflist C 126 k 1), it is often hard to follow the alchemical allegories in translation since sal niter is rendered "salitter."

51. Oswald Croll, *Philosophy Reformed and Improved*, trans. Henry Pinnell (London, 1657), "Admonitory Preface," p. 136.

52. *Mysterium Magnum*, p. 233.

53. *Confessio*, p. 48.

54. *Mysterium Magnum*, p. 231.

55. *Coelum Terrae*, p. 128.

56. Thomas Vaughan, *Anthroposophia Theomagica* (London, 1650), *Magical Writings*, p. 32.

57. J. Webster, *Academiarum Examen*, p. 28.

58. See Charles Webster, "English Medical Reformers of the Puritan Revolution: A Background to the 'Society of Chymical Physitians,'" *Ambix* 14 (1967): 16–41.

59. J. Webster, *Academiarum Examen*, p. 106.

60. Ibid., pp. 25, 32.

61. *The Journal of George Fox* ed. John L. Nickalls (London, 1975), pp. 333–34. The year is 1658.

62. Attacks upon "the language of the Beast" were a staple of sectarian sermons during the early 1640s.

63. George Fox, John Stubs, and Benjamin Furly, *A Battle-Door for Teachers and Professors to Learn Singular & Plural* (London, 1660), introduction, sig. A2v.

64. J. Webster, *Academiarum Examen*, p. 30.

65. See Richard Bauman's admirable survey, *Let Your Words Be Few: Symbolism of Speaking and Silence among Seventeenth-Century Quakers* (Cambridge, 1983).

66. Böhme, *Mysterium Magnum*, p. 238. Cf. the brethren's combination of mystic linguistic universalism with their declaration that "it hath been necessary that the *Fama* should be set forth in every ones Mother Tongue, because those should not be defrauded of the knowledg thereof, whom (although they be unlearned) God hath not excluded from the happiness of this Fraternity (*Confessio*, p. 42). The brethren's combination of hieratic mystery and demotic appeal spoke powerfully to unlettered English Puritans.

67. Was Ben Jonson the only vernacular source of information about the Rosicrucian controversy in Europe? Behmenist manuscripts already seem to have made their way across the Channel before the Civil Wars and may have been circulating among groups of devotees. See Hutin, *Les disciples anglais*, pp. 37, 194.

68. No synoptic account of this important subject has been written, but much may be gleaned from Keith Thomas, *Religion and the Decline of Magic* (New York, 1971).

69. Jakob Böhme, *Forty Questions concerning the Soul*, trans. John Sparrow (London, 1647), p. 149.

70. *Mysterium Magnum*, p. 233.

71. Fox, *Journal*, p. 27. Fox's indebtedness to Böhme is too complex for discussion here.

72. *Confessio*, p. 45.

73. Henry J. Cadbury, ed., *George Fox's "Book of Miracles"* (Cambridge, 1948).

74. Laurence Clarkson, *The Lost Sheep Found* (London, 1660), p. 32.

75. Note should be made, however of the place of Revelation in the shamanism of Eduardo Palomino; see Douglas Sharon, *Wizard of the Four Winds: A Shaman's Story* (New York, 1978), pp. 101–6.

76. Fox, *Journal*, p. 27.

77. "Godded with God" is the Familist formula of Hendrik Niclaes that undoubtedly influenced both Rosicrucians and Quakers. See Jean Dietz Moss, "Godded with God: Hendrik Niclaes and His Family of Love," *Transactions of the American Philosophical Society* (1981).

78. Joseph Wright, *A Testimony for the Son of Man* (London, n.d.) p. 78.

79. "They continued on their way, not answering in any other notes, but what were musical, "Holy, holy, holy, Lord God of Sabaoth: &c . . . but sometimes with such a buzzing melodious noise, that he could not understand what it was" (*The Grand Impostor Examined* [London, 1656], "To the Reader").

80. "It is the language with which Jonathan Swift, that strange Dean of St. Patrick's was thoroughly

familiar and which he used with so much knowledge and virtuosity" (Eugène Canseliet, *Fulcanelli, Master Alchemist: Le mystère des cathedrales,* trans. Mary Sworder [London, 1971], preface to the second edition, p. 18). I shall discuss mystical birdsong in greater detail in *Nature's Mystick Book.* See also Geza von Roheim, "The Language of Birds," *American Imago* 10 (1953): 3–14; René Guenon, "The Language of the Birds," in *The Sword of Gnosis,* ed. Jacob Needleman (Baltimore, 1974), 299–303.

81. Norman Penney ed., *The First Publishers of Truth* (London, 1907) p. 278.

82. On Solomon and Sheba, see H. St. John Philby, *The Queen of Sheba* (London, 1981), which contains materials familiar in Interregnum England; on Apollonius, see *The First Two Books of Philostratus, concerning the Life of Apollonius Tyaneus,* trans. Charles Blount (London, 1680), already popularized in Agrippa, *Occult Philosophy,* pp. 120–21; on Jesus see John Bulwer, *Chirologia; or, The Naturall Language of the Hand* (London, 1644), pp. 6–7. See further, for contemporary contexts of the birds' "most learned Original," Andrew Marvell, "Upon Appleton House," stanzas 71–72.

83. Butler, *Hudibras,* ed. John wilders (Oxford, 1967), Bk. 2, canto 3, lines 651–58. In his "Preface" to the manifestos Vaughan had emphasized the similarities between Apollonius and the Fratres R. C.

84. Butler, "An Hermetic Philosopher," *Characters,* ed. Charles Daves (Cleveland, 1970), pp. 145–46.

85. M. Bastiaensen, "Le don des langues," *La pensée et les hommes* 7 (1974): 230–45.

86. Böhme, *Mysterium Magnum,* p. 243.

87. For "tongues of men and angels" see 1 Corinthians 13:1. Most (though fortunately not all) modern scholars believe that Acts 2 must be interpreted in the light of Saint Paul's commentary on glossolalia; with the exception of heresiarchs and occultists, most earlier commentaters have not interpreted the two texts in conjunction.

88. Vaughan, "The Morning-watch," *Silex Scintillans* (London, 1650), p. 41. Gombrich, *"Icones Symbolicae,"* p. 190. For Webster's vision of the world as "a Pamphoniacal and musical instrument" in which "the language of birds and beasts" played its role, see *Academiarum Examen,* pp. 28–29, 31. The topic is most majestically handled by Robert Fludd in *Utriusque Cosmi . . . Historia* (Oppenheim, 1617).

89. Vaughan, *Magia Adamica,* in *Magical Writings,* p. 100.

90. Marvell, "Upon Appleton House," stanza 96. For a full discussion of this encounter between metaphysical poet and Quaker leader, see Ormsby-Lennon, *Nature's Mystick Book.*

91. William R. Shea, introduction to *Reason, Experiment, and Mysticism in the Scientific Revolution,* ed. M. L. Righini Bonelli and W. R. Shea (New York, 1975), pp. 7–9.

92. *The Assayer* (1623), in *Discoveries and Opinions of Galileo,* trans. Stillman Drake (New York, 1957), p. 237–38.

93. The flourish comes from the author's dedication" *Dialogue concerning the Two Chief World Systems,* trans. Stillman Drake, 2d ed. (Berkeley and Los Angeles, 1967), p. 3.

94. Galileo, quoting Cardinal Baronius, as discussed by Benjamin Nelson, "The Quest for Certitude and the Books of Scripture, Nature, and Conscience," in *The Nature of Scientific Discovery,* ed. Owen Gingerich (Washington, D.C., 1975), pp. 364–71.

95. "John Dee His Mathematicall Preface," in *The Elements of . . . Euclide,* by H. Billingsley (London, 1570), sigs. biir–v. For the text's resonance in Rosicrucian book mysticism, see Waite, *Rosy Cross,* p. 287.

96. Francis Bacon, *The Advancement of Learning,* ed. G. W. Kitchin (London, 1915), p. 209.

97. Thomas Browne, *Religio Medici* (London, 1643), p. 32.

98. "To the Reader," sigs. A2r–v.

99. Browne, *Religio Medici,* p. 48; cf. p. 24.

100. For this Aristotelian tradition see, inter alia, Ernst Robert Curtius, *European Literature and the Latin Middle Ages,* trans. Willard Trask (1953; reprint, New York, 1963), pp. 319–26; J. A. Mazzeo, *Renaissance and Seventeenth-Century Studies* (New York, 1964), pp. 29–59; William G. Madsen, *From Shadowy Types to Truth* (New Haven, 1968), pp. 126–46; Gabriel Josipovici, *The World and the Book* (London, 1971), pp. 25–51; Gombrich, *"Icones Symbolicae,"* pp. 123–91.

101. Hacking, *Emergence of Probability,* p. 41.

102. J. Webster, *Academiarum Examen,* p. 28.

103. Browne, *Religio Medici,* p. 48.

104. *Magia Adamica,* in Vaughan, *Magical Writings,* pp. 115–17.

105. Francis Bacon, "Historia Naturalis et Experimentalis," *Works,* ed. James Spedding, R. L. Ellis, and D. D. Heath (London, 1857–74), 5:132–33. The Latin text is in *Works,* 2:14–15. Bacon here provides a scientific gloss on Psalm 19:1–4 but he also glances at the "pure language" of Zephaniah 3:9, reminding us of the pronounced millenarian strain in his *Great Instauration.*

106. See Waite, *Rosy Cross,* p. 390.

107. The allusion to Moses is from Abraham Cowley's Pindaric ode "To the Royal Society," which

prefaced Thoms Sprat, *The History of the Royal Society of London* (London, 1667), stanza 5.

108. Ward and Wilkins, *Vindiciae Academiarum*, p. 46.

109. Barbara Shapiro, *JohnWilkins, 1614–1672: An Intellectual Biography* (Berkeley and Los Angeles, 1969), p. 59.

110. René Taton, "The Mathematical Revolution of the Seventeenth Century," in *Reason, Experiment and Mysticism*, ed. Bonelli and Shea, p. 228.

111. *An Essay towards a Real Character and Philosophical Language* (London, 1668), pp. 162–68.

112. Boyle Papers 7, fol. 285r, Royal Society, London, as quoted by James R. Jacob, *Robert Boyle and the English Revolution* (New York, 1977), p. 101.

113. Boyle Papers 8, fols. 123–38, as discussed by Jacob, *Robert Boyle,* pp. 98–104.

114. See Robert Boyle, *The Sceptical Chymist* (London, 1661).

115. Sprat, *History of the Royal Society,* pp. 370–71. The contexts of Royalist chiliasm are ably discussed by Michael McKeon, *Politics and Poetry in Restoration England* (Cambridge, Mass., 1975), pp. 231–57.

116. Sprat, *History of the Royal Society,* p. 318.

117. Rupert Hall, commenting upon Nelson, "Quest for Certitude," p. 377.

118. Robert Hooke, "A Discourse of Earthquakes," in *Posthumous Works,* ed. Richard Waller (London, 1705), p. 338. The "Discourse" dates from the late 1660s.

119. C. Webster, "English Medical Reformers," p. 32.

120. *The Scientist's Role in Society: A Comparative Study* (Englewood Cliffs, N.J., 1971), p. 73.

121. Ibid., pp. 73–74.

122. B. J. T. Dobbs, *The Foundations of Newton's Alchemy; or, "The Hunting of the Greene Lyon"* (Cambridge, 1975), pp. 62–92.

123. *Chymical, Medicinal, and Chyrurgical Addresses: Made to Samuel Hartlib* (London, 1655), addresses 5 and 1 respectively. On Boyle's authorship, see Margaret Rowbottom, "The Earliest Published Writing of Robert Boyle," *Annals of Science* 6 (1948–50): 376–89.

124. Webster, "English Medical Reformers," p. 32.

125. Samuel Boulton, *Medicina & Magica Tamen Physica: Magical but Natural Physick* (London, 1656), p. 5.

126. Eugenio Garin, "La nuova scienza e il simbolo del 'libro,'" *La cultura filosofica del rinascimento italiano* (Florence, 1961), pp. 462–63; A well-willer to Learning [i.e., Francis Lodwick], *A Common Writing* (London, 1647), title page.

127. Ward and Wilkins, *Vindiciae Academiarum*, p. 22.

128. George Dalgarno, *Didascalocophus; or, The Deaf and Dumb Man's Tutor* (Oxford, 1680), "To the Reader."

129. Dalgarno, *Didascalocophus,* "To the Reader."

130. Wilkins, *Essay,* "Epistle Dedicatory," Sig. B1r. Wilkins's dedicatee, like Charleton's in *A Ternary of Paradoxes,* was Viscount Brouncker.

131. Ibid., sig. A2v. For an Aristotelian reading of Wilkins's *Essay* see M. M. Slaughter, *Universal Languages and Scientific Taxonomy in the Seventeenth Century* (Cambridge, 1982). For the inadequacy of such a single-minded reading, see my review-essay, forthcoming in *Language and Society.* For an Aristotelian reading of Dalgarno's *Ars Signorum* see Wayne Shumaker, *Renaissance Curiosa* (Binghamton, N.Y., 1982) and for the limitations of such an approach see my review in *Modern Philology* 82 (1985): 417–19.

132. J. G. A. Pocock, "The Tower of Babel," *Times Literary Supplement,* 21 October 1983, p. 666.

133. Wilkins, *Essay,* "Epistle Dedicatory," sig. B1v.

134. Sprat, *History of the Royal Society,* p. 113. As usual, Sprat indulges in rhetoric, contradicting his earlier praise of the Royal Society's potential contribution to the improvement of "the Humour, and Wit, and Variety, and Elegance of Language" (ibid., p. 41). Of Sprat's own florid style, Samuel Butler commented tartly, "The Historian of Gresham Colledge, Indevors to Cry down Oratory and Declamation, while He uses nothing else," *Prose Observations,* ed. Hugh de Quehen (Oxford, 1979), p. 155.

135. *Philosophical Transactions* 6, no. 69 (25 March 1671):2088.

136. On the complex phenomenon of logophobia, see Roy Harris, "The Misunderstanding of Newspeak," *Times Literary Supplement,* 6 January 1984, p. 17.

137. See the classic studies by R. F. Jones collected in *The Seventeenth Century* (Stanford, 1951); more recently see Michael Hunter, *Science and Society in Restoration England* (Cambridge, 1981).

138. Essay 7, in Joseph Glanvill, *Essays on Several Important Subjects in Philosophy and Religion* (London, 1676), separately paginated, p. 39.

139. Ibid., p. 42.

140. Joseph Glanvill, *Plus Ultra; or, The Progress and Advancement of Knowledge since the Age of Aristotle* (London, 1668), p. 12, sig. B5v.

141. Samuel Parker, *A Discourse of Ecclesiastical Politie* (London, 1670), pp. 74–75.

142. Sprat, *History of the Royal Society*, p. 42.

143. Ibid., p. 37.

144. Böhme, *Signatura Rerum*, "Translator's Preface," sig. A3r.

145. Vaughan, *Anthroposophia Theomagica*, in *Magical Writings*, p. 35.

146. For the list see Gratacolle's work as reprinted in *Five Treatises of the Philosopher's Stone* (London, 1652), pp. 65–72. Gugliemo Grataroli was an Italian iatrochemist of the sixteenth century; for the original, see "Elixiorum varia composita et modus," *Verae Alchemicae artisque metallicae citra Aenigmata: Doctrina*, 2 vols. (Basel, 1561), 2:220–25.

147. Helmont, *Ternary of Paradoxes*, "The Translator's Supplement," p. 97.

148. Samuel Parker, *A Free and Impartial Censure of the Platonick Philosophie*, 2d ed. (Oxford, 1666), pp. 62, 73. For his related criticism of Böhme, see p. 67.

149. Parker's linguistic philosophy was thinly disguised Hobbism. Arguing that "Words do not naturally denote those Things which they are used to represent, but have their import Stampt upon them by Consent and Institution, and may, if Men would agree to it among themselves, be made Marks of Things quite contrary to what they now signife," Parker concluded that "the Sovereign Authority should take upon it self (as some Princes have done) to define the Signification of Words" (*Discourse*, p. 108).

150. Parker, *Censure*, p. 73.

151. Ibid.

152. Ibid., p. 75.

153. Frank Manuel, *The Changing of the Gods* (Hanover, 1983), p. 10.

154. Quoted ibid.

155. Heydon, *The Wise-Man's Crown: or, The Glory of the Rosie Cross* (London, 1664), sig. A7r.

156. Garin, "La nuova scienza," p. 462.

157. Quoted by Manuel, *Changing of Gods*, p. 11.

158. Ibid., p. 3

159. Ibid.

160. See Dobbs, *Foundations of Newton's Alchemy*.

161. Keynes MS 130, King's College, Cambridge. Herbert McLachlan, ed., *Newton: Theological Manuscripts* (Liverpool, 1950); Frank Manuel, *Isaac Newton Historian* (Cambridge, 1963); David Castilejo, *The Expanding Force in Newton's Cosmos as Shown in His Unpublished Papers* (Madrid, 1981).

162. Isaac Newton, Keynes MS 20, fol. 1v, King's College, Cambridge: "Democritus (a Graecian Adeptist) said there were certain birds (volatile substances) from whose blood mixt together a certain kind of serpent was generated wch being eaten (by digestion) would make man understand ye voyce of birds (ye nature of volatiles how they may be fixed)." Newton notes no source for his jotting. B. J. T. Dobbs has suggested that he was making notes from a tract from Michael Maier, but so far I have not been able to find the source. Newton possessed a copy of Ashmole's *Theatrum Chemicum Britannicum* (in the "Preface" to which alchemical birdsong is also discussed), but there are no relevant marginalia in his copy (in the E. F. Smith Library at the University of Pennsylvania).

163. The copy is in Yale University Library; quoted in Yates, *Rosicrucian Enlightenment*, p. 243.

164. J. E. McGuire and P. M. Rattansi, "Newton and the 'Pipes of Pan,'" *Notes and Records of the Royal Society* 21 (1966): 108–43. I owe the anecdote to my friend Jo Dobbs.

17

Renaissance Hieroglyphic Studies and Gentile Bellini's
Saint Mark Preaching in Alexandria

CHARLES DEMPSEY

The history of Renaissance hieroglyphic studies begins in Florence in the decade of the 1420s, and it begins with Poggio Bracciolini, Ambrogio Traversari, and, above all, Niccolò Niccoli. Indeed, of the latter the famous traveler and epigrapher Cyriacus of Ancona (who sent Niccolò a hieroglyphic inscription from his Egyptian journey of 1435) wrote that there was no one more interested than he in such matters. The single discovery of Horapollo's *Hieroglyphica* by Cristoforo de' Buondelmonti on the island of Andros in June 1419 has been greatly exaggerated in its significance, and in a way that has obscured much of the serious, and even beautiful, thought, both philological and poetic, devoted to hieroglyphs in the Renaissance. Buondelmonti's manuscript, the original text of which was probably written in the fourth century A.D. by an Egyptian from Alexandria named Horus Apollo, contained in Greek translation made by one Philippus no fewer than 189 descriptions of hieroglyphs, together with interpretations of their meanings. Though care must be taken to avoid falling into the opposite extreme of underestimating the significance of Horapollo in Renaissance scholarship, at the same time it can be said that the *Hieroglyphica* served at best as an extremely abridged dictionary of hieroglyphic symbols, that it was by no means the only source of such information available to Renaissance scholars (who used it with caution), and that it was certainly not the most important. It contained no statement of the linguistic or pictographic principles of hieroglyphs, no grammar or syntax, except as these could be deduced from Horapollo's definitions consulted in conjunction with information supplied by other, and much more frequently cited and familiar, classical authors. The discovery of Horapollo in short is quite certainly not, as has been claimed, equivalent in significance to the discovery of the Rosetta stone for the Renaissance theory of hieroglyphs, and this theory is neither wholly bizarre nor is it symptomatic of some sort of Egyptomania.

The humanists did not succeed in reading true Egyptian hieroglyphs, and history has characteristically not been kind to them for failing. But they were professional philologists of the first order, and neither their interest in hieroglyphs, nor their methods, nor even the symbolic they developed, is best considered primarily as evidence for Renaissance absorption in the strange, the occult, and the Hermetic. In my judgment, the Hermetic content to hieroglyphic interpretation, first arising in the theories of Pico and Reuchlin and further developed in the time of Athanasius Kircher, is a phenomenon that only becomes dominant after the Renaissance itself. Renaissance interest in hieroglyphs was itself predominantly humanistic and linguistic, and the practical expression of that interest lay in the historical justification given to a theory of symbolic expression that is so characteristic of the period, whether appearing in the form of military and amorous devices, emblematic expressions, allegorical attributes, or parabolic utterances. A Hermetic fascination with hieroglyphs, on the other hand, gains ascendancy in the later seventeenth and eighteenth centuries and can easily be discerned in the subjects of prints like Tiepolo's *Capricci* and *Scherzi,* where Egyptian mages are shown fingering magic amulets while contemplating human bones burning on altars, as well as in literary works such as Schiller's *Geisterseher.* It is this element that still colors the romantic view of ancient Egypt that survives today, giving rise to the legends surrounding the curse of King Tut, and that, as John Irwin has recently shown in his *American Hieroglyphics,* plays a profound role in the works of the American Renaissance, as, for example, in the symbolic structure of Hawthorne's novels and Melville's *Moby Dick,* centering upon the character of the Manichaean Ahab and his Parsi companion, and appearing in the famous hieroglyph of the doubloon nailed to the mast.

In fact, Renaissance interest in hieroglyphs is part of the humanist study of ancient languages and recovery of ancient letters. One might be pedantic and argue that Poggio's discovery of Ammianus Marcellinus at Saint Gall in January 1417 (more than two years before the finding of Horapollo) marks the true beginnings of hieroglyphic studies, but this, too, would be misleading. Rather, when Poggio returned to Florence with the manuscript of Ammianus (where it was transcribed by Niccolò), and when Buondelmonti sent Horapollo's *Hieroglyphica* to Niccolò (where it was read by Poggio and Ambrogio), both were adding new texts to the store of what was already known. Pliny, Lucan, Apuleius, and Macrobius were among these (leaving aside the reports of Isidore of Seville), and the emergence of hieroglyphic studies was then spurred by the convergence in Florence from the 1420s on of many manuscripts—Ammianus and Horapollo among them—containing a great deal of information and lore about hieroglyphs. Niccolò's famous manuscripts of the *Histories* and *Annals* of Tacitus must be mentioned, but especially important are the Greek manuscripts sent by Aurispa, Filelfo, and others—Herodotus, Diodorus Siculus, Strabo, Plutarch's *Moralia,* Plato, Plotinus, Proclus, and Iamblichus—all combine with other sources to give the true stimulus to hieroglyphic research. Especially important, too, is the part played by the Church fathers and early Church historians, in particular Eusebius of Caesarea and Clement of Alexandria, the unique surviving manuscript of whose *Stromata* was read by Politian and Ficino, and remains to this day in the Biblioteca Laurenziana.

Hieroglyphic study begins then with the recovery of texts, especially Greek texts. The next important event in the transmission and development of hiero- glyphic information and theory is the humanist translation of those texts. The relevant streams here descend from various sources, but mention should be made of Traversari's translations of the Greek fathers, especially Dionysius the Areopagite, whose mystical symbolism is fundamental to Renaissance concepts of hieroglyphic symbolism; the very important translations commissioned by Nich- olas V in Rome, notably of Diodorus by Poggio, Herodotus by Valla, and Eusebius by George of Trebizond; and the translations commissioned by Cosimo de' Medici from Ficino of various Platonic, Neoplatonic, and Hermetic texts. When Cyriacus went to Egypt in 1435 he took with him an abridged translation of Horapollo to aid him in his epigraphical researches, and this was disseminated in manuscript copies made by Michele Ferrarini. Giorgio Valla also made translations from Horapollo, as did Filippo Beroaldo the Elder of Bologna, who even compiled a short list of hieroglyphic signs taken from various authors that was printed in a *vocabularium* published for the use of grammar school students. Early in the sixteenth century Celio Calcagnini translated the whole of the *Hieroglyphica* for his nephew, to which he added more hieroglyphs taken from other sources; in Germany Joannes Stobaeus made use of a translation sent to Konrad Peutinger by Trebatius for the composition of the famous hieroglyphic inscription on Dürer's *Arch of Max- imilian*. Pirkheimer also made a translation of Horapollo, which was illustrated by Dürer and presented to the emperor in 1515.

It is really not surprising to find hieroglyphic studies rising out of philology (the natural home, after all, for the study of languages), and with the best that the century had to offer in the study of Latin, but especially of Greek, letters. Nor is it surprising to discover that research into hieroglyphs soon gravitated into the realm of scholars of the Near Eastern languages, notably Hebrew and Aramaic, which in the Renaissance was called Chaldean. In consequence of this it soon became known that ancient Egyptian was related to the Semitic tongues, that its demotic script read from right to left, and that the study of Coptic was to be important in order to provide a link between the languages of ancient and modern Egypt. My present concerns are only with the history of the earliest attempts at hieroglyphic decipherment. However, Coptic was to die out as a living language in the seven- teenth century, and had it not been for the study of it by scholars such as Athanasius Kircher (who is invariably characterized as the craziest of all the students of hieroglyphs), it is virtually certain that the Rosetta stone would never have yielded up its secrets. One of Kircher's primary conceptual errors, that there was a cabalistic foundation to the interpretation of hieroglyphs, derived from the very fact that hieroglyphs were studied in conjunction with Hebrew, and also from the fact that the most important ancient sources—Clement of Alexandria, Plotinus, Iamblichus, and even Horapollo—are products of the eclectic and mysti- cal philosophies of late antique and early Christian Alexandria. Indeed, the serious study of Hebrew among non-Jews had been inspired and profoundly affected by Pico della Mirandola's conviction that biblical interpretation would be deepened by the employment of rabbinical methods of exegesis, leading to the development of a Christian cabala. Cabalistic interpretation of words and letters as a kind of evolving symbolic, capable of expressing a broad and continually expanding spiritual meaning, fusing the thing expressed with the words and letters that express it, found much in common with Renaissance theories of hieroglyphic exegesis, and Kircher's methods are inherited from such earlier students of both Hebrew and hieroglyphics as Pico and Reuchlin.

Be that as it may, the remarkable and fundamental conceptual error made in the Renaissance was the distinction drawn between demotic and hieroglyphic as languages. The former was identified with the ordinary written and spoken Egyptian tongue, and hence seen as a conventional language; hieroglyphic was not identified with Egyptian at all, but was rather seen as a universal symbolic means of communication among the educated, a means, moreover, inextricably intertwined with speculation about the origins of language and the language of God himself. The symbolic foundation to hieroglyphic interpretation appears clearly in Giovanni Battista Alberti's observation, for example, that languages like Etruscan die, making its inscriptions no longer comprehensible, whereas hieroglyphics will always be accessible, but only to the learned. This error is extraordinary, and had remarkable consequences, and it is the more interesting insofar as Renaissance scholars certainly knew, thanks to Clement of Alexandria, that hieroglyphs served not only as ideograms but also as phonemes. Indeed, there are many Renaissance hieroglyphs that are formed on the principles of a phonetic rebus—Lorenzo Lotto, for example, represented in one of his portraits the letter *C* within a moon in order to give the sitter's name (Lu-ci-na), and Agostino Carracci composed an extended rebus to give the title of one of his engravings as "Ogni cosa vince l'oro." Nor were hieroglyphs considered only as pictograms. They embraced any kind of symbolic utterance: famous and often cited examples of hieroglyphic expression being Pythagoras's *aenigmata,* proverbs, allegorical speech, and the parables of Christ.

What is today the best-known form of Renaissance hieroglyph I will call the Neoplatonic form, and the locus classicus for its definition is in Plotinus and in Ficino's commentary to the passage. This form of hieroglyph Ficino conceived as an image that reveals in an instant "understanding, wisdom, and substance, given all at once, and not by discursive reasoning and deliberation." There are two especially beautiful Renaissance examples of such a hieroglyph. The first is the winged eye encircled by a laurel wreath that appears on Alberti's famous medal, and it is beautiful because on the one hand it is literally not translatable—that is, its meaning cannot efficiently be rendered in discursive form (and Alberti himself gave differing, though metaphorically related, interpretations of its signs)—but on the other hand its essential meaning of God-like intellect, judgment, swiftness, and glory, can be immediately sensed, in a flash as it were. The second hieroglyph, even more wonderful, appears in Politian's story of the blinding of Homer, the principal episode of the *Ambra.* It has recently been discovered that the source for Politian's account is a scholion to Plato's *Phaedrus* by Hermias, who reports the tale of Homer's going to the grave of Achilles, praying for a vision of the hero, and, when Achilles appeared before him, being blinded by the radiance of his armor. Politian the scholar discovered the story, but Politian the poet transformed it in a remarkable way, and in a way that encapsulates his revival of the ancient notion that Homer, the archetypal poet, is also the archetypal, and omniscient, philosopher (and this no doubt done partially in response to Socrates' challenge in the *Phaedrus* that poets must speak the truth—that is, be philosophers). Politian imagined Homer blinded, not by the flashing armor of Achilles, but by gazing full upon the shield fashioned for him by Hephaestus, on which was engraved the land, the seas, and the heavens, in short the whole of the universe. In that flashing instant, before his lights went out forever, there was hieroglyphically and indelibly impressed upon Homer's mind the image and understanding of all things, grasped at once, without the need for discursive reasoning, comprehended even as God understands and encompasses all things.

Direct evidence for Politian's scholarly interest in hieroglyphs has not survived, although there are tantalizing glimpses provided in his preface to Homer and in the writings of his pupil Crinito (who promised, but never wrote, a treatise on the subject). Valeriano, in his *Hieroglyphica* of 1556, acknowledged Politian and Crinito as among the most distinguished early students of hieroglyphs. The Neoplatonic form of hieroglyph has an important later history, in particular as it interested such students of Hebrew and the Christian cabala as Reuchlin and Giles of Viterbo, and also as regards the Hermetic tradition. If it should turn out, for example, that the famous medal of Federigo da Montefeltro, on which there appear hieroglyphic signs for Jupiter, Mars, and Venus together with the planetary signs of these gods, further were composed of an alloy of metals proper to each god, then there would be no doubt that hieroglyphic in this case is combined with magic. But I must leave this now, and turn to another form of Renaissance hieroglyph, one that was really far more influential than the Neoplatonic form (especially for the development of the literature of emblems and impresas). I shall name this the epigraphical form of hieroglyph.

Hieroglyphs, as the name implies, were distinguished from ordinary writing in part because they were sculptured or incised, placed on monuments (as Pliny says) to preserve the natural philosophy of the priests and (as Ammianus says) to record the vows and great deeds of kings. Hence the fact that the history of Renaissance hieroglyphic interpretation is closely bound up with the work of Renaissance epigraphers, including not only travelers like Cyriacus of Ancona and Fra Urbano Valeriano, but also artists like Mantegna and Gentile Bellini (who had himself seen the obelisks of Constantinople). From the study of actual hieroglyphs on the obelisks of Constantinople and Rome, as well as the images on certain Roman temple friezes (which were mistakenly thought to be hieroglyphs), a significant fact quickly emerged: Whereas the winged eye on Alberti's medal descends from the single images on Roman coins (which were also considered to be hieroglyphs), these hieroglyphs were multiple, arranged in series and with repeating combinations. That is to say, the evidence of Plotinus notwithstanding, they are in some sense discursive. Moreover, Ammianus Marcellinus expressly reports that hieroglyphs stand not only for whole concepts but also for single nouns and verbs, and Beroaldo the Elder added to this in his commentary to the *Golden Ass* of Apuleius, writing that the twining tendrils Apuleius describes connecting the hieroglyphs in a book carried by a priest of Isis actually functioned as adverbs and conjunctions. Clearly implied here is a form of discursive hieroglyph in which particular signs have a particular and understood definitive meaning, and are even governed by some sort of syntactical rule. If this is so, then it is clear that there were those who thought that hieroglyphs not only could be grasped in an intuitive flash, but also discursively read. It should then follow that there is a class of Renaissance hieroglyphs that can be read, and that were intended to be read by others conversant with the science. The implications of this are fascinating, but cannot be drawn until it is demonstrated that an epigraphical hieroglyph actually can be read.

My intent, therefore, is to propose a reading—really a decoding—of one such sequence of hieroglyphs, those represented by Gentile Bellini on the obelisk in his painting of *Saint Mark Preaching in Alexandria*. The basis for this reading is close comparison of Gentile's signs with the hieroglyphs that appear on several obelisks and a tomb described and illustrated in Francesco Colonna's romance entitled *Hypnerotomachia Polifili* (Venice: Aldus, 1499), published just six years earlier than the painting. This was undoubtedly the immediate source, not only for one or two of the particular hieroglyphs used by Bellini, but also, especially, for the manner by which he formed of them an extended rebus. Here the reader must be referred to Karl Giehlow's magisterial study of hieroglyphic lore in the Renaissance in order to comprehend something of the historical and intellectual context in which it was possible for the hieroglyphs of the *Hypnerotomachia* to be taken seriously as genuine and as a source. I will only interject that I think it can be shown (as Giehlow suspected, and as will appear in my arguments below) that they are genuine in the sense that they represent an attempt to compose new sentiments according to the rules of an ancient language, just as other humanists composed new poems and inscriptions in Latin and Greek. The same phenomenon appears in Dürer's woodcut portrait of the Emperor Maximilian, which is clearly based on Roman profile coin portraits surrounded by an inscription, an inscription in this case not in Latin but in hieroglyphs composed by Pirkheimer. Suffice it, however, for the moment to say that hieroglyphs were conceived on the basis of numerous ancient authorities to express ideas *non in verbis sed in rebus* (and hence very likely the origin of the word *rebus*); that much of the material contained in the

SAINT MARK PREACHING IN ALEXANDRIA, by Gentile Bellini. *(Courtesy of Brera, Milan.)*

Hypnerotomachia was accepted as truly antique in the sixteenth century (as witnessed by the inclusion of some of its inscriptions in Apianus's *Inscriptiones sacrosanctae veterum* of 1534 and in Boissard's *Topographia romana* of 1598); and that the hieroglyphs of the *Hypnerotomachia* were accepted as genuine by Beroaldo's student Filippo Fasanini (in the introduction to his translation of Horapollo's *Hieroglyphica* of 1517), by Alciati (who attended Fasanini's lectures on hieroglyphs at the University of Bologna, who invented his *Emblematum liber* in accordance with Fasanini's suggestion that hieroglyphs might be used to express sentiments and *motti* on badges, medals, shields, and so on, and who incorporated hieroglyphs from the *Hypnerotomachia* into his book), by Pirkheimer (who used them in preparing the hieroglyph inscription for Durer's *Arch of Maximilian*), and by none less than Erasmus of Rotterdam, who, as well as being convinced that they were authentic, was further persuaded that Colonna had at hand the lost hieroglyphic treatise (cited by Eusebius and excerpted in Tzetzes and the *Suda*) composed by the great scholar Chaeremon of Alexandria.

Bellini showed on the obelisk in his painting, reading from top to bottom, the following signs: a crooklike form and a circle, the soles of two sandals, the Roman letters *V.L.,* an owl, an eel (or less likely, a snake), an awl, and the old moon cradled within the full circle of the new. Strange as they are, and unconvincing as they are as representations of actual hieroglyphs, nevertheless every one of Bellini's figures (the Roman letters obviously excepted) is based on actual hieroglyphs that were known from the obelisks in Rome and Constantinople. Indeed, the vertical sequence of gigantic figures he showed finds it closest analogy in the inscription on the obelisk in the hippodrome in Constantinople, an object Bellini had certainly seen. Unfortunately, no Renaissance interpretation of this inscription or reading of its individual characters is known, even though it had been seen by Cyriacus and by Fra Urbano Valeriano, Pierio Valeriano's uncle and the man who inspired not only the *Hieroglyphica* but also, if Giehlow's argument is followed, very possibly the hieroglyphs of the *Hypnerotomachia* itself.

The sandal soles establish definitively the relationship of Bellini's hieroglyphs to the *Hypnerotomachia,* where they are used twice in hieroglyphic inscriptions—the first on the base of the elephant and obelisk, the second on the tomb of the lovers. In the former instance the sole is shown with an eye placed on it (the eye being the familiar hieroglyph for God or divinity, as Alberti noted in the *De architectura*), and its meaning is rendered by Colonna as *Deo subjectus,* deriving from the sole as an image indicating "trampling underfoot." This signification directly obtains in the use of the sole as a hieroglyph on the tomb of the lovers, the top line of which is translated in the *Hypnerotomachia* thus: "Diis manibus. Mors vitae contraria et velocissima cuncta calcat, suppeditat, rapit, consumit, dissolvit." This is expressed hieroglyphically by two eyes over a doubled face *(Diis manibus),* a spindle *(mors,* an allusion to the Fates), a lamp *(vita,* and the fact that it faces back toward the spindle expressing *contraria),* two arrows *(velocissima,* the opposed direction of the arrows repeating *contraria),* a globe with a sun and moon on it *(cuncta),* the sandal sole *(calcat, suppeditat),* a grappling hook *(rapit),* a flame *(consumit),* and a knife *(dissolvit).*

We now know the general concept expressed by Bellini in the sandal soles he

SAINT MARK PREACHING IN ALEXANDRIA (detail), obelisk with hieroglyphic inscription. *(Courtesy of Brera, Milan.)*

Hypnerotomachia Polifili (Venice, 1499), hieroglyphic inscription on base of elephant and obelisk. *(Photo by Karl Dimler.)*

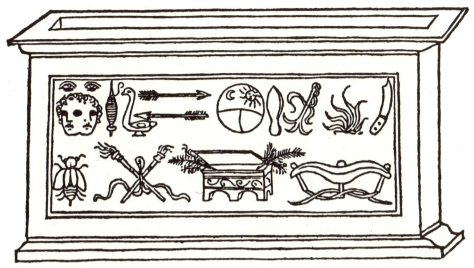

HYPNEROTOMACHIA, hieroglyphic inscription on tomb of the lovers. *(Photo by Karl Dimler.)*

placed on the obelisk, although we do not yet know what part of speech may be intended—nor can we, for Beroaldo notwithstanding, Renaissance hieroglyphs express ideas as things, not as words, and it is the translator who in the end renders these into a syntactical discursive sequence of nouns and verbs; thus, the same image is rendered in the *Hypnerotomachia* now as one part of speech, now as another, even though ribbons and vines joining signs do follow Beroaldo's commentary to Apuleius in expressing a conjunctive function. We do know, however, that the concept is plural, for there are two sandal soles, not one, and comparison with other hieroglyphs in the *Hypnerotomachia* shows that a doubled image invariably represents a plural. We have already seen this in the two eyes and doubled face, meaning *Diis manibus,* and another hieroglyph from the *Hypnerotomachia* shows two ibises and two architect's plumb lines in order to express *Aegyptii communi erexerunt.* As it happens, the doubling of a hieroglyphic sign does indicate a plural in ancient Egyptian writing, but the rationale for this in the Renaissance undoubtedly derived from the conventions of Roman epigraphical inscription, in which the repetition of letters is used to indicate a plural— *AVG.G.G.,* for example, means "the three Augustuses." And in fact the two architect's plumb lines that appear as a hieroglyph in the inscriptions composed for Agostino Carracci's funderal in 1603 were translated by Benedetto Morello (in a letter he wrote describing the obsequies to Cardinal Farnese) with the letters *P.P.,* meaning *posuerunt,* indicating that the members of the Carracci Academy were responsible for the building and placement of the catafalque. It is of course significant that the meaning of the plumb lines in 1603 *(posuerunt)* is the same as that of 1499 *(erexerunt).*

We can for the moment translate the sandal soles as "subjects," understanding this as a generic concept and not yet deciding what part of speech it will take. Moreoever, it would be possible to understand the sign as a metaphorically related

HYPNEROTOMACHIA, hieroglyphic dedication to Julius Caesar. *(Photo by Karl Dimler.)*

concept (as, for example, the provinces of a kingdom, or as slaves) according to the principles of hieroglyphic tropes, or metaphorically determined transfers of meaning, indicated by Diodorus and Clement of Alexandria. Diodorus, taking as his example the hieroglyph of the hawk as denoting swiftness, explains it thus: "The concept then portrayed is transferred, by the appropriate metaphorical transfer, to all swift things and to everything to which swiftness is appropriate." There is in fact a grain of truth in this so far as true hieroglyphs are concerned. As for the Renaissance, Alberti's hieroglyph of the eye incorporates the meaning of God (from Macrobius) and judgment (from Diodorus), the two terms standing in true metaphorical relationship, and hence express a notion of God-like judgment and omniscience. Colonna, too, uses the sandal soles to give the meaning *calcat, suppeditat,* and also to give the metaphorical extension of this meaning, *subjectus.*

Confirmation of the generic meaning we have proposed for the sole can be found in Pirkheimer's notes, where he drew a sandal sole and next to it wrote the word *subiecit.* And Pierio Valeriano, in a very interesting passage, records his uncle Fra Urbano's unhappiness with Colonna's rendering of the eye and sandal, thinking that the positioning of the eye directly on the sandal sole might inadvertently convey the meaning *divum contemptor.* This does not mean, however, that either Valeriano thought Colonna's hieroglyphs mere fictions. Pierio, in fact, who described both his uncle and Colonna as *juniores* in the new science of hieroglyphic study, goes on to write that the sole taken alone translates directly as *calcandi, supprimendique,* which of course agrees with Colonna's *calcat, suppeditat.* Moreover, Fra Urbano's *divum contemptor* follows from this meaning, and the objection is one based upon the placement of the eye in relation to the sole, not upon the meaning of either sign.

Several related uses of the sandal sole in Renaissance hieroglyphic inscriptions demonstrate the familiarity of the sign. It appears on the inscription on the extraordinary tomb of the Canon Hubert Mielemanns in Liège, dating to around 1558, to which we shall return shortly. The Frenchman Geoffroy Tory noted the sandal sole and eye in an inscription he saw on a Roman house facade some time between 1512 and 1517. The inscription as a whole, which clearly had been

composed entirely from two sources—the *Hypnerotomachia* and Horapollo's
Hieroglyphica—Tory described as follows: "Une teste de boeuf, ayant pendu aux
deux cornes deux hoes, puis une grenoille et au dessus d'elle ung oueil, en apres
une chaufrette pleine de feu, ung visage d'homme, ung vaisseau vuydant de l'eaue,
des violettes en ung pot, ung oeil sus une sole de soulier, une ancre de navire, une
grue tenant une pierre de l'ung de ses pieds et ung dauphin sus une lampe qui est
tenu d'une main." Although space does not permit a detailed demonstration, the
meaning of the inscription (potentially Lutheran) can be confidently rendered by
comparing it to the hieroglyphs on the base of the obelisk in the *Hypnerotomachia*
and adding signs from the *Hieroglyphica:* "The labor (or works) of man are
contemptible in the eye of God. By his divine love for the man who little by little
subjects his soul to God, He will take firm custody of his life and vigilantly
preserve it in safety." The German painter Hans van Aachen painted a picture of
the city of Sodom, in which there appears an obelisk inscribed with the sandal
soles (among other hieroglyphs), and this was circulated in an engraving made after
the painting by Raphael Sadeler. An especially interesting use of the sole appears
among the paintings by Polidoro da Caravaggio on the house facade of the Casa
Boniauguri in Rome, one of which (an allusion to the name of the house) showed
the story of Romulus and the omen of the vultures, in the background of which
there appeared an inscribed obelisk. The first three signs shown on the obelisk (the
composition is preserved in an engraving by Michele Crecchi) were the eye, the
sandal sole, and a bird—in light of the subject of the painting, undoubtedly
intended to be a vulture. The vulture was a very familiar hieroglyph in the
Renaissance, for Ammianus had mentioned it and expressly rendered its meaning
as *natura*. The meaning of the three hieroglyphs can thus be expressed as *Deo
subjectus natura,* in reference to natural phenomena acting as a sign from God, and
the separation of the eye from the sandal sole can be explained, perhaps, as
motivated by the desire to place the idea of God in the dominant position on the
obelisk; or perhaps (and more intriguingly) as an attempt to avoid the inadvertent
signification of *divum contemptor*. Lastly, two other instances of the sandal sole
should be mentioned. Luca Pacioli, in the *Divina proportione,* writes that on the
Roman obelisks could be seen Egyptian letters in the form of feathers, knives,
animals, sandal soles, birds, vases, and the like, and this is important for giving
evidence of the sandal sole and other hieroglyphs earlier than the publication of
the *Hypnerotomachia*. And finally, although it does not bear directly on my
present purposes, Paolo Giovio reports that in his youth a certain Bastiano del
Mancino wore on his cap the image of a small sandal sole, with a *T* emblazoned in
the middle of it and a pearl at the point of the toe; when asked its meaning he
answered, "Margherita te sola di cor amo." Now this is no doubt ridiculous, but an
important point emerges. Bastiano in fact used a familiar hieroglyph, but he used it
phonetically, and he used it in a manner by which Egyptian hieroglyphs do in fact
function phonetically—as rebuses—and in a way that Clement of Alexandria said
such hieroglyphs worked. Indeed, there is a class of ancient hieroglyph that
functions emblematically, the only difference being that Bastiano's puns are in
Italian, and not Egyptian. While this is, of course, a tremendous difference,
nonetheless the fact remains that Renaissance scholars were fully aware of the

principles of phonetic hieroglyphs. What they did not possess was the ancient language of Egypt.

To return to Bellini's obelisk, it can be determined by the same means of comparison that the eel (or snake) hieroglyph signifies hatred or envy. One is at first disconcerted to find that the snake appears in one hieroglyphic medallion in the *Hypnerotomachia* with the signification of *prudentia*, while two hieroglyphs on another medallion, described in the text as "uno cane et uno serpe," are translated as *amicitia et odium*. The identification of the serpent with prudence, which is of course biblical in derivation ("be prudent as the serpent"), is easy to explain, but it is extremely difficult to imagine any system of metaphorical transfer or broadening of meaning that could make one sign stand simultaneously for prudence and animosity. But here an interesting fact emerges. Among the group of hieroglyphs that could have been considered by Renaissance scholars as certainly identified on the basis of ancient authority, the most familiar snake character was the *ouroboros,* or tail-devourer, variously identified as the world, the year, time, and eternity. One source for this hieroglyph is Horapollo. Horapollo's definition of the hieroglyph of the eel, which does not bite its tail—which I cite from Trebatius's translation of 1515 (used by Pirkheimer) and from Fasanini's translation of 1517—is *omnibus inimicus,* deriving from the eel's customary avoidance of the company of other fish. *Inimicitia* is of course the antonym of *amicitia,* expressed by the hieroglyph of the dog in the *Hypnerotomachia* woodcut, and it is also an exact synonym for *odium,* the translation given by Colonna. In sum, I may claim here the small honor of being the first to emend a Renaissance hieroglyphic text. Colonna, in a slip of the pen, wrote *serpe* instead of *anguilla* when describing the hieroglyphs on the medallion. This means that the designs for the hieroglyphic inscriptions in the *Hypnerotomachia* existed before the actual writing of the text, and this strengthens the suspicion often expressed that Colonna was working with materials provided him by a hieroglyphic expert, perhaps Fra Urbano Valeriano.

The eel was in fact a very familiar hieroglyph in the earlier Renaissance, and its antipathy to other fish naturally led to an extension of the meaning of the sign to include *invidia.* In a well-known essay, early translated, *De odio et invidia,* Plutarch had pointed out that many considered the terms synonymous, though he distinguishes them. Filarete, in his *Trattato di architettura,* written in the first half of the 1460s, when discussing the obelisk in the Circus of Maxentius (now in Piazza Navona), mentions several hieroglyphic signs, among them the eye and the owl, and says that Francesco Filelfo had explained their meaning to him, but the only one he can remember is the eel, which means *invidia.* Filarete's memory, at least on this one point, did not fail him, for a letter written by Filelfo in 1444 to Scalamonti, the biographer of Cyriacus of Ancona, refers to Horapollo and specifically cites the eel as meaning envy. This signification is also given by Caelius Rhodiginus in his *Antiquae lectiones* of 1516 and by Alessandro Alessandri in the *Dies geniales* of 1522. A particularly amusing instance of the eel appears in the Roman sketchbook of Giovanni Antonio Dosio, one sheet of which shows an obelisk inscribed with various hieroglyphs taken from the ancient authors, and on which Dosio has clearly identified the eel as representing the *invidiosi.*

The hieroglyph of the owl can also be deciphered with reference to the *Hyp-*

nerotomachia, where it appears together with a lamp as the entire inscription on the broken pediment of the gate to the graveyard wherein the tomb of the lovers is found. Although the pediment is imagined and illustrated as broken, so that the bird (whose lower parts rather resemble an eagle) is partly destroyed, Colonna in the text calls it an owl: *bubone.* This is in itself an indication of the closeness with which hieroglyphic inscriptions were studied, for the true Egyptian hieroglyph is an eagle-owl *(bubo ascalaphus).* In the text the inscription is interpreted as *Vitae lethifer nuntius,* meaning the fatal, or death-bringing herald of life. The meaning of the lamp as life has already emerged in the discussion of the tomb of the lovers. It is a meaning sanctioned by antiquity, both by Plutarch and Apuleius, at least as Apuleius's description of the lamp-bearing priest in the procession celebrating Isis is explained in Beroaldo's commentary of 1500. The concomitant meaning of the owl as "death" (hardly surprising, though it might be noted that the Latin word for owl is *noctua*) can further be established by reference to the hieroglyphic inscription on the tomb of Hubert Mielemanns in Liège, one part of which is composed almost entirely of the hieroglyphs on the tomb of the lovers and the cemetery gate in the *Hypnerotomachia.* There are shown on the tomb an owl facing a lamp, a sole within a circle, a grappling hook, a flame, a knife, a globe and cross, and a spindle. It is certainly possible to read the opposition of the owl and lamp as *vitae lethifer nuntius* on the authority of Colonna's reading of the inscription on the cemetery gate, but it is also possible to consider the owl as a replacement for the spindle facing the lamp on the tomb of the lovers. Both the owl and the spindle signify *mors;* since the spindle appears with this meaning at the end of the inscription, the owl might have been substituted for it at the beginning in order to avoid repetition. The owl and the lamp would then mean, as had the spindle and lamp on the tomb of the lovers, *mors vitae contaria.* This, of course, perfectly reconciles with the succeeding five characters, which exactly follow the succeeding hieroglyphs on the tomb of the lovers—the sandal sole within a circle instead of next to a globe *(cuncta calcat, suppeditat),* the hook, flame, and knife again indicating snatching away, consuming and loosening *(rapit, consumit, dissolvit).* The globe and the cross with the spindle represent a variation on Colonna's theme. They clearly stand for the world and death, and one might therefore render the whole of the inscription in this way: "Mors vitae contraria: cuncta calcat, suppeditat, rapit, consumit; solvitur mundus morte." One might also render the inscription thus: "Vitae lethifer nuntius: cuncta calcat, suppeditat, rapit, consumit, dissolvit omnia mors."

It is important to stress at this point that a succession of Renaissance hieroglyphic signs expresses a series of ideas without grammatical relation, and that the burden of deciding what parts of speech to assign to each hieroglyph falls on the translator, whose job is to transform an ideographic sequence into a fully discursive one. Strictly speaking, the signs on the Mielemanns tomb carry only the following meanings: death, life, all, subject, grasp, consume, sever, world, and death. Moreover, even the particular identifications of individual hieroglyphs are only valid within quite broadly defined limits. The owl and lamp, by metaphoric extension, could also mean the opposition of darkness to light, or ignorance to knowledge (and Valeriano gives both "darkness" and "ignorance" as meanings of the owl), while the circle that has here been translated as "all" could as legit-

TOMB OF HUBERT MIELEMANNS, LIÈGE (after Tervarent).

imately be used to express the adverb *semper,* as it does in the most famous of all hieroglyphs from the *Hypnerotomachia,* the circle followed by a dolphin twined round an anchor, with the meaning *Semper festina lente.* The immediate problem is first to identify the broad concepts embodied in Bellini's hieroglyphs, and then to translate these into a syntactically coherent sequence. As with all translations, the particular wording and syntax employed will vary, although the broad sense of the passage should be accurately conveyed. So far I have isolated three broad concepts *in rebus:* subjects (the sandal soles); death, darkness, or ignorance (the owl); and hatred or envy (the eel).

We can now turn to the Roman letters *V.L.* that appear between the sandal soles and the owl on Gentile's obelisk. They are first of all interesting because of their form, which, while not so fine as the majuscules employed by his brother-in-law Mantegna, nevertheless show Bellini preoccupied with the forms of Roman lapidary inscription in the same way as were Mantegna and his follower Bernardo Parenzano (or Parentino), who only a few years earlier was at work on the many inscriptions and hieroglyphs that appeared in his extraordinary frescoes in the cloister of Santa Giustina in Padua. Nor is it so very odd that Bellini should have combined his hieroglyphs with Roman letters, for Mantegna and Parenzano did the same thing, and similar combinations appear in the *Hypnerotomachia.* The reason for this lies in the Renaissance notion that the Romans themselves used hieroglyphs on their temple friezes and on coins and medals, where they appear together with conventional inscriptions and familiar abbreviations. The dolphin and anchor, for example, derives from a coin of Titus, while the reverses of imperial coins are often inscribed with such forms as *S.C.,* for *Senatus consulto.* The Roman letters *V.L.* are themselves the common abbreviation for *votum libens,* although more usually they appear in some extended form such as *V.L.S., votum libens solvit,* meaning that a monument has been erected in willing fulfillment of a vow. Parenzano indeed employed such an inscription in his frescoes in Santa Giustina. The shorter form may also mean *vovit libens,* indicating the cheerful and unconstrained undertaking of a vow rather than the discharge of one. And according to Ammianus, it was the purpose of hieroglyphic inscriptions on obelisks to record just such vows: "The Egyptians, by engraving many kinds of beasts and birds . . . thereby registered the vows of kings, either promised or performed" *(promissa vel soluta vota regum monstrabant).*

The last two hieroglyphs on Bellini's obelisk are the carpenter's awl and the old moon cradled in the circle of the new, an image it seems possible to understand only as signifying a waning, or decline. The sign is in fact the Egyptian ideogram for the moon (as Clement of Alexandria accurately reports), and Eusebius says that the hieroglyph of the moon means fruitfulness (something also mentioned by Beroaldo). The old moon within the circle of the full moon of abundant fruitfulness would logically then represent the waning of that abundance, and this is in fact what Rabelais reports in his satire (though quite an accurate one) on the French mania for hieroglyphic expression, writing that the horned moon is employed for the devices of courtiers in order to indicate the waxing or the decline of a fortune. One need not worry about the distorting mirror of satire here, for Rabelais took his knowledge of the hieroglyph from Geoffroy Tory, and Aulus Gellius moreover reports that the Egyptian priests believed that garden vegetables grew with the waxing moon and shrank with the moon's decline. As for the awl—which recalls Diodorus Siculus's statement that the Egyptians composed their hieroglyphs not only from animals and parts of the body but also from "implements and especially carpenters' tools"—Giehlow has already suggested in passing that this stands for the cross (in the tau form), one of the most famous of all Egyptian hieroglyphs and one that especially engaged the attention of Christian theologians and historians. Giehlow was certainly right, and to show this I must turn to a different group of sources.

Although Bellini's painting has been known since the time of Ridolfi by the title of *Saint Mark Preaching in Alexandria,* properly speaking its subject is the establishment of the Church in Alexandria by Saint Mark, who remained there as the city's first bishop. The event is not recorded in the Bible, but is first mentioned in the *Historia ecclesiastica* of Eusebius (ca. 260–340), followed by Jerome (ca. 340–420), and further transmitted by the translators and continuers of Eusebius, notably Rufinus (ca. 345–410), Socrates Scholasticus (first half of the fifth century), and Cassiodorus (ca. 490–593). By Eusebius's reckoning, Saint Mark introduced Christianity into Egypt in the third year of Claudius's reign (that is, A.D. 43), only one year after Saint Peter established his see in Rome, and the year before Evodius was raised to the see of Antioch. The Church of Alexandria was thus second only to the Church of Rome in antiquity, and with regard to Gentile's painting, this is significant. The body of Saint Mark had centuries earlier been brought from Alexandria to Venice, where it was placed in the church of San Marco. The imposing building in the background of Bellini's painting bears obvious enough analogies to the architecture of San Marco (as well as to the Scuola di San Marco, for which the picture was painted). At the same time, Bellini's obelisk appears in exactly the same relation to this building as did the obelisk of Saint Peter's to its church, before Fontana's celebrated removal of it to the square in front of Saint Peter's later in the sixteenth century. Clearly intended here is a comparison of San Marco in Venice, which contained the body of the founder of the second most venerable see in antiquity, both to the Church he had established in Alexandria and to Saint Peter's itself, a comparison that implies a virtually equal standing with the see of Rome. This fusion of historical narrative with contemporary reference is consistent with the rest of Gentile's imagery, which shows Saint Mark in an impeccable antique toga preaching, not to the ancient Alexandrians, but to a crowd of Turkish men and women. Explicitly stated thereby is the hope of reconverting Alexandria, with Saint Mark as inspiration and example, and this hope of turning back the new paganism of Islam by Venetian Christians appears in the assembly of Venetian citizens, Gentile Bellini among them, who are portrayed attending the sermon of Saint Mark.

The painting was thus conceived as a historical picture, but one with a contemporary reference. And Bellini, although he had never seen Alexandria, expended some effort on historical and topographical accuracy. The camel and giraffe, for example, that appear in the background of his painting show his desire to render accurately the fauna of Egypt. Indeed, Phyllis Lehmann has recently shown that Bellini's depiction of the giraffe directly depends on one of the manuscripts recording Cyriacus of Ancona's visit to Egypt, wherein there appeared a drawing made by Cyriacus of a giraffe taken from the life. Other elements in the painting— Saint Mark's Roman toga, for example, and the high tower with the glass cockpit intended to represent the pharos of Alexandria, and the very obelisk I am discussing here—further demonstrate Gentile's concerns with topographical and antiquarian accuracy. As a matter of historical record, the building in the background, therefore, cannot be intended as the church established by Saint Mark in Alexandria, for Saint Mark is shown converting the Alexandrians from the old religion. It therefore follows that the building and the obelisks inscribed with hieroglyphs next to it are in reference to the ancient cult replaced by Christianity, and this was, of course, the great cult of Serapis in Alexandria.

With respect to this present attempt to read the hieroglyphs on the obelisk, the most valuable information about the cross hieroglyph appears in the accounts of the followers of Eusebius, namely Jerome, Rufinus, Socrates Scholasticus, and Cassiodorus. This occurs in the places where each of them discusses the hieroglyphs connected with the temple of Serapis, the Serapeum in Alexandria, when they tell of its destruction by the Patriarch Theophilus in A.D. 391 (after which the use of hieroglyphs in antiquity ceased forever). The information not only sheds light on the meaning of Gentile's hieroglyphs, but also helps to establish that his sources for the general conception of his painting lie primarily in the early *Scriptores historiae ecclesiasticae,* rather than in such later compilations as the *Legenda aurea,* something not surprising given the evident historical, antiquarian, and topographical care that he devoted to the painting.

In brief, both Rufinus (*Hist. eccles.* 2.29) and Socrates Scholasticus (*Hist. eccles.* 5.17) devote a chapter to the hieroglyph of the cross that appeared everywhere throughout the Serapeum in Alexandria, one of the greatest sanctuaries of late antiquity, the home of Serapis (who had been made patron of the Greek colony of Alexandria by Ptolemy I), and the fountainhead of the cult of Isis and Osiris that had had so great a following as one of the major religions of the Roman Empire. Rufinus reports that the hieroglyph of the cross signified *vita ventura,* "life to come," and Socrates Scholasticus reports the same, but then their accounts diverge in a manner that gives evidence of a lively controversy among the early Christians on the significance of the hieroglyph. Rufinus has it that the Egyptians received from their ancestors the tradition that the cross appeared in the Serapeum in order to indicate that the temple would stand until the time when a sign would come in which there was life, at the appearance of which the worship of Serapis would end. Socrates Scholasticus goes one step further, however, reporting that there are those who believe (though he does not) that the hieroglyph meant that the temple and worship of Serapis would be destroyed when the actual sign of the cross would appear, and in so saying he clearly indicates that, according to this belief, the Egyptian priests had foreknowledge of the coming of Christ. In any event, from these sources the discussion passed directly to scholars of the Renaissance.

First among these should be mentioned Ficino, the translator not only of Plotinus but also of Iamblichus's *De mysteriis,* an important source for the students of hieroglyphs. Ficino himself was, of course, profoundly convinced that the highest dogmas of Christianity were adumbrated in the ancient wisdom of Egypt, and it is hardly necessary here to elaborate upon the influence of his repetition and amplification of the attempts of the early fathers to reconcile Christianity with philosophy. Ficino's translation of the cross hieroglyph was *vita futura,* as one learns from a letter written to Corvinus in 1489: "Inter Aegyptiorum characteres crux una erat insignis, vitam eorum more futuram significans eamque figuram pectori Serapidis insculpebant." Crinito also mentions the hieroglyph of the cross in the *De honesta disciplina* of 1504, while Celio Calcagnini in a letter written between 1505 and 1517 says that the cross signified *spes futurae salutis,* thereby suggesting that the sign actually denoted salvation to the Egyptians. Other citations of the cross hieroglyph could be given, by Fasanini and Valeriano among others, but one is especially interesting. Although one would be justified in supposing that the form of the cross referred to is the *crux ansata* (or "cross of life") adopted by the Coptic Church from the ankh, or Egyptian life sign, Paulus Frellonius (who wrote a supplement to Valeriano's *Hieroglyphica*) reminds us that Saint Jerome specifically identified the sign with the tau cross (or *crux commissa*): "Narratur historiis ecclesiasticis, & D. Hieronymi commentariis, literam Hebraicam TAV salutes fuisse olim signum etiam Paganis ipsis habitum, quod parietibus templi Sarapidis passim visum est." In this passage clearly appears one foundation for a theoretical justification of hieroglyphic interpretation according to a mystical and cabalistic examination of the meaning of individual letters, but for my purposes the significant fact is that Saint Jerome attributes to the cross sign the meaning of salvation as well as of a life to come, and that it is his discussion of the tau cross that gives the meaning to Gentile's hieroglyph of the carpenter's awl.

We must now consider the hieroglyph with which the inscription on Bellini's obelisk begins. This is a crook-shaped outline with a circle next to it, and while it is quite likely an abstraction of the shepherd's staff that is, together with the ankh, an attribute of Serapis, I can find no real *comparandum* for it among Renaissance hieroglyphs. It is certainly not Arabic, and in fact the two signs are observed from actual Egyptian hieroglyphs. The circle is the ideogram for the sun, and hence also the phoneme *re.* The crook outline without question is a hieroglyph derived from the hieratic abbreviation of the earlier sign of the quail chick, and at the same time it is also similar in form to the ideogram for scepter. Plutarch reports, and Macrobius agrees, that the eye and scepter together was the hieroglyph for Osiris, and this sign was well known in the Renaissance. Nanni of Viterbo, for example, described the hieroglyph in his well-known forgery of an inscription to Osiris in Viterbo, and by the seventeenth century the eye and scepter of Osiris became the attributes of Divine Wisdom as described by Ripa in his *Iconologia* and portrayed by Andrea Sacchi in the Palazzo Barberini. It is best to be cautious about Gentile's sign, however, although I am convinced that it is invented from that shepherd's staff which is one of the attributes of Serapis.

Nevertheless, taken in the context of the hieroglyphs that follow it on the obelisk, the crook and circle can only stand for the maker of the vow—king or god—and if one takes Rufinus and the *Scriptores historiae ecclesiasticae* as guides, this can only be Serapis, the great patron deity of Alexandria, whose name would naturally appear first on the inscription. Ammianus reported, as we have seen, that such inscriptions recorded the vows of kings, and this was confirmed by Diodorus, who records inscriptions not only of the semilegendary king Sesostris (perhaps Ramses II) but also of Osiris himself. And it was Serapis who predicted, as the early Church writers affirm, a *vita ventura* when his worship would end, expressing this in the hieroglyph of the cross that appeared in the Serapeum. And it is indeed the fulfillment of that vow that is the subject of Bellini's painting, which shows Saint Mark establishing the Christian Church in Alexandria in place of the old religion. We may now attempt a translation of the message set forth in Gentile's hieroglyphs, first setting them forth as a sequence of ideas expressed *non in verbis sed in rebus:* Serapis, subjects, willing vow, death or ignorance, envy or hatred, life to come, and a declining fortune. Even without setting this sequence forth in discursive form, it is possible to see that the meanings of the hieroglyphs as established on the basis of the *Hypnerotomachia* and other Renaissance sources combine to express a message that conforms remarkably to the prophecy recorded by Rufinus and the early Church historians. This is in itself a remarkable confirmation of the meanings we have proposed for the individual hieroglyphs—for they combine to express a meaning that may be found independently in the legend of Saint Mark—and also a confirmation of the fact that the message of the obelisk was intended to be read. One may in consequence attempt a translation of the hieroglyphs, giving the ideographic sequence a syntactically discursive form: *Serapis subjectis suis vovit libens: ex ignorantia invidiaque in vita ventura fortuna sua decrescet.*

Such might well be the subject of the sermon that Saint Mark is preaching to the Alexandrians. Indeed, it is virtually certain that the message of the obelisk is his theme, for Gentile has placed him standing just beneath the obelisk in the painting (the inscription appearing almost like a cartoon bubble over his head), with the inescapable implication that Mark is expounding the mysteries engraved in the stone. Moreover, there is textual justification for believing this. Socrates Scholasticus, in his discussion of the hieroglyph of the cross in the Serapeum, discounts the view that the ancient Egyptians had actual knowledge of the coming of Christ himself, for this was a mystery hidden from the ages and generations, unknown to the Devil himself. However, he adds, the erroneous doctrine could in itself be seen as inspired by Divine Providence, for with the preaching of it many Alexandrians were converted and baptized. The justification for this mode of exegesis Socrates Scholasticus gives in the example of Paul, who, when preaching to the Athenians, was first inspired by Divine Providence to read aloud an inscription from one of their own altars, interpreting it in the light of Christian doctrine, and by doing this was able to win over many converts.

Such craftiness, worthy of Ulysses and sanctioned by the example of the divinely inspired Paul, the great preacher of mysteries, is surely not absent in Mark, the converter of the mystery-loving Alexandrians. However, I do not want to suggest that Gentile was cynical in his conception of Saint Mark preaching the ancient mysteries. Allusion has already been made to the humanist notion that the profoundest Christian beliefs were adumbrated in the wisdom of ancient Egypt, and indeed one need look no further than the *Hypnerotomachia* itself to find, in Colonna's words, the doctrine of "la Trinitate in figure hieroglyphe, cioè sacre lettere aegyptie," engraved upon an obelisk. I would suggest that in Bellini's Saint Mark one finds instead the prototype for Ficino's religious philosopher, preaching the ancient wisdom hidden in the stone, establishing the doctrine that would be explored by Origen and by his teacher, Clement of Alexandria. And, indeed, it is Clement who first stated in the *Stromata* that hieroglyphic expression encompasses the enigmas of Pythagoras, the symbolic utterances of Plato, the wisdom of the biblical proverbs, and the parables of Christ himself. Accordingly, the reading of the message on the obelisk could as well be: *Serapis subjectis suis vovit libens: ex ignorantia invidiaque in spe futurae salvationis* (or even *in signo crucis*) *fortuna sua decrescet.*

My purpose in this discussion has not been primarily to present an iconographical reading of a single painting, however interesting that may be, and I am afraid that a review of the full range of Renaissance hieroglyph expression, and a consideration of it as a theory of language and art, as philosophy and poetry, and as a universal symbolic must await another forum. It has been necessary as the first step to establish that there is at least one class of Renaissance hieroglyphs that can be read; if I have been able to do this, then I must leave it to the reader to consider the meaning of the discovery and writing of a language that could be understood by Fra Urbano Valeriano in Venice, Beroaldo and Fasanini in Bologna, Calcagnini in Ferrara, Crinito in Florence, Bessarion and Giles in Rome, Pirkheimer in Germany, and Tory and Thevet in France. I shall simply end by referring to a picture of a famous obelisk published by Thevet in his *Cosmographie du Levant,* together with its adaptation in a painting by Joachim van Beuckelaer.

The obelisk is in fact Cleopatra's Needle, which today stands on the Victoria Embankment in London. Thevet actually saw it in Alexandria, the only obelisk then still standing in the ancient city, and he had thought that it was erected to Alexander and stood next to Alexander's palace. It was only in the seventeenth century that the palace and obelisk were reattributed to Cleopatra. The hieroglyphs that his engraver has shown on the obelisk are especially interesting, because they quite certainly derive, not from the actual obelisk, but from the hieroglyphs that Cyriacus of Ancona (who had also visited Alexandria) claimed to have seen on it, sending them back to Italy, where immediately they became known to the circle of Scalamonti, Felice Feliciano, Mantegna, and Gentile Bellini. The first three signs are an eye (expressing divinity, in this case certainly referring to the divine Alexander, and in Beuckelaer's painting referring to the deified Augustus), an eel (envy or hatred), and an open right hand, which Diodorus as translated by Poggio said meant "liberality" (this is in fact true of the genuine Egyptian hieroglyph). The concept is plain. The obelisk is dedicated to "the divine Alexander, liberal to his enemies." Next there appears a vase (the soul) and a bucranium (labor), both easily identifiable on the basis of the *Hypnerotomachia.* The idea is expressed of Alexander's magnanimity and his great labors. The last three hieroglyphs are the knife (dissolution), an owl (death), and a cuirass (military triumph), and one learns that Alexander's great conquests have been cut short by death.

ECCE HOMO (detail), by Joachim van Beuckelaer. *(Courtesy of Nationalmuseum, Stockholm.)*

COSMOGRAPHIE DU LEVANT (Paris, 1575), obelisk with hieroglyphic dedication to Alexander the Great. *(Courtesy of the Folger Shakespeare Library.)*

Bibliographical Note

The foregoing paper has been excerpted from a larger study, and is accordingly printed as it was written, without notes. The interested reader may further consult the following publications:

Karl Giehlow, "Die Hieroglyphenkunde des Humanismus in der Allegorie der Renaissance," *Jahrbuch der Kunsthistorischen Sammlungen des Allerhöchsten Kaiserhauses* 32 (1915): 1–218, remains (in Wittkower's terms) the masterpiece *hors concours* of all studies of Renaissance hieroglyphics. See also L. Volkmann, *Bilderschriften der Renaissance: Hieroglyphik und Emblematik in ihren Beziehungen und Fortwirkungen* (Leipzig, 1923); E. Iversen, *The Myth of Egypt and Its Hieroglyphics in European Tradition* (Copenhagen, 1961); M. Pope, *The Story of Archaeological Decipherment from Egyptian Hieroglyphs to Linear B* (New York, 1975); L. Dieckmann, *Hieroglyphics: The History of a Literary Symbol* (Saint Louis, 1970); and P. Castelli, *I Geroglifici e il mito dell'Egitto nel Rinascimento* (Florence, 1979).

For Gentile Bellini's painting of *Saint Mark Preaching in Alexandria,* see P. W. Lehmann, *Cyriacus of Ancona's Egyptian Visit and Its Reflections in Gentile Bellini and Hieronymus Bosch* (Locust Valley, N.Y., 1977). For Beuckelaer's use of hieroglyphs, see K. Moxey, "The 'Humanist' Market Scenes of Joachim Beuckelaer: Moralizing Exempla or 'Slices of Life'?" in *Koninklijk Museum voor Schone Kunsten Antwerpen, Jaarboek* (1976), pp. 109–87. For hieroglyphic rebuses, E.-M. Schenck, *Das Bilderrätsel* (Hildesheim, 1974). For Fasanini, D. L. Drysdall, "Filippo Fasanini and His 'Explanation of Sacred Writing' (Text and Translation)," *Journal of Medieval and Renaissance Studies* 13 (1983): 127–55.

For Beroaldo and the study of Horapollo, R. Aulotte, "D'Egypte en France par l'Italie: Horapollon au XVIᵉ siècle," in *Mélanges à la mémoire de Franco Simone: France et Italie dans la culture européenne* (Geneva, 1970). For Poliziano and the hieroglyph of Achilles' shield, E. Cropper, "A Scholion by Hermias to Plato's *Phaedrus* and Its Adaptations in Pietro Testa's *Blinding of Homer* and in Politian's *Ambra,*" *Journal of the Warburg and Courtauld Institutes* 43 (1980): 262–65. For Lotto's hieroglyphs, D. Galis, "Concealed Wisdom: Renaissance Hieroglyhic and Lorenzo Lotto's Bergamo *Intarsie,*" *Art Bulletin* 62 (1980): 363–75.

And for an excellent summary introduction in English, based largely on Giehlow, see the lecture by R. Wittkower, "Hieroglyphics in the Early Renaissance," in *Allegory and the Migration of Symbols* (Boulder, Colo., 1977), pp. 114–28.

18

Freemasonic Imagery in a Venetian Fresco Cycle of 1716

DOUGLAS LEWIS

To discover a truly startling novelty in one aspect of a well-known masterwork from the Italian Renaissance is a somewhat infrequent phenomenon, especially when the work constitutes a major component in the oeuvre of so celebrated a genius as Andrea Palladio (1508–80). Yet one of that great architect's most significant and most characteristic buildings—a large country palace built in 1551–53 for the naval commander Zorzon Cornaro at the village of Piombino[1] near Castelfranco Veneto, in the mainland territories of the Venetian Republic (pl. 1)—contains an extensive early-eighteenth-century cycle of fresco paintings incorporating clear evidences of proto-Masonic, or even canonical Freemasonic imagery. The presence of this particular Hermetic element in such an unexpectedly early setting appears all the more astonishing in that the paintings are documented through a preliminary contract of 19 December 1716, already referring to a comprehensive iconographical program, whereas Freemasonry as an international movement only emerged from its hitherto somewhat unorganized obscurity into a more accessible and influential role in European affairs during the following year, with the establishment of the Grand Lodge in London in 1717.[2] Even through the succeeding two and a half centuries an aesthetically sophisticated use of Freemasonic imagery has been so extraordinarily rare as to suggest that the movement, once publicly declared and disseminated, has really not achieved any notable manifestations in the visual arts. For this reason the previously unsuspected existence of a major fresco cycle substantially organized according to Freemasonic themes, completed in a remote corner of Italy in the identical year as Freemasonry's emergence into public recognition in England, constitutes not only a chronological precedent of striking precocity (Freemasonic sympathizers have heretofore been documented in Italy only from 1731), but also an artistic innovation without apparent parallel even to the present day.[3] The further consideration that this exceptional iconographic and artistic rarity was commissioned by a highly placed aristocratic member of the politically closed and ultraconservative Venetian Republic[4] affords the final anomaly that justifies at least a brief announcement of such a surprising—and puzzling—innovation, so close to the cultural origins of the European Enlightenment.

The fresco cycle at Piombino (with its accompanying stucco enframements) has had one significant previous publication, an eight-page article by Nicola Ivanoff in 1950; but—again curiously—in this scholarly elucidation by a master of iconographic subtlety, among the ten panels illustrated, one of the biblical subjects is incorrectly identified, and the single allegorical figure is not named at all.[5] Indeed, the fact that so accomplished a student as Ivanoff, in visiting the Piombino villa and publishing its frescoes, should identify them only as a biblical cycle with figural allegories testifies to the continuing efficacy of their patron's Hermetic camouflage. It also offers a procedural methodology for a fuller interpretation, by demonstrating some of the ways in which this pictorial series differs from more standard biblical cycles.

The stuccos and paintings at Piombino were ordered in June and December of 1716 by the Venetian nobleman Andrea Antonio Giuseppe Cornaro (1672–1742), who in January of 1717—a fortnight after his forty-fifth birthday, and just as the cycle was getting under way—was elected a Procurator of Saint Mark, the highest subsovereign office and honor in the Venetian state (pl. 2).[6] His family (founded in A.D. 800, from which it was destined to survive exactly a thousand years) had owned Piombino as their principal country seat since 1422, and indeed its ancient privileges had been specially renewed in an unusual judicial review when Andrea was a child of four.[7] His father, Girolamo III Cornaro (1632–90), and his mother, Cornelia Cornaro (ca. 1650–1715), had taken up residence at Piombino—the estate being entailed in primogeniture—in 1670, three years after their marriage, following the deaths of Girolamo's elder brothers in 1667 and 1669; their own first son had been born in this latter year, but he died in 1695 at twenty-six, leaving the patron Andrea, their second son, as prospective owner at the age of twenty-three.[8] "Prospective" only, since although his father, Girolamo, had died in 1690, a younger uncle, Ferigo Prospero Cornaro, technically inherited it through the primogeniture, and remained much involved with Piombino until his death in 1708; but also (and most particularly) because Andrea's mother Cornelia Cornaro continued as de facto occupant for a full quarter-century after her husband's death, until her own demise on 15 November 1715.[9] Even when Andrea finally took possession of the house, however, his ownership was not untroubled. Within a few feet of the eastern wing of the Palladian structure there stood until the Napoleonic period an earlier house at Piombino (another Cornaro palace, rebuilt in 1540 by Sanmicheli), unhappily inherited from some Cornaro female cousins in the 1630s by an antagonistic branch of the Emo family.[10] At the moment of Andrea Cornaro's commissions, that older house was presided over by the crotchety and contentious seventy-four-year-old Leonardo Emo, who obsessed by his schemes for a second-rate watermill, filed lawsuit after lawsuit to protest Andrea's irrigation of the garden, its new fishponds, and the park.[11] This shadow, which quite literally hung over the eastern half of the Palladian house, seems frankly acknowledged in its frescoes, and provides one of the clues to their interpretation.

Turning to the more immediate content of these mural decorations, I might note that Andrea Cornaro inherited at Piombino one of Palladio's most handsome houses, but one whose unusual size had forestalled any previous attempts to paint it. Its sole cinquecento decoration had been a pantheon of ancestor portraits in life-size sculptured figures installed in the six niches of Palladio's great hall.[12] Its four large suites of three rooms each, flanking the central halls on both upper and lower floors (and independent of the utilitarian wings) (fig. 1), had remained as great luminous whitewashed spaces with plain ceilings. For eight of these rooms, Andrea ordered in his contract a cycle of historiated fresco panels (the biblical scenes) in large rectangles to cover the walls, and (in rectangles and occasional ovals) the centers of their vaulted ceilings; together with a second group of chiaroscuro figures to be painted in fictive relief in overdoor and ceiling medallions. (The contract tells nothing else, beyond the fact that sketches of all the prescribed panels were to be prepared from Andrea Cornaro's specifications, before the frescoes were begun.) For the remaining four bedrooms and upstairs hall, Andrea contented himself with figurated overdoor medallions alone, thereby creating a cooler, more luminous, and less intensely active effect on these more restful walls. The pictorial campaign has usually been judged one of the most successful in the Veneto, and even, strangely enough, one of the most attractive among the works of Palladio. Many Palladian houses retain their original white walls, so that nothing unique was lost in painting Piombino's; while it is equally true that the concept of an overall interior decoration of these buildings was by no means unusual either, since Palladio himself had recommended and evidently supervised the ornamental plastering and painting of many of his country houses, notably the ones decorated by Giambattista Zelotti at Lonedo and Fanzolo, and by Paolo Veronese at Maser.[13] But those original schemes by artists contemporaneous with Palladio had become revered antiques before a fourth-generation descendant of his Cornaro patron decided to adopt this policy by embellishing the whole interior of that family's villa as well.

Although the high quality of the new decorations clearly attests to Andrea Cornaro's enlightened and discriminating taste, both he and posterity are fortunate that his mother's long life prevented him from commissioning the Piombino frescoes some decade or fifteen years earlier than he did.[14] The great revival of Venetian painting in the early eighteenth century, of which the Piombino frescoes constitute a significant example, had only barely been prefigured by 1704 with Sebastiano Ricci's celebrated paintings on the vault of San Marziale in Venice;[15] and the next ten years were crucial not only to his and others' development of that compellingly radiant new style, but especially for its diffusion to the younger masters who were to become its supreme practitioners. Among these, when Andrea Cornaro was ready to make his selection in 1716 (having perhaps already found that he could not afford—or could not interest—the likes of Ricci or Piazzetta, who, with their followers Amigoni, Pellegrini, and Pittoni, if not already abroad, had at least begun to command international prices), his quest for an inexpensive new artist in the most up-to-date style would essentially have left him a choice between youngsters such as Gregorio Lazzarini's pupil Giambattista Tiepolo (1696–1770), or Antonio Balestra's student Mattia Bortoloni (1696–1750), each of whom at that moment was approaching his twentieth birthday.[16] It may be

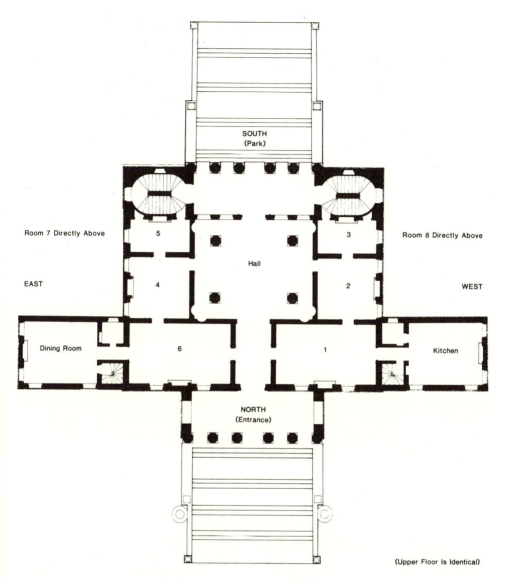

SOUTH
(Park)

Room 7 Directly Above

5

3

Room 8 Directly Above

Hall

EAST

4

2

WEST

Dining Room

6

1

Kitchen

NORTH
(Entrance)

(Upper Floor Is Identical)

FIGURE 1. VILLA CORNARO, PIOMBINO DESE (by Andrea Palladio, 1551–53): Common plan of both main floors, with *piano nobile* rooms numbered to coincide with Table of Locations of Frescoes in Appendix. *(Courtesy of author.)*

deceptively simple to assume that Andrea Cornaro's choice of the latter artist merely reflected the generally greater appeal of his master, Balestra, over Lazzarini. It is perhaps more indicative of Andrea's intimate understanding of the avant-garde to realize that Tiepolo was then (and for several years longer) painting in a rather darkly tenebrist style of heavy figural types mainly influenced by Piazzetta and Bencovich, while Bortoloni, even in his first works, was already confidently adopting the luminous pastel tonalities and the airy spatial amplitude of the new "light manner," which he was interpreting with figural, emotive, and compositional types derived from north Italian and northern European academic traditions, probably through models such as Maffei and Carpioni, and the fashionable Venetian-based French painter Louis Dorigny.[17]

It deserves to be emphasized that Andrea Cornaro's selection in 1716 of Mattia Bortoloni as his artist was, on several counts, a commendable choice. First, he could certainly not have found an economical and energetic young artist, willing to devote himself immediately to painting over a hundred large fresco panels in a rather remote country house for only four hundred ducats, who was any closer to the forefront of the revolutionary new Venetian style—and who, at that point, showed every promise of becoming recognized as one of its leaders. Second, these same considerations of stylistic precocity combine with the generally successful aspect of the finished ensemble to establish the Piombino cycle, executed in 1717, as one of the first extensive fresco demonstrations of the new style in the Veneto itself, deserving to be compared in character with Ricci's beautiful series of 1706–7 at the Palazzo Marucelli in Florence, and in quality ranking well above Celesti's work of 1705–7 at the Villa Rinaldi-Barbini (in Casella di Asolo in the Veneto), or even Pellegrini's in the Villa Alessandri at Mira, near Mestre (before 1708).[18] Third, it should be noted that Andrea Cornaro's personal discovery and initiating patronage of an untested apprentice is likely to have established a special relationship of dependence between executant and patron, which Andrea may have recognized as essential to insuring an absolute fidelity—such as an independent artist might well have resisted—to the iconographic program that he developed, as I shall show, with special care.

On 28 February 1716, then, barely three months after his mother's death had given him an assured mastery over their family's mainland palace, Andrea Cornaro signed a first contract with the Piombino stuccoist, Bortolo Cabianca, which functioned as a trial commission through the decoration of a small house that Andrea owned in the nearby university town of Padua.[19] Satisfied with the result, he signed a similar contract for the same experimental commission with the eventual painter of Piombino, on 30 April 1716.[20] Mattia Bortoloni at that point was only nineteen years old, and apparently had not yet had a real commission; Andrea Cornaro's knowledge of his extraordinary precocity may perhaps have derived from Bortoloni's family, for Mattia came from a village surrounded by extensive Cornaro estates in the southern Veneto (San Bellino in the Polesine), and a Cesare Bortoloni from nearby had borrowed 1,500 ducats from Andrea in 1714.[21] Andrea's preliminary commissions to decorate his house in Padua had involved contracting with Bortoloni "to fresco the ceiling of the upper hall, each of the framed compartments in the two rooms newly stuccoed, and all the friezes and overdoors in the four other rooms" adjoining. The contract specified unequivocally that "all . . . are to be done with diligence, a fine manner, and good taste; and, as regards both the subject paintings and the single figures, these are to be chosen by the Noble Messer Andrea"—by which it is very clear, even in this early demonstration cycle, that the patron was determined to maintain the closest possible supervision over the program. One is enabled shortly afterward to learn more about the details of this author-and-artist collaboration through the terms of the Piombino contract, which—Andrea evidently having been fully satisfied with the Paduan experiment—was drawn up in even more explicit terms, and signed by the painter (together with his surety Girolamo Mengozzi-Colonna) on 10 December 1716.[22] In its major provisions, Bortoloni agreed:

> First, that sketches shall be made for all the compartments, in the rooms [of the palace at Piombino] where it is intended to install paintings, with history subjects and single figures chosen by His Excellency.
> Second, one room shall be painted according to the sketches already made, and [then] inspected by His Excellency with all diligence and with close attention to judging [its] quality; and a continuation [of this system shall apply] in the other rooms.

Notwithstanding its significant place in the development of the light and graceful mode of the Venetian rococo, and its primacy in the oeuvre of its executing artist, the painted cycle at Piombino is far more important for its organization and its content than for its style. Of its two inventing personalities, Andrea Cornaro can lay claim to a substantially higher historical rank than Mattia Bortoloni—or rather in their remarkably significant and successful synthesis, Andrea's is always the controlling character. The first exceptional fact about the Piombino cycle, which sets it decisively apart from all its predecessors and contemporaries, is that among its more than one hundred separate fresco panels, not a single one is surrendered to those vapid cloudscapes of anonymous amorini which comprise such a consistent ingredient of late baroque decorative cycles in northern Italy. Instead every one of its hundred and four frames has a specific subject: forty-eight large narrative compositions represent biblical scenes (with forty from the Old Testament and eight from the New), while fifty-six smaller frescoes display emblematic or symbolic single figures, to which eight figural stuccos in the downstairs *camerini* and vestibule should be added.[23] Even more unusual, all hundred and twelve of these figural images are incorporated in a single iconographic sequence, whose component episodes are interrelated with the greatest care. The unifying thread is ostensibly provided by the large biblical subjects, which run in textual sequence from Genesis to Revelation. But an explicit commentary of considerable subtlety is provided as an expansion of their meaning, in the "hieroglyphic allegories alluding to the virtues shown in the narratives" (as one of Andrea's nephews accurately specified somewhat later, for an almost exactly derivative fresco cycle in the new family palace at Venice);[24] while yet another and more general level of meaning is to be discerned—now, alas, only fragmentarily—from the more esoteric connotations of the cycle as a whole. Andrea Cornaro's Piombino decorations thus display one immediate level of interest in the series of figural subjects, whose identifications are mostly straightforward enough to anyone who walks through the house with a Bible and a couple of emblem books. Beyond the experience of this first impression, however, a second and hidden order of meaning underlies all the images, and affords the crucial interpretative clue not only to their individual significance, but to their extremely unusual pattern of selection.

For the Piombino frescoes display a choice of subject matter that to the casual visitor, or even to the initially attentive student, seems exceedingly bizarre. Within a remote and tranquil country house—one of the most perfect paradigms of Renaissance calm, rationality, and ennobling spatial harmony—one discovers an interior bedizened with rococo fantasy by a biblical landscape of torment and testing (pls. 3, 6), of wilderness wandering and the plagues of Egypt (pl. 8), which contrasts in the sharpest possible way with Piombino's actual garden paradise outside. Even more disturbing are the figural allegories, especially upstairs, which oppose understandable emblems inspiring Christian Virtue (as in the large west bedroom) with a corresponding apartment disporting their reciprocal Vices, or flank them with a room nerve-rackingly presided over by the Fates, where Atropos perpetually reaches out to snip the thread of life. Rooms—which are concentrated on the east side of the house, and overlook the Emo palace next door—dedicated to Melancholy, Envy and Covetousness, or Idolatry, Miserliness, and Despair, provide the harrowing frame for a strangely limited series of New Testament images: Christ's four epiphanies (to the Shepherds, Magi, Doctors, and Gentiles); and in the corresponding western chamber, Holy Week without the Passion—which skips from the Last Supper to the Last Judgment, where the biblical cycle apocalyptically ends. Even among the much more extensive and regularly sequential Old Testament scenes downstairs, the omission of so many traditionally popular subjects for such strangely recondite ones is immediately apparent. From the narratives inspired by the earliest books alone are omitted such pictorially adaptable favorties as the stories of Melchizedek; of Leah and Rachel; the Joseph cycle, notwithstanding that Giuseppe was one of Andrea Cornaro's baptismal names; Jacob wrestling with the Angel; his ladder dream; the finding of Moses and the water from the rock, above all, through their obvious applicability to the water-rights imagery which—as in the figure of Drought in room 4—Andrea seems to have been developing against his Emo neighbors; the brazen serpent, Balaam's ass; and many more. The individual scenes and emblems that were selected can be studied in the illustrations, and through their complete listing in the Appendix; here, before investigating the nature of the Hermetic interests influencing the whole design, it may be well to demonstrate how intricately the Procurator Cornaro's concept operated, through the linked images in a single room.

The most appropriate demonstration group—both for posing fewest problems and for coming first—is provided by the long west room just inside the northern entrance door, to the right of the vestibule. One should pause to note that immediately upon entering this latter space the first two images that the visitor encounters, after having passed four thoroughly predictable stone figures of Jupiter and Hercules on the gateposts of the palace (pl. 1), and Zephyr and Flora on its north steps,[25] are sculptural as well, but of a substantially more esoteric import. Set in as overdoors amid the elaborate enframements modeled by Cabianca on twin portals opening left and right into the principal apartments, they are two beautiful stucco masks of a Satyr and a Sage, which may be taken to represent respectively Nature and Philosophy: the Satyr a reminder of the natural order, on the right, introduces the visitor into the west facade room where the pictorial sequence begins with man's natural state under the Fall; while the philosophic Sage, on the left, presides over the east facade room, the last and most diagnostic of the main floor series, with its frescoed triumph of Hermetic philosophy. Here at the very outset, then, one's first experience of the elaborate figural imagery at Piombino involves a conscious choice. As one may imagine its first visitors to have been guided by the patron himself, one may appropriately embark on a counterclockwise course by moving to the right;[26] and thus, by stepping under the satyric mask with its promise of hidden meanings, one enters the first episode of Andrea Cornaro's symbolic world in the story of Noah.

On the east or entrance wall of this long front room (pl. 3), Noah opens the whole cycle by reviewing the plans for the Ark, and he begins its construction. On the west wall opposite, he provisions and loads it. The largest wall panel, on the south side of the room opposite the windows, shows the godless abandoned to destruction as the Ark floats away—an example of the rather discouraging iconography of these radiant images. The large ceiling panel (pl. 4) presents the crucial episode of Noah's sacrifice to God at the moment of landing,[27] and this is reciprocated by God's promise of the binding character of their covenant in the rainbow, which is conceived as arching across the fireplace and windows between the two panels at the ends of the north wall. The one element of relief comes at the end, with Noah's uncovered drunkenness (the single scene that one might think appropriate to a relaxed country-house setting) being tucked anticlimactically into the southwest corner.

Set over the doors as personified emblems of the biblical narrative are four life-size figures symbolizing the forces one finds at work in the purgative drama of the Great Flood, painted within oval frames around which flutter pairs of stucco putti, who sustain looped and folded lengths of stucco draperies pulled back to reveal the allegorical figures. Beside the destruction of the godless appears Ripa's icon of the Wrath of God,[28] who brandishes his whip and shakes his thunderbolts in their direction; next (on the west) comes Retributive Justice, who stares with unnerving directness at the central furniture arrangement as if to threaten similar retribution for frivolities. These are further reproved by the inescapable figure of Divine Chastisement who stands over the fireplace as the centerpiece, both conceptually and physically, of the whole room (pl. 3). A large mirror is set in over the eighteenth-century mantel just beneath, and in contemplating Chastisement's raised whip it comes as something of a shock to find one's own reflected image superimposed on the panorama of drowning sinners opposite. This glimpse of their profound if belated penitence, however, leads through the interceding rainbow covenant to Peace, who crowns the entrance as one turns back to face the eastern door (pl. 3).

Above these preoccupying images is an especially subtle interplay of ceiling emblems (pl. 4). The point of commencement is symbolized by Sin (pls. 3, 4), representing man's state that provoked the Flood; there follow Affliction (his state within it) and Repentence—which is both the outcome of (here successive to) Affliction, and opposite of (here literally opposite to) Sin—and finally Courage or Strength,[29] which stands in exactly the same sequential and opposite relationship to Repentence and Affliction respectively, as well as forestalling Sin, so that the deadly dance does not encircle one's destiny yet again. The emblematic images mediate man's plight, too, as one reads them—more naturally—in verticals: Repentence softens the baleful stare of Retribution, divine Peace foretells the reward for forsaking Sin (pl. 3), and Strength stands as the ultimate proof against (or successful outcome of) Chastisement; only on the south, above the vast panorama of the damned, does Affliction still embody the inevitable punishments of the Wrath of God. Strangely enough it is exactly here, at the intersection of these three untempered tragedies, that Andrea Cornaro set a stucco cartouche bearing his own initials—the unique signature to the whole cycle—and thus sharply calls one back to a consideration of the specialized, personal meaning of this extraordinary iconography.

The curiousness of the patron's choices continues in the succeeding rooms, whose themes perhaps need only be summarized as extensions of the elaborate concetto elucidated in the first room. It is followed, in the western suite, with a square chamber (pls. 5, 6) and a smaller rectangular room (pl. 7) devoted to the stories of Abraham and Isaac, while the corresponding rooms across the sculpture hall, on the east side, depict Moses and the Israelites respectively in Egypt and on the Exodus (pl. 8). To this point the first five rooms represent a tight sequence from Genesis 6 to Exodus 32 (though with the unusual selections and notable omissions that I have already remarked), whereas the sixth installment of the biblical narrative, in the long east room to the left of the entrance door, jumps to David and Solomon (1 Kings, with 1 and 2 Chronicles), which makes of it a somewhat disconnected coda to the principal Old Testament imagery.

The vestibule entrance to this room is presided over by the piercing-eyed mask of the philosophic Sage, however, while Knowledge, Wisdom, and Truth beckon from the large allegorical medallions ahead and to the left and right as one enters (pl. 11); Virtue sits contemplatively enthroned between a victor's crown and a ducal cap at the focal point of the ceiling cove (pls. 9–11), as one raises one's eyes toward the delicate harmony of feathery white stucco rinceaux against a Wedgwood blue vault. So far, then, an unprecedented concentration of positive emblems serves principally to alert one to a major revelation; the fact that they promise Truth insures that one's scrutiny will be the more attentive. The investigation, proceeding upward (pl. 9), discovers a musical harmony[30] to augment the visual one. As King David sings and dances toward Jerusalem in the vanguard of a festival procession, there at the very center of the frescoed vault, riveting one's attention as the centerpiece of this first scene in the room's narrative decoration, appears the Ark of the Covenant—the holiest symbol of that same covenant of the rainbow secured by Noah's initial sacrifice long before, and painted at this precise spot on the twin ceiling of the inaugural room to the west.

This bracketing of the cycle with repetitive Arks is indicative enough, but the special character of the Piombino iconography is established explicitly in the two narrative scenes on the east wall (pl. 11), placed directly opposite the entrance door so as to catch the eye of every visitor immediately upon his coming into the room. They represent Solomon's principal artisan, Hiram of Tyre, crafting the altar for the Ark, and supervising the production of furnishings for the Temple; their excessively rare subjects do have scriptural precedents (the pertinent texts are 1 Kings 7:13–47, and 2 Chronicles 2:13–14, with 3:10 to 4:22), but they are so infrequently depicted as artistic images[31] as to imply immediately the promptings of a special interest. And their special meaning is not far to seek. Hiram of Tyre is the personality who stands at the heart of Freemasonry, as the supremely gifted master of the ancient world who was killed in a plot to gain the secrets of his genius—secrets which, in deference to this memory, are transmitted in occult or Hermetic form by the Craft itself. Here in these frescoes the rarely depicted antique artificer is shown literally surrounded by the cult symbols that remain familiar to Freemasons even today: the masonic aprons and trestle tables, angle irons and dividers, double-cube altars and seven-branched candelabra, ritual vessels and sacred images, all crafted by the legendary master whose mystery lies at the core of the ancient Craft.[32] After grasping his role as a key to the cycle in one's first view of this final and celebratory room, other images crowd around to confirm Andrea Cornaro's central iconography. The Ark itself, present explicitly or implicitly in almost every panel, is thus consistently paired off against the Noachite Ark in the parallel introductory room—a favorite theme of Freemasonry, which in fact acknowledges an important source of its modern ritual in the so-called Noachian Precepts.[33] The building of the Temple (indeed the wholly idiosyncratic concentration on architecture throughout all parts of the cycle) forms another justification for a lavish display of Masonic apparatus (pl. 12), culminating in the overtly symbolic depiction of the completed Temple (pl. 10), with its typically Masonic twin columns, its immense bronze purification vessel called the Molten Sea, and its detached altar approached by a sequence of three, five, and seven steps—an especially indicative detail, for which no scriptural source exists.[34]

Virtually every room in the Procurator Cornaro's intricately calculated scheme can be shown to display specific Masonic imagery. First, the broad divisions of the cycle, commencing with Noah and culminating with Hiram (as "masters of the Arks") is deeply significant. Within the story of Noah, so strange in itself for a retiring country house, an inordinate amount of attention is focused once more on building the Ark (pl. 3) and erecting the crucially symbolic masonry altar (pl. 4); and even the surrounding stuccos alternate the Masonic images of acacia and olive, palm branch and vase.[35] In the second room, the strangest (and largest) subject is explained by the old tradition, which saw the building of the Tower of Babel (pl. 5) as the true origin of the mason's craft, a tradition emphasized by the stonemasons' yard in the foreground of Bortoloni's fresco.[36] Covenants established on altars both rustic and Masonic occupy the adjacent north wall (pl. 6), while the Tower is warningly presided over by Prudence, one of the Freemasons' favorite Four Cardinal Virtues, which are painted in the ceiling medallions (pls. 5–6).[37] As one moves to the oppressions of the Israelites in Egypt (pl. 8), one finds further displays of Masonic construction, with trestle tables and dressed ashlar blocks as prominent as Aaron's symbolic rod or the newly sprouting dead tree, both components of Hermetic imagery.[38] In the wilderness the inscribed masonry altar and even the manna itself recall Masonic themes, while upstairs the Freemasons' special interest in the Three Theological Virtues accounts for their appearance twice, together with Hope, a third time, in association with the equally symptomatic images of Constancy and Eternity.[39]

The altogether astonishing thing about this esoteric cycle, which may seem from the foregoing description to be so consistent and complete, is that it constitutes by far the earliest large-scale cycle of Masonic visual imagery in any land. Indeed, it was painted in the very year—1717—to which modern Freemasonry traces its commencement, in the founding of the Grand Lodge at London. But early Freemasonic tendencies were both more various and more numerous than can be reconstructed from the official histories of its development after 1717. Specifically, it is established that closely related "Socratic Societies" organized by groups of "Pantheists" were to be found in Venice well before 1720;[40] but more up-to-date ideas of early northern European and especially English Freemasonry—which the Piombino cycle seems to reflect—could easily have reached Andrea Cornaro directly. His very close cousin Francesco Cornaro (who is documented during their youth to have spent several months visiting Andrea at Piombino in the 1690s) had been in London as Venetian ambassador to Queen Anne from 1705 to 1709.[41] On Francesco's journeys both to and from England he spent substantial time in Holland, where Masonic ideas were as widely discussed as in England, and perhaps were even affecting the graphic works of a refugee French printmaker, Bernard Picart.[42] Francesco Cornaro might possibly have brought back such prints to his cousin Andrea at Piombino (where he is reported to have visited on his way north),[43] but in any event their conversations about such developments, and possible perusal of clandestine manuscripts or even prints describing them, must have been intense. The useful fact that Francesco's father, Giovanni II Cornaro, then reigned as doge (1709–22) may have offered the presumed enthusiasts some degree of protection, but the 1720 commentator on "Socratic Societies" in places such as Venice enjoins that their pantheist members "shall not make . . . any, except the Brethren alone, or other ingenious, upright, and learned Men, Partakers of Esoterics."[44] This Hermeticism doubtless accounts for Andrea Cornaro's carefully veiled display of such new and unorthodox images, even at this distant country seat. His pictorial cycle gives the distinct impression that it could be quite satisfactorily read or explained on one level of meaning, as a biblical narrative and emblematic commentary, without raising any suspicions of irregularity; while for similar "Brethren, or other ingenious . . . and learned Men" who might be guided, for example, from the first room directly into the last, one look at its concentrated imagery should have been enough to establish the esoteric link with Andrea Cornaro's special interests—if indeed such a commonality existed in the visitor's experience—without risk of prior disclosure from either side.

The Piombino fresco cycle may thus have functioned, rather amazingly, as a silent diagnostic aid in identifying the free thinkers (of whom there were doubtless many more than the conservatives among his fellow Procurators would have liked to admit) among Andrea Cornaro's guests—as well, perhaps, as a setting for actual secret meetings of pantheistic or Masonic brethren, such as the author of the 1720 *Pantheisticon* goes on to describe after mentioning their earlier frequency in

Venice.[45] It must be cautioned that these proposals, advanced here as novelties to the literatures of both Italian fresco painting and the European Hermetic tradition, will have to be exhaustively tested by specialists in each of these fields against contemporary texts, both published and clandestine, and studiously compared with all comparable decorative cycles, before the present conclusions can be modified or confirmed. But for the moment, in the light of this analysis of its unifying inconography, the painted program at Piombino appears to be by far the earliest surviving document for an interest in Freemasonry in Italy. Indeed, its apparent uniqueness at this date as a private cycle of Hermetic iconography establishes a much broader stage for the intellectual and philosophic role of its patron, and places the neglected figure of Andrea Cornaro near the forefront of one aspect of the European Enlightenment.

PLATE 1. VILLA CORNARO, PIOMBINO DESE (by Andrea Palladio, 1551–53): North or Entrance Facade. On gate piers in foreground, Jupiter and Hercules (by an anonymous sculptor, probably ca. 1670s–80s). *(Photograph by Fototecnica, Vicenza.)*

PLATE 2. ANDREA ANTONIO GIUSEPPE CORNARO (1672–1742), Procuratore di San Marco de Supra (by
Antonio Luciani, 1716). *(Courtesy of Museo Civico Correr, Venice.)*

PLATE 3. WEST LONG ROOM, 1: East end with fresco panels (*left to right*) of Divine Chastisement, Noah reviewing the plans for the Ark, Sin (*ceiling medallion*), Peace (*overdoor*), Construction of the Ark, and The Ark escaping the destruction of the Flood (by Mattia Bortoloni, 1717). (*Photograph by Fototecnica, Vicenza.*)

PLATE 4. WEST LONG ROOM, 1: Ceiling with frescoes (*center*) of Noah's sacrifice after the Flood, and (*medallions, counterclockwise from left*) Sin, Affliction, Repentence, and Strength. (*Photograph by Fototecnica, Vicenza.*)

PLATE 5. WEST SQUARE ROOM, 2: East wall with frescoes *(left to right)* of Building of the Tower of Babel, Prudence *(ceiling medallion)*, and *(overdoor)* Female figure kneeling. *(Photograph by Fototecnica, Vicenza.)*

PLATE 6. WEST SQUARE ROOM, 2: North wall with frescoes *(left to right)* of Abraham reprieved from sacrificing Isaac, Justice *(ceiling medallion)*, Male (?) figure half-kneeling *(overdoor)*, and Parting of Abraham and Lot. *(Photograph by Fototecnica, Vicenza.)*

PLATE 7. West Small Room, 3: East end with frescoes *(left to right)* of Esau selling Jacob his birthright, Rebecca and Eliezer at the well, and *(ceiling)* Isaac hearing God's promise. *(Photograph by Fototecnica, Vicenza.)*

PLATE 8. EAST SQUARE ROOM, 4: Northwest corner with frescoes *(left to right)* of Equivocation? *(overdoor)*, Crossing of the Red Sea, the plagues of Egypt (death of the first-born), and *(overdoor)* Judgment?. *(Photograph by Fototecnica, Vicenza.)*

PLATE 9. EAST LONG ROOM, 6: Ceiling with frescoes (*center*) of David bringing the Ark into Jerusalem and (*medallions*), Allegorical figures of (*left and right*) Virtues and (*top and bottom*) Vices. (*Photograph by Fototecnica, Vicenza.*)

PLATE 10. EAST LONG ROOM, 6: North wall with frescoes (*left to right*) of the completed Temple, Solomon ordering the Temple constructed to the plan given him by David (*overmantel*), and Solomon dedicating the Temple. (*Photograph by Fototecnica, Vicenza.*)

PLATE 11. EAST LONG ROOM, 6: Southeast corner with frescoes (*left to right*) of Hiram of Tyre crafting the altar for the Ark, Virtue (*ceiling medallion*), Knowledge (*overdoor*), Hiram of Tyre crafting furnishings for the Temple, The Judgment of Solomon, Truth (*overdoor*) and Offerings before the Ark. (*Photograph by Fototecnica, Vicenza.*)

PLATE 11. EAST LONG ROOM, 6: Southeast corner with frescoes (*left to right*) of Hiram of Tyre crafting the altar for the Ark, Virtue (*ceiling medallion*), Knowledge (*overdoor*), Hiram of Tyre crafting furnishings for the Temple, The Judgment of Solomon, Truth (*overdoor*), and Offerings before the Ark. (*Photograph by Fototecnica, Vicenza.*)

Appendix

Table of Locations, Subjects, and Textual Sources of Frescoes and Figural Stuccos in the Villa Cornaro at Piombino, in the Veneto (executed 1716–1717)

VESTIBULE   North Entrance
Overdoors (stucco): above, urns garlanded with fruits and flowers
A.   Satyr mask   West overdoor
B.   Sage mask   East overdoor

1 WEST LONG ROOM   Large reception room/sitting room; north
                                             windows

Wall and ceiling panels: full color
1.   Noah reviewing the plans for the Ark   (Genesis 6:14–16, 22)   East wall, left
2.   Construction of the Ark   (Genesis 6:14–16, 22)   East wall, right
3.   Noah orders the provisioning of the   (Genesis 6:18, 21–22)   West wall, left
     Ark
4.   Embarkation of the birds and the   (Genesis 6:19–20,   West wall, right
     beasts   7:1–9)
5.   The Ark escaping the destruction of   (Genesis 7:10–12, 17–   South wall, left
     the Flood   18)
6.   Noah offers a sacrifice after the   (Genesis 8:18, 20)   Ceiling (reads
     Flood   facing south)
7,8. Noah and his sons witnessing the   (Genesis 9:12–17)   North wall, left
     convenant of the rainbow   and right
9.   The drunkenness of Noah   (Genesis 9:21–23)   South wall,
                                                                          right

Overdoors: rose and yellow on gold
A.   The Wrath of God   (Ripa)   South overdoor
B.   Retributive Justice   West overdoor
C.   Divine Chastisement   North
                                                                          overmantel
D.   Peace   East overdoor
Ceiling medallions: green and silver on gold
i.   Sin   East cove
ii. Affliction   South cove
iii. Repentance   West cove
iv. Strength   North cove
Ceiling stuccos: olive and laurel branches flanking cartouches and canopied urns; Andrea Cornaro's initials in a shield over panel 5.

2 WEST SQUARE ROOM   Reception room/sitting room; west windows
Wall and ceiling panels: full color
1.   The building of the Tower of Babel   (Genesis 11:2–4)   East wall
2.   God's Covenant with Abraham for   (Genesis [12:5–7 and]   South wall, left
     the Promised Land   17:1–21)
3.   The parting of Abram and Lot   (Genesis 13:2–11)   North wall,
                                                                          right
4.   King Abimelech of Gerar restoring   (Genesis 20:8, 14–15)   Ceiling (reads
     Sarah to Abraham   facing west)
5.   The Angel appearing to Hagar and   (Genesis 21:15–18)   South wall,
     Ishmael in the wilderness   right
6.   Abraham reprieved from sacrificing   (Genesis 22:9–12)   North wall, left
     Isaac
Overdoors: white and brown on gold (all except the overmantel much perished)

A.	[male (?) figure half-kneeling]	North overdoor
B.	[female figure kneeling]	East overdoor
C.	[female figure standing before a throne]	South overdoor
D.	[female figure seated against a tiered power] perhaps "The Glory of Princes"	(Ripa)	West overmantel

Ceiling medallions: blue and silver on white

i.	Fortitude	West cove
ii.	Justice	North cove
iii.	Prudence	East cove
iv.	Temperance	South cove

Ceiling stuccos: antique *imperator* busts with laurel crowns; rinceaux in lunettes

3 WEST SMALL ROOM   Writing room/west window

Wall and ceiling panels: full color

1.	Rebecca and Eliezer at the well	(Genesis 24:11–18)	East wall
2.	Esau selling Jacob his birthright for a mess of pottage	(Genesis 25:29–33)	North wall, right
3.	Isaac hearing God's promise on the site of the well of Sheba	(Genesis 26:23–33)	Ceiling (reads facing south)
4.	Rebecca and Jacob stealing from Isaac the blessing of Esau	(Genesis 27:15–29)	North wall, left

Overmanel panel formerly mirrored, now blank
Ceiling medallions (stucco): in the fields, masks, urns, and rinceaux

i.	Io recumbent, with Jupiter in a cloud (?)	East lunette
ii.	Venus (?) or a nymph beneath a tree	West lunette

GREAT HALL   Main reception room; south windows and door to park

Door surrounds (stucco): nonfigurated shell, frond, and flower motifs   East and west walls

4 EAST SQUARE ROOM   Reception room/sitting room; east windows

Wall and ceiling panels: full color

1.	Moses before the burning bush	(Exodus 3:1–6)	Ceiling (reads facing east)
2.	Oppressions of the Israelites in Egypt	(Exodus [1:11–14 and] 5:6–14)	South wall, left
3.	Moses and Aaron before Pharaoh and his sorcerers	(Exodus 7:10–12)	North wall, right
4.	The plagues of Egypt: the death of the first-born	(Exodus 12:29–30)	North wall, left
5.	Moses and Aaron leading the Israelites forth from Egypt	(Exodus 12:30–38)	South wall, left
6.	The crossing of the Red Sea	(Exodus 14:15–31)	West Wall

Overdoors: white and cream on violet gray

A.	Release? [striding female figure with flying drapery, pointing forward]	South overdoor
B.	Equivocation? [draped female figure seated, pointing to left and to right]	West overdoor
C.	Judgment? [draped female figure kneeling, pointing down]	North overdoor
D.	Drought: the privations of the Israelites in the wilderness of Shur	(Exodus 15:22)	East overmantel

Ceiling medallions: white and cream on gray

i.	Ingenuity or Genius (?)	(Ripa: *Ingegno?*)	East cove
ii.	(?) [draped female figure standing with open-handed gesture]	South cove

iii.   (?) [draped female figure seated, seen from back, holding wreath]   West cove
iv.   Fortitude [draped and hooded female figure standing with shield]   North cove
Ceiling stuccos: antique philosopher busts; rinceaux in lunettes

5 EAST SMALL ROOM   Sitting room/retiring room; east window
Wall and ceiling panels: full color
1.   Israelites collecting manna in the   (Exodus 16:1–35)   North wall,
       wilderness   right
2.   Joshua's battle with the Amalekites   (Exodus 17:8–13)   West wall
       at Rephidim, in the presence of
       Moses, Aaron, and Hur
3.   Sacrifice of Moses and the Israelites   (Exodus 24:4–6)   Ceiling (reads
       at Sinai   facing south)
4.   Worship of the golden calf, and   (Exodus 32:5–19)   North wall, left
       Moses breaking the tablets
Overdoors (amateur stuccos and monochrome painting)
A.   Fortitude [nude aged male figure reclining between a tree and a square   South
       tower]   overdoor, left
B.   Chastity [nude female figure crouching against a tree, pointing to a   South
       round tower]   overdoor,
                                                                            right
C.   Venus (?) seated on ground, being shot by Cupid (modern painting;   South
       formerly mirrored)   overmantel
Ceiling medallions (stucco): with masks, urns, and rinceaux in the fields
i.   Strife [flying putto with bow and arrow, and quiver on ground; leaf-   East lunette
       crowned and smiling masks]
ii.   Victory [flying putto with trumpet and banner; helmeted and   West lunette
       grimacing masks]

6 EAST LONG ROOM   Large reception room/sitting room; north
                                                  windows

Wall and ceiling panels: full color
1.   David bringing the Ark into   (1 Chronicles 15:1–28)   Ceiling (reads
       Jerusalem   facing south)
2.   David making offerings before the   (1 Chronicles 16:1–2)   South wall,
       Ark, and blessing the multitude   right
3.   The judgment of Solomon   (1 Kings 3:16–28)   South wall, left
4.   The building of the Temple   (2 Chronicles 2:1–3:2)   West wall, right
5.   Hiram (Huramabi) of Tyre crafting   (2 Chronicles 2:13–15;   East wall, left
       the altar for the Ark   3:10–4:22)
6.   Hiram of Tyre crafting furnishings   (2 Chronicles 2:13–15;   East wall, right
       for the Temple   3:10–4:22)
7.   The completed Temple   (2 Chronicles 3:1–5:1)   North wall, left
8.   Solomon dedicates the Temple   (2 Chronicles 5:11–   North wall,
                                                  7:2)   right
9.   The Israelites' festival of the   (2 Chronicles 8:12–13)   West wall, left
       Tabernacles
Overdoors: violet, lavender, and yellow on gold
A.   Solomon ordering the Temple   (1 Chronicles 28:11–   North
       constructed to the plan given him   12)   overmantel
       by David
B.   Knowledge (Scientia)   (Ripa)   East overdoor
C.   Truth [nude female figure seated, pointing to branch of laurel]   South overdoor
D.   Eternity? (or Providence?) [draped female figure with two orbs, one   West overdoor
       flaming]

Ceiling medallions: gold on plum and cerise

i.	(?) [heavily draped male figure pointing forward and up]	West cove
ii.	Lust (?) [aged male nude reclining, holding pitchfork]	North cove
iii.	Virtue [draped male figure seated, holding palm frond or branch]	East cove
iv.	Adultery [debauched male nude seated, with satyric smile, raising cup]	South cove

Ceiling stuccos: rinceaux flanking masked cartouches containing two doge's caps, one victor's wreath, and one eastern crown; Cornaro family arms in shield over panel 2.

7 EAST SMALL BEDROOM   Private bedroom/dressing room/retiring room; east window

Wall and ceiling panels: full color

1.	Adoration of the Shepherds	(Luke 2:7–16)	North wall, left
2.	Adoration of the Magi	(Matthew 2:9–11)	West wall
3.	Christ among the Doctors	(Luke 2:46–47)	North wall, right
4.	Christ and the woman of Samaria	(John 4:5–26)	Ceiling (reads facing south)

Overdoors: cerise and lavender on blue-gray

A.	Faith [draped female figure seen from behind, standing and holding Cross]	South overdoor, left
B.	Charity? [draped female figure kneeling and gesturing]	South overdoor, right
C.	Hope? [draped male figure seen from behind, seated and beckoning]	North overdoor

Ceiling medallions: pink and silver on blue-gray

i.	The Old Law? [draped aged male figure kneeling with gesture of disputation]	West lunette
ii.	The New Grace? [draped female figure semi-reclining and gesturing to right]	East lunette

8 WEST SMALL BEDROOM   Private bedroom/dressing room/retiring room; west window

Wall and ceiling panels: full color

1.	Christ entering Jerusalem on Palm Sunday	(Mark 11:1–10; Matthew 21:1–9)	East wall
2.	Christ cleansing the Temple	(Mark 11:15–17; Matthew 21:12–13; Luke 19:45–46)	North wall, right
3.	The Last Supper	(Mark 14:12–25; Matthew 26:17–29; Luke 22:7–38; John 13:12–35)	North wall, left
4.	The Last Judgment	(Revelation 4:2–5)	Ceiling (reads facing south)

Overdoors: pink and silver on gold

A.	Eternity [draped female figure semi-reclining and holding hoop]	South overdoor, left
B.	Constancy [draped and capped female figure holding shield on pedestal]	South overdoor, right
C.	Hope? [draped female figure semi-reclining and beckoning]	North overdoor

Ceiling medallions: cerise and silver on ocher

i.	(?) [draped female figure seen from behind, seated and pointing to right]	East lunette
ii.	(?) [draped female figure standing and pointing to right]	West lunette

GRAND SALONE   Main upper reception room; south windows and
                                    loggia; vestibule has north door and loggia
Overdoors: gold and cream on yellow-brown; THE SEASONS(?)

A. Spring(?) [draped female figure seated holding leafy wreath]   Vestibule, west
                                                                          overdoor
B. Summer   Salone, west
                                                                          overdoor
C. Autumn(?) [draped and swathed female figure seated holding leafy fruit]   Vestibule, east
                                                                          overdoor
D. Winter   Salone, east
                                                                          overdoor

WEST SQUARE BEDROOM   Bedroom/sitting room; west windows
Overdoors: white and cream on lime green; THE THREE FATES
A. Clotho (cartouche has stucco crown)   South overdoor
B. Lachesis   East overdoor

C. Atropos (cartouche has stucco   North overdoor
        crown)
D. Stuccos: two medallions amid rococo strapwork: running putto with   West
        raised arms, and oval mirror surmounted by plumes   overmantel

WEST LONG BEDROOM   Principal bedroom; north windows
Overdoors: white and cream on violet; THE THREE THEOLOGICAL VIRTUES
A. Faith   East overdoor
B. Charity   South overdoor
C. Hope   West overdoor

D. Stuccos: three medallions amid rococo strapwork: male portrait   North
        medal, running putto with raised arms, and oval mirror surmounted overmantel
        by flowers

EAST LONG BEDROOM   Second major bedroom; north windows
Overdoors: gold and yellow on brown ocher; THREE ANTI-THEOLOGICAL VICES
A. Idolatry [draped and turbaned male figure standing with gesture of   East overdoor
        disdain]
B. Avarice or Anger [draped male figure seen from back, standing with   South overdoor
        arms folded]
C. Despair [draped male figure seen from back, seated with arm raised   West overdoor
        fearfully]
D. Stuccos: three medallions amid rococo strapwork: female portrait   North
        medal, draped and helmeted(?) standing female figure, and oval   overmantel
        mirror surmounted by flowers

EAST SQUARE BEDROOM   Bedroom/sitting room; east windows

Overdoors: yellow and white on gold: A VICE AND TWO CARDINAL SINS
A. Melancholy [draped female figure leaning on masonry pier and   South overdoor
        holding globe; implements at feet]
B. Envy [draped female figure seated, bending and pointing forward]   West overdoor
C. Covetousness? [draped female figure seen from behind, standing and   North overdoor
        pointing forward]
D. Stuccos: two medallions amid rococo strapwork: running putto with   East
        raised arms, and oval mirror surmounted by plumes   overmantel

Notes

1. The village acquired a surname with the unification of Italy and has since been known as Piombino Dese; in the mid-nineteenth century (on 1 July 1853), it was transferred to the province of Padua from its former millennial association with Treviso.

For the Palladian palace itself, I have written a monograph that was commissioned in 1971 for the *Corpus Palladianum*, and was submitted to the Centro Palladiano in Vicenza in 1976, but has remained unpublished for lack of funds. In the meantime, the basic works are Giangiorgio Zorzi, *Le ville e i teatri di Andrea Palladio* (Venice, 1969), pp. 192–98; Douglas Lewis, "La datazione della villa Corner a Piombino Dese," in *Bollettino del Centro Internazionale di Studi di Architettura* (henceforth *Bollettino del CISA*), 14 (1972): 381–93; Lionello Puppi, *Andrea Palladio* (Milan, 1973), pp. 292–95; Douglas Lewis, *The Drawings of Andrea Palladio* (Washington, D.C., 1981), pp. 164–65; idem, "Andrea Palladio," in *Macmillan Encyclopedia of Architects* (New York, 1982) 3:345–62, esp. 357.

The thesis of this present essay was first announced in shorter form in a paper circulated on 31 March 1975 to the members of the Washington Renaissance Colloquium, and discussed before that group (through sponsorship by the Folger Institute of Renaissance and Eighteenth-Century Studies) on 16 April 1975. I am grateful for the opportunity to publish material from that earlier study in the Appendix here.

2. Four small Lodges in the City of London amalgamated on 24 June 1717 and began keeping public records. Many Masonic historians maintain the significance of the event to have been vastly overrated, but most acknowledge the utility of a watershed date between the inchoate decades of very sporadic archival materials, in the later seventeenth century, and the publicly acknowledged burgeoning of Freemasonry as an international movement in the 1720s and 1730s. See Douglas Knoop, G. P. Jones, and Douglas Hamer, *A Short History of Freemasonry to 1730* (Manchester, 1940); idem, *The Two Earliest Masonic Manuscripts* (Manchester, 1938); idem, *The Early Masonic Catechisms*, (Manchester, 1943); idem, *Early Masonic Pamphlets* (Manchester, 1945); and Knoop and Jones, *The Genesis of Freemasonry: An Account of the Rise and Development of Freemasonry in Its Operative, Accepted, and Early Speculative Phases* (Manchester, 1947). See also Harry Carr, "Freemasonry before Grand Lodge," chap. 1 in *Grand Lodge, 1717–1967* (Oxford, 1967), pp. 1–46; and Francis P. Castells, *English Freemasonry in Its Period of Transition, A.D. 1600–1700* (London, 1931).

3. For the earliest evidences published to date of Freemasonry in Italy: Carlo Francovich, *Storia della Massoneria in Italia dalle origini alla rivoluzione francese* (Florence, 1974), esp. pp. 41, 49, for a Lodge dating from 1731 in Florence (pp. 133–47 deal with Venice); Ernesto Baldi, *L'Alba: La prima Loggia massonica a Firenze* (Florence, 1959), esp. pp. 7–28; and Alberto Cesare Ambesi, *Storia della Massoneria* (Milan, 1971), with reference on p. 196 to a recently discovered ivory seal inscribed with Masonic emblems and dated "Naples, 1728"; further, on this one isolated testimony of Masonic interest in Italy (perhaps introduced into that port from England), between the date of the Piombino frescoes (1716–17) and that of the documented Lodge in Florence (1731–32), see Fulvio Bramato, *Napoli massonica nel settecento: Dalle origini al 1789* (Ravenna, 1980), p. 17 n.1.

For the rarity and generally low quality of Masonic iconography in the visual arts, see Erich J. Lindner, *Die Königliche Kunst im Bild: Beiträge zur Ikonographie der Freimaurerei* (The royal art illustrated: Contributions to the iconography of Freemasonry), transl. by Arthur Lindsay (Graz. 1976). passim, but esp. pp. 265–67, a useful bibliography on Masonic images in art. The one painting with a Masonic theme that I have found to approach the level of quality of the Piombino frescoes is an anonymous picture of ca. 1760 in the Deutsches Freimaurermuseum, Beyreuth, of "Solomon Showing the Queen of Sheba the Plan of the Temple Being Presented to Him by Hiram," in Peter Francis Lobkowicz, *Die Legende der Freimaurer* (Hamburg, 1971), frontispiece. The single intriguing title in recent periodical literature, "Masonic Wall Paintings," is a two-paragraph announcement of a provincial cycle of four panels painted in ca. 1864 by John J. Glendenning in Central City, Colorado; see Marian Talmadge and Iris Gilmore, *Antiques* 62, no. 5 (November 1952): 406–7.

4. On the conservatism of the Venetian Republic, in general and politically, see John Julius Norwich, *A History of Venice* (New York, 1982); and Frederic C. Lane, *Venice: A Maritime Republic* (Baltimore, 1973); and, with specific reference to the manifestation of this phenomenon in the fine arts, Francis Haskell, *Patrons and Painters* (London, 1963), pt. 3, Venice, pp. 243–383.

5. "Mattia Bortoloni e gli affreschi ignoti della villa Cornaro a Piombino Dese," *Arte Veneta* 4 (1950): 123–30; in Ivanoff's fig. 142, p. 129, the ceiling fresco in room 3 (here Appendix item 3.3, "Isaac Hearing God's Promise on the Site of the Well of Sheba," Genesis 26:23–33) is identified, in my view incorrectly, as "Il sogno di Giacobbe," Genesis 28:11–15; while my "Affliction" (room 1.2, identified in Edward A. Maser, ed., *The 1758–60 Hertel Edition of Ripa's "Iconologia,"* (New York, 1971), no. 58 is called by Ivanoff simply a "Chiaroscuro" (fig. 145, p. 130).

6. Born 1 January 1672 (1671 in the *more veneto* of the Republican calendar, hereafter rendered in

the form 1671/72 for the two ambiguous months of January and February), baptised 5 January, died 9 December 1742; elected Procuratore di San Marco de Supra, 20 January 1716/17 (for the latter date, see Museo Civico Correr, Venice—hereafter Museo Correr—MS P.D. B525, Cons. XI.E.6). For this and all following biographical data on the Cornaro family, my sources have been a careful comparison of the standard MS genealogies derived from Marco Barbaro, in the two redactions at the Museo Correr (Cod. Cicogna 510) and the Archivio di Stato di Venezia (Misc. Cod. 898), against an unusually full and accurate *Libro d'Oro* of two large MS volumes in a private collection in Venice, and checked wherever possible against original documents in the Cornaro family archive (preserved in many hundreds of *buste* in the Museo Correr).

 7. On 10 July 1676 (Museo Correr, MS P.D. c.2510/VI [25, 66]).

 8. Girolamo III Cornaro (25 June 1632–4 October 1690) and Cornelia Cornaro (ca. 1650–15 November 1715) married on 19 October 1667, following the death of Girolamo's brother Zorzi Carlo (b. 20 November 1623, d. shortly after 12 March 1667); Girolamo inherited the primogeniture at Piombino as a result of the death of his second brother, Cattarin Domenico Cornaro (27 October 1624–13 May 1669) in the heroic final defense of Candia. Their son, Cattarin Andrea, was born 29 August 1669 and died during September 1695; our protagonist Andrea Cornaro, who thus inherited Piombino, was the first in his immediate family to be born there, in January of 1672.

 9. Ferigo Prospero Cornaro (15 April 1638–24 August 1708); Cornelia Cornaro, daughter of Cav. Proc. Nicolò Cornaro, was born ca. 1650, dictated her last will on 14 November 1715 at her villa in Fiesso, and apparently died the following day (Museo Correr, MS P.D. c.2537/5,7).

 10. Douglas Lewis, "The Rediscovery of Sanmicheli's Palace for Girolamo [I] Cornaro at Piombino," *Architectura* 1 (1976): 29–35.

 11. Leonardo Emo (1642–1721) and his late brother Zorzi Emo (1644–1704) had jointly inherited the Sanmicheli palace at Piombino on 14 November 1684, as heirs of their mother Chiaro Emo and their aunt Marietta Cornaro Michiel (Private Archive, MS Index: *busta* 158, *mazzo* 112, *processo* 283; and *mazzo* 56, *processo* 30, p. 24). For Leonardo's lawsuits of 1715–21 against Andrea Corraro, see Museo Correr, MSS P.D. c.2738/6; c.2736/4 (41, 57, 61–62, 65); c.2736/6; and c.2242.

 12. Giuseppe Fiocco, "Camillo Mariani," in *Le Arti*, 3, no. 2 (December 1940): 74–86; Rodger Burns, *Camillo Mariani: Catalyst of the Sculpture of the Roman Baroque*, Ph.D. diss., Johns Hopkins University, 1979.

 13. Douglas Lewis, "Palladio's Painted Architecture," in *Vierhundert Jahre Andrea Palladio (1580–1980) Colloquium*, (Heidelberg, 1982), pp. 59–74; Giampaolo Bordigno Favero, *The Villa Emo at Fanzolo*, trans. D. Lewis, *Corpus Palladianum* 5 (University Park, 1972); Rodolfo Pallucchini, "Gli affreschi di Paolo Veronese," in *Palladio, Veronese e Vittoria a Maser* (Milan, 1960), pp. 69–83.

 14. Andrea Cornaro and his brother, Ferigo Antonio Alberto (6 June 1676–May 1743), were the youthful beneficiaries of a full partitioning of their late father's estate, in a series of divisions culminating in the spring of 1699 (Museo Correr, MSS. P.D. c.2204/III, IV; c.2430/3; c.2496/IV; c.2213/III; c.2216/II); their bachelor uncle, Federico Prospero, still technically held the primogeniture at Piombino until his death in 1708, but even before that date (and increasingly after it, though his mother remained in residence and de facto possession until her death in 1715), Andrea was the patron who made the most important decisions about the Piombino estate.

 15. Michael Levey, *Painting in Eighteenth-Century Venice* (London, 1959), esp. pp. 19–20; Rodolfo Pallucchini, *La pittura veneziana del settecento* (Venice, 1960).

 16. For the more fashionable history painters, see Pallucchini, *Pittura*, and Levey, *Painting*, pp. 13–52; for Tiepolo, a standard work is Antonio Morassi, *Complete Catalogue of the Paintings of G.B. Tiepolo* (London, 1962); for Bortoloni see notice by M. A. Novelli in *Dizionario Biografico degli Italiani* (Rome, 1974), 13 : 146–48; Ivanoff, "Bortoloni," passim; Pallucchini, *Pittura*, pp. 55–56; E. Martini, *La pittura veneziana del Settecento* (Venice, 1964), pp. 18–21; and the following note.

 17. For Maffei, see Levey, *Painting*, p. 138; and Haskell, *Patrons*, p. 248; on Dorigny, ibid., pp. 250–51, 268 (and for Carpioni, p. 393); for the relevance of all three to this context, see Ivanoff, "Bortoloni," pp. 124–25. Piazzetta and Bencovich are usefully compared (in relation to a painting by the latter of ca. 1710, whose principal figure of Saint Andrew was directly borrowed by Bortoloni for the Piombino Isaac ceiling—see note 5 above) in *Giambattista Piazzetta: Il suo tempo, la sua scuola*, exhibition catalog; (Venice, 1983), pp. 62–63, no. 6. Such a palpable influence from Bencovich's early Venetian phase on the very young Bortoloni has not, I think, previously been noticed.

 18. For all these Venetan cycles, see Mercedes Precerutti Garberi, *Affreschi settecenteschi delle ville venete* (Milan, 1968), pp. 67–68, figs. 57–61 (Piombino); and Rodolfo Pallucchini et al., *Gli affreschi nelle ville venete dal seicento all'ottocento*, 2 vols. (Venice, 1978), 1 : 218, and vol. 2, figs. 352–58 (Piombino, by Caterina Furlan).

 19. An architect's pair of fine measured drawings for the plans of both floors of Andrea's house at San Massimo in Padua survive in Museo Correr, MS P.D. c.857/16. For Cabianca's contract there of 28

February 1715/16, see ibid., c.2378/XXXVIII (though the document has apparently been lost since 1950); for his subsequent contract of 26 June 1716 at Piombino, see ibid., *pezzo* XXXVII (also lost, but transcribed in Ivanoff, "Bortoloni," pp. 129–30, item 2).

20. For the Paduan frescoes contract of 30 April 1716, see Museo Correr, MS P.D. c.2378/XXXVI (lost since 1950, but transcribed in Ivanoff, "Bortoloni," p. 129, item 1).

21. Bortoloni's birth date comes from P. Zani, *Enciclopedia metodologia* (Parma, 1822); cited by Ivanoff, "Bortoloni," p. 123, n. 1). As E. Riccomini has pointed out ("Un modelletto inedito," in *Arte Veneta* 22 [1968]: 200), there is no reason to doubt it. For Cesare "Bertoloni" or Bortoloni and his debt to Andrea Cornaro, see Museo Correr, MS P.D. c.2230/2, of 23 June 1714.

22. For the Piombino frescoes contract of 10 December 1716, see ibid., c.2378/41 (lost since 1950, but transcribed in Ivanoff, "Bortoloni," p. 130, item 3).

23. There are actually only thirty-eight Old Testament *narrative* scences, but two of the fifty-eight large single figure panels also represent biblical subjects: my Appendix numbers 4.D ("Drought," based on Exodus 15:22) and 5.A ("King Solomon with the Plan of the Temple," from 2 Chronicles 28:11–12). Thus these enumerations can be adjusted to forty and fifty-six respectively. Complete lists of all the frescoed and stuccoed images at Piombino can be found in the Appendix to this article, where the sequence of their generating biblical texts is given as well.

24. Contract between Cattarin Cornaro, the last of the family (23 May 1732–7 November 1802), and the painter Costantin Cedini, of 6 February 1782/3: "le sopraporte con puttini, e geroglifici allusivi alle virtù del sudetto" (i.e., the narrative cycle); Museo Correr, MS P.D. c.2523/II.

25. Jupiter and Hercules, appropriately for their high and commanding positions on the gateposts, would have symbolized Majesty and Strength; Zephyr and Flora, marking the transition from garden to palace on the long podia of the access stair, Fructification and Blossoming. The latter two sculptures may possibly be coeval with the stair ramps (probably of the 1670s or 1680s); the gatepost figures may have been contemporaneous and reused, or coeval with the walls, posts, and gates, evidently installed by Andrea Cornaro after 1715.

26. In an extremely helpful conversation of 1974 with Mr. Roy A. Wells, Editor and Master of the Quatuor Coronati Lodge, 27 Great Queen Street, Kingsway, London (for which I am especially grateful), I thought I had understood that a particular Masonic significance might attach to this *counterclockwise* arrangement of the room sequence at Piombino; but an official publication by the Masonic History Company—Albert Gallatin Mackey, *Symbolism of Freemasonry*, rev. Robert Ingham Clegg (Chicago, 1945), pp. 141–45, s.v. "Ritual Symbolism: circumambulation"—maintains that such symbolic movement should properly be performed *clockwise*, that is, with the participant's right side always turned toward an altar at the center. On such ambiguous points of interpretation the non-Masonic commentator (as I am unlucky enough to be) must simply register the dichotomy and hope for future elucidation.

27. A beautiful drawing for the left-hand seated woman in this fresco is preserved in California, and was brilliantly recognized as Bortoloni's by Alfred Moir, ed. *European Drawings in the Collection of the Santa Barbara Museum of Art* (Santa Barbara, 1976), pp. 188–89, where a useful résumé of other Bortoloni drawings is included.

28. Cesare Ripa, *Iconologia*, rev. G. Zaratino Castellini Romano (Venice, 1669), p. 224, "Flagella di Dio"; Maser, *Hertel Edition of Ripa*, no. 71, "Flagellum Dei" (The scourge of God).

29. Sin: Ripa, *Iconologia*, p. 477, and Maser, *Hertel Edition of Ripa*, no. 164; Affliction: see note 5 above; Repentance: I identify by gesture (clasped hands, upraised eyes) and context; Courage or Strength: has that figure's standard Lion (Maser, *Hertel Edition of Ripa*, nos 66 and 167), whose paw also has a ritual or symbolic character in Freemasonry.

30. Many commentators have emphasized the intimacy and excellence of this celebrated relationship between Masonry and music; the literature on this aspect of Mozart's *Magic Flute* alone is copious. Jacob Ernst, *Illustrations of the Symbols of Masonry* (Cincinnati, 1868), p. 291 (together with many subsequent writers), cites music's place among the Seven Liberal Arts and Sciences, which have long been crucial to Masonic ritual (see note 34 below). Charles Clyde Hunt, *Masonic Symbolism* (Cedar Rapids, 1939), has a chapter (48) on "Masonry and Music" (pp. 431–37). Knoop, Jones and Hamer's magisterial *Early Masonic Pamphlets*, pp. 12–17, has a much more valuable section on the earliest preserved Masonic songs.

31. Andor Pigler, *Barockthemen*, 2 vols. (Budapest, 1956), 1:164; Lindner, *Royal Art*, passim.

32. "The life and death of Hiram Abif [Hiram the Builder] could be said to constitute the cornerstone of Masonry" (John H. Van Gorden, *Biblical Characters in Freemasonry* [Lexington, Mass., 1980], p. 77); for this translation of the name, and one of the best analyses (among dozens) of Hiram's Dionysiac, redemptive character, see Mackey, *Symbolism*, pp. 17–19, 51–57, 230–47. For the ritual symbolism of the Masons' tools and equipment as shown in these frescoes, see ibid., pp. 89–98. The most important of these famous images in modern Masonry (in addition to the initiate's apron) are the

trestle board, the rough ashlar, and the perfect ashlar ("the three jewels"); the rule and the mallet (tools of the "first degree"); the square, level, and plumb (tools of the "second degree"); and the trowel (symbol of the "third degree). See also Colin F. W. Dyer, *Symbolism in Craft Freemasonry* (Shepperton, Middlesex, 1976), pp. 149–78, "The Working Tools"; and most specifically, Robert Ambelain, *Scala philosophorum; ou, La symbolique maçonnique des outils,* 3 ed. (Paris, 1982), esp. table, p. 190.

33. Most clearly summarized in Mackey, *Symbolism,* pp. 14–17, 20–25, and 354, quoting James Anderson's seminal *Constitutions of the Freemasons,* 2d ed (London 1738), p. 143, in turn quoting the so-called MS Old Charges, in which it was enjoined that Masons should "observe the moral law as true Noachidae." See especially Douglas Knoop and G. P. Jones, *Freemasonry and the Idea of Natural Religion* (Frome, 1942), pp. 9–10, "The Noachian Precepts"; for this crucial reference (see, e.g., notes 40, 44 and 45 below) I am greatly indebted to the kindness of my Folger Institute colleague Florence Sandler.

34. Alexander Horne, *King Solomon's Temple in the Masonic Tradition* (London, 1972), esp. p. 97; Mackey, *Symbolism,* pp. 20, 99–103; Dyer, *Symbolism,* pp. 72–82; Ernst, *Illustrations,* pp. 243, 285, 291, 309, 317, 337–38.

35. Salvatore Farina, *Gli emblemi araldici della Libera Muratoria* (Rome, 1973), p. 37, prescribes laurel on the right and olive on the left, as shown in the ceiling of Room 1 at Piombino; most other authors (e.g., Allen E. Roberts, *The Craft and Its Symbols* [Richmond, 1974], pp. 54–55) connect the olive's oil with the grape's wine and the wheat's grain, as the three elements with which a Masonic altar is properly consecrated. Acacia is the crucial resurrection symbol of Master Hiram (Mackey, *Symbolism,* pp. 200–265) and may very well be the plant actually shown in the sometimes unclear low relief stuccoes of the Piombino celings.

36. One of the precepts inherited from the Old Charges (see note 33 above) was that "at the making of the Tower Babilon there was the Craft of Masonry then first found." But Mackey (*Symbolism,* p. 14) maintains that Babel represented a secession from the basic truths of the Noachites, and cites an early ritual mentioning "the lofty tower of Babel, where language was confounded and Masonry lost" (p. 28). See my caveat to note 26 above. Lindner (*Royal Art,* p. 212, pl. 109), at any rate, notes usefully, though inaccurately—considering Piombino's date twenty-eight years earlier—that "the theme of the Tower of Babel probably appeared for the first time in *La Franç-Maconne,* 1744 . . . [but] the Tower soon disappeared from use as a symbol."

37. Dyer, *Symbolism,* p. 82, reports that in an eighteenth-century Masonic lecture from Lancashire, Justice is recommended to occupy an eastern position, Prudence western, Temperance southern, and Fortitude northern. In Room 2 at Piombino only Temperance complies with this advice, and the relationship of the Virtues to the lower narratives seems calculated to be more locally appropriate.

38. On Aaron's rod, see William Adrian Brown, *Facts, Fables and Fantasies of Freemasonry* (New York, 1968), pp. 50–52; Van Gorden, *Biblical Characters,* pp. 17–19; Lindner, *Royal Art,* p. 148, pl. 80; and most interestingly, Arthur Edward Waite, *Emblematic Freemasonry and the Evolution of Its Deeper Issues* (London, 1925), pp. 129–30. The new branch on the old stock refers Hermetically to Isaiah's prophecies, as I was reminded by Professor Jan van Norsten of the University of Leiden, in a conversation on 14 May 1975.

39. The Tetragrammaton is fully discussed in its Masonic context by Mackey, *Symbolism,* pp. 176–98. It is combined with the manna (as at Piombino) by Waite, *Emblematic Freemasonry,* pp. 129–30, and on an early-nineteenth-century print in Lindner, *Royal Art,* p. 148, pl. 80, where the Three Theological Virtues are also incorporated; Lindner, p. 94, pl. 43, shows Piombino's same Eternity image of a circling snake biting its tail, as a symbol in 1804 of the Mother Lodge Royal York of Friendship.

40. Knoop and Jones, *Freemasonry and the Idea of Natural Religion,* pp. 8–9, quote from the *Pantheisticon* of John Toland (1670–1722), published in Latin in 1720, and in English in 1751: in describing "Socratic Societies," Toland reports that "many of them are to be met with in . . . Venice also, in all the Cities of Holland, especially Amsterdam" (1751 e., p. 57). On the Low Countries, see the following note: on the date of composition of Toland's *Pantheisticon,* see note 44 below.

41. Francesco Cornaro inscribed at Piombino a record of his youthful sojourn, in quarantine from the plague:

> 1690 9 novembre
> Io franc° Corner venni à star
> à Piombin p il sospetto
> del contagio che fù a Ven[a]
> e mì fermo fin del 4 Genn[ro] seguete.

He was elected ambassador to England on 5 September 1703, left Venice on 1 July 1705 for Germany, reached the Hague by 4 September, stayed there during September and October 1705 to consult with his predecessor, Cav. Alvise II Mocenigo, arrived in London on 13 November 1705, and made his ceremonial entrance at Court on 23 April 1706. His father was elected Doge of Venice on 22 May 1709, and Francesco left England three months later, in August; his last dispatch is dated once more from the Low Countries, from Antwerp on 3 September 1709. On the importance of the Low Countries as a "workshop for [Hermetic] ideas," see Franco Venturi, *Utopia and Reform in the Enlightenment* (Cambridge, England, 1971), p. 66.

42. I am indebted for this suggestion to Dr. Margaret Candee Jacob, in her letter to me of 19 July 1975.

43. Nadal Melchiore, *Catalogo historico cronologico*, MS, Treviso, Biblioteca Comunale, p. 324; MS. 158c287 in Castelfranco, Biblioteca Comunale, p. 388.

44. Knoop and Jones, *Freemasonry and the Idea of Natural Religion*, p. 8, quoting from Toland, *Pantheisticon*, 1720/51. Venturi, *Utopia and Reform*, pp. 65–66 n. 1, points out that Toland sent to Vienna a first version of his *Pantheisticon* on 7 March 1712. Venturi's p. 69 discusses relations between England and Venice in our very period of 1714–19, during a phase of considerable Venetian creativity and influence.

45. As cited in preceding note. An example of the appeal of such Hermetic works to the Continental aristocracy of Andrea Cornaro's generation is afforded by the extraordinary enthusiasm of the French maréchal d'Estrées for a copy of Toland's *Pantheisticon* in 1722: ibid., p. 67. In considering the broader historical implications of the Piombino cycle, one might do well to remember, with Arthur Lindsay (foreword to English ed. of Lindner, *Royal Art*, P. vii), that "the intrinsically feudal social context of Freemasonry on the European continent has left its lasting imprint . . . [And] occasional persecution . . . has sometimes made Freemasonry rather less democratic, [but] more elitist, more secretive and occasionally even politically active."

19

The Utopian Exit of the Hermetic Temple;
or,
A Curious Transition in the
Tradition of the Cosmic Sanctuary

ROBERT JAN VAN PELT

The Problem

The year 1605 saw the publication of the second of what would ultimately be a three-volume commentary on the book of Ezekiel, *In Ezechielem explanationes* (Rome, 1594–1605). The authors of this major contribution both to biblical scholarship and to the history of printing were two Spanish Jesuits, Hieronymo Prado (1547–95) and Juan Bautista Villalpando (1552–1608). The latter, who had trained as an architect, was responsible for the detailed monumental reconstruction of the temple described in Ezekiel's vision. This reconstruction marked a historic moment in the long line of attempts to visualize the Jewish sanctuary as described in the books of Kings, Chronicles, and Ezekiel, as well as the writings of Flavius Josephus.[1] Never before had it been seen as such a perfect and elaborate complex; never before had a reconstruction envisaged so much architectural embellishment. Uniting biblical description with classical tradition, and imposing his own taste, Villalpando turned the temple into a paradigm of good architecture.

Villalpando's reconstruction was particularly important for two reasons. First, it offered a new theory of the orders of architecture. This system, with its Solomonic column, was adduced as the biblical origin of all the later Greek and Roman orders,[2] and became popular in the seventeenth century, when an increasing number of architects began to be dissatisfied with the prevailing theories of the five orders. Of greater moment was Villalpando's explicit claim that the proportions of the temple and its parts were in accordance with musical consonances. Unlike earlier theorists, Villalpando actually demonstrated his theory with the help of diagrams, which illustrated his thesis in elaborate detail.

The Solomonic order and the harmonic proportions of Villalpando's temple have attracted the attention of many scholars who have recently ventured to explore the (rather undefined) territory between architectural history and the history of ideas.

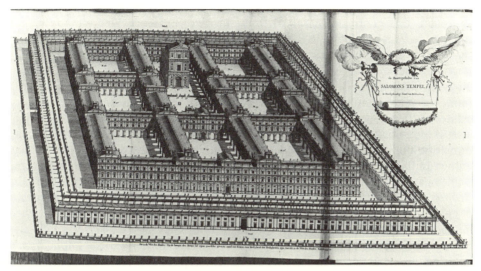

VILLALPANDO'S RECONSTRUCTION OF THE TEMPLE OF JERUSALEM as depicted in Willem Goeree's *Voor-bereidselen tot de bybelsche wysheid* (Amsterdam, 1690). *(Courtesy of the Warburg Institute.)*

Wittkower discussed Villalpando's reconstruction within the context of the influence of Neoplatonism on sixteenth-century architecture; his observations led to the more detailed study of Taylor in 1952.[3] With the ascent of Hermeticism after the publication of Frances Yates's *Giordano Bruno and the Hermetic Tradition,* Taylor reinterpreted his earlier conclusions within a Hermetic framework.[4] "Astrology, numerology, mystical geometry, anthropomorphism, the microcosm-macrocosm, the Pythagorean musical intervals, the mystical properties of colours and precious stones, the Cabala, and, of course, the Pseudo-Dionysian hierarchies" constitute the Hermetic influences on Villalpando's reconstruction of the temple.[5] Even though the great wave of studies that detected Hermeticism in virtually every aspect of sixteenth-century thought has subsided, it seems that Villalpando's temple will remain one of the most "Hermetic" examples of architecture produced in the sixteenth and seventeenth-centuries. I certainly feel that such a claim is justified on the basis of the architect's explicit manipulation of numbers to create a perfect whole. Villalpando's temple will provide again and again a new attraction for those who are intrigued by curious and fascinating mixtures of fact and fiction, magic and mystery, tradition and reform, in relation to the Hermetic traditions.

In this essay I shall define a new approach to the design of Villalpando's temple as an expression or illustration of Hermeticism. Rather than dwell on details of a possibly occult flavor, my discussion will concentrate on aspects of the design that reveal a Hermetic mode of thought. One of the problems with many of the attempts by architectural historians to discuss the influence of Hermeticism on architectural design and theory of the fifteenth, sixteenth, and seventeenth centuries is that in general they have not ventured beyond discussions of the esoteric or occult elements of certain designs. Statues of the planets or the four humors, for example, are immediately claimed to be Hermetic. These new "discoveries" of hidden symbolism confirm that architectural history ranks among the great intellectual disciplines. Few, however, have dared venture beyond this kind of narrow scholarly approach. This contrasts sharply with the history of science, where the influence of Hermeticism on scientific development is discussed in more general terms. In this essay, I would like to discuss the Hermetic tradition as consisting of a Hermetic mode of thought. This was not simply an amalgam of cabalism, numerology, astrology, and other relatively arcane branches of knowledge, but a basic frame of mind that gave these traditions room for expansion and reason for existence. It was a way of thinking that accepted, as a paradigm, the notion that man is potentially divine; through the manipulation of certain symbols he can transform the world and reconcile the opposites of a dispersed creation into a new union. Initiation into the meaning of these symbols was described in diverse traditions of ancient wisdom, and preserved in writings such as those of the *Corpus Hermeticus*. Hermeticism offered man a new perspective on the potential of earthly life, a perspective that became a vision of a classical millennium when mirrored in the rediscovery of the urban glories of imperial Rome. When I discuss the Hermetic mode of thought, I shall do so with regard to its social implications, ignoring the mysteries of the occultists and the secrets of the initiates.

The element of Villalpando's reconstruction that invites a more general discussion of the Hermetic mode of thought in architecture is a rather strange aspect of design: the simple fact that the building does not look like a temple at all. Until now, this has simply been accepted by architectural historians, but in fact the design reveals a clear departure from earlier reconstructions of the temple. Villalpando's design is closer to sixteenth-century notions of a palace or monastery, or seventeenth-century conceptions of an ideal city, than to a sanctuary. The relative insignificance of the temple building itself and the extraordinary importance of the palatial forecourts are the absolute antithesis of the Renaissance concept of a true religious structure, in which the holiest parts of the church were given proper architectural emphasis with a dome dwarfing the surrounding auxilary buildings. Hafenreffer's reconstruction of the temple of Ezekiel is a good example of this Renaissance idea.[6] Although he and Villalpando used precisely the same biblical data, Hafenreffer did not allow any secondary structure, whether gate or tower, to distract from or compete with the center of attention: the temple building itself. Villalpando's temple seems designed more for man than for God (or perhaps it was meant to provide space for a divine man). In any case, when one studies his vision of the temple, one can perceive that the divine flows into the terrestrial world in such a way that the main point of contact with the divine, the holy of holies in the main sanctuary, is somewhat deprived of its exclusive significance. This is of course very much in accordance with the message of Ezekiel's vision, and even more so with certain Hermetic concepts of the spiritual nature of matter.

In this context, it is important to note how Hermetic texts expressed the concept of matter spiritualized and man deified through the image of the magical city. In the prophecy in the *Asclepius,* one reads how

> the gods who exercise their dominion over the earth will be restored one day and installed in a City at the extreme limit of Egypt, a City which will be founded

towards the setting sun, and into which will hasten, by land and by sea, the whole race of mortal men.[7]

This ideal city of the future, the Hermetic New Jerusalem, has, as does its Hebrew paradigm, a predecessor—the city of Adocentyn, founded by Hermes Trismegistus. As prophesied in the *Asclepius,* Adocentyn was destined to decay with the rest of the Egyptian religion, but in the days of glory before its fall it represented a perfect synthesis of matter and spirit through magic.

There are among the Chaldeans very perfect masters in this art and they affirm that Hermes was the first who constructed images by means of which he knew how to regulate the Nile against the motion of the moon. This man also built a temple to the Sun, and he knew how to hide himself from all so that no one could see him, although he was within it. It was he, too, who in the east of Egypt constructed a City twelve miles long within which he constructed a castle which had four gates in each of its four parts. On the eastern gate he placed the form of an Eagle; on the western gate, the form of a Bull; on the southern gate the form of a Lion, and on the northern gate he constructed the form of a Dog. Into these images he introduced spirits which spoke with voices, nor could anyone enter the gates of the City except by their permission. There he planted trees in the midst of which was a great tree which bore the fruit of all generation. On the summit of the castle he caused to be raised a tower thirty cubits high on the top of which he ordered to be placed a light-house the colour of which changed every day until the seventh day after which it returned to the first colours. Near the City there was abundance of waters in which dwelt many kinds of fish. Around the circumference of the City he placed engraved images and ordered them in such a manner that by their virtue the inhabitants were made virtuous and withdrawn from all wickedness and harm.[8]

The *Picatrix* described how Hermes Trismegistus built both a temple and a city, and it is clear which enterprise the author of the text considered more important. The function of the castle in the city of Adocentyn is also revealing. As a bridge between matter and spirit, the castle served as the city's temple, but its gates led outward into the city, and not into its own holy of holies. Both the temple of the Sun and the castle temple led into the city; thus the Hermetic pinnacle of perfection was an urban dream. This is an image that shall be encountered many times in the following pages.

The Background

The origins of Villalpando's concept of the temple of God as a palace for man were rooted in contemporary social realities that, as shall be seen, caused a radical transformation in the perception of the meaning of the temple's holy of holies (a symbol of the divine world) and the forecourt (an allegory of the terrestrial world). By examining these realities one can understand the significance of Villalpando's reconstruction as a monument of man's changing relationship with the world, which was partly influenced by Hermeticism. Any discussion of this new world picture must note the three great inventions that were responsible (as Bacon had already observed) for creating the framework for the Renaissance: the printing press, gunpowder, and the magnet.[9] Ameliorating the spread of information, breaking the traditional feudal and ecclesiastical power structures, and encouraging voyages beyond the horizon, these mechanical discoveries transformed and enlarged the world. They also prepared the ground for the acceptance of such an essentially revolutionary doctrine as that proposed by the Hermetic philosophers. The availability of texts made possible a cult of ancient wisdom; cannons enlarged the scale of war and, concomitantly, gave rise to more lofty ideals of harmony and peace, to be achieved in the wake of a general reformation; and the discovery and conquest of new continents gave rise not only to new dreams of mastership over the earth, but also to those of mastership over nature. The culture of the printing press, gunpowder, and expansion overseas was the culture of an urban civilization. Only in cities was there the technical and scholarly expertise that made publishing feasible, and a demand for books that made it practicable; only cities offered both the space and the wealth necessary for the large-scale, expensive fortifications needed to withstand heavy bombardments during a siege; and only cities were able to launch the great commercial ventures that would change the face of the West and the East.

The city was the stage onto which the Hermetic philosopher projected his dreams: Bensalem, Christianopolis, the City of the Sun, and the city of Adocentyn. It was where academies met, with triumphal entries and processions moving slowly through the streets. The city was where the future was to be made, where the great instauration of the economy, the spread of knowledge and of society ordered according to the laws of nature was anticipated. But within the city walls one still finds the temple, a symbol of tradition, of the past, of arcane knowledge that was revealed only to the elect few, the place where priests and men were ordered according to the revealed laws of the Scriptures. The Hermetic philosopher took cognizance of the temple as well as of the city; to explain the world of this magus, I must describe it in terms of both. To comprehend the Hermetic city of perfection, one must observe the temple in its middle, and when contemplating the sanctuary of the Hermetic temple, one must remember the city that lies outside its gates. Thus, Villalpando's dream can only be understood in terms of the city.

Prior to examining the changing relation between city and temple in the Renaissance, I shall consider the two ancient cities that determined the concepts our ancestors had about the possible relation between the house of God and the houses of men. The first is Jerusalem, which derived its meaning and significance from the temple, a symbol of God's presence in and among the people of Israel. The city of Jerusalem was sometimes perceived as more important than its temple, as in the writings of Isaiah, for example, but even then it was a sort of supersanctuary for the whole of mankind. The way in which Jerusalem was ultimately an extension of its temple is clearly indicated by the sense of *place* it possessed: like the temple, Jerusalem was a holy place, a *templum,* elected by God; it could not be created anywhere but on Mount Zion. Thus, in contrast to Rome, Jerusalem was not a *polis* or *civitas* in the Greek or Roman sense. Rome was not a holy place, but an *idea* that existed through its citizens. When the Romans conquered an empire, the city of Rome expanded also. It was anything but a holy place, which is one of the reasons that temples were relatively unimportant within the republican and the imperial city. In this context it is significant that Ammianus Marcellinus, a soldier who visited Rome in 357, described the Pantheon (the most sophisticated of all Roman temples) as "a rounded city region, vaulted over in lofty beauty.[10] In the way they related to their respective temples, as in almost everything else, Jerusalem and Rome were diametric opposites.

With the collapse of urban life in the western part of the Roman Empire in the fifth and sixth centuries, the city lost much of its symbolic value. It survived throughout the early and High Middle Ages as a structure of an ideal, ordered life and as a symbol of human salvation thanks only to Augustine's spiritualization of the memory of Jerusalem and the concept of the Roman *civitas* in his *City of God*. However, the limited urban development of that time prevented this curious amalgam of memories of Jerusalem and Rome from becoming more than an abstract concept in obscure theological discussions." In a world in which cities were vague recollections of the past and towns were little more than disorderly collections of dwellings (architecturally insignificant in comparison with the great churches and abbeys), and in a society in which the local, isolated, and small commune could not compete with the international community of the Church, it made sense to use the image of the Church—both as a building and as a community—as a symbol of perfection and redemption. The Church, the mystical body of Christ, and the church building were understood to be the embodiment of the concept of the new temple of Jerusalem. Therefore the concepts of both the City of God and the heavenly city were subordinate to that of the universal temple; it was through that temple, church building, or Church as an institution, encompassing heaven and earth, that the City of God and the heavenly city were accessible and theoretically justified.[12] The medieval symbolic framework did not offer any space for the Hermetic dream of a utopian city, which shared its meaning with the temple rather than being subordinated to it. In short, the city of Adocentyn was meaningless as a symbol for medieval man.

In trecento Italy this quickly changed. The rise of new cities, new urban societies, and a new civic mentality signified that the concept of the heavenly city, the City of God that Augustine had seen as separate from the earthly city, was once again mirrored on earth. Hermann Bauer describes the abolition in Italy of the common fourteenth-century punishment of destroying the houses of convicts.[13] Contemporary aesthetic arguments were generally adduced in justification. The reason for the ban in Brescia in 1287, however, is quite revealing: the city should not be harmed as it is an image of paradise. The towns themselves increasingly became the image, theater, or instrument of salvation through the great processions and mystery and passion plays in which the city of Jerusalem was reconstructed. During these festivals, the temple, Paradise, Mount Sinai, and Bethlehem were set up together in the marketplace, with a ditch representing the river Jordan.[14] Outside the church building stood the theater of salvation. The relationship between Church and town could not but change; the Church now shared its original function as access and image of heaven with the town.

These developments had a lasting effect on the way worshipers perceived the meaning of the church building. Until the development of the town it was an image of the catholic universal Church, encompassing heaven and earth and offering access to another perfect reality. As cities began to grow, the church beame a civic monument first and foremost, deriving its meaning and legitimacy from the metropolis itself. In his study of church building around 1300, Wolfgang Gross has shown that this new meaning was expressed in contemporary attitudes toward the decoration of churches. According to Gross, Santa Croce in Florence was not meant to be an image of another reality and a spiritual entrance to the heavenly world; it was designed to be self-contained, revealing the manifold nature of this world unified in a single ideal entity.[15] Theological abstraction and mystic movement gave way to pictorial realism and self-satisfied rest. And while church paintings gained independence, predominating within the structure like windows to salvation, the architecture itself lost its anagogical meaning. Only in the designs of ideal cities, frequently represented on church walls, could the church building acquire new meaning as a home of images of perfection and salvation. Heaven on earth was imagined through the painted and described image. Thus, as Bauer concluded, a new concept of beauty in art was born as a surrogate for the anagogical.[16] From beauty in symbolism developed symbolism in beauty; paintings, not texts, became the paradigms of salvation.

These pictorial representations also made possible the creation of an architectural utopia: images of a perfect reality in the shape of images of a perfect town on earth. In the Renaissance, new philosophical concepts of man's power to transform his world (symbolized by the town) into a place of salvation and a world of perfection provided an additional impetus for utopian architecture. One of these new influences was undoubtedly Hermeticism. In that Hermeticism did not rely solely on speculation to achieve its ends, it differed fundamentally from other great intellectual traditions of the West. Manipulation of the physical world through magic, art, and science (terms that were synonymous in the Hermetic tradition) was not only acceptable, but nothing less than the keystone of the arch with which Hermetic philosophers hoped to span the gap between matter and spirit, thus creating a bridge from this world to a world of perfection.[17] In the philosophers' stone, alchemists foresaw the perfect union of matter and spirit, mortal and divine, and thus salvation. In utopian architecture, one finds the philosophers' stone of the community. Through buildings, laws, cosmic symbolism, and sometimes astral magic, individuals such as Tommaso Campanella, Andreä, and many others sought to create a perfect society in harmony with both the universe and the divine—a heavenly Jerusalem on earth. The phenomenon of the architectural utopia clearly reveals a Hermetic frame of mind. Whether the notion of the ideal town in the Renaissance was influenced by the description of Adocentyn in the *Picatrix,* which was said to have been written by Hermes Trismegistus, is another question. For my purposes, it is important only to note that the new vision of the divine man, capable of creating Paradise on earth, reinforced in the Renaissance the trecento shift in the importance of the church building. The ancient Stoic and Hermetic idea of the temple of the world, a concept that was highly polemical with regard to the man-made temple, was revived.[18] In the Renaissance the Church, symbolized by the temple, lost forever its definitive status as a gateway to heaven and became a transitory element within a new definitive symbol of salvation, perfection, and happiness: the ideal city.

My observations already indicate one possible approach to the meaning of Villalpando's design. To establish more specific conclusions, one must turn to the tradition of the cosmic temple in the Renaissance. I have attempted to define elsewhere the significance of the motif of the cosmic temple as the metaphysical model of man's means to salvation.[19] Initially given metaphysical coherence by Philo of Alexandria, the motif of the cosmic temple partly recalled the mythical symbolism of the temple of Jerusalem. This symbolism was derived from the meaning of Mount Moriah where, it was believed, heaven, earth, and underworld met. Philo's perception of the architectonic structure of the tabernacle, the mythical archetype of the temple as a cosmic stairway—as Jacob's ladder, reinterpreted the original symbolism. For Philo the forecourt was an image of the earth, the sanctuary the visible heaven, and the holy of holies the intelligible world. Man's task was to follow the high priest into the holy of holies, and find salvation in the apocalypse, the vision of the divine in darkness. Purification in the forecourt and rigorous philosophical training in the sanctuary were prerequisites; only thus could man attain wisdom in the holy of holies.[20]

This image of a road to salvation gained popularity in Christian theology. Some, like Clement of Alexandria and Origen, followed Philo's allegory quite literally. Others, such as an unknown author in the Epistle to the Hebrews and Augustine in his commentaries on the Psalms, related the symbolism of the cosmic temple and tabernacle to the fate of the whole community of believers. Through his crucifixion and ascension, Christ had opened the way for Christians to the holy of holies, a symbol of heaven and the triumphant Church. The militant Church was still in the sanctuary, but Christ's sacrifice assured access to the heavenly Church.[21] This simple symbol had given rise to far-reaching speculations, in which the temple and tabernacle became the framework for entire encyclopedias of knowledge. The temple/tabernacle architectural model was, in a great variety of ways, applied to different problems and systems of knowledge. All speculations, however, agreed on one important issue: The stairway to heaven represented in the temple led in only one direction. Once one entered the holy of holies, the place of salvation and heavenly Jeruselam, one remained there. This is understandable; man can only hope to join the saints in the triumphant Church after death; as Christianity never subscribed to the doctrine of reincarnation, there was no need for a means of return. The individual mystic, on the other hand, might perceive access to the holy of holies as his vision of God. This experience would, of necessity, be followed by a continuation of life on earth. But, with the great exception of Franz Rosenzweig, not even an allegory of return was created. Rosenzweig, at the end of his *Star of Redemption,* explained that nobody can live in the holy of holies; after the vision of God, which was little more than the attainment of self-knowledge, man must find his way back to the forecourt of the temple and return to everyday existence. "To walk humbly with thy God," wrote Rosenzweig, "the words are written over the gate, the gate which leads out of mysterious-miraculous light of the divine sanctuary in which no man can remain alive. Whither, then, do the wings of the gate

THE SYMBOLIC STRUCTURE OF THE TABERNACLE as depicted in Phillipe d'Aquin's *Discours du Tabernacle* (Paris, 1623). *(Courtesy of the British Library.)*

open? Thou knowest not? INTO LIFE."[22] This allegory, however, was written in the trenches in 1918, in a situation in which a good life on earth seemed more meaningful than the theological abstractions of the holy of holies. In medieval allegories of the mystic cosmic temple, descriptions of the return to life are not to be found.

As I have shown, the building of churches initially offered a route to heaven, as did the allegory of the temple. But when the city itself became an image of salvation in its own right, and when, as Carl Becker described, the heavenly city slowly shifted to earthly foundations and became a utopia, an image of a future state that could be built on earth, then (so to speak) both an exit from the holy of holies and a new interpretation of the forecourt—the location of the utopia—were needed.[23] Originally an ultimate goal, the holy of holies gradually became a station between the world of sin and the world of future perfection; it was given an exit door to return to the world!

The Evidence

In the Renaissance and the seventeenth century, traditional Christian allegories of the temple, as for example that by François de Sales,[24] did not describe any means of return from the holy of holies. On the other hand, a number of those allegories in which the traditional interpretation was flavored with Hermeticism included an exit from the holy of holies back into utopia. Individual examples varied, but one of the oddest was undoubtedly Campanella's *Civitas Solis*.[25] The design of the city described in this utopia has been discussed by numerous scholars.[26] The City of the Sun was round, with a temple at the center surrounded by seven concentric walls, on which palaces were built.[27] The walls were decorated with imges that provided a pictorial encyclopedia of the world. It is significant that the description of the decorative elements started with the temple, which symbolized astronomy. The first circle of walls—mathematics—was followed by the remaining circles until the outer perimeter with its portraits of great leaders, lawgivers, the ancient theologians, Jesus, the Apostles, and so on was reached. These were the visionaries and founders of the ideal society; it was here that terrestrial events were depicted. Thus, there was a clear progression from the abstract laws of the universe at the center of the scheme to those of the ideal society at its perimeter.

The description of the town proceeded outward from the temple which, in its architecture and decoration, was intended as an image of the universe. The center of the temple was a domed hall with seven lights representing the planets. The symbolism of the temple was significant in that it reflected that of the town, but while the cosmic meaning of the town was definitive in character and, one might say, eternal, that of the temple was only transitory in nature. This was reflected in Campanella's description of the most important annual religious holiday that was celebrated outside the temple.[28] Campanella explained that heaven was the real temple of God; the ancient Stoic notion of the *templum mundi* established the temple as a transitory monument.[29] It was also significant that the temple itself was used for private prayer. Public prayer, said on behalf of the whole community, was recited in the open by the high priest. Campanella's description of the annual sacrifice elucidated this relationship between temple and town, where the first was a kind of vestibule for the ideal society represented by the second.[30] Each year, one person volunteered to sacrifice himself for his fellow citizens to obtain redemption for the community. He was taken to the middle of the temple, where he was bound to a table and then hoisted upward through the oculus into a second area, which was also domed. This area was encircled with cells inhabited by monks, who fed the sacrificial volunteer for one month. When this period had expired and God had returned life to the volunteer—that is, the person was still alive—he was allowed to return to the community. The table was not lowered, as one would perhaps expect; the sacrificial volunteer climbed down a staircase outside the dome. The "victim" then became a priest and as such took his place in society.

This entire ritual was clearly inspired by the entry of the high priest into the holy of holies on the Jewish Day of Atonement.[31] As the priest moved from the sanctuary (a symbol of the perfect material world of the planets) to the intelligible world of God he passed through the gates of death. He survived this experience—a unique privilege. With one exception there was only a minor difference between the Jewish temple and that of the City of the Sun. The architecture of the latter more explicitly mirrored the cosmic symbolism both shared. For example, the holy of holies (a symbol of the supercelestial world of God) in the temple of the City of the Sun is not behind the main space that represented the planetary world, but above it. This was an absolutely literal interpretation of the notion that the divine world was "above" this world. The cosmic temple of the sun was radically different from the cosmic temple of Jerusalem in that it had an exit from the holy of holies above the starry vault of the main space. This was what may be described as a back door, providing access into the perfect world of the city. Originally a sinner, the sacrificial volunteer who survived the thirty days left the temple through this emergency exit a holy man. He did not join the saints in heaven, but resumed the burden of daily life.

I have already described the relationship between the temple and the city in Campanella's utopia. The peculiar details and ingenious technical solution of a concentric rather than linear structure of forecourt, sanctuary, and holy of holies certainly makes the description attractive. Other utopians wrestling with similar problems provided different solutions. In *Gargantua and Pantagruel,* Rabelais described two architectural structures in detail, the Abbey of Thélème, and the temple of the Dive Bouteille. Described at the end of the fifth book, the Dive Bouteille was a cosmic temple based on the descriptions of the Temple and Fountain of Venus in Francesco Colonna's *Hypnerotomachia Poliphili.*[32] Rabelais's temple was more of a palace of initiation than Colonna's Temple of Venus; and in the former, Hermetic overtones were strong.[33] Pantagruel and his companions were led to the oracle of the Dive Bouteille by a guide, or Lantern. Her light and knowledge illuminated the way. Before the pilgrims reached the entrance of the subterranean temple, they passed a vineyard; as the temple was dedicated to the Dionysian mysteries, they had to experience the physical pleasures and enjoyment caused by wine to attain truth. This was symbolized, as they passed through the vineyard, by covering their heads and filling their shoes with vine leaves. The pilgrims then descended a long, winding staircase with one hundred steps which, as Lantern informed them, equaled twice the sum of the Platonic lambda if the number eight was added to the total ($108 = 2 \times 54. 54 = 1 + 2 + 2^2 + 2^3 + 3 + 3^2 + 3^3$). It is of particular interest that the steps represented the two Platonic lambdas, indicating perhaps that one would ultimately return to the point of departure. The group first descended one step, then two, three, four. Then, as implicitly suggested, eight, nine, and twenty-seven. The last step, twenty-seven, repeated itself, followed by nine, eight, four, three, two, and returned to one. Not only did one return to the place of origin at the gateway of the temple below, but one passed through the lambda in the wrong direction. It would have been normal to start with twenty-seven, the male number of the earth, and from there climb to one and back again to the number twenty-seven. Now, instead, the pilgrims departed from one, the unity of God, the first cause of creation.

Other elements of this stairway were odd, too. For example, Lantern left them at the moment they entered the main space of the temple, where they were left to the priestess of the drunken fury Bacbuc. Normally one would have expected Bacbuc to precede Lantern, since even in the Dionysian furor the ultimate goal remained enlightenment, which was symbolized by Lantern. The direction of the winding stairs was also unusual. In traditional allegories in which mystery temples were used as stage sets for initiation, the initiates were requested to ascend rather than descend. Finally, the use of the great *tetraktys,* which determined the symbolism of the steps, seems to be out of place. The seven numbers, united in their first cause, are the causes of the order of the planetary worlds. These figures, as the ultimate cause of the cosmic order, belonged to the world of pure intellect, the supercelestial world, or the Platonic world of ideas. Knowledge of the numbers was not a prerequisite for initiation, but the ultimate revelation after having been granted access to the holy of holies. Perhaps, then, the winding staircase was not a porch but the temple's innermost sanctuary, and the vineyard was not a garden preceding the porch but the Paradise behind the holy of holies' exit. Perhaps the main element of satire in the temple of the Dive Bouteille is that the initiates were guided through the temple in the wrong direction. Perhaps the satire was not a joke at all, but an expression of a deeply religious, Hermetic vision of the temple as a cosmic ladder, a ladder leading back to life.

This temple had still further curious elements. At the center of the main sanctuary was a large fountain on a heptagonal base with seven columns made of different precious stones and crowned with statues of the planets made of various metals. The fountain was covered with a crystalline dome. A large lamp, brighter than the sun and illuminating the entire temple, hung above. It is significant that neither the fountain nor the lamp, whose Hermetic, cosmic, and alchemical symbolism have been discussed in detail by G. Mallary Masters, was given a major role in the initiation ceremony.[34] As Rabelais suggested, the water from the fountain was an elixer that deceived those who drank it into believing that they were tasting the wine of their choice. Thus the fountain brought confusion, not enlightenment. Initially it functioned as a decoy and not a symbol of the deepest mysteries. Similarly, the oracle imparted in the holy of holies (which only Panurge was allowed to enter) was an enigma. Later, the mystery was explained at the fountain in the middle of the main sanctuary.

Rabelais described this chapel of the oracle as lit by daylight shining through the walls, which added to its paradoxical meaning. While in mystery temples the holy of holies were normally dark, illuminated only by the light of the spirit, here the holy of holies was lit by natural light, as if it were the outside world, the forecourt. I would like to suggest that it is indeed the forecourt; thus Panurge was presented not with an answer but with a question, an enigma. As such it was a turning point in the allegory of the temple of the Dive Bouteille. Until that point the initiates had been descending, moving from understanding and the light of reason to deceit and illusion. Now, when Panurge left the holy of holies to attend the oracle at the fountain, the pilgrims began to ascend again. The elixer, which deceived upon arrival from the intelligible world, illuminated upon arrival from the mundane world as symbolized by the chapel of the oracle. At the fountain Panurge was smitten with what at first appeared to be irrational fury, and from this state reason emerged in the figure of Friar John. The founder of the Abbey of Thélème (the utopia inhabited by people able to control their will), Friar John was the hierophant who symbolically opened the door to the winding staircase, which the pilgrims had to ascend to return to the one. He led the initiates from the fountain, which represented the planets and their spheres, to their cause as symbolized by the seven numbers of the lambda. Indeed, upon leaving the temple they entered, as Jesse Zeldin has observed, a real but better world, symbolized by the Abbey of Thélème.[35] This was a world of enlightenment, directly ruled through the simple numerology of the seven numbers of the *tetraktys* and directly protected by a God who was characterized here (appropriately enough) in mathematical terms as an intellectual sphere, the center of which was everywhere and the circumference of which was nowhere.

The allegory of the temple of the Dive Bouteille is highly complex and multi-layered. What is important is the fact that it did not offer a one-way road to enlightenment, but was a dual carriageway that led first into this world, and then to a world of perfection, which was located at the top of the stairs, from whence the initiates had originally departed. The allegory represented the descent of the Hermetic Adam in creation as described in the *Poimandres* and the difficult road back to regain his lost divinity. The fountain was initially deceitful, as were the seven governors in the first part of the *Poimandres;* only after the experience of the terrestrial world in the chapel of the oracle did it play a more positive role, as did the governors in the latter half of the *Poimandres.* Thus in this story it was a Hermetic vision of man and of God that was elucidated. And just as ultimately within the Hermetic context the regained divinity of man has a terrestrial significance, since it can be attained here on earth, similarly the real holy of holies of the temple was not a terminal port, but a passage into a reformed and perfected world, symbolized by the abbey. It was a world that could be reached only when man had learned to control his fury through his will, where man, as Zeldin observed, would prove virtuous when left to his own natural powers.[36] Friar John represented that power; in many ways, he was the Hermetic ideal of the magus. The Abbey of

Thélème, onto which the holy of holies of the temple opened, was not a haven of security but "a real world in which man must assert his true, honorable self."[37] By leading the reader via the staircase back to the real world, transformed from a world of illusions where man had to be guided by the reason of another (Lantern) to a world that he could transform through his own will and natural powers, a world under the protection of the intellectual sphere of the Hermetic God, Rabelais created the ultimate Hermetic holy of holies: a place that derived its significance solely from the fact that it was a mere corridor between two gates—the gate of life and the gate of life transformed.

The more serious Renaissance and Seventeenth-century allegories of the cosmic temple reveal similar desires to provide an exit from the holy of holies into the real world. In fact, a biblical precedent for this notion was readily available. Ezekiel 47:1 explained:

> He brought me back to the entrance of the Temple, where a stream came out from under the Temple threshold and flowed eastwards, since the Temple faced east.

In his design for the Temple of Pansophia, first published in *Conatuum Pansophicorum Delucidatio* (1639), and translated into English by Hartlib in 1642 under the title *A Reformation of Schooles in Two Excellent Treatises,* Comenius exploited this image of water to create a means of return from the holy of holies. First he described the temple, with each court symbolizing part of his pansophical curriculum. Then came the holy of holies:

> The last, and most secret part of the Temple, called the Holy of Holies, shall be answered by the sixth part of *Pansophia,* wherein the God of Gods shall be seene inhabiting his owne eternity.[38]

For Comenius, the whole pansophical system was not intended merely as a preparation for the vision of God in the holy of holies. To the contrary, this sytem and the apocalypse together were to form the foundation of a new utopian society. One could not dwell in the holy of holies; one had to apply the knowledge acquired there to earthly activities, using it to transform and perfect the world. The vision in the holy of holies was, therefore, immediately followed by a description of the exit from the Temple of Pansophia, symbolized by the water that flowed from under the threshold.

> Lastly, from that river of waters issuing out of the Temple, and diffusing themselves over all the earth, we will derive the last part of the Pansophie, which unfolds the right use of the waters of true wisdome. I am not ignorant that by those waters proceeding out of Ezekiel's Temple, the course of the Gospell is disciphered to us. . . . Yet it is plainly as appears also, that wisdome is compared to waters. . . . Therefore in this last part of Pansophie it will be our work to consider of, and designe such channels, as may convey these waters abroad on every side, so that the vast Commons of humane affaires, together with the private garden plots of every ones soule, and the whole Paradise of the Church may be therwith watered.[39]

In Comenius's epistemology, the temple derived its meaning and justification as a structure from the issuing of the waters from the holy of holies, and not from a vision of God in this innermost chamber. Comenius did not want to build temples in the sky; he wanted a better society here on earth, to transform this world into Paradise. The exit from the temple therefore became more important than the entrance.

In the commentaries on Ezekiel, the waters usually symbolized the spread of the Christian Church. This motif was subsequently adopted by George Herbert in *The Temple,* a collection of his poems. In the first *(Church Porch)* of this three-part work, Herbert described the external aspects of Christian life. The second part, composed of numerous poems, he called the *Church.* This described the spiritual ascent of the writer. The third part, the *Church Militant,* related the history and tribulations of the Church on earth. Contrary to such theories as those of J. D. Walker, I do not believe that the tripartite arrangement of the work alludes to the division of the temple into porch (forecourt), sanctuary, and holy of holies.[40] Nor do I agree with Barbara Lewalski who, in rejecting Walker's thesis, has denied any strict architectural relationship between Herbert's edifice and the Jewish temple. It is she, however, who has offered a key to the true symbolism of Herbert's *Temple* as an architectonic temple with her observation that the heavenly kingdom was already symbolized at the end of the second part (the *Church*).[41] If one accepts that Herbert referred to the temple of Ezekiel, the symbol of Christianity par excellence, then one can certainly find parallels in the collection of poems with each of the architectural components. Herbert's *Porch* was the porch of the whole complex of the temple. Merely a series of didactic prescriptions and rules for how a Christian should behave, this poem did not trace any spiritual development. The *Church* itself encompassed the forecourt, the sanctuary, and the holy of holies. These are, of course, the three major stepping stones for the soul striving to reach God. Indeed, as Lewalski has noted, there is a clear development within the poems of this second part of *The Temple*. The first group of poems in the *Church* deals with conversion, struggle, repentance, and faith. This group begins (as one would expect) in the forecourt with the poem "Altar," and ends with the two poems "Repentance" and "Faith," which recapitulate the whole symbolism of the forecourt. The second group, from "Prayer (I)" to "The Crosse," progresses from the tribulations of the forecourt through the sanctuary to the Cross which, in traditional exegesis, was equated with the Veil before the holy of holies. The final group of poems, beginning with "Flowers" and closing with "Love (III)," symbolizes the holy of holies. Here one finds confidence, ease, and the author's anticipation of heaven. These poems suggest the heavenly kingdom, culminating in the heavenly banquet to which the soul is invited.[42] But for Herbert, as for Comenius, the achievement of entering the holy of holies was only a step on the way to transforming the whole world into Paradise. Hence the *Church* ends with the statement, "Glorie be to God on high, and on earth peace, good will towards men." Hence the account of the Church militant; the difficult struggle to transform the earth, the making of the new Jerusalem. This part of the volume is the water that flows under the threshold of the temple. Again one is brought from the exterior of the temple, to the porch, through the temple back to the outside world in the Church militant.

Comparable phenomena may be found in Bacon's concept of the cosmic temple. I have argued elsewhere that Bacon's *New Atlantis* was intended to be seen as the holy of holies of a temple, the sanctuary being the natural history published under the title *Sylva Sylvarum* with *New Atlantis* as the appendix.[43] The imagery in the *New Atlantis,* where Bacon referred repeatedly to the supercelestial world, and in the frontispiece to the volume containing both texts, suggests this interpretation.[44] This illustration depicts two Corinthian columns with a globe between them, labeled *mundus intellectualis.* Above the globe, between two cherubim and emitting light, is the name of God. The columns allude to those before the porch of the temple. The *mundus intellectualis* is the part of human understanding that is capable of rationalization and that can be related to Ficino's concept of the rational soul. This was ruled by the celestial world, the world of the sanctuary. Understanding is illuminated by the active intellect, which establishes general principles of research along with goals and aspirations. The active intellect would be aroused by the fable of *New Atlantis,* which described a supercelestial world; the imagery is thus relevant and appropriate.[45]

New Atlantis, however, was not simply part of Bacon's epistemology. It was also a utopia that demanded imitation. For Bacon, this utopia was not an end in itself. In the holy of holies in Bacon's temple, too, one finds a small door labeled exit. At the end of the fable, the father of the House of Solomon, who had revealed the secrets of utopia, bade the author farewell and gave him leave to publish the work for the good of other nations.[46] *New Atlantis* was thus transformed from a supercelestial fable, intended to illuminate the reader's understanding and guide him through the material of the *Sylva Sylvarum,* into an ordinary utopia in the forecourt of this world.

The few examples I have analyzed reaveal the same characteristics. The Holy of Holies was no longer a static realm beyond this world, the end of the road to heaven; to the contrary, it pointed back to earth, and to man's responsibility on earth. All of these texts mark a transitional phase in the history of man's attempt to understand his world with the help of architecture. From Philo to the late Middle Ages, the symbolism of the temple was simple. It offered a way out of this world and, through the unity of its architecture, linked the spiritual and material worlds. From the second half of the eighteenth century, the character of architecture as a model of thought is also clear. On the one hand the romantic (Masonic) temple of the world, a temple without structure, which was little more than a glorification of this world or of mankind.[47] And then there were the plans developed by architects to bring felicity and happiness through design, and to save the world by building ideal towns for ideal people.

Conclusion

These documents from the Renaissance and seventeenth century illuminate the evolution from one conception to the others and reveal how the heavenly Jerusalem and the holy of holies of the cosmic temple were given earthly foundations and an earthly goal. The symbolism of the temple as a cosmic stairway lost its definitive

FRONTISPIECE of Bacon's *Sylva Sylvarum*, first edition (London, 1627). *(Courtesy of the Warburg Institute.)*

character. The temple became a transitory symbol; the stairs led, as those in Rabelais's temple of the Dive Bouteille, ultimately back to their point of origin. But when one sees that the holy of holies was pulled down to earth, one can also understand why the traditional cosmic symbolism of the temple was moribund. By bringing the holy of holies down it was in fact demolished. Indeed, social and scientific development of the seventeenth and later centuries has been described metaphorically as the erection of a temple without a holy of holies. This is certainly apposite. Western man wants nothing more than, as Nathaniel Culverwell remarked,

> to lie in the Porch, at the Gate of the Temple called beautiful and be a door-keeper in the house of its God.[48]

But by guarding the door, one does not preserve the building within. And thus Comenius predicted, and Hegel concluded with reason, that

> indem so die Wissenschaft und der gemeine Menschen-verstand sich in die Hände arbeiteten, den Untergang der Metaphysik zu bewirken, so schien das sonderbare Schauspiel herbeigefürt zu werden, ein gebildetes Volk ohne Metaphysik zu sehen, wie einen sonst mannigfach ausgeschmückten Tempel ohne Allerheiligstes.[49]

The holy of holies would be pulled down in the centuries that followed the period between the trecento and the time of Herbert, Bacon, and Comenius. In their era, the forecourt and the holy of holies coexisted, albeit the forecourt had implicitly become more important than the innermost sanctum. This development in the traditional symbolism of the temple was splendidly mirrored in the vision of the temple in Villalpando's *In Ezechielem Explanationes*. This reconstruction emphasized the architecture of the forecourt. It was quite unparalleled, and was to influence subsequent designs well into the seventeenth century. The temple itself, containing the holy of holies and the sanctuary, was dwarfed by galleries, porticoes, and halls that surrounded the various forecourts. As I noted above, the design gave the impression of a large palace or a utopian town, comparable if not superior to the monolithic town designed by Andreä. Villalpando made the link between the plan of the temple and the utopian settlement explicit by planning the edifice in accordance with the encampment of the twelve tribes that originally surrounded the tabernacle in the desert. In Christian thought, this had been interpreted as the utopian concept of the Church, gathered in perfect order around Christ, the true tabernacle of God.[50] This concept is also evident in Villalpando's symbolic and cosmological interpretation of the temple. It is remarkable that he did not concentrate on the meaning of the sanctuary and the holy of holies, but on the palace that surrounded the courts. Before Villalpando, these structures had been only an allegory of the terrestrial world. Now, in their entirety, they carried the symbolism of the temple. The towers around the inner court before the temple symbolized the four elements; those in the outer precinct represented the signs of the zodiac, with the symbols of the planets in the adjacent courtyards. Thus can be seen the scheme of the Ptolemaic world in the central forecourt, which symbolized

& Gad. Ad Occidentem Ephraim, Manaſſes, & Beniamin. Ad Aquilonem denique Dan, Aſer, & Nephtali, vt ſubſequens caſtrorum Iſrael figura demonſtrat. Ex ijs autem quatuor principes Iudas, Ruben, Ephraim, & Dan, in angulis fixere tentoria: latera vero complebant binae illae numeratae ordine ſuo tribus.

Singuli porro duces exercitus vexilla ſua in aëra ſubſtulerunt, ac parentum, maiorumque ſtemmatis inſignia: quod illis verbis videtur à ſacro Textu indicari: *Singuli per turmas, ſigna, atque vexilla, & domos cognationum ſuarum.* Vel, vt habent Hebraea: Vnuſquiſque ſuper vexillum ſuum in ſignis domus patrum ſuorum caſtrametabuntur filij Iſrael. Sed inter omnia vexilla,

A illa potiſſimum eminebant, quae in quatuor caſtrorum angulis à quatuor primis principibus, quos enumeraui, erigebantur. Ad Orientem ſuper tabernaculum Naaſſon primogeniti Iadae vexillum effulgebat viridis coloris:in viridi namque lapillo, qui ſmaragdus appellatur, parentis ſui nomen deſcriptum erat in rationali iudicij, quod ſummus Sacerdos geſtabat in pectore: in quo, quaſi in Pontificia bulla, Iſraeliticae nobilitatis antiqua iura continebantur. In vexillo autem Iudae inſigne nobilitatis erat Leo: leoni enim comparauerat illum Iſrael, ſeu Iacob pater eius, quando nimirum tanquam omnium parens, & princeps ſingulis propria ſtemmata diſtribuit. vnde ex hoc reliqua licebit rimari.

Geneſ. 49. ℣. 9.

CASTRA TRIBVVM ISRAEL
CIRCA TABERNACVLVM
FOEDERIS·

OCCIDENS·

 Ephraim

 Manaſſes

 Beniamin

 Dan

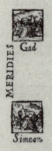 MERIDIES Gad

 Gerſonitæ

 Merarite

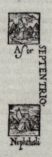 Aſer SEPTENTRIO·

Simeon

Caathitæ

Moyſes, et Aaron

Nephthali

 Ruben

 Zabulon

 Iſachar

 Iudas

ORIENS·

Ad Meridiem deinde eminebat ſupra tentorium Elizur filij Ruben rubrum colore vexillum, quod referebat ſardium rationalis lapillum, quod illi obtigerat: eius autem inſigne fuit humana facies; vt pote qui primogenitus eſſet, & veluti caput totius domus Iſrael.

Ad Occidentem ſupra tentorium Eliſama filij Ephraim vexillum collucebat aureum, chryſolithum referens rationalis, in quo deſcriptus erat: habebat vero pro inſigni nobilitatis vitulum, cui comparauerat eum Moyſes, cum tribus prophetice benedixit, haud ſecus quàm fecerat prius illorum parens Iacob: *Quaſi primogeniti tauri,* inquit, *pulchritudo eius &c. Hae ſunt multitudines Ephraim* &c. Denique ad Aquilonem ſuper tentorium Ahiezer filij Dan effulgebat diuerſi coloris vexillum, ex albo nimirum, & rubro colore permix-

Deuteron. 33. ℣. 17.

Tom. 2. Explanat. Pars 2.

B tum; iaſpidem referens eiuſdem rationalis. Hunc ſic interpellat parens Iacob: *Dan iudicabit populum ſuum ſicut & alia tribus in Iſrael. Fiat Dan coluber in via, ceraſtes in ſemita.* Quae ad ingenij acumen, & bellicam fortitudinem, atque induſtriam ſingularem referenda eſſe merito putarunt Doctores illi, qui cum Sancto Hieronymo arbitrati ſunt ad fortiſſimum Samſonem referendam eſſe huiuſmodi prophetiam. Quae duo cum maxime in aquila ſint conſpicua, propterea creditum eſt ab aliquibus, Dan; quòd ceraſtem in vexillo pingere recuſaret, aquilam effinxiſſe pro ſerpente. Aquilarum autem plura genera facit Plinius: Melaenaetos, inquit, à Graecis dicitur, eademque valeria, minima magnitudine, viribus praecipua, colore nigricans: ſola aquilarum foetus ſuos alit, ceterae, vt dicemus, fugant: ſola ſine

Geneſ. 49. ℣. 17.
S. Hierony. de trad. Hebraic. in.
Geneſ.
Euſeb. Emiſſenus.
Strabus.
Honcala.
Percerus in Genef.
Bellarminus. lib. 3. de Rom. Pont. cap. 12
Plinius lib 10. cap. 3.
& 4.

Qq 3 CA-

SOLIS LO-
cum ſibi ven-
dicat Dei ſe-
des.
Ecclesiastes
1. ῎. 6.
Iacob. 1. ῎.
17.
Malachi. 4.
῎. 2.
SOL IV-
ſtus, ideſt, iu-
ſte faciens di-
ſcernere.

hoc ipſo aedificio repraeſentatur, in planetarum
medio non eſt ſol ille : *Qui oritur, & occidit , &*
ad locum ſuum reuertitur : ibique renaſcens gyrat
per Meridiem , & reflectitur ad Aquilonem : ſed
verus ille luminum parens , *apud quem non eſt*
tranſmutatio , nec viciſſitudinis obumbratio. Sol ,
inquam , *iuſtitiae :* hoc eſt, Sol iuſtus, cuius lux
iuſte facit diſcernere, nec ei poteſt vlla oculorum
obeſſe aut hebetudo , aut aegritudo ; quippe
cum radijs ſuae miſericordiae omnes ſanat lan-
guores, & ſanitas in pennis eius. Hic igitur verus

A Sol Chriſtus, ſeptem ſplendens luminibus ſepti-
formis gratiae, quam effudit in nos abunde, tanquam in medio duodecim ſignorum , ſic olim in
medio tribuum populi Iſraelitici viſus eſt in figura , vt cum in medio duodecim Apoſtolorum
viſus fuiſſet in Iudaea Deus , adoraretur vt verus
creator caeli noui , nouaeque terrae: quatuor ſti-
patus veluti Cherubinis, Euangeliſtis ad quatuor
mundi plagas euangelizare tranſmiſſis . Quae
omnia , qua ex parte poterit , ſubſequens figura
indicabit.

ECCLESIA
Chriſti his
omnibus ſi-
gnis indica-
tur.

E O R V N D E M
C A S T R O R V M
DISPOSITIO, MVNDVM
referens, & Templum.

Geneſ. 48. ῎. 5. & Cap. 49. ῎. 4. 7. 9. 13. 14. 17. 19. 21. Deut. 33. ῎. 26.

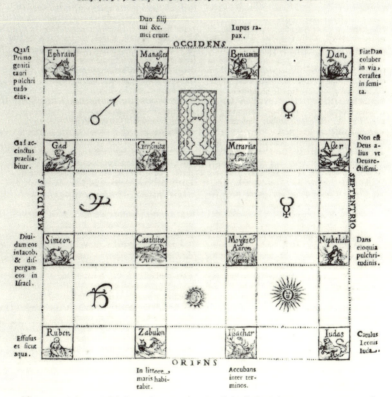

Neque vero in hoc aedificio humanis commo-
dis, & vtilitati dicato humana deeſſe potuit ſimi-
litudo, quaſi minoris cuiuſdam mundi, qui ex
quatuor conflatur humoribus, vt elementis mun-

dus, & duodecim ſtellis deducitur per ſeptem vitae huius aetates. quarum prima, & in imbecillio-
ri Lunari ſcilicet peracta , ſi ad dexteram diriga-
tur, non Mercurij inconſtans, variaque conditio ,
lubrici

the earth. The visible heavens and planets surrounded it. According to Villalpando, the supercelestial world was not found in the holy of holies, but at the center of the entire design; in the middle of the twelve signs of the zodiac. This was man's place on earth and also that of Christ who, according to Villalpando, was not the visible sun, but the real, spiritual sun.[51] Here, at the center, the terrestrial, celestial, and supercelestial worlds were united in Christ, the Hermetic magus par excellence. The temple was not presented as a stairway to heaven with no return, but as the philosophers' stone—the perfect conjunction of matter and spirit on the terrestrial world. Thus, in the general conception of the building and in the numerology of its proportions one sees a significant Hermetic influence on Villalpando's reconstruction of the temple.

In the celestial harmony that pervades the design through musical proportion, one perceives the means through which the extremes of heaven and earth were united. In the architectonics of the temple the invisible had become visible, the infinite finite. In the general layout and symbolism of the temple, one sees another *coincidentia oppositorum*. The temple is no longer a bridge between the extremes of sin and salvation, but a point of rest, which found its center in the central courtyard. There earth and the spiritual sun were united, man's soul and the world's soul were unified, the natural world of the four elements and the supernatural world of God joined. Around this center the celestial worlds and the terrestrial world danced, reformed through the architecture of the temple. Matter becomes spiritual, and the spirit material in an endless process of becoming. In this reintegration of the worlds into their primordial—undivided—state, the union of historical oposites as biblical revelation and classical Vitruvian canon were necessary, if relatively unimportant, aesthetic details within the whole Hermetic epistemology presented by the temple. In offering both a way up as well as an exit, in visualizing both a palace for God and a temple for man, Villalpando designed a powerful instrument of transformation that allowed the universe to interact in order to achieve the Hermetic dream of a general, world-encompassing reformation.

Until now, Villalpando's design has not been seen for what it really was: the perfect Hermetic Christian utopia. It is perhaps significant that his influence on church architecture was limited solely to decoration,[52] whereas in the planning of utopian communities,whether in monasteries, hospitals, places, or even new towns, there are numerous indications that his utopia had a strong conceptual influence.[53] The temple as depicted in the *In Ezechielem Explanationes* established a pattern for the great institutional buildings where men, often against their own will and with loss of dignity, were forced into basically inhuman patterns of existence. Just as modern science in many ways represents a perversion of the Hermetic dream to manipulate the world, so the communities, planned according to the revelations of Marx and Marcuse, are a perversion of the Hermetic ideals of a perfect and spiritual society symbolized in Villalpando's temple. The weakness of Villalpando's concept of God's sanctuary on earth was made patently clear in Louis Richeome's lyrical evocation of the temple sandwiched between a discussion on terrestrial and celestial music in his *Trois discours pour la religion catholique* (1597):

> Il faut croire, que ceste musique est richement remplie, & nombreusement riche, puis qu'ell est accordée pour le grand & celeste temple de la gloire de Dieu, & ou les Anges sont les choristes & chantres. Tout le temple terrestre, que iadis Salomon bastit à Dieu, estoit un choeur d'une tres-belle musique, aussi bien que le tabernacle de Moyse: Il n'y avoit en ce temple la edifice, muraille, autel, chapelle, porche, parvis, cour, allée, degrée, porte, fenestre, frontispice, cornice, architecture, frise, columne, chapiteau, piedestal, qui n'eust sa proportion, son octave, sa quinte, sa tierce, sa quarte, sa quiziesme, douziesme, dixiesme, ou autre nombre de musique en longueur, largeur, & hauteur, avec toutes ses partis & celles des autres par un rapport symetrique admirablement bien compassé, comme il est clair à voir en ceste belle description du temple faicté par Ezechiel, & tres doctement expliquée par Villalpando le Iesuite. De maniere qu'il ne se faut esmerveiller, si L'Escriture nous advise, que quand on le bastit, il n'y fut ouy aucum son de marteau, ou de scie, ou d'autres instruments de fer, pour donner aux plus sages une secrette leçon de plusieurs belles choses qui no sont propres de ce lieu, mais entre autres pour signifier que la musique de ceste belle fabrique est si bonne, qu'il ne falloit pas qu'elle fust destournée par ces bruits rudes de fer: moins encore se faut'il esmerveiller, si comme David, qui avoit preparé à son fils Salomon les materiaux du Temple, composa & laissa tant de beaux Hymnes, Pseaumes & motets, accordez sur le harpe, sur les psaltions, sur le regale & autres instruments pour representer la secrette musique s'iceluy temple faicte à la semblance de la musique celeste, dont nous parlons maintenant.[54]

In this early reaction to Villalpando's design, the occult harmony of the temple's proportions had become a goal in itself. The temple may have symbolically offered an exit from the holy of holies, but nobody would use it, because there was no necessity to enter the sanctuary any more. Many details of the decoration were listed, but neither the holy place nor the holy of holies was mentioned Thus in the zenith of the Hermetic-Christian dream one can see the nucleus of its destruction. Indeed, it was only a question of time until the Hermetic city/temple, a perfect union between biblical sanctuary and utopian town, between Jerusalem and Rome, between Ezekiel's vision and Vitruvius's canon, was demolished, leaving behind the empty shell of the profane city: a city without an emergency exit leading back to the divine.

Notes

This essay is written in grateful memory of many hours spent at 5 Coverts Road, Claygate. I would like to express my particular thanks to Betty Kingston and Rick Scorza for their assistance with its preparation.

1. Wolfgang Hermann, "Unknown Designs for the 'Temple of Jerusalem' by Claude Perrault," in *Essays in the History of Architecture Presented to Rudolf Wittkower* (London, 1967), pp. 143–58; Helen Rosenau, *Vision of the Temple: The Image of the Temple of Jerusalem in Judaism and Christianity* (London, 1979); B. Vogelsang, *Archaische Utopien* (Cologne, 1981).

2. See esp. the study of Juan Antonio Ramirez, *Edificios y suenos* (Malaga, 1983), pp. 149–50.

3. Rudolph Wittkower, *Architectural Principles in the Age of Humanism* (London, 1949); René Taylor, *El Padre Villalpando (1552–1608) y sus ideas esteticas*, Anales y Boletin de la Real Academia de San Fernando (Madrid, 1952).

4. René Taylor, "Architecture and Magic: Considerations on the Idea of the Escorial," in *Essays in the History of Architecture Presented to Rudolf Wittkower* (London, 1967), pp. 80–90; idem, "Hermeticism and Mystical Architecture in the Society of Jesus," in *Baroque Art: The Jesuit Contribution* (New York, 1972), pp. 63–97.

5. Taylor, "Hermeticism," p. 76.

6. Matthias Hafenreffer, *Templum Ezechielis* (Tübingen, 1613).

7. *Asclepius* 3.27d, quoted in Frances Yates, *Giordano Bruno and the Hermetic Tradition* (London, 1964), pp. 55–56.

8. *Picatrix* 4.3, as quoted in yates, *Bruno*, p. 54.

9. Francis Bacon, *The Works of Francis Bacon*, 14 vols., ed. J. Spedding, R. L. Ellis, and D. D. Heath (London, 1857–74): 4:114.

10. Ammianus Marcellinus *History*, 16.14; *Ammiani Marcellini Quae Supersunt*, 3 vols., ed. Johann Augustus Wagner a.o. (London, 1808), 1:93.

11. Only in the fifteenth-century, with the planning of Rome by Nicholas V do we see a first attempt to project the sacred tectonics of Jerusalem in a city: Rome. See Carroll William Westfall, *In This Most Perfect Paradise* (University Park, Pa., 1974).

12. Robert Jan van Pelt, *Tempel van de Wereld: De kosmische Symboliek van de Tempel van Salomo* (Utrecht, 1984), p. 152.

13. Hermann Bauer, *Kunst und Utopie: Studien über das Kunst- und Staatsdenken in der Renaissance* (Berlin, 1965), pp. 1–17.

14. Karl Young, *The Drama of the Medieval Church*, 2 vols., (Oxford 1933).

15. Wolfgang Gross, *Die abendländische Architektur um 1300* (Stuttgart, 1948), pp. 213–14.

16. Bauer, *Kunst und Utopie*, p. 17.

17. See Yates, *Bruno;* see also Frances A. Yates, "The Hermetic Tradition in Renaissance Science," in *Art, Science and History in the Renaissance*, ed. C. S. Singleton (Baltimore, 1968), pp. 255–74.

18. A.-J. Festugière, *La révélation d'Hermès Trismègiste*, 3 vols. (Paris, 1949), 2:233–37; van Pelt, *Tempel*, pp. 62–65.

19. Van Pelt, *Tempel*.

20. Robert Jan van Pelt, "Philo of Alexandria and the Architecture of the Cosmos," *A. A. Files* 4 (1983): 1–15.

21. Van Pelt, *Tempel*, pp. 142–44.

22. Franz Rosenzweig, *The Star of Redemption* (London, 1971), p. 424.

23. Carl L. Becker, *The Heavenly City of the Eighteenth-Century Philosophers* (New Haven, 1932), p. 49.

24. François de Sales, *Oeuvres complètes,* 4 vols. (Paris, 1836), 4:176–77.

25. Tommaso Campanella, *Civitas Solis Idea Reipublicae Philosophicae,* printed with *Realis Philosophiae Epilogisticae Partes Quator* (Frankfurt, 1623).

26. See, for example, L. Firpo, "La cité idéale de Campanella et la culte du soleil," in *Le soleil à la Renaissance* (Brussels, 1965), pp. 327–ff.

27. Campanella, *Civitas Solis*, pp. 418–22.

28. Ibid., pp. 454–56.

29. Van Pelt, *Tempel*, pp. 60–67.

30. Campanella, *Civitas Solis*, pp. 452–53.

31. Leviticus 16.

32. See discussion in G. Goebel, *Poeta Faber* (Heidelberg, 1971), pp. 38–41, 152–55.

33. G. Mallary Masters, "The Hermetic and Platonic Traditions in Rabelais' 'Dive Bouteille,'" *Studi Francesi* 10 (1966): 15–29. See also idem, *Rabelaisian Dialectic and the Platonic-Hermetic Tradition* (Albany, N.Y., 1969).

34. Mallary Masters "Dive Bouteille," pp. 23–25.

35. Jesse Zeldin, "The Abbey and the Bottle," *L'esprit créteur* 3 (1963): 73.

36. Ibid., p. 71.

37. Ibid.

38. J. A. Comenius, *A Reformation of Schooles* (London, 1642), p. 83.

39. Comenius, *Reformation,* p. 84.

40. J. D. Walker, "The Architectonics of George Herbert's Temple," *Journal of English Literal History* 29 (1962): 289–305.

41. Barbara Kiefer Lewalski, *Protestant Poetics and the Seventeenth-century Religious Lyric* (Princeton, 1979), p. 288.

42. Ibid., pp. 286–91.

43. Robert Jan van Pelt, "Through the Temple of Solomon to the Temple of Heaven: Bacon's *New Atlantis*," *Boletin de Arte* 2 (1981): 45–52.

44. See also Elizabeth McCutcheon, "Bacon and the Cherubim: An Iconographical Reading of the *New Atlantis*," *English Literary Renaissance* 2 (1972): 334–55.

45. For Bacon's epistemology, see K. L. Wallace, *Francis Bacon on the Nature of Man* (Urbana, Ill., 1967), pp. 96–ff. The frontispiece is discussed in M. Corbett and R. W. Lightbown, *The Comily Frontispiece: The Emblematic Title-page in England, 1550–1660* (London, 1979), pp. 188–89.

46. Bacon, *Works*, 3:155–56.

47. Van Pelt, *Temple*, pp. 316–18.

48. Nathaniel Culverwell, *An Elegant and Learned Discourse on the Light of Nature*, ed R. A. Greene and H. MacCallum (Toronto, 1971), p. 15.

49. G. W. F. Hegel, *Sämtliche Werke*, ed. H. Glockner, 27 vols. (Stuttgart, 1927–36), 4:14.

50. See, for example, the discussion in Francesco Giorgi, *L'harmonie du monde* (Paris, 1578), p. 572.

51. Villalpando, *Explanationes*, 2:469–71.

52. See for example Marcello Fagiolo, "Borromini in Laterano: 'Il Nuovo Tempio' per il Concilio universale," *L'arte* 13 (1971): 5–44.

53. G. M. Lechner, "Villalpandos Tempelrekonstruktion in Beziehung zu barocker Klosterarchitektur," in *Festschrift Braunfels* (Tübingen, 1977), pp. 223–37.

54. Louis Richeome, *Trois discours pour la religion catholique: des miracles, des saincts, et des images* (Bordeaux, 1597), pp. 19–20.

20

The Children of Hermes and the Science of Man

ANTOINE FAIVRE

Hermes, the Greek god, is clever at transforming things—for example, raw material like a tortoiseshell into a marvelous musical instrument. But even if I had this gift, I do not see how I could transform the precious stones that the participants at this symposium have brought before us into a synthetic stone, especially as those gems do not need to be transmuted. I will, therefore, not be so foolhardy as to present here a synthesis of what I have heard with you. Furthermore, the time at my disposal is longer than that allocated to my colleagues, and it would not be right for me to take advantage of the situation by giving a lecture that would essentially be historical, even though it is as historians that we are gathered here on the occasion of this colloquium on Hermeticism in the Renaissance. Since it is incumbent upon me to present my own thoughts at this final plenary session, I propose to do so in what some would consider a rough-and-ready form. I will take the risk of speaking at the same time of history and of certain fundamental problems that, according to me, confront men today. Let us first don the winged sandals and with Hermes Trismegistus travel through the centuries of modern history in the specific context of this colloquium; let us call the landscape that we shall observe Hermetica and modern Hermeticism (this last word having a broader sense than *Hermetism,* which, as Frances A. Yates used it, is restricted to the *Hermetica* and to the texts directly influenced or inspired by them). Then, in a second part, we shall forsake the Thrice-Greatest to ask ourselves: What is the place of the god Hermes today?

Hermetica and Modern Hermeticism

The Hermetica contain many elements that have been retained in modern Western Hermeticism: a state of mind, a philosophical attitude, a permanent reference to a mythical scenario of fall and reintegration.

424

This state of mind is, first of all, characterized by a taste for eclecticism. The Alexandrine Hermetica of the second and third centuries A.D., and those of the preceding period, are the result of diverse contributions, of disparate philosophies blended in a melting pot, the theoretical and doctrinal coherence of which is scarcely perceptible. What is apparent in these texts is rather an avid curiosity, ready to feed upon diverse traditions. Similarly, for sixteenth-century Hermeticists, the *philosophia perennis* continued to be the postulate it was during the preceding eras. This state of mind is also characterized by a preference for will, on a human as well as divine level. In fact, in the Hermetica, the notion frequently arises that God's activity is his will, and that his essence consists in "willing" all things. God has great need of men, whose proofs of human admiration, adoration, praise, reverence, are the delight of heaven and of celestial beings. Similarly, German theosophy emphasizes the primacy of the will in God, and in this respect the influence of Jakob Böhme on German philosophy up to Hegel, Schopenhauer, and even beyond is well known. In pagan gnosis, the will is a necessary attribute of all who would see the light; the would-be philosopher must *want to know,* and it is his will that he calls upon when he evokes intermediary or heavenly spirits.

The state of mind that is here under discussion is also characterized by an apparent contradiction between two different ways of approaching gnosis. The Hermetica stress equally the importance of two paths that would appear opposites, one optimistic and the other pessimistic. What is called gnostic optimism considers the universe as divine. Since God reveals himself in all things, man can become God-like; by contemplating and understanding the universe, he can reach the divine, unite with God by absorbing a representation of the universe within his own *mens.* Gnostic pessimism, on the contrary, rejects the world as evil. Both of these tendencies are represented in modern Hermeticism, the second consisting in strongly emphasizing the consequences of the Fall on the present state of nature. Such an apparent contradiction is rich in dialectical tension, and I would like to emphasize that it is not uncommon to find it in the works of one and the same theosophist, for example Saint-Martin. There is nothing astonishing in this, since these attitudes are but complementary ways of seeing the universe, both suggesting that in the final analysis man possesses divine powers that must be regenerated and utilized. It is thus difficult to determine whether a given theosophist is optimistic or pessimistic. A fundamental pessimism would be that of a theosophist who believes in a power of evil ontologically equal to the power of good, but this is hardly ever the case in modern Hermeticism. In any event, both attitudes should be interpreted as a hermeneutical tension rather than a contradiction within the *Corpus.*

These reflections on optimistic and pessimistic attitudes make it easier to understand the philosophical premises of the Hermetica and of modern Hermeticism. In these traditions there is no absolute dualism. For example, what is called "moist nature" in the Poimandres is not presented as an ontological principle; there is deprivation, but not a complete break. This applies equally well, in modern tradition, to Jakob Böhme and other theosophists. There could not be a real dualism, especially as the world below, so complex, is in homological and analogical touch with the worlds above, which are also extremely complex. In the treatise *Nous to Hermes,* Nous addresses Hermes in order to teach him how to attain Gnostic experience. One gets there, he says, by reflecting the universe in one's own spirit; the adept must learn to seize the divine essence of the material universe and imprint it within his psyche. It is possible to do this because man possesses a divine intellect. It is thus understandable that there is frequently, though often in a very implicit way, a prolific use of mirror symbolism in Hermesian tradition; this theme was reactualized in the Middle Ages by the famous text of the *Tabula Smaragdina* (printed for the first time in 1541). Böhme, then Baader after Novalis, combine these speculations on the speculum with all kinds of considerations on light, the prism, and colors.

The universe, conceived as a system of analogical and dynamic relationships, like a text to be read, decoded, is obviously one of the biggest common denominators within this vast current of thought. An entire aspect of European literature reflects this, but if European romanticisms have done a great deal to accredit this vision of the world, it must be remembered that this vision is often expressed in the Hermetica, numerous texts of which teach the possibility of a knowledge of God through contemplation of the world. The germ of Paracelsus's thought is already contained in the *Kyranides*. This tendency affirms: *colit qui novit,* and this is what will be called pansophy in the seventeenth century. Of course this tendency is linked in the Hermetica to another apparently opposite, but finally complementary tendency, that God, unknowable, reveals himself through prayer and religion *(novit qui colit).* In the twilight of the Middle Ages, *Pistis* and *Sophia*—belief and knowledge—try to reconcile themselves, each to the other; Paracelsus tries to reconcile Christian mysticism with Neoplatonic tradition and with a real philosophy of nature, preparing the way for Rosicrucian thought and eighteenth-century Illuminism.

Because the universe is a forest of symbols, it is natural to wish to examine closely all that it contains. Whereas Aristotelianism had a tendency to be interested in the general, the Hermetica showed an extremely pronounced taste for the particular, for the hidden face and form in beings and in objects. Thus the *Kyranides* dominates the whole of Hellenistic and Greco-Roman literature of the *mirabilia,* emphasizing especially the relationships among the seven planets, metals, plants. It is this tradition that has been reactivated by the Paracelsianism so ably studied by Allen G. Debus. Thanks to Paracelsianism, one also sees experimental science making real progress, as abstract theories increasingly make way for concrete experimentation. Influenced by this new Hermesian approach, science is no longer disinterested; it looks for practical applications and ceases to neglect the particular in favor of the general. Another manifestation of this major aspect of modern Western Hermeticism is the romantic *Naturphilosophie,* especially in Germany during the second half of the eighteenth and the first half of the nineteenth centuries. Novalis, G. H. von Schubert, H. Steffens, J. W. Ritter, and many others try, through their research and their writings, to understand and reveal the hidden structure of things by a synthetic approach, but always using nature as a point of departure. It happens, for instance with Schelling, that theory precedes experimentation, but one is not conceivable without the other, which constantly revitalizes an active mind and imagination applied to decoding all the given premises of reality. The discoveries of chemistry, physics, and particularly the new experiments dealing with oxygen, galvanism, and electricity, lead to a form of cosmology or cosmosophy that brings to mind, although in a different style, the harmonies of the world of Renaissance Hermeticism.

Thus one of the main characteristics common to the Hermetica and to the entire modern Hermesian current is this taste for the concrete, tied to a philosophy of incarnation. The nightmare of Illuminism in the eighteenth century is not the thought of Condorcet or Rousseau, but pure abstraction, the disincarnate systems of certain representatives of "Light," or of *Aufklärung*. The Hermetica teach that "there is nothing invisible, even among the incorporeals," because the reproduction of matter is "an eternal operation." The incarnation is "a force in action"; there must necessarily exist bodies that serve as vessels and as instruments of immortal and eternal forces *(Tract XI, Asclepius; Fragment IV, Stobaeus)*.

The third major point of agreement between Hermetica and modern Hermeticism is a permanent reference, implicit or explicit, to the mythic themes of Fall and reintegration. To retell the myth and draw philosophical and practical consequences from it, to reenact it through a narrative or by an inspired commentary, is the task of theosophy. It is interesting to note that the theme of man's Fall by the inducement of the tangible—a very common theme in Christian theosophy at least since Böhme—exists in the Poimandres where one sees that the incarceration of Adam in the tangible was due to eros *(Kore Kosmou; Asclepius)*. It is also interesting to remember that this text is the first among all the Hermetica in their traditional presentation; thus the collection starts with a basic mythic narrative, so that one is plunged, from the start, into theosophy. The Fall calls forth a regenerative work, and the characteristic of all Hermesian gnosis is to put the emphasis on human power and will in the climb or reascension. From the Hermetica to the Hermeticism of the twentieth century, each human being is considered to be a potential magus who, by his intellect, can accomplish marvelous actions. One does not talk so much of the man *below* God, as of man *and* God. Remember here Pico, the *Monas hieroglyphica* of John Dee, and Christian theurgy; the angels that one can evoke are considered to be man's ancient servants, as man before the Fall was directly in the presence of God. The Order of the Elect Cohens, of Martines de Pasqually, is one of the last examples of this kind of theurgic practice.

Apart from "popular Hermetism" as Festugière used to say, represented by astrology and other occult sciences, there is erudite Hermetism, which is what principally interests me here, and which revolves entirely around the idea that man can discover the divine, on one hand because of theurgic practices, and on the other hand by establishing a mystical relationship between the universe and humanity. One of the basic concepts of Hermetism (Hermetica as well as modern Hermeticism) is that one can regain his divine essence, lost since the Fall, by renewing his links with the divine *mens*. This aspect was strongly emphasized during the Renaissance. The divine essence enclosed within man is not such as to be freed or regenerated at random, but only through very precise means, among which are initiations of different sorts. What is taught during these initiations always leads, even by indirect means, to a belief in an astrological cosmos, even though modern astrology tends more and more to separate itself from initiation processes and to become exclusively a special form of occultism. There is finally in the Hermetica the idea that, thanks to man, the earth, too, is capable of improving itself, of rediscovering its glorious state of before the Fall, of becoming truly *active*. An extremely fruitful idea that a text of Saint Paul (Romans, 8:19–22) has greatly helped to propagate is that man dragged nature down with him in his Fall, and consequently nature is capable of being regenerated with man's help. Here is a possible basis for an ecology founded on metaphysics.

A few reminders concerning the word *Hermeticism* in modern times are doubtless necessary at this point. Obviously, the word does not always appear where this state of mind, these doctrines, and these practices are apparent. In 1614, Casaubon demonstrated that the Hermetica are not so ancient as had been thought, and consequently, until the beginning of the nineteenth century, the word *Hermeticism* had rather a bad connotation. Gradually, *Hermes* and *hermeticism* came more and more to refer to alchemy or theosophy—or esotericism in the modern sense of the term. The example of Germany is particularly interesting. In general, the Germans had little part in the golden age of European hermetism, which lasted from Ficino to Kircher. Agrippa had written before the Reformation and Kircher had composed his main works in Rome. During this period humanism made only slight progress in Germanic lands, hampered by the barrier that Lutheranism had erected against it. Alexandrian hermetism, by its very nature, and as a legacy of ancient Greek literature and thought, remained a subject of study for the humanists. As a consequence, the authors of almost all the great commentaries on the *Corpus* were French and Italian.

What is most remarkable is that Germanic hermeticism (not Hermetism) of the sixteenth and seventeenth centuries was essentially "barbaric," in the sense that it did not owe much to the ancient legacy and developed in a more or less autonomous fashion. Hermes Trismegistos was the object of a particular veneration in Valentin Weigel and Cornelius Agrippa, although they made little use of the *Hermetica*. Paracelsus, J. Böhme, J. G. Gichtel, and most of the representatives of early *Naturphilosophie*, in other words the whole theosophical current that had chosen Germany as its protector, owed practically nothing to hermetism. This remained so, despite similarities of thought, a few publications of extracts from the *Hermetica*, and occasional references in the works of theosophers and Rosicrucians. One may well wonder if the discovery made by Casaubon did not result, either as a consequence, reaction, or compensation, in the reinforcement of the belief in a tradition, all the more secret or primordial because one could no longer date it. The Rosicrucian vogue, which appeared at the same time as Casaubon's revelation, can perhaps be partially accounted for by such a reaction, as the historian R. C. Zimmermann has recently suggested.

In the Germanic countries, Hermetism at the end of the seventeenth century and at the beginning of the eighteenth appears to have been a manifestation of humanism as well as of esotericism. Not until the beginning of the Enlightenment did Humanism really appear there. One interesting presentation of Hermes Trismegistos at the time was a book by Christian Kriegsmann, published in 1684 at Tübingen, *Conjectaneorum de germanicae gentis origine, ac conditore, Herme*

Trismegiste, qui S. Moysi est Chanaan . . . Liber unus. In it the author endeavored to demonstrate by philological arguments that Hermes was the founder of the Germanic peoples. A large place is also given to Hermes Trismegistos in the works of Johann Heinrich Ursinus (*De Zoroastre bactriano, Hermete Trismegisto,* 1661) and Olaus Borrichius (*Hermetis Aegyptiorum,* 1674). In the same period, the title of Ehregott Daniel Colberg's work, *Das Platonisch Hermetische Christentum* (1690–92), was a vague reference to both spiritualists and theosophists, against whom the author took up arms, reserving only four pages of his huge book for Hermes himself. A little later, Gottfried Arnold made almost no mention of hermetism in his voluminous history of sects and heresies, and Johann Heinrich Zedler's dictionary, which appeared around 1730, gave only a vague definition of it. Nevertheless, 1706 saw the first complete German translation of the *Poimandres* in Hamburg, with commentaries, by Aletophilus (W. von Metternich ?), under the title *Erkenntnüsz der Natur und des sich darin offenbahrenden Gottes,* while Johann Albrecht Fabricius began to publish his monumental *Bibliotheca Graeca* (1705–28), one of the first great surveys of Hellenism in Germany, in which Hermes is much discussed. And Johann Jacob Brucker devoted an entire volume of his popular *Historia critica philosophiae* (1743) to hermetism—and hermeticism (theosophy, rosicrucianism, etc.). Later on, both in Germany and elsewhere one can see a reason for the development of hermetism and hermeticism in the second half of the eighteenth century in the following fact: Popular philosophy had spread the idea of reason and of a divine love everywhere apparent (for example, and the work is significant, by Abbot Antoine Noël La Pluche, *Spectacle de la nature,* 8 vols. [1737–50]); however, as of about 1750, the sensualism and materialism that develop more and more make one forget this reason and this divine love, leading by way of reaction or rather as a compensation, to a more marked taste for esotericism.

In the nineteenth century, the word *Hermeticism* reappears, associated with Orphism and Pythagoreanism. This, with preromanticism and romanticism, is the time of its real rebirth. Among the authors less often cited than others, and not to speak of German romanticism, let me mention here *La Thréicie* of Quintus Aucler (year 7), which recalls the most beautiful passages of *De Harmonia Mundi* of Giorgia; and in the same vein, in 1806, Pierre Jacques Devismes's *Pasilogie,* where one rediscovers cosmic musical harmonies comparable to those of Giorgi and Fludd.

There is not enough time to speak of the different forms of the rebirth of Hermeticism in modern times, especially of the ways in which pagan Hermetic wisdom and cabalistic thought were utilized in the nineteenth and twentieth centuries in order to revitalize the Jewish and Christian religions. I will cite only three major transpositions of this type. First, that of Hasidism by Martin Buber, profoundly marked by the cabala; then, the work of Franz von Baader, who took up and refashioned the thought of Böhme and Saint-Martin in an original and creative way, without betraying any of their fundamental doctrinal elements. Finally, the transposition, in the domain of modern psychology, of Western Hermeticism by C. G. Jung, who greatly contributed to the awareness in our times of the eminently formative and therapeutic aspects of these doctrines for man today. From all of this there emerges an impression of something that is multiformed, yet

sufficiently united in its substance to allow us now to examine the specific forms
that, in the midst of these currents, clothe the activity of the god Hermes, this god
of exchanges and relationships, this god generous with universal and specific
knowledge.

Hermes' Place Today

What then, in the second half of our century, is Hermes' place, or what are the
conditions for his return? The Renaissance has done a great deal, especially by the
study of the Hermetica, to keep alive the presence of the god with the caduceus,
but what is happening today? In my opinion the beneficial presence of Hermes is
perpetually menaced by three dangers. First of all, by partial or nonexistent
erudition. Many works are published on the occult sciences, witchcraft, and secret
societies, but all too often their content could not be more vague, or else constitute
a pure and simple betrayal of historical reality, when reference is made to the texts
of the past. To stick to the example of a well-known popularizer of the nineteenth
century, I will only refer to the indignation of a real scholar like Gershom Scholem
when confronted with the whimsical documentation of Eliphas Lévi, whose merit
after all, lies elsewhere. Today, historical forgery flourishes, as well as reprints of
poorly researched studies, important books badly reprinted or, even when presented in facsimile, not preceded by any introductory notes for the enlightenment
of the reader. I am also thinking of forgery of another sort, coming under what one
calls disguised Evehmerism, of those malicious writers who, attempting to "disoc-
cult the occult," think it fit to reduce mythical premises to "rational" events, such
as Erich von Däniken's book *Chariot of the Gods,* which interprets biblical
hierophanies as traces of extraterrestrial visits. In an excellent work (*The Unfinished Animal,* 1977), Theodor Roszak had given a juicy list of such examples
that take us further away from a veritable analogical hermeneutics of the Scriptures. In *hermeneutics* there is Hermes, but *hermêneuein,* "to explain," is an *explicatio* quite different from that furnished by the new *Hermocopides* or Multi-
lators of Hermes (to pick up on the image furnished by the events in Athens in the
year 415 B.C.). In the sense in which Hermeticism is also alchemy, one speaks of it
as of an empirical manner of obtaining energetic results for purely utilitarian ends.
Finally the third danger, like the second, consists of a confusion of goals. It is
confusion that reigns in many circles, especially in the United States but also
elsewhere, between initiatic symbolism as a means of spiritual knowledge, and the
simple—and legitimate—need for psychic integration. There is today a real hunger
for initiations, for real fairs of the occult, of which Theodor Roszak has ably
spoken in order to describe what is the cruelest deficiency in this domain, the
absence of reference to myth—in the positive and spiritually formative sense of the
word *myth.* It is often difficult in this jungle of societies and of diverse groupings of
new religious movements that multiply everywhere and especially in California,
where some even call themselves Gnostics and refer sometimes explicitly to
Hermetism, to distinguish between those which emerge from a real religious (that

is to say, mystical) consciousness, and those that translate into a simple need for individual and collective therapy. Mass media produce a profusion of pseudoinitiatic discourse, but since all of this remains in a state of fragmentation, one is dealing most frequently with the forms of discourse or of images that are more often fantastical than psychologically and spiritually formative or structuring.

And yet, this wild imagining testifies to the need of escaping from an official imagining, that is to say, from a schizomorphic regime of images of which one realizes more and more the inadequacies. New medicines, new therapies, are oriented toward an imaginary (in the positive sense of the term) that is better able to respond to the complexity of reality. This fusion of therapy and traditional sciences, such as one sees in the best of cases (for example, in the work and teaching of Carl Gustav Jung), is no doubt one of the positive developments of our times. If a practitioner and thinker like Jung can recover the heritage of Hermeticism, in the sense of hermetism as well as of all alchemy in general, it is because he has seen the necessity for the anthropos to live with the myth in its complete and individual form. The Hermeticists of the Renaissance had understood that the reading of the myth is the key to an understanding of art and poetry as well as of science and technology. They placed the myth in their field of knowledge. There was, therefore, room among them for Hermes, whereas today it is Prometheus who reigns, even without our knowledge or when one does not invoke him by name. The risk that our age must take, if it wishes to see the birth of a new humanism, consists of relearning the place of myth and mystery in our lives and in our field of knowledge. This indispensable task was undertaken by the authors of the Hermetica, who mythologized the cosmos; by those of the Renaissance, an age that corresponded to a powerful remythologization. *Remythologization* does not mean the creation of false myths but the refusal of them; it is not sacrificing to ancient or new idols but refusing to idolize history, that is to say, refusing to succumb to the ideologies and pseudophilosophies of history. If Hermeticism today has a role to play, it is that of demystifier so as to remythify.

To regain the sense of myth, whether within the framework of a constituted religion or outside it, is also to learn or relearn how to read. What a beautiful lesson so many of the thinkers of the Renaissance teach us, those who knew how to read the book of the world, of man and of theophanies! They had understood that language starts with reading and passes through it—the reading of myths, of anthropos and of the cosmos. Is not the art of memory, so well studied by Frances A. Yates, first of all a means of reading the world so as to interiorize it and, in some sense, to rewrite it within the self? But if it is true that language starts by reading, it must be recognized that, in our age, one no doubt speaks too much of the writing. Formal linguistics exalt writing as a primary premise for decoding, whereas man is above all *homo legens*. Writing, Gilbert Durand once remarked, is only the consequence, the "reduced description" of reading. And Hermesian reading, which is what I am talking about, is an open, in-depth reading, one that lays bare the metalanguages for us, that is to say, the structures of signs and correspondences that only symbolism and myth make it possible to conserve and transmit. To read, to find the depth of things—by looking in the right place. There is a search for depth in Karl Marx, because of the notion of infrastructure, but I do not see that it is applied where appropriate. And the Freudian distinction between the latent content and an apparent symptom also bears witness to an effort tending toward reductionism. The Hermesian spirit is the one that looks for depth where it is, a living place so poetically indicated in the *Emerald Table,* that breviary of profoundness. Baudelaire, in his sonnet of *Correspondances* extolled one aspect of this depth:

> Comme de longs échos qui de loin se confondent
> Dans une ténébreuse et profonde unité
> Vaste comme la nuit et comme la clarté
> Les parfums, les couleurs et les sons se répondent.

A Hermesian reading of the world is necessarily a plural reading. The caduceus of Hermes is plural because it is constituted of a bipolarity whose symbolism reflects back to a ternary. Hermes is the antitotalitarian god par excellence. The currents of thought that interest us here and that go back to him exalt an ethic of completeness rather than one of perfection; an ethic, a philosophy, of plural totality, which signifies a refusal to objectify the problems of the spirit (for example, of evil) into simplistic or abstract concepts that flatten the soul; which also signifies a recognition of the multilayered and hierarchical character of the elements that constitute the human psyche. What psychoanalysis rediscovered, traditional thinkers had always known and repeated: that we have within us different qualitative levels. It is not only a question of the distinctions among body-soul-spirit, or shadow-persona-anima, but also of what, for example, the psychologist Rafael Lopez Pedraza (*Hermes and His Children,* 1977) says: that there are several gods in sexuality and not just one, contrary to a narrow perspective. The caduceus of Hermes is also the *tertium datur,* the refusal to stay blocked in the logic of identity and in its corollaries of noncontradiction and exclusion of third parties. Today, this plurality is made evident by, among other things, the effort of all who contribute to the establishment of a planetary dialogue by deprovincializing ethnology (Mircea Eliade) and by showing what is common and irreducible in the great traditions of the Gnosis and the Sacred (Seyyed Hossein Nasr, *Knowledge and the Sacred,* 1981). To maintain the dialogue between even the most scientific modern experiment and traditional symbolism is what Fritjof Capra (*The Tao of Physics,* 1975) and others after him have done. There are those who, following Friedrich Schlegel who revealed the Orient to Europe, today study symbols, myths, archetypes, and make of comparative mythology a science that leads to knowledge. Alchemy opens a new epistemology (René Alleau), and C. G. Jung has found a place within the modern psyche for the occult and religious heritage of the world.

Is this a new *ratio,* opposed to the one that has held sway until now in our Promethean and triumphant civilization? Rather, it is a different but nonetheless complementary *ratio,* which integrates without excluding, which dynamizes without reducing. The crisis in our human sciences is due, without any doubt, to the abandonment in anthropology (in the wider sense of the term) of this *ratio hermetica* and particularly of the principle of similarity that hermeticism knew so well how to conserve. German culture was for centuries in our modern history the best conservator of this principle. This *ratio hermetica* means saying first of all that nature is pluralistic and that these pluralities are concrete things. The baroque and romanticism are in Germanic countries the two great creative and truly original moments of which these people were capable, and it is doubtless no accident that the one and the other correspond to a considerable recrudescence of Hermesian thought and activity. From German culture, inspired by this Hermesian science, comes in particular the idea, set out at the beginning of our century by Spengler, of the pluralism of cultures and civilizations; next to the idea of growth and progress, there appears that of decline, of fall. And when Spengler links the time of each organism to the "qualities of the species to which it belongs," one remembers Paracelsus expounding the theory of the *Kraftzeit* "fixed by God for each species." If, on the other hand, pure, official, exact science, teaches objective disinterest, laic neutrality, the *ratio hermetica* teaches a pragmatic interest, a subjectifying interest. Medicine, astrology, magic must "operate" concretely since the Paracelsian type of High Science is the knowledge of concrete facts, of *mirabilia.* There is no question of neglecting the other sicence, naturally, but of simultaneously using both; of not throwing out, as Kepler said, the baby with the bathwater (that is to say, in its context, not to throw overboard astrological knowledge under the pretext that astronomical knowledge is being verified). The *ratio hermetica* also adds a principle of similitude, or participation in entity forces, to the causal determination of Aristotle. The mediator Hermes-Mercurius plays here an essential role inasmuch as either with him or by him the complete break between the subject and object disappears. Unification is brought about by the mediation of an energy principle that is seen to assure order in the cosmos and unification of the subject. This is to show how much Hermeticism can today facilitate comprehension of a multiple reality which, far from limiting itself to a project of flat rationality, would associate the flesh and the flame, as these beautiful lines of Péguy suggest:

> et le surnaturel est lui-même charnel
> Et l'arbre de la Grâce et l'arbre de la Nature
> Se sont étreints tous deux comme deux lourdes lianes
> Par-dessus les piliers et les temples profanes.
> Ils ont articulé leur double ligature.

Is this not at the same time a way of evoking the caduceus? Of recognizing in Mercurius the mediator par excellence, capable of unlocking antagonistic dualisms that bear witness to a schizomorphic, and thus diminished, imaginary? Mediations between the body and the spirit, sky and earth, God and the World (this is *anima mundi*), passion and reason, the ego and the id, eros and thanatos, animus and anima, heaviness and grace, spirit and matter. Hermeticists have always looked for the epiphanies of the earth to experience the divine in the world. If they see the body as a magical object, mystically linked to the planets and to the elements of nature, it is because they find sense everywhere in things and transcend the illusion of banality, a poetic task par excellence. This path is certainly more poetic than ascetic, but if asceticism is the source of technological progress, it is not necessarily a model to follow to experience totality.

Hermeticists had understood that there is everywhere sense in the concrete. In the twentieth century, Gaston Bachelard, thanks to whom the imaginary reestablished its credentials, has affirmed as a postulate that scientific concepts and explanations derive from the pragmatic and not the other way around. In fact, the fear of or the refusal of sense corresponds today to a convulsive jump by Prometheus, who wants to work for man's benefit by using a usurped light, a torch that is not nature's and that he invents as needed. But the refusal of sense leads to the agnosticism of the great abstracts, to formalist structuralism for example, since saying that it can only be found in formal relations, in abstract form, in the exchange of empty signs, is to recoil from sense. Oriented almost entirely toward formalism, linguistics today leads to a consideration of language as being shut off from the outside, without links outside itself, without heuristics. Solipism, atomization, incommunicability are the ransom of our episteme since the eighteenth century, whereas Hermes shows the path of otherness, of living diversity, of communication of souls. This otherness, as well as its opposite—shutting out of the outside—are found in our arts and our literature, according to whether Narcissus or Prometheus reigns as absolute master, or whether, on the contrary, Hermes favors and stimulates living relationships within art and literature. Prometheus without Hermes is dangerous, but so are Narcissus and Dionysius. A God, like a child, must not be left alone when he plays. The warning thrown out by Nietzsche in *Die Geburt der Tragödie* (1872) has shown itself to be even more incontrovertibly true than one had thought. The experience of the dramas of the twentieth century thus deserves to be taken advantage of; if this could be done, monotheistic ideologies would have ceased to live. This is so because monotheism without counterpart runs the risk of being transformed into a dangerous philosophical abstraction devoid of links with reality—the words *monotheism* and *polytheism* being used here of course without a theological sense; for example, I call the Christian belief in angels polytheism. Pagan gods and Judeo-Christian myths can go well together in a healthy soul, in the same way that they got along well together during the Renaissance, that period of abounding health and supreme vitality. Dom Pernéty, in the middle of the eighteenth century, was one of those, and they were numerous, who understood this and reminded us of it when it was about to be forgotten. Similarly, Gershom Scholem has convincingly shown how and why the sudden development of the cabala in the thirteenth century was a reaction against an abstract form of rabbinism that was prevalent at the time.

The magia, understood as a search for the unity of man with nature, teaches us an active manner of being and having, rather than a method of manipulation. What one calls tradition is not for me a sort of immutable depository, an invariable doctrinal body, but a perpetual rebirth. The tragedy of a culture occurs when everything is perceived in the form of an empty and abstract concept. This could well be our tragedy.

Select Bibliography

Bonardel, Françoise. *L'hermétisme*. Paris, 1985.

Durand, Gilbert. *Science de l'homme et tradition*. Paris, 1975.

——. *Figures mythiques et visages de l'oeuvre*. Paris, 1979.

Faivre, Antoine. *Accès de l'esotérisme occidental*. Paris, 1986.

——. *L'esotérisme au XVIIIème siècle en France et en Allemagne*. Paris, 1974.

Nock, Arthur Darby, and André-Jean Festugière, ed. and trans. *Corpus Hermeticum*. 4 vols. Paris, 1954–60.

Festugière, André-Jean. *La révélation d'Hermès Trismégiste*. 3 vol. Paris, 1949.

Nasr, Seyyed Hossein. *Knowledge and the Sacred*. New York, 1981.

Roszak, Theodor. *The Aquarian Frontier and the Evolution of Counsciousness: The Unfinished Animal*. New York, 1975.

Sladek, Mario. *Fragmente der hermetischen Philosophie in der Neuzeit*. Frankfurt, 1984.

Tuveson, Ernest Lee. *The Avatars of Thrice Great Hermes: An Approach to Romanticism*. Lewisburg, Pa., 1982.

Yates, Frances A. *Giordano Bruno and the Hermetic Tradition*. London, 1964.

——. *The Art of Memory*. London, 1966.

Zimmermann, Rolf Christian. *Das Weltbild des jungen Goethe*. 2 vols. Munich, 1969–79.

Contributors

Brian Copenhaver
Professor of History
Oakland University
Rochester, Michigan

Allen G. Debus
Morris Fishbein Professor of the History of Science and Medicine
University of Chicago

Charles Dempsey
Professor of Italian Renaissance and Baroque Art
The Johns Hopkins University
Baltimore, Maryland

B. J. T. Dobbs
Professor of History
Northwestern University
Evanston, Illinois

Leland L. Estes
Assistant Professor of History
Chapman College
Orange, California

Antoine Faivre
Ecole des Hautes Etudes. Sciences Religieuses
Sorbonne, Paris

Edward A. Gosselin
Professor of History
California State University at Long Beach
Editor of *The History Teacher*

WILLIAM C. GRESE
Bloomington, Illinois

MOSHE IDEL
Professor of Jewish Thought
Hebrew University
Jerusalem, Israel

KARIN JOHANNISSON
Associate Professor of History of Science and Medicine
Uppsala University, Sweden

DOUGLAS LEWIS
Curator of Sculpture and Decorative Arts
National Gallery of Art
Washington, D.C.
Visiting lecturer
Georgetown University, Washington, D.C.

INGRID MERKEL
Associate Professor of Modern Languages
The Catholic University of America
Washington, D.C.

HUGH ORMSBY-LENNON
Professor of English Literature
Villanova University
Villanova, Pennsylvania

G. S. ROUSSEAU
Professor of English and Eighteenth-Century Studies
University of California at Los Angeles

JOHN SCARBOROUGH
Professor, History of Medicine and Pharmacy
School of Pharmacy
University of Wisconsin at Madison

WAYNE SHUMAKER
Professor Emeritus of English
University of California at Berkeley

ROBERT JAN VAN PELT
Assistant Professor of Cultural History
University of Waterloo
Waterloo, Ontario, Canada

BRIAN VICKERS
Professor of English Literature
Director of the Centre for Renaissance Studies
Eidgenössische Technische Hochschule
Zurich, Switzerland

D. P. WALKER
Late Emeritus Professor of History of the Classical Tradition
The Warburg Institute
University of London, England

PAOLA ZAMBELLI
Professor of the History of Philosophy
University of Florence, Italy